MERCANTILE LAW

AUSTRALIA
The Law Book Company Ltd.
Sydney : Melbourne : Brisbane

CANADA AND U.S.A.
The Carswell Company Ltd.
Agincourt, Ontario

INDIA
N. M. Tripathi Private Ltd.
Bombay

ISRAEL
Steimatzky's Agency Ltd.
Jerusalem : Tel Aviv - Haifa

MALAYSIA, SINGAPORE AND BRUNEI
Malayan Law Journal (Pte.) Ltd.
Singapore

NEW ZEALAND
Sweet & Maxwell (N.Z.) Ltd.
Wellington

PAKISTAN
Pakistan Law House
Karachi

CHARLESWORTH'S

MERCANTILE LAW

THIRTEENTH EDITION

by

CLIVE M. SCHMITTHOFF,

LL.M., LL.D. (Lond.), Dr. jur. (Berl.), Drs. h.c. (Marburg and Berne),
Hon. F.I.Ex.
of Gray's Inn, Barrister
Visiting Professor at the City University and the
University of Kent in Canterbury;
Hon. Professor at the Ruhr-Universität Bochum

and

DAVID A. G. SARRE, M.A.

of the Middle Temple, Barrister

LONDON
STEVENS & SONS
1977

First Edition	–	–	– (1929)	By His Honour Judge Charlesworth
Second Edition	–	–	– (1931)	,, ,, ,,
Third Edition	–	–	– (1934)	,, ,, ,,
Second Impression	–	– (1935)	
Third Impression	–	–	– (1936)	
Fourth Edition	–	–	– (1938)	,, ,, ,,
Fifth Edition	–	–	– (1942)	,, ,, ,,
Sixth Edition	–	–	– (1945)	,, ,, ,,
Second Impression	–	– (1946)	
Third Impression	–	–	– (1947)	
Fourth Impression	–	– (1947)	
Fifth Impression	–	– (1948)	
Sixth Impression	–	– (1948)	
Seventh Edition	–	–	– (1949)	,, ,, ,,
Second Impression	–	– (1951)	
Eighth Edition	–	–	– (1955)	,, ,, ,,
Second Impression	–	– (1957)	
Ninth Edition	–	–	– (1960)	By Clive M. Schmitthoff and
Second Impression	–	– (1961)	David A. G. Sarre
Tenth Edition	–	–	– (1963)	,, ,, ,,
Eleventh Edition	–	–	– (1967)	,, ,, ,,
Second Impression	–	– (1969)	
Third Impression	–	– (1971)	
Twelfth Edition	–	–	– (1972)	,, ,, ,,
Second Impression	–	– (1974)	
Third Impression	–	– (1974)	
Translated into French	–	– (1976)	
Thirteenth Edition	–	– (1977)	,, ,, ,,
Second Impression	–	– (1979)	

*Published in 1977 by
Stevens & Sons Limited of
11 New Fetter Lane, London
and printed in Great Britain
by Richard Clay (The Chaucer
Press) Ltd, Bungay, Suffolk*

ISBN Hardback 0420 45320 2
Paperback 0420 45050 5

PREFACE

THIS book is primarily intended as a textbook for students. It has always attempted by using illustrative cases to explain how the principles of law are applied to the problems which arise in the conduct of business.

The book has been brought up to date by the inclusion of references to new decisions of the court and to new statutes enacted since September 1971 when the preceding edition went to press. Among the new statutes taken into account are the Carriage of Goods by Sea Act 1971, the Contracts of Employment Act 1972, the European Communities Act 1972, the Fair Trading Act 1973, the Supply of Goods (Implied Terms) Act 1973, the Consumer Credit Act 1974, the Insurance Companies Act 1974, the Sex Discrimination Act 1975, the Policyholders Protection Act 1975, the Employment Protection Act 1975, the Arbitration Act 1975, the Race Relations Act 1976, the Insolvency Act 1976, the Restrictive Trade Practices Act 1976 and the Companies Act 1976.

In the present edition the whole text has been thoroughly revised and an arrangement has been adopted which is designed to assist the student in his work. Two new chapters have been added, namely in Part 1, which deals with Contracts, a chapter on Terms of the Contract, and in Part 3 a chapter on Consumer Credit. As in the previous edition, each chapter is followed by a Select Bibliography in which the reader is referred to the leading textbooks and to important articles in the *Law Quarterly Review*, the *Cambridge Law Journal*, the *Modern Law Review*, the *Journal of Business Law*, and the *International and Comparative Law Quarterly*. In my experience as a law teacher, serious-minded students require this help and library facilities have improved so much everywhere that there should be no difficulty of access to these sources.

The various branches of Mercantile Law have now become highly specialised subjects. If the editors had attempted to treat all the subjects which recently have come into existence or have been profoundly affected by recent legislation, the publication of this edition would have been unduly postponed. For that reason they called in the assistance of eminent specialists whose help is gratefully acknowledged. The following have assisted in the preparation of this edition:

Professor Christopher S. Axworthy (Bibliography),
Mr. Christopher M. C. Cashmore (Common Carriers, Carriage by Land),

Mr. Paul Davies (Contract of Employment),
Mr. A. P. Dobson (Sale of Goods, Hire-purchase, Consumer Credit),
Dr. John H. Farrar (Bankruptcy),
Mr. Stephen Walzer (Monopolies, Restrictive Trade Practices and Resale Prices).

The overall task of co-ordinating the specialist contributions with the material prepared by the editors and of presenting the whole work as an integrated textbook remained with the editors.

The present edition is again jointly edited by my friend David A. G. Sarre, a valued colleague on the editorial board of the *Journal of Business Law*, and myself. Our co-operation proceeded in perfect harmony and mutual understanding. Mr. Sarre's erudition, skill and imaginative appreciation of the reader's point of view have made a most valuable contribution to the production of our joint work.

The law is stated as on May 1, 1977.

10 South Square,   CLIVE M. SCHMITTHOFF
Gray's Inn,
WE1R 5EU.

CONTENTS

xii   *Contents*

TABLE OF CASES

TABLE OF STATUTES

PART 1: CONTRACT

CHAPTER 1

NATURE OF CONTRACT

DEFINITION OF CONTRACT

A CONTRACT is an agreement which will be enforced by the law.

This definition is satisfied when the following elements are present—

1. There must be an agreement. Since nobody can agree with himself (though he may resolve to do or not to do an act), there must be at least two parties to an agreement. One of them will make an offer, and the other will indicate its acceptance. When offer and acceptance correspond in every respect, there is agreement between the parties.

2. The parties must intend their agreement to result in legal relations. This means that the parties must intend that if one of them fails to fulfil a promise undertaken by the agreement, he shall be answerable for that failure in law.

    It is evident that not all agreements are intended to produce legal consequences. If, *e.g.* John agrees to lend his cycle to his friend Paul but later refuses to let him have it, an action for damages will not lie against John because the two friends did not contemplate, when entering into the agreement, that it should be enforceable in law. Similarly, if a father fails to pay his son the promised pocket money, it is obvious that the son cannot sue the father. The former agreement is of purely social character, the latter is a domestic arrangement. Neither of these agreements qualifies as a contract.

3. English law is not content with these two requirements. It requires further that either consideration must be present or that the contract should be under seal.

4. The parties must have capacity to contract.

5. The reality of the contract must not be affected by circumstances which render the contract unenforceable, voidable, void or illegal.

All these elements of a valid contract will be considered in detail

1

in the following chapters, with the exception of the second one, *i.e.* the intention of creating legal relations, which it is convenient to treat here.

Intention of Creating Legal Relations

It has already been seen that the intention to create legal relations is an element necessary for the formation of a contract. Both parties must have this intention but what matters is not what they had in mind when concluding the contract, but whether reasonable persons would draw the conclusion from their words and actions that they want to be legally bound. If the parties indicate expressly or impliedly that they do not wish their agreement to be binding on them, the law would accept and respect their intention. But where there is agreement the burden of proof that it is not intended to have legal effect is on the party asserting this, and this onus is a heavy one.

Domestic agreements

Engagements of purely domestic or social nature are often not intended to be binding in law but are intended to rely on bonds of mutual trust and affection.

A husband who was a Civil Servant in Ceylon came to England with his wife. When his leave was nearing its end and he had to return to Ceylon, he promised his wife who on the doctor's advice had to remain in England a household allowance of £30 a month until she joined him in Ceylon. Later the parties separated and the wife sued for the allowance. *Held*, domestic agreements such as these were outside the realm of contract altogether: *Balfour* v. *Balfour* [1919] 2 K.B. 571.

A husband and a wife, whose marriage was unhappy, hoped that their relationship would improve if the husband bought her a car. The husband acquired a car on hire-purchase terms and agreed that the registration book should be put into the wife's name and that she should have possession of the car. In spite of this arrangement, the marriage continued to be unhappy and the parties separated. *Held*, applying the rule in *Balfour* v. *Balfour*, *ante*, the husband, and not the wife, was entitled to the car because the arrangement between them was of purely domestic character: *Spellman* v. *Spellman* [1961] 1 W.L.R. 921.

A mother who lived in Trinidad wanted her daughter to study for the English Bar and after completion of her studies to practise as a lawyer in Trinidad. At a time when mother and daughter were very close, the mother bought a house in London to enable the daughter to reside there during her studies. Later differences arose and the mother claimed possession of the house. *Held*, that the arrangements in relation to the house were made without contractual intent and that the mother was entitled to possession of the house: *Jones* v. *Padavatton* [1969] 1 W.L.R. 328.

On the other hand, even if the parties are in a domestic or social relationship but intend their agreement to have legal consequences, an enforceable contract is concluded

A husband had formed an attachment to another woman and the spouses intended to separate. They negotiated in the husband's car about some arrangement for the future. Before the wife left the car she insisted that the husband gave her a written statement according to which in consideration of her paying the mortgage on the family home (which was in the name of her husband) he should transfer that house into her sole ownership. The wife paid the mortgage and asked for the transfer of the house. *Held*, the rule in *Balfour* v. *Balfour* did not apply. In that case the parties reached their agreement when they lived in amity but in the present case they negotiated at arms' length as they had decided to separate and reasonable persons would regard their agreement as intended to be binding in law. The wife was entitled to the house: *Merritt* v. *Merritt* [1970] 1 W.L.R. 1211.

Brian and his two brothers Peter and Barrie were directors of a family company engaged in the building trade. Serious disputes arose between the three brothers and, as the company needed additional finance, it took up a loan from a finance house. That loan was secured by way of a mortgage on the company's property. The three brothers had large individual loan accounts with the company and agreed in writing between themselves that if one of them voluntarily resigned his directorship, his loan account with the company should be forfeited immediately and the money be used towards the repayment of the loan given by the finance company. Brian voluntarily resigned his directorship. *Held*, Brian's argument that the agreement between the three brothers was only of domestic character was not sound and therefore the rule in *Balfour* v. *Balfour* applied. Owing to the dissensions between the brothers the family relationship had already been destroyed and nothing but the biological tie remained. The written agreement between the brothers was intended to create legal relations and Brian could not recover his loan account, but the company could not rely on the contract between the brothers because it was a stranger thereto (see p. 152, *post*), *Snelling* v. *John G. Snelling Ltd.* [1973] 1 Q.B. 87.

The parties, a widow, her grandmother, and the widow's lodger, agreed to "go shares" with respect to a newspaper competition. Sellers J. *held* that they intended to create legal relations, *viz.* to form an informal syndicate and that the recipient of the prize money had to share it with the others: *Simpkins* v. *Pays* [1955] 1 W.L.R. 975.

Commercial agreements

The parties may agree that their agreement, although couched in legal terms, shall not be binding in law but shall be binding "in honour only."

The R Company made an agreement with the C Company whereby they were appointed agents for the sale of paper supplied by the C Company. One clause in the agreement was, "This arrangement is not entered into as a formal or legal agreement and shall not be subject to legal jurisdiction in the law courts." *Held*, no contract was made between the parties: *Rose & Frank Co.* v. *Crompton Bros. Ltd.* [1925] A.C. 445.

A condition expressly negativing the intention of creating legal relations is not contrary to public policy, but is binding.

A sued the promoters of a football pool for £4,335 which he claimed to have won. The pool was subject to a condition that it was not to be legally enforceable. *Held*, the claim failed: *Appleson* v. *Littlewood Ltd.* [1939] 1 All E.R. 464.

Collective agreements

The Trade Union and Labour Relations Act 1974, s. 18, (1) to (3), provides that a collective agreement between a trade union and an employer (or an employers' association) is conclusively presumed not to have been intended by the parties to be legally enforceable, except if the following two conditions are satisfied:

    (a) the agreement is in writing, and
    (b) it contains a statement that the parties intend it to be a legally enforceable contract.

Terms prohibiting or restricting the right to strike

Even if the collective agreement constitutes a legally enforceable contract, according to the provisions just explained, any terms which prohibit or restrict the right of an employee to engage in a strike or other industrial action, are unenforceable, except if those terms are expressly incorporated into the individual contract of employment with the employee, and the collective agreement itself satisfies the following four conditions:

    (a) it is in writing, and
    (b) contains a provision expressly stating that those terms may be incorporated into the contract of employment with the employee, and

(c) the collective agreement is reasonably accessible to the employee at his place of work and can be consulted during working hours, and

(d) each of the contracting trade unions is an "independent trade union," *i.e.* a trade union which is not under the control of the employer

(section 18 (4)).

In common law

In common law a collective agreement is not normally enforceable because it is usually not intended to create legal relations (*Ford Motor Co.* v. *Amalgamated Union of Engineering and Foundry Workers* [1969] 2 Q.B. 303).

Ex gratia payments

The promise of an *ex gratia* payment is ambiguous; it might mean that, without recognising a pre-existing legal liability, the promise should create an enforceable legal obligation.

E, a pilot employed by S, was promised an *ex gratia* payment on termination of his services. He left the employment of S. *Held*, the promise of an *ex gratia* payment was enforceable in law: *Edwards* v. *Skyways Ltd.* [1964] 1 W.L.R. 349.

The promise of a garage owner selling a particular brand of petrol to give purchasers of petrol, by way of an advertising gift, a coin showing the image of a prominent footballer and on the reverse the name of the petrol company, is not intended to create a legal relationship (*Esso Petroleum Co. Ltd.* v. *Customs and Excise Commissioners* [1975] 1 W.L.R. 406, 410).

Without prejudice negotiations

It happens sometimes that the parties attempt to settle a dispute in "without prejudice" negotiations. If agreement is reached on some issues but not on all, the question is whether the agreement was merely a step in the negotiations intended to be binding only on the conditions that final settlement will be reached on all outstanding points, or whether the intention was that the agreement, as far as it went, should be binding in any event, and the settlement of the outstanding issues should be left to further negotiations or judicial decision.

A work accident had occurred in which a fitter was injured. The fitter's solicitor and the agent for the employers' insurers agreed in "without prejudice" negotiations that the liability of the employers should not exceed 50 per cent. but they could not reach agreement on the valuation of the fitter's claim. The fitter started proceedings and the employers (who were the defendants for procedural reasons) denied liability. *Held*, the 50/50 agreement reached in the "without prejudice" negotiations was intended to be binding although the parties had not reached agreement on the quantum of the plaintiff's claim: *Tomlin* v. *Standard Telephones and Cables Ltd.* [1969] 1 W.L.R. 1378.

Too Vague Agreements

The agreement may be so vague as to show that the parties did not intend to be bound in law.

The company agreed with V that, on the expiration of V's existing contract, they would favourably consider an application by V for a renewal of his contract. *Held*, the agreement was not intended to bind the company to renew their contract with V and imposed no obligation on them to renew it: *Montreal Gas Co.* v. *Vasey* [1900] A.C. 595.

A husband who had left his wife agreed to pay her £15 a week "as long as he had it." *Held*, that although husband and wife could enter into a legally binding agreement, the vague terms which were used indicated an intention not to create legal obligations: *Gould* v. *Gould* [1970] 1 Q.B. 275 (Lord Denning M.R. gave a strong dissenting judgment).

The parties agreed that the buyers should acquire land of approximately 51½ acres at £500,000. Of the purchase price, £250,000 was to be paid upon first completion, £125,000 12 months later, and the balance of £125,000 thereafter, and on occasion of each completion " a proportionate part of the land" should be transferred to the buyers. *Held*, the power to release "a proportionate part of the land" was an element of substance which left the whole contract uncertain: *Bushwall Properties Ltd.* v. *Vortex Properties Ltd.* [1976] 1 W.L.R. 591.

An agreement to agree on some future date may likewise be too vague, see p. 21 *post*. But if an agreement intended to create legal relations contains a term which is meaningless, that term may be disregarded by the court and the contract is binding, see pp. 22–23, *post*.

SELECT BIBLIOGRAPHY

Books

	Treitel *The Law of Contract* (4th ed., 1975)	M. P. Furmston, *Cheshire & Fifoot's* *Law of Contract* (9th ed., 1975)
Definition of Contract	1–6	19–20
Intention of creating *Legal Relations*	97–104	102–111

Schmitthoff, C. M., *Commercial Law in a Changing Economic Climate* (1977).

Articles

Hepple, B. A., "Intention to create Legal Relations" [1970] C.L.J. 122–137.

Ingham, T., "Intention to create Legal Relations" [1970] J.B.L. 109–116.

CHAPTER 2

FORMATION OF CONTRACT

THE essence of contract is that there should be an **agreement** between the contracting parties. This agreement is normally constituted by one party making an **offer** and the other indicating its **acceptance.** The acceptance must correspond to the offer in all material aspects.

The negotiations between the parties need not always lead to a contract. Inquiries may be made or offers invited but no offer may be made or, if one is made, it need not be accepted.

Before the concepts of offer and acceptance can be considered in detail, it is necessary to distinguish certain statements preliminary to the offer from the offer itself.

STATEMENTS PRELIMINARY TO AN OFFER

An offer must be distinguished from
1. an invitation to make an offer; and
2. a declaration of intention.

Invitation to make an offer

An invitation to make an offer is not an offer which is capable of being turned into a contract by acceptance. An advertisement is normally only intended to be an invitation to treat, *i.e.* to negotiate. Further, a shopkeeper who displays goods in his window with a ticket on them stating a price, does not make an offer, but merely invites the public to make an offer to buy the goods at the price stated. Therefore, if a customer enters the shop, tenders the price and demands the article, the shopkeeper is not bound to sell it to him. The demand of the customer is the offer which the shopkeeper is free to accept or reject as he pleases.

Goods were sold in B's shop under the self-service system. Customers selected their purchases from shelves on which goods were displayed, put them into a wire basket supplied by B and took them to the cash desk where they paid the price. *Held*, the contract was made, not when the customer put the goods in the basket, but when the cashier accepted the offer to buy and received the price: *Pharmaceutical Society* v. *Boots* [1953] 1 Q.B. 401.

P advertised in the column "Classified Advertisements" of the periodical *Cage and Aviary Birds* "Quality British . . . bramblefinch hens." T ordered a bramblefinch hen and enclosed his cheque, and P supplied him with the bird. The Protection of Birds Act 1954, s 6 (1) makes it an offence to sell, *offer for sale*, or have in his possession for sale these birds, except in specified cases. P was accused of having committed the offence of *offering for sale* a bramblefinch hen, by inserting the advertisement into the periodical. *Held*, P was not guilty because the advertisement was not an offer to sell. "When one is dealing with advertisements and circulars, unless they indeed come from manufacturers, there is business sense in their being construed as invitations to treat and not offers for sale": *per* Lord Parker C.J. in *Partridge* v. *Crittenden* [1968] 1 W.L.R. 1204.

Note that if P had been accused of *having in his possession for sale* the bird, he would have been convicted.

British Car Auctions were in business as auctioneers of motor cars. Their standard conditions provided that no contractual relationship should ensue between the auctioneers and the buyer but that any contract resulting from the auction should be directly between the seller and the buyer. British Car Auctions auctioned a Morris 1100 car which undoubtedly was unroadworthy. They were accused under section 68 of the Road Traffic Act 1960 which made it an offence "to offer to sell" an unroadworthy car. *Held*, at an auction the bidder, and not the auctioneer, made the offer and that offer was accepted by the fall of the auctioneer's hammer (see p. 268, *post*. The charge was dismissed: *British Car Auctions Ltd.* v. *Wright* [1972] 1 W.L.R. 1519.

A prospectus to subscribe to the shares or debentures of a company is often in the nature of an invitation to make an offer (see Companies Act 1948, s. 455); the application for shares or debentures is the offer and the allotment by the company is the acceptance.

Declaration of intention

A declaration by a person that he intends to do a thing gives no right of action to another who suffers loss because the former does not carry out his intention. Such a declaration only means that an offer is to be made or invited in the future, and not that an offer is made now.

An auctioneer advertised in the newspapers that a sale of office furniture would be held at Bury St. Edmunds. A broker with a commission to buy office furniture came down from London to attend the sale, but all the furniture was withdrawn. The broker thereupon sued the auctioneer for his loss of time and expenses. *Held*, that a declaration of intention to do a thing did not create a binding contract with those who acted upon it, so that the broker could not recover: *Harris* v. *Nickerson* (1873) L.R. 8 Q.B. 286.

THE OFFER

How an offer is made

The offer may be express, or implied from conduct. Examples (1) and (2) below are illustrations of express offers, and example (3) of an implied offer. The person making the offer is called the *offeror*, and the person to whom it is made is called the *offeree*. In examples (1) and (2) A is the offeror.

Examples—(1) A offers to sell his motor cycle to B at the price of £100. B promises to pay £100 for the motor cycle.

(2) A advertises in a newspaper offering £5 reward to anyone who returns his transistor radio. B brings the radio to A.

(3) A bus goes along the street. This is an offer on the part of the transport enterprise to carry passengers at the published fares. The offer is accepted when a person gets on the bus with the intention of becoming a passenger.

An offer may be made to a definite person, to the world at large, or to some definite class of persons. An offer to a definite person can only be accepted by that person and by no one else. An offer to the world at large can be accepted by anyone. Examples (2) and (3) above are illustrations of this. An offer to some definite class can only be accepted by a member of that class.

Carbolic Smoke Ball Co. offered by way of reward £100 to anyone who contracted influenza after using their smoke ball as prescribed; the offer stated that they had lodged £1,000 with "the Alliance Bank, Regent Street, showing our sincerity in this matter." Mrs. Carlill used the smoke ball as prescribed but, notwithstanding, contracted influenza. She claimed £100. *Held*, the company was bound to pay. The company raised four defences. (1) that this was an offer made to the public; on this point Bowen L.J. said: "Why should not an offer be made to all the world which is to ripen into a contract with anybody who comes forward and performs the condition?" (2) that the promise of £100 was merely an advertising puff not intended to create legal relations; the court rejected this argument on the ground that the company had declared it had lodged £1,000 to meet its obligations. (3) that Mrs. Carlill had not notified the company of her acceptance; the court rejected this contention on the ground that if the offeror expressly or impliedly intimated in his offer that it would be sufficient to act on his offer without communicating acceptance to him, performance of that condition was a sufficient acceptance without notification. (4) that the promise to pay £100 was not supported by consideration; this argument failed because, in the judgment of the court, the inconvenience of applying the smoke ball to one's nostrils as prescribed was sufficient consideration: *Carlill* v. *Carbolic Smoke Ball Co.* [1893] 1 Q.B. 256.

All offers must be communicated

All offers must be communicated to the offeree before they can be accepted. The offeree cannot accept an offer unless he knows of its existence, because he cannot accept it without intending to do so, and he cannot intend to accept an offer of which he is ignorant. If A offers by advertisement a reward of £5 to anyone who returns his transistor radio, and B, finding the radio, brings it to A without having heard of the offer of the reward, he is not entitled to the £5.

An offer is only made when it actually reaches the offeree and not when it would have reached him in the ordinary course of post.

A, by letter dated September 2, offered goods to B "receiving your answer in course of post." The letter was misdirected and did not reach B until the 5th, when the offer was immediately accepted. The acceptance reached A on the 9th, but on the 8th A sold the goods to X. *Held*, there was a good contract between A and B, because the offer was immediately accepted on its receipt by B: *Adams* v. *Linsdell* (1818) 1 B. & Ald. 681.

However, if the date of the letter or other facts, *e.g.* the date of the postmark, had given the offeree warning that there was an unforeseen delay in transmission, the decision would probably have been different.

Lapse of offer

An offer lapses—

1. On the death either of the offeror or the offeree before acceptance. Death after acceptance does not affect the obligations arising from a contract unless they are of a personal nature.

K offered to redeem certain annuities payable to V on payment of £6,000 and sent a draft deed of release to V's solicitors. V, who lived in Holland, executed the release on January 12 and died on January 17, but her death was not known to her solicitors in London until January 31. On January 24 V's solicitors told K of V's acceptance of the offer and K paid them £6,000. In an action to recover the money paid, *held*, (1) the offer lapsed by the death of V before the communication of the acceptance on January 24; (2) V's death revoked the authority of her solicitors to notify her acceptance to K: *Kennedy* v. *Thomassen* [1929] 1 Ch. 426.

2. By non-acceptance within the time prescribed for acceptance by the offeror.

3. When no time for acceptance is prescribed, by non-acceptance

within a reasonable time. What is a reasonable time depends on the nature of the contract and the circumstances of the case.

On June 8, M offered to take shares in the R Company. He heard nothing until November 23, when he received a letter of acceptance. M refused to take the shares. *Held*, M was entitled to refuse, as his offer had lapsed before November 23 and so could not be accepted: *Ramsgate Victoria Hotel Co.* v. *Montefiore* (1866) L.R. 1 Ex. 109.

The reason why the offer lapses is that the offeree is regarded as having refused it if he has not accepted it within a reasonable time. If the offeree indicates within a reasonable time that he accepts the offer but sends a formal letter of acceptance later, the offeror cannot claim that his offer has lapsed by effluxion of time.

A council offered school premises for sale by tender. On August 26, 1964 a company submitted a tender offering to buy the premises. On September 15, 1964 the council replied accepting the company's offer. Various formalities had to be complied with, and on January 7, 1965 the council posted a formal letter of acceptance but on the same day the company sent the council a letter withdrawing the offer. *Held*, the contract of sale was concluded on September 15, 1964. In the alternative, if it was not concluded on that date, it was still open to acceptance, and had been validly accepted, on January 7, 1965: *Manchester Diocesan Council for Education* v. *Commercial & General Investments Ltd.* [1970] 1 W.L.R. 241.

Revocation of offer

An offer may be revoked in accordance with the following rules—

1. An offer may be revoked at any time before acceptance.[1]

There is, however, a statutory exception to this rule, when an application for shares in or debentures of a company is made in pursuance of a prospectus issued generally. Such an application cannot be revoked until after the third day after the opening of the subscription lists (Companies Act 1948, s. 50 (5)).

An offer is irrevocable after acceptance.

2. Revocation does not take effect until it is actually communicated to the offeree. Communication for this purpose means that the revocation must actually have reached the offeree.

---

[1] If the offer is made in an international sale to which the Uniform Law on the Formation of Contracts for the International Sale of Goods applies, the offer is binding if:
(1) made for a fixed time, or
(2) otherwise indicating that it is firm or irrevocable:
Uniform Laws on International Sales Act 1967, Sched. 2, Art. 5 (2); see p. 264, *post*.

A by letter of October 1 offered to sell goods to B in New York. B received the offer on the 11th and immediately telegraphed his acceptance. On the 8th, A wrote revoking his offer, and this was received by B on the 20th. *Held*, the revocation was of no effect until it reached B, and a contract was made when B telegraphed: *Byrne* v. *Van Tienhoven* (1880) 5 C.P.D. 344.

F handed to H a written option on some property at £750. The next day F posted a withdrawal of the offer. This was posted between 12 and 1 and did not reach H until after 5 p.m. In the meantime H at 3.50 p.m. had posted an acceptance. *Held*, (1) although the offer was not made by post, yet the parties must have contemplated the post as a mode of communicating the acceptance; (2) F's revocation was of no effect until it actually reached H and did not operate from the time of posting it; (3) a binding contract was made on the posting of H's acceptance: *Henthorn* v. *Fraser* [1892] 2 Ch. 27.

The communication need not have been made by the offeror. It is enough that the offeree learns of the revocation from a source which he believes to be reliable.

X agreed to sell property to Y by a document which stated "this offer to be left over until Friday, 9 a.m." On the Thursday X contracted to sell the property to Z. Y heard of this from B, and on Friday at 7 a.m. he delivered to X an acceptance of his offer. *Held*, Y could not accept X's offer after he knew it had been revoked by the sale of the property to Z: *Dickinson* v. *Dodds* (1876) 2 Ch.D. 463.

3. Apart from international sales to which the Uniform Laws on International Sales Act 1967 applies (see p. 262 n., *ante*), if the offeror agrees to keep his offer open for a specified time, he may nevertheless revoke it before the expiration of that time, unless—

(a) the offer has in the meantime been accepted before notice of revocation has reached the offeree; or

(b) there is consideration for keeping the offer open.

Rejection of offer

An offer is rejected—

1. If the offeree communicates his rejection to the offeror.

2. If the assent of the offeree is qualified or is subject to conditions. In that case the assent constitutes the rejection of the original offer, combined with a counter-offer (see below, under "Acceptance must be absolute and unqualified," p. 14, *post*).

THE ACCEPTANCE

Acceptance only possible if offer still in force

The acceptance must be made while the offer is still in force, and before the offer has lapsed, been revoked or rejected.

Once the acceptance is complete, the offer has become irrevocable.

Acceptance must be absolute and unqualified

Only an absolute and unqualified assent to all the terms of the offer constitutes an effective acceptance. If the offer requires the offeree to promise to do or pay something, the acceptance must conform exactly to the offer; if the offer requires an act to be done, the precise act and nothing else must be done. If the "acceptance" varies the terms of the offer it is a counter-offer, and not an acceptance of the original offer.[2]

M offered land to N at £280. N replied accepting, and enclosing £80 with a promise to pay the balance by monthly instalments of £50 each. *Held,* no contract, as there was not an unqualified acceptance: *Neale* v. *Merrett* [1930] W.N. 189.

N, a Canadian company, negotiated with F, of North Wales, for the purchase of an amphibian aircraft. F sent the following telegram: "Confirming sale to you Grummond Mallard aircraft . . . Please remit £5,000. . . ." N replied: "This is to confirm your cable and my purchase Grummond Mallard aircraft terms set out your cable. . . . £5,000 sterling forwarded your bank to be held in trust for your account pending delivery. . . . Please confirm delivery to be made thirty days within this date." *Held,* N's telegram was not an acceptance of F's offer because it introduced two new terms, one as to payment because F had asked for £5,000 to be paid in advance and N offered this sum to be released by the bank on delivery; and another as to the time of delivery which, according to F's offer, was a reasonable time but, according to N's purported acceptance, was within thirty days. N's telegram was a counter-offer which had not been accepted by F. No contract: *Northland Airliners Ltd.* v. *Dennis Ferranti Meters Ltd., The Times,* October 23, 1970.

A conditional acceptance is not an acceptance.

---

[2] If the offer is made in an international sale to which the Uniform Law on the Formation of Contracts for the International Sale of Goods applies, an acceptance which contains additional or different terms that do not materially alter the offer constitutes a valid acceptance with the proposed modifications, unless promptly objected to by the offeror: Uniform Laws on International Sales Act 1967, Sched. 2, Art. 7 (2); see p. 264, *post.*

Communication of acceptance

Here two cases have to be distinguished— *Silence*

1. On principle, an unexpressed acceptance or an unmanifested assent to an offer does not result in a contract. The acceptance must be communicated in writing, by words or by conduct. What constitutes communication of an acceptance will be considered in the following sections; it will be seen that different rules apply to the communication of an acceptance in instantaneous contracts and in contracts by post.

F offered by letter to buy his nephew's horse for £30, saying "If I hear no more about him, I shall consider the horse is mine at £30." The nephew did not reply, but he told the auctioneer who was selling his horses not to sell that particular horse because it was sold to his uncle. The auctioneer inadvertently sold the horse. *Held*, F had no claim against the auctioneer because the horse had not been sold to him, his offer of £30 not having been accepted: *Felthouse* v. *Bindley* (1862) 11 C.B.(N.S.) 869.

If the offeror prescribes or indicates a particular method of acceptance and the acceptor accepts in that way, there will be a contract, even though the offeror does not know of the acceptance. If, for example, the offeror requires the offeree to accept by advertisement in a particular column of a certain newspaper, the acceptance will be communicated when the advertisement is published, whether or not the offeror reads it.

Failure to accept in the prescribed method may mean there is no contract.

X, of London, offers Y, of New York, some shares, the acceptance to be by telex. Y accepts by airmail letter. That acceptance would be insufficient because it did not comply with the terms of the offer.

But if the offeror prescribes only acceptance within a stated time, and not by a particular method, only the time requirement has to be complied with; thus, a request for acceptance "by return of post" relates only to the time, but not to the method, of acceptance and the offer may be accepted by telegram or by verbal message: *Tinn* v. *Hoffman & Co.* (1873) 29 L.T. 271.

2. If, however, the offer is one which is to be accepted by being acted upon, no communication of the intention to accept is necessary, unless communication is stipulated for in the offer itself. If an offer of reward is made for finding a lost dog, the offer is accepted by

finding the dog, and it is unnecessary before beginning to search for the dog to give notice of acceptance of the offer.

Carlill v. *Carbolic Smoke Ball Co.* [1893] 1 Q.B. 256; on p. 10, *ante.*

Acceptance

The basic principle is that a statement addressed by one party to another is effective in law only if **communicated** to him. That principle applies to acceptances in the same manner as to offers, notices and other statements.

"Communication" means that the addressee must have been able to take notice of the statement in question. If it is in writing and has reached the addressee, the statement is duly communicated, even if for one reason or another he has not read it.

A distinction is drawn between an acceptance in an instantaneous contract and one in a contract by post.

Acceptance in instantaneous contracts

In the case of instantaneous communications, namely, communications between parties present, or communications by telephone or telex, the contract is complete only when the acceptance is received by the offeror and not merely when transmitted (*Entores Ltd.* v. *Miles Far East Corpn.* [1955] 2 Q.B. 327).

Where, according to the terms of the contract, a party is entitled to withdraw from the contract if the other party fails to make punctual payment, the notice of withdrawal, if given by telex, is effective when received by the party in default (*The Brimnes* [1975] Q.B. 929).

Acceptance in contracts by post

Where contracts are made by letter, telegram or cable they are said to be made by post. In such a case it depends on the intention of the parties whether the general rules for the communication of a statement shall apply, *i.e.* whether the postal acceptance shall be communicated to the offeror, or whether the mere posting of such an acceptance, and not its arrival at the address of the offeror, shall be sufficient.[3] Normally the intention of the parties will be that an

[3] If the acceptance by post is made in an international sale to which the Uniform Law on the Formation of Contracts for the International Sale of Goods applies, mere posting is not sufficient but the acceptance must be communicated to the offeror: Uniform Laws on International Sales Act 1967, Sched. 2. Art. 6 (1); see p. 264, *post.*

acceptance by post shall be duly communicated to the offeror, but in exceptional circumstances it can be inferred from the terms of the offer that the mere posting of the acceptance shall be sufficient.

Dr. Hughes gave Holwell Securities an option on his house. The option agreement stated that "the said option shall be exercisable by notice in writing to the intending vendor." Holwell Securities posted a letter to Dr. Hughes purporting to exercise the option but that letter never arrived. *Held*, the option was not duly exercised because the parties had not dispensed with the communication of the notice whereby it was exercised: *Holwell Securities Ltd.* v. *Hughes* [1974] 1 W.L.R. 155.

Exceptional circumstances in which the parties have contemplated that the post may be used can be inferred even if the offer itself was not made by post. If the parties have admitted an acceptance by posting, it is complete as soon as the letter of acceptance is posted, prepaid and properly addressed, whether it reaches the offeror or not; if the letter is lost or delayed in the post the contract is nevertheless made although the offeror may be quite ignorant of that fact.

G applied for shares in a company. A letter of allotment was posted but never reached G. *Held*, G was a shareholder in the company: *Household Fire Insurance Co.* v. *Grant* (1879) 4 Ex.D. 216.

But if the acceptance, instead of being properly posted, is handed to a postman to post, the contract is not complete until the acceptance is actually received by the offeror (*Re London and Northern Bank* [1900] 1 Ch. 220).

Acceptance subject to contract

An acceptance subject to contract means that the parties do not intend to be bound until a formal contract is prepared and signed by them.

C and D signed an agreement for the purchase of a house by D "subject to a proper contract" to be prepared by C's solicitors. A contract was prepared by C's solicitors and approved by D's solicitors, but D refused to sign it. *Held*, there was no contract as the agreement was only conditional: *Chillingworth* v. *Esche* [1924] 1 Ch. 97.

Unless there is an agreement to the contrary, the contract is made either when the formal contract is signed by both parties or, if each party is to sign a separate counterpart of the contract, when the separate counterparts so signed are exchanged. If the exchange is to be made by post, the contract is not concluded before the later of the two counterparts is posted.

B sold a house to E "subject to contract." The contract was agreed
between the solicitors, and the parties were ready to exchange the counterparts. E signed his part and posted it to B, but B did not post his part.
Held, no contract: *Eccles* v. *Bryant* [1948] Ch. 93.

The words "subject to" do not in all cases indicate that the parties
do not intend to be bound until the event referred to has happened.
While normally the phrase "subject to the purchaser obtaining a
satisfactory mortgage" indicates that there is no binding contract
because that term is too uncertain to give it a practical meaning
(*Lee-Parker* v. *Izzet* (No. 2) [1972] 1 W.L.R. 775), exceptionally a
similar phrase has been interpreted by the court as meaning that the
purchaser cannot withhold his satisfaction unreasonably and that
there is already a binding contract (*Janmohamed* v. *Hassam*, *The
Times*, June 11, 1976).

An acceptance subject to an identified contract already in existence makes a contract.

A house was offered for sale by auction, but not sold. Later, X
wrote to Y offering £350 and saying that if this offer was accepted he
would "sign contract on auction particulars." Y accepted the offer
"subject to contract as agreed." *Held*, X was bound by the auction
particulars although he did not sign them: *Filby* v. *Hounsell* [1896]
2 Ch. 737.

An agreement subject to contract must be distinguished from an
agreement between the offeror and the offeree which is only to
become effective on the approval of a third party, as where X agrees
to sell and Y to buy a piece of land subject to Z's approval. Here,
there is a binding contract from which neither X nor Y can withdraw
until Z approves or disapproves within the time stated in the contract
or within a reasonable time.

SOME SPECIAL CASES

Options

An option is a conditional contract to do something. For
example, A, the owner of a piece of land, may, in consideration of
£100, give B an option to buy the land within six months at a certain
price. An option is only binding on the person giving it, if it is
supported by consideration or expressed in a deed.

In the example just given, there are two contracts. The first is the
option agreement whereby A *allows B to buy* the land within the time

and upon the terms stated in that contract; if A purports to revoke the option, B can nevertheless exercise it and compel A to sell the land to him. The second is the contract whereby B actually *buys* the land from A; that contract is conditional upon B exercising the option granted him in the first contract.

An option has been described as a **unilateral contract** because it imposes only an obligation on the promisor but the promisee is not bound and will never be bound if he fails to exercise the option. If the promisee exercises it, a **synallagmatic contract,** *i.e.* a contract whereby each party undertakes obligations to the other, is constituted and both parties are bound. The option must be exercised within the time stated therein; if no time is stated, a condition is implied that it has to be exercised within a reasonable time (*United Dominions Trust (Commercial) Ltd.* v. *Eagle Aircraft Services Ltd.* [1968] 1 W.L.R. 74, see p. 280, *post*).

The notice to exercise the option must be communicated to the person who granted the option (*Holwell Securities Ltd.* v. *Hughes* [1974] 1 W.L.R. 155, see p. 17, *ante*).

Tenders

A tender is an offer. The acceptance of a tender has different legal results, depending on the terms of tender which are accepted. Examples of these different types of tender are as follows—

1. The accepted tender may result in a contract by which the buyer undertakes to buy all the goods in the tender from the tenderer.

Example—A requires 1,000 tons of coal. He invites tenders and B's tender is accepted. There is then a contract for the sale of 1,000 tons of coal from B to A.

2. The accepted tender may result in a standing offer to supply goods as and when required by the buyer. When the buyer gives an order there is a contract.

A railway company invited tenders for such iron articles as they might require for a year. W tendered and his tender was accepted. Orders were given and supplied for some time, but during the currency of the tender, W refused to execute an order given. *Held*, as W's tender had been accepted he could not refuse to supply goods within the terms of the tender: *G.N. Ry.* v. *Whitham* (1873) L.R. 9 C.P. 16.

If the buyer gives no order or does not order the full quantity of goods set out in the tender, there is no breach of contract.

P signed a tender addressed to the London County Council (L.C.C.) agreeing, on acceptance, to supply all the goods specified in the schedule to the extent ordered and in any quantity. Quantities were set out in the schedule and stated to be those estimated as the probable requirements for the period of the contract. P's tender was accepted, but the L.C.C. did not order the estimated amounts. P claimed he was entitled to supply goods to the full amount in the schedule. *Held*, the L.C.C. were under no obligation to order any goods, but that P was bound to deliver goods as and when they were ordered: *Percival Ltd.* v. *L.C.C.* (1918) 87 L.J.K.B. 677.

3. The buyer may not be bound to take any specified quantity, but bound to buy all the goods he needs. Such a contract is broken if the buyer does need some of the goods and does not take them from the tenderer.

Example—X invites tenders for his usual requirements of certain goods, and agrees to take his requirements from the person whose tender is accepted. If Y's tender is accepted, X must order all goods of the stated kind he requires from Y, but if he requires none there is no breach of contract. X's "requirements" means what he needs in his own business, and Y is not obliged to supply X with goods for resale: *Kier* v. *Whitehead Iron Co.* [1938] 1 All E.R. 591.

Rewards

It has already been observed that the offer of a reward is accepted by acting upon the offer and that prior notice of acceptance is not required (see pp. 15–16, *ante*). The offer of a reward, like an option, is a unilateral contract.

On the other hand, where the act for which the reward is promised is done in ignorance of the promise of the reward, the latter cannot be claimed because there can be no acceptance without knowledge of the offer.

The Government of Western Australia offered a reward of £1,000 for information leading to the arrest and conviction of the murderers of two police officers. C saw the offer but forgot it and later gave the necessary information. *Held*, C was not entitled to the reward: *R.* v. *Clarke* (1927) 40 C.L.R. 227 (an Australian case).

THE AGREEMENT

When offer and acceptance correspond in every respect, the parties have reached agreement, or, as it is said, there is *consensus ad idem* (consent on the same [points]). A valid contract has come into existence, provided that the other requirements set out on p. 1, *ante*, are present.

The terms of the contract are, thus, settled by the parties them-selves in their agreement, within the law. This is called **the doctrine of freedom of contract.**

Sometimes, however, it is not easy to determine whether nego-tiations between the parties resulted in an agreement.

Agreement to agree in future

If the parties have not agreed upon the terms of their contract but have made an agreement to agree in future, there may be no contract. There cannot be a contract to make a contract, if there is a material term of the future contract which is not agreed, expressly or by implication. The terms must be "definite or capable of being made definite without further agreement of the parties."

O agreed to buy from S a motor-van giving another van in part-exchange. The contract provided "This order is given on the under-standing that the balance of the purchase price can be had on hire-purchase terms over a period of two years." *Held*, no contract, as the words "on hire-purchase terms" were too vague to be given a definite meaning: *Scammel* v. *Ouston* [1941] A.C. 251.

Tolaini, who wanted to develop a site in Hertfordshire, agreed with Courtney, a company of building contractors, that Courtney would introduce them to persons providing the necessary finance, upon the understanding that they would employ Courtney as their building con-tractors. Tolaini were to instruct their quantity surveyor "to negotiate fair and reasonable contract sums" with Courtney. Negotiations took place but broke down and Tolaini placed the contract with another firm of builders. *Held*, in a building contract the price was of such fundamental importance that there was no contract unless it was agreed by the parties or there was an agreed method of ascertaining it, independent of negotiations between the parties: *Courtney & Fairbairn Ltd.* v. *Tolaini Brothers (Hotels) Ltd.* [1975] 1 W.L.R. 297.

The contract may contain machinery for ascertaining the terms of the future contract, and then there is a binding contract. Such machinery may be provided either by allowing the court to fill the gap in the contract or by giving an arbitration tribunal power to do so (*Sweet & Maxwell Ltd.* v. *Universal News Services Ltd.* [1964] Q.B. 699).

F sold land to a motor company for the purposes of their business. The sale was subject to an agreement that the company should buy all their petrol from F at a price to be agreed by the parties from time to time, and that any dispute should be submitted to arbitration. The price was never agreed, and the company refused to buy from F. *Held*, there was a binding contract to buy petrol of reasonable quality at a reasonable price to be determined in case of dispute by arbitration: *Foley* v. *Classique Coaches Ltd.* [1934] 2 K.B. 1.

S agreed to supply F with broiler chicken for five years. The contract provided that S should supply 30,000 to 80,000 chicken per week during the first year but failed to specify the number of chicken to be delivered in the second and subsequent years. The contract contained a clause according to which any difference between the parties as regards performance should be referred to an arbitrator. *Held*, as far as the supply of chicken for the second and subsequent years was concerned, the contract was binding because the number of chicken to be delivered could be ascertained by arbitration: *F. & G. Sykes (Wessex) Ltd.* v. *Fine Fare Ltd.* [1966] 2 Lloyd's Rep. 205.

Further, the modern tendency is for the courts to uphold a contract freely negotiated and intended to be binding, whenever they can give business efficacy to it, and not to hold it void for uncertainty. Thus a clause that there should be "suitable arbitration" is not void on the ground that it is too vague (*Hobbs Padgett & Co. (Reinsurance) Ltd.* v. *J. C. Kirkland* [1969] 2 Lloyd's Rep. 547, see p. 544, *post*). Also, an agreement by which a person was given the first option of purchasing certain land "at a figure to be agreed" has been held not to be void for uncertainty because the vendor, if desirous to sell the land, would have to offer it to the person to whom the option was given at a price at which he was bona fide willing to sell it (*Smith* v. *Morgan* [1971] 1 W.L.R. 803).

Meaningless terms

There is a distinction between a term which has yet to be agreed and a term which has no meaning. A meaningless term can be disregarded.

N ordered 3,000 tons of steel bars at £45 14s. 5d. a ton from S. S accepted and wrote, "I assume that the usual conditions of acceptance will apply." There were no usual conditions of acceptance. *Held*, a binding contract: *Nicolene Ltd.* v. *Simmonds* [1953] 1 Q.B. 543.

If, however, upon the proper construction of the contract, it can be said that the parties have attributed a common meaning and intention to a clause which, on its face, is meaningless, the courts will give effect to the intention of the parties and uphold the clause. 'Thus, the insertion of the phrase "also Paramount Clause" into a charterparty is not meaningless but imports the Hague Rules relating to Bills of Lading into the charterparty (*Nea Agrex S.A.* v. *Baltic Shipping Co. Ltd.* [1976] Q.B. 933.

The parties attached to a charterparty a typed slip stating: "Paramount Clause. This bill of lading shall have effect subject to the Carriage of Goods by Sea Act of the United States . . . 1936, which shall be incorporated herein." The Act provided in section 5 that it should not be applicable to charterparties. *Held*, that according to the common meaning and intention of the parties the words "bill of lading" on the slip meant "charterparty," and that the Act of 1936, so far as regulating the rights and liabilities of the parties, was incorporated into the charterparty, but that section 5 of the Act was to be disregarded as meaningless: *Adamastos Shipping Co. Ltd.* v. *Anglo-Saxon Petroleum Co. Ltd.* [1959] A.C. 133.

A clause providing for "suitable arbitration" is not meaningless; its meaning is explained on p. 544, *post*.

SELECT BIBLIOGRAPHY

Books

	Treitel	*Cheshire & Fifoot*
Invitation to make an offer	7–11	26–32
Offer	7–12	26–32
Withdrawal of Offer	32–34	50–54
Lapse of Offer	35	55
Rejection of Offer	34	33–34
Acceptance	12–32	32–49
Tenders	11, 13	39–41
Rewards	26–30	47–49
Agreement	7–45	19–61

Article

Hudson, A. H., "Retraction of Letters of Acceptance" (1966) 82 L.Q.R. 169–173.

CHAPTER 3

TERMS OF THE CONTRACT

THE undertakings and promises contained in the contract are known as the **terms of the contract.** They have to be distinguished from **representations** which are made before the contract is entered into and are not intended to form an integral part of it.

The parties will usually state the terms which they consider material expressly in their contract and little difficulty exists to ascertain these **express terms.** Sometimes, however, they consider a term as so obvious that they fail to express it in their contract and in these cases it becomes necessary to imply a term in order to give efficacy to their contractual intention; these **implied terms** and in particular the stringent legal requirements for admitting such an implication are considered later, see p. 28, *post*.

In simple contractual undertakings the terms of the contract are classified into **conditions** and **warranties.** However, these categories are not exhaustive; there exist also terms which can be evaluated only in the light of the events that have actually occurred; these terms produce in some events the effect of a broken condition and in others that of a broken warranty; they are referred to as **complex terms** or intermediate terms.

In modern commercial practice **standard contract forms** are often used. They are of two types. They may be **model contracts** aimed at the simplification and standardisation of contract terms; here the parties are free to alter the suggested terms of contract and to adapt them to their requirements; model contract forms are used particularly frequently in the commodity trade. The other type of standard contracts are **contracts of adhesion** which are imposed by the economically stronger party on the weaker party and place before him the choice to take it or leave it; these terms make a mockery of the principle of freedom of contracting because they are not open to negotiation.

Contracts sometimes contain **exemption clauses** by which a party, who proposes the contract, seeks to obtain exemption from some or all liabilities imposed on him by the common law. These exemption clauses have attracted the attention of the legislator and the courts and will be discussed later, see p. 29, *post*.

Conditions and warranties

A condition is a vital term of a contract, going to the root of the contract, a breach of which entitles the injured party, if he is so minded, to rescind the contract and to claim damages for non-performance. It is defined by Fletcher Moulton L.J. in *Wallis* v. *Pratt* [1910] 2 K.B. 1012 as an obligation "which goes so directly to the substance of the contract, or, in other words, is so essential to its very nature, that its non-performance may fairly be considered by the other party as a substantial failure to perform the contract at all."

Owners let their steamship *Mihalis Angelos* to charterers under a voyage charter for a voyage from Haiphong, North Vietnam, to Hamburg or another port in Europe. The cargo was to consist of the mineral apatite. The charterparty stated that the vessel was "now trading and expected ready to load under this charter about July 1, 1965," and that, should the vessel not be ready for loading on July 20, the charterers had the option of cancelling the contract of charterparty. In June and July 1965, the transport of apatite from the mines of Haiphong was prevented by bombings of the U.S.A. Air Force. On July 17, 1965, the charterers cancelled the charterpolicy. The ship was delayed on her journey to Haiphong and could not have reached that port on or before July 20. The owners claimed damages from the charterers for repudiation of the charterparty. *Held*, (1) the clause that the ship was "ready to load" about July 1, 1965, was a condition and the charterers were entitled to cancel the contract on July 17 on the ground that that condition was broken; (2) even if the charterers had not been entitled to cancel on July 17 and by their repudiation of the charterparty had committed an anticipatory breach of contract, the owners would not have suffered a loss because the charterers would beyond doubt have cancelled on July 20: *Maredelanto Compania Naviera S.A.* v. *Bergbau-Handel GmbH; The Mihalis Angelos* [1971] 1 Q.B. 164.

A warranty is not a vital term in a contract, but one which is merely subsidiary, a breach of which gives no right to rescind but only an action for damages for the loss which he has suffered. It may be made orally or in writing. It is described in the Sale of Goods Act 1893 as an agreement "collateral to the main purpose of " the contract, and by Fletcher Moulton L.J. in *Wallis* v. *Pratt* as an "obligation which, though it must be performed, is not so vital that a failure to perform it goes to the substance of the contract."

B agreed to sing for G, the director of the Italian Opera in England, during certain dates and to arrive in London six days before the commencement of the engagement for rehearsals. He arrived only two days before, and G thereupon refused to be bound by the contract. *Held*, the stipulation was not a condition, and the contract could not be rescinded on its breach: *Bettini* v. *Gye* (1876) 1 Q.B.D. 183.

Whether a term in a contract is a warranty or condition is a question of the intention of the parties to be deduced from the circumstances of the case. The use by the parties of the terms "warranty" and "condition" is not conclusive of their meaning. Thus, the term "condition" may be used as a lawyer's term of art or in its common meaning as simply denoting a stipulation, and when ascertaining what meaning the parties intended to give to that term, a reasonable meaning should be attributed to it (*Wickman Machine Tool Sales Ltd.* v. *L. Schuler A.G.* [1972] 1 W.L.R. 840). In the Marine Insurance Act 1906 the term "warranty" is used as meaning what is here described as a "condition."

Complex terms

Complex or intermediate terms combine the nature of a condition and a warranty in so far as in some events the breach of such undertaking may entitle the innocent party to rescind the contract and in other events the breach entitles him only to claim damages but does not entitle him to rescind the contract. These terms can only occur in synallagmatic contracts, *i.e.* contracts in which each party undertakes obligations to the other (*per* Diplock L.J. in *United Dominions Trust (Commercial) Ltd.* v. *Eagle Aircraft Services Ltd.* [1968] 1 W.L.R. 74, 82; see p. 19, *ante*).

An illustration of a complex term is, *e.g.* the shipowner's undertaking in a charterparty to provide a seaworthy ship; "it can be broken by the presence of trivial defects easily and rapidly remediable as well as by defects which must inevitably result in total loss of the vessel": Diplock L.J. in *Hongkong Fir Shipping Co. Ltd.* v. *Kawasaki Kisen Kaisha Ltd.* [1962] 2 Q.B. 26. The unseaworthiness of the ship may, according to the nature of the defect, go to the root of the contract and then entitles the charterer to rescind the contract, or it may be of such trivial consequence that the charterer has to abide by the contract and can only claim damages if he has suffered a loss. Although the Sale of Goods Act 1893 distinguishes between conditions and warranties, the principle embodied in the *Hongkong*

Fir Shipping Co. Ltd. case applies to contracts for the sale of goods just as to all other contracts; consequently, the term in a contract of sale that "shipment to be made in good condition" can be interpreted as not referring to a condition within the meaning of that Act, nor as a warranty strictly called, but may be one of those intermediate stipulations which gives the buyer no right to reject the goods unless the breach goes to the root of the contract: *Cehave N.V.* v. *Bremer Handelsgesellschaft mbh; The Hans Nord* [1976] Q.B. 44, see p. 234 *post*.

Even if the breach of contract is merely due to the negligence of a party, the event resulting from that breach might be so serious that it deprives the other party of substantially the whole benefit of the contract and makes the breach a fundamental breach of contract; in such a case one has likewise to consider the ensuing event rather than the nature of the breach: *Harbutt's "Plasticine" Ltd.* v. *Wayne Tank and Pump Co. Ltd.* [1970] 1 Q.B. 447, 211, 472; see pp. 34–35, *post*.

Collateral contracts of warranty

It happens sometimes that a party (X) is induced by an undertaking of another (Y) to enter into a contract with a third party (Z). X, a customer, may decide to acquire on hire-purchase a second-hand car from Y, a car dealer, relying on Y's warranty that the car is in good working order. Y will then sell the car outright to a finance company (Z) which will enter into a hire-purchase contract with X (p. 279, *post*). Here there are two contracts: the contract of hire-purchase between X and Z, and a collateral contract of warranty between X and Y; if the car is not in good working order, X can claim damages from Y for breach of the collateral contract.

B negotiated with the defendants for the purchase of a second-hand car described by the defendants to be in perfect condition and good "for thousands of trouble-free miles." In reliance on this statement B decided to buy the car on hire-purchase terms. The defendants sold it outright to a finance company which granted B hire-purchase terms. The car was not in a satisfactory condition. *Held*, that B had a claim in damages against the defendants for breach of the collateral contract of warranty: *Brown* v. *Sheen & Richmond Car Sales Ltd.* [1950] 1 All E.R. 1102 (similar: *Andrews* v. *Hopkinson* [1957] 1 Q.B. 229).

W. chrysanthemum growers, were assured by the defendants that B.W. sand supplied by them would conform to a certain analysis and, consequently, be suitable for propagation of chrysanthemum. W then requested H, a firm dealing in builders' material, to purchase B.W. sand from the defendants and to resell it to them. The sand was unsuitable for the propagation of chrysanthemum. *Held*, that W were entitled to damages from the defendants for breach of the defendants' undertaking that the sand was suitable: *Wells (Merstham) Ltd.* v. *Buckland Sand & Silica Ltd.* [1965] 2 Q.B. 170 (similar: *Shanklin Pier Ltd.* v. *Detel Products Ltd.* [1951] 2 K.B. 854).

Esso Petroleum sought to find a tenant for a new petrol service station in Southport. The local manager of Esso, who had 40 years' experience in the petrol trade, induced Mr. Mardon to become tenant by representing that the estimated annual consumption would be 200,000 gallons. This estimate was erroneous because the planning authority had not allowed the pumps to face the main street, but it had never been revised. The actual throughput in the first 15 months was only 78,000 gallons. Mr. Mardon who had sunk all his capital in the business suffered heavy loss. *Held*, the statement as to the potential throughput was a collateral warranty whereby Mr. Mardon was induced to enter into the contract of becoming tenant of the petrol station. In addition, Esso were liable under the rule in *Hedley Byrne & Co. Ltd* v. *Heller and Partners Ltd.* (see p. 75, *post*). Mr. Mardon recovered damages: *Esso Petroleum Co. Ltd.* v. *Mardon* [1976] Q.B. 801. (The Misrepresentation Act 1967 (see pp. 75, 82, *post*) was not in force at the relevant time.)

The correct measure of damages as between a hirer under a hire-purchase agreement and a dealer whose warranty has induced him to enter into the agreement with the finance company is the whole damage suffered by the hirer, including his liability under the contract with the finance company, and is not limited to the difference in value between the goods as warranted and as in fact they are: *Yeoman Credit Ltd.* v. *Odgers* [1962] 1 W.L.R. 215.

Implied terms

It may be presumed that the parties to a contract have expressed in it every material term and accordingly that there is no necessity to imply additional terms. A term will be implied, however, if it is necessary to carry out the presumed intention of the parties and is so obvious that the parties must have intended it to apply to the contract and therefore thought that it was unnecessary to express it. The term's implication must be *necessary* to give that efficacy to the contract which the parties intended: *The Moorcock, post*.

The owner of *The Moorcock* agreed with the defendant wharfingers that his vessel should be discharged and loaded at their wharf and for that purpose should be moored at a jetty which belonged to the wharfingers and extended into the river Thames. When the tide ebbed and the vessel took the ground, it struck a ridge of rock and was damaged: *Held*, the contract contained an implied undertaking on the part of the wharfingers that it was reasonably safe for the vessel to be berthed at the jetty: *The Moorcock*, (1889) 14 P.D. 64.

M agreed to buy from C a house which was in course of erection by C. *Held*, there was an implied warranty that the house should be built in a workman-like manner and of proper materials and should be fit for habitation: *Miller* v. *Cannon Hill Estates Ltd.* [1931] 2 K.B. 113.

A term will not be implied merely because it would be reasonable to imply it, contracts being made by the parties themselves and not by the courts. An implied term cannot override an express term.

In some instances, in the interest of consumer protection, statutory terms implied by enactments cannot be excluded by agreement of the parties. Provisions prohibiting the exclusion of statutory implied terms are contained in the Supply of Goods (Implied Terms) Act 1973, with respect to terms implied by the Sale of Goods Act 1893 into contracts of sale (see p. 241, *post*) and, by the 1973 Act, into contracts of hire-purchase (see p. 283, *post*).

EXEMPTION CLAUSES

It follows from the doctrine of freedom of contract that the parties, on principle, may agree that in certain contingencies one of them shall be exempt from the liability imposed by the law. This rule is, however, subject to qualifications required by public policy or statute law. Thus, a term exempting a party from liability in the event of his committing a fraud against the other party to the contract is void because it infringes public policy. Further, the Supply of Goods (Implied Terms) Act 1973 prohibits certain exemption clauses in consumer sales and restricts them in other sales (see p. 241, *post*) and also prohibits certain exemption clauses in some hire-purchase transactions (see p. 283, *post*). Also, a carrier by sea cannot contract out of the liability imposed by the Carriage of Goods by Sea Act 1924 because that statute prohibits it (see p. 462, *post*).

The courts do not favour exemption clauses in contracts, although they have to respect the liberty of the parties to agree on their own contract terms.

Written contracts containing exemption clauses

Written contracts may contain exemption clauses although the offeree is ignorant of them. Tickets issued by railway and bus companies, cloakroom tickets and many contracts set out in printed documents contain numerous terms, of many of which the party receiving the document is ignorant. If a passenger on a train receives a ticket on the face of which is printed "this ticket is issued subject to the by-laws, regulations and conditions contained in the publications and notices of and applicable to British Railways," the regulations and conditions referred to are deemed to be communicated to him, and he is bound by them whether or not he has read them.

T, who could not read, took an excursion ticket on the railway. On the front of the ticket was printed "for conditions see back," and on the back was printed that the ticket was issued subject to the conditions in the time-tables. The time-table could be purchased and only one was available at the booking-office. T did not read the conditions or attempt to buy a time-table. One of the conditions was that the railway company would not be liable for personal injuries to passengers. T was injured in a railway accident, and the jury found that reasonable steps had not been taken to bring the conditions to T's notice. *Held*, T was bound by the conditions as there was no evidence on which the jury could arrive at their finding. That there might have been difficulty in getting a time-table was immaterial: *Thompson* v. *L.M. & S. Ry.* [1930] 1 K.B. 41.

If, however, it can be shown that—
1. the offeree did not know that the document contained the terms of the contract, and
2. reasonable notice of them was not given to him,

he will not be bound by the terms.

R booked her passage on a ship and received a ticket folded so that no writing was visible until it was opened. On the ticket was printed "this ticket is issued and accepted upon the following conditions," one condition being that the shipowners' liability for loss was limited to $100. R knew there was printing on the ticket, but did not know that the printing contained conditions relating to the contract. *Held*, R was not bound by the conditions as she did not know of their existence, and, having regard to the smallness of the type in which they were printed, the failure to call attention to them, and the stamping of red ink across them, the shipowners had not given reasonable notice of them: *Richardson* v. *Rowntree* [1894] A.C. 217.

M arranged for his car to be taken in D's ferry from Islay, in the Hebrides, to the mainland. The contract was made orally without anything being said about exemption of D from liability for the car, but on previous occasions M had been given on conclusion of the contract a note stating that the carriage was at owner's risk. Owing to the negligence of D's servants, the ferry sank and the car was lost. *Held*, that the exemption clause in the previous contracts could not be imported into the present oral contract and D could not rely on the (previous) exemption clause: *McCutcheon* v. *David Macbrayne Ltd.* [1964] 1 W.L.R. 125.

When there is a business document given by one party and received by the other as the document containing the terms of the contract, the offeror is under no obligation to call the offeree's attention to all the terms of the document, unless the terms are printed in such a manner or are in such a position as to mislead a reasonably careful business man.

R ordered four lots of timber from N's traveller. The traveller left a sold note setting out the sale and containing a clause "Goods are sold subject to their being on hand and at liberty when the order reaches the head office." N did not deliver the timber, and, on being sued by R, pleaded the clause set out above. R did not know of the clause and had not read it. *Held*, R was bound by the clause, unless it was so printed that from its position in the document and the size of the type an ordinary careful business man, reading the document with reasonable care, might miss it: *Roe* v. *R. A. Naylor Ltd.* [1971] 1 K.B. 712.

When the offeree has signified his acceptance by signing a document presented by the offeror, the offeree cannot plead ignorance of the terms of the offer, in the absence of fraud or misrepresentation, even if he is in fact ignorant of them.

The proprietress of a café bought an automatic cigarette vending machine from the defendants. She signed a document which contained a number of clauses in small print, amongst them a clause excluding "any express or implied condition statement or warranty, statutory or otherwise, not stated therein." She refused to pay the price on the ground that the machine did not work and contended *inter alia*, that she was not bound by the exclusion clause as she had not read it. *Held*, the clause was binding on her: *L'Estrange* v. *F. Graucob Ltd.* [1934] 2 K.B. 394.

If the contractual document is signed as a result of the offeree's oral misrepresentation of one of its terms, the offeree will not be able to rely on that term.

C took a dress to D to be cleaned and was asked to sign a receipt which contained, among other terms, a clause, "This article is accepted on condition that the company is not liable for any damage howsoever arising." C asked why she had to sign and was told that D would not accept liability for damage to beads or sequins. She then signed. The dress was returned stained. *Held*, D could not rely on the clause, because C's signature was obtained by misrepresentation of the effect of the document: *Curtis* v. *Chemical Cleaning & Dyeing Co.* [1951] 1 K.B. 805.

Similarly, if at the time when the contract is made a person gives an oral promise which cannot be reconciled with a term in the printed contract, the oral promise takes priority over the printed clause.

M left his car in N's garage. Contrary to the rules of the garage, the car attendant who took the car over told M he must not lock the car. M informed the attendant that there was valuable property in the car and the attendant promised to lock the car after he had moved it. By the terms of the ticket which the attendant gave M, N excluded responsibility for the loss of contents of the car. A suitcase containing valuables was stolen from the car. *Held*, N was liable. Though the attendant had no *actual* authority to promise to lock the car, he had *ostensible* authority to make a statement concerning the safety of the car and its contents. The printed exclusion clause was repugnant to the express oral promise and could not be relied upon by N: *Mendelsohn* v. *Normand Ltd.* [1970] 1 Q.B. 177.

Where printed conditions in a contract are repugnant to a binding oral promise they do not provide exemption from liability for breach of that promise: *J. Evans & Son (Portsmouth) Ltd.* v. *Andrea Merzario Ltd.* [1976] 1 W.L.R. 1078 (see p. 36, *post*).

Oral contracts containing exemption clauses

An exemption clause may likewise be contained in an oral contract but the person who wishes to rely on the clause must prove strictly that the other party had clear notice of the clause when entering into the contract. Denning L.J. observed in *Olley* v. *Marlborough Court Ltd.* (p. 33, *post*): "The best way of proving it is by a written document signed by the party to be bound. Another way is by handing him before or at the time of the contract a written notice specifying its terms and making it clear to him that the contract is on those terms. A prominent public notice which is plain for him to see when he makes the contract or an express oral stipulation would, no doubt, have the same effect. But nothing short of one of these three ways will suffice."

Interpretation of exemption clauses

When interpreting exemption clauses, the courts "lean against them," *i.e.* will allow a party to escape from his liability under it only if the words of the clause are perfectly clear, effective and precise.

An exemption clause cannot be introduced into the contract unilaterally after it is made

Thus, a hotel proprietor who contracts at the reception desk to accommodate a guest cannot rely on an exemption clause displayed in a bedroom and stating that the proprietor shall not be responsible for articles stolen unless handed to him for safe custody.

The plaintiff and her husband took a room in a residential hotel owned by the defendants. At the reception desk they were asked to pay a week in advance. They did so and went to their bedroom in which a notice was displayed stating that the proprietors did not hold themselves responsible for the loss or theft of articles unless handed to the manageress for safe keeping. Owing to the negligence of the defendants' personnel, a stranger gained entrance into the hotel and stole articles from the plaintiff's room when she was absent. *Held*, the defendants were liable. The contract was concluded at the reception desk and the terms of the notice in the bedroom were not incorporated in it: *Olley* v. *Marlborough Court Ltd.* [1949] 1 K.B. 532.

Similarly, an attempt to introduce an exemption clause in a receipt would not make it a term of the contract and is not binding on the person who receives it.

C hired a chair from the council, paid for it and was given a ticket which he put in his pocket unread. The chair collapsed and C was injured. The ticket had a clause that the council were not to be liable for accidents or damage. *Held*, this was not binding on C: *Chapelton* v. *Barry U.D.C.* [1940] 1 K.B. 532.

Thornton wished to park his car in a multi-story automatic car park belonging to the defendants. A traffic light at the entrance of the car park showed red. A ticket was extruded from a machine. When Thornton took the ticket the light turned green and the car was taken up. When Thornton collected the car, an accident occurred and Thornton was injured. The defendants pleaded that the ticket contained a notice in small print that it was issued "subject to the conditions of issue as displayed on the premises," and that these conditions, displayed inside the garage, contained a clause exempting the defendants from liability for personal injury. Thornton had not read the small print. *Held*, the exempting clause in the conditions did not protect the defendants. (1) Lord Denning M.R. held that the contract was concluded when Thornton positioned his car at the appointed place and the light turned green, and the ticket was only a receipt which could not alter the terms of the contract; (2) all three judges of the Court of Appeal agreed that the defendants had failed sufficiently to bring to the notice of Thornton the limitation of liability: *Thornton* v. *Shoe Lane Parking Ltd.* [1971] 2 Q.B. 163.

Effect of exemption clause

The doctrine of fundamental breach

A clause exempting a party from his common law liability is subject to the ordinary rules of construction of a contractual term. Normally it will have to be construed as not protecting a party who has committed a **fundamental breach of contract**, *e.g.* a party who, having sold a car for use on the road, delivers a car which is wholly unroadworthy. But, in some contracts, an exemption clause may have to be construed as applying even to a case of fundamental breach, namely when the language of the clause is sufficiently clear to indicate an intention of the parties that it shall apply in that contingency. These rules of construction were developed by the House of Lords in *Suisse Atlantique Société d'Armement Maritime S.A.* v. *N.V. Rotterdamsche Kolen Centrale* (see pp. 35–36, *post*).

In the following cases the rule of construction was applied that a party who was guilty of a fundamental breach was not intended to be protected by the exemption clause.

Wallis wished to buy a second-hand Buick car which was in excellent condition. Arrangements were made with a finance company which had never seen the car and Wallis entered into a hire-purchase contract with the finance company; the contract provided that no condition or warranty was given that the car was roadworthy. The former owner brought the car to Wallis at night and when Wallis inspected it he found that it had been towed to his premises, parts were missing and the engine was so defective that the car would not go. Wallis refused to accept the car. Karsales to whom the finance company had assigned its rights sued Wallis, relying on the exemption clause. *Held*, that the plaintiffs could not rely on the exemption clause which could not be construed as covering the case of fundamental breach that had occurred here, namely that the car would not go at all: *Karsales (Harrow) Ltd.* v. *Wallis* [1956] 1 W.L.R. 936.

A bought a new motor cycle from F, a hire-purchase company. The contract provided that the cycle was supplied "subject to no conditions whatsoever express or implied" and "not . . . subject to any condition that the same is fit for any particular purpose." The cycle was seriously defective and these defects could not be remedied in the factory; they made the cycle unroadworthy. *Held*, the series of defects in their accumulation constituted a fundamental breach. A was entitled to repudiate the contract and F could not rely on the exemption clauses: *Farnworth Finance Facilities Ltd.* v. *Attryde* [1970] 1 W.L.R. 1053.

W contracted to design and install equipment in H's factory for storing and dispensing heavy wax which had to be liquefied under heat for manufacturing purposes. The contract provided that the total liability of W in case of direct damage to H's property should be limited to the value of the contract which was £2,330. Owing to W's negligence, a wholly unsuitable heating system was installed and switched on without supervision. The heating system burst into flames and the whole factory of H burnt down. *Held,* W were in fundamental breach, having regard to the quality and consequences of their breach of contract (applying the *Hong Kong Fir* principle, see p. 26, *ante*). Consequently, the clause limiting W's liability did not apply and they were liable for the whole loss which amounted to £151,420: *Harbutt's "Plasticine" Ltd.* v. *Wayne Tank and Pump Co. Ltd.* [1970] 1 Q.B. 447.

See also *Alexander* v. *Railway Executive* [1951] 2 All E.R. 442 (p. 375, *post*).

While in the preceding cases, as a matter of construction of the contract, the court held that the exemption clause was not intended to protect a party guilty of fundamental breach, "it cannot be said as a matter of law that the resources of the English language are so limited that it is impossible to devise an exclusion clause which will apply to at least some cases of fundamental breach. . . ." (*per* Lord Reid in *Suisse Atlantique, post*). This is particularly true if the contract under review is not a contract of adhesion (see p. 24, *ante*) but a carefully negotiated contract between parties of equal bargaining power, although even in this case the exemption clause does not apply if the quality and consequences of the breach are so grave that the parties cannot have intended the guilty party to rely on it in the events which have happened; this is demonstrated by *Harbutt's "Plasticine"* (*ante*). In *Suisse Atlantique* (*post*) the House of Lords held, in fact, that no fundamental breach had occurred and that the demurrage clause in the charterparty which it had to consider was not an exemption clause at all but was a clause stating only the calculation of agreed damages in the event of delay in loading and unloading of the chartered ship, but as the effect of fundamental breach had been argued exhaustively before the House, it used the opportunity to express its views on this important problem.

Charterers agreed to charter the m.v. *Silvretta* "for a total of two years consecutive voyages" between the East Coast of the United States of America and Europe. A demurrage of 1,000 dollars a day was provided in the charterparty for excess of the lay time allowed for loading and unloading. The vessel made eight round voyages. The owners claimed that six to nine more voyages could have been made if the charterers had loaded and discharged the vessel with reasonable dispatch and that, the charterers being in fundamental breach, they could recover damages in excess of the stipulated demurrage. *Held,* where delay was due to detention of the vessel on loading or unloading, the demurrage payments were the only damages recoverable: *Suisse Atlantique Société d'Armement Maritime S.A.* v. *Rotterdamsche Kolen Centrale* [1967] 1 A.C. 361.

Where the breach of contract is not deliberate but is due to an honest, though negligent, error, it will normally not constitute a fundamental breach of contract.

D, garage proprietors, excluded their liability for negligent loss or misdelivery of garaged cars. D handed over H's car to a fraudulent person who told D that H had asked him to collect the car. *Held*, D was protected by the exemption clause. The misdelivery was not a fundamental breach of contract as it was not deliberate but due to an honest, though negligent mistake: *Hollins* v. *J. Davy Ltd.* [1963] 1 Q.B. 844.

Exemption clauses repugnant to main object of contract

Further, if an exemption clause is **repugnant to the main object** and intent of the contract, it is invalid.

A clause in a bill of lading absolving a carrier from liability if he delivered the goods to a person unable to produce a bill of lading would be repugnant to the main object of the contract of carriage by sea: *Sze Hai Tong Bank Ltd.* v. *Rambler Cycle Co. Ltd.* [1959] A.C. 576.

The plaintiffs contracted with the defendants, road hauliers, that the latter should carry a load of copper wire from London to Glasgow. The transport manager of the defendants, without knowledge or consent of the plaintiffs, sub-contracted the carriage to a man who telephoned, giving the name of a non-existing firm. No adequate check was made of the man's credentials and he disappeared with the copper wire. *Held*, (1) the defendants were not entitled to sub-contract without consent of the plaintiffs, and (2) even if they were entitled to sub-contract, the manner of sub-contracting amounted to a deliberate interference, without justification, with the plaintiffs' rights and constituted a fundamental breach of contract and a conversion of the goods: *Garnham, Harris & Elton Ltd.* v. *Alfred W. Ellis (Transport) Ltd.* [1967] 1 W.L.R. 940.

Merzario, a freight forwarder, gave Evans, one of his customers, an oral promise that a container carrying an injection moulding machine would be shipped below deck on a voyage from Italy to England. Owing to an oversight, the container was shipped on deck and lost when the ship encountered a swell. Merzario contended that the printed terms and conditions exempted him from liability. *Held*, (1) the oral promise amounted to an enforceable contractual promise, and (2) the oral promise overrode the printed conditions: *J. Evans & Son (Portsmouth) Ltd.* v. *Andrea Merzario Ltd.* [1976] 1 W.L.R. 1078.

SELECT BIBLIOGRAPHY

Books

Terms of Contracts	Treitel	Cheshire & Fifoot
Express Terms	120–128	113–121
Implied Terms	128–135	121–135
Exemption Clauses	137–165	144–169
Proposals for Reform	166–167	—
Breach of Condition	537–542	135–144
Breach of Warranty	537–542	135–144

Articles

Burrows, J. F., "Contractual Co-operation and the Implied Term" (1968) 31 M.L.R. 390–407.

Coote, B., "Exception Clauses—Three Aspects" [1972] C.L.J. 53–58.

Dawson, F., "Fundamental Breach of Contract" (1975) 91 L.Q.R. 380–405.

Drake, C. D., "Fundamentalism in Contract" (1967) 30 M.L.R. 531–546.

Egan, B., "Standard Contracts" [1968] J.B.L. 204–212.

Greig, D. W., "Condition—Or Warranty?" (1973) 89 L.Q.R. 93–106.

Jenkins, D., "The Essence of Contract" [1969] C.L.J. 251–272.

Johnston, K. F. A., "More Exemptions, Not Less" [1967] J.B.L. 133–138.

Legh-Jones, P. N. and Pickering, M. A., "Harbutt's Plasticine Ltd. *v.* Wayne Tank and Pump Co. Ltd." (1970) 86 L.Q.R. 513.

Legh-Jones, P. N. and Pickering, M. A., "Fundamental Breach: The Aftermath of Harbutt's Plasticine" (1971) 87 L.Q.R. 515–531.

Spencer, J. R., "Signature, Consent and the Rule in L'Estrange *v.* Graucob" [1973] C.L.J. 104–122.

Treitel, G. H., "Exclusion Clauses—Possible Reform" [1967] J.B.L. 200–209, 334–345.

Treitel, G. H., "Fundamental Breach" (1966) 29 M.L.R. 546–556.

CHAPTER 4

FORM OF CONTRACT

CONTRACTS are of two kinds, namely **contracts under seal** and **simple contracts.** A fundamental difference exists between these two types of contract: all simple contracts require **consideration** (see p. 42, *post*) but no consideration is required for contracts under seal.

The expression "simple contracts" is a technical legal phrase denoting contracts requiring consideration. Simple contracts include **contracts which require a writing,** either for their validity or as evidence, and **oral contracts,** *i.e.* contracts which can be made by word of mouth.

Further, circumstances might exist in which a party has enriched himself unjustly at the expense of another and it appears to be appropriate to afford the latter a right to restitution. These cases cannot be classified under the category of contract because the element of consent is manifestly absent, nor do they fall under the heading of tort or trust. They are known as **quasi-contracts** and will also be considered in this chapter.

Consequently, the subject-matter of this chapter will be treated under four headings:

1. contracts under seal;
2. contracts which require a writing;
3. consideration; and
4. quasi-contracts.

CONTRACTS UNDER SEAL

A contract under seal, also called a deed or a specialty contract, is a contract which is in writing and is signed, sealed and delivered.

In modern practice the formal requirements of a deed are treated with some laxity. The seal is usually affixed before execution; it may be printed or written on the document, often surrounded by a circle, or it may consist of a small wafer which can be purchased from a stationer. The deed must be signed by the party intending to be bound by it; this is provided by the Law of Property Act 1925, s. 73. The deed is regarded as delivered if the grantor intends unconditionally to be bound by it, even if he retains the document in his actual possession; physical delivery is no longer required. A deed takes effect from the date when it is delivered in the legal sense just explained.

A deed is known as an **escrow** when it is delivered subject to a condition, or until a certain time has elapsed, and it then takes effect only on the fulfilment of that condition or the expiration of that time. A document delivered as an escrow cannot be recalled by the person who executed it while the condition on which it depends has not been discharged (*Beesly* v. *Hallwood Estates Ltd.* [1961] Ch. 105), and he is bound when the condition is fulfilled (*Vincent* v. *Premo Enterprises (Voucher Sales) Ltd.* [1969] 2 Q.B. 609).

The following must be made under seal—

1. Contracts made without consideration.
2. Conveyances of the legal estate in land or any interest in land, including leases of land for more than three years.
3. A transfer of a British ship, or any share therein.

A right of action under a contract under seal is barred in twelve years, while a similar right under a simple contract is barred in six years; see p. 148, *post*.

CONTRACTS WHICH REQUIRE A WRITING

In some cases the contract itself must be expressed in a writing and would be invalid if not contained in a written document.

In other cases the contract is perfectly valid if made orally but if a dispute arises and it is necessary to prove its existence or contents in court, on principle at least only written evidence of the contract and its terms is admitted.

Contracts required to be in writing

The following contracts are only valid if in writing—

1. Bills of exchange and promissory notes (Chaps. 19 and 20, *post*).
2. Contracts of marine insurance (Chap. 24, *post*).
3. Bills of sale (p. 382, *post*).
4. Acknowledgments of statute-barred debts (p. 150, *post*).
5. Further, hire-purchase contracts, credit sales or conditional sales governed by the Hire-Purchase Act 1965 are not normally

enforceable by the owner unless they are in writing and have been signed by the hirer or buyer and by, or on behalf of, all other parties to the agreement (Chap. 16, *post*). Further, the Consumer Credit Act 1974, s. 60, provides that regulated agreement shall satisfy the form prescribed by regulations made by the Secretary of State. Such regulations which will be made by statutory instrument, have not been issued to date (November 15, 1976) but, when issued, are likely to require the written form for all regulated agreements.

6. A person is not liable to pay for an entry relating to him in a directory unless he, or his agent, has signed an order complying with the requirements of the Unsolicited Goods and Services Acts 1971 and 1975.

Contracts required to be evidenced by a note or memorandum in writing

Certain contracts are only enforceable if they can be proved by written evidence. The meaning of an unenforceable contract is explained on p. 63, *post*. The written evidence must satisfy the requirements of the statutes postulating this method of proof. The contracts falling into this category are—

1. Contracts of guarantee (Statute of Frauds 1677, s. 4).
2. Contracts for the sale or other disposition of land or any interest in land (Law of Property Act 1925, s. 40).

A **contract of employment** need not be in writing nor need it be evidenced by a writing but the Contract of Employment Act 1972 provides that an employer must give his employees written particulars of the main terms of employment, if the contract is not in writing (see p. 168, *post*).

The Statute of Frauds 1677

The Statute of Frauds 1677, s. 4, provided originally that no action could be brought in respect of five types of contracts unless the contract was evidenced by a note or memorandum in writing signed by the party to be charged or his agent. By the Law of Property Act 1925, the provisions of the Statute of Frauds relating to contracts for the sale or other disposition of land or any interest therein were repealed and re-enacted in section 40 of the Act of 1925, and by the Law Reform (Enforcement of Contracts) Act

1954 the other cases except that of contracts of guarantee were repealed. Today the Statute of Frauds applies only to the contract of guarantee, defined by the statute as "any special promise to answer for the debt, default or miscarriage of another person." The contract of guarantee must be distinguished from the contract of indemnity which need not be evidenced by a note or memorandum in writing. The distinction is explained on p. 384, *post*.

The note or memorandum in writing required by the Statute of Frauds and the Law of Property Act

The following rules apply to the note or memorandum required by the Statute of Frauds 1677 and the Law of Property Act 1925 as evidence of the contract—

1. It need not be made at the time of the formation of the contract, but may be made at any time before action is brought. This is because the memorandum is not the contract itself, but merely evidence of it, the contract being good but unenforceable in the absence of writing.

2. It must contain the names of the parties or a sufficient description of them.

3. The subject-matter must be described so that it can be identified, and all material terms of the contract must be stated.

4. The consideration must appear, except in contracts of guarantee. In the latter case section 3 of the Mercantile Law Amendment Act 1856 dispenses with the necessity for setting out the consideration in writing, although it must be present.

5. It may be comprised in several documents, but they must be connected on the face of them. The correspondence between the solicitors of the parties containing the essential terms of the oral agreement may be a good "note or memorandum in writing" (*Law v. Jones* [1974] Ch. 112).

6. It must be signed by the party to be charged or his agent. It is only the party against whom the contract is being enforced who need sign. The signature may be printed or stamped and may be at the beginning, middle or end of the document.

If there is no memorandum the contract cannot be enforced except in certain cases where there has been **part performance**. This exception relates almost entirely to contracts for the sale and leasing of land.

CONSIDERATION

Definition

Consideration is some benefit received by a party who gives a promise or performs an act, or some detriment suffered by a party who receives a promise. It may also be defined as "that which is actually given or accepted in return for a promise." It was defined by the court in *Currie* v. *Misa* (1875) L.R. 10 Ex. 153 as "some right, interest, profit or benefit accruing to one party, or some forbearance, detriment, loss, or responsibility given, suffered or undertaken by the other," but to this definition there should be added that the benefit accruing or the detriment sustained was in return for a promise given or received.

Examples—(1) A receives £5 in return for which he promises to deliver goods to B. Here, the money A receives is consideration for the promise he makes to deliver the goods.

(2) C promises to deliver goods to D, and D promises to pay for the goods when they are delivered. Here, the benefit C receives is D's promise to pay, and in return for it he promises to deliver the goods.

(3) X lends a book to Y and Y promises to return it. Here, the advantage is entirely on Y's side, but X suffers a detriment in parting with his book, and this is consideration to support Y's promise to return it.

Executed and executory consideration

When the act constituting the consideration is completely performed the consideration is said to be executed. In example (1) above, the payment by B to A is an executed consideration. When the consideration takes the form of a promise to be performed in the future, it is executory. In example (2), the consideration is executory. An executed consideration is therefore an *act* done by one party in exchange for a promise made or act done by the other; an executory consideration is a *promise* made by one party in exchange for a promise made or act done by the other.

General rules on consideration

Consideration required for all simple contracts

Consideration is necessary for the validity of every contract not under seal. Even contracts in writing require it. "A promise without consideration is a gift; one made for consideration is a bargain."

✗ *Consideration must be of some value but need not be adequate*

Consideration need not be adequate or equivalent to the promise, but it must be of some value. It is a matter for the parties themselves to determine what they consider is the proper value of their acts or promises. If the courts were to embark on an inquiry as to the adequacy of the consideration in all contracts which came before them, their task would be endless. If, for example, X engages Y as his clerk at a salary of £50 a week it would be a difficult, if not impossible, task in most cases for the courts to ascertain whether the salary was adequate to Y's work, or whether Y's services were worth the salary. In all cases, therefore, the courts only concern themselves with the presence of consideration, and assume that the parties themselves have attended to its value.

A promised to pay certain bills if B would hand over a guarantee to him. B handed the guarantee over and it turned out to be unenforceable. *Held*, as A had received what he asked for, there was consideration for his promise, although the guarantee was of smaller value than he had supposed: *Haigh* v. *Brooks* (1839) 10 A. & E. 309.

Inadequacy of consideration may be evidence of fraud.

✗ *A promise to perform an existing obligation is not sufficient consideration, but a promise to do something different is good consideration.*

Payment of a smaller sum of money is not a satisfaction of an agreement to pay a larger sum, even though the creditor agrees to take it in full discharge. If A owes B £100, and B agrees to take £75, there is no consideration for the forgiveness of £25.

Mrs. Beer obtained a judgment against Dr. Foakes for £2,090. Dr. Foakes asked for time to pay and the parties agreed that Mrs. Beer would not "take any proceedings whatsoever on the judgment" if Dr. Foakes paid that amount in stated instalments. After Dr. Foakes had paid off the debt, Mrs. Beer sued him on the judgment for interest. Dr. Foakes pleaded the agreement but Mrs. Beer replied that her promise to forego interest was not supported by consideration. *Held*, she was entitled to recover interest: *Foakes* v. *Beer* (1889) 9 App. Cas. 605.

The practical effect of this remarkable rule is considerably reduced by the following—

(a) An agreement without consideration intended to create legal relations, which to the knowledge of the promisor has been acted on by the promisee, although it cannot be enforced, is binding on the promisor so that he will not be allowed to act inconsistently with it.

In 1937 C let to H a block of flats for ninety-nine years at £2,500 a year. In 1940, owing to war, very few flats were let and C agreed to reduce the rent to £1,250. In 1945, C sued for arrears of rent at the rate of £2,500. *Held*, as the agreement for the reduction of rent had been acted upon C could not claim the full rent, but that it was only operative during the conditions which had given rise to it. As the flats had been fully let in 1945 the full rent was payable from then: *Central London Property Trust* v. *High Trees House* [1947] K.B. 130.

On the other hand, in these circumstances the creditor is not bound by his acceptance of the smaller sum if his agreement was obtained in an inequitable manner.

D, builders, had a claim for £482 against R. R's wife, knowing that D were in financial difficulties, offered £300 in full settlement, adding that if D would not take that sum, they would get nothing. D accepted reluctantly. *Held*, that D could recover £182 as the debtor's wife had "held the creditor to ransom": *D & C Builders Ltd.* v. *Rees* [1966] 2 Q.B. 617.

(b) An agreement by the creditor to take something different in kind, as a bill of exchange, or a smaller sum paid before the larger becomes due, gives the debtor a good discharge. In this case the accord (agreement) is accompanied by satisfaction (consideration); on discharge of the contract by accord and satisfaction see p. 126, *post*.

Consequently, if X owes B £50, payable on June 1, his obligation will be legally discharged by an agreement on the part of B to take £40 on May 10.

When a debtor makes an agreement with his creditors to compound his debts, although he is satisfying a debt for a larger sum by the payment of a smaller, the consideration is the agreement by the creditors with each other, and with the debtor, not to insist upon their full claims (*Good* v. *Cheesman* (1831) 2 B. & Ad. 328).

If a person makes a claim upon another in good faith whether or not the claim is likely to succeed, the withdrawal of his claim is valuable consideration so as to support a promise to pay him money (*Callisher* v. *Bischoffsheim* (1870) L.R. 5 Q.B. 449). Similarly, if an action has been commenced by one who honestly believes he has a claim upon another, a compromise of that claim is made for valuable consideration.

On the other hand, an agreement to perform an existing obligation made with the person to whom the obligation is already owed, is not made for consideration. Thus, if C owes D £100, payable on December 1, and subsequently promises to pay it punctually if D will give him discount, there is no consideration for his promise, because he is already legally bound to pay it punctually. But if the promise is made to a stranger to the contract, there is consideration for the promise, because the promisor imposes a new obligation upon himself which can be enforced by the stranger.

A wrote to his nephew, B, promising to pay him an annuity of £150 in consideration of his marrying C. B was already engaged to marry C. On his marriage with C, *held*, the fulfilment of B's contract with C was consideration to support A's promise to pay the annuity: *Shadwell* v. *Shadwell* (1860) 9 C.B.(N.S.) 159.

Consideration must be legal

An illegal consideration makes the whole contract invalid.

Consideration must not be past

A past consideration is one which is wholly executed and finished before the promise is made. It must be distinguished from an executed consideration which is given at the time when the promise is made.

Examples—(a) X gives Y £50 and Y promises to go to Paris to transact some business for X. This is an executed consideration, since the promise to go to Paris is given at the time the £50 is handed over.

(b) Y, without any arrangement with X, goes to Paris and transacts some business for X. On his return, X promises to pay Y £50 for his services in Paris. This is a past consideration because Y's services have been rendered before X has agreed to accept and pay for them.

A sold a horse to B and, after the sale was completed, promised that the horse was free from vice. It was in fact vicious. *Held*, the previous sale was no consideration for the promise, which was therefore unenforceable: *Roscorla* v. *Thomas* (1842) 3 Q.B. 234.

If services are rendered under circumstances which raise an implication of a promise to pay for them, the subsequent promise to pay is merely the fixing of the price (*Stewart* v. *Casey* [1892] 1 Ch. 104). Accordingly, if in circumstances in which he may expect a remuneration (*e.g.* because he is a solicitor) Y at the request of X goes to Paris on X's business, but without any prior promise of remuneration from X, and on his return X promises to pay him £50, this will be regarded as the agreed price of Y's services which X had impliedly promised to pay before Y went to Paris.

Consideration must move from the promisee

This means that the person to whom the promise is made must furnish the consideration.

At a time when the law did not restrict resale price maintenance, Dunlop who were wholesale tyre manufacturers sold tyres to X under a contract whereby X agreed not to sell the tyres below Dunlop's list prices and, as Dunlop's agent, to obtain from other traders an agreement similar to that which he had entered into. X sold to Selfridge, who agreed with X not to sell below list prices. They broke this contract and Dunlop sued for its breach. *Held*, assuming that X was the agent of Dunlop when he obtained the price maintenance stipulation from Selfridge, Dunlop could not enforce the contract because no consideration moved from them: *Dunlop Pneumatic Tyre Co. Ltd.* v. *Selfridge & Co. Ltd.* [1915] A.C. 847.

This rule is based on the principle that a stranger to the contract cannot sue on it, a rule known as the doctrine of privity of contract (see p. 152, *post*). The rule in *Dunlop* v. *Selfridge* was reaffirmed by the House of Lords in *Scruttons Ltd.* v. *Midland Silicones Ltd.* [1962] A.C. 446, below.

In that case S, who were stevedores employed by a shipping company in the unloading of a cargo belonging to M as consignees, damaged the cargo, causing a loss of £593. In an action by M against S for that sum, S, who had been employed by the shipping company as independent contractors and not as agents, sought to rely on a clause in the contract of carriage (and stated in the bill of lading) whereby the liability of the carriers was limited. *Held*, S were strangers to the contract of carriage and could not rely on the clause limiting the liability.

It was again asserted by the House of Lords in *Beswick* v. *Beswick* (*post*), in spite of repeated determined attacks on it by Lord Denning M.R. who declared it to be a nineteenth-century innovation.

Peter, a coal merchant, entered into a written contract with his nephew John, whereby Peter sold his business to John. The contract provided that after the death of Peter the nephew should pay the widow (who was not a party to the agreement) an annuity of £5 a week. Peter died and the nephew refused to pay her. *Held*, (1) the widow was entitled to the amount as the administratrix of Peter's estate, (2) but she could not enforce the obligation in her personal capacity as she was not a party to the contract: *Beswick* v. *Beswick* [1968] A.C. 58.
Also *Snelling* v. *John G. Snelling Ltd.* [1973] Q.B. 87, see p. 3, *ante*.

Similarly,

When an employer takes out a personal accident group insurance covering his employees, the latter cannot sue the insurance company on the contract of insurance, since they are not a party to it: *Green* v. *Russell* [1959] 1 Q.B. 28.

The rule in *Dunlop* v. *Selfridge* is subject to a number of exceptions, some real and others apparent, in which an action by a stranger to the contract is admitted. The first two of the following are true exceptions, the others merely apparent exceptions.

(a) Under the Resale Prices Act 1976, s. 26, where goods are sold by a supplier subject to a price maintenance condition, which is not unlawful under the Act (see p. 327, *post*), that condition may be enforced by the supplier against any trader who, though not a party to the sale, subsequently acquired the goods, as if he had been a party to the sale. The section does not give the supplier a right of action against a person who acquires goods for consumption and not for resale.

However, where section 26 applies, the third person who acquired the goods must have done so with notice of the condition and for the purpose of resale.

The notice requirement of the section must be strictly construed. Its effect is that no trader should be in a worse position than if he had been a party to the original contract. Express notice of the actual terms and conditions to be enforced is required (*Goodyear Tyre & Rubber Co. (Great Britain) Ltd.* v. *Lancashire Batteries Ltd.* [1958] 1 W.L.R. 857).

(b) The Road Traffic Act 1972, s. 148(4) provides that in the case of compulsory third-party motor insurance persons specified in the motor insurance policy may sue the insurer directly although they are not parties to the contract of insurance (which is concluded between the car user and the insurer).

(c) In a contract made by an agent the principal (whether named or unnamed, see pp. 195–196, *post*) can sue on the contract; he is in fact the contracting party who acted through the instrumentality of the agent.

Thus, where a man arranges with a travel agent a family holiday for himself and the members of his family and the contract is broken because hotel accommodation is unsatisfactory, he can claim damages for discomfort suffered by himself and the members of his family because, as far as the latter are concerned, he contracted as their agent (*Jackson* v. *Horizon Holidays Ltd.* [1975] 1 W.L.R. 1468).

(d) If a contract constitutes a trust relationship under which a trust fund is created in the hands of one of the contracting parties in favour of a third party, the latter can sue the trustee in case of breach of trust.

X promised Y out of moneys he owed him to pay £500 to Z, Y's brother, and informed Z of this promise. Later X refused to pay and Z's action against him was successful on the ground that X held the £500 in a trust for Z. It was immaterial that the fund consisted merely of a monetary obligation and not of identifiable money: *Shamia* v. *Joory* [1958] 1 Q.B. 448.

The Married Women's Property Act 1882, s. 11, provides that if a man insures his own life for the benefit of his wife or children, the policy shall create a trust in favour of the persons therein named; a similar provision applies to a wife who insures her life for the benefit of the husband or children.

(e) The assignee of a debt or chose in action may in certain circumstances sue the original debtor (see p. 153, *post*).

(f) The holder of a negotiable instrument may sue the acceptor and all parties to the bill who became parties prior to the giving of consideration by him (see p. 340, *post*).

QUASI-CONTRACTS

When one person has been enriched at the expense of another under such circumstances as to call for restitution. the law imposes an obligation on him to make repayment. Such cases are called quasi-contracts, because, although there is no contract or agreement between the parties, they are put in the same position as if there were a contract between them. The following are the principal cases of quasi-contracts—

Where one person has paid money for the use of another

This occurs when A pays money which B is liable to pay at the implied request of B, as where a tenant pays his landlord's rent to prevent a distress by a superior landlord, or where one person's goods are taken in execution for another's debt. In such cases there is an obligation on the party benefited to repay the amount paid for his benefit.

G imported skins from Russia and stored them in W's bonded warehouse. The skins were stolen without any negligence on W's part. After the theft, the customs demanded duty from W, which W were bound to pay. W paid and sued G for what they had paid. *Held*, G was liable as W had been compelled by law to pay money for which G was liable: *Brooks Wharf* v. *Goodman Bros.* [1937] 1 K.B. 534.

An account stated

This is an admission of indebtedness, from which the law may imply an undertaking to pay, *e.g.* an IOU. More correctly, it is where two parties in account with each other agree a balance. There is then a new contract by the party in debit to pay the balance, the consideration being the discharge of the items on each side of the account. An action can be brought on the account stated without going into all the transactions which led up to it.

Where money has been paid on a consideration which has wholly failed

If the consideration supporting a party's payment has totally failed, *i.e.* if he has received nothing at all for his money, he is entitled to recover his money. If *e.g.* X pays Y £300 for a colour television set but Y fails to supply the set, X can recover the £300 which he paid. An illustration of a claim for repayment on the ground of total failure of consideration is *Comptoir d'Achat* v. *Luis de Ridder* [1949] A.C. 293, see p. 267, *post*.

If the failure of consideration is not total but only partial, the quasi-contractual remedy is not available but the remedy is an action for damages for breach of contract.

Where money has been paid under a mistake of fact

Money paid under a mistake of fact can be recovered.

L was employed by the L.C.C. who agreed, on L's being called up for the R.A.F., to pay him the difference between his service pay and his civil wages. L agreed to inform the L.C.C. of any increase in his pay, but omitted to do so and in consequence was overpaid. *Held*, the overpayments could be recovered: *Larner* v. *L.C.C.* [1949] 2 K.B. 683.

Money paid under a mistake of law cannot be recovered.

M, an officer in the R.A.F., was entitled to a gratuity, the amount of which depended on the construction of certain regulations. H, an army agent and banker, mistook the meaning of the regulations, and credited M with a larger gratuity than he was entitled to. M did not know of the mistake and spent the money. *Held*, H could not recover the excess paid, as his mistake was not a mistake of fact: *Holt* v. *Markham* [1923] 1 K.B. 504.

A mistake as to the existence of a private right, such as a right of property, is a mistake of fact, but a mistake as to the construction of a contract is a mistake of law.

If the mistake of fact is induced by the fraud of a third person, the payment can nevertheless be recovered.

B owed W. & G. Ltd. £5,000 which he was unable to pay. He falsely represented to J that he was the agent of a motor company and induced J to pay him £5,000 as a deposit for the purchase of motor-cars. This payment was made by a cheque drawn by J in favour of W. & G. Ltd. who were represented by B as being interested in the motor company. B handed the cheque to W. & G. Ltd. in payment of his debt, and they received it in good faith and in ignorance of B's fraud. *Held*, J could recover the £5,000 from W. & G. Ltd. as money paid under a mistake of fact: *R. E. Jones Ltd.* v. *Waring & Gillow Ltd.* [1926] A.C 670.

Where money has been had and received by one party to the use of
    another

This occurs when one person has wrongfully obtained money to which another is entitled or when a servant or an agent obtains money from another by the use of his master's or his principal's property. In such cases, the law compels the payment of the money so obtained.

R, a sergeant in the Army, received large sums of money from M for sitting in uniform in the front of loaded lorries as they went through Cairo, so that the lorries were not inspected. *Held*, the Crown, as his employer, was entitled to the money, because R had obtained it by the use of his uniform and the opportunities and facilities attached to it: *Reading* v. *Att.-Gen.* [1951] A.C. 507.

It also occurs where a man's money is taken from him without his authority and is received by another, even in good faith and for value, who has notice of the want of authority.

P, B's sole executor, fraudulently drew cheques on the executor's banking account signed "P, executor of B, decd." L cashed them for P, who used the money for his own purposes. *Held*, L must have known of P's want of authority and must refund the amount of the cheques: *Nelson* v. *Larhold* [1948] 1 K.B. 339.

Quantum meruit claims

A claim on a *quantum meruit* is likewise of quasi-contractual nature, but it is convenient to consider claims falling under this heading later (see p. 145, *post*).

Where the equitable doctrine of specific restitution applies

Goods may be stolen and subsequently acquired by a purchaser acting in good faith, *i.e.* being unaware that he has acquired stolen property. If the purchaser, acting in good faith, improves the value of the goods by expending his money or labour and later the rightful owner asks for specific restitution of his property, equity requires that the owner shall recompense the purchaser for the improvement of the goods.

Mr. Bennett entrusted his Jaguar car which was worth £400 or £500 to Mr. Searle for repair which was to cost £85. Mr. Searle was a rogue who used the car for his own purposes and smashed it in a collision. Mr. Searle then sold the car in its damaged condition to Mr. Harper for £75 which was all it was worth in that state. Mr. Harper repaired the car and put it into good order, expending £226·47 for labour and material. Later Mr. Bennett claimed the car from Mr. Harper and the latter was prepared to return it to Mr. Bennett but claimed to be recompensed for the £226·47 spent on it. *Held*, Mr. Harper as innocent purchaser was entitled to recover the value of the improvements he had done to the car: *Greenwood* v. *Bennett* [1973] Q.B. 195.

SELECT BIBLIOGRAPHY

Books

	Treitel	Cheshire & Fifoot
Form of Contract	105–119	174–201
Consideration	46–96	62–101
Quasi-Contract	703–706	631–663

Articles

Chloros, A. G., "The Doctrine of Consideration and the Reform of the Law of Contract" (1968) 17 I.C.L.Q. 137–166.
Clarke, M., "Bankers Commercial Credits among High Trees" [1974] C.L.J. 260–292.

CHAPTER 5

CAPACITY TO CONTRACT

MINORS

A MINOR, as an infant is described in the Family Law Reform Act 1969, s. 12, is a person who has not reached the age of majority. That age was reduced from 21 to 18 years by the Act of 1969, s. 1. A person attains majority at the commencement of his eighteenth birthday (s. 9 (1) of the 1969 Act).

Contracts made by a minor may be—

✗1. binding during minority,
⟩2. voidable,
✗3. void, or
✗4. unenforceable against the minor both during and after minority. (On the difference between unenforceable, voidable and void contracts, see p. 63, *post*.)

Binding contracts

A minor is bound by contracts—

⟨ (a) for necessaries, and
(b) of educational character, if they are for his benefit.

✗ "A minor may bind himself to pay for his necessary meat, drink, apparel, necessary physic, and such other necessaries, and likewise for his good teaching and instruction, whereby he may profit himself afterwards" [Co.Litt. 172a].

Necessaries

The term "necessaries" is not restricted to things which are required to maintain a bare existence, such as bread and clothes, but includes articles which are reasonably necessary to the minor having regard to his station in life. A watch, for example, and such things as a transistor radio or a motor cycle may well be considered to be necessaries, but not articles of mere adornment and luxury. An engagement ring may be a necessary, but not a diamond necklace bought for the minor's fiancée. Goods are not the only necessaries. The hire of a car may be a contract for necessaries.

When the necessaries are goods, the minor is only liable when the goods are—

(i) suitable to his condition in life;
(ii) necessary to his requirements at the time of sale;
(iii) necessary to his requirements at the time of delivery (Sale of Goods Act 1893, s. 2); and
(iv) goods with which he was not sufficiently supplied at the time of sale and delivery.

A minor must pay a reasonable price for necessaries supplied to him. Although the goods supplied may be within the class of necessaries, they may not be necessary to the particular minor, because any of the four requirements set out above are not fulfilled.

I, a minor who was an undergraduate at Cambridge, bought eleven fancy waistcoats from N. He was at the time adequately provided with clothes. *Held*, the waistcoats were not necessaries, and I was not liable to pay for any of them: *Nash* v. *Inman* [1908] 2 K.B. 1.

Educational contracts for the minor's benefit

Not every contract for the benefit of a minor is binding on him. But contracts for his education, service or apprenticeship, or for enabling him to earn his living (other than trading contracts) are binding unless they are detrimental to the interests of the minor.

D, a minor who was a professional boxer, held a licence from the British Boxing Board, under the terms of which his money was to be stopped if he was disqualified. In a boxing match he was disqualified and the Board withheld the money. D sued to recover it. *Held*, the contract was for his benefit and was binding on him: *Doyle* v. *White City Stadium* [1935] 1 K.B. 110.

C, a minor aged 19, the son of a wealthy and world-famous comedian from whom he had become estranged, applied for National Assistance for himself, his wife and child. C signed a contract with publishers for the publication of his autobiography, which contract he later sought to avoid. *Held*, the contract was binding on the minor, for it was similar to a contract of service in that it would enable him to earn his living and support his family, and it was a contract for his benefit: *Chaplin* v. *Leslie Frewin* (*Publishers*) *Ltd.* [1966] Ch. 71.

A contract relating to the minor's education which is not detrimental to his interests can be enforced although it is to be performed in the future, *e.g.* a contract by a minor billiards player to tour and play billiards matches with a well-known expert (*Roberts* v. *Gray* [1913] 1 K.B. 520).

In these cases, if the contract as a whole is for the benefit of the minor it will be binding on him, although particular parts of it, such as a restrictive covenant not to compete with his employer, may be against his interests. If, however, the clauses in the agreement which are adverse to the minor's benefit are clearly severable from the rest, the minor will not be bound by the adverse clauses.

Similarly, an arbitration clause in an apprenticeship deed has been held to be for the minor's benefit and to be binding on him (*Slade* v. *Metrodent Ltd.* [1953] 2 Q.B. 112, see p. 541, *post*).

A contract of apprenticeship is a contract of special character. If it is broken by the master, the apprentice can claim damages not only for his loss of earnings for the remainder of his training period, but also for the diminution of his future prospects (*Dunk* v. *George Waller & Son Ltd.* [1970] 2 Q.B. 163).

When a minor is engaged in trade, contracts entered into by him in the way of his trade, however much for his benefit they may be, are not binding on him. He is therefore not liable to pay for goods bought for trading purposes, or, if he is a haulage contractor, for a motor-lorry obtained under a hire-purchase agreement (*Mercantile Union Guarantee Corp. Ltd.* v. *Ball* [1937] 2 K.B. 498).

Voidable contracts

When a minor acquires an interest in a subject of a permanent nature, which imposes a continuous liability on him, the contract cannot be enforced against him during minority. But after he attains full age, it will be binding on him unless he avoids it within a reasonable time (*Edwards* v. *Carter* [1893] A.C. 360). Examples of these contracts are: leases, partnerships and the holding of shares in a company.

A fortnight before attaining his majority a minor took a lease of a flat. Three years later he was sued for current rent. *Held*, he was liable, as the lease was voidable, not void, and was binding on him unless repudiated within a reasonable time of attaining majority: *Davies* v. *Beynon-Harris* (1931) 47 T.L.R. 424.

A minor who was a partner in a partnership took no steps to avoid the partnership upon attaining his majority; he was held liable for the debts of the partnership incurred after he came of age (*Goode* v. *Harrison* (1821) 5 B. & Ald. 147).

Void contracts

The Infants Relief Act 1874, s. 1, enacts that all contracts, whether by specialty or by simple contract, entered into by minors—

(a) for the repayment of money lent or to be lent; or
(b) for goods supplied or to be supplied (other than contracts for necessaries); and
(c) all accounts stated with minors

shall be absolutely void. The Betting and Loans (Infants) Act 1892 renders void any agreement made by a person after he comes of age to pay a loan contracted during minority.

The effect of these statutes is to make absolutely void all the contracts set out above.

B, a minor, had an overdraft with the bank. X and Y guaranteed it. The bank sued X and Y for payment. *Held*, as the loan by the bank to B was void, X and Y could not be liable: *Coutts & Co.* v. *Browne-Lecky* [1947] K.B. 104.

Even if the minor has induced the other party to the contract to enter into it by fraudulently representing that he was of full age, he cannot be sued either in contract or in tort for fraud, because to allow the injured party to sue for fraud would be giving him an indirect means of enforcing the void contract.

S, a minor, by fraudulently representing himself to be of full age, induced L to lend him £400. He refused to repay it and L sued him for (a) fraudulent misrepresentation, or, alternatively, (b) money had and received to S's use. *Held*, the Infants Relief Act 1874 made the contract absolutely void, and S was not liable to repay the £400. The two claims by L were indirect ways of enforcing this void contract and they failed: *R. Leslie Ltd.* v. *Sheill* [1914] 3 K.B. 607.

Contracts falling under the Infants Relief Act 1874 cannot be ratified by the minor after full age, even though there is a fresh consideration for the ratification. This is the result of section 2 of the Act, according to which—

"No action shall be brought whereby to charge any person upon any promise made after full age, to pay any debt contracted during infancy, or upon any ratification made after full age, of any promise or contract made during infancy, whether there shall or shall not be any new consideration for such promise or ratification after full age."

K, during minority, became indebted to stockbrokers. After K attained his majority, the stockbrokers sued him for the debt and K compromised the action by accepting two bills for £50 each. In an action on the bills. *Held*, K was not liable, as the transaction amounted to a promise by K after full age to pay a debt contracted during minority: *Smith* v. *King* [1892] 2 Q.B. 543.

The minor may, however, make an entirely fresh contract after attaining full age. If it is a fresh contract based on a new offer and acceptance, and is not merely a ratification of the old contract, the new contract will be binding.

A minor is not liable on a cheque (*Hutley* v. *Peacock* (1913) 30 T.L.R. 42), but it is thought that he would be so liable if the cheque is given in performance of an obligation arising from a binding contract.

Recovery by and against the minor

If a minor has taken the benefit of a void contract for the sale of goods he cannot retain the goods and recover the money he has paid for them.

X, a minor, agreed with Y to become the tenant of a house and to pay £102 for the furniture therein. He paid £68 on account, and after occupying the house and using the furniture for some months, sued to recover the money he had paid. *Held*, he could not recover money paid for something he had used: *Valentini* v. *Canali* (1889) 24 Q.B.D. 166.

Money paid by a minor under a void contract can be recovered by him only if there has been a complete failure of consideration.

S, a minor, agreed to take 500 £1 shares in a company and paid 10s. on each share. She received no dividend on the shares. While still a minor she repudiated the contract and brought an action (1) to recover the money she had paid, and (2) for a declaration that she was not liable for future calls. *Held*, (1) as the shares had some market value S could not recover money already paid, but (2) was not liable for future calls: *Steinberg* v. *Scala* (*Leeds*) *Ltd.* [1923] 2 Ch. 452.

Similarly, if a minor delivers goods under a void contract he cannot recover them back unless there is a total failure of consideration. Inadequacy of consideration is not enough (*Pearce* v. *Brain* [1929] 2 K.B. 310).

If a minor by fraud obtains goods, but not money, he may be ordered by the court to return such of the goods as are in his possession and are unpaid for (*Stocks* v. *Wilson* [1913] 2 K.B. 235). Apparently, if he obtains goods without fraud and does not pay for

them, he cannot be compelled either to pay for them or to return
them. Similarly, if a minor who is a trader agrees to sell goods and
receives payment for them, he cannot be compelled to refund the
money or to deliver the goods in the absence of fraud (*Cowern* v.
Nield [1912] 2 K.B. 419).

Minor's liability in tort for acts committed in connection with contracts

It has already been seen that a minor who by fraudulent misrepresentation procured a contract void by virtue of the Infants
Relief Act 1874, s. 1, cannot be made liable in tort for the fraud
because this would be an indirect means of enforcing the void
contract (*R. Leslie Ltd.* v. *Sheill*; p. 55, *ante*).

Where the performance, and not the conclusion, of the contract
is in issue it is, however, sometimes possible to make a minor who
cannot be made liable in contract liable in tort. The test is whether
the act done by the minor was done in performance of the contract,
though wrongfully, or whether it was something never contemplated
by the contract at all.

A minor hired a mare and injured her through immoderate riding.
Held, he was not liable: *Jennings* v. *Rundall* (1799) 8 T.R. 335.

A minor hired a radio set and in breach of contract parted with
it to X. *Held*, he was liable, because his parting with the set was outside
the contract altogether: *Ballet* v. *Mingay* [1943] 1 K.B. 281.

CORPORATIONS

A corporation is an artificial person created by law. It is distinct
from the individual persons who are members of the corporation,
and has a legal existence separate and apart from them.

Salomon, a boot manufacturer, was the owner of a profitable business.
At a time when he and his business were perfectly solvent, he converted
his business into a company limited by shares. He took 20,000 shares and
his wife and five children took one each (at that time the minimum number
of shareholders in all companies was seven). No other shares were issued.
Salomon also received a debenture to the amount of £10,000 which was
secured by a charge on all the assets of the company. Later the company
became insolvent. *Held*, the debenture took priority over the unsecured
creditors. The "one man company" was a person different in law from
the controlling shareholder: *Salomon* v. *Salomon & Co. Ltd.* [1897]
A.C. 22.

A corporation may be (a) a body incorporated by royal charter;

(b) a company formed by special Act of Parliament; or (c) a company registered under the provisions of the Companies Acts 1948 to 1976.

Lifting the veil

In company law, in exceptional cases the veil of corporateness is lifted and the separate personality of the company is disregarded. Examples of these exceptions are:

(a) In some cases the legislature has lifted the veil, *e.g.* in requiring holding and subsidiary companies to prepare group accounts;
(b) if the controlling shareholder uses the company as his agent; or
(c) if the corporate form is abused for an unlawful or improper purpose.

Mr. Lipman agreed to sell some property to Mr. and Mrs. Jones. Mr. Lipman did not want to perform the contract and sold and transferred the property to a private company that was wholly owned and controlled by him. The purpose of that transaction was to defeat the purchasers' claim for specific performance. *Held*, the private company was a sham to avoid enforcement of the equitable remedy of specific performance and an order for specific performance was granted against Mr. Lipman and the private company: *Jones* v. *Lipman* [1962] 1 W.L.R. 832.

Contractual capacity of a corporation

The contractual capacity of a corporation is limited—

1. By natural possibility, *i.e.* by the fact that it is an artificial and not a natural person. A corporation can only contract through an agent, and therefore it cannot enter into any contract of a strictly personal nature. For example, it cannot be the treasurer of a friendly society (*Re West of England and South Wales District Bank* (1879) 11 Ch.D. 768), and it cannot act as a solicitor, doctor or accountant.

2. By legal possibility, *i.e.* by the restrictions imposed on the powers of a corporation on its formation. In the case of a body incorporated by royal charter, the charter sets out the powers of the corporation. If those powers are exceeded, the crown may forfeit the charter, or a member of the corporation may obtain an injunction restraining the corporation from doing an act which will be a ground for forfeiture (*Jenkin* v. *Pharmaceutical Society* [1921] 1 Ch. 392). But the *ultra vires* doctrine which, as we shall see presently, applies

to companies incorporated by a special Act of Parliament or under the Companies Acts 1948 to 1976, does not apply to corporations created by royal charter.

The ultra vires doctrine

According to general principles of law, in the case of corporations formed by special Act of Parliament, their contractual capacity is limited by the statutes governing them. "Whenever a corporation is created by Act of Parliament . . . I am of opinion not only that the objects which the corporation may legitimately pursue must be ascertained from the Act itself, but that the powers which the corporation may lawfully use in furtherance of those objects must either be expressly conferred or derived by reasonable implication from its provisions" (*per* Lord Watson in *Baroness Wenlock* v. *River Dee Co.* (1885) 10 App.Cas. 354). If the contractual capacity is exceeded, the contract is *ultra vires* and void, and cannot be made valid or ratified, even if each member of the corporation agreed to the making of the contract.

A municipal council was authorised by certain Acts to establish baths, wash-houses and bathing places. It established a municipal laundry. A ratepayer objected and applied for an injunction. *Held*, the injunction had to be granted as the council had acted *ultra vires*: *Att.-Gen.* v. *Fulham Corporation* [1929] 1 Ch. 440.

The doctrine of *ultra vires*, however, "ought to be reasonably, and not unreasonably, understood and applied, and whatever may fairly be regarded as incidental to, or consequential upon, those things which the legislature has authorised, ought not (unless expressly prohibited) to be held, by judicial construction, to be *ultra vires*" (*per* Lord Selborne in *Att.-Gen.* v. *G. E. Ry.* (1880) 5 App.Cas. 473).

In the case of companies created under the Companies Acts 1948 to 1976, or their predecessors, the *ultra vires* doctrine likewise applied. The company could only contract for the objects set out in the memorandum of the company. If these objects were exceeded, the company acted *ultra vires* and a contract purported to be made by it was void. Moreover, the company itself could plead that it had acted *ultra vires* and thus avoid the contract, though the party with which it had contracted was unaware that the contract was *ultra vires*.

By the European Communities Act 1972, s. 9 (1) the operation of the *ultra vires* doctrine was greatly restricted in the case of companies but was not abolished entirely. Section 9 (1) provides:

"In favour of a person dealing with a company in good faith, any transactions decided on by the directors shall be deemed to be one which it is within the capacity of the company to enter into, and the power of the directors to bind the company shall be deemed to be free of any limitation under the memorandum or articles of association; and a party to the transaction so decided on shall not be bound to enquire as to the capacity of the company to enter into it or as to any such limitation on the powers of the directors, and shall be presumed to have acted in good faith unless the contrary is proved."

Today the *ultra vires* doctrine applies in the case of companies only in the following cases:

1. The contracting party has not acted in good faith, *i.e.* has actual notice that the contract is *ultra vires*; or
2. the directors did not approve the transaction; or
3. the contracting party (but not the company) can plead that the company had no capacity to enter into the contract.

A company was incorporated with the principal objects of providing entertainment, services and facilities for foreign visitors. The objects clause provided, *inter alia*, that the company should have power to borrow money and it ended with a declaration that each of the various objects and powers stated in the objects clause should be independent objects of the company. Initially the company pursued its principal objects. Its shares and management were then transferred into other hands and it carried on pig breeding as its sole business. The defendant bank, which knew that the objects of the company did not include the business of pig breeding, granted the company a loan, but the pig breeding business was a disastrous failure and the company was wound up. *Held*, the bank could not recover the loan as it was given for a purpose known to be *ultra vires*. The authority in the memorandum to borrow money was not an independent object of the company but was merely a power which could not be exercised for a purpose which was not legal: *Introductions Ltd.* v. *National Provincial Bank Ltd.* [1970] Ch. 199. This decision is not overruled by the European Committees Act 1972, s. 9 (1) because the bank did not act in good faith.

Form of contracts concluded by corporations

At common law all contracts by corporations had, on principle, to be made under seal. This is the result of the artificial character of the corporation; "the seal is required as authenticating the concurrence of the whole body corporate."

This "age-old requirement of the common law" was found to be inconvenient in modern conditions and has been abolished by statute.

1. If the corporation is incorporated under the Companies Acts 1948 to 1976, or one of their predecessors, it can, by its agents, contract in the same manner as a natural person can contract (Companies Act 1948, s. 32).
2. If the corporation is not incorporated under the Companies Acts, *e.g.* if it is a municipal corporation, it can likewise contract in the same manner as a natural person (Corporate Bodies' Contracts Act 1960, s. 1 (1)).

In the result all corporations can today make contracts in the same form as is available to private persons.

UNINCORPORATED BODIES

Associations of persons which are not incorporated, such as clubs or societies, contract through an agent. The committee or other persons authorising the agent to contract are liable, but the members are not liable, unless the rules provide that the agent is authorised by them.

MENTALLY DISORDERED AND DRUNKEN PERSONS

Contracts made by mentally disordered persons, more briefly referred to by the Mental Health Act 1959 as "mental patients," are valid unless these persons are placed under the jurisdiction of the court (below); but if the other party knew that he was contracting with a person who, by reason of the unsoundness of his mind, could not understand the nature of the contract, the contract is voidable at the option of the patient.

L sued S on a promissory note. S pleaded that he was insane at the time he made it. *Held,* for the defence to succeed S must prove (1) that he was insane at the time, and (2) that L knew of his insanity: *Imperial Loan Co.* v. *Stone* [1892] 1 Q.B. 599.

A person may suffer from delusions, and yet be capable of understanding the nature of the transaction into which he is entering. In such a case the contract is valid, although the other party may have known of the delusions (*Birkin* v. *Wing* (1890) 63 L.T. 80). A contract made during mental disability can be ratified in a lucid interval.

If a person is incapable by reason of mental disability to manage his property and affairs, the court may assume jurisdiction to manage them; this jurisdiction is exercised by certain judges of the Chancery Division and the master and deputy master of the Court of Protection (Mental Health Act 1959). If the property of the patient is under the control of the court, the patient cannot dispose of it by a contract; such a contract would not be binding on the court or the patient but the court has power to affirm it and in that case the other party is bound by it (see *Baldwyn* v. *Smith* [1900] 1 Ch. 588).

Contracts made by persons who were so drunk at the time as not to understand what they were doing are voidable at the option of the person who was drunk, provided the other party knew of his condition (*Gore* v. *Gibson* (1845) 14 L.J. Ex. 151). The burden of proof in this, as in the case of mental patients, is on the party suffering from the incapacity to prove the knowledge of the other party. A contract made by a man when drunk can be ratified when he is sober.

B agreed to buy some houses from M. At the time he was too drunk to know what he was about, but he ratified the contract when he became sober. *Held*, the contract was binding: *Matthews* v. *Baxter* (1873) L.R. 8 Ex. 132.

Both mentally disordered and drunken persons are liable for necessaries supplied to them. In such a case they are bound to pay a reasonable price for the necessaries (Sale of Goods Act 1893, s. 2).

SELECT BIBLIOGRAPHY

Books

	Treitel	*Cheshire & Fifoot*
Capacity of Infants	367–395	401–422
Void and Voidable Contracts	374–388	408–417
Corporations	397–403	423–430

CHAPTER 6

REALITY OF CONTRACT

UNENFORCEABLE, VOIDABLE, VOID AND ILLEGAL CONTRACTS

AN arrangement between two parties which, on first impression, appears to satisfy all requirements of a valid contract (p. 1, *ante*) may, on closer examination, be found to lack reality because it is affected by a defect which renders the contract

  a. unenforceable;

  b. voidable;

  c. void; or

  d. illegal.

An **unenforceable** contract is one which is valid but cannot be enforced by action because of some technical defect, such as the absence of a note or memorandum in writing required by the Statute of Frauds 1677, s. 4 (as far as it still applies; see p. 40, *ante*) or the Law of Property Act 1925, s. 40, or lapse of the time for bringing an action required by the Limitation Act 1939.

This defect is not serious; it must be pleaded by the defendant if the court is to take notice of it. Further, where a note or memorandum in writing is required by a statute, that requirement can be satisfied at a later date and the contract can thus be rendered enforceable, but even while it cannot be enforced it may have important collateral effects.

M agreed to buy a house from L and paid L £200 as a deposit. M later on repudiated the contract and refused to complete. The contract was unenforceable as there was no memorandum in writing to satisfy the Statute of Frauds (now Law of Property Act 1925, s. 40). M sued L to recover his deposit. *Held*, M failed. He had paid a deposit under a contract which was valid although it could not be enforced, and as he had broken this contract he could not recover his deposit. The action was not to enforce the contract, but merely to recover money paid in respect of it: *Monnickendam* v. *Leanse* (1923) 39 T.L.R. 445.

A **voidable** contract is one which one of the parties can put an end to at his option. His option can be exercised without reference to the other party, so that the contract is binding if he elects to treat it as binding, and void if he elects to treat it as void. A contract might *e.g.* be voidable if one of the contracting parties has been

63

induced by misrepresentation, or by duress or undue influence to enter into the contract.

Example—A by innocent misrepresentation induces B to make a contract with A. The contract is binding on A, unless B chooses to set it aside. B can set aside the contract or not at his option, but A has no option to set it aside.

A voidable contract must be distinguished from a contract terminable at the will of one of the parties. The latter kind of contract does not suffer from an inherent defect but is terminated in accordance with its terms, *e.g.* if A is employed by B subject to a week's notice on either side, and B gives a week's notice, the contract comes to an end when the notice expires but it is not a voidable contract.

A **void** contract is one which is without legal effects. It is a complete nullity in law and confers no rights on either party. Examples of a void contract are a contract of a minor to buy goods which are not necessaries, a contract which is declared to be void by section 18 of the Gaming Act 1845 or a "contract" in which, owing to a genuine mistake, there is an absence of true agreement between the parties. Collateral contracts connected with a void contract are valid and enforceable in court.

Example—Two bookmakers form a partnership for the purpose of betting. Even if the betting contracts with the clients of the partnership are void, the partnership contract itself is valid and one of the partners may obtain a court order for an account against the other.

An **illegal** contract is affected by the most serious defect of all. Not only is the contract itself void but collateral contracts tainted by the illegality may likewise be void. That applies even to a collateral contract with a third party who knew of the illegal character of the main contract (*Pearce* v. *Brooks* (1866) L.R. 1 Ex. 213, on p. 98, *post*).

Mistake

Mistakes which do not affect the validity of the contract

The mere fact that one of the parties to a contract acted under a mistake does not, as a general rule, affect the validity of the contract. A contract is only void on the ground of mistake when the mistake is such that there was never any real agreement between the parties, or, if there was a real agreement, it was only entered into because the parties both made the same mistake on some vital matter, and would never have made the agreement at all unless they had both made that mistake. There is no mistake so as to avoid the contract in the following cases—

1. Mistake by one party of the expression of his intention.

H contracted with the N Corporation for the erection of a number of houses. In calculating his price for the houses, H by mistake deducted a particular sum twice over. The Corporation affixed its seal to the contract which correctly represented its intention, but did not correctly represent H's intention. *Held*, the contract was binding: *Higgins Ltd.* v. *Northampton Corporation* [1927] 1 Ch. 128.

2. Mistake as to the meaning of a trade description, when goods are sold under that trade description.

H bought a quantity of kapok, described as "Sree" brand, from B, both parties thinking that goods of that brand were pure kapok. In fact, kapok of the "Sree" brand contained an admixture of cotton. Kapok of the "Sree" brand was delivered but proved to be unsuitable for H. *Held*, the mistake did not affect the validity of the contract: *Harrison & Jones Ltd.* v. *Bunten & Lancaster Ltd.* [1953] 1 Q.B. 646.

R received an order from a customer abroad for "feveroles." He asked P what that was and both parties thought it meant "horse beans." R then bought a quantity of goods described in the contract as "horse beans" from P and sent them to his customer who rightly rejected them as not being feveroles. *Held*, there was a binding contract for the sale of horse beans between R and P: *Frederick E. Rose (London) Ltd.* v. *William H. Pim Jnr. & Co. Ltd.* [1953] 2 Q.B. 450.

3. A mistake or error of judgment. If A buys an article thinking that it is worth £100, when it is only worth £50, the contract remains good and A has to bear the loss of his own ignorance of the true value of the article.

4. A mistake by one party of his ability to perform it. If X agrees to build ten houses by July 1, but finds it is impossible to complete them before September 1, he has mistaken his ability to perform the contract, but nevertheless cannot escape from the contractual obligation he has undertaken.

Mistakes which render the "contract" void

In cases of genuine mistake, as defined above, there is no contract between the parties, and the "contract" is therefore void.

Mistake avoids the contract in the following cases—

Χ *Mistake as to the nature of the contract itself*

If a person signs a contract in the mistaken belief that he is signing a document of a fundamentally different character, there will be mistake which renders the contract void. The mistaken party can successfully plead *non est factum* (it is not my deed[1]). The essential point is that the consent, a necessary requirement of contract, is missing.

M, an old man of feeble sight, indorsed a bill of exchange for £3,000 thinking it was a guarantee. *Held*, as he was not negligent in indorsing the bill he was not liable: *Foster* v. *Mackinnon* (1869) L.R. 4 C.P. 704.

K was to be released from his hire-purchase agreement with a finance company on the understanding that the dealer found a purchaser for the car. The dealer sold the car to H on hire-purchase terms and asked K to sign a document which he described as a release note. The document was in fact an indemnity obliging K to pay if H defaulted. When K signed, the document, apart from its lower portion, was covered by other papers on the dealer's desk. *Held*, K was not bound by his signature: *Muskham Finance Ltd.* v. *Howard* [1963] 1 Q.B. 904.

The principle on which the plea of *non est factum* is founded is this: A person of full age and understanding who signs a document evidently intended to have legal effect is bound by his signature and cannot avoid it by claiming that he did not read the document, or did not inform himself of its purport or effect, or that he relied on the word of another who read it over to him or explained it. The strictness of this rule is mitigated by the plea of *non est factum* which is admissible only if the signer can prove that the document which he signed is fundamentally different, as regards character or effect, from that which he intended to sign; in that case the signer can avoid the contract. The plea of *non est factum* is thus available only within narrow limits and the onus is on the person who wishes to rely on it. These are the rules which apply to persons of full age and understanding; if the signer of the document was illiterate, blind or lacking in understanding, the law is more easily prepared to give relief, if consent is truly lacking and the signer acted carefully. The plea of *non est factum* is not admissible if the signer acted carelessly because "a person who signs a document, and parts with it so that it may come into other hands, has a responsibility, that of the normal man of prudence, to take care what he signs, which, if

---

[1] The expression "deed" is not used here in a technical sense but denotes every written document signed by the person raising this plea.

neglected, prevents him from denying his liability under the document according to its tenor" (*per* Lord Wilberforce in *Saunders* v. *Anglia Building Society, post*). (This case is more generally known by its name in the Court of Appeal, *Gallie* v. *Lee*.)

G intended to give her nephew her house on condition that he would allow her to live there for life. She knew that her nephew wanted to raise money on the house and that Lee, her nephew's business associate, was to help him in that respect. Lee and her nephew asked her to sign a document. She had broken her spectacles and asked what it was and was told that it was a deed of gift of the house to her nephew. She executed the document in that belief. The document was, in fact, an assignment of the house (which was leasehold property) by G to Lee for £3,000 which was never paid nor intended to be paid. Lee mortgaged the house for £2,000 to the defendant building society. *Held*, G could not plead *non est factum* and could not recover the title deeds of the house. *Saunders* v. *Anglia Building Society* [1970] 3 W.L.R. 1078.

The defence of *non est factum* is likewise not available where a party signs a contractual document in blank and the other party completes it falsely, provided that the element of consent of the first party is not entirely missing.

Mr. Western bought a second-hand Ford Corsair from a dealer. He agreed with him that the price should be £550 and the deposit £34 which Mr. Western paid. The parties further agreed that Mr. Western should have the car on hire-purchase terms and Mr. Western signed the documents offered him by the dealer in blank. The dealer completed the documents, showing the purchase price as £730, and not £550, and the deposit as £185, and not £34; further, the document evidenced a loan agreement and not a hire-purchase contract. The plaintiff finance company accepted the documents as sent in by the dealer. Mr. Western, when receiving copies, noticed the difference but did not complain because on the figures he was not substantially worse off than agreed with the dealer. *Held*, when sued by the finance company, Mr. Western could not plead *non est factum*: *United Dominions Trust Ltd.* v. *Western* [1976] Q.B. 513.

Non est factum cannot be successfully pleaded if dissimilar documents produce a similar legal effect and "the object of the exercise" is achieved, albeit by legal means different from those which the signer had in mind. This point was mentioned by the court incidentally, but not as its main reason, in *United Dominions Trust Ltd.* v. *Western*, *ante*.

H intended to raise money on the security of her car. She signed certain documents in blank and without reading them. The documents did not provide for a loan on the security of her car, but they resulted in a so-called refinancing agreement, whereby H purported to sell her car to a dealer who resold it to the plaintiff finance company which, in turn, let H have her car (which never left her possession) on hire-purchase terms. H claimed to repudiate the arrangement. *Held*, she could not succeed on *non est factum*, but she succeeded on other grounds: *Mercantile Credit Co. Ltd.* v. *Hamblin* [1965] 2 Q.B. 242 (for details see Schmitthoff, *Sale of Goods*, 2nd ed., p. 99).

B was induced by C's fraud to execute a deed. This deed mortgaged some land to C and contained a covenant by B to pay £1,000. B knew that the deed disposed in some manner of the land, but he did not know that it was a mortgage and he did not read it. *Held*, in the hands of an innocent assignee for value the deed was enforceable against B: *Howatson* v. *Webb* [1907] 1 Ch. 537.

Mistake as to the identity of the person contracted with

If A intends to contract with B, but finds he has contracted with C, there is no contract if the identity of B was a material element of the contract and C knows it. A's offer is addressed to B but accepted by C who knows that he cannot accept it; there is no agreement.

Blenkarn, by imitating the signature of a reputable firm called Blenkiron, induced X to supply him with goods on credit. *Held*, as X never intended to contract with Blenkarn there was no contract between them and an innocent purchaser of the goods from Blenkarn did not get a good title: *Cundy* v. *Lindsay* (1878) L.R. 3 App.Cas. 459.

In *Cundy* v. *Lindsay* the deception was effected by letter but the situation may be different if the deceived person deals with the fraud face to face: *Phillips* v. *Brooks Ltd., post*.

This principle only holds good, however, when the personality of the contracting party is of importance. If, in the illustration given earlier, A intends to contract with B, but would have been content with C as long as he got performance of the contract, a contract with C in mistake for B is binding. But if C knows that A does not intend to contract with him, the contract is void.

B, the managing director of a theatre, gave instructions that a ticket was not to be sold to S. S knew this, and asked a friend to buy a ticket for him. With this ticket S went to the theatre, but B refused to allow him to enter. *Held*, no contract, as the theatre company never intended to contract with S: *Said* v. *Butt* [1920] 3 K.B. 497.

If A is prepared to sell to anyone who will pay his price and C pretending to be B, comes into his shop and buys, there is a contract between A and C.

N went into a jeweller's shop and represented himself to be Sir G B, a person of credit and stability. The jeweller sold him a ring for which N gave a cheque purporting to be signed by Sir G B. The cheque was a forgery and the ring was subsequently pawned. *Held*, the pawnbroker had a good title to the ring, because the contract between the jeweller and N was good until the jeweller disaffirmed it: *Phillips* v. *Brooks Ltd.* [1919] 2 K.B. 243.

Here the jeweller intended to contract with the person he saw in the shop, N, the representation by N that he was Sir G B only affecting the question of payment. Had N paid cash there would undoubtedly have been a sale, and there was equally a sale, though a voidable one, when he paid by forged cheque. If a person is deceived by another actually present before him, the contract is normally only voidable (*Lewis* v. *Averay* [1972] 1 Q.B. 198) but exceptionally even in this situation the contract may be void.

I. and her two sisters were joint owners of a car which they advertised for sale. X bought it and began to write out a cheque for the price. I. told X that the sale was for cash, that the owners were not prepared to accept a cheque and that the sale was cancelled. X replied that he was H, a reputable business man, giving an address which was checked by one of I.'s sisters. I. believed X to be H and let him have the car in exchange for his cheque. X had nothing to do with H and the cheque was dishonoured. The car was acquired by L in good faith for value. *Held*, the owners intended to sell their car only to H and their offer was only addressed to him; X was incapable of accepting the offer and the owners could recover the car from L: *Ingram* v. *Little* [1961] 1 Q.B. 31.

Mutual[2] mistake as to the identity of the thing contracted for

If A makes an offer to B about one thing, and B accepts, thinking that A is referring to another thing of the same name, the contract is void because there is no *consensus ad idem.*

E agreed to buy from F a cargo of cotton to arrive "ex *Peerless* from Bombay." There were two ships called *Peerless* sailing from Bombay, one sailing in October and the other in December. E meant the earlier one and F the later. *Held*, there was no contract: *Raffles* v. *Wichelhaus* (1864) 2 H & C. 906.

The result is the same even if the mistake was caused by the negligence of a third party.

[2] *Mutual* mistake occurs where the two contracting parties mean different things; *common* mistake occurs where they mean the same thing which, however, is different from reality. Mutual mistake: A means a black car and B a white one. Common mistake: A and B mean a black car but the car, is in fact, white.

X by telegram ordered three rifles. Owing to the telegraph clerk's mistake, the message was transmitted as "the" rifles. From previous negotiations this was understood to mean fifty rifles, and that number was dispatched. *Held*, there was no contract between the parties: *Henkel* v. *Pape* [1870] L.R. 6 Ex. 7.

If a code message is understood in one sense by the sender and in another by the recipient, there is no contract. If the message is ambiguous it is for the party relying on it to show that it is so clear that the other party cannot be heard to say that he misunderstood it: *Falck* v. *Williams* [1900] A.C. 176.

Common mistake as to the existence of the thing contracted for

If both parties believe the subject-matter of the contract to be in existence, but in fact at the time when the contract is made it is non-existent, there is no contract.

In a contract for the sale of specific goods if the goods, unknown to the seller have perished before the contract, the contract is void: Sale of Goods Act 1893, s. 6.

G agreed to assign to H a policy of assurance upon the life of L. L had died before the agreement was made. *Held*, no contract: *Scott* v. *Coulson* [1903] 2 Ch. 249.

Common mistake as to the fundamental subject-matter of the contract

If the parties have made a contract on the mistaken assumption that there exists a state of affairs which is of such fundamental importance to them that they would not have made the contract had it not existed, the contract is void.

It should be noted that not every common mistake produces that effect, even if it concerns a matter of importance to the parties. The doctrine of common mistake relating to the foundation of the contract is interpreted restrictedly and applies only if, in the words of Lord Atkin in *Bell* v. *Lever* [1932] A.C. 161 (see *post*), the state of affairs which exists in reality "makes the contract something different in kind from the contract in the . . . state of facts" that the parties erroneously assumed to exist.

If, *e.g.* there was no mistake when the contract was made but facts subsequently come to light which, though important, do not destroy the identity of the subject-matter as it was when the contract was made, the contract is not void.

B and S were employed by L under agreements for a fixed time.

Later, L paid B and S £50,000 to be discharged from these agreements. B and S had been making secret profits, which would have entitled L to dismiss them without notice, but this was unknown to L at the time the £50,000 was paid. The jury negatived fraud on the part of B and S. *Held*, L could not recover the £50,000. There was no mistake on either side as to the contracts which were being released. The fact that L could have obtained a release on much cheaper terms did not, in the absence of fraud or breach of warranty, render the contract void: *Bell* v. *Lever Bros. Ltd.* [1932] A.C. 161.

Further illustrations of common mistake which, though affecting an important aspect of the contract, were not regarded to be fundamental, are *Harrison & Jones Ltd.* v. *Bunten & Lancaster Ltd.* and *Frederick E. Rose (London) Ltd.* v. *William H. Pim Jnr. & Co. Ltd.*, both on p. 65, *ante*, and further *Leaf* v. *International Galleries*, on p. 261, *post*.

Since the effect of the doctrine of common mistake relating to the foundation of the contract is restricted in common law, equity has intervened and grants discretionary relief where the mistake is not sufficiently fundamental in the eyes of the common law but, nevertheless, serious; in these cases, however, the contract is not void (as in cases in which the common law doctrine applies) but voidable

B granted S the lease of a flat at a yearly rental of £250. Both parties believed erroneously that, as the result of structural alterations, the flat was not subject to rent control. The tenant claimed a declaration that the lease was under rent control, and the landlord counter-claimed for rescission of the lease on the ground of common fundamental mistake. *Held*, the lease was subject to rent control: the common mistake of the parties was one of fact and not of law; the lease was voidable at the instance of the landlord: *Solle* v. *Butcher* [1950] 1 K.B. 671.

G bought a house from B for £850. Both parties believed that a tenant who was in occupation of the house was a statutory tenant, whereas he was not protected and could have been compelled to quit on notice. The value of the house, with vacant possession was £2,250. *Held*, the parties were under a common mistake of fundamental nature. While at common law the contract was not void, equity would grant relief and treat the contract as voidable. The seller was entitled to rescind the contract: *Grist* v. *Bailey* [1967] Ch. 532.

M, who could not drive and had no licence, took out a car insurance with the defendant company. He stated in the proposal, contrary to the truth, that he had a provisional licence and that the car would be driven by himself and his two sons both of whom had licences. The car was involved in an accident when driven by the younger son. The insurance company agreed to pay £385 for the damage to the car but later sought to avoid the compromise on the ground that M's statements in the proposal form were untrue. *Held*, that, when concluding the compromise agreement, both parties were under the common fundamental mistake that M had a valid claim under the insurance policy and that in the circumstances the agreement was voidable and could be set aside by the company: *Magee* v. *Pennine Insurance Co. Ltd.* [1969] 2 Q.B. 507.

Mistake as to the promise of one party known to the other

The general rule is that if a person makes a mistake as to the offer of the other party to the contract, the contract is nevertheless binding upon him. "If, whatever a man's real intentions may be, he so conducts himself that a reasonable man would believe that he was assenting to the terms proposed by the other party, and that other party upon that belief enters into the contract with him, the man thus conducting himself would be equally bound as if he had intended to agree to the other party's terms" (*per* Blackburn J. in *Smith* v. *Hughes* (1871) L.R. 6 Q.B. at p. 607 (see *post*)).

S sold H a quantity of oats, a sample of which S had shown H. The oats were new oats but H who had inspected the sample erroneously thought that he was buying old ones. The price was high for new oats but oats were very scarce at that season. *Held*, H's mistake was irrelevant unless S positively knew that H wanted to buy old oats only: *Smith* v. *Hughes* (1871) L.R. 6 Q.B. 597.

If, however, in the last case, S had *known* that H had made a mistake in accepting his offer, there would have been no contract.

An auctioneer was selling tow and hemp. A lot of tow was put up for which M, thinking it was hemp, made a bid. The bid was extravagant for tow, but reasonable for hemp. From the price bid the auctioneer knew that the bid was made under a mistake. *Held*, there was no contract: *Scriven Bros. & Co.* v. *Hindley & Co.* [1913] 3 K.B. 564.

The same point is illustrated by the following case.

M, after declining an offer from P to buy certain property for £2,000, wrote to P offering to sell it for £1,250. This was a mistake for £2,250. P, immediately on receipt of the offer, wrote accepting it. *Held*, the contract would not be specifically enforced as P had snapped at an offer he perfectly well knew to be made by mistake: *Webster* v. *Cecil* (1861) 30 Beav. 62.

Rectification

If the parties were in agreement on all important terms but by mistake wrote them down wrongly, rectification of the written document may be ordered. To obtain rectification it must be proved—

1. there was complete agreement between the parties on all important terms;
2. the agreement continued unchanged until it was reduced into writing; and
3. the writing did not express what the parties had already agreed.

U owned two adjoining pieces of land, plots 1 and 2. Behind plot 1, but forming part of it, was a yard used with plot 2. P bought plot 1, excluding the yard, and Q bought plot 2, with the yard. By mistake, plot 1 was conveyed to P without the yard being excluded, and plot 2 was conveyed to Q without any mention of the yard. *Held*, the deeds could be rectified, so that the yard was conveyed to Q and not to P: *Craddock Bros.* v. *Hunt* [1923] 2 Ch. 136.

The object of rectification is "to bring the written document executed in pursuance of an antecedent agreement into conformity with that agreement" (*per* Warrington L.J. in *Craddock Bros.* v. *Hunt, ante*). It is sufficient to show a continuing common intention in regard to a particular provision or aspect of the antecedent agreement, although, until the written instrument is executed, a binding contract cannot be said to exist between the parties. But strong and convincing proof is required that the concluded instrument does not represent the common accord of the parties, and that is particularly the case if rectification is claimed merely on the strength of a continuing common intention and not on that of a complete contract.

A father agreed with his daughter to transfer his house and car hire business to her in consideration of her paying him a small weekly pension and defraying certain of his household expenses, including gas, electricity and coal bills and the cost of a home help for the invalid mother. The written agreement provided that the daughter should "discharge all expenses" in connection with the house in which she and the parents lived in separate households in self-contained flats. The daughter met the expenses for the father's gas, electricity and coal and for the home help for some time but refused to continue paying them after differences had broken out; she relied on the wording of the written agreement. *Held*, there was a common continuing intention that the expenses in dispute should be paid by the daughter and the written agreement had to be rectified by writing a clause to that effect into it: *Joscelyne* v. *Nissen* [1970] 2 Q.B. 86.

Exceptionally, rectification may be ordered if a party provides

convincing proof that he believed a particular term to be included
in the contract but that the other party, without informing him,
omitted or varied that term, well knowing that he still believed the
term to be included (*A. Roberts & Co. Ltd.* v. *Leicestershire County
Council* [1961] Ch. 555).

Recovery of money paid under a mistake

Money paid under a mistake of fact can normally be recovered,
but money paid under a mistake of law is usually unrecoverable.
In the former case the action is founded on quasi-contract (see pp.
49–50 *ante*).

MISREPRESENTATION

Representations distinguished from terms of contract

It happens often that the actual conclusion of the contract is
preceded by negotiations between the interested parties. These
negotiations might not be smooth: one party might be eager to
contract while the other might be reluctant. A statement of fact
which one party makes in the course of the negotiations with a
view to inducing the other to enter into the contract and to conclude
it is known as a representation; if such statement is false, it is a
misrepresentation.

It is characteristic of a misrepresentation that it is made **before**
the parties conclude the contract, and made just for the purpose of
inducing one of them to accept contractual obligations. Such
statement must be distinguished from a statement actually embodied
in the contract which forms part of the **terms** of the contract (see
p. 24, *ante*).

From the point of view of the person to whom the statement
is made, the distinction is between merely relying on what was
said in the negotiations or contracting that the statement is true.

H, rubber merchants, in reply to B's question told B that they were
bringing out a rubber company. B asked if it was all right, and H said
they were bringing it out. B therefore said that was good enough for
him and bought 5,000 shares from H at a premium. The shares depreciated
and B claimed damages. The jury found the company was not a rubber
company but negatived fraud. *Held*, the statement that the company was
a rubber company was not a term of the contract of sale of the shares,
nor was there a contractual collateral warranty that the company was a
rubber company: *Heilbut, Symons & Co.* v. *Buckleton* [1913] A.C. 30.

W sold a Morris car to O. C. Ltd. Before the sale W told the representative of O. C. Ltd. that the car was a 1948 Morris and produced the registration book that showed 1948 as the year of first registration. W's mother had bought the car second-hand as a 1948 model. The car was, in fact, a 1938 model and the registration book was forged, unknown to all parties concerned. *Held*, W's statement was a representation and not a term of the contract; as the misrepresentation was innocent, the buyer could not recover damages: *Oscar Chess Ltd.* v. *Williams* [1957] 1 W.L.R. 370.

The circumstances may show that a statement of fact which first was merely a representation was then embodied by the parties into the contract as a term of it (*Couchman* v. *Hill* [1947] K.B. 554; see p. 233, *post*). Even if the misrepresentation has become a term of the contract, such as a condition or a warranty, the remedy of rescission for innocent misrepresentation is available to the misled party (Misrepresentation Act 1967, s. 1 (*a*)); he can, of course, always rescind if the misrepresentation was fraudulent. The remedies for breach of conditions and warranties have been discussed earlier (p. 25, *ante*).

The basis of the law of misrepresentation

The rules of the common law and equity on misrepresentation have been considerably affected by two events: the Misrepresentation Act 1967 and the decision of the House of Lords in *Hedley Byrne & Co. Ltd.* v. *Heller and Partners Ltd.* [1964] A.C. 465.

The Misrepresentation Act 1967 altered these rules, as far as the law of contract was concerned. The main features of the Act are that it divides innocent misrepresentation into the two categories of negligent misrepresentation and misrepresentation which is not negligent and that it equates negligent misrepresentation to fraudulent misrepresentation in many respects. Another provision of the Act states that, if a misrepresentation has occurred, it is presumed that it was made negligently, so that the burden of proving that it was not negligent rests on the defendant.

Hedley Byrne & Co. Ltd. v. *Heller and Partners Ltd.* is a decision in the law of torts. The House of Lords extended the rule in *Donoghue* v. *Stevenson* [1932] A.C. 562, by holding that a person who made a negligent statement might be liable for financial loss suffered by the person to whom the statement was made, if he possessed special skill and competence and owed the person who suffered the loss a duty to apply these qualities when making the statement; he is not, however, liable in these circumstances if he excludes his responsibility. Unlike the situation under the Misrepresentation Act 1967, however, the burden of proving negligence falls on the plaintiff.

Hedley Byrne, advertising agents, were instructed by Easipower Ltd., one of their clients, to conclude advertising contracts which would involve Hedley Byrne in personal liability to the advertisers. They made inquiries about the creditworthiness of Easipower with Heller, who were merchant bankers. Heller gave a favourable reply but stipulated that it was "without responsibility." In reliance on that statement Hedley Byrne placed the advertising contracts on behalf of Easipower and, when the latter went into liquidation, became personally liable for £17,000. Hedley Byrne contended that Heller had acted negligently.

The House of Lords, without deciding on Heller's alleged negligence, held that a negligent though honest misrepresentation could give rise to an action in tort for negligence, where no contractual or fiduciary relationship existed between the parties, but only if the person making the statement owed a duty of care to the person to whom the statement was made; such duty was owed if the person making the statement possessed special skill and judgment and he knew or ought to have known that the other party relied on these qualities. In the result, the House of Lords held that there was no liability on Heller as there was an express disclaimer of liability: *Hedley Byrne & Co. Ltd.* v. *Heller and Partners Ltd.* [1964] A.C. 465.

The rule established in *Hedley Byrne* covers the following proposition: "If a man, who has or professes to have special knowledge or skill, makes a representation by virtue thereof to another—be it advice, information or opinion—with the intention of inducing him to enter into a contract with him, he is under a duty to use reasonable care to see that the representation is correct, and that the advice, information or opinion is reliable. If he negligently gives unsound advice or misleading information or expresses an erroneous opinion, and thereby induces the other side to enter into a contract with him, he is liable" (*per* Lord Denning M.R. in *Esso Petroleum Co. Ltd.* v. *Mardon* [1976] Q.B. 801). The same principles must apply if the person who has or professes to have special knowledge or skill by his advice negligently induces the other side to enter into a contract with a third party. The rule in *Hedley Byrne* applies not only to professional advisers but also to other persons, *e.g.* those who are in a special relationship to the adviser or those who have a financial interest in the transaction on which they advise. It also covers pre-contractual negotiations (*Esso Petroleum Co. Ltd.* v. *Mardon*, see p. 28, *ante*), but here it is more easy for the advised to recover damages under the Misrepresentation Act 1967 (see *post*). The rule never applies to advice given only casually or in a social context (*Mutual Life and Citizens' Assurance Co. Ltd.* v. *Evatt* [1971] A.C. 793).

Innocent and fraudulent misrepresentation

Requirements of misrepresentation

A misrepresentation is relevant if it satisfies the following requirements:

1. it must be a representation of a material fact,
2. made before the conclusion of the contract with a view to inducing a party to enter into the contract,
3. with the intention that it should be acted upon by the party to whom it is addressed,
4. it must actually have been acted upon and must have induced the contract, and
5. it must have been false, either to the knowledge of the person making it or without his knowledge.

If the person who made the statement honestly believed it to be true, the **misrepresentation** was **innocent.** There are two types of innocent misrepresentation: *innocent but negligent misrepresentation* which occurs if the person making the statement had no reasonable ground to believe it to be true, and *innocent and not negligent* misrepresentation which occurs if he had reasonable ground to believe it to be true.

If the person making the statement did not honestly believe it to be true, the **misrepresentation** was **fraudulent.**

In the following the requirements of misrepresentation will be considered more closely.

1. The representation must be one of fact, and not of general opinion or of intention. Mere puffing or commendatory statements by traders as to their wares are not representations of fact. For example—

(a) A statement that a second-hand car is good value is a statement of opinion.
(b) A statement that the car has only run 6,000 miles is a statement of fact.
(c) A statement that the car is the best model ever produced by the makers is puffing.

If statement (b) is untrue and the person making it knows it to be untrue, the remedies for fraudulent misrepresentation are available, p. 81, *post*). Whether the statements (a) and (c) are true or not has no effect on the contract, subject to the rule in *Hedley Byrne* (see p. 76, *ante*).

Although, as a general rule, a statement of opinion or intention is not a statement of fact, yet if it can be proved that no such opinion or intention were held, the remedies for fraudulent misrepresentation are available, because "the state of a man's mind is as much a fact as the state of his digestion" (*per* Bowen L.J. in *Edgington* v. *Fitzmaurice* (1885) 29 Ch.D. 483). The difficulty in such cases is chiefly one of proof. Moreover, if the facts are not equally known to both parties, a statement of opinion by the one who knows the facts better may be a statement of a material fact, for it may be implied that he knows facts which justify his opinion (*Brown* v. *Raphael* [1958] Ch. 636).

Misrepresentation of a general rule of law is irrelevant, but misrepresentation of particular rights, such as the existence and contents of a private Act of Parliament, is a misrepresentation of fact (*West London Commercial Bank* v. *Kitson* (1884) 13 Q.B.D. 363).

2. The representation must have been made before the conclusion of the contract with a view to inducing the other party to enter into the contract. This requirement has already been explained when the distinction between representations and terms of the contract was discussed (p. 74, *ante*).

3. The representation must be made with the intention that it should be acted upon by the person to whom it is addressed.

Z, on the faith of statements appearing in the prospectus of a company, bought some shares in a company from a holder of them. Some of the statements were false, and Z thereupon sued the directors. *Held*, the statements were only intended to mislead the public into being original subscribers of the shares from the company. As Z was not an original subscriber, but had purchased the shares later from a subscriber, he was not within the class intended to be misled, and therefore could not maintain the action: *Peek* v. *Gurney* (1873) L.R. 6 H.L. 377.

If, however, it can be shown that the statements in the prospectus were intended to induce persons to buy in the market, those persons can sue for the damage they have suffered (*Andrews* v. *Mockford* [1896] 1 Q.B. 372).

While it is doubtful whether, in view of modern issuing techniques, *Peek* v. *Gurney* would be decided in the same way today as it was a hundred years ago (see the criticism in Gower's *Modern Company Law*, 3rd ed., p. 320), the principle is undoubtedly correct that if A induces B by fraudulent misrepresentation to buy land or chattels and B resells them to C, C has no right to claim the remedies for fraudulent misrepresentation directly against A because the original misrepresentation spent itself when B sold the land or chattels to C.

Gross asked Grace Rymer Investments Ltd. to find a suitable shop for her to purchase as an investment. Grace Rymer were induced by misrepresentation to purchase a shop themselves from certain sellers and then resold the shop to Gross. The shop was conveyed directly from the sellers to Gross, who suffered loss as the result of the original misrepresentation. *Held*, even if the misrepresentation was fraudulent (which, according to the finding of the judge of first instance was not the case), Gross could not rescind the conveyance of the shop on the ground of the sellers' misrepresentation because the right to rescind was not an equity which ran with the land and the effect of the misrepresentation had spent itself when Grace Rymer sold the shop to Gross: *Gross* v. *Lewis Hillman Ltd.* [1970] Ch. 445.

4. The representation must actually have been acted upon and must have induced the contract.

If the party to whom the misrepresentations are made does not rely upon them, but relies instead upon his own skill and judgment, or upon his own inquiries and investigations, he cannot bring an action. For example, if C offers a business to D for sale, representing the takings to be £500 a week, and D, after investigating the books, decides as a result of that investigation to buy the business, D will not be able to sue C upon his fraudulent representation as to the takings. But if D relies even partly on C's representation, C will be liable for fraud.

T bought a cannon from H. The cannon being defective, H plugged the hole. T did not examine the cannon, and, on using it, it burst. *Held*: as the plug had not deceived T, he could not refuse to pay for the cannon, *Horsfall* v. *Thomas* (1862) 1 H. & C. 90.

The fact that the party misled had the means, of which he did not avail himself, of discovering the falseness of the representation is immaterial because he was entitled to rely on the representation made to him by the other party.

In the negotiations for the sale of X's business to Y, X represented

that his takings were £300 a year and produced papers to Y which, he
said, bore out his statement. Y bought the business without examining
the papers. If he had examined them, he would have discovered that
X's statements were false. *Held*, as Y had relied on X's statements he
could rescind the contract and it was no defence to say that he had the
means of discovering their untruth: *Redgrave* v. *Hurd* (1881) 20 Ch.D. 1.

Innocent misrepresentation

Innocent misrepresentation occurs where the false statement has
been made honestly, whether made negligently or not, but, as will be
seen later, the remedies for negligent misrepresentation differ from
those for non-negligent misrepresentation.

An innocent misrepresentation is presumed to have been made
negligently. The onus is on the person making the statement to
prove "that he had reasonable ground to believe and did believe
up to the time the contract was made that the facts represented were
true" (Misrepresentation Act 1967, s. 2 (1)). The test of negligence
is thus—as always—the objective one of reasonableness. A person
of unusual simplicity of mind who makes a statement which he
believes to be true but which any reasonable man would not make
without further investigation of the facts, is liable for negligent
misrepresentation; it will be seen that the remedies for that type of
misrepresentation are the same as those for fraudulent misrepresentation.

A representation which is true when made but, to the knowledge
of the party making it, becomes untrue before the contract is entered
into must be corrected. If it is not, the contract can be rescinded.

In negotiating a sale of a medical practice in January, X represented
the takings to be at the rate of £2,000 a year. In May, when the contract
was signed, the takings had, owing to X's illness, fallen to £5 a week.
Held, the contract could be rescinded owing to X's failure to disclose
the fall in the takings: *With* v. *O'Flanagan* [1936] 1 Ch. 575.

Fraudulent misrepresentation

"Fraud is proved," said Lord Herschell in *Derry* v. *Peek* (1889)
14 App.Cas. 337, 374, "when it is shown that a false representation
has been made:

1. knowingly; or
2. without belief in its truth; or
3. recklessly, careless whether it be true or false."

A misrepresentation is not fraudulent if the person who made it honestly believes it to be true.

A tram company had statutory powers to run trams by animal power, and, with the consent of the Board of Trade, by steam power. A prospectus was issued inviting the public to apply for shares and stating that the company had the right to use steam power. The Board of Trade refused its consent to the use of steam power and the company was wound up. *Held*, as the directors honestly believed the statement in the prospectus they were not guilty of fraud: *Derry* v. *Peek* (1889) 14 App.Cas. 337. (As a result of this case the law relating to the liability of directors for false statements in the prospectus was altered.)

For the ascertainment of fraud, the test of honest belief is purely subjective; the question is not whether the belief that the statement was true could be reasonably entertained on an objective consideration of its truth or falsity, but the test is whether the person who made the statement believed it to be true in the sense in which he understood it albeit erroneously when it was made.

The defendants induced the plaintiffs by a false statement to subscribe to a company in Kenya. The company was a failure and the plaintiffs who had lost their money claimed damages for fraudulent misrepresentation. *Held*, there was no fraudulent misrepresentation as the defendants honestly believed the statements to be true in the sense in which they made them: *Akerhielm* v. *De Mare* [1959] A.C. 789.

Absence of reasonable grounds for belief in the truth of a fact may, however, tend to show that in fact the belief was not held.

If the representation be made knowing it to be false the fact that it was made from an honest motive will not prevent it from being a fraud. Where, therefore, X accepted without authority a bill of exchange drawn on Y, honestly believing that Y would confirm his act, he was held liable for fraud (*Polhill* v. *Walter* (1832) 3 B. & Ald. 114).

Remedies for fraudulent and innocent misrepresentation

Remedies for fraudulent misrepresentation

They are—

1. a claim for damages by the misled party, if he has suffered a loss. This claim is founded on the common law tort of deceit and may be combined with any of the two following:—
2. rescission of the contract by the misled party.

3. refusal of the misled party to perform the contract.
4. although this is not a remedy for fraudulent misrepresentation, it should be added that the misled party has always the right to affirm the contract, if he so wishes.

Remedies for innocent but negligent misrepresentation

The remedies are the same as in the case of fraudulent misrepresentation but—

1. the right to claim damages is not founded on the common law but is statutory; it arises under the Misrepresentation Act 1967, s. 2 (1).

Mr. and Mrs. Spence were the joint owners of a house in London. Without authority from his wife and without her consent, Mr. Spence sold the house to Mr. Watts. Mrs. Spence refused to agree to the sale. *Held*, Mr. Spence was liable to Mr. Watts under the Misrepresentation Act 1967, s. 2 (1) because at the time of the sale he was well aware that his wife had not consented and he falsely represented to Mr. Watts that he was entitled to sell the house: *Watts* v. *Spence* [1976] Ch. 165.

2. Further, although the misled party would be entitled to rescind the contract, the judge (or arbitrator) has a discretionary power to declare the contract as subsisting and to award damages in lieu of rescission (section 2 (2)), but these damages have to be taken into account when the damages to which the misled party is entitled under section 2 (1) are calculated (section 2 (3)).

Remedies for innocent and not negligent misrepresentation

They are—

1. rescission of the contract by the misled party, but the judge (or arbitrator) has a discretionary power to declare the contract as subsisting and to award damages in lieu of rescission (section 2 (2)).
2. refusal of the misled party to perform the contract,
3. affirmation of the contract.
4. it should be noted that the misled party has no *right* in common law or under the statute to claim damages; all he can do is to invoke the *discretionary power* of the judge to award damages in lieu of rescission.

The right to damages

Damages can be demanded, as stated earlier, in the case of fraudulent and negligent misrepresentation. It is thought that the measure of damages is the same in both cases although the former is founded on the common law and the latter on the statute.

The discretionary power to award damages in lieu of rescission

The judge (or arbitrator) has this power in the case of negligent and of innocent but not negligent misrepresentation. He should exercise it "if of opinion that it would be equitable to do so, having regard to the nature of the misrepresentation and the loss that would be caused by it if the contract were upheld, as well as to the loss that rescission would cause to the other party" (section 2 (2)).

Rescission of the contract

A contract induced by innocent or fraudulent misrepresentation is voidable at the option of the party misled. The guilty party cannot set up his own wrong as a ground for repudiating the contract.

The party who has been misled may rescind the contract either by his own act or by bringing an action for rescission. The general rule is that the party wishing to rescind must communicate his intention to the other party. An exception is admitted where a contract has been induced by fraudulent misrepresentation and the party guilty of the fraud has absconded with the intention of avoiding communication; in such a case the innocent party may rescind the contract by overt means falling short of communication or re-possession, *e.g.* by informing the police (*Car and Universal Finance Co. Ltd.* v. *Caldwell* [1965] 1 Q.B. 525, see pp. 251–252, *post*).

The injured party loses the right of rescission in the following circumstances—

(a) If, in the exercise of his discretionary power, the judge (or arbitrator) declares the contract as subsisting and awards damages in lieu of rescission (section 2 (2)).

(b) If, with knowledge of the misrepresentation, he takes a benefit under the contract or in some other way affirms it.

(c) If the parties cannot be restored to their original positions.

The L Syndicate sold nitrate works to the L Company under a contract which contained misleading particulars. The company sued for rescission of the contract. *Held*, owing to the alteration of the property consequent

on its being worked by the company, the position of the parties had been
so changed that they could not be restored to their original positions, and
therefore the contract could not be rescinded: *Lagunas Nitrate Co.* v.
Lagunas Syndicate [1899] 2 Ch. 392.

The same result obtains where a person is induced by false
statements in the prospectus to take shares in a company, and
before he rescinds the contract the company goes into liquidation.
In such a case it is too late to rescind the contract. If the shares
have merely fallen in value, rescission can be obtained.

A broker employed to buy shares on behalf of a client fraudulently
pretended to do so, while in fact selling shares of his own to the client.
On discovering this, the client brought an action for rescission. At the
time of the purchase the shares were worth nearly £3 each, but at the
date of the commencement of the action they had fallen to 5s. *Held*,
the contract could be rescinded because the same shares could be handed
back, the deterioration in value being immaterial: *Armstrong* v. *Jackson*
[1917] 2 K.B. 822.

In the case of fraud, lapse of time alone does not prevent the
contract from being rescinded as long as the action is brought
within six years of the time when the fraud was or with reasonable
diligence could have been discovered: Limitation Act 1939, s. 26.

(d) If a third party has acquired for value rights under the
contract.

If A obtains goods from B by fraud and pawns them with C,
B cannot rescind the contract on learning of the fraud so as to
be able to recover the goods from C (*Phillips* v. *Brooks* [1919]
2 K.B. 243; see p. 69, *ante*).

(e) The fact that the contract has been performed does not
deprive the misled party of his right to rescind. The rule in *Seddon*
v. *North Eastern Salt Co.* [1905] 1 Ch. 326, which supported the
contrary view has been abolished by the Misrepresentation Act
1967, s. 1 (*b*).

Refusal of the injured party to perform the contract

The misled party can either refuse to perform his part or he
can resist a suit for specific performance or an action for damages
brought against him on account of it.

Misrepresentation and exemption clauses

A term of a contract which excludes or restricts

(a) the liability of a party for misrepresentation, or

(b) any remedy of a party for misrepresentation

is null and void, except in so far as admitted by the court (or arbitrator) as being fair and reasonable in the circumstances of the case (Misrepresentation Act 1967, s. 3).

This section only limits clauses excluding or restricting liability for misrepresentations made by a party or his agent, but it does not qualify the right of a principal publicly to limit the otherwise ostensible authority of his agent (*Overbrooke Estates Ltd.* v. *Glencombe Properties Ltd.* [1974] 1 W.L.R. 1335).

Estoppel by conduct

An innocent misrepresentation may give rise to an action for damages through the **doctrine of estoppel.** Estoppel means that a person is prevented (or estopped) from denying the truth of a statement which he has made.

The basis of estoppel is, in the words of Lord Denning M.R. (in *Panchaud Frères S.A.* v. *Etablissements General Grain Co.* [1970] 1 Lloyd's Rep. 53, 57, see p. 266, *post*) "that a man has so conducted himself that it would be unfair or unjust to allow him to depart from a particular state of affairs which another has taken to be settled or correct."

To set up an estoppel there must be—

(a) a representation of fact intended to be acted on by the person to whom it was made;

(b) action taken upon it by that person;

(c) detriment to that person by acting on it.

Two parcels of cans of frozen eggs were shipped on O's ship under a bill of lading, signed by the master, stating that they were shipped "in apparent good order and condition." They were delivered damaged. *Held*, as against the consignees of the eggs, O was stopped from proving that the parcels were already damaged when they were shipped, and consequently O was liable for the damage: *Silver* v. *Ocean Steamship Co.* [1930] 1 K.B. 416.

Here, the cause of action was that O had damaged the eggs during transit, but the statement that they were in good order on shipment was an essential fact to be proved. Had there been no

such statement in the bill of lading, the consignee would not have
paid for the eggs. It was because the statement (which may have
been false) was made that damages were payable.

The plaintiff, Peter Cremer, an importer in West Germany, bought a
quantity of tapioca roots from a seller in Bangkok for shipment from
Thailand to Bremen on c.i.f. terms. When the goods were loaded in the
Dona Mari, a vessel owned by the defendants, the chief officer noticed a
bitter smell which indicated that the tapioca was mouldy, and he claused
the mate's receipts "not quite dry." The clausings were not transferred
to the bills of lading which were issued clean. The plaintiff and a buyer
who had acquired part of the consignment paid against the clean bills of
lading. When on arrival it was discovered that the tapioca was mouldy,
they claimed damages from the defendant shipowners. *Held*, the shipowners were estopped by the issue of clean bills of lading from relying on
the pre-shipment condition of the goods: *Cremer and Others* v. *General
Carriers S.A.* [1976] 1 W.L.R. 341.

As owners, Moorgate Mercantile Co. Ltd., a finance company, let
a car to Mr. McLorg on hire-purchase terms. Owing to some oversight,
they failed to register the agreement with Hire Purchase Information Ltd.
(H.P.I.) with which the great majority of hire-purchase agreements were
registered. Later Mr. Twitchings who contemplated buying the car from
Mr. McLorg inquired from H.P.I. whether there was any hire-purchase
agreement registered against the car, Mr. McLord having concealed that
fact, Mr. Twitchings received a negative reply from H.P.I. He then
purchased the car and resold it. The finance company sued Mr. Twitchings
for damages for conversion. *Held*, that the finance company was not
estopped by the negative reply of H.P.I. because H.P.I. were not their
agents and, even if they had been agents, the terms of the reply of H.P.I.
excluded an estoppel: *Moorgate Mercantile Co. Ltd.* v. *Twitchings* [1976]
Q.B. 225.

DISCLOSURE OF MATERIAL FACTS

Silence not a misrepresentation

The general rule of the common law is that mere silence is not
a misrepresentation. In general, a contracting party is not bound to
disclose to the other material facts which he knows will influence him
in coming to a decision about the contract; even if he knows that
the other party is ignorant of an important fact or if he thinks
that the other party is under some misapprehension, he is under no
obligation to enlighten him (*Smith* v. *Hughes*, p. 72, *ante*). This
rule has not been affected by the Misrepresentation Act 1967.

In contracts of sale of goods, this rule is summed up in the maxim "*caveat emptor*," but its harshness is greatly modified by the Sale of Goods Act 1893 which implies certain conditions into every contract of sale (ss. 12–15) (see p. 234, *post*).

Duty to disclose

Exceptionally, however, in the following cases, a party is under a duty unasked to disclose all material facts.

1. When in the course of the negotiations a party makes a representation of fact which is true when made but which, before the contract is concluded, becomes untrue to the knowledge of the party who made it, that party is bound, without being asked, to correct his former representation to the other party (see p. 80, *ante*).

2. If part only of a state of facts is disclosed, and the undisclosed part so modifies the part disclosed as to render it, by itself, substantially untrue, there is a duty to disclose the full facts. For example, if an accountant reporting on accounts says that the accounts are correct, subject to some observations which he makes, there is a duty on the person disclosing the report not only to quote that part which says that the accounts are correct, but also to reveal that the correctness is subject to qualifications. In such a case, the statement of part of the report represents by implication that the part is complete, and that there is nothing more to disclose.

A prospectus contained statements, which were true, that the company had paid dividends every year between 1921 and 1927. In fact during each of those years the company had incurred substantial trading losses, and was only able to pay the specified dividends by the introduction into the accounts of non-recurring items such as repayments of excess profits duty, adjustment of income tax, reserves and the like. No disclosure was made of these trading losses. *Held*, the prospectus was false, because it put before intending investors figures which apparently disclosed the existing position of the company, but in fact hid it, and K, a director, who knew that it was false, was guilty of fraud: *R. v. Kylsant* [1932] 1 K.B. 442.

3. Contracts *uberrimae fidei*. They require further explanation.

Contracts of utmost good faith

Contracts of utmost good faith (*uberrimae fidei*) constitute the most important exception to the general rule that silence does not amount to misrepresentation. These are contracts in which one party alone has full knowledge of the material facts and therefore the law imposes on him a duty to disclose these facts to the other party.

Contracts of utmost good faith *are*—

 1. contracts of insurance;
 2. contracts for the allotment of shares in companies;
 3. contracts of family arrangement;
 4. certain contracts for the sale of land; and
 5. contracts of suretyship and partnership in some respects.

1. In insurance contracts there is an obligation on the assured to disclose to the insurer all material facts. These are facts which would influence the judgment of a prudent insurer in fixing the premium or determining whether he will take the risk. Failure to fulfil this obligation renders the contract voidable at the option of the insurer. It is irrelevant that the assured did not appreciate the materiality of the fact which he failed to disclose. (See Chaps. 23 and 24, *post*.)

2. When the public is invited to subscribe for shares or debentures in a company, a prospectus must be issued. The prospectus must disclose the various matters set out in the Companies Act 1948, s. 38. The omission to disclose any of these matters may render those responsible for the prospectus liable in damages (*Re South of England Natural Gas Co.* [1911] 1 Ch. 573).

3. When members of a family make arrangements for the settlement of the family property, each member of the family must make full disclosure of every material fact within his knowledge (*Gordon* v. *Gordon* (1816) 3 Swanst. 400).

4. In contracts for the sale of land, there is normally no duty to make disclosure, except that the vendor is under the obligation of disclosing every defect in his title, such as the existence of restrictive covenants affecting the user of the land. This, however, is in reality not a case of a duty to disclose but one of inability to perform because, if the vendor has undertaken to convey an unencumbered title to the purchaser and cannot do so, he has failed to perform his contract.

5. Suretyship and partnership, though often described as contracts of utmost good faith, are not properly so described. In both cases, *after* the contract has been made there is a duty to disclose every material circumstance affecting the relationship between the parties, but there is no such duty *before* the contract is entered into.

DURESS AND UNDUE INFLUENCE

A contract entered into under duress or undue influence is voidable at the option of the party coerced or influenced, because his consent to the making of the contract is not freely given.

Duress at common law had a much narrower meaning than undue influence in equity. They are now merged in one another, and prevent a contract from being made when it is entered into under compulsion, physical or moral, or under some persuasion which the law regards as unfair. A contract is voidable under this head when there is—

1. Actual or threatened physical violence or imprisonment.
2. Threatened criminal proceedings.

The person threatened need not be the actual contracting party, but may be the husband or wife or near relative of the party.

K sued G on a contract made in France, which K had coerced G into making by threats of prosecuting G's husband for a criminal offence which he had committed. *Held*, G was not liable, as her consent was obtained through duress: *Kaufman* v. *Gerson* [1904] 1 K.B. 491.

3. Implied threat of criminal proceedings.

W's son forged the company's signature to a guarantee. In exchange for the forged guarantee, M obtained a valid guarantee from the company, because, as M knew, W's state of health was such that the prosecution of his son would be likely to endanger his life. The company was W's family company. No actual threat of prosecution was made. *Held*, the guarantee was obtained by undue influence and was voidable: *Mutual Finance Ltd.* v. *John Wetton & Sons* [1937] 2 K.B. 389.

4. Wrongful detention or threatened seizure of property.

H owned a market and claimed tolls from M, a produce dealer. M refused to pay, and H seized his goods, whereupon M paid and continued to pay yearly under protest. H's right to tolls was subsequently declared illegal. *Held*, M could recover the payments made: *Maskell* v. *Horner* [1915] 3 K.B. 106.

5. A fiduciary relationship between the contracting parties.

"There are two well-established classes of undue influence. The first is where the donee stands in such a fiduciary relation to the donor that a presumption of undue influence arises which prevails unless rebutted by the donee; and secondly where undue influence is established independently of such a presumption" (*per* Ungoed-Thomas J. in *Re Craig, decd.* [1971] Ch. 95).

Cases of undue influence "tend to arise where someone relies on the guidance or advice of another, where the other is aware of that reliance and where the person upon whom reliance is placed obtains, or may well obtain, a benefit from the transaction or has some other interest in it being concluded. In addition, there must, of course, be shown to exist a vital element which in this judgment will for convenience be referred to as confidentiality" (*per* Sir Eric Sachs in *Lloyds Bank Ltd.* v. *Bundy* [1975] Q.B. 326, 341).

The defendant, Mr. Herbert Bundy, an elderly farmer, and his only son had been customers of the local country branch of the plaintiffs, Lloyds Bank, for many years. Mr. Bundy wished to assist his son in the promotion of the son's company called M. J. B. Plant Hire Ltd. The company was indebted to Lloyds Bank and the defendant had guaranteed the company's overdraft and secured it by a charge on his house. Subsequently the manager of the local branch made the continuance of the overdraft dependent on the defendant giving the bank a further charge to full value of his house. The defendant who trusted the bank manager implicitly agreed to his proposal. The bank manager had failed to advise the defendant to seek independent legal advice. The plaintiff bank tried to sell the defendant's house and claimed possession. *Held*, the bank, in the circumstances of the case, was under a duty of confidentiality to the defendant and exercised undue influence. The defendant could avoid the guarantee and the charge: *Lloyds Bank* v. *Bundy* [1975] Q.B. 326.

It should not be inferred from this case that the relationship between bank and customer is invariably of a fiduciary character. That is not so; all that *Lloyds Bank* v. *Bundy* establishes is that in exceptional circumstances that relationship may be of that character.

Undue influence is presumed in transactions between parent and child, solicitor and client, trustee and *cestui que trust*, guardian and ward, and physician and patient. In all these cases the presumption may be rebutted. The most effective way of rebutting this presumption is by showing that the other party had independent legal advice; even this, however, will not be effective unless the legal adviser had full knowledge of all the relevant circumstances.

A Malay woman of great age and wholly illiterate made a deed of gift of valuable property in Singapore to her nephew, who managed her affairs. She was advised by her lawyer, who did not know that the gift constituted practically the whole of her property and did not tell her that she could equally benefit her nephew by will. *Held*, the gift should be set aside on the ground of undue influence: *Inche Noriah* v. *Shaik Allie Bin Omar* [1929] A.C. 127.

A widow of more than 70 years who owned a house took a lodger. The lodger ingratiated himself with her and she reposed such trust and confidence in him that she made him virtually the manager of her affairs and eventually transferred her house to him for the purpose of preventing her nephew from turning him out. It was orally agreed that the house would remain her property during her life although it was registered in the lodger's name. The lodger sold the house to a purchaser who was unaware of the true position and did not know that the widow continued to live in the house in actual possession. The widow sued the purchaser for the return of the house. *Held*, (1) the lodger held the house in trust for the widow; (2) in the alternative, undue influence was presumed as the lodger had acquired a position of trust and confidence with respect to the widow; (3) the purchaser in good faith was not protected by virtue of the Land Registration Act 1925 because he was aware that the widow was in actual possession. The claim of the widow was successful: *Hodgson* v. *Marks* [1971] Ch. 892.

No presumption of undue influence exists between an engaged couple (*Zamet* v. *Hyman* [1961] 1 W.L.R. 1442) or between husband and wife (*Howes* v. *Bishop* [1909] 2 K.B. 390). Undue influence may, however, be proved to exist in fact in this as in other cases, and when it is proved, the contract is voidable.

A third party contracting with notice of the exercise of undue influence by another is in no better position than if he had exercised undue influence himself.

B, a married woman, under the undue influence of her mother, entered into improvident moneylending contracts for her mother's benefit. The moneylenders knew all the circumstances between B and her mother. *Held*, the moneylenders were in no better position than the mother, and the contracts were voidable: *Lancashire Loans Ltd.* v. *Black* [1934] 1 K.B. 380.

MONEYLENDING CONTRACTS

The statutory provisions relating to this subject are contained in the Moneylenders Acts 1900–1927, which, however, will be superseded by the Consumer Credits Act 1974 (Chap. 17), when fully operative.

Under the Moneylenders Act 1900 the court has power to reopen moneylending transactions when—

1. the interest charged is excessive or the amounts charged for bonuses or commission are excessive; and
2. the transaction is harsh and unconscionable, or is otherwise such that a court of equity would grant relief.

If the interest exceeds the rate of 48 per cent. per annum, there is a presumption that it is excessive, and that the transaction is harsh and unconscionable, but the court may be satisfied that interest at a smaller rate is excessive (Moneylenders Act 1927, s. 10).

No moneylending contract is enforceable unless a note or memorandum of the contract is in writing signed by the borrower personally, and a copy of it is sent to the borrower within seven days of the making of the contract. The note or memorandum must contain all the terms of the contract, the date of the loan, the principal, and the interest charged expressed either as a rate per cent. per annum or the rate represented by the interest charged in the manner calculated in the Act (Moneylenders Act 1927, s. 6). An action by a moneylender to recover money lent must be brought within 12 months from the date when the cause of the action accrued, unless the borrower gives an acknowledgment in writing or is beyond the seas at the date of the accrual of the cause of action (Moneylenders Act 1927, s. 13).

A moneylender is a person who carries on the business of moneylending. Moneylenders must be licensed and a licence can only be obtained by persons holding a certificate granted by the petty sessional court for the district in which the moneylender's business is to be carried on. The certificate must show the moneylender's true name and the name under which and the address at which he is authorised to carry on business.

Friendly societies, banks, insurance companies, and persons bona fide carrying on any business not having for its primary object the lending of money, but in the course of which, and for the purpose of the business, money is lent, are not moneylenders (Moneylenders Act 1900). A hire-purchase finance house may be a banker by repute and consequently not a moneylender (*United Dominions Trust Ltd.* v. *Kirkwood* [1966] 2 Q.B. 431). In order to resolve any uncertainty whether a person is a banker and not a moneylender, the Department of Trade is authorised to issue a certificate to that effect, and that certificate is conclusive evidence that the person is a banker for the purposes of the Moneylenders Acts 1900 and 1927 (Companies Act 1967, s. 123).

Where an unregistered moneylender makes an illegal loan and later another person who has full knowledge of the illegality of that loan lends the borrower money to enable him to repay the illegal loan, the second loan is also tainted by the illegality of the first loan and is unenforceable (*Spector* v. *Ageda* [1973] Ch. 30). But where the claim by an unregistered moneylender for the return of the money is the subject of a bona fide settlement between the parties which includes a compromise of the question whether or not the Moneylenders Acts apply, it is not open to the debtor to reopen the question of illegal moneylending in an action on the settlement (*Binder* v. *Alachouzos* [1972] 2 Q.B. 151).

SELECT BIBLIOGRAPHY
Books

	Treitel	Cheshire & Fifoot
Unenforceable Contracts	105–119	174–201
Mistake	168–212	205–244
Remedies—Rectification	202–208	221–223
Recovery of money paid under mistake of fact	—	641–647
Rescission	198–202	217–221
Misrepresentation	213–269	243–285
Remedies—Rescission	241–257	263–273
Damages	233–241	273–276
Duress & Undue Influence	270–276	285–294
Money Lending	276–277	—

See also Stoljar S. J., *Mistake and Misrepresentation, A Study in Contractual Principles*, Sweet & Maxwell 1968, as a reference book.

Articles

Atiyah, P. S., and Treitel, G. H., "Misrepresentation Act 1967" (1967) 30 M.L.R. 369–388.

Beatson, J., "Duress as a Vitiating Factor in Contract" [1975] C.L.J. 97–115.

James, P. S., "Innocent Misrepresentation: An Unanswered Challenge" [1963] J.B.L. 207–220, 319–335.

Stoljar, S. J., "A New Approach to Mistake in Contract" (1968) 28 M.L.R. 265–285.

Stone, J., "The Limits of *Non est Factum* after Gallie *v.* Lee" (1972) 88 L.Q.R. 190–224.

Chapter 7

ILLEGAL CONTRACTS

A CONTRACT which is illegal is void. The illegality may be present—

1. in the formation of the contract, *e.g.* when an unlicensed moneylender makes a loan;
2. in the performance of the contract, *e.g.* a contract to commit a crime;
3. in the consideration for the contract; or
4. in the purpose for which the contract is made, *e.g.* if a motor boat is hired for the purpose of smuggling drugs into the country.

Contracts are illegal because they are forbidden by statute or because they are contrary to public policy, which is a common law concept. A contract is contrary to public policy when it is in the public interest that it should not be enforced.

Illegality is a matter of degree, varying according to the gravity of the legal prohibition. Two general categories of illegal contracts can be distinguished: some illegal contracts contain an element of obvious moral turpitude, *e.g.* an agreement to commit a crime; in others such taint is absent, *e.g.* in a contract in restraint of trade. The courts treat contracts of the latter category more leniently than contracts of the former class; in particular, collateral agreements not tainted by illegality of the former type are not void.

In addition, an act rendered illegal by statute might be committed in performance of an otherwise perfectly legal contract. Here a question of interpretation of the statute arises: Was it the intention of Parliament to preclude a party from enforcing the contract or was it only intended that other consequences should ensue, *e.g.* the imposition of a penalty? In the latter case the contract would remain enforceable. Later, when the effect of illegality will be considered, this type of illegality will require special attention (see p. 113, *post*).

The following contracts are illegal—

Contracts tending to injure the public service

These include agreements for the sale of public offices or for the assignment of salaries of public officials or of pensions granted for public services. A contract to procure a title of honour for reward is also void.

> The secretary of the College of Ambulance promised Col. Parkinson that if he made a large donation to the college, which was a charitable institution, he would receive a knighthood. The Colonel made a large donation, and, not receiving his knighthood, sued for the return of his money. *Held*, the action failed because the contract was against public policy and illegal: *Parkinson* v. *College of Ambulance Ltd.* [1925] 2 K.B. 1.

A contract by a person to use his position and influence with the Government to procure a benefit for another is void as being against public policy (*Montefiore* v. *Menday Motor Components Ltd.* [1918] 2 K.B. 241), as is also a contract to restrain a person from serving in the naval or military forces of the country (*Re Beard* [1908] 1 Ch. 383).

Contracts tending to impede the administration of justice

Contracts relating to criminal prosecution and bankruptcy

An agreement to stifle a prosecution for a criminal offence is void, because the public has an interest in the proper administration of justice. If, however, the offence was one for which the injured party could sue and recover damages as well as one which could be the subject of criminal proceedings, an agreement for compromise will be valid. An agreement between a prisoner and a person who has gone bail for him to indemnify him against the bail is void, as tending to defeat the object for which bail was granted (*R.* v. *Porter* [1910] 1 K.B. 369).

A contract tending to defeat the bankruptcy law is void.

> M owed J £852 and promised that if J would tell M's trustee in bankruptcy that the money was a present, M would, notwithstanding, still be J's debtor. *Held*, the agreement was void: *John* v. *Mendoza* [1939] 1 K.B. 141.

Contracts of maintenance and champerty

Maintenance has been defined as "improperly stirring up litigation and strife by giving aid to one party to bring or defend a claim without just cause or excuse" (*per* Lord Denning M.R. in *Re Trepca Mines Ltd.* (*No.* 2) [1963] Ch. 199, 219). Champerty is an arrangement whereby a person obtains a promise of a share in the proceeds of an action in return for providing evidence or financial assistance to

the person who conducts the litigation. Contracts having maintenance or champerty as their object tend to pervert the course of justice
and are illegal.

It is not maintenance, however, when the person giving assistance
is a near relation, or acts from motives of charity, or has a common
interest with the person assisted. In modern law, "common interest"
is interpreted widely; a person who has "a legitimate and genuine
business interest in the result of an action" must be taken to have
such interest (*Martell* v. *Consett Iron Co. Ltd.* [1955] Ch. 363).

Maintenance and champerty are no longer criminal offences or
torts, but the abolition of criminal and civil liability has not affected
the rule that contracts aimed at these activities are illegal. (Criminal
Law Act 1967, ss. 13 (1) (*a*) and 14.)

Contracts ousting the jurisdiction of the courts

A contract purporting to oust the jurisdiction of the court in a
question of law is illegal as being contrary to public policy and consequently void.

Thus, an arbitration agreement prohibiting the parties from
requiring the arbitration tribunal to state a special case for the
opinion of the court on a question of law is void (*Czarnikow* v. *Roth,
Schmidt & Co.* [1922] 2 K.B. 478, see p. 547, *post*). Similarly, a clause
in a lease that a surveyor's certificate as to the contribution of a
lessee towards expenses shall be final and not subject to any challenge
whatsoever, is void, as the clause relates not only to questions of fact
but also to questions of law (*Re Davstone Estate Ltd.'s Leases* [1969]
2 Ch. 378).

Contracts of trading with the enemy

At common law, and also by virtue of the Trading with the
Enemy Act 1939, all contracts made with a person voluntarily
residing in enemy territory in time of war are illegal unless made with
the licence of the Crown. "Contracts made directly with enemies as
contracting parties are declared illegal on the ground of public policy
based upon one of two reasons, either that the further performance
of the contract would involve intercourse with the enemy, or that the
continued existence of the contract would confer upon the enemy an
immediate or future benefit" (*per* Russell J. in *Re Badische Co. Ltd.*
[1921] 2 Ch. 331).

But war does not expropriate; accrued rights of an enemy are preserved and kept in suspense until the war is over; often their administration is entrusted to an administrator of enemy property during the war (*Arab Bank Ltd.* v. *Barclays Bank* [1954] A.C. 495).

Contracts to commit a criminal offence or a civil wrong

An agreement to defraud the inland revenue by tax evasion is illegal and cannot be relied upon in a court of law (*Napier* v. *National Business Agency Ltd.* [1951] 2 All E.R. 263; see p. 115, *post*). The same principle applies to an agreement to defraud a local rating authority.

A let a flat to R at a rent of £1,200 a year. With the object of getting a low rateable value for the flat, two written agreements were entered into, one purporting to let the flat for £450 a year, the other being an agreement by R to pay £750 a year for services in connection with the flat. A sued R for an instalment of £750. *Held*, the agreement, being made to defraud the rating authority, was void, and A failed: *Alexander* v. *Rayson* [1936] 1 K.B. 169.

An agreement to take shares in a company in order fraudulently to induce the public to believe that there is a market for the shares is an indictable conspiracy and is illegal (*Scott* v. *Brown* [1892] 2 Q.B. 724). Similarly, an agreement by the proprietors of a news-paper to indemnify the printers against claims arising out of libels published in the newspaper is void (*W. H. Smith & Son* v. *Clinton* (1908) 25 T.L.R. 34). Further, an insurance policy indemnifying the assured against legal liability for accidents caused by him cannot be enforced because, even if the event was an "accident," it was caused by a deliberate and unlawful assault by the assured (*Gray* v. *Barr*, below).

Gray had an affair with Barr's wife. Barr, armed with a loaded shot-gun, went to Gray's farm to search for his wife. In a struggle with Gray, Barr fell down the stairs, the gun was involuntarily discharged, and the shot killed Gray. Barr was acquitted of murder and manslaughter. The administrators of Gray's estate sued Barr for damages under the Fatal Accidents Acts and Barr, by way of third party proceedings, claimed to be indemnified by the Prudential Assurance under an accident liability policy. *Held*, (i) Barr was liable for having caused Gray's death by gross negligence; (ii) the killing was not an "accident" within the meaning of the insurance policy; (iii) even if the killing was an "accident," it was caused by the deliberate and unlawful act of the assured, and it was therefore against public policy to admit a claim for indemnity against the insurance company: *Gray* v. *Barr* [1971] 2 Q.B. 554 (C.A.).

The suicide of the assured, if sane at the time, rendered the sum assured irrecoverable at a time when suicide was a crime.[1]

B insured his life under a policy which provided that the policy should be void if the assured committed suicide whether sane or insane within a year of the policy. Nine years after, while he was sane, B committed suicide. *Held*, the sums assured could not be recovered because, suicide then being a crime, it was against public policy that a man or his estate should benefit from his own crime: *Beresford* v. *Royal Insurance Co.* [1938] A.C. 586.

An agreement to perform in a foreign and friendly country an act which is illegal in that country, is void in English law as a matter of public policy based on international comity.

In 1927, when the United States was subject to Prohibition and the sale and importation of alcoholic liquors were illegal, a partnership was formed in England for the purpose of smuggling whisky into the States, in contravention of the American Prohibition legislation. In proceedings between the partners in the English courts, *held*, the partnership agreement was illegal in English law: *Foster* v. *Driscoll* [1921] 1 K.B. 470.

S agreed to sell and deliver jute bags to R, both parties contemplating and intending that the goods would be shipped from India and be made available in Genoa so that R might import them into South Africa. Both parties knew that the law of India prohibited the direct or indirect export of goods from India to South Africa. The proper law of the contract was English law. S repudiated the contract. *Held*, the contract was likewise illegal in English law: *Regazzoni* v. *K. C. Sethia (1944) Ltd.* [1958] A.C. 301.

Immoral contracts

Contracts relating to sexual immorality, such as agreements for future illicit cohabitation, are void. Contracts in consideration of past illicit cohabitation are made for no consideration, but are not illegal. Moreover, collateral contracts good in themselves will become void if they are knowingly made to further an immoral purpose.

A let a cab on hire to B, a prostitute, knowing that it was to be used for immoral purposes. *Held*, A could not recover the hire: *Pearce* v. *Brookes* (1866) L.R. 1 Ex. 213.

Agreements between husband and wife for future separation, and between a married man, with a woman who knows him to be

[1] Suicide ceased to be a crime by virtue of the Suicide Act 1961, s. 1.

married, for marriage after his wife's death are void (*Wilson* v. *Carnley* [1908] 1 K.B. 729), but a contract made between decree nisi and decree absolute for marriage after the dissolution of the existing marriage is valid (*Fender* v. *Mildmay* [1938] A.C. 1).

Contracts affecting the freedom of marriage

Contracts in general restraint of marriage are void, as also are contracts unreasonably affecting freedom of choice in marriage. But contracts restraining marriage with a particular person, or otherwise only partially restraining marriage, are valid.

Marriage brokage contracts, that is, contracts to introduce men and women to each other with a view to their subsequent marriage, are void.

Miscellaneous contracts contrary to public policy

A contract by a newspaper proprietor not to comment on the conduct of a particular person is void. "For a newspaper to stipulate for a consideration that it will refrain from exercising its right of commenting upon fraudulent schemes, when it is the ordinary business of the company to comment upon fraudulent schemes, is in itself a stipulation which is quite contrary to public policy, and which cannot be enforced in a court of law" (*per* Atkin J. in *Neville* v. *Dominion of Canada News Co. Ltd.* [1915] 3 K.B. 556).

A contract unduly fettering the liberty of the individual is void. Where, therefore, a man agreed with a moneylender not to change his residence, or his employment, or to consent to a reduction of his salary, or to part with any of his property, or to incur any obligations on credit, or any obligations, legal or moral, without the consent of the moneylender, it was held that the contract was void (*Horwood* v. *Millar's Timber Co.* [1917] 1 K.B. 305). But where a father, whose son was of dissolute habits, agreed to pay his son's debts, and the son, in consideration thereof, agreed not to go within 80 miles of London, it was held that the contract was binding, because the object of the restriction was to reform the son (*Denny's Trustee* v. *Denny* [1919] 1 K.B. 583).

Contracts in restraint of trade

A contract in restraint of trade is one which restricts a person, wholly or partially, in the carrying on of his trade or business. All such contracts are prima facie void and will only be enforced if they are reasonable. They may be divided into two classes: 1, those protecting a proprietary interest, and 2, those restraining competition.

1. A contract in restraint of trade which is intended to protect a proprietary interest, *e.g.* on the sale of the goodwill of a business or to prevent a servant from revealing trade secrets, will be enforced if it is—

(a) reasonable with reference to the party against whom it is made; and

(b) reasonable with reference to the public.

N was an inventor and a manufacturer of guns and ammunition. He sold his business to a company and agreed that for twenty-five years he would not manufacture guns or ammunition in any part of the world. *Held*, the agreement was binding: *Nordenfelt* v. *Maxim Nordenfelt Gun Co.* [1894] A.C. 535.

If a restraint is wider than is reasonably necessary to protect the party in whose interest it is imposed, the courts will refuse to alter it to what would have been a proper limit. But if an agreement has several clauses, some valid and others void, the court will, if the valid clauses can be **severed** from the void, enforce those clauses which are valid if the severance does not affect the meaning of the remaining part of the contract.

S carried on business as an estate agent in Dartmouth and in Kingsbridge. He employed S J as clerk and negotiator at the Kingsbridge office. S J signed a covenant whereby he undertook for three years not to set up in business within a radius of the Dartmouth or of the Kingsbridge offices of S. After termination of the contract of employment S J forthwith opened an office of his own within the five-mile radius of Kingsbridge. *Held*, the restraint, as agreed, was too wide, as S J had never worked at the Dartmouth office. However, the Dartmouth restraint was severable from the Kingsbridge restraint, which was not too wide. While the former was invalid, the latter had to be upheld: *Scorer* v. *Seymour Jones* [1966] 1 W.L.R. 1419.

The plaintiff company, T. Lucas & Co. Ltd., manufactured a binder and filler used in the production of processed meat products. They employed the defendant, Mr. Mitchell, as a sales representative in Greater Manchester. The service contract provided that Mr. Mitchell should not "deal" in similar goods, or "solicit" orders for them, or "supply" them within the allocated area for 12 months after termination of his employment. Mr. Mitchell terminated his employment with Lucas and at once began to canvass on behalf of a rival firm a considerable number of customers of Lucas in the Greater Manchester area. *Held*, the restraint relating to "dealing" was wider than was necessary to protect the legitimate interests of Lucas and was therefore invalid, but it could be severed from the restraint relating to "soliciting" and "supplying." An injunction was granted to Lucas against the solicitation and supply by Mitchell: *T. Lucas & Co. Ltd.* v. *Mitchell* [1974] Ch. 129.

Amoco Australia was an oil company operating in Australia. Amoco contracted with Rocca that the latter should build a service station on their land and lease it to Amoco who would underlease it to Rocca. The underlease contained tying covenants with respect to the supply of petrol and oil by Amoco, which constituted an unreasonable restraint. The headlease contained a provision that it should be independent of any other agreement. *Held* by the Privy Council (on appeal from the Supreme Court of South Australia), (1) covenants in restraint of trade in a lease had to be treated on the same principles as such terms in contracts; (2) the restraint in the underlease was not severable from the other covenants in the underlease; (3) the headlease and the underlease were parts of a single commercial transaction and the statement in the headlease that it should be independent was not true; (4) consequently, the invalidity of the underlease rendered the headlease also invalid as it could not be severed from the underlease: *Amoco Australia Pty. Ltd.* v. *Rocca Bros. Motor Engineering Co. Pty. Ltd.* [1975] A.C. 561.

If a contract in restraint of trade is reasonable as between the parties, the onus of showing that it is unreasonable in the public interest is, in common law, a very heavy one. It will only be discharged if it creates "a monopoly calculated to enhance prices to an unreasonable extent" (*Att.-Gen. of Australia* v. *Adelaide S.S. Co.* [1913] A.C. 781). "But an ill-regulated supply and unremunerative prices may, in point of fact, be disadvantageous to the public. Such a state of things may, if it is not controlled, drive manufacturers out of business, or lower wages, and so cause unemployment and labour disturbance. It must always be a question of circumstances, whether a combination of manufacturers in a particular trade is an evil from a public point of view" (*per* Lord Haldane in *N. W. Salt Co.* v. *Electrolytic Alkali Co.* [1914] A.C. 461). In modern cases, however, a narrower meaning is attributed to the requirement that the contract must not be unreasonable "in the public interest." That concept appears to refer to a *legal* principle or proposition, rather than to *economic* theories. ". . . reasonableness in the interest of the public refers to the interests of the public as recognised in a principle or proposition of law and not to the interests of the public at large. . . . For my part, I prefer to decide that the restraints relied on in our case are reasonable in the interests of the public, not on balance of existing or possible economic advantages and disadvantages to the public but because there is, in conditions as they are, no unreasonable limitation of liberty to trade" (*per* Ungoed-Thomas J. in *Texaco Ltd.* v. *Mulberry Filling Station Ltd.* [1972] 1 W.L.R. 814, 828).

The categories of restraint of trade are not closed. The doctrine is not limited to contracts between employer and employee, vendor and purchaser of a business, and combinations to restrict trading activities. The doctrine may apply to restrictions intended to promote trade, to restrictions on part only of a multiple business and to restrictions in a trade or service contract during the subsistence of the trading or service. It may also apply to restrictions imposed on trade on a particular piece of land where the effect is to restrict the trader's liberty to trade or to restrictions preventing a person from exploiting his earning power if the party for whose benefit these restrictions are stipulated has made use of his superior bargaining power.

A **solus agreement** whereby a garage proprietor binds himself to buy all his petrol from an oil company is not necessarily in restraint of trade and bad, for in view of existing arrangements for the distribution of petrol, the widespread incidence of solus agreements and the necessity for oil companies to protect their trade outlets, such an agreement might be reasonable. It depends on the nature and duration of the restrictions imposed on future liberty to trade.

M, who was negotiating to buy a garage, signed as a condition of the sale a solus agreement with P, an oil company. The agreement provided, *inter alia*, that M would obtain all petrol from P and sell no other brand of petrol, that M would advertise only P's lubricating oil and use only that oil in the lubricating bay, that M would not sell or otherwise dispose of the garage without first giving P first refusal and then only to a person willing to enter into a solus agreement in similar terms, and that the agreement was to continue for 12 years although it could be determined before on three months' notice once 600,000 gallons of P's petrol had been sold. *Held*, (i) as the agreement operated as a restriction on the way in which M could carry on his trade on his own land—P having no interest by way of mortgage, lease or sale in respect of that land—the doctrine of restraint of trade applied; (ii) the restriction of M's power to dispose of his property, the period of restriction and the restriction of the lubricating oils were all unreasonable restrictions; (iii) as these provisions were not severable, the agreement as a whole was in unreasonable restraint of trade and unenforceable: *Petrofina (Great Britain) Ltd.* v. *Martin* [1966] Ch. 146.

The doctrine of restraint also applies to mortgages. Accordingly, if in contract to the situation in the *Petrofina* case, there is a mortgage of the premises in question in favour of the oil company, the court may regard the solus and loan agreements and the mortgage as constituting one transaction and the decision will turn on whether or not the restrictions, including any prohibition or restriction on redemption of the mortgage, are reasonable; a restriction of four years and five months was held to be reasonable to afford adequate protection to the oil company in maintaining a stable system of distribution, but a tie of 21 years was held to be excessive and void (*Esso Petroleum Co. Ltd.* v. *Harper's Garage (Stourport) Ltd.* [1968] A.C. 269). The doctrine of restraint does not, however, apply to leases; here the solus agreement and the lease are treated as one transaction and the restraint can be extended for the whole duration of the lease (*Total Oil Great Britain Ltd.* v. *Thompson Garages (Biggin Hill) Ltd.* [1972] 1 Q.B. 318).

2. A contract *merely* in restraint of competition is unenforceable.

"Such a restraint has . . . never been upheld, if directed only to the prevention of competition or against the use of the personal skill and knowledge acquired by the employee in his employer's business": *per* Lord Parker in *Morris* v. *Saxelby* [1916] 1 A.C. 668, 710.

But if the restraint, although against competition, is necessary to protect the employer against any improper use by the employee of the knowledge he has acquired in the service of his employer, *e.g.* trade connections, trade secrets, or confidential information, it will be enforced provided that it is no wider than is reasonably necessary to effect that purpose.

A, a tailor, employed B as his assistant under a contract by which B agreed on the termination of his employment not to carry on business as a tailor within 10 miles of A. *Held*, the agreement was merely to prevent B from using such skill as he possessed in competition with A and was therefore void. "An employer may not, after his servant has left his employment, prevent that servant from using his own skill and knowledge in his trade or profession, even if acquired when in the employer's service": *per* Younger L.J. in *Attwood* v. *Lamont* [1920] 3 K.B. 571.

X was a solicitor at Tamworth and Y was successively his junior clerk, articled clerk and managing clerk. In his contract of service Y agreed, on leaving X's employment, not to practise as a solicitor within seven miles of Tamworth. *Held*, the agreement was good, because Y during his service with X had become acquainted with the details of the business of X's clients, and therefore he could be restrained from using that knowledge to the detriment of X: *Fitch* v. *Dewes* [1921] 2 A.C. 158.

The extent of the protection depends on (a) the nature of the employer's business. and (b) the business position of the employee. A wider protection will be upheld, for instance, in the case of a manager of a business than in the case of a subordinate. Thus, a wider protection will be upheld where the employee has had personal contact with customers in cash transactions, and the business was not primarily conducted over the telephone on a credit basis (*S. W. Strange Ltd.* v. *Mann* [1965] 1 W.L.R. 629).

If the employee, in an attempt to evade a contract in restraint of trade, forms a company to carry on business as a cloak or sham to enable him to break the contract, an injunction will be granted to restrain the company as well as the employee from breaking the contract (*Gilford Motor Co.* v. *Horne* [1933] Ch. 935).

There is no confidential relationship in respect of which the master is entitled to protection between a reporter and a newspaper proprietor (*Leng* v. *Andrews* [1909] 1 Ch. 763); a canvasser and a clothing company (*Mason* v. *Provident Clothing Co.* [1913] A.C. 724); an estate agent and his clerk (*Bowler* v. *Lovegrove* [1921] 1 Ch. 642); a motor salesman and a firm of motor-car dealers (*Vincents of Reading* v. *Fogden* (1932) 48 T.L.R. 613).

It is, in practice, extremely difficult to frame restrictions which will adequately protect a trade connection and which will not at the same time cover some cases where the breach will not injure it; an employee cannot claim that a restraint is too wide by referring to situations which were clearly outside the contemplation of the parties when entering into the contract, although, on a literal interpretation, they might fall under the restraint clause.

A dairy agreed with a roundsman that after termination of his contract he should not serve for one year any person who was a customer of the dairy with "milk or dairy produce." The roundsman left the employment of the dairy and immediately started to operate a milk round covering the same area for a competitor. The dairy applied for an injunction, and the roundsman contended that the restraint was too wide as it would have prevented him from serving dairy produce, such as butter and cheese, in a grocery shop. *Held*, the restraint was valid because it had to be construed as relating only to the future activities of the defendant as a milk rounds-man: *Home Counties Dairies Ltd.* v. *Skilton* [1970] 1 W.L.R. 526.

It follows that such a restraint must be read in the context of the business in relation to which it was entered and must not be given an artificial and extended meaning.

Ann Francis worked as a ladies hairdresser in the establishment of

Marion White Ltd. She signed an agreement which provided that after termination of her employment she would not accept employment with a competitive enterprise within half a mile of the place where she was last employed for three months, the restraint to be valid for 12 months. Ann Francis was dismissed for a valid reason and a week later entered employment with a rival hairdresser within the prohibited area. It was argued on her behalf that the restraint was too wide because it would have prevented her from working for a rival as receptionist or bookkeeper. *Held*, the restraint was not too wide. The covenant aimed only at her active participation in the hairdressing aspects, if read in the business context of her employment: *Marion White Ltd.* v. *Francis* [1972] 1 W.L.R. 1423.

A servant who copies the names and addresses of his employer's customers for use after he has left his employment can be restrained from using the list, apart from any express restriction in his contract of service (*Robb* v. *Green* [1895] 2 Q.B. 315). Similarly, if he retains a secret process in his memory he can be restrained from disclosing it (*Amber Size and Chemical Co.* v. *Menzel* [1913] 2 Ch. 239). A skilled man with access to his employer's secrets must not work for a rival firm on similar work in his spare time.

H employed D on highly skilled work with access to their manufacturing data. In his spare time D worked for P on similar work in competition with H. *Held*, D was in breach of his duty to be faithful to H and could be restrained from working for P: *Hivac Ltd.* v. *Park Royal Scientific Instruments Ltd.* [1946] Ch. 169.

If an employee is wrongfully dismissed from his employment, the employer, having broken the contract, cannot rely on it so as to enforce a restrictive agreement against the servant (*General Billposting Co.* v. *Atkinson* [1909] A.C. 118). The court will refuse the contract-breaker an interlocutory injunction on the equitable ground that "he who comes to equity must do equity and come with clean hands" (*Consolidated Agricultural Suppliers Ltd.* v. *Rushmere, The Times*, 30 June, 1976).

The principles applying to a restraint on an employee imposed for the benefit of an employer apply also if the restraint is contained in a contract between two employers with respect to their employees.

Two companies manufacturing similar products agreed that neither would, without the written consent of the other, employ any person who had been a servant of the other during the previous five years. *Held*, the restraint was too wide and, consequently, void: *Kores Manufacturing Co. Ltd.* v. *Kolok Manufacturing Co. Ltd.* [1959] Ch. 108.

3. A contract is in restraint of trade if a person, by making use of his superior bargaining power, imposes unfair restrictions on another

person's ability to exploit his earning power. This principle, in essence, underlies the whole doctrine of restraint of trade.

Mr. Macaulay (formerly Mr. Instone), a song writer, entered into an agreement with Schroeder Music Publishing Co. Ltd., a powerful firm of publishers of music, whereby he gave Schroeder the exclusive right to publish his songs for five years, with an automatic extension to 10 years if his songs were successful. The publishers did not undertake to publish the song writer's songs but promised him a royalty if they published and sold them. The agreement, which was on a standard form prepared by the publishers, further provided that the publishers could terminate it but no corresponding right was given to the song writer. *Held*, the agreement constituted an unreasonable restraint of trade and was contrary to public policy. It was an unfair restriction on the earning power of the song writer, obtained by the publishers who had made use of their superior bargaining power: *A. Schroeder Music Publishing Co. Ltd.* v. *Macaulay (formerly Instone)* (known as *Instone* v. *A. Schroeder Music Publishing Co. Ltd.*) [1974] 1 W.L.R. 1308.

In a similar case the Court of Appeal refused to grant publishers of music an interlocutory injunction against the song writer (*Clifford Davis Management Ltd.* v. *W.E.A. Records Ltd.* [1975] 1 W.L.R. 61).

4. The decision of a trade association to restrict the trading activities of its members is subject to the rules governing a restraint of trade.

The Pharmaceutical Society of Great Britain decided that existing pharmacies should not extend their trading activity to non-traditional goods. Boots objected. *Held*, that the Society's decision was a restraint of trade and contrary to public policy, and the objection of Dickson (who was the retail director of Boots) had to be upheld, since no attempt had been made to justify the restraint: *Dickson* v. *Pharmaceutical Society of Great Britain* [1966] 1 W.L.R. 1539.

5. The principles relating to restraint of trade are also applicable to restrictions in a partnership agreement purporting to apply after dissolution of the partnership or expulsion of a partner from it. In the case of a partnership of **general medical practitioners** regard must be given to section 35(1) of the National Health Services Act 1946 which prohibits the sale of goodwill of a general medical practice or any part of it (*Macfarlane* v. *Kent* [1965] 1 W.L.R. 1019). Where medical practitioners are in general medical practice as partners, a covenant purporting to prohibit a partner after retirement from engaging in practice as a "medical practitioner" would be too wide, as it would prevent him from practising as a medical consultant

(*Lyne-Pirkis* v. *Jones* [1969] 1 W.L.R. 1293; *Peyton* v. *Mindham* [1972] 1 W.L.R. 8).

6. Normally the question whether a term of a contract constitutes an unreasonable restraint of trade has to be decided by reference to the wording of the term, construed in the context of the business which it is designed to protect. But a clause which, on its face, is innocent may, in connection with other clauses of the agreement, produce a restrictive effect and then has to be treated as an unreasonable restraint (*Stenhouse Australia Ltd.* v. *Phillips* [1974] A.C. 391 (P.C.)). Moreover, a restraint clause which, at its inception, is not unreasonable cannot be enforced so long as the person in whose favour it is stipulated carries out his own obligations under the contract in a discriminatory manner which causes hardship to the person restrained.

Shell U.K. Ltd. had a reasonable and, on principle, enforceable solus agreement with Lostock Garage Ltd., a small garage in Cheshire. Under the agreement Shell were obliged to supply the garage with petrol. In December 1975 there was a price war in petrol. Shell operated a support scheme enabling garages which had suffered a drop in sales of 40,000 gallons in 1975 to sell petrol at a cut price. Lostock did not profit from that scheme because, being a small garage, its drop was only 13,000 gallons. Lostock was thus faced with a situation in which all garages in the neighbourhood, including those supplied by Shell, sold petrol at a cut price but Lostock was bound by the solus agreement to sell at a higher price. Lostock then began to buy petrol from a cheaper source. *Held*, so long as Shell discriminated against Lostock, the restraint was not enforceable: *Shell U.K. Ltd.* v. *Lostock Garage Ltd.* [1976] 1 W.L.R. 1187.

Restrictive trade practices and resale prices
This subject is treated in Chap. 18, *post.*

Gaming contracts
By section 18 of the Gaming Act 1845—
   1. contracts by way of gaming or wagering are null and void and
   2. no action can be brought to recover money won upon any wager.

By the Gaming Act 1892 any promise, express or implied—
   1. to pay any person any sum of money paid by him in respect of any contract rendered null and void by the Gaming Act 1845; or

    2. to pay any sum of money by way of commission, fee, reward, or otherwise in respect of any such contract, or of any services in connection therewith;

is null and void and no action can be brought to recover any such sum of money.

A **wagering contract** is not illegal, but the law gives no assistance in enforcing it, and it is therefore a void contract.

A wager is an agreement between two parties that upon the happening or ascertainment of some uncertain event, one party shall pay a sum of money to the other, which party is to pay depending on the issue of the event. Neither party must have any other interest in the contract than the sum he shall win or lose. If either of the parties may win but cannot lose, or may lose but cannot win, it is not a wagering contract.

In contracts on the Stock Exchange and other commercial exchanges, if the parties intend that no stock or goods shall be delivered, but that "differences" only shall be accounted for, then the contracts are void as being wagers. The fact that it is provided that either party may require completion of the purchase does not prevent this result (*Universal Stock Exchange* v. *Strachan* [1896] A.C. 166). If, however, the contracts genuinely contemplate the transfer of stock or goods, but the parties, instead of carrying out the actual bargain, agree that the difference between prices shall be paid instead, the contracts will be enforceable.

B, a metal broker, acted for S in speculative transactions on the London Metal Exchange. The contracts were legally enforceable, but neither party expected to have to take or give delivery. A balance was struck when the account was closed and the difference paid by B, who sued S to recover the amount. *Held*, the transactions, though speculative, were not gaming contracts and B could recover from S: *Barnett* v. *Sanker* (1925) 41 T.L.R. 660.

A **contract of gaming** is a wager upon any game, such as a horse-race or a football-match. Gaming is largely regulated by the Gaming Act 1968 but the Act does not apply where—

    (a) the game involves playing or staking against a bank, whether the bank is held by one of the players or not;

    (b) the nature of the game is such that the chances in the game are not equally favourable to all the players; or

    (c) the nature of the game is such that the chances in it lie wholly or partly between the players and some other person, and those chances are not as favourable to the players as they are to the other person (Gaming Act 1968, s. 2).

The prohibition of gaming does not apply where—

(i) the gaming takes place on a domestic occasion in a private dwelling or in a hostel, hall of residence or similar establishment which is not carried on by way of trade or business and the players consist exclusively or mainly of residents or inmates of that establishment (section 2 (2) of the Act of 1968);

(ii) the gaming takes place in licensed premises or at a club or a miners' welfare institute which is duly registered (section 1 (1)). These licensed or registered premises are strictly controlled;

(iii) special provisions apply to gaming machines, gaming at entertainments not held for private gain, and gaming which constitutes the provision of amusements with prizes (section 1 (2));

(iv) certain types of gaming, such as dominoes and cribbage, are exempted from the prohibition of gaming in public places, *e.g.* in public houses (section 6).

The Gaming Act 1968 draws a distinction between "hard gaming" and bingo and contains relaxations in favour of bingo club premises (section 20).

A competition which has no element of skill, and does not satisfy the statutory requirements, is an unlawful lottery. In deciding whether a competition is a lottery or not, a realistic view must be taken and regard must be had to the way in which the competition is conducted (*Singette Ltd.* v. *Martin* [1971] A.C. 407).

A wagering contract is more comprehensive than a gaming contract, and includes all kinds of wagers. A contract of insurance is not a wagering contract, because the insured must have an insurable interest in the subject-matter insured before the contract is made. The effect of this is that he stands to lose on the happening of the event insured against, quite apart from the contract of insurance.

The following points should be noted—

1. An agent employed to make wagering contracts must hand over to his principal any winnings he has received (*De Mattos* v. *Benjamin* (1894) 63 L.J.Q.B. 248), but he cannot compel his principal to reimburse him losses he has paid away on his behalf: Gaming Act 1892.

2. Money paid to a stakeholder to abide the result of a wager can be recovered from him at any time before it has been paid away (*Burge* v. *Ashley and Smith Ltd*. [1900] 1 Q.B. 744). This is so even if the person demanding the return of the money has lost the wager, provided that the demand is made before the money has been paid over.

3. Money knowingly lent for the purpose of gaming in England cannot be recovered (*Carlton Hall Club* v. *Laurence* [1929] 2 K.B. 153); but if it is lent to make bets in a country where betting is lawful it can be recovered (*Saxby* v. *Fulton* [1909] 2 K.B. 208). Money lent to pay bets already lost cannot be recovered (*Macdonald* v. *Green* [1951] 1 K.B. 594), but if it is lent to enable the loser to pay such bets, though not so as to bind him to do so, it can be recovered (*Re O'Shea* [1911] 2 K.B. 981). Where chips are issued to members of a club a member's promise to repay any gaming losses through a weekly account is void (*C.H.T. Ltd* v. *Ward* [1965] 2 Q.B. 63). Licensed clubs are prohibited from allowing any form of credit for gaming (except the cashing of cheques) by section 16 of the Gaming Act 1968.

4. A new contract to pay money lost by a wager cannot be enforced, whether there is fresh consideration or not, if the intention of the parties in making it is to enable the money so lost to be recovered.

H owed £3,635 to W for lost bets. An order was made by Tattersalls that H should pay £635 within fourteen days and the remainder by monthly instalments of £100. H failed to comply with the order, but gave W a cheque for £635 and a promise to pay the instalments in consideration of W not enforcing the order. The instalments were not paid. *Held*, H was not liable to pay, in spite of the fresh consideration, as W's action was to recover money won upon a wager which was prohibited by the Gaming Act 1845, s. 18: *Hill* v. *William Hill* (*Park Lane*) *Ltd.* [1949] A.C. 530.

5. **Securities given for gaming contracts** are deemed to be given for an illegal consideration. They are therefore void as between the parties, but holders in due course who are not aware of their origin can sue upon them: Gaming Act 1835. Securities given for other wagering contracts are given for no consideration, and, therefore, although they are void as between the parties, they can be sued upon by third parties to whom they have been assigned without their having to prove ignorance of their origin.

6. Numerous enactments not mentioned here, notably the Betting and Gaming Act 1960 and the Gaming Act 1968, contain

detailed provisions for the use of premises as licensed betting offices, the licensing and registration of bookmakers and their agents, the provision of amusements with prizes, amusement machines and other matters.

7. **Lotteries** are subject to special regulation, mainly contained in the Lotteries and Amusements Act 1976. Lotteries which do not constitute gambling are unlawful, except as provided by that Act (section 1). The Act admits, subject to specified conditions, exceptions in the case of small lotteries incidental to entertainments such as a bazaar, sale of work, fête, dinner, dance, sporting or athletic event or other entertainment of a similar character (section 3); private lotteries (section 4); lotteries arranged by charitable or similar societies (section 5); or local authorities (section 6).

Effect of illegality

Contracts tainted by illegality are normally void

The effect of illegality on a contract is to render it void, the maxim being *ex turpi causa non oritur actio*. The law gives no assistance of any kind to the guilty party in such a case, and consequently he cannot recover any money paid or goods supplied under such a contract, nor can he sue for damages or the price of goods if, in order to be successful, he has to rely on his own illegality (*Yin* v. *Sam* [1962] A.C. 304).

B a tobacconist, was put on the stop-list by a tobacco association for breach of its rules. Concealing his identity and by means of an agent, he induced S to sell him cigarettes, and paid £72 19s. 0d. for them. Later S suspected the fraud and refused to deliver the cigarettes. *Held*, B could not recover the £72 19s. 0d. paid, because it was paid for an illegal purpose, namely, to obtain goods from S by false pretences: *Berg* v. *Sadler* [1937] 2 K.B. 158.

When an action is admitted although unlawfulness or illegality has occurred

The rule that the courts will not entertain an action founded on, or brought in connection with, an illegal contract is subject to the following exceptions:

1. Where the parties are not *in pari delicto* the innocent party may recover anything he has paid under the contract. For example, when a person was induced by fraud to take over some insurance policies on a life in which he had no insurable interest (such a contract being illegal), he was entitled to recover the premiums he had paid under

the illegal contract (*Hughes* v. *Liverpool Victoria Friendly Society* [1916] 2 K.B. 482).

2. Where the illegal purpose has not been carried out, one party to the contract may repent his illegal purpose and if he does so before performance takes place the law will assist him. If, however, non-performance is due, not to his repentance but to other causes, the law will not assist him.

X wanted to send his wife to Italy for her health. He agreed with Y that Y should provide her in Italy with Italian currency to the value of £150, contrary to the Exchange Control Act 1947, and deposited shares with Y as security for repayment. X's wife went to Italy, but Y failed to supply the currency. *Held,* as the contract was illegal and the failure of the contract was Y's conduct and not X's repentance, the action failed: *Bigos* v. *Bousted* [1951] 1 All E.R. 92.

3. **The Race Relations Act 1976** makes it unlawful to discriminate against a person on the ground of colour, race or ethnic or national origins in a number of specified situations. These situations are in the employment field (see p. 180, *post*); education; the provision of goods, facilities or services; or in the disposal or management of premises. It is also unlawful to publish or cause to be published discriminatory advertisements (section 29). The Act admits, however, important exceptions in which such discrimination is not unlawful.

The Act further provides that a term of contract shall be void if it provides for anything unlawful by the Act; where it provides for discrimination which is not unlawful but not authorised by the Act, it is unenforceable against the person against whom it is directed, but this provision is subject to certain exceptions (section 72). In the employment field, the industrial tribunals have jurisdiction to administer remedies, including the award of compensation (sections 54–56). In other situations jurisdiction is vested in the courts and the Commission for Racial Equality may apply to the County Court for an injunction against persistent offenders (section 62).

4. **The Sex Discrimination Act 1975** renders unlawful certain kinds of sex discrimination and discrimination on the ground of marriage and establishes the Equal Opportunities Commission with the function of working towards the elimination of such discrimination.

5. **The Trade Descriptions Acts 1968 and 1972,** which provide criminal sanctions in the case of false trade descriptions (see p. 271, *post*), provide that a contract for the supply of goods shall not be void

or unenforceable by reason only of a contravention of the Act of 1968 (section 35). If such a contravention constitutes a misrepresentation, the normal civil remedies for misrepresentation (see p. 81, *ante*) are available.

Illegal act committed in the course of performance of a legal contract

It happens sometimes that in the course of performance of a perfectly legal contract an act is committed which is made illegal by statute but which is not directly connected with the object of the contract. Here a question of interpretation of the statute in question arises. If it is the intention of the legislature that the illegality in performance shall result in the prohibition of the whole contract, no action can be brought on it. That is, in particular, the case if both parties know that the chosen mode of performance contravenes the statutory prohibition.

The plaintiffs were manufacturers of heavy engineering equipment known as tube banks. They arranged with the defendants, a small company of road hauliers, for the carriage of two tube banks from Stockton-on-Tees to Hull for shipment to Poland. Contrary to the regulations made under the Road Traffic Act 1960 each of the tube banks, which weighed 25 tons, was loaded on a vehicle which had an unladen weight of 10 tons. According to the regulations, the maximum total weight allowed was 30 tons and that limit was, to the knowledge of both parties, exceeded by five tons. In addition, the load was top heavy and unsuited to be carried in the vehicles in question. On the road, one of the vehicles toppled over and the load was damaged. In an action for damages, *held*, that, although the contract was lawful in its inception, its performance was illegal to the knowledge of both parties and consequently the plaintiffs could not recover damages from the defendants: *Ashmore, Benson, Pease & Co. Ltd.* v. *A. V. Dawson Ltd.* [1973] 1 W.L.R. 828.

On the other hand, if Parliament intended that the illegality should only have other consequences, *e.g.* the guilty person should be liable to a penalty, the contract is not tainted by the illegality and remains enforceable in a court of law.

The *St. John*, which was registered in Panama, carried a consignment of grain from the United States to England. When the ship arrived in Birkenhead it was found that she was overloaded and that her loadline was submerged. This was an offence under the Merchant Shipping (Safety and Loadlines Conventions) Act 1932. The defendants who were holders of a bill of lading refused to pay the freight on the overloaded portion of the cargo. *Held*, on the true construction of the Act of 1932, contracts for the carriage of goods were not within its ambit and the defendants were liable to pay the retained part of the freight: *St. John Shipping Corporation* v. *Joseph Rank Ltd.* [1957] 1 Q.B. 267.

A arranged with S to carry a consignment of whisky from Leeds to London docks. The goods were stolen in transit owing to the negligence of S. In an action for damages by A, S pleaded that the contract of carriage was illegal because S's van was not licensed to carry the goods. *Held*, the defence failed; the contract was not *ex facie* illegal and public policy did not require the court to refuse aid to A who did not know that the contract would be performed illegally: *Archbolds (Freightage) Ltd.* v. *S. Spanglett Ltd.* [1961] 1 Q.B. 374.

A landlady let an unfurnished room in her house to a tenant. She gave her a rent book which did not contain all the information required by the Landlord and Tenant Act 1962 and the Rent Book (Forms of Notice) Regulations 1965, and thereby she committed an offence. She sued the tenant for arrears of rent, but the tenant contended that she was precluded from recovering the rent owing to the insufficiency of the rent book. *Held*, the landlady could recover the rent. She had not to rely on the rent book as an essential ingredient of her cause of action and the rent book was only a statutory requirement collateral to the contract. It was not the intention of Parliament, when requiring a rent book in a specified form, that a landlord who failed to comply with this requirement should be precluded from recovering the rent: *Shaw* v. *Groom* [1970] 2 Q.B. 504.

Certain land situated in Richmond, Surrey, was owned by Curragh Investments Ltd., a company incorporated in the Isle of Man, which in England was treated as an overseas company but had failed to register the documents required to be registered under sections 407 and 416 of the Companies Act 1948. The company sold the land to the defendant. The latter, having discovered the company's failure to register the documents, refused to perform the contract of sale. *Held*, (1) no question of illegality of the contract arose because there was no nexus or link between the contract and the statutory requirements which were infringed; and (2) even if the vendor was in breach of sections 407 and 416, there was no justification for the purchaser to refuse the performance of the contract: *Curragh Investments Ltd.* v. *Cook* [1974] 1 W.L.R. 1559.

Severance of illegal parts

If only part of a contract is illegal, the whole contract will not be void if the illegal part can be severed from the rest of the contract.

Mr. Ailion, the lessee of a flat which he occupied as a protected tenant, agreed to assign the remainder of his lease to Mr. Spiekermann and his wife. The rent was £850 per annum and the purchasers agreed to pay £3,750 for certain furniture which was worth much less; the purchase price for the furniture thus contained a premium prohibited by the Rent Act 1968. *Held*, the illegal element, *i.e.* the premium, was severable.

Consequently, the lease was valid and the Spiekermanns were entitled to specific performance, but without payment of the illegal premium represented by the excess purchase price of the furniture: *Ailion* v. *Spiekermann* [1976] Ch. 158.

If, however, the whole purpose of the contract is an illegal one, the court will not make a new contract for the parties by attempting to cut out those portions which are illegal and enforce the rest.

N was employed as secretary and accountant at a salary of £13 a week with £6 a week expenses. Both parties knew his expenses were less than £1 a week. *Held*, the contract was to evade tax and was illegal. It was impossible to sever the part dealing with salary from the part dealing with expenses, so that the whole was unenforceable: *Napier* v. *National Business Agency Ltd.* [1951] 2 All E.R. 264.

Passing of title under a fully executed illegal contract

If a contract of sale or a similar transaction is illegal, the buyer cannot claim the goods from the seller because to do so he would have to rely on the illegal contract and the court will not assist him in its enforcement.

The position is, however, different if the illegal contract has been fully executed and the seller has transferred the title to the goods to the buyer. Title can pass under an illegal contract and when it has passed the buyer has the normal remedies of an owner; he can, in particular, sue in trespass or detinue (*Singh* v. *Ali* [1960] A.C. 167) or in conversion (*Belvoir Finance Co. Ltd.* v. *Stapleton, post*).

The plaintiffs, a finance company, bought cars and hired them out to a car hire company on hire-purchase terms which were illegal to the knowledge of both parties because the deposit paid by the car hire company was much smaller than prescribed by the hire-purchase regulations then in force. The car hire company, of which the defendant was assistant manager, sold the cars (which had never been delivered into the possession of the plaintiffs) without authority of the plaintiffs. *Held*, although the hire-purchase contracts were illegal, they were fully executed and a valid title to the cars had passed under them to the plaintiffs. Their claim for damages for conversion against the defendant was successful: *Belvoir Finance Co. Ltd.* v. *Stapleton* [1971] 1 Q.B. 210.

SELECT BIBLIOGRAPHY

Books

Treitel 286–319, 345–336.
Cheshire & Fifoot 295–319, 364–398.

Articles

Buckley, R. A., "Implied Statutory Prohibition of Contracts" (1975) 38 M.L.R. 535–542.

Buckley, R. A., "Participation and Performance in Illegal Contracts" (1974) 25 N.I.L.Q. 421–429.

Dawson, F., "Contracts in Restraint of Trade: Meaning and Effect" (1974) 90 L.Q.R. 455–463.

Graupner, R., "Sole Distributorship Agreements—A Comparative View" (1969) 18 I.C.L.Q. 879–895.

Heydon, J. D., "The Frontiers of the Restraint of Trade Doctrine" (1969) 85 L.Q.R. 229–251.

Shand, J., "Unblinkering the Unruly Horse: Public Policy in the Law of Contract" [1972] C.L.J. 144–167.

CHAPTER 8

DISCHARGE OF CONTRACT

A CONTRACT may be discharged by—
1. performance,
2. agreement,
3. acceptance of breach, or
4. frustration.

PERFORMANCE

If both parties have performed what they agree to do under the contract, the contract is discharged. Performance must be strictly in accordance with the terms of the contract to be a discharge.

Time

Time for performance may be fixed in the contract. In that case, the contract must be performed within that time when time is of the essence of the contract. Time is of the essence of the contract when the parties have expressly said so in the contract or when the circumstances of the contract show that they intended it to be so. In mercantile contracts which provide for *performance* in a specified time the general rule is that the contract must be performed in that time, otherwise it is broken. Stipulations as to time of *payment*, however, are not as a rule of the essence of the contract in the absence of a contrary intention. The Sale of Goods Act 1893, s. 10, applies this rule to contracts of sale of goods.

If no time for performance is agreed, performance is to be made within a reasonable time,

The requirement that performance at the agreed or a reasonable time shall be of the essence of the contract can be waived by showing indulgence, but normally the strictness of the contract can be restored by notice or, if the circumstances indicate such an intention, even without a notice (see p. 124, *post*).

Tender

Tender is an offer of performance in accordance with the terms of the contract. If such a tender is made but the other party refuses to

accept it, the party tendering is free from liability under the contract
if the tender was made under such circumstances that the party to
whom the tender was made had a reasonable opportunity of examining the goods or money tendered. The object of tender is to show
that the party tendering was ready and willing to perform his obligations under the contract and was only prevented from doing so by the
act of the other party. Accordingly, if goods are tendered by the
seller and refused by the buyer, the seller is free from liability. A
tender of money, on the other hand, only discharges the tenderer if it
is followed by payment of the sum tendered into court on action
being brought.

In tender of money the exact amount owed must be tendered
without any request for change. Legal tender are Bank of England
notes for any amount (Currency and Bank Notes Act 1954, s. 1);
gold coins for any amount; coins of cupro-nickel or silver exceeding
10 pence in value up to 10 pounds, coins of cupro-nickel or silver of
not more than 10 pence in value up to five pounds only, coins of
bronze up to 20 pence only (Coinage Act 1971, s. 2).

Tender by cheque or other negotiable instrument is not good
tender, unless the creditor does not object to the form but only to the
amount tendered. Tender must be unconditional and must comply
with the conditions of the contract as to time, place and mode of
performance. It may be made "under protest" so as to reserve the
right of the payer to dispute the amount.

Payment

Payment of the amount due under a contract is a discharge.
Payment of a smaller amount is not a discharge, unless it is made at
an earlier date or in a different manner from that prescribed by the
contract, *e.g.* at the debtor's instead of the creditor's place. The
following points should be noted—

1. Payment to an agent is a good discharge if the agent is authorised or held out as having authority to receive payment.

2. Payment to one of several joint creditors discharges the debt.

3. Payment by a third party is not a discharge, unless it was made
by the third party as agent for the debtor or has been ratified by the
debtor. The agency or the ratification may be implied.

S was R's tenant and C was R's agent to collect the rent. S owed
£260 arrears, but C, knowing that R was old and poor, accounted to
R as if the rent had been paid. C distrained and it was argued that the

distress was wrongful because R had been paid. *Held*, C's payments to R were not made as agent for S, S was a debtor and the distress was lawful: *Smith* v. *Cox* [1940] 2 K.B. 558.

4. A receipt is evidence, but not conclusive evidence of payment. It is therefore always open to the person who has given the receipt to show either that he has not in fact received payment or that the receipt was given by mistake or obtained by fraud. Again, payment may be proved by parol evidence although no receipt was taken, or, if taken, has been subsequently lost.

The practice of not giving receipts unless asked for is common today because it is provided by the Cheques Act 1957, s. 3, that an unindorsed cheque which appears to have been paid by the banker on whom it is drawn shall be evidence of the receipt of the money by the payee.

5. Payment by negotiable instrument is, in the absence of any agreement to the contrary, a conditional payment only; that is, the creditor, on the dishonour of the negotiable instrument, may sue either on the original contract or on the negotiable instrument. Pending payment or dishonour of the instrument, the creditor's right of action is suspended. A creditor is not bound to take a negotiable instrument in payment of a debt, but may insist on payment in cash.

6. Payment by post is not a good payment in the event of the letter being lost in the post, unless the creditor requested the debtor to pay by post.

C had bought goods from P for many years and had always paid him by cheque through the post, without any objection being made by P. One of C's cheques was lost in the post. *Held*, there was no payment, because there was nothing from which a request by P for payment by cheque could be inferred so as to make the loss during transmission by post fall upon him: *Pennington* v. *Crossley & Son* (1897) 77 L.T. 43.

Even a request to pay through the post does not absolve the debtor from paying in a reasonable manner and in accordance with business practice.

An insurance company sent to M a written notice for payment of £48 and asking him "when remitting" to return the notice. M sent £48 in Treasury notes by registered post and the letter was stolen. *Held*, there was no payment. Although the words "when remitting" authorised M to pay by post, they did not authorise him to depart from usual business methods and send so large a sum as £48 in notes: *Mitchell-Henry* v. *Norwich Life Insurance Society* [1918] 2 K.B. 67.

Where there is a request by the creditor or an agreement between the parties that payment should be made by post, payment is established by posting even though the letter be lost in the post. (*Thairlwell* v. *G.N. Ry.* [1910] 2 K.B. 509).

N, a milliner, wrote to R, a customer, saying "the favour of a cheque within a week will oblige." R sent a cheque by post, but it was stolen in transit and cashed by the thief. In an action by N, *held*, N's letter to R was a request to pay by post, and the posting of the letter with the cheque was a good payment: *Norman* v. *Ricketts* (1886) 3 T.L.R. 182.

When periodical payments have to be made under a contract, evidence is admissible to prove the method of payment accepted by the parties. If the method is by post, delay in the post excuses late payment.

Hire under a charterparty was payable in London on the 17th of each month, the owners having a right to cancel in default of prompt payment. The practice was to pay by cheque posted to a London bank. cheque was sent in time to arrive on Sept. 27, but was late owing to postal delay caused by war. The owners cancelled the charterpolicy. *Held*, payment was made in time: *Tankexpress* v. *Compagnie Financière Belge des Petroles* [1949] A.C. 76.

7. A settled account is an arrangement whereby two persons, with mutual debits and credits, strike a balance which they agree represents the financial results of their transactions. On payment of a settled account the transactions cannot be reopened. There is no settled account when one party only renders an account which is accepted and paid by the other.

A appointed R their sole licensees for the manufacture and sale of their road-making specialities, payment to be made by R of royalties on the materials they manufactured under the licence. A were given power to inspect accounts. For many years R submitted statements showing the materials manufactured and made payments accordingly which A accepted. A applied for inspection of R's books over the period of the licence. *Held*, the principle of settled account did not apply where the whole account was to be rendered by one party to the other, and A could inspect R's books for the six years before action: *Anglo-American Asphalt Co.* v. *Russell & Co.* [1945] 2 All E.R. 324.

A bank is entitled to combine several accounts of a customer, even if kept at different branches (*Barclays Bank Ltd.* v. *Okenarhe* [1966] 2 Lloyd's Rep. 87), and to set off credits in one against debits in another. This right of combination is analogous to the general lien of the banker (see p. 380, *post*). But this right of combination may be excluded by an agreement, express or implied, to keep the accounts separate.

H had a loan account with W Bank. This account was overdrawn by £11,339. H had also a trading account with the L Bank which was operated on a credit basis and out of which the wages for H's employees were paid. In April 1968 H agreed with W that H should transfer the trading account from L to W and that the accounts should then be operated on the following basis: the loan account should become No. 1 account and should be frozen, and the trading account should become No. 2 account which had to be constantly kept in credit and to which the interest for the loan on No. 1 account should be debited; W agreed to adhere to this arrangement for four months, in the absence of materially changed circumstances. On the morning of June 12, 1968 H paid a cheque drawn in its favour of £8,611 into No. 2 account. In the afternoon of the same day H went into voluntary winding up and a liquidator was appointed. W claimed to combine No. 1 and No. 2 accounts and to set off the credit of £8,611 on No. 2 account against H's debit of £11,339 on No. 1 account, but the liquidator contended that W was not entitled to combine the accounts, that the £8,611 had to be used for the benefit of the general creditors, and that W had to prove for the £11,339 as an unsecured creditor. W argued that the debit on the No. 1 account could be set off against the credit on the No. 2 account because the two items amounted to "mutual dealings" within section 31 of the Bankruptcy Act 1914, which was applicable by virtue of section 317 of the Companies Act 1948. H argued that W had contracted that the two accounts should not be combined. *Held*, (1) there were "mutual dealings" within section 31 and that section was mandatory and could not be contracted out; and (2) even if it was possible to contract out of section 31, the agreement between W and H, on its true construction, had only been intended to be operative while H was a going concern and consequently had come to an end: *National Westminster Bank Ltd.* v. *Halesowen Presswork & Assemblies Ltd.* (known as *Halesowen Presswork & Assemblies Ltd.* v. *National Westminster Bank Ltd.*) [1972] A.C. 785.

If a bank receives a cheque payable to a company which is its customer on condition that the cheque shall only be used for the payment of dividend declared by the company and it places the proceeds of the cheque into a special dividend account, it has received the cheque in pursuance of a fiduciary relationship or trust and cannot combine the dividend account with the other accounts of the customer; if the customer is wound up before the dividend is paid, there is a resulting trust for the benefit of the drawer of the cheque and the bank must repay the money to him (*Quistclose Investments Ltd.* v. *Rolls Razor Ltd.* [1970] A.C. 567).

Appropriation of payments

When a debtor owes several debts to the same creditor and a payment is made, it is a question to which debt the payment should be appropriated. The rules are—

1. The debtor can appropriate, expressly or by implication, provided he does so at the time of payment. For example, if the debtor owes £100 and £57, and sends a cheque for £57, it will be an implied appropriation, in the absence of anything to the contrary, to the second debt. A cheque for £50 would be unappropriated by the debtor and would bring into operation the next rule.

2. In the absence of an appropriation by the debtor, the creditor can appropriate at any time. A creditor can appropriate the debtor's payment to a debt which the creditor cannot enforce by action because it is statute-barred, or if it is a guarantee, which he cannot prove in the form required by the Statute of Frauds 1677, but the creditor cannot appropriate the debtor's payment to a debt which is illegal.

S was an unregistered dentist who could not recover any fee for performing a dental operation, but could sue for the price of materials supplied. S's bill against P was £45, £20 for services and £25 for materials supplied. P paid £20 without appropriating it. In an action by S, *held*, (i) S could appropriate the £20 to the payment of his professional fees; (ii) the appropriation could be made by S for the first time in the witness box: *Seymour* v. *Pickett* [1905] 1 K.B. 715.

3. In the case of a current account there is "no room for any other appropriation than that which arises from the order in which the receipts and payments take place and are carried into the account. Presumably, it is the sum first paid in that is first drawn out. It is the first item in the debit side of the account that is discharged or reduced by the first item on the credit side; the appropriation is made by the very act of setting the two items against each other": *per* Sir William Grant in *Clayton's Case* (1816) 1 Mer. 572.

Example—X guarantees Y's account with the bank. When Y is overdrawn up to £1,000, X revokes his guarantee as to future transactions. The bank keeps the old account going and Y pays in various sums amounting to £1,000, but draws out sums equal to that amount. As soon as Y has paid in £1,000, the liability of X to the bank will be extinguished, because these payments in will be appropriated by the rule in *Clayton's* case to the satisfaction of the overdraft existing when they were paid in. See *Deeley* v. *Lloyds Bank Ltd.* [1912] A.C. 756.

This rule only applies to current accounts, but it is not confined to banking accounts. It includes "current accounts for goods supplied and work done rendered periodically with a balance carried forward" (*per* Scrutton L.J. in *Albermale Supply Co. Ltd.* v. *Hind & Co.* [1928] 1 K.B. 307, 319). It does not mean that when an account containing several items is rendered by the creditor, a payment by the debtor "on account" is appropriated to the first item on the account. In such a case the creditor can appropriate as stated in the second rule (*The Mecca* [1897] A.C. 286).

In spite of the rule in *Clayton's* case, the balance owed on current account is a single and undivided debt and for that reason payment constitutes part payment of that debt within the meaning of the Limitation Act 1939 and revives the whole outstanding balance (*Re Footman, Bower & Co. Ltd.* [1961] Ch. 443).

Waiver

It is a common experience in commercial practice that a party does not insist on its strict contractual rights but, when requested by the other party, shows some indulgence. Thus, a contract of sale may provide for delivery on February 1 but the buyer may ask the seller to defer delivery until March 1. Or a building contract may provide for payment within one month after completion of the work and, the work being completed on April 1, the owner may ask the builder to agree to payment on May 15.

If in these cases the party who agrees to the relaxation of the strict terms of contract receives consideration, a **variation** of the contract takes place and the new agreement is binding on both parties.

More difficult, from the legal point of view, but more frequent in practice is the case where an indulgence shown by a party is not supported by consideration. Here the doctrine of **waiver** applies. The courts have evolved the following rules.

1. The party in whose favour the indulgence has been exercised cannot later claim that the other party has not performed his obligations in time. If, *e.g.* the contract of sale provides for delivery on February 1 but, by request of the buyer, the seller postpones delivery until March 1 and then tenders the goods, the buyer cannot refuse acceptance on the ground that the goods ought to have been tendered on February 1 (*Levey* v. *Goldberg* [1922] 1 K.B. 688).

2. The party who grants indulgence is also bound by his under-

taking. "If one party, by his conduct, leads another to believe that the strict rights arising under the contract will not be insisted upon, intending that the other should act on that belief, and he does act on it, then the first party will not afterwards be allowed to insist on the strict rights when it would be inequitable for him to do so" (*per* Denning L.J. in *Plasticmoda S.p.A.* v. *Davidsons (Manchester) Ltd.* [1952] 1 Lloyd's Rep. 527). This rule, which is an extension of the rule in *Central London Property Trust Ltd.* v. *High Trees House Ltd.* ([1947] 1 K.B. 130, see p. 44, *ante*), has been developed from the equitable principle of estoppel by conduct.

A contract for the sale of flour to a buyer in Greece provided for payment under a banker's confirmed documentary credit, each shipment to be a separate contract. The buyer opened an unconfirmed credit. The sellers did not at first reject that credit but made some shipments and received payment under it. Later they cancelled the contract on the ground that the credit was not confirmed. *Held*, (i) by accepting payment under the unconfirmed credit the sellers had waived the right to insist on a confirmed credit; (ii) in spite of their acceptance of the unconfirmed credit, they could still have given the buyer reasonable notice of their insistence that the credit must be confirmed for future shipments; (iii) they could not cancel the contract without such notice: *Panoutsos* v. *Raymond Hadley Corporation of New York* [1917] 2 K.B. 473.

3. If no time limit is provided for the forbearance, the party who has agreed to relax the strict terms of the contract can unilaterally restore them. This is normally done by giving the other party notice of reasonable length that the indulgence is over.

C agreed to sell to O a Rolls-Royce chassis with a body built on it, delivery to be made by March 20. It was not delivered then. O pressed for delivery and finally said in June that he would not accept delivery after July 25. Delivery was not made then and O bought another car. Delivery was offered in October but O refused it. C sued for the price. *Held*, the action failed. O had waived the original time for delivery but was entitled, on giving reasonable notice, again to make time of the essence of the contract: *Charles Rickards Ltd.* v. *Oppenhaim* [1950] 1 K.B. 616.

But such notice is not essential. It is not required if it is clear from the circumstances that the time of relaxation is over and the strictness of the contract is restored (*Tool Metal Manufacturing Co. Ltd.* v. *Tungsten Electric Co. Ltd.* [1955] 1 W.L.R. 761).

AGREEMENT

A contract may be discharged by agreement in any one of the following ways: (a) release, (b) new agreement, (c) accord and satisfaction, and (d) provision for discharge contained in the contract itself.

Release

At any time before the performance of a contract is due, or after a breach of the contract has taken place, a release of the obligations under the contract may be granted by deed. Such a deed dissolves the contract and is binding, whether or not it is based on consideration.

New agreement

A contract may be rescinded by a new agreement between the parties at any time before it is discharged by performance or in some other way. Discharge by mutual agreement can only take place as long as there is something to be done by each party to the contract; if one party has completely performed all his obligations under the contract, discharge must be either by release under seal or by accord and satisfaction (*per* Parke B., *Foster* v. *Dawber* (1851) 6 Ex. at p. 851). An exception to this is a bill of exchange, which can be discharged in writing or by delivering the bill to the acceptor (Bills of Exchange Act 1882, s. 62). In the case of a contract completely executed by one party, there is no consideration for his discharging the other party from his obligations under the contract.

The agreement for rescission may be either express or implied. Non-performance for a long period may lead to an inference of abandonment.

In September 1913, X agreed to sell to Y 50 dozen skins "delivery as required." By September 1914, Y had from time to time requested delivery of 20 dozen which had been duly delivered, but no more deliveries were asked for until July 1917. *Held*, an inordinate delay having taken place, the parties must be taken to have abandoned the contract: *Pearl Mill Co.* v. *Ivy Tannery Co.* [1919] 1 K.B. 78.

A contract in writing may be rescinded or varied by an oral agreement. Similarly, a contract under seal may be rescinded or varied by a simple contract (*Berry* v. *Berry* [1929] 2 K.B. 316). But a contract which is required by statute to be in writing, can be rescinded (*Morris* v. *Baron* [1918] A.C. 1), but cannot be varied by an oral agreement; *Goss* v. *Nugent* (1833) 5 B. & Ad. 58.

Accord and satisfaction

Accord and satisfaction occurs when after a contract is concluded a party obtains the release from his contractual obligation by giving or promising a consideration other than that which the other party is bound to accept under the contract. The agreement is known as accord and the consideration as satisfaction.

Accord without satisfaction is no discharge of a contract or of a right of action arising from the contract. The satisfaction may, however, consist of a promise which, as has been seen (p. 42, *ante*) is good consideration, and an accord supported by such consideration amounts to an enforceable agreement.

"It is still the law that a mere accord without satisfaction does not put an end to an existing liability after breach, but I think it amounts to an agreement which can be enforced by a claim for damages if it is broken by one of the parties when the other has shown his readiness to perform the terms of the agreement": Greer L.J. in *British Russian Gazette* v. *Associated Newspapers* [1933] 2 K.B. 616, 650.

The agreement of a creditor to accept a smaller sum than is due to him is accord without satisfaction (*Foakes* v. *Beer* [1889] 9 App. Cas. 605; see p. 43, *ante*), but the agreement of a creditor to accept a smaller sum than is due to him in consideration of something to which he was not entitled under the original contract is a valid accord and satisfaction and, as such, is binding on both parties.

Provision for discharge in the contract

The contract may contain a term providing for its termination on the non-fulfilment of a condition, the happening of an event or on the exercise by one or either of the parties of a power to terminate it. The non-fulfilment of a **condition precedent** gives a right to the party in whose interest the condition was imposed to terminate the contract.

T sold a horse to H warranting that it had hunted with the B hounds and giving H the right to return it by a certain date if it did not comply with the warranty. The horse had not hunted with the B hounds and H returned it in time, but in the meantime it had been injured through no fault of H. *Held*, H was given a right to terminate the contract and T had to accept the injured horse: *Head* v. *Tattersall* (1871) L.R. 7 Ex. 7.

The contract may contain a term releasing the parties from liability on the happening of a certain event. Such a term is a **condition subsequent.**

G chartered a vessel from S by a charterparty under which S agreed to go to Hamburg and load coals, with an exception in the case of "restraints of princes and rulers." War broke out between France and Germany, and Hamburg was blockaded, so that S refused to load a cargo. *Held,* S was released by the exception in the charterparty: *Geipel* v. *Smith* (1872) L.R. 7 Q.B. 404.

The contract may contain a term giving either party a power to terminate it. Examples are a lease that can be terminated by notice to quit or a contract of employment with power to either party on giving notice to end the contract. Contracts of employment are subject to special regulations which will be considered later (see Chap. 12, *post*).

ACCEPTANCE OF BREACH

A party to a contract may commit a breach of that contract
- (a) by repudiating his liability under the contract before the time for performance is due;
- (b) by his own act disabling himself from performing the contract; or
- (c) by failing to fulfil his obligations when purporting to perform the contract.

Breach always entitles the injured party to bring an action for damages. It may also entitle him to treat the contract as discharged, but he can only treat it as discharged on proving that the breach is either of the entire contract or of some term which is so vital that it goes to the root of the contract. The breach must be such as to show that the party in default has repudiated his obligations under the contract.

Repudiation before time for performance

Before the time for performance arrives a party to the contract may declare his intention of not performing the contract. This is called a repudiation of contract or an anticipatory breach. In such a case the other party is not bound to wait until the actual time for performance has arrived, but may immediately treat the contract as discharged and sue for damages.

B engaged C as a courier, his services to start on June 1. On May 11
B told C he would not require his services. C, before June 1 arrived,
brought an action against B. *Held*, he was entitled to do so: *Hochster*
v. *De La Tour* (1853) 2 E. & B. 678.

K promised to marry F on the death of his, K's, father. The father
still living, K informed F that he would not marry her on his father's
death. F sued him at once for breach of promise (which was then actionable as breach of contract). *Held*, F was entitled to accept K's repudiation of the contract to marry her and to bring her action for breach of
promise at once: *Frost* v. *Knight* (1872) L.R. 7 Exch. 111.

Acceptance of repudiation

A minor breach of contract, such as a short delay in payments
likely to be made later does not amount to repudiation, but "the
case would be quite different if the defendants' breaches had been
such as reasonably to shatter the plaintiffs' confidence in the defendants' ability to pay for the goods" (*per* Salmon L.J. in *Decro-Wall
International S.A.* v. *Practitioners in Marketing Ltd.* [1971] 1 W.L.R.
361).

Repudiation by one party does not of itself discharge the contract.
The contract is only discharged when the repudiation is accepted by
the other party (*Heyman* v. *Darwins Ltd.* [1942] A.C. 356). If the
repudiation is not accepted, the contract remains in existence. The
party in default may then change his mind and proceed with performance, or it may be that some supervening event occurs which relieves
him from further performance.

Under a charterparty X agreed to load a cargo of wheat on Y's ship
at Odessa within a certain number of days. On the arrival of the ship, X
refused to load a cargo. Y would not accept this refusal and continued to
demand a cargo. Before the last day for loading had expired, the Crimean
War broke out, rendering performance of the contract illegal. *Held*, Y had
no cause of action against X, because he had refused to accept X's breach
of contract as a discharge, and the contract had, in the meantime, become
discharged by something beyond the control of either party: *Avery* v.
Bowden (1856) 6 E. & B. 953.

If the injured party accepts the repudiation, he is entitled to the
same damages as he could have claimed if the contract had been
broken on due date. But if the injured party would not have been
able to perform himself on due date and consequently would then
have been in breach himself, he cannot claim any damages for the
anticipatory breach of contract by the other party.

Maredelanto Compania Naviera S.A. v. *Bergbau-Handel G.m.b.H.; The Mihalis Angelos* [1971] 1 Q.B. 164, see p. 25. *ante.*

In the case of the repudiation of part of the contract, it is a question of construction whether the part repudiated is so vital as to entitle the other party to treat the whole contract as discharged.

Disability

If a party to a contract by his own act disables himself from performing the contract, the other party can treat the contract as discharged. For example, in *Synge* v. *Synge* [1894] 1 Q.B. 466, a man agreed before marriage to settle a house on his wife after marriage. He subsequently conveyed the house to a third person, and it was held that his wife could bring an action for breach of contract, although it was not beyond the bounds of possibility that he might have repurchased the house and then settled it upon her.

X chartered from Y a steamer which was being built. After the ship was built Y sold it to Z free from the charterparty. *Held*, Y by selling the steamer had repudiated the charterparty and was liable in damages: *Omnium d'Enterprises* v. *Sutherland* [1919] 1 K.B. 618.

Breach in performance

During the performance of a contract one party may either fail or refuse to perform his duties under the contract. In such a case, if the failure or refusal amounts to a repudiation of the whole contract, the other party may treat the contract as discharged by breach.

C agreed to supply the railway company with 3,900 tons of railway chairs. After 1,787 tons had been delivered the company told C that no more were required. *Held*, C could bring an action at once without showing an actual delivery: *Cort* v. *Ambergate Ry.* (1851) 17 Q.B. 127.

In contracts of sale of goods the breach of any of the implied conditions set out in the Sale of Goods Act 1893, ss. 12–15, entitles the buyer to rescind the contract.

FRUSTRATION

The principle

When the common object of the contract can no longer be achieved because, in the light of the circumstances, a situation fundamentally different from that contemplated when the parties entered into the contract has unexpectedly emerged, the contract is at an end, for otherwise the parties would be bound to perform a contract which they did not make.

An unexpected turn of events which does not create a fundamentally different situation does not enable a party to refuse the performance of the contract on the ground that the contract is frustrated. In particular, frustration cannot be pleaded merely because the performance of the contract has become more difficult or more costly than expected, or will result in a loss rather than the anticipated profit, or even has become impossible.

It should be noted that impossibility, as a general rule, does not excuse from performance. "Frustration is a doctrine . . . very rarely relied upon with success. It is, in fact, a kind of last ditch, and . . . it is a conclusion which should be reached rarely and with reluctance" *per* Harman L.J. in *Gaon (Albert D.) & Co.* v. *Société Interprofessionelle des Oléagineux Fluides Alimentaires* [1960] 2 Q.B. 318, 370). In short, the discharge of a contract by frustration is the exception, and not the rule.

Circumstances in which the contract is not frustrated

Where a party gives an absolute undertaking

A contract to perform something that is obviously impossible, *e.g.* to build a castle in the air, is void because there is no real consideration for the contract, but an absolute undertaking is binding though it might be difficult or even impossible to perform.

> Finnish exporters sold a quantity of ant eggs to English buyers, "delivery: prompt, as soon as export licence granted." The sellers were unable to obtain the export licence and failed to ship the goods. *Held*, the sellers were liable for breach of contract; they had undertaken absolutely that they would obtain the export licence: *Cassidy (Peter) Seed Co. Ltd.* v. *Osuustukkauppa I.L.* [1957] 1 W.L.R. 273.

> A sold to B 70 standards of Finland birch timbers to be delivered at Hull from July to September 1914. No deliveries were made before August when the war broke out and disorganised transport, so that A could not get any timber from Finland. *Held*, B was not concerned with the way in which A was going to get the timber to fulfil his contract, and the impossibility of getting timber from Finland did not discharge A: *Blackburn Bobbin Co.* v. *Allen & Sons* [1918] 2 K.B. 467.

Where the change is not fundamental

Builders contracted with Fareham Council to build 78 houses for a fixed sum within a period of eight months. Owing to lack of adequate supplies of labour it took the builders 22 months to complete the work.

The costs of building having risen, the builders claimed that their contract with the council was frustrated and that they were entitled to a higher sum than the agreed sum on a *quantum meruit*. *Held,* what had taken place was an unexpected turn of events which made the contract more onerous than had been contemplated, but this did not operate to frustrate the contract: *Davis Contractors* v. *Fareham U.D.C.* [1956] A.C. 696.

Before the closure of the Suez Canal on November 2, 1956, sellers in the Sudan sold a quantity of groundnuts to a German company; the terms were shipment c.i.f. Hamburg, November/December 1956. The normal shipment which was via the Suez Canal became impossible because the Canal was closed but shipment via the Cape of Good Hope was still possible. The sellers failed to ship the goods. *Held,* the sellers were liable for breach of contract; the change in circumstances was not fundamental and did not amount to frustration, inasmuch as the contract provided only for a time of shipment but not of arrival: *Tsakiroglou & Co. Ltd.* v. *Noblee Thorl G.m.b.H.* [1962] A.C. 93.

In April 1967 the charterers chartered *The Captain George K* for a voyage from Mexico to India. The charterparty provided in Clause 21 that the master should give estimated dates of arrival 96 hours before due to arrive off Suez and 96 hours after passing Suez. On June 13, when the ship approached Suez, she was informed that the Canal was closed (owing to the Six Days War between Egypt and Israel). The ship then proceeded via the Cape of Good Hope. If she had passed through the Canal, she would have covered 9,700 miles but in fact she covered 18,400 miles. The owners claimed additional freight for the extended voyage as a *quantum meruit*, contending that the contemplated voyage was frustrated. *Held,* the difference between the contemplated voyage via Suez and the actual voyage via the Cape amounted only to the difference in expense and for that reason was insufficient to produce frustration: *Palmco Shipping Inc.* v. *Continental Ore Corporation; The Captain George K.* [1970] 2 Lloyd's Rep. 21.

Circumstances in which the contract is frustrated

Statutory interference

A contract which is contrary to law at the time of its formation is void. But if, after the making of the contract, owing to an alteration of the law or the act of some person armed with statutory authority, the performance of the contract becomes impossible, the contract is discharged.

D leased some land to B and covenanted that he would not erect any but ornamental buildings upon the adjoining land. A railway company, under statutory powers, took this adjoining land and built a railway station on it. *Held,* D was excused from performance of his covenant, because the railway company's statutory powers had rendered it impossible: *Baily* v. *De Crespigny* (1869) L.R. 4 Q.B. 180.

X sold to Y a specific parcel of wheat in a warehouse in Liverpool. Before delivery and before the property in the wheat passed to Y, the wheat was requisitioned by the Government under statutory powers. *Held*, as delivery was being rendered impossible by the lawful requisition of the wheat by the Government, X was excused from performance of the contract: *Re Shipton, Anderson & Co. and Harrison Bros. & Co.'s Arbitration* [1915] 3 K.B. 676.

On the other hand, if at the time of the making of the contract compulsory powers are in existence, the exercise of which may affect the contract, a party knowing of those powers cannot rely on the fact that they are subsequently exercised as a defence to his breach of contract. The exercise of the compulsory powers was an event which might have been anticipated and guarded against in the contract (*Walton Harvey Ltd.* v. *Walker and Homfrays Ltd.* [1931] 1 Ch. 274).

If a contract to be performed in a foreign country becomes illegal owing to a change in the law of that country, the contract is discharged (*Ralli* v. *Campania Naviera* [1920] 2 K.B. 287).

The destruction of a specific object necessary for the performance of the contract

The contract may contemplate the continued existence of a particular thing as essential to the contract, so that if it ceases to exist the contract cannot be performed.

Caldwell let a music-hall to Taylor for a series of concerts on certain days. The music-hall was burnt down before any of the days arrived. *Held*, Caldwell was excused from performance. "In contracts in which the performance depends on the continued existence of a given person or thing, a condition is implied that the impossibility of performance arising from the perishing of the person or thing shall excuse the performance": *per* Blackburn J. in *Taylor* v. *Caldwell* (1862) 3 B. & S. 826.

The destruction of the essential object need not be total, as long as it is sufficient to prevent the contract from being carried out.

A sold to N a cargo of cotton seed to be shipped by a specified ship in a named month. Before the time for shipping arrived, the ship was so damaged by stranding as to be unable to load by the agreed time. *Held*, the contract was discharged: *Nickoll and Knight* v. *Ashton, Eldridge & Co.* [1901] 2 K.B. 126.

If A, in the case just quoted, had not named the ship on which the cargo was to be loaded in his contract, he would not have been excused from performance by the destruction of the ship on which he had intended, in his own mind, to load the cargo.

When specific goods are sold and, before the property passes to the buyer, they perish without the fault of either party, the contract is avoided (Sale of Goods Act 1893, s. 7).

Fundamental change in circumstances

It has already been seen that only events which are of such gravity that they result in a fundamentally different situation from that contemplated by the parties when they entered into the contract can be regarded as frustrating events; a mere unexpected turn of events is insufficient.

Frustration occurs if the following three requirements are satisfied—

1. an event occurs which was outside the contemplation of the parties;

The *Kingswood* was chartered to go to Port Pirie and load a cargo for Europe. Before she arrived, there was a violent explosion of one of her boilers, and she was unable to perform the charter. The cause of the explosion was unknown. *Held*, the explosion "frustrated" the contract; the shipowners did not have to negative negligence, the charterers had to prove it: *Joseph Constantine Line* v. *Imperial Smelting Corpn.* [1942] A.C. 154.

A ship was chartered to go with all possible dispatch from Liverpool to Newport and there load a cargo for San Francisco. The vessel was stranded on the way to Newport and could not be repaired for some months. *Held*, the delay put an end, in a commercial sense, to the commercial venture entered upon and the contract was discharged: *Jackson* v. *Union Marine Insurance Co.* (1873) L.R. 10 C.P. 125.

2. the contract, if performed, would thereby be made a different contract from that entered into. This is really the decisive requirement: if a fictitious person, "the officious bystander," had told the parties what would happen, and the parties had replied: "of course, if that event happens the contract is off," only then this requirement is satisfied.

D contracted with M to construct a reservoir within six years, with power for M's engineers to grant an extension of time. After two years the Government, acting under statutory powers, required D to cease work on the contract. D did so and claimed that this put an end to the contract. *Held*, the interruption created by the Government's action was of such a character and duration as to make the contract, when resumed, different from the contract when broken off, and discharged it: *Metropolitan Water Board* v. *Dick, Kerr & Co. Ltd.* [1918] A.C. 119.

3. the event is one for which neither party was responsible.

N chartered O's trawler to use it for trawling. A licence was necessary, but N could not get one, as they already had three licences, which was their full allowance. *Held*, N's failure to get a licence did not excuse them from performance because it was their own act in appropriating the licences to their other trawlers which frustrated the contract: *Maritime National Fish Ltd.* v. *Ocean Trawlers Ltd.* [1935] A.C. 524.

Frustration, when it occurs, automatically brings the contract to an end. No notice or other action by either party is required to terminate it.

It is doubtful whether the doctrine of frustration applies to leases (*Cricklewood Property Co.* v. *Leighton's Investment Trust* [1945] A.C. 221).

Personal incapacity in contracts where the personal qualifications of one of the parties are important

C who was 16 years old was employed as the drummer by the Barron Knights band under a contract for a term of five years. His duties were, when the band had work, to play on seven nights a week. C fell ill and the doctor ordered that he was only fit to play on four nights a week. Thereupon the band terminated his contract. *Held*, that in the business sense it was made impossible for C to continue his contract and that the contract was properly terminated: *Condor* v. *The Barron Knights Ltd.* [1966] 1 W.L.R. 87.

In the case of the employment of a servant for a fixed period, the temporary illness of the servant will not discharge the contract.

Mr. Marshall was employed as a shipyard fitter by Harland & Wolff. He was absent from work for 18 months owing to illness and received no wages during that time. It was not the policy of the employers to terminate employment on grounds of illness. The employers decided to close down the shipyard and gave Mr. Marshall four weeks notice of dismissal. They argued that he was not entitled to redundancy payment because the contract of employment was terminated by frustration caused by his inability to work. *Held*, since it was the policy of the employers not to terminate employment during illness of the employee and the latter might recover and resume work, the contract was not frustrated. Mr. Marshall was entitled to redundancy payment: *Marshall* v. *Harland & Wolff Ltd.* [1972] 1 W.L.R. 899.

If, however, such illness goes to the root of the whole contract, it will discharge the contract (*Poussard* v. *Spiers* (1876) 1 Q.B.D. 410).

Whether wages are payable during sickness depends on the

terms of the contract. In the absence of an express term wages will only be payable if there is an implied term to pay based on what the parties intended (*Petrie* v. *MacFisheries Ltd.* [1940] 1 K.B. 258).

Effect of discharge by frustration

This is governed by the Law Reform (Frustrated Contracts) Act 1943 as follows—

1. All sums paid to any party in pursuance of the contract before it is discharged are on principle, recoverable. Sums payable cease to be payable.

English sellers agreed to sell machinery to Polish buyers for £4,800, one-third of which was to be paid with order. The buyers paid £1,000 only. Before delivery was due, Germany occupied Poland. *Held*, the contract was discharged by frustration, buyers could recover £1,000 paid and were not liable to pay the balance of £600: *Fibrosa etc.* v. *Fairburn etc.* [1943] A.C. 32 (which was decided before the 1943 Act came into operation).

If the payee has incurred expenses, before the time of discharge, in performing or for the purpose of performing the contract, the court may allow him to retain or recover from the payer the whole or part of these expenses where it considers it just.

Example—A ship repairer repairs a ship, but before completion of the repairs the ship is destroyed by fire. He may be allowed to retain his expenses, including his overhead expenses.

2. Where one party has, by reason of anything done by the other party to the contract, obtained a valuable benefit (other than the payment of money), that other party may recover from him such sum as the court considers just.

Payments under contracts of insurance are to be disregarded in considering the sum to be retained or recovered under 1 or 2 above.

3. The Act does not apply to—
   (a) Contracts containing a provision to meet the case of frustration.

   But a clause providing for a reasonable extension of time in case performance is hindered or delayed does not prevent frustration by reason of war, because war involves indefinite delay and in that case the Act applies.
   (b) Contracts which are not governed by English law.
   (c) Charterparties (except time charterparties or charterparties by way of demise).

(d) Contracts for the carriage of goods by sea.

(e) Contracts of insurance.

(f) Contracts for the sale of specific goods which have perished before the risk has passed to the buyer (Sale of Goods Act 1893, s. 7), and any other contracts of sale where the contract is frustrated by reason of the fact that the goods have perished. The second category, unlike the first, extends to cases in which the risk has already passed to the buyer.

SELECT BIBLIOGRAPHY

Books

	Treitel	*Cheshire & Fifoot*
Performance	524–570	522–532
Agreement	—	533–543
Acceptance of Breach	571–582	568–580
Frustration	583–616	544–567

Articles

Beck, A., "The Doctrine of Substantial Performance: Conditions and Conditions Precedent" (1915) 38 M.L.R. 413–428.

Devlin, Lord, "Treatment of Breach of Contract" [1966] C.L.J. 192–215.

Hudson, A. H., "Prorating in the English Law of Frustrated Contracts" (1968) 31 M.L.R. 535–543.

Lloyd, M. G., "Ready and Willing to Perform: the Problem of Prospective Inability in the Law of Contract" (1974) 37 M.L.R. 121–133.

Treitel, G. H., "Some Problems of Breach of Contract" (1967) 30 M.L.R. 139–155.

CHAPTER 9

REMEDIES FOR BREACH OF CONTRACT

WHEN a contract is broken, the injured party may have several courses of action open to him. These are—
1. to refuse further performance of the contract;
2. to bring an action for damages;
3. to sue on a *quantum meruit*;
4. to sue for specific performance;
5. to sue for an injunction.

REFUSAL OF FURTHER PERFORMANCE

If one party has broken his contract, the other party may treat the contract as rescinded and refuse further performance. By treating the contract as rescinded he makes himself liable to restore any benefits he has received, *e.g.* if he has agreed to sell goods and has received all or part of the price, he must return it, unless it is a term of the contract that he need not do so (*Dies* v. *British and International Mining Corpn.* [1939] 1 K.B. 724). A deposit paid by the purchaser need not be repaid if the sale goes off by the purchaser's default, but a sum given in part payment of the price is returnable (*Howe* v. *Smith* (1884) 27 Ch.D. 89). If the breach has only been a breach of warranty, the injured party must perform his part, although he has a right of action for damages.

DAMAGES

Whenever there is a breach of contract by one party, the other is entitled to bring an action for damages. If in fact he has sustained no loss from the breach he will not be entitled to substantial damages but can only claim nominal damages, *i.e.* damages which recognise that he has had a legal right infringed.

By a c.i.f. contract the buyers, an Italian firm, bought a quantity of Brazilian yellow maize from the sellers, a Brazilian company. The price was $64 per 1,000 kilos delivered weight. When the goods arrived in Trieste, part of them were found to be damaged and the buyers rejected them. Negotiations ensued and eventually the buyers bought the goods

137

which were stored in Trieste at $51.40 per 1,000 kilos. The buyers claimed damages for breach of contract on the ground that the goods were damaged on arrival. *Held*, the purchase of the consignment at $51.40 formed part of a continuous course of dealing between the same parties in respect of the same goods and the profit which the buyers had made by their eventual purchase extinguished their alleged loss which was purely fictitious: *Pagnan & Fratelli* v. *Corbisa Industrial Agropacuaria Ltda.* [1970] 1 W.L.R. 1306.

On February 19, 1974 Lazenby Garages sold a second-hand BMW 2002 car to Mr. Wright for £1,670. On the following day Mr. Wright cancelled the purchase. Lazenby continued to offer the car for sale and sold it on April 23, 1974 for £1,770. Lazenby claimed £345 from Wright as the difference between their buying price and the price which Mr. Wright was obliged to pay, on the ground that they had lost a sale. *Held*, a second-hand car, unlike new cars, was a unique article which had no "available market" within section 50 of the Sale of Goods Act 1893. In the circumstances the cases relating to new cars, such as *Thompson Ltd.* v. *Robinson* (*Gunmakers*) *Ltd.* [1955] Ch. 177 (see p. 259, *post*), did not apply. Lazenby had suffered no loss and could not recover damages: *Lazenby Garages Ltd.* v. *Wright* [1976] 1 W.L.R. 459.

Calculation of damages

If he has sustained loss, he is entitled to substantial damages, which are calculated in accordance with the following rules—

1. The injured party is to be placed in the same financial position as if the contract had been performed. This is called the doctrine of restitution (*restitutio in integrum*).

C agreed to carry S's machine to Guernsey, but owing to their delay, the machine arrived a week late. S proved no loss of profit. *Held*, S's damages were (1) £20, one week's depreciation of the machine; (2) £10, interest on the capital cost, maintenance and wages: *Sunley Ltd.* v. *Cunard White Star Ltd.* [1940] 1 K.B. 740.

The measure of damages is the value of performance to the plaintiff, not the cost of performance to the defendant. In the contract of sale of goods the measure of damages when there is an available market for the goods is the difference between the market price at the date of the breach and the contract price. If therefore, the market price is equal to or below the contract price the plaintiff will be in the same financial position as if the contract had been performed, and so will only be entitled to nominal damages (see p. 259, *post*).

A sale to a merchant who has bought for resale makes no difference to the measure of damages where there is a market. If goods of special manufacture are sold and it is known they are to be resold and cannot be bought in the market, loss of profit is the measure of damages. In string contracts, where the seller knows the merchant is not buying for resale generally but for resale of those specific goods and no others, loss of profit is the right measure (*Kwei Tek Chao* v. *British Traders & Shippers Ltd.* [1954] 2 Q.B. 459).

In accordance with the doctrine of restitution, in calculating damages the tax liability of the person who suffers a breach of contract may have to be taken into account. In an action in tort for injuries from negligence or in contract for wrongful dismissal where the loss of the plaintiff consists wholly or in part in a loss of earnings, which would attract income tax, the amount of that tax must be deducted from his damages because otherwise he would obtain more than restitution (*British Transport Commission* v. *Gourley* (below); and *Parsons* v. *B.N.M. Laboratories Ltd.* [1964] 1 Q.B. 95).

G, a civil engineer, was injured in a railway accident for which the British Transport Commission accepted liability. The damages for earnings, actual and prospective, were agreed to be £37,720 but, if income-tax and surtax, to which G was liable, were taken into account they would be reduced to £6,695. *Held*, it would be unrealistic to ignore the tax element; if the tax liability were not taken into account G would receive more than he had lost. Consequently, the B.T.C. had only to pay the lower amount: *British Transport Commission* v. *Gourley* [1956] A.C. 185.

If there is an anticipatory breach of contract (see p. 127, *ante*) the injured party can claim the same amount of damages as he could have claimed if the contract were broken on due date, but if the injured party himself would have been in breach on due date, so that the other party could have treated the contract as repudiated, he can recover nothing (*Maredelanto Compania Naviera S.A.* v. *Bergbau-Handel G.m.b.H.*; *The Mihalis Angelos* [1971] 1 Q.B. 164, see p. 25, *ante*).

2. Subject to the preceding rule, the damages must be such as were reasonably foreseeable, when the contract was made, as liable to result from the breach of the contract. This principle was laid down in *Hadley* v. *Baxendale* (*post*). The purpose of the rule in that case is to establish that damages can only be recovered if they are caused by a proximate cause but not if they are caused by an event that is too remote.

A mill belonging to X had a broken shaft, and X delivered the shaft to

Y, a carrier, to take to a manufacturer to copy it and make a new one. Y delayed delivery of the shaft beyond a reasonable time, as a result of which the mill was idle for a longer period than should have been necessary. X did not make known to Y that delay would result in a loss of profits. *Held,* Y was not liable for loss of profits during the period of delay: *Hadley* v. *Baxendale* (1854) 9 Ex. 341.

Loss of profits for non-delivery or delayed delivery may be recovered when the party in breach could reasonably have contemplated that it was not unlikely or that there was a serious possibility that such loss will be incurred.

V bought from N a boiler for use in his laundry. Delivery was to be made on June 5 but was not made until November 8. V claimed (1) loss of the profit the laundry would have made had the boiler been delivered in time; (2) loss of profit from some highly profitable dyeing contracts. *Held,* (1) the laundry profits lost were recoverable, as N must have contemplated their loss if there was delay, but (2) the loss on the dyeing contracts, which could not have been contemplated, could not be recovered: *Victoria Laundry* v. *Newman Industries* [1949] 2 K.B. 528.

Charterers chartered the s.s. *Heron II* to carry a cargo of white sugar from Constanza to Basrah. The normal length of the voyage was 20 days. The shipowner deviated in his own interest and thereby prolonged the voyage by nine days. At Basrah there was, as the shipowner knew, a market for white sugar. During the nine days, the market fell and the charterers suffered a loss of more than £4,000. *Held,* the charterers could recover that sum from the shipowners by way of damages for breach of the contract of carriage by sea. The very existence of a "market" for a commodity implied that prices fluctuated and the likelihood that the market price may fall was reasonably foreseeable by the shipowner: *C. Czarnikow Ltd.* v. *Koufos* [1969] 1 A.C. 350.

3. Although not arising naturally from the breach, if the damages may reasonably be supposed to have been in the contemplation of both parties at the time when they made the contract as the probable result of the breach of it, they may be recovered.

P bought from L some copra cake. P resold the copra cake to B, who resold it to dealers, and they in turn resold it to farmers, who used it for feeding cattle. The copra cake was poisonous and cattle fed on it died. Claims were made by the various buyers against their sellers, and P claimed against L the damages and costs he had had to pay to his purchaser. *Held,* as it was within the contemplation of the parties that the copra cake was to be used for feeding cattle, P was entitled to succeed in his claim: *Pinnock Bros.* v. *Lewis & Peat Ltd.* [1923] 1 K.B. 690.

If unusual damages are likely to be sustained as the result of a breach of contract, their nature should be communicated to the other party before the contract is made, so that he contracts subject to the prospective liability.

H contracted to deliver boots for the French Army at a price above the market price. He delivered them to the railway company to be carried, and owing to their delay the purchasers rejected them. *Held*, although H was entitled to ordinary damages for delay, he could not recover the loss he had sustained through the loss of a price above market price unless he could show that the railway company had undertaken to be liable for such loss: *Horne* v. *Midland Ry*. (1873) L.R. 8 C.P. 131.

4. The damages must be caused by the proximate cause and must not be too remote.

Following the litigation in *Harbutt's "Plasticine" Ltd.* v. *Wayne Tank and Pump Co. Ltd.* [1970] 1 Q.B. 447 (see pp. 34–35, *ante*), Wayne, who had been held liable to pay £151,420, claimed to be covered by their insurance with the Employers Liability Insurance. The policy contained an exception clause stating that the insurers should not be liable if the damage was "caused by the nature or condition of any goods . . . sold or supplied by . . . the insured." *Held*, the damage had two causes, first the wholly unsuitable nature of the heating system installed by Wayne, and secondly that Wayne's employee switched on the heating system overnight without proper attention. The first cause fell within the exception clause, but not the second. The first cause was the proximate or dominant cause and that was sufficient to bring into operation the exception clause: *Wayne Tank and Pump Co. Ltd.* v. *Employers Liability Assurance Corpn. Ltd.* [1974] Q.B. 57.

5. The fact that damages are difficult to assess does not prevent the injured party from recovering them.

H advertised a beauty competition, by which readers of certain newspapers were to select 50 ladies, from whom H himself would select 12 and for whom he would provide theatrical engagements. C was one of the 50, and, by H's breach of contract, she was not present when the final selection was made. *Held*, although it was problematic whether she would have been one of the selected 12, and although it was difficult to assess damages, C was entitled to have the damages assessed: *Chaplin* v. *Hicks* [1911] 2 K.B. 786.

The difficulty in assessing damages is enhanced if the damages are for disappointment or mental distress but even in these cases the court has to express them in monetary values.

Mr. Jarvis booked a 15 day Christmas Winter sports holiday in Switzerland with Swan Tours. Contrary to the promises of the travel agency, there was no houseparty at the hotel, the skiing facilities were inadequate and there were other disappointments. *Held*, Mr. Jarvis was entitled to damages compensating him for loss of entertainment and enjoyment. The damages were fixed at £125: *Jarvis* v. *Swans Tours Ltd.* [1973] Q.B. 233.

Mr. Cox, an industrial metallurgical engineer, had differences with his employers, Philips Industries Ltd. He was removed without notice to a position of less responsibility but at the same salary. He became depressed, anxious, frustrated and ill. *Held*, the relegation of Mr. Cox to a position of lesser responsibility was a breach of contract and he could recover damages for the vexation, frustration and distress suffered by him. The damages were assessed in £500: *Cox* v. *Philips Industries Ltd.* [1976] 1 W.L.R. 638.

6. Vindictive or exemplary damages, that is, damages awarded by way of punishment, cannot be awarded for breach of contract, and even in an action founded on tort an award of exemplary damages is anomalous (*Cassell & Co. Ltd.* v. *Broome*, known as *Broome* v. *Cassell & Co. Ltd.* [1972] A.C. 1027).

A was wrongfully dismissed by G from his employment and he claimed (1) damages for his injured feelings for having been dismissed from his employment, and (2) damages for the manner of his dismissal. *Held*, they were not recoverable: *Addis* v. *Gramophone Co.* [1909] A.C. 488. (The difference between this case and *Cox* v. *Philips Industries Ltd.* (*ante*) is that Mr. Cox could not claim damages for wrongful dismissal as he had been paid the appropriate compensation.)

7. It is the duty of the injured person to take reasonable steps to minimise the damages. "The fundamental basis is compensation for pecuniary loss naturally flowing from the breach; but this first principle is qualified by a second, which imposes on a plaintiff the duty of taking all reasonable steps to mitigate the loss consequent on the breach and debars him from claiming any part of the damage which is due to his neglect to take such steps" (*per* Lord Haldane *British Westinghouse Electric and Manufacturing Co.* v. *Underground Electric Ry.* [1912] A.C. 673, 689). The reason for this rule is that the injured party "can recover no more than he would have suffered if he had acted reasonably, because any further damages do not reasonably follow from the defendant's breach" (*per* Scrutton L.J. *Payzu Ltd.* v. *Saunders* [1919] 2 K.B. 581, 589). He is not bound to spend money on a risky venture or to risk his commercial reputation in order to minimise the loss.

B was employed by a partnership consisting of four members for a period of two years certain. After six months the partnership was dissolved through the retirement of two of the partners, the business being carried on by the other two. The continuing partners were willing to continue B's employment on the same terms, but B declined. *Held,* although the dissolution of the partnership operated as a wrongful dismissal of B, he was only entitled to nominal damages as he had suffered no loss: *Brace* v. *Calder* [1895] 2 Q.B. 253.

A person who is wrongfully dismissed, cannot "sit in the sun" but must reasonably attempt to obtain alternative equivalent employment (*Denmark Productions Ltd.* v. *Boscobel Productions Ltd.* [1969] 1 Q.B. 699).

A person who has suffered damage has not performed his obligation reasonably to minimise damages if instead of replacing a damaged chattel at the market price he has it repaired at a cost exceeding its market value; he cannot recover such excess by way of damages (*Darbishire* v. *Warren* [1963] 1 W.L.R. 1067).

8. The parties may agree in their contract that in case of breach the damages shall be a fixed sum or be calculated in a specified manner; such damages are *liquidated* damages. Damages are *unliquidated* when they are not assessed by agreement of the parties and a party seeks to recover such an amount as the court may hold is the proper measure of damages; in this case the amount of damages recoverable is uncertain until the court has given its ruling.

In the case of liquidated damages, no more and no less can be claimed than the agreed sum and the injured party is entitled to recover that amount without proving actual loss.

W agreed to erect a plant for C by a certain date, and also agreed to pay £20 for every week they took beyond that date. They were 30 weeks late, and C claimed £5,850, their actual loss from the delay. *Held,* W had only agreed to pay £20 a week for delay and were not liable for more: *Cellulose Acetate Silk Co.* v. *Widnes Foundry* [1933] A.C. 20.

Liquidated damages and penalties

When a contract provides that, on a breach, a fixed sum shall be payable by the party responsible, it is a question of construction whether this sum is a penalty or liquidated damages. The distinction is important, because if it is a penalty only the actual damage suffered can be claimed, while if it is liquidated damages the sum fixed can be recovered.

The rules for distinguishing a penalty from liquidated damages are—

1. The use of the words "penalty" or "liquidated damages"

in the contract is not conclusive. The court will ascertain whether a sum is in truth a penalty or liquidated damages.

A professional footballer received an injury during a match. He was insured against this risk and the underwriters paid him £500 for total disablement, having first obtained from him an undertaking that he would repay this sum by way of "a penalty" if he took part in a professional football match thereafter. The footballer infringed this undertaking. *Held,* the sum was not a penalty and the footballer had to return it: *Alder* v. *Moore* [1961] 2 Q.B. 57.

2. The essence of a penalty is the payment of money stipulated as *in terrorem* of the offending party; that is to say, its intention is to compel the performance of the contract by providing something by way of punishment if the contract is not performed; the essence of liquidated damages is a genuine pre-estimate of damage.

3. It is a penalty if the sum is extravagant and unconscionable compared with the greatest loss that could conceivably be proved to have followed from the breach.

Under a hire-purchase agreement in respect of a motor car the purchase price was £558, H paid a deposit and four instalments amounting to £302, but failed to pay the fifth instalment. L terminated the agreement, retook possession of the car and sold it for £270. L claimed £122 under a clause making H liable to pay in respect of "depreciation" a sum sufficient to bring his total payments up to £425 which was approximately three-quarters of the purchase price. *Held,* the sum of £425 was not a genuine pre-estimate of damage but was an extravagant and extortionate sum held *in terrorem* over the head of the hirer; it was a penalty and as such not recoverable: *Lamdon Trust Ltd.* v. *Hurrell* [1955] 1 W.L.R. 391.

A term of a contract of hire by which the hirer agrees to pay to the owners of the goods a percentage of the balance of the outstanding rentals in the event of his breach of the contract is not a penalty if such percentage is not extravagant and unconscionable (*Robophone Facilities Ltd.* v. *Blank* [1966] 1 W.L.R. 1428).

4. It is a penalty if the breach consists of not paying a sum of money by a certain time, and the sum fixed is greater than the sum to be paid.

Example—B agrees to pay C £100 on June 1, and, if he fails to make the payment at the stipulated time, to pay £150 as liquidated damages. The extra £50 will be a penalty and irrecoverable.

5. When a single sum is made payable on the occurrence of one or more of several events, some of which may occasion serious and

others trifling damage, there is a presumption (but no more) that the sum is a penalty.

F agreed to act at K's theatre and to conform to all the regulations of the theatre. Each party agreed on breach by either of them of the agreement to pay £1,000 as liquidated damages. F broke the contract, and the jury assessed the damages at £750. *Held*, the £1,000 was a penalty because it was payable even if F had broken any of the smallest regulations of the theatre, and K could only recover £750: *Kemble* v. *Farren* (1829) 6 Bing. 141.

6. The fact that the consequences of the breach make an accurate pre-estimation of the damages almost impossible does not prevent the sum from being liquidated damages.

Before the passing of the Resale Prices Act 1964[1] (see p. 327, *post*), N agreed with D not to sell motor tyres at less than D's list prices, and to pay £5 by way of liquidated damages for every tyre sold in breach of the agreement. *Held*, the £5 was liquidated damages and the whole of it was recoverable: *Dunlop Pneumatic Tyre Co. Ltd.* v. *New Garage Ltd.* [1914] A.C. 79.

In a case like this, the contrast is not between the price of the article and the sum fixed as damages, but between the sum fixed and the probable amount of the damages.

Interest

Interest is recoverable in the following cases—

1. Where there is an express agreement to pay it.
2. Where there is an implied agreement to pay it, resulting from the course of dealing between the parties or from trade usage (*Re Anglesey* [1901] 2 Ch. 548).
3. Upon overdue bills of exchange and promissory notes.
4. By the Law Reform (Miscellaneous Provisions) Act 1934 the court may allow interest at such rate as it thinks fit on all claims for debt or damages from the date when the claim arose to judgment. Interest upon interest cannot be given.

The measures of damages for failure to pay money by a due date is, as a general rule, interest at the market rate.

QUANTUM MERUIT

Where there is a breach of contract, the injured party, instead of suing for damages, may claim payment for what he has done under the contract. His right to payment does not arise out of the original

[1] Which preceded the Resale Prices Act 1976 now in force.

146 Remedies for Breach of Contract

contract, but is based on an implied promise by the other party arising from the acceptance of an executed consideration. This is termed a *quantum meruit*. Cases of *quantum meruit* fall under the category of quasi-contracts (see p. 51 *ante*).

The claim on a *quantum meruit* arises—

1. When one party abandons or refuses to perform the contract.

P was engaged by C to write a book to be published by instalments in a weekly magazine. After a few numbers had appeared the magazine was abandoned. *Held*, P could recover on a *quantum meruit* for the work he had done under the contract: *Planché* v. *Colburn* (1831) 8 Bing. 14.

2. When work has been done and accepted under a void contract.

C was employed as managing director by a company under a written contract. The contract was not binding, because the directors who made it were not qualified. C rendered the services and sued for remuneration. *Held*, he could recover on a *quantum meruit*: *Craven-Ellis* v. *Canons Ltd.* [1936] 2 K.B. 403.

Lump sum contracts

A lump sum contract is one where the intention of the parties is that complete performance must take place before payment can be demanded. Failure to make complete performance prevents any payment being recovered either under the contract or on a *quantum meruit*.

S agreed with H to erect buildings for £565. He did work to the value of £333 and then abandoned the contract. H thereupon completed the contract. *Held*, (i) S could not recover anything under the original contract because he was only entitled to payment on completion of the work; (ii) S could not recover on a *quantum meruit* based on H's acceptance of his work, because H had no option but to accept the work, and no fresh contract to pay could be implied from his acceptance: *Sumpter* v. *Hedges* [1898] 1 Q.B. 673.

But where there is a lump sum contract which is completely performed, though insufficiently and badly, the person who has performed the work can recover the lump sum, less a deduction for his bad work (*Dakin & Co. Ltd.* v. *Lee* [1916] 1 K.B. 566).

X agreed to decorate Y's flat and to fit a wardrobe and a bookcase for the lump sum of £750. The work was done, but Y complained of faulty workmanship, the cost of remedying which being £294. *Held*, X could recover from Y £750 less £294: *Hoenig* v. *Isaacs* [1952] 1 All E.R. 176.

Specific Performance

Instead of or in addition to awarding damages to the injured party, a decree for specific performance may be granted. Specific performance means the actual carrying out by the parties of their contract, and in a proper case the court will insist on the parties carrying out their agreement (*Beswick* v. *Beswick* (see p. 46, *ante*)).

This remedy, however, is discretionary, and will not be granted in any of the following cases—

1. Where damages are an adequate remedy.
2. Where the court cannot supervise the execution of the contract, *e.g.* a building contract.
3. Where the contract is for personal services (see Trade Union and Labour Relations Act 1974, s. 16; p. 173, *post*).
4. Where one of the parties is a minor.
5. In contracts to lend money.

Specific performance is usually granted in contracts connected with land or to take debentures in a company. In the case of the sale of goods, it can only be granted in the case of specific goods and is not ordered as a rule unless the goods are unique and cannot easily be purchased in the market.

Although the court will not order specific performance of a contract for personal services, it may order that such a contract be entered into (*C. H. Giles & Co. Ltd.* v. *Morris* [1972] 1 W.L.R. 307).

Injunction

An injunction is an order of the court restraining a person from doing some act. It will be granted to enforce a negative stipulation in a contract where damages would not be an adequate remedy. Even if there is no express negative stipulation, one may be inferred.

G agreed to take the whole of the electric energy required by his premises from the plaintiffs. *Held*, this was in substance an agreement not to take energy from any other person and it could be enforced by injunction: *Metropolitan Electric Supply Co.* v. *Ginder* [1901] 2 Ch. 799.

In a contract for personal services a clear negative stipulation will be enforced by injunction in a suitable case.

W agreed to sing at L's theatre and nowhere else. *Held*, she could be restrained by injunction from singing for Z: *Lumley* v. *Wagner* (1852) 5 De G.M. & G. 604.

N, a film actress, agreed to act exclusively for W for a year and for no one else. During the year she contracted to act for X. *Held*, she could be restrained by injunction: *Warner Bros.* v. *Nelson* [1937] 1 K.B. 209.

Like specific performance, injunction is an equitable remedy, and is only granted if, in all the circumstances, it is just and equitable to do so.

LIMITATION OF ACTIONS

Time for bringing actions

An action will be barred unless it is brought within the period laid down in the Limitation Acts 1939 to 1975. The Acts do not extinguish the right; they have no substantive effect but bar only the procedural remedy. The defence of limitation is only relevant when it is pleaded by the party entitled thereto. The court will not reject a claim *ex officio* on the ground that it is statute-barred.

Periods of limitation

The periods of limitation are—

1. Actions founded on simple contract, six years after the cause of action accrued (section 2 (1)).

2. Actions upon a deed, 12 years after the cause of action accrued (section 2 (3)).

3. Actions brought to recover land, 12 years after the cause of action accrued, except in the case of the Crown, when the time is 30 years (section 4).

4. Special provisions apply to an action for damages for personal injuries, whether founded on tort or the breach of a contractual or statutory duty. In such a case the period of limitation is, on principle, three years (section 2A) but the court has power to override the time limit (section 2D).

In actions concerning the payment of money, time begins to run from the moment the right of action arose, *e.g.* breach or non-payment. When money is lent and no time for payment is specified, time runs from the date of the loan. If a date for payment is specified, time runs from that date. In a bill or a note payable on demand, time runs from the date of the making of the bill or note and not of the demand. Where a customer has paid money into a current account with a bank, time begins to run when a demand for payment has been made (*Joachimson* v. *Swiss Bank Corporation* [1921] 3 K.B.

111); in the case of a deposit account, where the customer has to give notice of his intention to withdraw, the period of limitation begins to run from the expiration of the notice. In actions for personal injury, time begins to run from the date on which the cause of action accrued or the date, if later, of the plaintiff's knowledge (section 2 A (4)).

If the plaintiff is a minor or a mentally disordered person when the cause of action accrued, time does not begin to run until the disability has ceased to operate. Once time has begun to run, no subsequent disability on the part of the person entitled to the cause of action prevents it from continuing to run (section 22).

The fact that the court offices are closed on a particular day does not lead to an extension of the period of limitation; that period expires on the earlier date on which the court offices were open (*Pritam Kaur* v. *S. Russell & Sons Ltd.* [1973] Q.B. 336).

Effect of fraud or mistake (section 26).
When—
1. the action is based on the fraud of the defendant or his agent; or
2. the right of action is concealed by the fraud of the defendant or his agent; or
3. the action is for relief from the consequences of a mistake; time does not begin to run until the plaintiff either has or with reasonable diligence could have discovered the fraud or mistake. "Fraud" in section 26 is not limited to common law fraud or matters of dishonesty or moral turpitude. It includes "equitable fraud," *i.e.* conduct which is unconscionable, having regard to the special relationship of the parties, but it does not cover mere negligence (*Kitchen* v. *Royal Air Force Association* [1958] 1 W.L.R. 563, 572).

In 1921 L bought plum trees from B warranted as "Purple Pershore." In 1928 L discovered that they were not "Purple Pershore," and sued for damages for breach of warranty. B pleaded the Statutes of Limitation (the forerunner of the Limitation Act 1939). *Held*, fraudulent misrepresentation and fraudulent concealment of the breach of warranty on the part of B were good defences to this plea: *Lynn* v. *Bamber* [1930] 2 K.B. 72.

In 1961 Mr. King agreed to have a house built by Victor Parsons & Co. To the knowledge of the builders, but not of Mr. King, the foundations of the house were built on a disused chalk pit and were not underpinned sufficiently. In 1968 cracks appeared and the house was found to be unsafe for human habitation. In 1969 Mr. King commenced proceedings against the builders. *Held*, the defence of limitation failed because there had been unconscionable concealment constituting fraud within section 26: *King* v. *Victor Parsons & Co.* [1973] 1 W.L.R. 29.

If property obtained by fraud or mistake is subsequently bought for valuable consideration by a person who neither knew nor had reason to believe that a fraud or mistake had occurred, it cannot be recovered nor can its value be claimed from the purchaser in good faith (section 26, proviso (see *Eddis* v. *Chichester Constable* [1969] 2 Ch. 345, see p. 188, *post*)).

Fresh accrual of action (sections 23–25)

A right of action to recover a debt or other liquidated pecuniary claim (whether on simple contract or upon a deed) has a fresh accrual when there is—

1. An acknowledgment in writing signed by the person liable or his agent, and made to the person whose claim is being acknowledged.

   The acknowledgment need not contain or imply a promise to pay; or

2. Payment in respect of the debt or claim made by the person liable or his agent to the creditor or his agent.

   The payment may be a payment of interest or a part-payment of principal or interest.

When there is an acknowledgment or a payment, time runs from the date of the acknowledgment or the last payment.

There is no fresh accrual of a right of action by acknowledgment or part payment unless the claim is for an amount which can be quantified in figures or is liquidated in the sense that it can be ascertained without further agreement of the parties (*Good* v. *Parry* [1963] 2 Q.B. 418); thus there is no fresh accrual of a right of action for unliquidated damages. Where the claim is for a debt, *i.e.* it is a liquidated claim, an acknowledgment under the Act need not identify the amount of the debt but may acknowledge a general indebtedness, provided that the amount of the debt can be ascertained by extraneous evidence (*Dungate* v. *Dungate* [1965] 1 W.L.R. 1471).

Part payment of the balance of a current account cannot be set off against the oldest debts in the account under the rule in

Clayton's case, but is an acknowledgment of the whole amount of the outstanding balance (see *Re Footman, Bower & Co. Ltd.* [1961] Ch. 443, on p. 123, *ante*).

SELECT BIBLIOGRAPHY

Books

	Treitel	Cheshire & Fifoot
Damages	617–671	588–611
Quantum Meruit	703–706	657–660
Specific Performance	678–697	612–619
Injunction	691–697	615–619
Limitation of Actions	—	619–627

Articles

Barton, J. L., "Penalties and Damages" (1976) 92 L.Q.R. 20–26.

James, P. S., "Foresight at Sea" [1968] J.B.L. 303–310.

Macleod, J. K., "Damages: Reliance on Expectancy Interest" [1970] J.B.L. 19–37.

Stoljar, S. J., "Normal, Elective and Preparatory Damages in Contract" (1975) 91 L.Q.R. 68–85.

Treitel, G. H., "Specific Performance and Third Parties" (1967) 30 M.L.R. 687–693.

Yates, D., "Damages for Non-Pecuniary Loss" (1973) 36 M.L.R. 535–541.

CHAPTER 10

OPERATION, ASSIGNMENT AND INTERPRETATION OF CONTRACT

PRIVITY OF CONTRACT

IN common law, a contract cannot impose liabilities upon one who is not a party to the contract.

X sold to Y some rubber heels packed in a box, in the lid of which was a notice that the heels were sold on the express agreement that they were not to be resold below certain prices. Z bought the heels from Y with notice of the agreement, but resold them below the prices. *Held*, as there was no contract between X and Z, X could not enforce the agreement: *McGruther* v. *Pitcher* [1904] 2 Ch. 306. But now see the Resale Prices Act 1976, p. 327, *post*.

Except as stated earlier (p. 47, *ante*), a contract cannot confer rights upon one who is not a party to the contract.

G married H, and their fathers, L and M, agreed each to pay a sum of money to G on a particular date, and that G should have power to sue for the sums. G sued L's executors for the sum. *Held*, he could not do so, as he was a stranger to the contract: *Tweddle* v. *Atkinson* (1861) 1 B. & S. 393.

Although no rights are conferred, benefits obtained by one who is not a party to the contract can be retained.

S was employed by a company. On the termination of his employment it was agreed between S and the company that the company should make certain payments to S during his life and after his death other payments to his wife and daughter. S became bankrupt and died, and his trustee in bankruptcy claimed from his widow all sums paid to her by the company. *Held*, the claim failed, as the company fulfilled its contractual obligations in paying the widow, although she could not compel payment: *Re Schebsman* [1944] Ch. 83.

A contract imposes a duty on third parties not to induce any of the contracting parties to commit a breach of contract.

L engaged W, an opera singer, to sing in his theatre for a season, and G, knowing of this contract, induced W to break it and to sing for him. *Held*, L could recover damages from G: *Lumley* v. *Gye* (1853) 2 E. & B. 216.

If a third party induces another to terminate a contract in a lawful manner, *e.g.* by giving notice, he will not be liable to an action. It is not actionable to induce a person by peaceful means not to enter into a contract with another, but if physical violence or threats are used, the person using them may be sued.

Special provisions apply to **trade disputes.** The Trade Union and Labour Relations Act 1974[1] provides (section 13) that an act done by a person in contemplation or furtherance of a trade dispute shall not, in principle, be actionable in tort; this protection extends to the tort of intimidation, *i.e.* the threat that a contract of employment will be broken or another person be induced to break such a contract (section 13 (1) (*b*)). Trade unions and employers' associations and their officials and members are afforded far-reaching immunity from actions in tort (section 14). Peaceful picketing is admitted (section 15). It is further provided that the courts shall not compel an employee to do any work or attend at any place of employment, by ordering specific performance of a contract of employment or by issuing an injunction restraining a breach or threatened breach of such a contract (section 16).

ASSIGNMENT OF CONTRACT

Liabilities under a contract cannot be assigned without the consent of the other party to the contract. They can only be assigned by novation which, as will be seen, requires the consent of the other party.

Rights under a contract can normally be assigned but highly personal rights, *e.g.* those arising from a contract of service, cannot be assigned, except by consent of the other party to the contract.

On the amalgamation of companies the court has power to order "the transfer to the transferee company of the whole or any part of the under-taking and of the property or liabilities of any transferor company" (Companies Act 1948, s. 208 (1) (*a*)). Such order does not include an assignment of a contract of service because an employee is free to choose his employer and the right to the employee's services cannot be transferred without his consent: *Nokes* v. *Doncaster Amalgamated Collieries Ltd.* [1940] A.C. 1014.

The assignment of rights under a contract is carried out by—

1. Novation.
2. Legal assignment.
3. Equitable assignment.
4. Assignment by operation of law.

[1] Amended by the Trade Union and Labour Relations (Amendment) Act 1976.

Novation

This is a new contract between the parties, whereby the creditor at the request of the debtor agrees to take another person as his debtor in the place of the original debtor. The effect of novation is to release the original debtor from his obligations under the contract and to impose those obligations on the new debtor. Novation frequently arises in partnership on a change in the membership of the firm when the creditors, expressly or by implication, agree to accept the liability of the new firm and to discharge the old firm.

M insured his life with the B N Association. The Association became amalgamated with the E Society and ceased to carry on business, and a memorandum was indorsed on M's policy that the E Society would be liable for the policy money. Subsequent premiums were paid to the E Society. *Held*, there was a complete novation, and, on the winding up of the two companies, M had no right of proof against the B N Association: *Re European Assurance Society* (1876) 3 Ch.D. 391.

Legal assignment

By the Law of Property Act 1925, s. 136, all debts and other legal things in action—*choses in action*—may be assigned, but the assignment must be—
1. in writing, signed by the assignor;
2. absolute and not purporting to be by way of charge only;
3. followed by express notice in writing given to the debtor, trustee, or other person from whom the assignor would have been entitled to claim such a debt or thing in action.

A *chose in action* is a right of property which can only be enforced by action and not by taking physical possession, as can be done with *choses in possession*. Choses in action include rights arising under a contract.

An assignment to be absolute must be of the whole interest of the assignor and not of a portion of it, so that the debtor will not be inconvenienced by having to seek out two creditors. It is absolute although it is by way of mortgage or by way of trust. Conditional assignments and assignments of part of a debt are not absolute.

A schoolmaster assigned to a moneylender so much of his salary as should be necessary to repay the sums borrowed from the moneylender. *Held*, this was not an absolute assignment but it was an assignment purporting to be by way of charge only: *Jones* v. *Humphreys* [1902] 1 K.B. 10.

The notice informing the debtor of the assignment need not state the date of the assignment (*Van Lynn Developments Ltd.* v. *Pelias Construction Co. Ltd.* [1969] 1 Q.B. 607). An assignment of which no notice has been given, does not operate as a legal assignment under section 136 of the Law of Property Act, but operates only as an equitable assignment (*Warner Bros. Records Inc.* v. *Rollgreen Ltd.* [1976] Q.B. 430).

The assignment takes effect subject to any defences or claims open to the debtor against the assignor existing at the time of his receipt of the notice of assignment. This is expressed by saying that the assignee takes "subject to equities." The defences or claims, however, must arise out of the contract itself to which the assignment relates. Further, a set-off founded on damages for fraud inducing the debtor to enter into the contract cannot be made against an innocent assignee (*Stoddart* v. *Union Trust Ltd.* [1912] 1 K.B. 181).

The effect of the assignment is to transfer to the assignee—
1. The legal right to the debt or chose in action;
2. all legal and other remedies for the same;
3. the power to give a good discharge without the concurrence of the assignor.

The assignment of a legal chose in action does not require consideration (*Re Westerton* [1919] 2 Ch. 104).

Equitable assignment

An assignment which does not comply with the requirements of a legal assignment may still be valid as an equitable assignment, as long as the intention to assign is clear. If the intention is clear, no particular formalities are necessary and the assignment need not be in writing. Notice to the debtor need not be given to perfect the assignee's title, but it should be given—
1. Because the debtor can set up any defences against the assignee which he had against the assignor up to the date of his receipt of the notice. If, therefore, he makes a payment to the assignor before he receives notice of assignment, this payment is good as against the assignee.
2. To gain priority over any subsequent assignee without notice of his assignment.

It is no objection to an equitable assignment that part only of a debt is assigned or that it includes future debts.

K. agreed with B, who financed him, that the purchase price of all goods sold by K should be paid direct to B. K sold goods to D, B gave notice to D to pay the price to B, but D disregarded the notice and paid K. *Held*, there was an equitable assignment of the price, and D was liable to pay B notwithstanding that they had already paid K: *Brandt* v. *Dunlop Rubber Co.* [1905] A.C. 454.

An equitable assignee cannot enforce the right assigned by action without joining the legal owner (*Performing Right Society* v. *London Theatre of Varieties Ltd.* [1924] A.C. 1).

An equitable assignment which is complete does not require consideration, but an incomplete equitable assignment made without consideration is ineffective (*Re McArdle* [1951] Ch. 669).

An equitable assignment of a legal chose in action must be distinguished from the assignment of an equitable chose in action. Examples of the latter are: a claim by a beneficiary against his trustee, and a claim by a legatee against an executor.

Contracts involving the personal credit, ability or other personal qualifications of a party cannot be assigned, either legally or equitably. Examples are: a contract to paint a picture, or a contract of service. Even a contract for the sale of goods may be incapable of being assigned on this ground.

B agreed to supply K, a cake manufacturer, with all the eggs he required for a year. K transferred his business to a company to which he assigned the benefit of his contract with B. B refused to supply the company. *Held*, he was entitled to refuse, as the contract was a personal one, referring to the number of eggs K would require personally, and so could not be assigned without B's consent: *Kemp* v. *Baerselman* [1906] 2 K.B. 604.

The following are transferred at law in accordance with the statutes relating to them and not in the manner laid down in the Law of Property Act 1925, s. 136—

1. Bills of exchange and promissory notes according to the Bills of Exchange Act 1882.
2. Shares in companies registered under the Companies Acts 1948 to 1976, according to those Acts.
3. Bills of lading according to the Bills of Lading Act 1855.
4. Policies of marine insurance according to the Marine Insurance Act 1906.
5. Policies of life assurance according to the Policies of Assurance Act 1867.

Assignment by operation of law

Contracts are assigned by operation of law on—
1. death, and
2. bankruptcy.

Death of a party passes all his rights and liabilities under a contract to his personal representatives. The only exceptions to this are contracts of personal service and contracts involving personal skill.

Bankruptcy passes all rights and liabilities to the bankrupt's trustee in bankruptcy (see p. 493, *post*).

INTERPRETATION OF CONTRACT

The general principle on interpretation of contracts was, in the older view, to ascertain the actual intention of the parties to the contract. The modern view is to ascertain "what each [party] was reasonably entitled to conclude from the attitude of the other" (*per* Lord Reid in *McCutcheon* v. *David Macbrayne Ltd.* [1964] 1 W.L.R. 125, 128). An objective standard is thus substituted for a subjective one.

If a contract is reduced by the parties into writing, the general rule is that it cannot be varied by parol evidence. The exceptions to this rule are—

1. Parol evidence may be given to show that the written contract was made subject to a condition.

P agreed to sell a share in an invention to C. A written agreement was drawn up setting out the agreement, but it was verbally agreed that it should not be binding unless X approved the invention. X did not approve. *Held*, parol evidence of X's non-approval could be given: *Pym* v. *Campbell* (1856) 6 E. & B. 370.

2. If the whole contract was not intended to be put into writing, parol evidence can be given of the additional terms. If the whole contract is required by statute to be in writing, this exception does not apply, and no parol evidence incorporating terms can be given.

A granted to B the lease of a house for three years. The terms were arranged, but B refused to hand over the counterpart which he had signed unless he was assured that the drains were in order. A gave this assurance. The lease did not refer to the drains, which were bad. *Held*, B could give parol evidence of the warranty as to the drains, because it was collateral to the lease and did not contradict it: *De Lassalle* v. *Guildford* [1901] 2 K.B. 215.

3. Parol evidence can be given to prove the rescission of a written contract. This applies even to contracts required by statute to be in writing (*Morris* v. *Baron & Co.* [1918] A.C. 1).

4. Parol evidence can be given to explain a latent but not patent ambiguity.

A patent ambiguity is an ambiguity which is apparent on the face of the document. If in a cheque the amount is stated to be "one hundred pounds" in words and "£150" in figures, the ambiguity is patent. In such a case no evidence can be given to show which is correct, the law conclusively presuming in favour of the words as against the figures.

A latent ambiguity is one which is not apparent. For example, if two men have the same name or if a man agrees to buy "your wool," parol evidence can be given to identify the man in the one case and to show the quantity and the quality of the wool in the other.

5. Parol evidence can be given to prove a trade usage or a local custom.

Thus, where in a charterparty the charterer agrees to take the cargo from alongside the ship at his own expense, parol evidence is admissible to show where "alongside" is according to the custom of a particular port.

SELECT BIBLIOGRAPHY
Books

	Treitel	*Cheshire & Fifoot*
Privity of Contract	416–450	434–452
Assignment	451–480	493–517
Interpretation	128–135	121–135

Articles

Millner, M. A., "*Jus Quaesitum Tertio*: Comparison and Synthesis" (1967) 16 I.C. L.Q. 446–463.

Palmer, N. E., "The Stevedore's Dilemma: Exception Clauses and Third Parties" [1974] J.B.L. 101–118, 220–224.

Chapter 11

CONFLICT OF LAWS

When a contract is made between persons or companies residing in different countries, or is made in one country to be performed in another, the question arises whether the contract is to be governed by English law or by the law of some other country. The solution of this question pertains to the subject known as private international law or conflict of laws. The following rules apply—

1. The capacity of a party to contract is governed by the law of his domicile, that is, of the country where he makes his home. For example, in the case of a Frenchman living permanently in France, the law of France determines his capacity to contract.

2. The formalities of the contract are governed by the law of the country where the contract is made, known as the *lex loci contractus*. If, therefore, the law of that country requires the contract to be made under seal or in some other way, the contract will not be enforced in England unless that requirement is complied with, although English law may not require the same formalities in the case of similar contracts made in England.

3. When a contract made abroad is sued upon in England, it must be proved in the manner required by English law. If, therefore, it is required to be evidenced in writing by some statute, this requirement must be complied with.

X entered into a contract of service with Y in France. The contract was not to be performed within a year, and had to be proved by a note or memorandum in writing to comply with the Statute of Frauds (since repealed on this point). According to French law, the contract was valid without writing. *Held*, the requirement of writing being a rule of procedure, the contract could not be enforced as the rule was not satisfied: *Leroux* v. *Brown* (1852) 12 C.B. 801.

Similarly, all matters of procedure are governed by English law and the English Limitation Acts 1939 to 1975 apply.

4. The essential validity, interpretation and discharge of the contract is governed by the law which the parties intend shall apply. That law is called **the proper law of the contract.** The intention of the parties may be expressly stated in the contract, by the insertion of a clause to the effect that the contract shall be governed by, *e.g.*

English law, or may be implied by the surrounding circumstances. The parties may subject the contract to a law with which the contract is not connected, provided that their choice is bona fide and legal and does not contravene public policy (*Vita Food Products Inc.* v. *Unus Shipping Co.* [1939] A.C. 277, 290).

When there is no stipulation in the contract, express or implied, indicating the law governing the contract the proper law of the contract is the law with which the contract has the closest and most substantial connection. Matters to be considered are: the law of the country where the contract was made, the law of the country where it is to be performed, the form of the contract and the language in which it is written.

When the contract is to be performed in the country in which it is made, the presumption is that the law of that country is the law of the most real connection (*Jacobs* v. *Credit Lyonnais* (1884) 12 Q.B.D. 589).

When the contract is made in one country and is to be performed wholly or partly in another, the presumption is that the law of the place of performance is the law with which the contract is most closely connected.

B in Gibraltar offered to sell anchovies f.o.b. Gibraltar to D at Malta, and D accepted by letter posted in Malta. On delivery of the anchovies, D claimed to be entitled to reject them and his right to do this depended on whether the law of Gibraltar or Malta applied to the contract. *Held*, although from the posting of the letter of acceptance in Malta the contract was made in Malta, the place of performance was Gibraltar and therefore the law of Gibraltar applied: *Benaim & Co.* v. *Debono* [1924] A.C. 514.

Where the contract contains an arbitration clause, the presumption is that the law of the place at which the arbitration is to be held shall be the law applicable to the contract because the arbitrator is assumed to apply the law with which he is best acquainted.

A Swedish shipping line sold the s.s. *Montrose* to Greek buyers. The contract contained an arbitration clause stating that any dispute should be decided by arbitration in the City of London. *Held*, the proper law of the contract of sale was English law: *Tzortzis* v. *Monark Line A/B* [1968] 1 W.L.R. 406.

But this presumption is rebutted by the surrounding circumstances if the arbitration tribunal which the parties have chosen does not have a permanent location and is constituted *ad hoc*, or if other circumstances point to another law as that of the closest connection.

A Tunisian company and French shipowners negotiated a contract through brokers in Paris for the transport of crude oil from one Tunisian port to another. The contract was in the form of a printed tanker voyage charter in English and provided that the contract should be governed by the laws of the flag of the vessels carrying the goods and disputes should be settled by arbitration in London. The French owners had four or five ships flying the French flag but they were not large enough to carry the cargo. Therefore the owners chartered other ships flying the Norwegian, Swedish, Liberian, French and Bulgarian flag respectively. *Held*, the proper law of the charterparty was French law. The arbitration clause was no more than one indication of the proper law which may, and in the present case did, give way to other indications: *Cie Tunisienne de Navigation S.A.* v. *Cie d'Armement Maritime S.A.* [1971] A.C. 572.

The law applicable to the arbitration procedure may be different from the substantive law governing the contract (*Whitworth Street Estates (Manchester) Ltd.* v. *James Miller & Partners Ltd.* [1970] A.C. 583).

There is a presumption that bonds issued by a government are governed by the law of that government (*Bonython* v. *Commonwealth of Australia* [1951] A.C. 201), and that an insurance policy is governed by the law of the head office of the insurance company at which the proposal of the assured has been accepted (*Rossano* v. *Manufacturers Life Insurance* [1963] 2 Q.B. 352). A contract of carriage by sea is governed by the law stated in the clause paramount of the bill of lading.

5. A distinction is drawn between the money of account and the money of payment. The money of account is the currency in which, according to the intention of the parties, the purchase price is to be measured. The money of payment relates to the mode of payment in which the obligation to pay the purchase price is to be discharged. If, on the date of settlement, the value of the money of payment has depreciated in relation to the money of account, more currency in the denomination of the money of payment has to be acquired to pay the money of account.

Woodhouse, of London, purchased a quantity of cocoa from the Nigerian Produce Marketing Co. The price was expressed in Nigerian currency. The Nigerian sellers agreed that the British seller might pay in pounds sterling. Before the date of payment, the pound sterling was devalued but the Nigerian currency was not devalued. *Held*, Nigerian currency was the money of account and pounds sterling the money of payment. Consequently, the British buyers had to pay the Nigerian sellers more in pounds sterling in order to discharge the liability for the price of the cocoa: *Woodhouse A.C. Israel Cocoa Ltd. S.A.* v. *Nigerian Produce Marketing Co. Ltd.* [1972] A.C. 741.

6. Special rules apply to contracts having a foreign element which are illegal according to English or foreign law.

A contract will not be enforced in England—

(a) If its object is to perform in a foreign and friendly country an act illegal in that country: see *Foster* v. *Driscoll* and *Regazzoni* v. *K. C. Sethia* (*1944*) *Ltd.*, both on p. 98, *ante*.

A Spanish ship was chartered to carry jute from Calcutta to Barcelona at a freight which exceeded the legal maximum fixed by the law of Spain. On arrival at Barcelona, the receivers paid the legal maximum, and the owners sued the charterers for the balance of freight. The charterparty was an English contract to be construed according to English law. *Held*, as the payment of the balance was illegal in Spain, where it ought to have been made, it could not be recovered in England: *Ralli Bros.* v. *Compania Naviera Sota y Aznar* [1920] 2 K.B. 287.

A contract concerning the exchange of the currency of one country for that of another and contravening the exchange control regulations of a foreign country which is a member of the Bretton Woods Agreements is an "exchange contract" within the meaning of the Bretton Woods Agreements Act 1945 and, as such, unenforceable in the English courts if either party was a resident of the foreign country in question: *Sharif* v. *Azad* [1967] 1 Q.B. 605. But a contract which is not a monetary transaction and is, in essence, a commercial contract for the sale or purchase of merchandise or commodities is not an exchange contract within the meaning of the Bretton Woods Agreements although the price is expressed in foreign currency (*Wilson, Smithett & Cope Ltd.* v. *Terruzzi* [1976] Q.B. 683).

(b) A contract which is valid where it is made will not be enforced in England if it is illegal by English law or if it is contrary to English ideas of public policy or morality.

O gave a cheque drawn on an English bank to M in Algiers to pay debts incurred by O in playing baccarat in Algiers. The consideration was legal according to French law, but illegal under section 1 of the Gaming Act 1835. *Held*, an action on the cheque was not maintainable: *Moulis* v. *Owen* [1907] 1 K.B. 746.

7. A contract relating to the title to land abroad will not be enforced or maintained in England: *British S. Africa Co.* v. *Companhia de Moçambique* [1893] A.C. 602.

Judgments in foreign currency

The English courts normally award damages or order the recovery of debts only in English currency.

If, however, payment is stipulated in favour of a foreign party in a foreign currency, the English courts have jurisdiction to give judgment ordering the defendant to pay in the foreign currency in question. If the judgment in foreign currency has to be executed in England, it is necessary to convert the amount ordered to be paid into pounds sterling. The rate of conversion is that prevailing at the date when the court gives the plaintiff leave to levy execution against the defendant's assets.

Mr. Miliangos, who carried on business in Switzerland, sold a quantity of polyester yarn to George Frank (Textiles) Ltd., a company in England. The purchase price was fixed in Swiss francs. Frank failed to pay. *Held*, the English courts had jurisdiction to order payment of the price in Swiss francs: *Miliangos* v. *George Frank (Textiles) Ltd.* [1976] A.C. 443.

Similarly, in appropriate cases an award in foreign currency can be made in claims for damages (*Jean Kraut A.G.* v. *Albany Fabrics Ltd.* [1976] 3 W.L.R. 872), in case of bills of exchange expressed in foreign currency (*Barclays Bank International Ltd.* v. *Levin Brothers (Bradford) Ltd.* [1976] 3 W.L.R. 852), in arbitration proceedings (*Jugoslavenska Oceanska Plovidba* v. *Castle Investment Co. Inc.* [1974] Q.B. 292), in salvage proceedings (*The Halcyon the Great* [1975] 1 W.L.R. 515), and in other cases in which the contractual obligation is expressed in foreign currency.

SELECT BIBLIOGRAPHY

Books

G. C. Cheshire and P. M. North, *Cheshire's Private International Law* (9th ed., 1974).

R. H. Graveson, *The Conflict of Laws* (7th ed., 1974).

J. H. C. Morris, *The Conflict of Laws* (1971).

Articles

Cheshire, G. C., "International Contracts for the Sale of Goods" [1960] J.B.L. 282–286.

Counter, K. N. S., "Improper Views of Proper Law" [1970] J.B.L. 198–203.

Counter, K. N. S., "The Proper Law of Contract—A Re-examination" [1965] J.B.L. 326–333.

Inglis, B. D., "The Doctrine of Forum Conveniens & Choice of Law in Conflict of Laws" (1965) 81 L.Q.R. 380–394.

Jaffey, A. J. E., "Offer and Acceptance and Related Questions in the Conflict of Laws" (1975) 24 I.C.L.Q. 603–616.

Mann, F. A., "Amended Sale of Goods Act 1893 and the Conflict of Laws" (1974) 90 L.Q.R. 42–54.

Sassoon, D. M., "Choice of Tribunal and the Proper Law of Contract" [1964] J.B.L. 18–24.

Wyatt, D., "Choice of Law in Contract Matters—A Question of Policy" (1974) 37 M.L.R. 399–416.

PART 2: CONTRACT OF EMPLOYMENT, AGENCY AND PARTNERSHIP

CHAPTER 12

CONTRACT OF EMPLOYMENT

Nature of the contract of employment

THE contract of employment is a contract of service and not for services. Under a contract of service a man places his labour at the disposal of another and a relationship is constituted which in past days was called that of master and servant. In the contract for services, on the other hand, a man who operates an independent business agrees to carry out a task for another and the relationship is that of employer and independent contractor. X's chauffeur is his employee, but a taxi-driver is an independent contractor. If Y wants to build a garage on his land, he has two courses open: he can employ a bricklayer and other tradesmen under contracts of employment or he can entrust the work to a builder as an independent contractor.

The distinction between contracts of employment and those with independent contractors is sometimes not easy to draw. In older decisions the test of control and supervision was held to be decisive and it was thought that a contract was one of employment if the employer had power to control the manner of work, if he had the right to say, not only what should be done, but also how and when it should be done. In modern law it is recognised that the control test can not be the exclusive criterion and that a contract of employment may also exist in cases in which the employer has no ability or right to control the method of work, *e.g.* in the employment of a professional man, such as a surgeon employed by a hospital board. Lord Denning advanced the following test which is supplemental to the control test: "one feature which seems to run through the instances is that under a contract of service a man is employed as part of the business and his work is done as an integral part of the business; whereas under a contract of services his work, although done for the business, is not integrated into it but is only accessory to it" (*Stevenson, Jordan & Harrison* v. *Macdonald and Evans* [1952] 1 T.L.R. 101).

Unfortunately, the test of whether a workman is an "integral part" of another's business is not easy to apply. In recent cases the courts have usually endorsed the approach of considering all the factors pointing one way or the other and then of attempting to reach a "common sense" decision (*Challinor* v. *Taylor* [1972] I.C.R. 129; *Construction Industry Training Board* v. *Labour Force Ltd.* [1970] 3 All E.R. 220; *Global Plant Ltd.* v. *Secretary of State* [1972] 1 Q.B. 139). The label that the parties themselves have attached to the relationship may be a relevant factor, but certainly is not a conclusive one (*Fergusson* v. *John Dawson Ltd.* [1976] 1 W.L.R. 1213).

In spite of the difficulties of making the distinction between a contract of service and one for services, the distinction is a crucial one, for many rights and duties, both at common law and by statute, hinge upon it. At common law an employer is under a general vicarious liability for the torts of his employees committed in the course of their employment, whereas his liability in respect of his independent contractors is much more limited. A clearly established set of terms is usually implied by common law into the contract of employment (see p. 170, *post*), whereas the terms implied into the contract with an independent contractor are likely to depend much more on the circumstances of the particular contract. The new statutory protections conferred upon employees, considered *passim* in this chapter, are generally confined to those working under a contract of employment. Finally, the incidence of health and safety, social security and tax legislation is very different in respect of employees and independent contractors.

Excluded classes of employees

The common law of the contract of employment applies uniformly to nearly all classes of employee, although Crown employees and perhaps certain other public employees may be under special disabilities. The statutory protections discussed later in more detail are subject, however, to a number of specific exceptions. Besides the fact that the statutes do not always bind the Crown, short service employees are not usually covered, although the length of service required before protection is acquired varies from statute to statute, being, for example, two years in the case of the Redundancy Payments Act, six months for unfair dismissal protection, and four weeks for minimum periods of notice. Part-time employees are often excluded, as are close relations of the employer and employees working ordinarily outside Great Britain. Again the details vary from statute to statute.

Legal machinery for resolving disputes about the contract of employment

Questions concerning the common law of the contract of employment have traditionally been settled by the ordinary civil courts, in the first instance by the county courts or the High Court. Beginning with the Redundancy Payments Act 1965, however, disputes about the new statutory structure of employment law have been referred in the first instance to **industrial tribunals**. Industrial tribunals have a lawyer as chairman, but also two lay "wingmen" who each have an equal voice with the chairman, even on points of law. The two wingmen are chosen for their experience in industry respectively on the employee's side and on the employer's side. The tribunals are expected to be informal, speedy and cheap. The tribunals are not bound by strict rules of procedure or of evidence. Legal aid is not available before tribunals, but the right of representation is not confined to lawyers. Trade union and employers' association officials, personnel managers, and indeed anyone who can bring himself within the category of "friend" of the applicant or respondent may appear and present a case, as well as the party himself. Travel and modest subsistence payments are made to witnesses and representatives other than lawyers. Costs are normally to be awarded against a losing party only if he has acted frivolously or vexatiously. Appeal from an industrial tribunal lies on a point of law only to the Employment Appeal Tribunal (EAT) in London. This body also is of tripartite composition, the chairman being a High Court judge. From the EAT appeals lie in the ordinary way to the Court of Appeal and the House of Lords. In recent enactments a conciliation stage, involving independent conciliation from the Advisory, Conciliation and Arbitration Service, has been added before the dispute even reaches an industrial tribunal.

The industrial tribunals now handle individual disputes under numerous statutes, notably the Redundancy Payments Act 1965, Contracts of Employment Act 1972, Trade Union and Labour Relations Act 1974 and 1976, Employment Protection Act 1975, Equal Pay Act 1970, and in the employment area, the Sex Discrimination Act 1975 and Race Relations Act 1976. Section 109 of the Employment Protection Act also provides that jurisdiction over a limited category of claims arising out of the common law of the contract of employment may also be conferred upon the industrial tribunals.

Formation of the contract of employment

The contract of employment may be embodied in a written document, may be wholly oral, may need to be deduced from the parties' conduct, or may be partly in one of the forms and partly in another. Although it is not usually problematic whether or not there is a contract, where the contract is not written it is often difficult to be sure of its precise terms. This is not merely because proof of an oral agreement is more difficult, but, more important, because in an oral hiring very little may have been expressly agreed between the parties. In *Fergusson* v. *John Dawson Ltd.* (see p. 166, *ante*), "the plaintiff came with four other Irishmen already working for the defendants, and he asked, or perhaps one of his friends asked, if he could 'come along.' " Mr. Murray's evidence [the site agent] is: "I said he could start on Monday and that was it. But I did inform him . . . we were working as a lump labour force."

To supplement what has been expressly agreed between the parties the law may treat rules derived from various other sources as part of the contract of employment. Such sources include the employer's works rules, relevant collective agreements, custom and practice, and terms implied by common law or by statute. But whether any terms from these sources have in fact been incorporated into a particular contract of employment may be very uncertain. With regard to the first three sources the basic question is whether the parties have implicitly agreed to incorporation, a question that may be very difficult to answer when the employee is first hired, but which may become clearer later "as particular questions of the rights and obligations of the parties arose during the progress of the work" (*per* Megaw L.J. in *Fergusson* v. *John Dawson Ltd.*, above).

Contracts of Employment Act

Since even lapse of time may not make the contents of the contract clear, Parliament in 1963 attempted a modest degree of formalisation of the contract of employment. By what is now section 4 of the Contracts of Employment Act 1972 (as amended), except in the case of certain written contracts, an employer must provide his employees with a written statement of the particulars of certain terms of the contract within 13 weeks of the commencement of the employment.

The terms in question relate to the parties to the contract, the date employment began, pay, hours of work, holidays, incapacity for work, pensions, notice required by the employee to terminate the contract, and the employee's job title. If the contract in question contains no such provisions on any of these matters, the particulars must so state. The employee must also be informed of changes in these terms by amendments to the written particulars. In addition, the written particulars must be accompanied by a note specifying the disciplinary rules applicable to the employee, the person to whom application for redress of grievances may be made, and the grievance procedure (if any) available to the employee.

The written particulars do not constitute the contract of employment nor ought they to be treated as conclusive evidence of its terms. Thus the employee may apply to an industrial tribunal under section 8(2) of the Act seeking to have the written particulars issued to him by his employer amended so as to correspond with the terms of his contract. The tribunals and the courts do, however, often lose sight of the distinction between the particulars and the contract, and sometimes the failure of an employee to object to the particulars which have been issued to him is used to raise a form of estoppel against him when he later seeks to dispute their accuracy (*Soutar* v. *Fisher* (1975) 10 I.T.R. 38). In this way the particulars become another source of terms for the contract of employment.

The main impact of the written particulars, however, has been as a method whereby terms from the other sources mentioned above may be incorporated into the contract of employment. Section 4(5) provides that the particulars themselves need not contain the details of the terms, but may instead "refer the employee to some document which the employee has reasonable opportunities of reading in the course of his employment or which is made reasonably accessible to him in some other way." Thus, the particulars may refer to a collective agreement or the works rules, so making it clear that parts of these documents have been incorporated into the contract of employment. Indeed, if the written particulars refer generally to, say, a collective agreement, the effect may be to incorporate into the contract of employment parts of the collective agreement which deal with matters beyond those which must be covered in the written particulars.

The employee's statement under the Contracts of Employment Act said that his terms and conditions of employment were those set out in the memorandum of agreement for the steel erecting industry concluded between the Engineering Employers' Federation and the Constructional Engineering Union. The court's interpretation of the memorandum was that steel erectors could be required to work anywhere in the country. Because the statement incorporated the memorandum in the contract of employment, the employer could require the employee to move to another site when work finished at the current site, even though geographical mobility is not one of the terms of employment of which the Act requires employees to be informed. *Stevenson* v. *Teesside Bridge and Engineering Ltd.* [1971] 1 All E.R. 296.

Of course, not all the terms of the collective agreement will be appropriate for incorporation in the individual contract of employment, *e.g.* those intended to affect only the relations between the parties to the collective agreement. Also, a special procedure must be followed if terms are to be incorporated from the collective agreement which prohibit or restrict the employee's freedom to engage in industrial action; see Trade Union and Labour Relations Act 1974, s. 18(4).

Terms implied by common law

With the transformation since 1963 of the contract of employment into a contract by incorporation (via the written particulars), customary practices, on the one hand, and terms implied by common law, on the other, have been afforded a more restricted scope as sources for the contract of employment. Nevertheless, certain categories of implied term were strongly established by judicial decision in the nineteenth and first half of the twentieth centuries and will normally be treated as part of the contract unless contradated by something expressly agreed or incorporated. The most important of these implied terms are briefly noted below. Moreover, the potential creativity of the implied term has not been destroyed, as witness the recent cases which have suggested (but not established) a right to strike (*Morgan* v. *Fry* [1968] 2 Q.B. 710) and a right to work (*Langston* v. *A.U.E.W.* [1974] I.C.R. 180).

1. Co-operation

It is an implied term that both parties to the contract should facilitate the performance of their mutual obligations under it. This principle is useful as an aid to the interpretation of particular contractual obligations, but there is a risk that the contract will become removed from the reality of the situation if the principle is used to import obligations into the contract.

The railway unions called their members out on a "work-to-rule," *i.e.* the employees, contrary to their usual practices, meticulously observed the requirements of their employer's rule book, with the result that the working of the railways was extensively disrupted. The employees were held to be in breach of their contracts of employment. The judges gave slightly varying reasons for their conclusions, but the better view seems to be that the deliberate non co-operation involved in the work-to-rule was at the basis of the decision: *Secretary of State for Employment* v. *ASLEF (No. 2)* [1972] ICR 19.

The employee's duty to obey all lawful and reasonable orders of the employer may also be viewed under this heading.

Pepper was employed as head gardener by Major Webb. Pepper worked satisfactorily for three months but then his work and his manners towards his employer deteriorated. One day the employer asked Pepper about the arrangements for the greenhouse in his absence over the weekend and Pepper replied: "I couldn't care less about your bloody greenhouse or your sodding garden," and walked off. He was dismissed summarily. *Held*, the dismissal was justified. The plaintiff's remark and conduct, taken against the background of his previous disobedience and insolence, clearly indicated an intention to repudiate the contract of employment: *Pepper* v. *Webb* [1969] 1 W.L.R. 514.

But compare *Wilson* v. *Racher* [1974] I.C.R. 428, where an isolated instance of obscene language by a gardener who was provoked by his employer was held not to justify summary dismissal.

2. *The employee owes the employer a duty of fidelity*

In particular, a skilled man must not work with a rival firm in his spare time on similar work if the competition would seriously damage the employer's business.

Hivac Ltd. v. *Park Royal Scientific Instruments Ltd.* [1946] Ch. 169, see p. 105, *ante.*

Further both before and after termination of the contract he must not make use of confidential information which came to his knowledge during his employment (see p. 105, *ante*).

3. *Duty of care*

Both parties are under a duty to take care in the performance of the contract. The employer must take reasonable care for the safety of his employees in the course of their employment and in particular must provide safe tools, a safe place of work, a safe system of working and select properly skilled fellow employees. This duty may be regarded as arising in tort or as an implied term of the contract of employment. The employer is not only liable for his own failure to use due care and diligence. The Employer's Liability (Defective Equipment) Act 1969, reversing the rule in *Davie* v. *New Merton Board Mills Ltd.* [1959] A.C. 604, provides that an employer shall be liable in negligence if an employee in the course of employment is injured in consequence of defective equipment being used for the purposes of the employer's business and the defect is attributable wholly or partly of a third party, such as the maker of the equipment, whether the third party is identified or not, but without prejudice to the law of contributory negligence and to any remedy by way of contribution or in contract or otherwise which is available to the employer in respect of the injury. An agreement between employer and employee to exclude or limit the employer's liability under the Act would be void.

The employee must exercise reasonable skill and care in the performance of his duties. From this the law has deduced an implied duty upon the employee to indemnify the employer in respect of the consequences of his negligent conduct.

> Lister was employed by a company as a lorry driver. He was accompanied by his father, a co-employee. When Lister backed his lorry into a yard, he knocked down his father who had previously alighted from the lorry and injured him. The company was held to be vicariously liable to the father in damages and by the present action claimed to recover damages from Lister for breach of the implied term of his contract of employment that he would use reasonable skill and care in driving. *Held*, the company was entitled to succeed: *Lister* v. *Romford Ice and Cold Storage Co. Ltd.* [1957] A.C. 555.

Terms implied by statute

Terms implied into the contract of employment by statute, unlike those implied at common law, operate so as to override anything agreed to the contrary between the parties themselves. Thus, under the Equal Pay Act 1970 the contract of employment is deemed to include an equality clause, which operates where a person of one sex is employed on like work (*i.e.* broadly similar work) with a person of the other sex or on work rated as equivalent under a job evaluation scheme. In such circumstances the equality clause will operate so as to equalise upwards the terms and conditions of employment of employees involved, irrespective of what has been specifically agreed between employer and employee unless the difference between the two sets of terms and conditions is explicable as "genuinely due to a material difference other than a difference of sex."

Statutory labour standards

Other statutory enactments, although not operating as implied terms, confer rights upon the employee irrespective of what his contract provides. A large number of such rights has been created by the Employment Protection Act 1975 and only the most important of these can be briefly noted here.

(i) A right to a guaranteed minimum payment from the employer where the employee is not entitled to contractual remuneration because he cannot be provided with work (ss. 22–29).

(ii) A right to remuneration from the employer where the employee is suspended on medical grounds under the health and safety legislation and is not entitled to contractual remuneration (ss. 19–33).

(iii) A right to maternity pay from the employer and to return to work within 29 weeks of the date of confinement (ss. 34–52).

(iv) A right to time off from work (with pay) to carry out trade union duties, and without pay to take part in trade union activities or public duties (ss. 57–60).

(v) A right to an itemised pay statement (ss. 81–84).

(vi) A right to a written statement upon request of the reason for dismissal (70).

Termination of the contract

1. *By notice*

At common law the contract of employment may be terminated by either party for any reason or for no reason upon giving notice of a reasonable length, unless the contract is one for a fixed term or unless it specifically restricts the reasons for which it may be terminated. Since the ordinary contract of employment is one of indefinite duration and without restrictions upon the reasons for termination, the common law puts the employee in particular in a weak legal position. However, by section 1 of the Contracts of Employment Act 1972 the minimum period of notice that must be given by an employer to terminate such a contract is one week if the employee has been continuously employed by the employer for at least four weeks. The

Contract of Employment

notice period rises to two weeks once the employee has two years' continuous employment and increases thereafter by one week for each additional year of continuous employment up to a maximum of 12 weeks' notice. The minimum period of notice required of the employee is one week after four weeks' continuous employment, but it does not thereafter increase. If the reasonable period of notice required of either employer or employee at common law is longer than the statutory minimum, then the common law period will be the operative one, as in *Hill* v. *C. A. Parsons Ltd.* [1972] 1 Ch. 305 where Lord Denning thought that a chartered engineer of 35 years' continuous employment was entitled at common law to at least six months' notice and perhaps even a year. Equally, the contract itself may, and often does, fix periods of notice for either employer or employee that are longer than the statutory minima.

2. *Summary termination*

Either party may lawfully terminate the contract summarily, *i.e.* without giving any notice, if the other party has committed a serious breach of the contract. Whether the breach is sufficiently serious to justify summary termination has to be answered in the context of each particular contract and few general guidelines can be discerned from the cases. The judges have tended to view any suggestion of dishonesty or disobedience on the employee's part particularly strictly. For a pair of contrasting decisions on disobedience, see *Pepper* v. *Webb* and *Wilson* v. *Racher* (see, p. 171, *ante*).

The manager of a betting shop openly, but without his employer's knowledge, took £15 out of the till, put in an I.O.U. for the money and used the money to place a bet of his own elsewhere. On the next day he repaid the £15. The manager knew the employer would not have given permission for him to borrow the money. When the employer discovered what had happened he dismissed the manager without notice and was held justified in so doing because the manager's conduct, even if not dishonest, was inconsistent with the continuance of the confidential relationship between them. *Sinclair* v. *Neighbour* [1967] 2 Q.B. 279.

3. *Remedies at common law*

The employer acts in breach of contract if he terminates it by giving shorter notice than the employee is entitled to or if he dismisses summarily in a situation in which he is not entitled to do so, as in *Wilson* v. *Racher*. Only in very rare circumstances will the common law require the employer to reinstate a wrongly dismissed employee because the contract of employment is regarded as one of a very personal nature. The damages remedy at common law is also very limited, as is notably illustrated by the rule that even in the case of wrongful summary dismissal damages in respect of loss of earnings are limited to earnings during the period of notice required to terminate the contract, on the assumption that the employer would have given the employee proper notice to terminate the contract if he had not dismissed him summarily. Further, the common law has developed no general requirement that the employee be given a hearing before dismissal or the reason for his dismissal, whether the termination is by notice or summarily. Finally, as we have seen, a dismissal on due notice is generally lawful. To mitigate these defects in the common law Parliament has created the quite separate statutory concept of *unfair* dismissal (as opposed to *wrongful* dismissal) with its own system of remedies.

4. *Unfair dismissal*

By virtue of Schedule I to the Trade Union and Labour Relations Act 1974, an employee who is dismissed, whether summarily or by notice, whether in breach of contract or not, may challenge the dismissal before an industrial tribunal on the grounds it was unfair. The definition of dismissal is further extended to include the expiration of a fixed-term contract without its being renewed and termination of the contract by the employee where this is in response to a serious breach of contract by the employer.

In general, the dismissal, as defined, will be held to be fair only if the employer, upon whom the burden lies, shows, first, that the reason for the dismissal is capable of being considered a fair one. For this purpose he must show that the reason related to the employee's capability, qualifications or conduct, or was that the employee was redundant or was that the employee could not continue to be employed without a breach "of a duty or restriction imposed by or under an enactment," or was "some other substantial reason of a kind such as to justify the dismissal of an employee holding the position which that employee held." Secondly, the employer must show that in the circumstances of the case it was reasonable of him to treat the reason as a sufficient reason for dismissal. Thus, smoking in a forbidden area would be a reason capable of being considered a fair one (as relating to the employee's conduct), but might not in the circumstances justify dismissal if, for example, the employer had in practice condoned smoking in this area on previous occasions. A dismissal might also be treated as unfair on procedural grounds, *e.g.* dismissing an employer without giving him a chance to explain his conduct, or on grounds of bad personnel management, *e.g.* dismissing an employee for bad workmanship without giving him a prior warning and a chance to improve his standard of work.

Certain reasons for dismissal are declared by the statute automatically to be unfair. In this category fall dismissal for joining an independent trade union or taking part in its activities at any appropriate time or for refusing to join a non-independent trade union. Dismissal for not joining an independent trade union is automatically unfair only if there is a closed shop (union membership agreement) in force and the employee objects on grounds of religious belief to being a member of any trade union whatsoever. Indeed, in the absence of such religious objection, dismissal for not joining an independent trade union in a closed shop situation is automatically deemed to be a fair reason for dismissal. In the above cases the automatically unfair reason for dismissal is labelled by the statute "an inadmissible reason." By section 34 of the Employment Protection Act 1975 dismissal on grounds of pregnancy is automatically unfair, unless the employee is thereby incapable of doing her work or her continued employment would be in breach of an enactment. Such an unfair reason is not, however, also an inadmissible one.

By section 53 of the Employment Protection Act 1975 an employee has a right not to have unfair disciplinary action short of dismissal taken against him for, in effect, an inadmissible reason. There is no more general right to be treated fairly in the matter of discipline short of dismissal.

Certain reasons for dismissal are automatically fair. Besides dismissal in a closed shop situation, such automatically fair reasons include dismissal of employees on strike or locked out by their employer, unless not all the strikers or those locked out are dismissed by the employer. The policy is not to use the law to restrict the economic sanctions each side may apply to the other in the course of an industrial dispute, unless there is prima facie evidence of victimisation. Dismissal on grounds of national security is also, in effect, treated as automatically fair.

The remedies for an employee found to have been unfairly dismissed are now contained in the Employment Protection Act 1975, ss. 71–80. If the employee so wishes and if the tribunal so decides, the tribunal may order that the employer reinstate or re-engage the employee. However, an employer who does not obey the order is not in contempt of court. He can refuse to take the employee back but will be liable to pay him by way of penalty an "additional award" of between three months' and six months' pay in the ordinary case or of between six months' and one year's pay in the case of a dismissal for an inadmissible reason or a dismissal contrary to the Sex Discrimination or Race Relations Acts. The employer is not liable to pay the penalty if he can show that it was not practicable to comply with the tribunal's order.

Where the tribunal does not order reinstatement or re-engagement or that order is not obeyed, it must make an award of compensation to the employee. This consists of two parts. First, a "basic award," essentially equivalent to a redundancy payment (see p. 178, *post*) to reflect the employee's loss of accrued redundancy rights. This award is not payable to the extent that as a result of the dismissal the employee does in fact receive a redundancy payment. Secondly, a "compensatory award" designed to compensate the employee for the loss he has suffered as a result of the dismissal. Loss of earnings is not confined to the notice period, as at common law, although there is a ceiling of £80 on the weekly earnings that will be taken into account and an overall limit of £5,200 on the compensatory award. Other pecuniary losses can be taken into account in this award, *e.g.* loss of pension rights or of benefits in kind. The amount of the compensation will obviously depend heavily upon how soon the employee is likely to obtain another comparable job.

The total award may be reduced if the employee has failed to mitigate his loss or if the employee has contributed to his own dismissal. There is a form of interim relief available before the full hearing at the tribunal in the case of an employee who claims to have been dismissed for joining or taking part in the activities of an independent trade union.

Redundancy

The Redundancy Payments Act 1965 has provided for payment of lump sums by way of compensation to those dismissed on grounds of redundancy who have at least two years' continuous employment with the employer who dismisses them. Dismissal is defined as for unfair dismissal. Redundancy arises where the employer dismisses because (i) he has ceased or intends to cease to carry on the business for the purposes of which the employee was employed, or (ii) he has ceased or intends to cease to carry on that business in the place where the employee was employed, or (iii) the requirements of the business for employees to carry out work of a particular kind in the place where the employee was employed have ceased or diminished or are expected to do so. The Act also covers in certain circumstances those who are laid-off or put on short time and who as a consequence decide to terminate their employment.

Compensation for redundancy is essentially backward looking. Consequently, unlike unfair dismissal, the amount of the payment in respect of redundancy is not in general reduced if the employee immediately obtains another job. However, if the dismissing employer makes the employee an offer to re-employ him within a certain time-limit either on the same terms and conditions as previously or on suitable alternative terms and conditions and, in either case, the employee unreasonably refuses the offer, then he will not be entitled to a redundancy payment. Where there is a change in the ownership of the business, a concept that has proved very difficult to operate in practice, the new owner of the business is placed in the shoes of the former owner for the purposes of the offers described above. If the employee actually accepts an offer of employment made by the employer within the relevant time limits, he is treated as not having been dismissed by the employer, whether the offer was of suitable alternative employment or not.

Standing by themselves, these provisions put in a very difficult position an employee who receives an offer of doubtfully suitable, alternative employment. If he accepts the offer, he cannot claim a redundancy payment because he has not been dismissed even though the tribunal might have held the employment to be unsuitable; if he rejects the offer, he may lose his payment if the tribunal holds the offer to be one of suitable alternative employment. An amendment introduced by the Employment Protection Act gives the employee the benefit of a trial period before he has to decide finally whether to accept the offer.

The amount of the redundancy payment, where such is due, is obtained by multiplying the number of completed years of continuous employment the employee has with the employer (subject to a maximum of 20) by the amount of a week's pay (subject to a maximum of £80) or a week and a half's pay in the cases of years of employment over the age of 40. The period of continuous employment is calculated for redundancy purposes basically according to the complex provisions of Schedule 1 to the Contracts of Employment Act 1972, which indeed is generally used to determine the length of continuous employment where this is necessary under the other statutes discussed in this chapter. The provisions of this Schedule cannot be discussed here in detail, but we may briefly note that it allows certain breaks in employment (*e.g.* on grounds of sickness) to be ignored and occasionally service with a previous employer to be aggregated with that with the dismissing employer (*e.g.* on a transfer of the business).

The amount of a week's pay is calculated in accordance with Schedule 4 to the Employment Protection Act 1975, which again is generally used for this purpose in the statutes discussed in this chapter. The schedule is designed to reflect the employee's pay at the date of dismissal, but differing provisions have to be made for those with normal working hours and those without, those whose pay varies with the amount of work done and those whose pay does not, and so on.

The employer may recover a rebate of half the payment from the Redundancy Fund, which is financed by a payroll levy on all employers.

The Redundancy Payments Act 1965 is concerned solely with compensating those who have in fact been made redundant. Part IV of the Employment Protection Act goes further by requiring an employer who is contemplating redundancies to consult in advance with the unions recognized by him as representing the employees affected on the reasons for the proposed redundancies and the methods of selecting the employees to be dismissed. In addition, section 61 of the Act gives the individual employee the right to reasonable time off from work after having been given notice of dismissal on grounds of redundancy but before the dismissal takes place in order to look for new employment or make arrangements for training for future employment.

Insolvency

A frequent cause of dismissal is the insolvency of the employer. Here the employee runs a special risk that the employer will not be able to pay to him or on his behalf the various sums due. Sections 61 to 69 of the Employment Protection Act 1975 strengthen the employee's position, notably by empowering the Secretary of State to pay some of the sums due out of the Redundancy Fund, the Fund then taking the risk that these sums will not be recoverable from the former employer.

Discrimination

Under the Sex Discrimination Act 1975 and the Race Relations Act 1976 it is unlawful (i) to treat a person less favourably than another on sexual or racial grounds, and (ii) to apply a condition or requirement uniformly to all persons if the requirement puts one sex or a racial group at a disadvantage, and if the requirement cannot be justified on non-sexual or non-racial grounds. An example of (ii) with regard to women would be a requirement that all applicants for a job as a bank cashier be six feet tall. Unlawful discrimination may be committed at the point of hiring, during the course of the employment, or at its termination. Individual complaints in the employment field are heard by industrial tribunals, which may award compensation and recommend action the respondent should take within a specified period to obviate the adverse impact upon the complainant of the discriminatory act. With regard to dismissal the remedies under these Acts overlap in a complicated way with the unfair dismissal remedies. The Equal Opportunities Commission and the Commission for Racial Equality have powers to play a broader enforcement role in the employment field.

SELECT BIBLIOGRAPHY

Books

S. D. Anderman, *Unfair Dismissal and the Law* (1973).

C. D. Drake, *Labour Law* (2nd ed., 1973).

M. R. Freedland, *The Contract of Employment* (1976).

C. Grunfeld, *The Law of Redundancy* (1971).

B. A. Hepple and Paul O'Higgins, *Employment Law* (2nd ed., 1976)

K. W. Wedderburn, *The Worker and the Law* (2nd ed., 1971).

K. Whitesides and G. Hawker, *Industrial Tribunals* (1975).

J. C. Wood, *Cooper's Outline of Industrial Law* (6th ed., 1972).

Articles

Davies, P. L., "Employee Representation on Corporate Boards and Participation in Corporate Planning" (1975) 38 M.L.R. 254–273.

Donaldson, J., "Judge's Eye View of Industrial Relations and the Law" (1975) 6 Cambrian L. Rev. 10–19.

Reynolds, B., "Compensation for Unfair Dismissal" (1973) 36 M.L.R. 424–430.

Simitis, S., "Workers Participation in the Enterprise: Transcending Company Law?" (1975) 38 M.L.R. 1–22.

Schmitthoff, C. M., "Employee Participation and the Theory of Enterprise" [1975] J.B.L. 265–272.

Williams, K., "Job Security and Unfair Dismissal" (1975) 38 M.L.R. 292–310.

CHAPTER 13

AGENCY

AN agent is a person who is employed for the purpose of bringing his principal into contractual relations with third parties. The agent does not make contracts on his own behalf, and consequently it is not necessary that he should have full contractual capacity. A minor or a bankrupt may be an agent. The principal, however, must have full contractual capacity: if he does not have it, he cannot make a contract by employing an agent who does.

CREATION OF AGENCY

Agency may be created by—
1. express agreement;
2. implication or conduct; or
3. necessity.

Express agreement

An agent may be expressly appointed either verbally or in writing. The appointment may be made verbally even though the contract which the agent is authorised to make has to be in writing. No particular form is required unless the agent is to make a contract under seal, in which case he must be given authority under seal, called a power of attorney. Powers of attorney are governed by the Powers of Attorney Act 1971.

Implication or conduct

If one person by words or conduct holds out another as having authority to make contracts on his behalf, he will be bound by such contracts as if he had expressly authorised them. For instance, if he habitually pays for goods ordered by another, the implication will be that that other is his agent; or, as it is sometimes expressed, he is estopped by his conduct from denying the fact of agency (*Summers* v. *Solomon* (1857) 7 E. & B. 879).

An estate agent was instructed by the owners to find a purchaser for a private hotel. He did so and accepted from the prospective purchaser a small deposit "as agent" of the owners. *Held*, although the estate agent was not expressly given authority to accept deposits, he had acted within the ostensible scope of his authority (*Ryan* v. *Pilkington* [1959] 1 W.L.R. 403).

When a husband and wife are living together, the wife is presumed to have her husband's authority to pledge his credit for necessaries, judged according to their style and standard of living. The presumption can, however, be rebutted by the husband proving that—

1. he expressly forbade his wife to pledge his credit; or
2. he expressly warned the supplier not to supply his wife with goods on credit; or
3. his wife was already sufficiently supplied with goods of the kind in question; or
4. his wife was supplied with a sufficient allowance or sufficient means for the purpose of buying such goods without pledging the husband's credit; or
5. the order, though for necessaries, was excessive in extent or, having regard to the husband's income, extravagant.

A wife was supplied with clothes to the value of £215 and the husband refused to pay for them. On his being sued by the tradesman, the husband proved that he paid his wife £960 a year as an allowance. *Held*, the husband was not liable (*Miss Gray Ltd.* v. *Cathcart* (1922) 38 T.L.R. 562).

If the husband has been in the habit of paying his wife's bills with a particular supplier, his wife's agency will be implied by his conduct, and he can only escape liability by expressly informing the supplier that his wife's authority is revoked. If the supplier gave credit to the wife personally and not to the wife as her husband's agent, the husband is not liable. In this connection, it is to be noted that the former rule that if a wife saved money from a housekeeping allowance made by the husband, such money belonged to the husband, has been changed by the Married Women's Property Act 1964 with the result that, in the absence of any agreement to the contrary, such money is to be treated as belonging to the husband and wife in equal shares.

Partners are each other's agents for making contracts in the ordinary course of the partnership business.

Necessity

Agency of necessity occurs when a person is entrusted with another's property and it becomes necessary to do something to preserve that property. In such a case, although the person who is entrusted with the property has no express authority to do the act necessary to preserve it, because of the necessity such an authority is implied. For example, if a horse is sent by train and on its arrival there is no one to receive it, the railway company, being bound to take reasonable steps to keep the horse alive, is the agent of necessity of the owner for the purpose of sending it to a livery stable for the night (*G. N. Ry.* v. *Swaffield* (1874) L.R. 9 Ex. 132).

The master of a ship in case of necessity can pledge the ship as security for the cost of repairs necessary to enable her to continue the voyage, provided that (1) there was a reasonable necessity according to the ordinary course of prudent conduct to pledge the ship; (2) the amount was advanced expressly for the use of the ship; and (3) the money was expended on the ship (*Arthur* v. *Barton* (1840) 6 M. & W. 138). If there is an agent of the shipowner on the spot, the master has no such authority (*Gunn* v. *Roberts* (1874) L.R. 9 C.P. 331).

But before any agency can be created by necessity, three conditions must be satisfied—

1. It must be impossible to get the principal's instructions.

Tomatoes were consigned by S from Jersey to London. The ship delivered them at Weymouth three days late and, owing to a railway strike, the tomatoes could not be unloaded until two days later. When unloaded they were found to be bad and the railway company decided to sell them locally. No communication was made to S. *Held*, the railway company were liable in damages to S, as they should have communicated with him and asked for his instructions as soon as the ship arrived: *Springer* v. *G.W. Ry.* [1921] 1 K.B. 257.

2. There must be an actual and definite commercial necessity for the creation of the agency.

In 1915 and 1916 S, as agents for P, bought skins to the value of £1,900 to be dispatched to P, a fur merchant in Bucharest. P paid for the skins. Owing to the occupation of Rumania by the German forces it was impossible to send the skins to P or to communicate with him. In 1917 and 1918 S sold the skins, which had increased in value. *Held*, as the skins were not likely to deteriorate in value if properly stored, there was no necessity for the sale, and S was liable in damages to P: *Prager* v. *Blatspiel Stamp & Heacock Ltd.* [1924] 1 K.B. 566.

Generally, there is no agency of necessity unless there is a real emergency, such as may arise out of the possession of perishable goods or of livestock requiring to be fed (*Sachs* v. *Miklos* [1948] 2 K.B. 23).

3. The agent of necessity must act bona fide in the interests of all parties concerned.

It is not possible to define all the situations in which an agency of necessity arises, but such an agency will be implied more easily when there is an existing agency which requires extending to provide for unforeseen events not dealt with in the original contract, than when there is no such agency (*per* Scrutton L.J. in *Jebara* v. *Ottoman Bank* [1927] 2 K.B. 254).

The law admitted also a wife's agency of necessity: when she was deserted or justified in leaving her husband and had inadequate means of support she could pledge her husband's credit for necessaries but these rules were subject to important exceptions. The Matrimonial Proceedings and Property Act 1970, s. 41 (1), provides that the rules conferring on a wife authority, as agent of necessity of her husband, to pledge his credit or to borrow money on his credit are abrogated, but, on granting a decree of divorce, nullity or judicial separation, or thereafter, the court may order a party to the marriage to pay a a lump sum to the other party for the purpose of enabling that other party to meet any liabilities or expenses reasonably incurred in maintaining himself or herself or any child of the family (s. 2 (2) (*a*) of the Act of 1970).

RATIFICATION

If an agent has no authority to contract on behalf of a principal or exceeds such authority as he has, the contract is not binding on the principal. The principal may, however, afterwards confirm and adopt the contract so made; this is known as ratification.

The effect of ratification is to render the contract as binding on the principal as if the agent had been properly authorised beforehand. Ratification relates back to the original making of the contract.

A contract can only be ratified under the following conditions—

1. The agent must expressly have contracted as agent. If, having no authority in fact, he merely intended to contract as agent and did not disclose his intention to the other party, *i.e.* if without authority he purports to act for an undisclosed principal (see p. 196, *post*), no ratification is possible.

R, authorised by K to buy wheat at a certain price, exceeded his authority and bought at a higher price from D. R bought in his own name, but intended to buy for K. K agreed with R to take the wheat at the price, but failed to take delivery. *Held*, K was not liable to D, as he could not ratify R's contract: *Keighley, Maxsted & Co.* v. *Durant* [1901] A.C. 240.

2. The contract can only be ratified by the principal who was named or ascertainable when the contract was made. If the principal was named, he can ratify the contract even if the agent never intended that he should so so, but wanted to keep the benefit of the contract for himself (*Re Tiedemann* [1899] 2 Q.B. 66).

3. The agent must have a principal who was in actual existence at the time of the contract.

K, a wine-merchant, agreed to sell wine to B, who was acting as agent for a hotel company which was about to be formed. *Held*, B was personally liable on the contract and no subsequent ratification by the company could relieve him from liability unless K agreed to release him: *Kelner* v. *Baxter* (1866) L.R. 2 C.P. 175.

But a person who signed a contract as a director of a company before the grant of the certificate of incorporation cannot sue the other party to the contract in his own name: *Newborne* v. *Sensolid* (*Great Britain*) *Ltd.* [1954] 1 Q.B. 45.

The preceding two cases concern so-called **pre-incorporation contracts**, *i.e.* contracts purported to be made on behalf of a company before it has come into existence as a legal person. The European Communities Act 1972, s. 9 (2) provides that such a contract shall, subject to any agreement to the contrary . . . have effect as a contract entered into by the person purporting to act for the company or as agent for it, and he shall be personally liable on the contract accordingly. *Palmer's Company Law* (22nd ed., 1976), Vol. I, para. 27–03 expresses the view that this provision of the European Communities Act 1972 has not affected the rule in *Kelner* v. *Baxter*, *supra*, but has overruled the decision in *Newborne* v. *Sensolid* (*Great Britain*) *Ltd.*, *supra*, because, in the words of section 9 (2), the contract shall have effect as a contract entered into by the person purporting to act for the company or as agent for it, and the additional words "and he shall be personally liable on the contract accordingly" are disjunctive; however, until the courts have given their ruling the question has to be regarded as an open one.

4. The principal must have had contractual capacity at the date of the contract and have it at the date of ratification. If the principal was, for example, an enemy at the date of the contract there can be

no valid ratification (*Boston Deep Sea Fishing and Ice Co. Ltd.* v. *Farnham* [1957] 1 W.L.R. 1051).

5. The principal must, at the time of ratification, have full knowledge of the material facts or intend to ratify the contract whatever the facts may be (*Marsh* v. *Joseph* [1897] 1 Ch. 213).

Ratification may be either expressed or implied by the conduct of the principal.

AUTHORITY OF THE AGENT

Actual and ostensible authority

An agent may have actual or ostensible authority. Actual authority is the authority given him by the principal expressly or by implication or conduct, or conferred on him by law, as in the case of agency by necessity. "Ostensible or apparent authority in the authority of an agent as it *appears* to others. It often coincides with actual authority . . . . But sometimes ostensible authority exceeds actual authority. For instance, when the board appoint the managing director, they may expressly limit his authority by saying he is not to order goods worth more than £500 without the sanction of the board. In that case his actual authority is subject to the £500 limitation, but his ostensible authority includes all the usual authority of a managing director. The company is bound by his ostensible authority in his dealings with those who do not know of the limitation" (*per* Lord Denning M.R. in *Hely-Hutchinson* v. *Brayhead Ltd.* [1968] 1 Q.B. 549).

Mr. Blaine was the secretary of the defendants Fidelis Furnishing Fabrics Ltd. In his capacity as secretary Mr. Blaine purported to hire expensive self-drive cars from the plaintiffs, Panorama Developments (Guildford) Ltd. Mr. Blaine had no actual authority from the defendants to hire these cars and used them for his own purposes. *Held*, as company secretary Mr. Blaine had ostensible authority to act for the company in administrative matters, such as car hire, and the defendants were liable for the outstanding charges: *Panorama Developments (Guildford) Ltd.* v. *Furnishing Fabrics Ltd.* [1971] 2. Q.B. 711.

General and special agents

The extent of an agent's authority may be either expressed in the terms of his appointment or implied by the circumstances of the case. When an agent is employed to conduct a particular trade or business he has implied authority to do whatever is incidental to such trade or business: he is termed a general agent. A special agent is one who is employed to make only a particular contract. The managing director of a company is the general agent of the company, but if a man sends a friend to bid for him at an auction the friend is the special agent of the sender.

We have already seen that in the case of a general agent his acts are binding on the principal if they are within the scope of his ostensible authority, although they may be outside the scope of his actual authority. A private limitation of the ostensible authority will not be binding unless it is known by the other party to the contract.

H, the owner of a public-house, sold it to F, who retained H as its manager. W, who knew nothing of F, sold cigars to H, for the use of the public-house. He had been expressly forbidden by F to purchase cigars on credit. Being unable to obtain payment from H, W sued F. *Held*, (1) as the cigars were such as would usually be dealt in at such a public-house, H was acting within the scope of his implied authority as manager in ordering them; (2) F could not, as against W, set up any secret limitation of that authority: *Watteau* v. *Fenwick* [1893] 1 Q.B. 346.

An authority given to an agent to sell goods does not of necessity imply authority to receive payment of the price (*Butwick* v. *Grant* [1942] 2 K.B. 483).

The effect of fraud

If an agent, acting within the scope of his authority, has notice of a fraud committed by a third party with whom he negotiates and eventually contracts, the principal, even if acting in good faith, is treated as having notice of the fraud.

C was a trustee and life tenant of an old master painting. In January 1951 he sold the painting to B in breach of trust and retained the purchase price. B, who was an agent for a consortium of art dealers, had notice that C was only a trustee and that he sold the painting in fraud. The art dealers resold and delivered the painting to a purchaser in U.S.A. After C's death in 1963 the other trustees discovered the fraud and sued the art dealers for conversion. They relied on the Limitation Act 1939 since more than six years had passed since the sale of the painting but the trustees replied that the period of limitation had not begun to run as the action was based on fraud (s. 26 of the 1939 Act). *Held*, the art dealers were affected with B's knowledge of C's fraud and could not rely on the defence of limitation: *Eddis* v. *Chichester Constable* [1969] 2 Ch. 345.

Types of Agent

Estate agents

Estate agents may receive a deposit from the intending purchaser either as agents of the vendor or in an independent capacity, *e.g.* as stakeholders. The liability of the vendor to return the deposit if the agent is unable to do so arises only if the vendor has authorised the agent to receive a deposit on his behalf. If the vendor has given the agent no actual authority, there would be no liability because the estate agent does not have ostensible authority to receive a deposit as agent of the vendor.

Where an estate agent authorised to act for the vendor of land receives a deposit from an intending purchaser, he does so as an agent of the vendor, unless there is a clear agreement that he should receive it only as stakeholder for both parties. If, before the conclusion of a contract, an agent becomes insolvent or misappropriates a deposit received by him as agent of the vendor, the vendor is liable for the return of the deposit: *Goding* v. *Frazer* [1966] 3 All E.R. 234.

If, on the other hand, the deposit was received by the agent not as agent of the vendor—*e.g.* as "stakeholder"—the vendor is not liable for the return of the deposit: *Sorrell* v. *Finch* [1976] 2 W.L.R. 833.

If an estate agent, pending the conclusion of a contract, receives a deposit as "stakeholder," he is under an obligation to repay the money on request unless and until a contract is concluded. On the other hand, as he receives such deposit not as trustee but in a contractual or quasi-contractual capacity, he does not have to account for any interest earned on the deposit: *Potters* v. *Loppert* [1973] Ch. 399.

Auctioneers

An auctioneer is an agent to sell goods at a public auction.

On a sale by auction there are three contracts—

1. Between the owner of the goods (the vendor) and the highest bidder to whom the goods are knocked down (the purchaser). This is a simple contract of sale to which the auctioneer is not a party.

2. Between the owner of the goods (the vendor) and the auctioneer. The vendor entrusts the auctioneer with the possession of the goods for sale by auction. The understanding is that the auctioneer should not part with the possession of them to the purchaser except against payment of the price: or, if the auctioneer should part with them without receiving payment, he is responsible to the vendor for the price. The auctioneer has, as against the vendor, a lien on the proceeds for his commission and charges.

3. Between the auctioneer and the highest bidder (the purchaser). The auctioneer has possession of the goods and has a lien on them for the whole price. He is not bound to deliver the goods to the purchaser except on receiving the price in cash; or, if he is willing to accept a cheque, on receiving a cheque payable to himself, the auctioneer for the price. If he does allow the purchaser to take delivery without paying the price the auctioneer can, as he has a special property in the goods, sue in his own name for the full price. If the highest bidder refuses to take delivery of the goods the auctioneer can sue him for the price.

An auctioneer's implied authority is to sell without a reserve price, and therefore a sale by him below the reserve will be binding on his principal even if the principal had instructed him not to sell below a definite price. On the other hand if the auctioneer states that the sale is subject to a reserve, but by mistake knocks the article down at a price below the reserve, the sale is not binding on the owner. In the latter case the buyer is informed that there is a limitation on the auctioneer's authority, and therefore bids can only be accepted subject to the reserve being reached (*McManus* v. *Fortescue* [1907] 2 K.B. 1). The buyer will be entitled to sue the auctioneer for damages for breach of warranty of authority (p. 193, *post*) (*Fay* v. *Miller Wilkins & Co.* [1941] Ch. 360).

An auctioneer, on a sale of specific goods, does not warrant his principal's title to the goods (*Benton* v. *Campbell, Parker & Co. Ltd.* [1925] 2 K.B. 410).

Factors

A factor is a mercantile agent who, in the customary course of his business as such agent, has authority either to sell goods, or to consign goods for the purpose of sale, or to buy goods, or to raise money on the security of goods (Factors Act 1889, s. 1 (1)). He has a general lien on goods in his possession and on the proceeds of sale of such goods for the balance of account between himself and his principal.

The owner is bound by the acts of the mercantile agent as follows—

1. If the agent has possession of goods, or of the documents of title to goods, with the consent of the owner, any sale, pledge, or other disposition of them, made in the ordinary course of business is binding on the owner, whether or not the owner authorised it (s. 2 (1)).

F owned a motor car and delivered it to H, a mercantile agent, for sale at not less than £575. H sold the car for £340 to K, who bought in good faith and without notice of any fraud. H misappropriated the £340 and F sued to recover the car from K. *Held*, as H was in possession of the car with F's consent for the purposes of sale, K got a good title: *Folkes* v. *King* [1923] 1 K.B. 282.

S pledged bills of lading with L to secure advances. At the request of S, L handed the bills to S in exchange for trust receipts, by which S agreed to sell the goods, represented by the bills, as trustees for L. S wrongly pledged the bills with B, who acted in good faith, as security for a loan. *Held*, B had a good title under section 2: *Lloyds Bank* v. *Bank of America Association* [1938] 2 K.B. 147.

If the purchaser from a mercantile agent wishes to claim a good title against the owner it is for him to prove that—

(a) the agent, as such, was in possession of the goods with the consent of the owner. If a person is in possession of goods only under a hire-purchase agreement, the goods are not in the possession of a mercantile agent "as such" (*Belvoir Finance Co. Ltd.* v. *Harold G. Cole & Co. Ltd.* [1969] 1 W.L.R. 1877, 1881);

(b) in selling them the agent was acting in the ordinary course of business of a mercantile agent; and

(c) he had not, at the time of the sale, notice that the agent had no authority to make the sale (*Stadium Finance Ltd.* v. *Robbins* [1962] 2 Q.B. 664).

A mercantile agent does not sell a car in the ordinary course of business unless he sells the registration book with it; but the purported sale of a car with its registration book does not confer a good title on the purchaser if the agent (though having the car with the consent of the owner) obtained the registration book only by larceny or by a trick (*Pearson* v. *Rose and Young Ltd.* [1951] 1 K.B. 275).

It should, however, be remembered that although the Factors Act codified and amplified the common law so far as it applied to mercantile agents, it does not derogate from it (s. 13). Consequently, in cases where the true principal not only puts an agent in possession of the goods and other signs of title, but also expressly authorises him to sell as principal, the question as to whether the factor sold in the ordinary course of business is relevant only in so far as it throws light upon the bona fides of the buyer (*Lloyds & Scottish Finance Ltd.* v. *Williamson* [1965] 1 W.L.R. 404).

2. If the mercantile agent pledges goods as security for an antecedent debt, the pledgee acquires no further right to the goods than the factor has against his principal at the time of the pledge (s. 4).

3. If the mercantile agent pledges goods in consideration of the delivery of other goods, or of a document of title to goods, or of a negotiable security, the pledgee acquires no right in the goods pledged beyond the value of the goods, documents or security when so delivered in exchange (s. 5).

4. If the mercantile agent has received possession of goods from their owner for the purpose of consignment or sale, and the consignee has no notice that he is not the owner, the consignee has a lien on the goods for any advances he has made to the agent (s. 7).

Confirming houses

In the export trade, when a supplier receives an order from a customer abroad, he sometimes asks for confirmation of that order by a person in the supplier's country. The confirmer "adds confirmation or assurance to the bargain which has been made by the primary contractor" and is personally liable to the supplier if the buyer abroad fails to perform the contract.

Turkish buyers placed a considerable order for radio sets with S, and C confirmed the order. After receipt of part of the consignment the buyers refused to take delivery of the balance. *Held*, C was liable for damages for non-acceptance: *Sobell Industries Ltd.* v. *Cory Bros. & Co. Ltd.* [1955] 2 Lloyd's Rep. 82.

A confirmer has a particular, but not a general, lien on the goods or documents of title of his overseas principal (*Tellrite Ltd.* v. *London Confirmers Ltd.* [1962] 1 Lloyd's Rep. 236).

If the confirmer fails to pay, the seller has still his claim for the purchase price against the buyer.

Brokers

A broker is an agent who is employed to buy or sell on behalf of another. He differs from a factor by not having possession of goods, and consequently he has no lien and he cannot sue in his own name on the contract. Brokers who are members of a stock exchange or a commercial exchange or other similar institution have an implied authority to make their contracts subject to the rules of such institution, but beyond that they have no implied or presumed authority of any kind. Brokers are not liable to their principal for the failure of a buyer to pay the price.

Del credere agents

A *del credere* agent is an agent employed to sell goods who undertakes that purchasers he procures will pay for any goods they take. He only undertakes that they will pay, and does not make himself liable to his principal if his buyer refuses to take delivery (*Gabriel & Sons* v. *Churchill and Sim* [1914] 3 K.B. 1272).

BREACH OF IMPLIED WARRANTY OF AUTHORITY

A person who professes to act as agent, but has no authority from the alleged principal or has exceeded his authority, is liable in an action for breach of warranty of authority at the suit of the party with whom he professed to make the contract (*Collen* v. *Wright* (1857) 8 E. & B. 647). The action is based, not on the original contract, but on the implied representation by the agent that he had authority to make the original contract. Points to note—

1. The action can only be brought by the third party, not by the principal.

2. The agent is liable whether he has acted fraudulently or innocently, and even if his authority has been terminated, without his knowledge, by death or mental disorder of the principal.

Solicitors were instructed by T to defend threatened proceedings on his behalf. Before the proceedings started, T, without the solicitors' knowledge, became insane. This revoked their authority (p. 206, *post*). The solicitors delivered a defence and then learnt that T was insane. The plaintiffs asked for the defence to be struck out and for the solicitors to pay the costs. *Held*, the solicitors, by acting for T, had impliedly warranted that they had authority to do so, and therefore they were liable for the costs: *Yonge* v. *Toynbee* [1910] 1 K.B. 215.

3. The agent is not liable if his lack of authority was known to the third party, or if it was known that he did not warrant his authority or if the contract excludes his liability.

S signed a charterparty "by telegraphic authority as agents." Owing to a mistake in the telegram the rate of freight offered was wrong, and S was sued for breach of warranty of authority. *Held*, on its being proved that by mercantile usage the form of signature negatived liability S was not liable: *Lilly* v. *Smales* [1892] 1 Q.B. 456.

4. If the principal gives ambiguous instructions and the agent

acts on them bona fide and in a reasonable way, he will not be liable
to an action for breach of warranty of authority even if he has
interpreted them wrongly.

X sent a telegram to Y as follows: "You authorise fix steamer prompt
loading 3,000 tons coal Newport Cagliari Messina or Palermo 20 shil-
lings." In pursuance of this, Y let a ship on charter to Z. X repudiated
this on the ground that this authority to Y was to hire a ship, not to let
one. *Held*, if the telegram were ambiguous, (1) Y had acted bona fide and
reasonably in interpreting it as he had done; (2) X would be responsible to
Z for the interpretation which his agents had bona fide and reasonably
placed upon ambiguous instructions; but (3) the actual charterparty
entered into was outside the authority in whatever way the telegram was
read, and Y was liable to Z for breach of warranty of authority: *Weigall &
Co.* v. *Runciman & Co.* (1916) 85 L.J.K.B. 1187.

5. The agent warrants his authority not only when he purports
to contract on behalf of another, but also when, purporting to act
as an agent, he induces a third party to enter into any transaction
with him on the faith of such agency.

One of two trustees of stock standing in the joint names in the books
of the Bank of England sold it under a power of attorney, to which the
signature of the co-trustee was forged. S, a stockbroker, bona fide acting
upon this power of attorney, induced the bank to transfer the stock to the
buyer. *Held*, S had impliedly warranted his authority to the bank, and
was therefore liable to indemnify the bank against the co-trustee's claim
for restitution: *Starkey* v. *Bank of England* [1903] A.C. 114.

6. The measure of damages for breach of warranty of authority
is the actual loss sustained. For example, if directors of a company
issue debentures which they had no power to issue, the measure of
damages is the value of genuine debentures. If the company was
insolvent so that the debentures would be worthless, the measure
of damages will be nil, but if the debentures would have been worth
their face value, the measure of damages will be that value.

EFFECT OF CONTRACTS MADE BY AGENTS

The effect of a contract made by an agent varies according to the
circumstances under which the agent contracted.

Where the agent contracts as agent for a named principal

In this case the agent incurs neither rights nor liabilities under
the contract (*Gadd* v. *Houghton* (1876) 1 Ex. D. 357). Exceptions to
this rule—

1. Where the agent executes a deed in his own name he is liable on the deed (*Plant Engineers Ltd.* v. *Davies* (1969) 113 S.J. 484).

2. Where the agent signs a bill of exchange in his own name he is liable on the bill.

3. Where the agent is in fact the principal but contracts as agent he is liable on and can enforce the contract.

4. Where the custom of a trade makes the agent liable.

It was once thought that an agent contracting on behalf of a foreign principal was personally liable, but it is now settled that there is no presumption of liability on the part of the agent. (*Teheran-Europe Co. Ltd.* v. *S. T. Belton Ltd.* [1968] 2 Q.B. 545, below.)

Where the agent contracts as agent for an unnamed principal

In this case the agent discloses the existence, but not the name, of his principal. As the agent expressly contracts as agent he cannot be personally liable on the contract.

A charterparty was made between X as agent of a shipowner and "J. M. & Co., charterers," and was signed "for and on behalf of J. M. & Co. (as agents), J. A. M." It provided for payment by the "charterers" of demurrage in the event of the ship being detained beyond the stipulated time. X knew when the charterparty was signed that J. M. & Co. were acting as agents for another, but they did not know who the principals were. In an action by the shipowner against J. M. & Co. for demurrage, *held*, having signed as agents, J. M. & Co. were not liable as principals to pay demurrage, although they were described as charterers in the charterparty: *Universal Steam Navigation Co. Ltd.* v. *James McElvie & Co.* [1923] A.C. 492.

Teheran-Europe was a company incorporated in Iran. Their buying agents in England were Richards Marketing. Richards Marketing negotiated with the defendants Belton for the supply of 12 air compressors, new and unused, "for their clients." Eventually they bought the goods and indicated that they were for shipment to Iran but did not disclose the name of their principals. Teheran-Europe complained that the goods were not in conformity with the contract and claimed damages from the defendants. *Held*, (1) the plaintiffs were unnamed principals and, as such, could sue the defendants directly; there was no rule in modern English commercial law that that principle did not apply if the principal was a foreigner residing abroad; (2) the defendants had not broken the implied condition of section 14 (1) of the Sale of Goods Act 1893 because, when deciding whether the goods were suitable for the Iranian market, the plaintiffs relied on their own skill and judgment and not on that of the defendants as sellers: *Teheran-Europe Co. Ltd.* v. *S. T. Belton* (*Tractors*) *Ltd.* [1968] 2 Q.B. 545.

If, however, the agent does not, on the face of the contract, show that he is merely an agent, he will incur personal liability, and the third party may sue either him or his principal at his option. Descriptive words, *e.g.* on the heading of notepaper or following a signature, such as "broker" or "manager," are not sufficient of themselves to negative personal liability. Furthermore, an agent who contracts in his own name but has failed to indicate clearly that he was doing so in his capacity of agent might not cease to be contractually bound even if it is proved that the other party knew, when the contract was made, that he was acting as agent; thus, a receipt signed by estate agents without describing themselves as agents of the seller may constitute a sufficient memorandum in writing adequately identifying the contracting parties, *i.e.* the purchaser and the estate agents, to satisfy the requirements of section 40 (1) of the Law of Property Act 1925 (*Davies* v. *Sweet* [1962] 2 Q.B. 300).

Where the agent contracts as agent for an undisclosed principal

In this case the agent discloses neither the existence nor the identity of the principal; he contracts with the third party as if he were the principal. Here—

1. The undisclosed principal has the right to intervene and claim, and if necessary sue, the third party directly. If he makes use of this right, he renders himself personally liable to the third party; and

2. the third party, after having discovered the principal, has an option. He may elect to hold liable and sue either the principal or the agent.

If the third party unequivocally elects to hold either the principal or the agent liable he cannot afterwards change his mind and sue the other. Commencement of proceedings against either is prima facie evidence of such election, but if that evidence is rebutted this does not bar subsequent proceedings against the other (*Clarkson Booker Ltd.* v. *Andjel* [1964] 2 Q.B. 775). On the other hand, obtaining judgment against either is conclusive evidence, even if unsatisfied, and bars proceedings against the other.

The ordinary rules that an undisclosed principal can intervene and that the third party can elect to sue the principal directly apply also where the undisclosed principal is a foreigner residing abroad; this fact is only one of the elements taken into consideration when determining whether he can sue (*cf. Teheran-Europe Co. Ltd.* v. *S. T. Belton* (*Tractors*) *Ltd.*, p. 195, *ante*).

The rights of the undisclosed principal to intervene and of the third party to elect are not available—

1. If their exercise would contravene the express or implied terms of the contract concluded between the third party and the agent, *e.g.* if the third party relied on the personal skill or solvency of the agent (*Greer* v. *Downs Supply Co. Ltd.* [1927] 2 K.B. 28);

2. if the agent was not authorised or exceeded his authority (*Keighley, Maxsted & Co.* v. *Durant* [1901] A.C. 240, see pp. 185–186, *ante*).

Where the rights relating to the undisclosed principal can be duly exercised, the principal can be met with any defence which was available to the third party against the agent before the third party discovered the existence of the principal.

M employed B & Co. as his agents to collect a debt from X. To do this B & Co. properly employed F, who collected the debt. B & Co. owed F money, and F, not knowing at the time he was employed that B & Co. were agents, claimed to set off the debt against the money owed him by B & Co. *Held*, he was entitled to do so: *Montagu* v. *Forwood* [1893] 2 Q.B. 350.

If the third party did not believe the agent to be a principal, he cannot set off any claim he has against the agent against the principal.

C knew that X, when he contracted in his own name, did so sometimes on his own account and sometimes as agent. X, as agent for D, sold goods to C without disclosing his agency. *Held*, C could not set off as against D a debt owed him by X because he did not believe that X was contracting as a principal: *Cooke* v. *Eshelby* (1887) 12 App.Cas. 271.

If an agent borrows money without his principal's authority and applies it in payment of his principal's debts, the lender of the money is entitled to recover the loan as money had and received by the principal to the lender's use (*Reversion Fund and Insurance Co.* v. *Maison Cosway Ltd.* [1913] 1 K.B. 364).

A principal is liable for the frauds and other wrongs of the agent committed in the course of his employment. The test is, was the agent employed to do honestly and carefully the thing he has done fraudulently or negligently? If so, then the principal is liable.

L who owned cottages and money lent on mortgage consulted G & Co., solicitors. She was seen by S, their managing clerk, who fraudulently induced L to sign deeds, which in fact transferred the cottages and the mortgage to S. S realised these assets and absconded. *Held*, G & Co. were liable for the fraud of S: *Lloyd* v. *Grace, Smith & Co.* [1912] A.C. 716.

Knowledge of the agent that the third party has committed a fraud, affects the principal (*Eddis* v. *Chichester Constable* [1969] 2 Ch. 345, see p. 188, *ante*).

RIGHTS AND DUTIES BETWEEN PRINCIPAL AND AGENT

Duties of agent

The duties of an agent are—

1. To exercise due diligence in the performance of his duties and to apply any special skill which he professes to have. If he is employed to sell, it is his duty to obtain the best price reasonably obtainable, and his duty does not cease when he has procured an offer which has been conditionally accepted.

K employed W to sell a house. On May 29 W received an offer of £6,150 from E and communicated it to K, who wrote accepting it "subject to contract." On June 3 D offered £6,750 to W, who did not communicate this to K, and on June 8 a written contract between K and E was signed. *Held*, W had committed a breach of duty towards K in not communicating D's offer and was liable to pay K the difference between the two offers: *Keppel* v. *Wheeler* [1927] 1 K.B. 577.

He must disclose to his principal anything coming to his knowledge which is likely to influence the principal in the making of the contract.

H was employed by P to sell the lease of P's premises. P had reason to believe that his superior landlord would not consent to the premises being used for a tailoring business. Several tailors were anxious to buy the lease, and H obtained from the landlords an assurance that they would consent to a tailoring business being carried on. He concealed this from P and so induced him to sell for a lower figure than he otherwise would have done. *Held*, H was not entitled to his commission, as he had not properly carried out his duty: *Heath* v. *Parkinson* (1926) 42 T.L.R. 693.

2. To render an account when required.

3. Not to become principal as against his employer. This is part of the more general duty that an agent must not let his interest conflict with his duty.

A employed a stockbroker, J, to buy some shares for him. J sent a contract note to A purporting to show that the shares had been bought, but the note was in fact a sham, and J really sold his own shares to A. *Held*, A could rescind the contract: *Armstrong* v. *Jackson* [1917] 2 K.B. 822.

4. Not to make any profit beyond the commission or other remuneration paid by his principal. So, for example, an agent is accountable to his principal for any profit which he makes, without the principal's consent, out of

—any property, with which he has been entrusted by his principal: *Shallcross* v. *Oldham* (1862) 2 Johns & Hem. 609;
—a position of authority, to which he has been appointed by his principal: *Reading* v. *Att.-Gen.* [1951] A.C. 507 (see p. 50, *ante*);
—any information or knowledge, which he has been employed by his principal to collect or discover, or which he has otherwise acquired for the use of his principal: *Lamb* v. *Evans* [1893] 1 Ch. 218 and *Regal (Hastings) Ltd.* v. *Gulliver* [1942] 1 All E.R. 378, H.L. The reason for this is that such information or knowledge is the property of his principal, just as an invention would be: *Triplex Safety Glass Co.* v. *Scorah* [1938] Ch. 211 and *Sterling Engineering Co. Ltd.* v. *Patchett* [1955] A.C. 534.

An agent is, however, not so accountable when the information or knowledge is not of a special or secret character and he is not dealing with the property of his principal: *Nordisk Insulinlaboratorium* v. *C. L. Bencard* (1934) *Ltd.* [1953] Ch. 430. This is because the agent cannot be prevented from taking advantage of an opportunity of earning money, although it is an opportunity which comes his way because of his employment as agent, provided he does not use his principal's property or break his contract by so doing: *Aas* v. *Benham* [1891] 2 Ch. 244, C.A.

If an agent does make a secret profit or takes a bribe from the party with whom he contracts on behalf of his principal, the result is that the principal has the right to do all of the following—

(a) The principal may recover the amount of the secret profit from the agent: *Reading* v. *Att.-Gen.* [1951] A.C. 507 (see p. 50, *ante*).
(b) The principal may refuse to pay the agent his commission or other remuneration.

A instructed R to sell property and agreed to pay him £50 commission. R sold and received £100 from the purchaser as deposit, of

which he paid £50 to A, retaining the other £50 in payment of his commission with A's consent. A learnt that R had also received £20 as
commission from the purchaser and sued to recover this £20 and also the
£50 he had paid R. *Held*, he was entitled to recover both sums: *Andrews*
v. *Ramsay & Co.* [1903] 2 K.B. 635.

   (c) The principal may dismiss the agent without notice (*Boston
       Deep Sea Fishing and Ice Co.* v. *Ansell* (1888) 39 Ch.D. 339).
   (d) The principal may sue the agent receiving and the third
       party giving the secret payment for damages for any loss he
       may have sustained through entering into the contract, with-
       out deducting the amount of the secret payment he has
       recovered from the agent.

The S Corporation invited tenders for coal. L agreed with X, the
corporation's manager, to pay X 1s. a ton if his tender was accepted, and
accordingly quoted 1s. a ton higher than he otherwise would have done.
Held, the corporation could recover not only the 1s. a ton received by X,
but also 1s. a ton as damages for the loss they sustained through entering
into the contract: *Salford Corporation* v. *Lever* [1891] 1 Q.B. 168.

   (e) The principal can repudiate the contract, whether or not the
       secret payment had any effect on the agent.

B agreed to buy horses from S if they were passed as sound by B's
veterinary surgeon. They were so passed, and B sent S a cheque for the
price. Subsequently the horses were found unsound and were returned
and the cheque stopped. The veterinary surgeon had been bribed by S.
S sued on the cheque. *Held*, B was not liable on the cheque in consequence
of the bribe given by S, and that it was immaterial what effect the bribe
had on the veterinary surgeon: *Shipway* v. *Broadwood* [1899] 1 Q.B. 369.

   (f) Both the agent and the person paying the bribe are guilty of a
       criminal offence under the Prevention of Corruption Act
       1906.

Where a person assumes the character of agent, *i.e.* takes it
upon himself to act as if he were the duly authorised agent of
another, he is liable to account to that other, as principal, for any
profit made out of the property of that other person (*Phipps* v.
Boardman [1967] 2 A.C. 46).
   Before an agent can recover a commission from two principals
whose interests are inconsistent he must make the fullest disclosure
to each of his principals of his own position, and must obtain the
consent of each of them to the double employment (*Fullwood* v.
Hurley [1928] 1 K.B. 498).

5. Not to delegate his authority.

The relation between the principal and his agent being a personal one, the agent cannot employ another to do it for him except in the ordinary way of business, as by employing clerks and assistants. Delegation may take place in case of necessity or where it is customary or sanctioned by the principal (*De Bussche* v. *Alt* (1878) 8 Ch.D. 286). An estate agent who has been appointed "sole agent" has no implied authority to appoint a sub-agent: *John McCann & Co.* v. *Pow* [1974] 1 W.L.R. 1643.

6. Not to disclose confidential information or documents entrusted to him by his principal: *Weld-Blundell* v. *Stephens* [1920] A.C. 956. This is part of the agent's general duty of good faith. During the agency the agent must not act against the principal's interest.

A fire broke out in the warehouse of the defendants. They instructed the plaintiffs to act for them in preparing the claim under the fire insurance policy. The defendants gave H, the director of the plaintiffs, confidential information about the policy and allowed him to visit one of their customers whose books were destroyed in the fire but forbade him to disclose certain information relating to their, the defendants' policy. H disclosed the confidential information to the customers. The defendants terminated their contract with the plaintiffs and claimed damages. *Held*, the defendants were entitled to terminate the contract for breach of confidence and were also entitled to damages: *L. S. Harris Trustees Ltd.* v. *Power Packing Services* (*Hermit Road*) *Ltd.* [1970] 2 Lloyd's Rep. 65.

An agent owes no duty to disclose to his principal that he has committed a breach of his own duty, *e.g.* that he has been taking secret commissions (*Bell* v. *Lever Bros. Ltd.* (pp. 70–71, *ante*)).

The burden of proving breach of duty by the agent is on the principal (*Gokal Chand-Jagan Nath* v. *Nand Ramm Das-Atma Ramm* [1939] A.C. 106).

Duties of principal

The duties of the principal are—

1. To pay the agent the commission or other remuneration agreed.

The amount of the commission and the terms under which it is payable depend entirely on the terms of the contract between the parties. There is no general rule by which the rights of the agent or the liabilities of the principal under commission contracts are to be

determined, but when an agent claims commission from a principal
three basic principles apply—

    (a) When an agent claims that he has earned the right to com-
mission the test is whether on the proper interpretation of
the contract between the principal and the agent the event
has happened on which commission is to be paid.

    (b) There are no special principles applicable to commission
contracts with estate agents.

    (c) Contracts under which a principal is bound to pay com-
mission for an introduction which does not result in a sale
must be expressed in clear language (*Ackroyd & Sons* v.
Hasan [1960] 2 Q.B. 144).

The event on the happening of which commission is payable
may be any event fixed on by the parties. The following are examples
of such events, with the implications. If the agent is to be paid a
commission—

    (a) on the sale of a particular thing, he is entitled to his com-
mission if the thing is sold to a purchaser whom he has introduced, although he may not have negotiated the terms of the
sale and although the terms were accepted contrary to his
advice (*Burchell* v. *Gowrie and Blockhouse Collieries Ltd.*
[1910] A.C. 614). He must, however, have been the effective
cause of the sale, although he need not be the first who
introduced the purchaser (*Nightingale* v. *Parsons* [1914]
2 K.B. 621).

    (b) on a sale being completed, it is not enough to find a purchaser
who signs an agreement to purchase but refuses to complete
or to pay the purchase-money (*Martin* v. *Perry* [1931] 2 K.B.
310). In such an event the vendor is not obliged to sue for
specific performance to enable the agent to obtain his commission (*Boots* v. *E. Christopher & Son* [1952] 1 K.B. 89).
If the vendor refuses to complete, the agent is entitled to his
commission (*Fowler* v. *Bratt* [1950] 2 K.B. 96). If the purchaser is able and willing to complete but signs an agreement
"subject to contract" and the vendor refuses to complete, no
commission is payable (*Luxor (Eastbourne) Ltd.* v. *Cooper*
[1941] A.C. 108). Neither is it payable if the vendor refuses
to sign the contract (*Jones* v. *Lowe* [1945] 1 K.B. 73).

    (c) if he introduces a person "willing and able to purchase":
he is not entitled to commission if he introduces one who is

willing to purchase subject to contract or subject to satisfactory survey (*Graham & Scott (Southgate) Ltd.* v. *Oxlade* [1950] 2 K.B. 257).

(d) if he introduces a person ready, able and willing to purchase: it is payable when a person who is able to purchase is introduced and expresses readiness and willingness by an unqualified offer to purchase, though such offer has not been accepted and could be withdrawn: *Christie Owen & Davies* v. *Rapacioli* [1974] Q.B. 781.

(e) if a "prospective purchaser" is found, the agent is entitled to commission if he finds a person who in good faith seriously contemplates the purchase and makes an offer, though, in the end, he might not be ready, willing and able to purchase (*Drewery and Drewery* v. *Ware-Lane* [1960] 1 W.L.R. 1204).

A contract by which the owner of a house, wishing to dispose of it, puts it in the hands of an estate agent on commission terms, is not (in the absence of specific provisions) a contract of employment in the usual sense; for no obligation is imposed on the agent to do anything. The contract is merely a promise binding on the principal to pay a sum of money upon the happening of a specified event, which involves the rendering of some service by the agent (*Luxor (Eastbourne) Ltd.* v. *Cooper* [1941] A.C. 108). Nevertheless, the ostensible authority of an estate agent invited to find a purchaser for premises or a lessee for premises does not extend to entering into any contractual relationship on behalf of the person instructing him in respect of the premises (*Hill* v. *Harris* [1965] 2 Q.B. 601).

When property is entrusted to an agent to sell there is, in the absence of any stipulation to the contrary, an implied term that the owner himself may sell or employ other agents to sell the property (*Brinson* v. *Davies* (1911) 105 L.T. 134). But if an agent is employed as "sole agent" no other agent can be employed, although the owner may still sell the property himself without paying commission (*Bentall, Horsley and Baldry* v. *Vicary* [1931] 1 K.B. 253).

If a manufacturer appoints a merchant his "sole selling agent," there is no contract of agency at all if the merchant buys the goods from the manufacturer and markets them. In such a case, the manufacturer cannot sell his goods to anyone except the merchant (*Lamb & Sons* v. *Goring Brick Co.* [1932] 1 K.B. 710).

When an agency has been created for a fixed time, but is revoked before the expiration of that time, the agent is entitled to damages

for being prevented from earning his commission if there is an
obligation, express or implied, on the part of the principal to continue the agency for that time.

If the employment is one of agency merely, with no service and
subordination, and the agent can act for other principals also, there
is in general no obligation on the part of the principal to supply the
agent with the means of earning his commission; but if the contract
is one of service, then the commission is merely intended to be in the
place of salary, and the contract cannot be determined without compensation to the servant.

F was appointed sole agent for the sale of R's coals in Liverpool for
seven years. F could determine the contract if R did not supply 75,000
tons a year and R could determine it if F did not sell 50,000 tons a year.
After four years, R sold the colliery. *Held*, there was no implied term
that R should not sell the colliery in the seven years and F was not entitled
to damages: *Rhodes* v. *Forwood* (1876) 1 App.Cas. 256.

G, a shirt manufacturer, employed T as agent, canvasser and traveller
to sell such goods as should be forwarded to him. The agency was for
five years determinable by either party at the end of that time by notice.
At the end of two years G's factory was burned down and he did not
resume business. *Held*, T was entitled to damages as there was a definite
agreement to employ him for five years: *Turner* v. *Goldsmith* [1891] 1 Q.B.
544.

X, a broker, effected a charter for a steamship for 18 months, but
after four months of the charter had run the owner sold the ship to the
the charterer and the charterparty was cancelled. The charterparty
provided for payment of a commission of two and a half per cent. to X on
the hire paid and earned under the charterparty. *Held*, X could not recover
commission for the remaining 14 months, as there was no implied term
that the owner should not put an end to the charterparty by selling
the ship to the charterer: *French & Co. Ltd.* v. *Leeston Shipping Co. Ltd.*
[1922] 1 A.C. 451.

If the sale had been made for the express purpose of defeating
the agent's right to commission the principal could not have relieved
himself from liability. An agreement to pay commission to an agent
if a sale is effected at one price does not bind the principal to pay any
commission if a sale is effected at a lower price.

In 1920 H, shipbrokers, negotiated a charterparty with K for five
years, one of the terms being that K could purchase the ship at any time
during the charter for £125,000. H's principals agreed to pay H three and
a half per cent. commission on the sale. In 1921 K bought the ship for
£65,000, and H claimed three and a half per cent. on this sum from his
principals. *Held*, as the sale had taken place at a different price from that

set out in the charterparty, H was not entitled to any commission: *Howard Houlder & Partners Ltd.* v. *Manx Isles SS. Co.* [1923] 1 K.B. 110.

Commission may be payable even after the termination of the agency. This, however, is exceptional. "Prima facie the liability to pay commission . . . ceases as to future trade with the cessation of the employment in the absence of a reasonably clear intention to the contrary" (*per* McCardie J. in *Marshall* v. *Glanvill* [1917] 2 K.B. 87, 92). An agreement to pay on "repeat" orders may show this intention (*Levy* v. *Goldhill* [1917] 2 Ch. 297). So may an agreement to pay commission as long as the principal does business with the customers introduced (*Wilson* v. *Harper* [1908] 2 Ch. 270). An agent who received an advance on his commission from his principal is normally bound to account for any excess on termination of his contract (*Bronester* v. *Priddle* [1961] 1 W.L.R. 1294).

2. To indemnify the agent for acts lawfully done and liabilities incurred in the execution of his authority.

C employed X, a broker, to make speculative purchases of cotton for him, and became heavily indebted to X owing to the fall of prices in the cotton market. X, as he was entitled to do, closed the account by selling the cotton which he had bought for C. X was personally liable on the contracts and the sale of cotton resulted in a loss. *Held*, X was entitled to be indemnified by C: *Christoforides* v. *Terry* [1924] A.C. 566.

The agent loses his right to an indemnity if he acts beyond his authority or performs his duty negligently.

F asked D, his stockbroker, the price of some stock ex dividend. D quoted the price, which was cum dividend, but negligently omitted to tell this to F. F, thinking the price was ex dividend, authorised D to sell. D sold and, in due course under the rules of the London Stock Exchange, had to pay the dividend to the purchaser. *Held*, D was not entitled to be indemnified by F: *Davison* v. *Fernandes* (1889) 6 T.L.R. 73.

TERMINATION OF AGENCY

Agency is terminated by—
    1. the act of the parties; and
    2. operation of law.

By act of the parties

The contract of agency can be terminated by mutual agreement between the parties, but the authority of the agent can be revoked

at any time by the principal. If the revocation is a breach of his
contract with the agent, the principal will be liable to pay damages
for loss of the agent's commission or other remuneration. The
power of the principal to revoke the authority of the agent is limited
in two directions—

1. If a principal has allowed an agent to assume authority, a
revocation of that authority will only be effective as against third
parties, if the third parties are informed of the revocation of authority. For example, if B is the agent of C to collect debts due to
C, and C revokes B's authority and then B, ostensibly on C's behalf,
collects a debt from X who has previously paid B as C's agent,
the payment will be good as between X and C unless X knew at the
time of payment that B no longer had authority to collect debts.

2. If the principal has given the agent an authority coupled with
an interest, the authority is irrevocable. An example of such an
authority is where X sells the goodwill and book-debts of his
business to Y and appoints Y his agent to collect the debts due to
the business. In such a case, as the book-debts form part of the
consideration for the sale, X cannot revoke the authority he has
given to Y.

The mere appointment of an agent to collect debts for five years
on a commission is not an authority coupled with an interest
(*Doward, Dickson & Co.* v. *Williams & Co.* (1890) 6 T.L.R. 316).

By operation of law

The authority of an agent is revoked by the principal—
  (a) having died;
  (b) becoming bankrupt;
  (c) becoming mentally disordered; or
  (d) becoming an enemy.

Although the mental disorder of the principal revokes the
authority of the agent, the principal will be bound by contracts made
with third parties who have no notice of that incapacity.

A wife was given authority by her husband to buy goods from D.
The husband became mentally disordered, but the wife continued to buy
from D, who did not know of the husband's incapacity. *Held*, the husband
was liable to pay for the goods: *Drew* v. *Nunn* (1879) 4 Q.B.D. 661.

When the principal becomes an enemy the authority of the
agent ceases on the ground that it is not permissible to have inter-

course with an enemy, and the existence of the relationship of principal and agent necessitates such intercourse.

S & Sons were sole agents for a German firm in Great Britain for
the sale of machines on a commission basis. *Held*, the outbreak of war
between England and Germany terminated the agency: *Stevenson & Sons
Ltd.* v. *Akt. für Cartonnagen-Industrie* [1917] 1 K.B. 842.

SELECT BIBLIOGRAPHY

Book

G. H. L. Fridman, *The Law of Agency* (4th ed., 1976).

Articles

Fridman, G. H. L., "Establishing Agency" (1968) 84 L.Q.R.
224–244.

Higgins, P., "Equity of the Undisclosed Principle" (1965) 28 M.L.R.
167–179.

Hill, D. J., "Some Problems of the Undisclosed Principal" [1967]
J.B.L. 122–132.

Hill, D. J., "The Commission Merchant at Common Law" (1968)
31 M.L.R. 623–641.

Hudson, A. H., "Agents for Foreign Principals" (1966) 29 M.L.R.
353–365.

Reynolds, F. M., "Election Distributed" (1970) 86 L.Q.R. 318–347.

Reynolds, F. M., "Personal Liability of an Agent" (1969) 85
L.Q.R. 92–103.

Schmitthoff, C. M., "Agency in International Trade" 129 *Recueil
des Cours, Académie de Droit International* (Vol. 1, 1970), 108–203.

CHAPTER 14

PARTNERSHIP[1]

PARTNERSHIP is "the relation which subsists between persons carrying on business in common with a view of profit" (s. 1). But the relation between members of any company registered under the Companies Acts 1948 and 1967 or incorporated under an Act of Parliament or by Royal Charter is not partnership.

The feature which distinguishes a partnership from a company is incorporation. A company is a legal entity distinct from the members forming the company, while a partnership has no legal existence apart from its individual members. The strictness of this principle is mitigated by the rule that a partnership may sue or be sued under its firm name (Rules of the Supreme Court 1965, Order 81, rule 1); if the partnership is the plaintiff, the defendant may require it to disclose the names and addresses of all partners (*ibid.* rule 2).

A partnership cannot consist of more than twenty persons (Companies Act 1948, s. 434), but this limitation does not apply to firms of solicitors, accountants, stockbrokers and stockjobbers, patent agents, and certain firms carrying on the business of estate agents, actuaries, chartered engineers and building designers (Companies Act 1967, s. 120, and statutory instruments made thereunder). Further, a banking partnership, which under the 1948 Act could not consist of more than 10 persons, may now, by virtue of the 1967 Act, consist of up to 20 persons, provided each partner is authorised by the Department of Trade to be a member of such a partnership (s. 119).

A club or society, such as a cricket club, or a social club, or a debating society, is not a partnership because it is not formed to make profit. The members of such institutions are not liable for debts incurred by the committee without their authority, and are not bound to contribute to the losses of the club beyond the amount of their subscription as laid down in the rules (*Wise* v. *Perpetual Trustee Co.* [1903] A.C. 139).

A partnership is formed by contract, either express or implied.

[1] References in this chapter are, unless the contrary is expressed, to the Partnership Act 1890.

The contract may be in writing or verbal or it may have to be inferred from the conduct of the parties. Even where there is no agreement of partnership, a person may incur the liabilities of a partner if he holds himself out, or allows himself to be held out, as a partner. In determining whether a partnership does or does not exist, regard must be had to the following rules—

1. Joint or part ownership does not of itself create partnership, whether the owners do, or do not, share any profits made by the use of the thing owned. The differences between co-ownership and partnership are—

(a) Partnership is necessarily the result of agreement, co-ownership is not, *e.g.* X may by his will leave his house to Y and Z jointly. Y and Z are co-owners of the house, but not partners, although the rent will be shared equally between them.

(b) Partnership necessarily involves the working for profit, co-ownership does not.

(c) A partner cannot transfer his share of the partnership to a third party without the consent of his partners. One co-owner can transfer his share without the other co-owner's consent.

(d) A partner is the agent of the partnership to bind the firm. A co-owner has no implied authority to bind the other co-owners.

2. The sharing of **gross returns** does not of itself create a partnership, whether or not the persons sharing in the returns have a common interest in the property from which the returns are derived. It is not even evidence of partnership.

3. The sharing of **profits** is prima facie evidence of partnership, but the receipt of a share of profits, or of a payment varying with the profits of a business, does not **of itself** make the recipient a partner in the business. This means that the sharing of profits, without more, proves a partnership, but this may be rebutted by proving other facts which show that the parties did not intend to be partners. In particular, there is no partnership in the following cases—

(a) Where a person receives a debt or other liquidated amount by instalments out of the profits of a business.

(b) Where a servant or agent is engaged in a business and is remunerated by a share in the profits.

(c) Where a widow or child of a deceased partner receives a portion of the profits by way of annuity.

(d) Where a person has lent money to a person engaged or about to engage in business, and receives a rate of interest varying with the profits or a share of the profits. Such a contract must be in writing signed by or on behalf of the parties thereto.

(e) Where a person has sold the goodwill of a business, and in consideration of the sale receives a portion of the profits.

In cases (d) and (e) above, if the person carrying on business becomes bankrupt, the lender of the money and the vendor of the business are postponed until all the other creditors are paid in full (s. 3).

If losses as well as profits are shared, the evidence of partnership is stronger, but it is not conclusive, and in every case the question of partnership depends on the intention of the parties.

A debtor assigned his business to trustees for the benefit of his creditors. The trustees carried on the business with the object of paying off the creditors out of the profits of the business. *Held*, the creditors were not partners in the business: *Cox* v. *Hickman* (1861) 8 H.L.C. 268.

Persons who intend to form a company and are working together prior to its formation are not normally partners; they do not carry on a business in common with a view to profit but are engaged in the preparation of the company's business.

M and B agreed to go into business together and to form a limited company which would carry on business in M's restaurant. B ordered certain goods from the plaintiffs; these goods were intended to be used by the company when incorporated. B was adjudicated bankrupt and the plaintiffs sued M, contending that he was a partner of B. *Held*, M and B were never partners because they never intended to carry on business in partnership. All they did was work preparatory to the business to be carried on by the company when formed: *Keith Spicer Ltd.* v. *Mansell* [1970] 1 W.L.R. 333.

Executors carrying on business under the terms of their testator's will are not partners (*Re Fisher & Sons* [1912] 2 K.B. 491).

The term "salaried partner" is not a term of art. It is, however, widely used to describe a person who is held out to the world as being a partner by, for example, including his name with those of the partners on the firm's notepaper but who receives a salary rather than a share of the profits; although he may also receive a bonus or some other sum dependent upon the profits. By holding him out as being a partner, the partners make themselves liable for his acts vis-a-vis third parties as if he were one; but this does not of itself mean that he is a partner vis-a-vis the partners themselves and not just an employee. To decide this one has to look at the substance of the relationship between the parties, not merely the label attached to it: *Stekel* v. *Ellice* [1973] 1 W.L.R. 191.

CREATION OF PARTNERSHIP

A partnership is illegal when it is formed for an illegal purpose.

In the case of an illegal partnership, no action can be brought for a breach of it, no account of profits will be ordered, and no proceedings can be brought in respect of it (*Foster* v. *Driscoll* [1929] 1 K.B. 470; see p. 98, *ante*).

Capacity to enter into partnership is governed by the ordinary law of contract. An alien can enter into a valid partnership with a British subject, but if he becomes an enemy owing to the outbreak of war, the partnership is dissolved.

A minor can enter into partnership, and the contract is binding on him unless he repudiates it before or within a reasonable time of his attaining full age. If he repudiates it, he is not liable for partnership debts contracted while he was a minor.

THE FIRM NAME

Persons who have entered into partnership with one another are collectively called a firm (s. 4), but the firm name, as such, is only a short way of expressing the names of all the partners, and the firm itself has no separate legal existence.

Brown, Jones, Robinson and Smith may carry on business in partnership as "Brown & Co." or "The City Stationers," but these two titles are merely aliases for the surnames of the four partners.

Partners may sue and be sued in the firm name; any name may be selected as the firm name, subject to the requirements of the **Registration of Business Names Act 1916**, which, as amended by the Companies Act 1947, s. 116, empowers the registrar to refuse registration of a business name which is in his opinion undesirable. A partnership may call itself a "company," but it must not use the word "limited" as the last word of its name, under a penalty of £5 a day (Companies Act 1948, s. 439).

By the Registration of Business Names Act 1916 every firm having a place of business in the United Kingdom and carrying on business under a business name which does not consist of the true surnames of all partners who are individuals without any addition other than the true Christian names of individual partners or the initials of such Christian names, must be registered. On registration the following particulars must be supplied—

1. The business name.
2. The general nature of the business.
3. The principal place of business.
4. The present Christian name and surname and any former name and surname of each partner.
5. The nationality of each partner.
6. Any other business occupation of the partners.

Registration must be effected within 14 days of the commencement of business, and any change in the constitution of the firm must also be registered within 14 days of the change. On registration being effected, a certificate is issued, which must be exhibited in a conspicuous position at the firm's principal place of business. Failure to comply with this renders each partner liable to a fine.

By the same Act, every firm which is required to be registered must mention in legible characters in all trade catalogues, trade circulars, show cards and business letters on which the business name appears, the present Christian names or the initials thereof and present surnames, any former Christian names and surnames, and the nationality, if not British, and the nationality of origin, where the nationality has been changed, of all the partners of the firm. Non-compliance with this requirement renders each member of the firm liable to a fine.

If a firm which ought to have registered under the Act has failed to do so, although any contract made while it was in default can be enforced against it, it cannot itself enforce it against the other party. It may, however, apply for relief against this disability to the court which, if satisfied that—

1. the default was accidental; or
2. it was due to inadvertence or some other sufficient cause; or
3. on other grounds, it is just and equitable to grant relief,

may grant relief on such conditions as it thinks fit to impose. This relief may be retrospective (*Re Shaer* [1927] 1 Ch. 355).

RELATIONS OF PARTNERS TO PERSONS DEALING WITH THEM

Every partner is the agent of the firm and his partners for the purpose of the business of the firm. The acts of every partner who does any act for carrying on in the usual way business of the kind carried on by the firm bind the firm and his partners unless (s. 5)—

1. the partner so acting has no authority to act for the firm in that matter; and
2. the person with whom he is dealing either knows that he has no authority or does not know or believe him to be partner.

Subject to the limitation just mentioned, every partner has implied authority to bind the firm by—

1. selling the goods of the firm;
2. purchasing on the firm's behalf goods of the kind usually employed in the firm's business;
3. receiving payment of the firm's debts and giving receipts for them; and
4. engaging servants for the partnership business.

In **trading firms** a partner may further—

5. accept, make and issue negotiable instruments in the firm's name;
6. borrow money on the firm's credit and pledge the firm's goods to effect that purpose; and
7. instruct a solicitor in an action against the firm for a trade debt (*Tomlinson* v. *Broadsmith* [1896] 1 Q.B. 386).

A trading firm is one which carries on the buying and selling of goods.

B and M carried on business in partnership as proprietors and managers of picture houses. The partnership deed prohibited a partner from borrowing money on behalf of the firm. M borrowed money from H, representing that it was not required for partnership purposes. *Held*, the firm was not liable for the debt, because it was not a trading firm, and M had therefore no implied authority to borrow on the firm's behalf: *Higgins* v. *Beauchamp* [1914] 3 K.B. 1192.

A partner may not, however, bind the firm by deed unless he is expressly authorised by deed, and he may not bind the firm by a submission to arbitration (*Stead* v. *Salt* (1825) 3 Bing. 101).

The firm and all the partners are bound by any act relating to the firm's business done in the firm's name, or in any other way showing an intention to bind the firm, by any person authorised, whether a partner or not (s. 6). A partner has not, however, implied authority to bind the other partners in another business.

D & Co. were a partnership consisting of D, T and L and carrying on the business of produce dealers. D was the only active partner. To cover the possibility of loss, D asked M, the plaintiff, whether M was prepared to buy a consignment of potatoes ex s.s. *Anna Schaar* as a joint venture, *i.e.* on the basis of sharing profits and loss, and M agreed. M contended that the joint venture was itself a partnership between him and D & Co., and sued T and L for half his share in the profits arising from that venture. *Held*, the contention of M was correct and the venture was concluded by D for the partnership and could not be considered as "another" business; consequently, D bound not only himself but also T and L: *Mann* v. *D'Arcy and Others* [1968] 1 W.L.R. 893.

If a partner pledges the credit of the firm for a purpose apparently not connected with the firm's ordinary business, the firm is not bound unless he was specially authorised by the other partners (s. 7). The partner himself is personally liable, and his act may subsequently be ratified by the firm. Again, if it has been agreed between the partners that any restrictions shall be placed on the power of any of the partners to bind the firm, no act done in contravention of the agreement is binding on the firm with respect to persons having notice of the agreement (s. 8). With respect to persons having no notice, the firm will be bound, notwithstanding the restriction, if the act done is within the ordinary course of business of the firm.

The firm is liable for torts or **wrongs** of each partner if committed in the ordinary course of the firm's business or with the authority of the other partners (s. 10).

A partner in a firm, whose business it was to obtain by legitimate means information about the business contracts of competitors, bribed the clerk of a rival to break his contract of service by betraying his master's secrets. The bribe came out of the firm's money, and the profits went into their assets. *Held*, as the partner had done illegitimately that which it was part of his business to do legitimately, the firm were liable for his act: *Hamlyn* v. *Houston & Co.* [1903] 1 K.B. 81.

If a partner acting within the scope of his apparent authority receives the property of a third person and misapplies it, or if the firm in the course of its business receives the property of a third person and, while it is in the firm's custody, a partner misapplies it, in each case the firm is liable to make good the loss (s. 11).

The liability of each partner in respect of the firm's **contracts** is **joint** (s. 9). Their liability in respect of the firm's **wrongs** is **joint and several** (s. 12).

Examples—A and B are partners. X sues A on a contract of the firm and recovers judgment against him, but the judgment is unsatisfied owing to A's lack of means. X cannot sue B, because B is liable jointly with A. *Kendall* v. *Hamilton* (1879) 4 App.Cas. 504.

A and B are partners. X sues A on a wrong for which the firm is responsible and recovers judgment which is unsatisfied. X can bring an action against B for the unsatisfied balance of his claim, because B's liability is joint and several.

The estate of a deceased partner is liable severally for the debts and obligations of the firm so far as they remain unsatisfied, but subject to the prior payment of his separate debts.

Liability of person by "holding out"

A person may be liable like a partner for the debts of the firm although he is not in fact a partner, if he by words spoken or written or by conduct represents himself or knowingly allows himself to be represented as a partner in the firm. His liability in such a case is only to those persons who have, on the faith of such representation, given credit to the firm (s. 14); he is not liable, therefore, for the torts or wrongs of the firm, because such a liability does not depend on giving credit (*Smith* v. *Bailey* [1891] 2 Q.B. 403).

B carried on business as M W & Co., and employed M W as the manager of the business. *Held*, these facts amounted to a holding out that M W was a partner: *Bevan* v. *The National Bank Ltd.* (1906) 23 T.L.R. 65.

A holding out which makes a person liable as a partner to a third person, does not necessarily establish that he and the person holding him out are, in fact, partners *inter se* though it provides some evidence tending to point to a partnership (*Floydd* v. *Cheney* [1970] Ch. 602).

When a partner dies and the partnership business is continued in the old firm name, the continued use of that name or of the deceased partner's name as part of it does not of itself make his estate liable for any partnership debts contracted after his death (s. 14 (2)).

M was a partner in a firm. The firm ordered goods in M's lifetime, but delivery was not made until after M's death. *Held*, M's estate was not liable for the price in an action for goods sold and delivered as there was no debt due in respect of the goods in M's lifetime: *Bagel* v. *Miller* [1903] 2 K.B. 212.

CHANGE OF PARTNERS

When a person is admitted as a partner into an existing firm he does not thereby become liable to the creditors of the firm for anything done before he became a partner (s. 17 (1)). The new firm may take over the old firm's liabilities, but this of itself does not give the creditors any right to sue the incoming partner. This right may be acquired by novation (see p. 154, *ante*), which is an agreement, express or implied, between the creditor, the new firm and the old firm by which the original contract between the creditor and the old firm is discharged by the acceptance of the liability of the new firm.

A partner who retires from the firm remains liable for the partnership debts contracted while he was a partner. He may, however, be discharged from liability by an agreement between himself, the new firm and the creditors, and this agreement may either be an express one or be inferred from the course of dealing (s. 17).

For the debts of the firm incurred *after* his retirement he is liable to persons who (s. 36) (a) dealt with the firm before his retirement, unless he has given them notice that he is no longer a partner; (b) had no previous dealings with the firm, unless he has either given notice of his retirement or had advertised it in the *London Gazette*. He is not liable, however, to persons who had no previous dealings with the firm and did not know him to be a partner.

C and I dissolved partnership, but no notice was given or advertisement published. After the dissolution, C ordered goods from T using the firm's old notepaper which showed I as a partner. T did not know I was a partner before the dissolution: *Held*, I was not liable to T: *Tower Cabinet Co. Ltd.* v. *Ingram* [1949] 2 K.B. 397.

The estate of a partner who dies or becomes bankrupt is not liable for partnership debts contracted after the date of the death or bankruptcy.

A continuing guarantee given to a firm or to a third person in respect of the transactions of a firm is, in the absence of agreement to the contrary, revoked as to future transactions by any change in the constitution of the firm (s. 18).

RELATIONS OF PARTNERS TO ONE ANOTHER

The relations of the partners to one another are usually governed by articles of partnership. If there is no written partnership agreement, their relations are governed by the course of dealing among themselves. In any event, their relations, whether governed by written articles or defined by the Partnership Act, may be varied by the consent of all the partners either given expressly or inferred from a course of dealing (s. 19).

The practice of a firm in making out their balance sheets was to treat the loss occasioned by any asset turning out bad as attributable to the year in which it was discovered to be bad. A partner died, and after the balance sheet had been made out various assets were found to be irrecoverable. *Held*, the estate of the deceased partner was entitled to the value of his share as shown in the balance sheet, without any deduction for the losses subsequently ascertained: *Ex p. Barber* (1870) L.R. 5 Ch. 687.

Partnership property

Partnership property must be applied exclusively for the purposes of the partnership and in accordance with the partnership agreement (s. 20 (1)).

Partnership property is—

1. Property originally brought into the partnership stock.
2. Property acquired, whether by purchase or otherwise, on account of the firm or for the purposes and in the course of the partnership business (s. 20).
3. Property bought with money belonging to the firm, unless the contrary appears (s. 21).

William Wray carried on business in partnership with his two sons and T under the name of "William Wray." On his death, his widow was made a partner and the old firm name was continued. A house was subsequently bought and paid for out of partnership moneys, and was conveyed to "William Wray." *Held*, the house was partnership property, and belonged to the four partners as joint tenants: *Wray* v. *Wray* [1905] 2 Ch. 349.

Where co-owners of an estate in land which is not partnership property are partners as to profits made by the use of that land and buy other land out of the profits to be used in the like manner, the land so bought is not partnership property. Such land belongs to

the co-owners in the same shares as they have in the original land
(s. 20 (3)).

Partners in a business borrowed money on the security of freehold
premises of which they were tenants in common, and expended the
money in adding a part of those premises to adjoining workshops in
which the business was carried on, and of which the partners were co-
owners. *Held*, the addition to the workshops was not a partnership
property: *Davis* v. *Davis* [1894] 1 Ch. 393.

Where land has become partnership property, it is treated as
between the partners as personal and not as real estate (s. 22). Such
land is usually conveyed to the partners (not exceeding four) on
trust for sale and to hold the proceeds of sale and the rents and
profits until sale as part of the partnership property. On the retirement of a partner, such partner will retire from the trusts and a new
partner when admitted will be appointed an additional trustee.

The partnership property is not liable to be taken in execution
except on a judgment against the firm. The only remedy of a creditor
of a partner in his private capacity, and not as a member of the
firm, against the partnership property is to obtain an order charging
that partner's interest in the partnership property and profits with
the amount of the debt. The creditor may also get a subsequent
order appointing a receiver of the debtor partner's share of the
profits. When a charging order is obtained in this manner, the other
partners may redeem the interest charged, or, if a sale is directed,
purchase it (s. 23); they also have an option to dissolve the partnership (s. 33 (2)).

Rights and duties between partners

The rights and duties of the partners among themselves, and the
interest taken by them in the partnership property, depend on
agreement, express or implied. Subject to any such agreement the
following rules apply (s. 24)—

1. All partners are entitled to share equally in the capital and
profits and must contribute equally to losses whether of capital or
otherwise. The rule is in no way affected by the amount of time
given by the partners to the business of the firm.

2. No partner is entitled to interest on capital before the ascertainment of profits.

3. No partner is entitled to remuneration for acting in the
partnership business even if the partners have worked unequally.

4. Every partner may take part in the management of the partnership business.

5. No person can be introduced as a partner without the consent of **all** existing partners. This is because partnership is presumed to be founded on mutual confidence, and an incompetent or dishonest partner may cause heavy loss to his fellow partners. Articles of partnership sometimes contain a provision allowing one of the partners to introduce a new partner, usually his son or near relative. In such a case the consent of the other partners is given in advance by their signing the articles.

Partnership articles between B and R gave B power to introduce into the partnership any of his sons on their attaining 21. His son S attained 21 and B therefore proposed to make him a partner. R refused to consent. *Held*, R could not prevent S from being a partner as the clause in the articles operated as a consent: *Byrne* v. *Reid* [1902] 2 Ch. 735.

If under the partnership articles a partner is entitled to nominate by his will a person to succeed him in the partnership, the person nominated cannot enforce the nomination, as he is not a party to the partnership agreement (*Franklin and Swathling's Arbn.* [1929] 1 Ch. 238).

6. Any difference arising as to **ordinary matters** connected with the partnership business may be decided by a majority of the partners; but no change may be made in the **nature of the partnership business** without the consent of all.

The majority of the partners, in exercising their powers, must do so in good faith, and after giving consideration to the views of the minority. It is not competent for a majority to act without consulting the minority.

7. A majority of partners cannot expel a partner unless a power to do so has been reserved by the articles (s. 25).

8. A partner is entitled to be indemnified by the firm in respect of payments made and liabilities incurred—

(a) in the ordinary and proper business of the firm; or

(b) in or about anything necessarily done for the preservation of the business or property of the firm.

If, for example, a partner, to save the firm's credit, has paid its debts out of his own pocket, he is entitled to an indemnity.

9. A partner making, for the purpose of the partnership, any advance beyond the amount of capital which he has agreed to subscribe is entitled to interest on that amount at five per cent.

10. The partnership books are to be kept at the place of business of the partnership (or the principal place, if there is more than one) and every partner may, when he thinks fit, have access to and inspect and copy any of them. A partner can have the books examined on his behalf by an agent.

Partnership articles provided that proper books of account should be kept. *Held*, any partner was entitled to have the books examined on his behalf by an agent, provided (i) the agent was one to whom no reasonable objection could be taken by the other partners, and (ii) the agent would undertake not to make use of the information obtained except for the purpose of confidentially advising his principal: *Bevan* v. *Webb* [1901] 2 Ch. 59.

In addition to the above, every partner is under a duty to his fellow partners—
- (a) To render true accounts and full information on all things affecting the partnership (s. 28).
- (b) To account to the firm for any benefit derived by him, without the consent of the other partners, from any transaction concerning the partnership, or from any use by him of the partnership property, name or business connection (s. 29 (1)).

X, Y and Z were partners. X without the knowledge of Y and Z obtained for his own benefit the renewal of the lease of the business premises; that lease belonged to the partnership. *Held*, the lease so renewed was partnership property: *Featherstonhaugh* v. *Fenwick* (1810) 17 Ves. 298.

Each partner must also disclose any secret profit made in dealing with the firm, and account for that profit to the firm.

B and C were partners, and C was employed to buy sugar for the firm. C, without B's knowledge, sold goods of his own to the firm at the market price and made a considerable profit. *Held*, he must account to the firm for the profit made: *Bentley* v. *Craven* (1853) 18 Beav. 75.

If one partner sells his share of the partnership business to another partner, and the purchaser knows, and is aware that he knows, more about the partnership accounts than the vendor, then the purchaser must disclose his knowledge to the vendor, otherwise the sale is voidable at the vendor's option (*Law* v. *Law* [1905] 1 Ch. 140).
- (c) Not to compete with the firm.

Any partner, without the consent of the others, carrying on a competing business must account to the firm for all profits so made (s. 30). There is nothing, however, in the absence of an agreement to the contrary, to prevent a partner from carrying on a non-competing business which does not involve the use of the firm's property.

A partner is not entitled to remove partnership documents and other confidential information behind the back of the other partners from the partnership offices for use elsewhere (*Floydd* v. *Cheney* [1970] Ch. 602).

Assignment of share in partnership

If a partner mortgages or assigns his share in the partnership, the mortgagee or assignee is not entitled to interfere in the management of the partnership business, or to require any partnership accounts, or to inspect the partnership books. All he is entitled to is to receive the share of profits to which the assigning partner would otherwise be entitled, and he must accept the account of profits agreed to by the partners (s. 31).

A, B and C were partners under partnership articles which made no provision for the payment of salaries to any of them. A charged his share to X. Subsequently, A, B and C made an agreement under which, in consideration of their doing more work for the business, they received salaries. *Held*, as the agreement was a bona fide one it was binding on X: *Re Garwood's Trusts* [1903] 1 Ch. 236.

In the case of a dissolution of partnership, the assignee is entitled to the share of the assigning partner, and, in order to ascertain that share, he is entitled to an account (s. 31 (2)).

One of two partners mortgaged his share in the partnership to X. Afterwards, without the mortgagee's consent, the partners agreed to a dissolution on the terms that the partner who had mortgaged should sell his share to his co-partner for a sum less than the mortgage debt. *Held*, the agreement was not binding on X, who was entitled to an account on the dissolution of the partnership: *Watts* v. *Driscoll* [1901] 1 Ch. 294.

DISSOLUTION OF PARTNERSHIP

A partnership may be dissolved by order of the court, but there are many cases when dissolution occurs without any order. A dissolution occurs without any order of the court by—

1. Expiration or notice (s. 32). Subject to any agreement between the partners, a partnership is dissolved—

   (a) if entered into for a fixed term, by the expiration of that term;

(b) if entered into for a simple adventure or undertaking, by the termination of that adventure or undertaking;

(c) if entered into for an undefined time, by any partner giving notice of dissolution to the others. Such a partnership is a partnership at will and may be determined at any time on notice. Where the partnership was originally constituted by deed, notice in writing is required (s. 26), but in other cases verbal notice is sufficient.

M and E were partners under an agreement which provided that the partnership should be terminated "by mutual arrangement only." *Held*, one partner could not terminate the partnership without the consent of the other: *Moss* v. *Elphick* [1910] 1 K.B. 846.

2. Bankruptcy or death (s. 33). Subject to any agreement between the partners, a partnership is dissolved by the death or bankruptcy of any partner. Often, however, the partners do not want the death, bankruptcy or retirement of one partner to dissolve the partnership, so it is frequently provided in the partnership deed that in such event the continuing partners shall have the option of purchasing the share of that partner at a valuation.

If one partner sends notice of dissolution to the other partner, and dies before the other partner receives the notice, the partnership is dissolved by death and not by notice (*McLeod* v. *Dowling* (1927) 43 T.L.R. 655).

3. Charge (s. 33). If one partner suffers his share to be charged for his separate debt, the others have the option of dissolving the partnership.

4. Illegality (s. 34). If an event happens which makes it unlawful for the business of the firm to be carried on or for the members of the firm to carry it on in partnership, the partnership is dissolved.

A, resident in England, and B, resident in Utopia, are partners. War breaks out between England and Utopia. The partnership has become unlawful and is dissolved automatically on the outbreak of war.

On application by a partner **the court** may decree a dissolution of the partnership in the following cases (s. 35, as amended)—

1. When a partner is incapable by reason of mental disorder of managing and administering his property and affairs (Mental Health Act 1959, s. 103 (1) (*b*)).

2. When a partner, other than the partner suing, becomes in

any other way permanently incapable of performing his duties under the contract of partnership.

3. When a partner, other than the partner suing, has been guilty of conduct calculated to affect prejudicially the carrying on of the business.

C and E were partners, and C was convicted of travelling on the railway without a ticket and with intent to defraud. *Held*, as the conviction was for dishonesty, it was calculated to be detrimental to the partnership business: *Carmichael* v. *Evans* [1904] 1 Ch. 486.

4. When a partner, other than the partner suing, wilfully or persistently commits a breach of the partnership agreement, or otherwise so conducts himself that it is not reasonably practicable for the other partners to carry on the business in partnership with him.

It is a ground for dissolution under this head if one of the partners keeps erroneous accounts and omits to enter receipts, or refuses to submit his dealings to the examination of his co-partners and if there is continued quarrelling between the partners, or such a state of animosity between them that all mutual confidence is destroyed.

5. When the business of the partnership can only be carried on at a loss.

6. Whenever the court thinks it just and equitable to dissolve the partnership. This provision enables the court to decree a dissolution in any case not specifically covered by the first five cases if it thinks it equitable to do so, *e.g.* when the partnership has reached a deadlock.

W and R, who had traded separately as tobacco and cigarette manufacturers, agreed to amalgamate and form a private company. W and R were the directors and had equal voting power. After a time the relations between them became so strained that neither would speak to the other, communications having to be conveyed between them through the secretary of the company. The company had made and continued to make large profits. *Held*, a deadlock had arisen which would be a clear ground for dissolution in the case of a partnership, and as this was, in substance, a partnership in the guise of a private company, it was just and equitable that the company should be wound up: *Re Yenidje Tobacco Co. Ltd.* [1916] 2 Ch. 426.

On dissolution any partner may give public notice of dissolution, and can compel the other partners to sign the necessary notices of dissolution (s. 37). The effect of a dissolution is to revoke the power of each partner to bind the firm, except to complete transactions begun, but not finished, at the time of the dissolution, and to do what may be necessary to wind up the partnership affairs (s. 38).

A surviving partner carried on business in the partnership name and continued the partnership banking account, which was overdrawn at the death of the deceased partner, and remained overdrawn until the final winding up of the business. To secure the overdraft he deposited with the bank the title deeds of partnership real estate. *Held*, as the deposit was made for the purpose of winding up the partnership estate, it was binding on the executors of the deceased partner: *Re Bourne* [1906] 2 Ch. 427.

To wind up the partnership, the court may appoint a receiver and manager. A receiver receives the income and pays the necessary expenses, while a manager manages the business with the object, as a rule, of its being sold as a going concern.

Notwithstanding the dissolution of a partnership, where assets remain undistributed, the duty of good faith between the parties continues. Thus, where a leasehold interest had been a partnership asset and the assets of a dissolved partnership remained undistributed, one of the former partners could not acquire the reversion for himself without giving his former partners the opportunity of sharing in the acquisition: *Thompson's Trustee in Bankruptcy* v. *Heaton* [1974] 1 W.L.R. 605.

Application of partnership property on dissolution

On dissolution each partner is entitled to have the partnership property, including the goodwill, sold, and the proceeds applied in payment of the debts and liabilities of the firm. In the case of the bankruptcy of any of the partners the rule is that the partnership estate is applicable in the first instance in payment of the partnership debts, and the separate estate of each partner in payment of his separate debts. A surplus of the separate estates is dealt with as part of the partnership estate. A surplus of the partnership estate is dealt with as part of the separate estate of each partner in such proportion as he shares in the partnership estate (Bankruptcy Act 1914, s. 33 (6)).

A and B were partners and became bankrupt. A's private debts are £1,000, and B's £1,500. The partnership debts are £5,000, and the assets £6,000. The partnership creditors will be paid in full, and the surplus £1,000 will be divided among the private creditors of A and B in proportion to their rights in the partnership property.

If the partnership assets are insufficient to discharge the debts and liabilities of the firm, the partners must bear the deficiency in the proportion in which they were entitled to share profits. The order of application of assets to meet losses is—

1. Out of profits.
2. Out of capital.
3. By the partners individually in the proportion in which they were entitled to share profits (s. 44 (*a*)).

Apart from this, the assets, including any sums contributed by the partners to make up losses or deficiencies of capital, are applied (s. 44 (*b*))—

1. In paying the debts and liabilities of the firm to persons who are not partners.

2. In paying each partner rateably what is due from the firm to him for advances as distinguished from capital.

When a partnership was wound up, a partner brought an action against the other partners for the recovery of a loan made by him to the partnership. *Held*, the action was misconceived and had to be dismissed. A partner advancing money to the partnership was advancing some of the money to himself, and the only way in which the money could be recovered was by proceedings for taking the accounts of the partnership, as provided by s. 44 (*b*) (2): *Green* v. *Hertzog* [1954] 1 W.L.R. 1309.

3. In paying each partner rateably what is due to him in respect of capital.

4. The ultimate residue, if any, to be divided among the partners in the proportion in which profits are divisible.

If the assets are sufficient to pay (1) and (2), above, but insufficient to repay to each partner his full capital, the deficiency in the capital is to be borne by the partners in the proportion in which profits are divisible.

G, M and W were partners on the terms that profits should be divided equally. The capital was contributed unequally, G contributing more than M. On a dissolution, the assets, though sufficient to pay the creditors, were insufficient to repay the capital in full. *Held*, the true principle of division was for each partner to be treated as liable to contribute a third of the deficiency, and then to apply the assets in paying to each partner rateably his share of capital: *Garner* v. *Murray* [1904] 1 Ch. 57.

If one partner has paid a premium on entering into a partnership for a **fixed term** and the partnership is dissolved before the expiration of the term, otherwise than by the death of a partner, the court may order the return of such part of the premium as may be just, having regard to the terms of the partnership and the time it has continued, unless (s. 40)—

1. the dissolution is due to the misconduct of the partner who paid the premium; or
2. the partnership has been dissolved by an agreement containing no provision for a return of the premium.

When a partnership is rescinded on the ground of the fraud or misrepresentation of one of the partners, the partner entitled to rescind is entitled (s. 41)—

1. to a lien on the partnership assets, after the liabilities have been discharged, for any sum he has paid for a share of the partnership and for any capital he has contributed;
2. to stand in the place of any of the firm's creditors for any payments he has made to them to discharge the firm's liabilities;
3. to be indemnified by the person guilty of the fraud or misrepresentation against all the firm's liabilities.

When a partner dies or retires and the surviving partners carry on the business of the firm without any settlement of account with the late partner or his estate, the outgoing partner or the estate of the deceased partner may—

1. claim such share of the profits made since the dissolution as is attributable to his share of the assets; or
2. claim interest at five per cent. on his share of the partnership assets (s. 42).

C and M carried on business in partnership. On C's death the partnership was dissolved, but M carried on the business for a further period. In an action to decide how the profits earned since C's death should be divided, *held*, C's estate was entitled to a share in such part of the profits as were attributable to the user of the partnership assets, proportionate to his share in the total partnership assets, and that inquiries should be made to ascertain what part of the profits had been earned otherwise than through the user of the partnership assets, including goodwill, an allowance being made to M for his management of the business: *Manley* v. *Sartori* [1927] 1 Ch. 157.

R and A were partners in selling petrol at a service station in Ceylon. A gave notice terminating the partnership, but before its termination procured new agreements with the petrol company giving him the sole agency, and after termination continued trading on the partnership property under his own name. R discovered the new agreements and claimed an account for his share in the profits. *Held*, R was entitled thereto under section 42 of the Partnership Act 1890 (which applied in

Ceylon). Further, R's claim was also justified by virtue of section 29 which likewise applied: *Pathirana* v. *Pathirana* [1967] 1 A.C. 233.

Goodwill

Goodwill is the benefit arising from a firm's business connection or reputation. It is defined by Lord Elton in *Cruttwell* v. *Lye* (1810) 17 Ves. 335 as "the probability that the old customers will resort to the old place." This definition is not complete, and must be supplemented by that given by Wood V.-C. in *Churton* v. *Douglas* (1859) Johns. 174: "Goodwill must mean every advantage—every positive advantage, if I may so express it, as contrasted with the negative advantage of the late partner not carrying on the business himself—that has been acquired by the old firm, or with any other matter carrying with it the benefit of the business." On a purchase of goodwill the purchaser usually obtains the premises of the old firm and the right to use the name of the old firm and, in all cases, the right to represent himself as the successor of the old firm. Goodwill is a partnership asset and on the death or retirement of a partner it does not survive to the continuing partners, but must be bought by them. If, on a dissolution of partnership, the goodwill is not sold, each of the partners is entitled to carry on business under the name of the old firm, provided he does not expose his former partners to any risk of liability (*Burchell* v. *Wilde* [1900] 1 Ch. 551). For this reason, when there is an agreement that on dissolution the partnership assets, including goodwill, shall be taken by one partner at a valuation, the goodwill must be valued on the footing that the outgoing partner is entitled to carry on a similar business.

The rights and duties between the vendor and the purchaser of goodwill, in the absence of agreement to the contrary, are—

1. The vendor may carry on a similar business to that sold in competition with the purchaser, but he must not use the old firm name or represent himself as continuing the old business.

2. The vendor may not canvass the customers of the old firm or solicit any customer of the old firm to deal with him (*Trego* v. *Hunt* [1896] A.C. 7).

3. The vendor may advertise the fact that he is carrying on business as long as he does not offend the two preceding rules (*Labouchere* v. *Dawson* (1872) L.R. 13 Eq. 322).

B, C and J D carried on a business as J D & Co. J D retired and B and C carried on the business under a new name with the addition of "late **J D & Co.**" **J D** formed a new firm carrying on the same kind of business in premises adjoining the old firm's premises in the name of **J D & Co.**, and circularised the old firm's customers. *Held*, (1) he could carry on his new business in competition with the old firm and in the immediate vicinity, but (2) although his name was **J D**, he could not carry on his new business in the name of **J D & Co.**, and (3) he could be restrained by the old firm from canvassing their customers: *Churton* v. *Douglas* (1859) Johns. 174.

4. Unless the right to use the old firm name is expressly assigned, the purchaser of the goodwill must not use that name so as to expose any of the partners in the old firm to liability (*Townsend* v. *Jarman* [1900] 2 Ch. 698).

When a partnership is dissolved on the terms of one partner taking over the assets, the other partners must not solicit the customers of the firm.

A partnership between X and Y was dissolved on the terms that Y retained the "assets." Goodwill was not specifically mentioned. *Held*, the assets included goodwill, and X could be restrained by injunction from canvassing the customers of the old firm: *Jennings* v. *Jennings* [1898] 1 Ch. 378.

When the deed of partnership provides that on the death of a partner the surviving partner shall acquire the deceased partner's share of the assets, an injunction will be granted to restrain an executor of the deceased partner from soliciting customers of the firm (*Boorne* v. *Wicker* [1927] 1 Ch. 667).

When the assignment of the goodwill of a business is involuntary, as on the sale by the trustee in bankruptcy of the business carried on by the bankrupt, the purchaser cannot restrain the bankrupt from canvassing his old customers (*Walker* v. *Mottram* [1881] 19 Ch. D. 355). Similarly, if a debtor has assigned all his property to a trustee for the benefit of his creditors, he cannot be restrained by the trustee from canvassing his old customers (*Farey* v. *Cooper* [1927] 2 K.B. 384).

LIMITED PARTNERSHIPS

Under the Limited Partnerships Act 1907 limited partnerships, which may be described as a cross between a partnership and a limited company, may be formed. They are not very common, owing to the superior advantages of private limited companies.

The limitation on the maximum number of partners discussed

earlier in respect of ordinary partnerships (see p. 208, *ante*) likewise
applies to limited partnerships, but at least one of the partners must
be a **general** partner and one a **limited** partner. The partnership
must be registered by sending to the registrar of joint stock companies the following particulars—
1. The firm name.
2. The general nature of the business.
3. The principal place of business.
4. The full name of each partner.
5. The term, if any, for which the partnership is entered into and
   the date of its commencement.
6. A statement that the partnership is limited and the description
   of every limited partner as such.
7. The sum contributed by every limited partner, and whether
   paid in cash or otherwise.
Every change in these particulars must also be registered.

A **limited partner** is one who contributes a stated amount of
capital or property and who is not liable for the firm's debts beyond
that amount. He must not withdraw his capital, otherwise he
becomes liable for the firm's debts to the amount withdrawn. The
rights and duties of a limited partner are—
1. He may not take part in the management of the partnership
business. If he does so, he becomes liable for all the firm's debts
and liabilities during that period. He has no power to bind the firm.
2. He may inspect the firm's books and examine into the state
and prospects of the partnership business and may advise with the
partners thereon.
3. His death, bankruptcy or mental disorder does not dissolve
the partnership.
4. He can assign his share with the consent of the general
partners.
5. He cannot dissolve the partnership by notice.

Any partner who is not a limited partner is a **general** partner.
The general partners manage the partnership business and by a
majority can decide differences arising out of the ordinary conduct
of the partnership business. They can also introduce a new partner
without the consent of the limited partners. A general partner may
become a limited partner by registering the change with the registrar
and by advertising it in the *London Gazette*. The change is of no
effect until it is advertised.

230 *Partnership*

In the event of a dissolution of the partnership, its affairs are wound up by the general partners, unless the court otherwise orders. The Bankruptcy Act 1914 applies to limited partnerships as if they were ordinary partnerships.

SELECT BIBLIOGRAPHY

Books

C. D. Drake, *Law of Partnership* (1972).
Underhill's Principles of Partnership Law (9th ed., 1971).

Articles

Fitzpatrick, P. G., "Why not a Partnership Floating Charge?" [1971] J.B.L. 18.
Morse, G. K., & Tedd, R. H., "Partnership Companies" [1971] J.B.L. 261–267.

PART 3: SALE OF GOODS, HIRE-PURCHASE AND CONSUMER CREDIT

CHAPTER 15

THE SALE OF GOODS[1]

A CONTRACT of sale of goods is a contract whereby the seller transfers, or agrees to transfer, the property in goods to the buyer for a money consideration called the price (s. 1 (1)).

The term "goods" includes all chattels personal, other than things in action and money (s. 62). Chattels personal are to be distinguished from chattels real, which are chattels attached to or forming part of the land. Chattels personal, on their part, are subdivided into things in possession and things in action (see p. 154, *ante*). "Goods" are thus all things in possession, with the exception of money used as currency of the realm.

Timber, for example, is not comprised in the term "chattels personal" if it is sold as growing timber, but if it is sold as timber severed from the land it is "chattels personal." A ship or aircraft is "goods." "Goods" also includes goods to be manufactured or acquired by the seller after the making of the contract of sale. These are called "future goods."

The consideration for the sale must be money, otherwise the contract is one of barter or exchange. There is nothing to prevent, however, the consideration from being partly in money and partly in goods or some other articles of value, *e.g.* when a dealer, in selling a new car, takes an old car in part exchange.

A contract of sale must be distinguished from a contract for work and materials. A contract of sale contemplates the delivery of a chattel; but if the substance of the contract is for the exercise of skill and the delivery of the chattels is only subsidiary, there is not a sale of goods.

If a picture dealer engages an artist to paint a picture for the dealer to sell in the ordinary way of business, there is a contract

---

[1] References to statutes in this chapter are, unless the contrary is expressed, to the Sale of Goods Act 1893.

231

of sale of goods, but if a person who is not a dealer commissions an artist to paint a portrait, the contract is not one of sale.

> G commissioned R, an artist, to paint a portrait of X for 250 guineas. R supplied the canvas and other materials. *Held*, a contract for work and materials and not sale of goods: *Robinson* v. *Graves* [1935] 1 K.B. 579.

The distinction is of importance, because a contract of sale of goods is governed by the Sale of Goods Act 1893 while a contract for work and materials is not (see p. 242, *post*).

A contract for the sale of goods must also be distinguished from a contract of hire.

> A price list for "Lucozade" showed the retail price as 2s. 6d. plus 3d. on the bottle. *Held*, the goods which were sold were the contents of the bottles, while the bottles themselves were not sold but merely hired: *Beecham Foods Ltd.* v. *North Supplies (Edmonton) Ltd.* [1959] 1 W.L.R. 643.

FORM OF THE CONTRACT

A contract of sale of goods may be in writing (with or without seal) or by word of mouth or partly in writing and partly by word of mouth or may be implied by the conduct of the parties (s. 3).

SUBJECT-MATTER OF THE CONTRACT

The goods which form the subject of a contract of sale may be either existing goods or goods to be manufactured or acquired by the seller after the making of a contract of sale. Where the property in the goods is transferred when the contract of sale is concluded (see p. 243, *post*), the contract is called a **sale**; where the property is to be transferred after the conclusion of the contract of sale, the contract is called an **agreement to sell** (s. 1 (3)). If, in a contract for the sale of specific goods, the goods have, without the seller's knowledge, perished at the time when the contract was made, the contract is void (s. 6). The same result obtains in the case of an indivisible parcel of specific goods if part only of the goods have perished at the time when the contract is made.

> X sold to Y 700 bags marked "E.C.P." and known as lot 7 of Chinese groundnuts, lying in a specified warehouse. At the time of the sale there were, unknown to both parties, only 591 bags, 109 bags having been stolen. *Held*, the contract was void: *Barrow, Lane & Ballard Ltd.* v. *Phillip, Phillips & Co.* [1929] 1 K.B. 574.

The price may be fixed by the contract or may be determined by the course of dealing between the parties. In the absence of either of these, the buyer must pay a reasonable price, the amount of which is determined by the circumstances of each particular case (s. 8).

CONDITIONS AND WARRANTIES

The distinction between conditions and warranties has already been explained when the **terms of the contract** were considered (see p. 24, *ante*). The Sale of Goods Act 1893 is, as far as the contract of sale is concerned, founded on this distinction.

A **condition** is a stipulation in a contract going to the root of the contract. It is "of the essence" of the contract. A breach of condition gives rise to a right to treat the contract as repudiated (s. 11). A **warranty** is a stipulation which is not of such importance as to go to the root of the contract, but is collateral to the main purpose of the contract, the breach of which gives rise to a claim for damages, but not to a right to reject the goods and treat the contract as repudiated (s. 62). Whether a term is a condition or warranty, depends on the construction of the particular contract of sale (s. 11 (1) (*b*)).

On a breach of condition the buyer may, if he chooses, bring an action for damages only instead of treating the contract as repudiated (s. 11 (1) (*a*)), but he is limited to such an action for damages if he has accepted the goods or any part thereof, unless there is a term in the contract to the contrary (s. 11 (1) (*c*), as amended by the Misrepresentation Act 1967, s. 4).

In the catalogue at a sale by auction a heifer was described as "unserved." Both the owner and the auctioneer confirmed this in answer to a question by the bidder. The printed conditions of sale excluded liability for misdescription. The heifer was not unserved and died. *Held*, the seller was liable in damages for breach of warranty, the special warranty overriding the printed conditions of sale: *Couchman* v. *Hill* [1947] K.B. 554.

Stipulations as to time of payment are not deemed to be of the essence of a contract of sale, unless a different intention appears from the terms of the contract (s. 10; see p. 117, *ante*).

Decisions since the Sale of Goods Act 1893 was passed have shown that the division of terms into conditions and warranties is not exhaustive (see p. 24, *ante*). The same principles apply to contracts of sale of goods as to other contracts (see pp. 26–27, *ante*). Thus, whilst the Sale of Goods Act implies certain conditions into a contract of sale of goods, the breach of a term which is not a condition, could nevertheless give rise to a right to treat the contract as repudiated. Whereas in the case of a condition even a trivial breach gives rise to such a right, in the case of an intermediate term (*i.e.* something less than a condition) the actual breach must be looked at. If that breach "goes to the root of the contract" or deprives the other party of "substantially the whole benefit of the contract," then the latter is entitled to treat the contract as repudiated.

A written contract to sell fruit pellets contained the express stipulation, "Shipment to be made in good condition." In fact some of the pellets were not in good condition when shipped. However, they were, on arrival, still fit to be used for the purpose the buyer had intended and, although they were worth less than they should have been, they could still have been re-sold at a reduced price. *Held*, the buyers were not entitled to reject the goods. On the facts the sellers were not in breach of either of the conditions implied by section 14 of the Sale of Goods Act as to fitness for purpose and merchantable quality (see below). The express stipulation in the contract was not a condition and the sellers' breach of it had not been serious enough to go to the root of the contract. Therefore the buyers were entitled only to damages: *Cehave N.V.* v. *Bremer Handelsgesellschaft m.b.h.; the Hansa Nord* [1976] Q.B. 44.

Implied Terms

Several highly important conditions and warranties are implied by the Sale of Goods Act in every contract of sale. The Supply of Goods (Implied Terms) Act 1973 made certain amendments to sections 12, 13, and 14 of the Sale of Goods Act which deal with these implied terms. References to those sections will therefore be references to them as amended by the 1973 Act. The biggest change wrought by the 1973 Act has been to make it difficult and sometimes impossible for the seller to contract out of liability for breach of one of these terms (see p. 241, *post*).

The terms implied by the Sale of Goods Act are:

1. *Title*

There is an implied condition that the seller shall have a right to sell the goods (s. 12 (1) (*a*)). If, therefore, the seller has no title, he is liable in damages to the buyer.

R bought a motor-car from D and used it for four months. D had no title to the car, and consequently R had to surrender it to the true owner. R sued to recover the total purchase price he had paid to D. *Held*, he was entitled to recover it in full, notwithstanding that he had had the use of the car for four months: *Rowland* v. *Divall* [1923] 2 K.B. 500.

If the goods delivered can only be sold by infringing a trade mark, the seller has broken the condition that he has a right to sell the goods (*Niblett Ltd.* v. *Confectioners' Materials Co. Ltd.* [1921] 3 K.B. 387).

There are implied warranties, (i) that the goods are free from any charge or encumbrance not disclosed or known to the buyer before the contract is made, and (ii) that the buyer will enjoy quiet possession of the goods (s. 12 (1) (*b*)).

In a contract made before May 1970 the seller sold the buyers some road marking machines. Unknown to them, another company was in the process of patenting their own road marking apparatus under the Patents Act which gave them rights to enforce the patent from November 1970. In 1972 this company brought a patent action against the buyers. The buyers then claimed against the sellers for breach of the implied condition as to title and breach of the implied warranty as to quiet possession. *Held*, (i) the sellers were not liable for breach of the implied condition because at the time of the sale they had had every right to sell, (ii) the sellers were liable in damages for breach of the implied warranty as to quiet possession because that was an undertaking as to the future: *Microbeads A. C.* v. *Vinhurst Road Markings* [1975] 1 W.L.R. 218.

Section 12 (2) governs an exceptional situation—namely where the seller has or may have a limited ownership and it is clearly intended that he will transfer only that limited ownership to the buyer. Here there is no implied condition that the seller has the right to sell the goods. This would be the case for example where there is some doubt as to whether the seller has complete ownership in the goods and where the buyer and seller therefore agree that the seller will transfer to the buyer only such ownership as the seller has. The seller may still be liable in respect of the implied warranties relating to freedom from charges and encumbrances and to quiet possession, except that he will not be liable in respect of charges or encumbrances of which the seller had been unaware at the time the contract was made (s. 12 (2)).

2. Description

Where there is a sale of goods by description, there is an implied condition that the goods shall correspond with the description (s. 13 (1)). Goods are sold by description when the buyer contracts in reliance (though not necessarily exclusive reliance) on the description.

M sold to L 3,100 cases of Australian canned fruits, the cases to contain 30 tins each. M delivered the total quantity, but about half the cases contained 24 tins, and the remainder 30 tins. L rejected the goods. There was no difference in market value between goods packed 24 tins and goods packed 30 tins to the case. *Held*, as the goods delivered did not correspond with the description of those ordered, L could reject the whole: *Re Moore & Co., and Landauer & Co.* [1921] 2 K.B. 519.

If the buyer does not see the goods, he must be buying by description. Even if he does see them he may be buying them by description.

G went to M's shop and asked for some men's underwear. Some woollen underwear was shown to him and he bought it. *Held*, a sale by description: *Grant* v. *Australian Knitting Mills Ltd.* [1936] A.C. 85.

A buyer responded to an advertisement describing a car for sale as a "1961" model. He inspected the car before buying it. After buying it he discovered that the car consisted of half a 1961 model and half of an earlier car. *Held*, the seller was liable under section 13, since the buyer had relied at least to some extent on the description: *Beale* v. *Taylor* [1967] 1 W.L.R. 1193.

Even goods selected by the buyer for himself—for example from the shelves of a supermarket—may nevertheless be bought by description (s. 13 (2)). Reliance by the purchaser on the description is the requirement.

A buyer can not be compelled to accept goods which do not comply with the description, even though they are not defective in quality. If, for example, the seller could supply only staves varying between half an inch and nine-sixteenths of an inch thick, he should not have contracted to supply staves "half an inch" thick (*Arcos* v. *Ronaasen* [1933] A.C. 470). The question is whether the goods correspond with their description, not whether they are merchantable or of good quality. The key to section 13 is identification.

The sellers, X, supplied herring meal consisting of herrings plus preservative under a contract to sell "herring meal" which was wanted by the buyers, Y, for use as an ingredient in compounding animal feed to be sold to Z who wanted it to feed to mink. Unfortunately the herrings and preservative together had suffered a chemical reaction making the meal poisonous to mink. *Held*, (1) there had been no addition of goods outside the contract description and therefore the meal supplied corresponded with the description "herring meal"; (2) the feed was not of merchantable quality (see below) because it had an ingredient which was toxic. *Ashington Piggeries Ltd.* v. *Christopher Hill Ltd.* [1972] A.C. 441 (for the liability of Y to Z see pp. 240, *post*).

Where there is a sale of goods by sample as well as by description the goods must correspond with the description as well as the sample (s. 13 (1)).

N agreed to sell to G some oil described as "foreign refined rape oil, warranted only equal to sample." N delivered oil equal to the quality of the samples, but which was not "foreign refined rape oil." *Held*, G could refuse to accept it: *Nichol* v. *Godts* (1854) 10 Ex. 191.

3. *Merchantable quality*

Where the seller sells goods in the course of a business there is an implied condition that the goods are of merchantable quality (s. 14 (2)). The fact that the condition is implied only when the seller sells in the course of a business means that in the absence of an express statement or undertaking a private seller will not be liable in respect of the quality of the goods. The carrying on of a profession and the activities of a government department, a local authority or a statutory undertaking are all regarded as businesses (s. 62 (1) as amended by the Supply of Goods (Implied Terms) Act 1973). There are two further exceptions from the condition as to merchantable quality. The condition is not implied in respect of defects specifically drawn to the buyer's attention before the making of the contract (s. 14 (2) (*a*)). Similarly, if the buyer examines the goods before the contract is made, the condition is not implied in respect of defects which that examination ought to reveal (s. 14 (2) (*b*)). In these two exceptional cases, the condition is still implied in respect of defects other than those which were drawn to the buyer's attention or which ought to have been revealed by his examination.

Goods are of merchantable quality if they are as fit for the purpose or purposes for which goods of that kind are commonly bought as it is reasonable to expect having regard to any description applied to them, the price and all other relevant circumstances (s. 62 (1A) of the Sale of Goods Act as amended by the Supply of Goods (Implied Terms) Act 1973). Thus it must be asked "What quality is it reasonable to expect in the circumstances?" It is not reasonable normally to expect that the goods will comply with the laws of some foreign country (*Sumner, Permain & Co.* v. *Webb & Co.* [1922] 1 K.B. 55). It is reasonable to expect Coalite not to contain explosive (*Wilson* v. *Rickett, Cockrell & Co. Ltd.* [1954] 1 Q.B. 598). There can be liability under s. 14 (2) in respect of second-hand goods, for it is reasonable to expect a certain standard of quality—the exact standard depending upon the price and description of the goods in question. A minor repair required to a second-hand car some weeks after the purchase would not indicate that the car had not been of merchantable quality when purchased (*Bartlett* v. *Sydney Marcus Ltd.* [1965] 1 W.L.R. 1013). If the goods supplied are useless for any purpose for which goods of that description are usually used then they are probably not of merchantable quality. On the other hand, if they are still suitable for some of the purposes for which goods of that description are usually used and could be re-sold for the same or very nearly the same price as if they were suitable for every such purpose, they will remain of merchantable quality.

The buyer of "industrial fabric" found it unsuitable for making into dresses but that it was suitable for other industrial purposes; as such it was commercially saleable, though at a slightly reduced price. *Held*, it was of merchantable quality: *Brown (BS) & Son Ltd.* v. *Craiks Ltd.* [1970] 1 W.L.R. 752 (and see also *Cehave N.V.* v. *Bremer Handelsgesellschaft m.b.h.*, p. 234, *ante*).

Ashington Piggeries Ltd. v. *Christopher Hill Ltd.* [1972] A.C. 441; see p. 236, *ante*.

4. *Fitness for purpose*

Where the seller sells goods in the course of a business and the buyer expressly or by implication makes known to the seller any particular purpose for which the goods are being bought, there is an implied condition that the goods are reasonably fit for that purpose (s. 14 (3)). Like the condition as to merchantable quality, this condition does not apply to the private seller who does not sell in the course of a business. The purpose for which the goods are required need not be expressly made known to the seller if it is impliedly made clear by the circumstances.

A, a milk dealer, supplied F with milk which F and his family consumed. Even though A had taken all reasonable precautions to prevent contamination of the milk, it contained typhoid germs which infected F's wife who died as a result. *Held*, the purpose for which the milk was supplied was sufficiently made known to A by its description; since it was clearly unfit for human consumption A was liable for breach of condition: *Frost* v. *Aylesbury Dairy Co. Ltd.* [1905] 1 K.B. 608.

Vacwells, who made transistors, bought from BDH some ampoules of boron tribromide which were marked "harmful vapour." Two of Vacwells' chemists washed the ampoules in a sink, to remove the labels. A violent explosion occurred, killing one of the chemists, injuring the other, and causing considerable damage to the premises. The chemical boron tribromide reacted violently to water; apparently one of the chemists had dropped an ampoule in the sink, the ampoule had broken and the chemical had come into contact with water. The dangerous propensity of the chemical was unknown to BDH and the chemists of Vacwells. *Held,* the chemical was not fit for the use for which it was required because the ampoules did not bear labels drawing attention to the danger which would ensue if the chemical was brought into contact with water: *Vacwell Engineering Co. Ltd.* v. *BDH Chemicals Ltd.* [1969] 1 W.L.R. 927.

McAlpines bought four carbon-dioxide fire extinguishers from Minimax. A fire broke out in a timber hut erected by McAlpines on a site. Two of the fire extinguishers were in the hut. When applied to the fire, they exploded, allegedly greatly adding to the damage. *Held,* the fire extinguishers were not fit for the purpose for which they were required: *McAlpine & Sons Ltd.* v. *Minimax Ltd.* [1970] 1 Lloyd's Rep. 397.

Mrs. Griffiths purchased a tweed coat which caused her to suffer dermatitis. She had an unusually sensitive skin and there was nothing in the coat that would have affected anyone with a normal skin. *Held,* since the plaintiff's skin abnormality had not been made known to the seller, the seller was not liable: *Griffiths* v. *Peter Conway Ltd.* [1939] 1 All E.R. 685.

It is possible for there to be liability in respect of second-hand goods, although a minor defect will not normally attract liability.

In 1972 the plaintiff paid £390 for a 1964 Jaguar car with 82,000 miles on the mileometer. He drove it 2,000 within three weeks of purchase and then the engine seized up. At the time of the sale the engine must have been nearing the point of failure. *Held,* this was not a minor defect and the seller was in breach of the condition that the car should be reasonably fit for the purpose of being driven on the road: *Crowther* v. *Shannon Motor Co. Ltd.* [1975] 1 W.L.R. 30.

If it is clear from the circumstances that the buyer did not rely or that it was unreasonable for him to rely on the seller's skill and judgment, the condition is not implied (s. 14 (3); *Teheran-Europe Co. Ltd.* v. *S. T. Belton (Tractors) Ltd.* [1968] 2 Q.B. 545 (see p. 195, *ante*)). However, such a situation will not often arise since the courts will generally infer reliance from the fact that a buyer has gone to a particular shop in confidence that the proprietor has selected his stock with skill and judgment (*Grant* v. *Australian Knitting Mills Ltd.* [1936] A. C. 85).

Where the buyer relies on his own skill and judgment in one respect but relies on those of the seller in another respect, the buyer

will still be able to rely on the implied condition if the unfitness of
the goods relates to the sphere of reliance placed on the seller. Thus
it was held in *Ashington Piggeries Ltd.* v. *Christopher Hill Ltd.*
[1972] A.C. 441 p. 236, *ante* (where the sellers made the goods to
the specification of the buyers), that the sellers were liable for breach
of the condition of fitness for a particular purpose because the unfitness of the goods as feeding stuff for the minks of the buyers arose
from an event within the sphere of reliance, *i.e.* as to the quality of
the ingredients of the feeding mixture.

5. *Sample*

Where the sale is agreed to be a sale by sample:
(a) the bulk must correspond with the sample in quality (s. 15
(2) (*a*));
(b) the buyer must have a reasonable opportunity of com-
paring the bulk with the sample (s. 15 (2) (*b*)); and
(c) the goods must be free from any defect rendering them
unmerchantable, which a reasonable examination of the
sample would not reveal (s. 15 (2) (*c*)). A buyer is not
expected to carry out every test that might be practicable.
"Not extreme ingenuity, but reasonableness, is the statutory
yardstick" (*per* Edmund Davies J. in *Godley* v. *Perry*, see
below).

G, a boy of six, bought a plastic catapult from P, a stationer. G used
the catapult properly but it broke in his hands as it was made in an
indifferent manner and part of it ruptured G's eye. P had bought a quantity of these catapults from B, a wholesaler, by sample and P's wife had
tested the sample, before placing the order, by pulling back its elastic.
Held, G could recover from P because (a) the catapult was not fit for its
purpose; and (b), the sale being by description, it was not of merchantable
quality. Further, P could recover from B since the defect of the goods
could not be discovered by reasonable examination of the sample (s. 15
(2) (*c*)): *Godley* v. *Perry* [1960] 1 W.L.R. 9.

6. *Sample and description*

Where there is a sale by sample as well as by description, the
goods must correspond both with the sample and the description
(s. 13 (1)). A sale is not prevented from being a sale by description
by reason only that, being exposed for sale or hire, the goods are
selected by the buyer (s. 13 (2)).

Exclusion of implied terms

The Supply of Goods (Implied Terms) Act 1973 has considerably amended section 55 of the Sale of Goods Act 1893 and has thereby severely curtailed the ability of the buyer and seller to exclude or limit the liability of the seller under the terms implied by sections 12–15 of the Sale of Goods Act. Section 55, as amended, draws a distinction between consumer sales and other contracts of sale of goods, but the provisions of section 55 as amended can be excluded by the parties in contracts for the international sale of goods (s. 61 (6); see *p.* 262, *post*). In the case of a **consumer sale**, any clause or agreement exempting the seller from liability under sections 12–15 is void (s. 55 (3) and (4)). A consumer sale is one made by a seller in the course of a business where the goods are of a type ordinarily bought for private use or consumption and are sold to someone who is not buying or holding himself out as buying in the course of a business (s. 55 (7)). Thus the following are not consumer sales: a sale by a private individual; a sale by a manufacturer to a wholesaler or a retailer; a sale by a wholesaler to a retailer. Also auction sales and sales by competitive tender are not consumer sales (s. 55 (7)).

In the case of non-consumer sales, any clause or agreement exempting the seller from liability under section 12 (title) is void (s. 55 (3)). However, a clause or agreement exempting the seller from liability under section 13 (description), section 14 (merchantable quality) or section 15 (sample) is not completely void but it will not be enforceable to the extent that it would not be fair or reasonable to allow reliance upon it (s. 55 (4)). In determining whether it would be fair or reasonable to allow reliance on the exempting clause, regard must be had to all the circumstances and to such questions as: whether the seller had a monopoly over the supply of the goods in question; whether he gave the buyer the opportunity of buying the goods without agreeing to the exempting clause; whether the buyer was aware of the existence of the clause; whether the clause was a harsh one exempting from all or only part of the liability under sections 13–15; whether the goods were made to a special order of the buyer (s. 55 (5)).

Four further points must be made in relation to section 55:

(i) It deals only with clauses and agreements exempting from liability under sections 12–15. Thus a clause exempting from an express stipulation in the contract will not be affected by it. Such a

242   *The Sale of Goods*

clause will have effect subject only to the rules of common law
relating to exempting clauses (see p. 29, *ante*).

(ii) A clause which is not rendered void or unenforceable by
section 55 is still subject to the rules of the common law relating to
exempting clauses, including those relating to a fundamental breach
of contract (see p. 34, *ante*).

In the catalogue at a sale by auction a heifer was described as "unserved." Both the owner and the auctioneer confirmed this in answer to a
question by the bidder. The printed conditions of sale excluded liability
for misdescription. The heifer was not unserved and died. *Held*, the
seller was liable in damages for breach of warranty, since as a matter or
common law the special warranty overrode the printed conditions of sale:
Couchman v. *Hill* [1947] K.B. 554.

(iii) An order made under the Fair Trading Act 1973, s. 22 (see
p. 274, *post*) is designed to prevent the giving to the buyer wrong or
misleading information about his rights under the Sale of Goods
Act. It makes it a criminal offence for someone in the course of a
business to display at a place where consumer transactions are
effected (*e.g.* a shop or garage) a notice of an exempting clause which
is void under section 55 of the Sale of Goods Act. Also, from
November 6, 1977, it will similarly be an offence for someone in the
course of a business to publish such a notice in any advertisement or
to supply goods bearing any such notice. From November 1, 1978
it will be an offence for someone in the course of a business to supply
goods bearing any statement about the seller's liability in respect of
description, quality or fitness for purpose unless the statement also
makes it clear that the statement does not affect the statutory rights
of the consumer.

(iv) Like the rest of the Sale of Goods Act, s. 55 applies only to
contracts of sale of goods and not to contracts for services.

Contracts for work done and materials supplied

In such contracts terms analogous to those in the Sale of Goods
Act are implied as to the good quality and fitness for purpose of
the goods supplied, unless the circumstances are such as to indicate
that those terms are excluded (*Young and Marten Ltd.* v. *McManus
Childs Ltd.*, below).

S, a dentist, made a denture for D's wife. *Held*, it was an implied
condition that the dentures would fit the patient: *Samuels* v. *Davis* [1943]
1 K.B. 526.

M instructed B, motor repairers, to repair his motor-car. B obtained from the makers new connecting rods and fitted them to M's car. One of them broke. *Held*, if M relied on B's skill and judgment, there was an implied condition that the rods were fit for the purpose: *Myers* v. *Brent Cross Service Co.* [1934] 1 K.B. 46.

A lady who knew that she was allergic to a particular hair dye, developed dermatitis as a result of having her hair dyed with that substance. She did not disclose her allergy to the hairdresser. *Held*, the hairdresser was not liable for breach of the implied condition as to the fitness of the hair dye since that condition extended only to the dyeing of the hair of a normal person: *Ingham* v. *Emes* [1955] 2 Q.B. 366.

The respondents were building new houses and they sub-contracted the roofing work to the appellants, specifying that "Somerset 13" tiles were to be used. These tiles were obtainable from only one manufacturer. After the work was completed, a previously latent defect appeared in the tiles. *Held*, the appellants were liable in damages for breach of the implied term that they would be of good quality. The fact that the tiles were specified by the respondents and were obtainable from only one manufacturer was not a circumstance excluding the implied term: *Young and Marten Ltd.* v. *McManus Childs Ltd.* [1969] 1 A.C. 454.

TRANSFER OF THE PROPERTY BETWEEN SELLER AND BUYER

It is important to know the precise moment of time at which the property in the goods passes from the seller to the buyer, because—

1. in case of the destruction of the goods by fire or other accidental cause it is necessary to know which party has to bear the loss; and
2. in case of bankruptcy of either seller or buyer it is necessary to know whether the goods belong to the trustee of the bankrupt or not.

The property in the goods means the ownership of the goods, as distinguished from their possession.

Specific goods

In a sale of specific or ascertained goods the property passes to the buyer at the time when the parties intend it to pass. The intention must be gathered from the terms of the contract, the conduct of the parties, and the circumstances of the case (s. 17). Specific goods are goods identified and agreed upon at the time the contract is made. Unless a contrary intention appears, the following rules are applicable for ascertaining the intention of the parties (s. 18)—

1. Where there is an unconditional contract for the sale of

specific goods in a deliverable state, the property passes to the buyer when the contract is made (Rule 1 of s. 18). Deliverable state means such a state that the buyer would be bound to take delivery of them.

The defendants bought carpet from the plaintiffs. When the carpet was delivered to the showrooms where it was to be laid, it was sent away for stitching. It was returned the next day in heavy bales and stolen. *Held*, the carpet in bales was not in a deliverable state. Consequently Rule 1 did not apply and the property remained in the plaintiffs. The defendants were not liable for the price: *Philip Head & Sons* v. *Showfronts* [1970] 1 Lloyd's Rep. 140.

Although according to Rule 1 the fact that the time of delivery or the time for the payment of the price is postponed does not prevent the property from passing when the contract is made, commercial practice is different in the case of sales in a cash and carry shop or a supermarket; here the intention of the parties is normally that property shall pass when the price is paid.

L selected goods in C, a cash and carry shop, and placed them into a wire basket. The price of the goods was £185. At the cash desk the till showed only £85 because, if the goods were worth over £100, the price recorded on the face of the till returned to zero. The manager who operated the till did not notice the error and demanded only £85 which L paid, knowing that it was not the true price and that a mistake had occurred. He was accused under the Larceny Act 1916 for having stolen goods to the value of £100, the property of C. *Held*, L had to be acquitted. The intention of the parties was that the property in the goods should only pass when the price was paid, but nevertheless the property in the unpaid goods likewise passed to L when the manager, a duly authorised person, handed them out to L: *Lacis* v. *Cashmarts* [1969] 2 Q.B. 400 (It should be noted that the Larceny Act 1916 is now repealed and that L might have been convicted under the Theft Act 1968).

2. Where there is a contract for the sale of specific goods not in a deliverable state, *i.e.* the seller has to do something to the goods to put them in a deliverable state, the property does not pass until that thing is done and the buyer has notice of it (Rule 2 of s. 18).

3. Where there is a contract for the sale of specific goods in a deliverable state, but the seller is bound to weigh, measure, test or do something with reference to the goods for the purpose of ascertaining the price, the property does not pass until that thing is done and the buyer has notice of it (Rule 3 of s. 18).

4. When goods are delivered to the buyer on approval or "on sale or return," the property therein passes to the buyer—

(a) when he signifies his approval or acceptance to the seller, or does any other act adopting the transaction.

K delivered jewellery to W on sale or return. W pledged it with A. *Held*, the pledge was an act by W adopting the transaction, and, therefore the property in the jewellery passed to him, so that K could not recover it from A: *Kirkham* v. *Attenborough* [1897] 1 Q.B. 201.

If K when he delivered the jewellery to W had done so on the terms that it was to remain his property until settled for or charged, the property would not have passed to W until either of those events had happened (*Weiner* v. *Gill* [1906] 2 K.B. 574).

(b) if he retains the goods, without giving notice of rejection, beyond the time fixed for the return of the goods, or, if no time is fixed, beyond a reasonable time (Rule 4 of s. 18).

A contract can be a contract for the sale or return of goods within this Rule, whether or not the recipient of the goods under the contract intended to buy them himself or sell them to third parties (*Poole* v. *Smith's Car Sales* (*Balham*) *Ltd.* [1962] 1 W.L.R. 744).

5. Rule 5 of section 18 refers to unascertained goods and is explained in the next paragraph.

Unascertained goods

The property in unascertained goods does not pass until the goods are ascertained (s. 16). Unascertained goods are goods defined by description only, *e.g.* 100 tons of coal, and not goods identified and agreed upon when the contract is made. The property in unascertained or future goods sold by description passes to the buyer when goods of that description and in a deliverable state are unconditionally appropriated to the contract, either by the seller with the assent of the buyer or by the buyer with the assent of the seller (Rule 5 (1) of s. 18). The buyer's assent may be either express or implied and be given either before or after appropriation is made.

G sold to P 140 bags of rice, the particular bags being unascertained. On February 27 P sent a cheque for the price and asked for a delivery order. G sent a delivery order for 125 bags from a wharf, and wrote saying that the remaining 15 bags were ready for delivery at his place of business. P did not send for the 15 bags until March 25, when it was found they had been stolen, without any negligence on G's part. P sued to recover from G the price he had paid for the 15 bags. *Held*, he could not succeed, because G had appropriated the 15 bags to the contract, and P's assent to the appropriation was to be inferred from his conduct in not objecting. The property in the 15 bags had therefore passed to P: *Pignataro* v. *Gilroy* [1919] 1 K.B. 459.

F, a Costa Rican company, bought from T, an English company, 85 bicycles under a contract providing that T should ship them in June 1953. F paid the purchase price in advance. In July 1953 a receiver was appointed for T, and all the assets, including the bicycles, became charged to the receiver. F alleged that as the bicycles had been duly packed into cases, marked with their name, were registered for consignment, and shipping space was reserved for them in a named ship, this setting aside of the goods constituted an unconditional appropriation to which they had assented by letter and that, by virtue of section 18, Rule 5, the property had passed to them. *Held*, the intention of the parties was that the property should pass on shipment and that, as there was no appropriation within section 18, Rule 5, the action failed: *Federspiel* v. *Charles Twigg* [1957] 1 Lloyd's Rep. 240.

If there is a sale of a quantity of goods out of a larger quantity, *e.g.* of 10 tons of scrap iron out of a heap in X's yard, the property will only pass on the appropriation of the specified quantity by one party with the assent of the other. If the buyer has told the seller to send the goods by rail or some other mode of carriage, he will be deemed to have given his assent in advance to the subsequent appropriation by the seller of the goods he has put on rail. Delivery by the seller of goods to a carrier in pursuance of the contract will normally be an appropriation sufficient to pass the property in the goods (Rule 5 (2) of s. 18). When the seller's warehouseman has separated a specified part from bulk and authorises the buyer's collection driver to load that part, that authorisation is an unconditional appropriation of that part and property in it passes to the buyer (*Wardar's (Import & Export) Ltd.* v. *W. Norwood & Sons Ltd.* [1968] 2 Q.B. 663).

Sometimes it is the seller who assents to an unconditional appropriation by the buyer. At a petrol station, property in the petrol passes when the petrol is put into the customer's car. If the attendant puts it in, that is an unconditional appropriation by the seller with the buyer's assent (*Edwards* v. *Ddin* [1976] 1 W.L.R. 942). If the customer puts it in (*i.e.* at a self-service garage), that is an unconditional appropriation by the buyer with the seller's assent.

Reservation of property

The property in goods, whether specific or unascertained, does not pass if the seller reserves a right of disposal of the goods. Apart from an express reservation of the right of disposal, the seller is deemed to reserve the right of disposal in two cases—

1. Where goods are shipped and by the bill of lading the goods are deliverable to the order of the seller or his agent (s. 19 (2)).

2. Where the seller sends a bill of exchange for the price of the goods to the buyer for his acceptance, together with the bill of lading, the property in the goods does not pass to the buyer unless he accepts the bill of exchange (s. 19 (3)).

Passing of risk

Unless otherwise agreed, goods remain at the seller's risk until the property has passed to the buyer, after which they are at the buyer's risk, whether delivery has been made or not. But if delivery has been delayed through the fault of either the buyer or the seller, the goods are at the risk of the party at fault (s. 20).

Where in a contract of sale which involves sea transit the seller fails to give the buyer sufficient notice to enable him to insure— assuming that the duty to insure does not fall on the seller—the goods travel at the seller's risk (s. 32 (3)).

SALE BY PERSON NOT THE OWNER

As a general rule, the sale of an article by a person who is not, or has not the authority of, the owner gives no title to the buyer (s. 21 (1); *nemo dat quod non habet*). The buyer will be obliged to give the article up to the true owner, generally without any recompense from him. An innocent purchaser will be entitled to be recompensed to the extent that he spent money improving the goods before he discovered they were not his.

B owned a Jaguar car which he entrusted to S for S to do some repairs to it. S did not do so but instead used it for his own purposes and had a crash in it. Without any authority S sold the car in its damaged state for £75 to H, an innocent purchaser. H spent £226 on repairing the car. H sold it to a finance company. *Held*, B was entitled to possession of the car but that B must pay £226 to H: *Greenwood* v. *Bennett* [1973] 1 Q.B. 195.

The rule that a buyer can not acquire ownership from someone who himself has neither ownership nor the owner's authority to sell, is subject to the following important exceptions—

Estoppel

If the true owner stands by and allows an innocent buyer to pay over money to a third party, who professes to have the right to sell an article, in the belief that he is becoming the owner of it, the true owner will be estopped from denying the third party's right to sell (s. 21 (1), end). This is in harmony with the related doctrine of estoppel by conduct discussed earlier (see p. 124, *ante*).

X, the owner of machinery in Y's possession, which was taken in execution by Z, abstained from claiming it for some months, and conversed with Z's attorney without referring to his claim, and by those means impressed Z with the belief that the machinery was Y's. Z sold the machinery. *Held*, X was estopped from denying that the machinery was Y's: *Pickard* v. *Sears* (1837) 6 A. & E. 469.

M, the owner of a Bedford van, wanted to buy a Chrysler car from C, a car dealer, but was unable to pay the deposit. M and C agreed that M should submit proposal forms to the plaintiff finance company according to which M applied to acquire both vehicles from the company on hire-purchase terms; M stated in the forms that both vehicles were the property of C. The object of this joint misrepresentation was to use the money obtained on the Bedford van for the payment of the deposit on the Chrysler car. The plaintiff company accepted the proposal for the Bedford van but rejected that for the Chrysler car. *Held*, M was estopped from denying that C was the owner of the van: *Eastern Distributors Ltd.* v. *Goldring* [1957] 2 Q.B. 600.

An estoppel can be raised against someone only if he can be shown either to have intended to deceive or else to have owed a legal duty of care.

The plaintiffs were a finance company which owned a car. They let the car under a hire purchase agreement to M. Before completing his instalments, M without authority sold the car to the defendant, a motor dealer. The plaintiffs and the defendant were both members of H.P.I., an organisation where finance companies register their hire purchase agreements so that any dealer member can, before buying a second hand car, check with H.P.I. to see if the car is the subject of a registered hire purchase agreement. On this occasion the plaintiffs had carelessly failed to register the hire purchase agreement so that the defendant had been told by H.P.I. that there was no hire purchase agreement registered in connection with this particular car. The defendant claimed that the plaintiffs were estopped from denying that M was the owner of the car. *Held*, the plaintiffs were not estopped, because they did not owe any legal duty to join H.P.I. and, having joined, did not thereby come under any legal duty to take care to register their hire purchase agreements: *Moorgate Mercantile Co. Ltd.* v. *Twitchings* [1976] Q.B. 225 (C.A.). (It should be noted that H.P.I. has since written into its terms of membership for finance houses an absolute obligation to register all their hire purchase agreements.)

Sale by factor

Under the Factors Act 1889 mercantile agents, who are not the owners of goods, can in certain circumstances sell them and give a good title to the buyer (p. 190, *ante*).

Sale by possessor of goods or documents of title to them

If a person who has sold goods continues or is in possession of the goods or of the documents of title to them, any sale or pledge by him to a buyer or pledgee who takes the goods in good faith without notice of the previous sale will give a good title to the buyer or pledgee (s. 25 (1)).

The effect of this is that if X, a shopkeeper, sells, *e.g.* hi-fi equipment to Y and promises to deliver it, and before delivery sells and delivers it to Z, Z will get a good title to the equipment, notwithstanding that the property had, before his purchase, passed to Y. This result ensues even if the seller, who retains uninterrupted possession of the goods, does so no longer as seller but as a bailee (*Worcester Works Finance Ltd.* v. *Cooden Engineering Co. Ltd.* [1972] 1 Q.B. 182).

Again, if a person who has bought or agreed to buy goods obtains, with the seller's consent, possession of the goods or of the documents of title to them, any sale or pledge by him to a buyer or pledgee who takes in good faith and without notice of any lien or other claim of the original seller against the goods will give a good title to the buyer or pledgee (s. 25 (2)).

X sold copper to Y and sent him a bill of lading indorsed in blank, together with a draft for the price. Y was insolvent and did not accept the draft, but he handed the bill of lading to Z in fulfilment of a contract for sale of the copper to him. Z paid for the copper and took the bill of lading without notice of X's right as unpaid seller. X stopped the copper *in transitu*. *Held*, as Y was in possession of the bill of lading with X's consent, he could give a good title to Z: *Cahn* v. *Pockett's Bristol Channel Co.* [1899] 1 Q.B. 643.

Section 25 (2) applies not only to cases in which the buyer transfers the actual document of title in his possession with the consent of the seller, for the purpose of this subsection is to protect an innocent person in his dealings with the buyer who appears to have the right to deal with the goods. In such cases the subsection provides that any transfer of the goods or documents of title held by the buyer to a person acting in good faith and without notice of any want of authority on the part of the buyer should be as valid as if expressly authorised by the seller. This position is to be contrasted with that under the proviso to section 47 which relates to the loss by an unpaid seller of his right of lien or stoppage *in transitu* (see p. 257, *post*); that provision applies only where a document is transferred to the buyer and the same document is then transferred by him to the person who takes in good faith and for valuable consideration (*D. F. Mount Ltd.* v. *Jay and Jay (Provisions) Co. Ltd.* [1960] 1 Q.B. 159).

A person who obtains goods under a **hire-purchase agreement** (p. 277, *post*) is not necessarily a person who has bought or agreed to buy goods within the section. If he has merely an option to purchase he cannot dispose of the goods so as to give a good title to the transferee, but if he is under an obligation to purchase he can do so.

B let on hire to M a motor-car, M agreeing to pay hire at £15 a month for 24 months. By the hiring agreement, M could at any time within 24 months purchase the car by making the amount of the hire paid equal to £424. During the hiring M pledged the car with C. In an action by B to recover it from C, *held*, M having only an option of purchase could not give a good title to C: *Belsize Motor Supply Co.* v. *Cox* [1914] 1 K.B. 244.

If a motor vehicle is under a hire-purchase or conditional sale contract and the hirer or buyer sells it to a private purchaser before the payment of the last instalment, the title of the purchaser who acquires the car in good faith and without notice of the hire-purchase or conditional sale contract is protected (see p. 294, *post*).

Sale in market overt

Where goods are sold in market overt, according to the usage of the market, the buyer obtains a good title to the goods, provided he buys them in good faith and without notice of any defect or want of title on the part of the seller (s. 22 (1)).

Market overt means, in the City of London, every shop in which goods are exposed for sale, for such things only as are usually sold in the shop. For example, a sale of jewellery in a hatter's shop is not a sale in market overt. Moreover, the sale must be by and not to the shopkeeper (*Hargreave* v. *Spink* [1892] 1 Q.B. 25). A sale in a showroom to which the general public is not generally admitted is not a sale in market overt (*Clayton* v. *Le Roy* [1911]

2 K.B. 1031). Neither is a sale which takes place other than during the daylight hours between sunrise and sunset (*Reid* v. *Commissioner of Police of the Metropolis* [1973] 1 Q.B. 551).

Outside the City of London market overt means a market held on days prescribed by charter, custom or statute as market days, and is limited to the place where, by charter, custom or statute, the market is held. What is a sale in market overt depends on the custom of the market.

H had a motor-car under a hire-purchase agreement from F. In breach of this agreement, H took the car to Maidstone market and handed it to auctioneers to sell at the market. The car was not sold by the auctioneers but, later that day, H sold it to B. *Held*, as the usage of the market allowed sales to be made privately in the market after an auctioneer had failed to sell, the sale was in market overt and B had a good title: *Bishopgate Motor Finance Corpn.* v. *Transport Brakes Ltd.* [1949] 1 K.B. 322.

Sale by person with voidable title

If the seller has a voidable title to goods and his title has not been avoided at the time of the sale, the buyer acquires a good title to the goods, provided that he did not know of the seller's defect of title and bought in good faith (s. 23).

For example, if A by fraud obtains goods from B, A has only a voidable title to the goods, and B can, on discovering the fraud, rescind the contract. If A, **before** B rescinds the contract, sells to C, who buys in good faith and in ignorance of the fraud, C will get a good title (see *Phillips* v. *Brooks* [1919] 2 K.B. 243; p. 69, *ante*). On the other hand, if A, **after** B has rescinded the contract, sells the goods to C, the latter does not acquire a good title unless C is protected by one of the exceptional provisions protecting the purchaser in good faith, such as section 25 (2) of the Sale of Goods Act 1893 (p. 249, *ante*) or sections 2 or 9 of the Factors Act 1889 (p. 249, *ante*).

On January 12, 1960, Caldwell, the owner of a Jaguar car, was persuaded to sell and deliver the car to a rogue who gave Caldwell a car of much lower value and a cheque. On the next morning Caldwell ascertained that the cheque was worthless and at once asked the police and Automobile Association to recover his car. The rogue sold the car to a person who did not acquire it in good faith, and only on January 15 the car was acquired by a purchaser in good faith. It passed through several hands and eventually was acquired by the Car and Universal Finance Co. Ltd., which acted in good faith. *Held*, that while normally the rescission of a voidable contract must be communicated to the other contracting party, that was not necessary if—as in the present case—the other party, by deliberately absconding, put it out of the power of the rescinding party to communicate. Consequently, Caldwell had rescinded the contract on January 13 and the finance company had not acquired a title to it: *Car and Universal Finance Co. Ltd.* v. *Caldwell* [1965] 1 Q.B. 525.

Stolen goods

Where goods have been stolen and the thief is convicted of any offence with reference to the theft (whether or not the stealing is the gist of the offence), the court by which the offender is convicted may order anyone having possession or control of the goods to restore them to the person entitled thereto (Theft Act 1968, s. 28 (1) (*a*)). Section 24 of the Sale of Goods Act 1893 is repealed by the Theft Act (Sched. 3, Pt. III).

PERFORMANCE OF THE CONTRACT

It is the duty of the seller to deliver the goods and of the buyer to accept and pay for them, in accordance with the contract of sale (s. 27). Unless otherwise agreed, payment and delivery are concurrent conditions, that is, they both take place at the same time as in a cash sale over a shop counter (s. 28).

Delivery

Delivery is the voluntary transfer of possession from one person to another. It may be actual or constructive. Delivery is constructive when the goods themselves are not delivered, but the means of obtaining possession of the goods is delivered, *e.g.* by delivering the key of a lock-up garage where the sold car is kept or the bill of lading which will entitle the holder to receive the goods on the arrival of the ship.

Whether the seller has to send the goods to the buyer or the buyer has to take them from the seller depends on the terms of the contract. In the absence of any such terms, **the rules as to delivery are—**

1. The place of delivery is the seller's place of business, if he has one, and, if not, his residence. But if the contract be for the sale of specific goods which, to the knowledge of both parties, are in some other place, then that place is the place of delivery (s. 29 (1)).

2. Where the seller is bound to send the goods to the buyer, but no time for sending them is fixed, they must be sent within a reasonable time (s. 29 (2)). Delivery must be at a reasonable hour.

3. If the goods are in possession of a third party, there is no delivery until such third party acknowledges to the buyer that he holds the goods on his behalf (s. 29 (3)). Such an acknowledgment is called attornment.

4. Where the seller is authorised or required to send the goods to the buyer, delivery to a carrier, whether named by the buyer or not, for the purpose of transmission to the buyer is prima facie delivery to the buyer. But the seller must make a reasonable contract with the carrier, otherwise the buyer may decline to treat the delivery to the carrier as delivery to himself. Where the carriage involves sea transit, the seller must give sufficient notice to the buyer to enable him to insure, otherwise the goods will be at the seller's risk (s. 32).

5. If the seller agrees to deliver goods to the buyer at a place other than that where they are when sold, the buyer must, in the absence of agreement to the contrary, take a risk of deterioration necessarily incident to the course of transit (s. 33).

Similarly, if the seller agrees to deliver goods at the buyer's premises and, without negligence, delivers them there to a person apparently authorised to receive them, and that person misappropriates them, the loss must fall on the buyer and not on the seller (*Galbraith & Grant Ltd.* v. *Block* [1922] 2 K.B. 155).

6. The expenses of putting the goods into a deliverable state must be borne by the seller (s. 29 (5)).

When the seller is ready and willing to deliver the goods and requests the buyer to take delivery and the buyer does not comply with his request within a reasonable time, the buyer is liable to the seller for—

1. any loss occasioned by his neglect or refusal to take delivery; and
2. a reasonable charge for the care and custody of the goods (s. 37).

Acceptance

Acceptance is deemed to take place when the buyer (s. 35)—

1. intimates to the seller that he has accepted the goods; or

2. does any act to the goods which is inconsistent with the ownership of the seller;

P sold barley to B by sample, delivery to be made at T railway station. B resold the barley to X. The barley was delivered at T, and B, after inspecting a sample of it, sent it on to X. X rejected it as not being according to sample, and B claimed to be entitled to reject it. *Held*, B's act in inspecting a sample and then ordering the barley to be sent on was an acceptance, and he could not afterwards reject it: *Perkins* v. *Bell* [1893] 1 Q.B. 193.

or 3. retains the goods, after the lapse of a reasonable time, without intimating to the seller that he has rejected them.

When goods are delivered to the buyer which he has not previously examined he is not deemed to have accepted them unless and until he has had a reasonable opportunity of examining them. He is entitled to demand of the seller a reasonable opportunity of examining them (s. 34), and the rule mentioned under 2, above, is dependent on the buyer being given such an opportunity of examination (Misrepresentation Act 1967, s. 6 (2)). He may, however, accept them at once, although a reasonable time for making an examination has not elapsed (*Hardy & Co.* v. *Hillerns and Fowler* [1923] 2 K.B. 490).

If the seller sends the buyer a larger or smaller quantity of goods than he ordered, the buyer may (s. 30)—

1. reject the whole;
2. accept the whole; or
3. accept the quantity he ordered and reject the rest.

The contract was for the sale of 4,000 tons of meal, 2 per cent. more or less. The sellers delivered meal greatly in excess of the permitted variation. *Held*, the buyers could reject the whole: *Payne and Routh* v. *Lillico & Sons* (1920) 36 T.L.R. 569.

What the buyer accepts he must pay for at the contract rate.

Where the contract is for the sale of "about" so many tons, or so many tons "more or less," the seller is allowed a reasonable margin. If, however, he exceeds that margin the buyer cannot be compelled to accept the goods.

If the seller delivers, with the goods ordered, goods of a wrong description, the buyer may accept the goods ordered and reject the rest, or reject the whole (s. 30 (3)).

Where the contract provides that "each shipment shall be deemed as a separate contract," the seller has an option: he may treat the contract as indivisible or he may make separate deliveries, in which case the contract becomes severable. The seller exercises this option by his mode of performance.

The seller shipped goods from Hongkong c.i.f. Liverpool, "each shipment under this contract [to] be deemed as a separate contract." He shipped the goods in one ship but under two bills of lading dated the same day and invoices, each of these documents relating to half of the consignment. The buyers accepted one half and purported to reject the other. *Held*, there was one indivisible contract and, having accepted part of the consignment, the buyers had lost the right to reject the other: *J. Rosenthal & Sons Ltd.* v. *Esmail* [1965] 1 W.L.R. 1117.

If a buyer has a right under his contract to reject goods, he is not bound to return the rejected goods to the seller, but it is sufficient if he intimates to the seller that he refuses to accept them (s. 36.)

INSTALMENT DELIVERIES

Unless he has agreed to do so, a buyer can not be compelled to take delivery by instalments. When there is a contract for the sale of goods to be delivered by stated instalments which are to be separately paid for, and either buyer or seller commits a breach of contract, it is a question depending on the terms of the contract and the circumstances of the case whether the breach is a repudiation of the whole contract or a severable breach merely giving a right to claim for damages (s. 31).

If a breach is of such a kind as to lead to the inference that similar breaches will take place with regard to future deliveries, the contract can be at once repudiated by the injured party. For example, if the buyer fails to pay for one instalment under such circumstances as to suggest that he will not pay for future instalments, or the seller fails to deliver goods of the contract description under similar circumstances, the contract can be repudiated.

X sold to Y 1,500 tons of meat and bone meal of a specified quality, to be shipped 125 tons monthly in equal weekly instalments. After about half the meal was delivered and paid for, Y discovered that it was not of the contract quality and could have been rejected, and he refused to take further deliveries. *Held*, Y was entitled to do so, as he was not bound to take the risk of having put upon him further deliveries of goods which did not conform to the contract: *Robert A. Munro & Co.* v. *Meyer* [1930] 2 K.B. 312.

The tests to be applied are: first, the ratio quantitatively which the breach bears to the contract, and, secondly, the degree of probability or improbability that such a breach will be repeated.

X bought from Y Co. 5,000 tons of steel to be delivered 1,000 tons monthly. After the delivery of two instalments, but before payment was due, a petition was presented to wind up Y Co., and X refused to pay unless the sanction of the court was obtained, being under the erroneous impression that this was necessary. *Held,* the conduct of X in so refusing payment did not show an intention to repudiate the contract so as to excuse the liquidator of Y Co. from making further deliveries: *Mersey Steel & Iron Co.* v. *Naylor* (1884) 9 App.Cas. 434.

RIGHTS OF UNPAID SELLER AGAINST THE GOODS

An unpaid seller of goods, even though the property in the goods has passed to the buyer, has (1) a lien for the price, (2) if the buyer is insolvent, a right of stoppage *in transitu* after he has parted with possession of the goods, (3) a limited right of resale (s. 39).

(A lien)

A lien is a right to retain possession of goods, until payment of the price. It is available when (s. 41)—

1. the goods have been sold without any stipulation as to credit;
2. the goods have been sold on credit, but the term of credit has expired;
3. the buyer becomes insolvent.

A lien is lost (s. 43)—

1. when the goods are delivered to a carrier for the purpose of transmission to the buyer, without reserving the right of disposal;
2. when the buyer or his agent lawfully obtains possession of the goods; or
3. by waiver.

(A right of stoppage in transitu)

The right of stoppage *in transitu* is a right of stopping the goods while they are in transit, resuming possession of them and retaining possession until payment of the price. It is available when (s. 44)—

1. the buyer becomes insolvent; and
2. the goods are in transit.

The buyer is insolvent if he has ceased to pay his debts in the ordinary course of business or cannot pay his debts as they become

due. It is not necessary that he should have committed an act of
bankruptcy (s. 62).

Goods are in transit (s. 45) from the time they are delivered to a
carrier for the purpose of transmission to the buyer until the buyer
takes delivery of them. The goods are still in transit if they are
rejected by the buyer. If goods are ordered to be sent to an intermediate place from which they are to be forwarded to their ultimate
destination, the transit is at the end if fresh instructions have to be
sent to the intermediate place before the goods can be forwarded,
but otherwise the goods are still in transit. The transit is at an end
in the following cases—

(a) If the buyer obtains delivery before the arrival of the goods
at their destination.

(b) If, after the arrival of the goods at their destination, the
carrier acknowledges to the buyer that he holds the goods
on his behalf, even if a further destination of the goods is
indicated by the buyer.

(c) If the carrier wrongfully refuses to deliver the goods to the
buyer.

When the goods are delivered to a ship chartered by the buyer,
whether they are in possession of the master of the ship as carrier
or as agent for the buyer is a question depending on the circumstances of the case (s. 45).

The seller exercises his right of stoppage *in transitu* either by
taking possession of the goods or by giving notice of his claim to
the carrier in whose possession the goods are. On notice being
given to the carrier he must redeliver the goods to the seller, who
must pay the expenses of the redelivery (s. 46).

Effect of sale by buyer

The seller's right of lien or stoppage in transitu is not defeated
by any sale or pledge except in the three following situations (s. 47)—

1. The seller has assented to the sale or pledge by the buyer.
2. The buyer disposes of the goods in a situation falling within
one of the exceptions to the *nemo dat* principle (see p. 247,
ante).
3. The buyer transfers to a bona fide purchaser a document of
title (*e.g.* a bill of lading) which the buyer has acquired from
the seller (s. 47 proviso).

X bought from Y a shipment of nuts, and Y sent to X the bill of lading. X handed the bill of lading to Z in return for a loan, and then became insolvent. Y attempted to stop the nuts *in transitu*, but Z claimed them. *Held*, Z had a good title to the nuts, which defeated Y's right to stoppage *in transitu: Leask* v. *Scott Bros.* (1877) 2 Q.B.D. 376.

A right of resale

The exercise of the right of lien or of stoppage *in transitu* does not rescind the contract or give the seller a right of resale. If, however, an unpaid seller who has exercised either of these rights does resell the goods, the buyer obtains a good title to them as against the original buyer (s. 48 (2)).

The seller can resell the goods—

1. Where the goods are of a perishable nature.

2. Where he gives notice to the buyer of his intention to resell and the buyer does not within a reasonable time pay or tender the price.

3. Where the seller expressly reserves a right of resale in case the buyer should make default.

If the seller should sustain any loss on the resale he can recover it from the buyer as damages for breach of contract.

A right of withholding delivery

If the property in the goods has passed to the buyer, the unpaid seller has a right of lien as described above. If, however, the property has not passed, the unpaid seller has a right of withholding delivery similar to and co-extensive with his right of lien (s. 39 (2)).

ACTIONS FOR BREACH OF THE CONTRACT

1. The **seller**, in addition to his rights against the goods set out above, has two rights of action against the buyer.

For the price

An action for the price lies when the property in the goods has passed to the buyer (s. 49 (1)). When the price is payable on a day certain irrespective of delivery, an action for the price may be brought although the property in the goods has not passed and the goods have not been appropriated to the contract (s. 49 (2)).

C sold to O a quantity of leather f.o.b. Liverpool, the goods being unascertained at the date of the sale. O instructed C to send the goods to Liverpool for shipment on the "K" and C did so. The "K" and other ships substituted could not take the leather, which remained at the docks for two months. C brought an action against O for the price. *Held*, as the property in the goods had not passed to O, and there was no agreement as to the price being payable on a day certain, irrespective of delivery, C could not sue for the price: *Colley v. Overseas Exporters* [1921] 3 K.B. 302.

When the property in the goods has not passed, the proper remedy of the seller in the case of a breach of contract is the one following.

For non-acceptance

An action for damages for non-acceptance lies when the buyer refuses or neglects to accept the goods. The measure of damages is the loss resulting from the buyer's breach of contract. This is the loss of profit on the sale when the goods have a fixed retail price and the supply exceeds the demand.

⸱ R contracted to buy a Vanguard motor car from T, who were car dealers. R refused to accept delivery. There was no shortage of Vanguards. *Held*, T were entitled to damages for the loss of their bargain, *viz.* the profit they would have made, as they had sold one car less than they otherwise would have sold: *Thompson Ltd. v. Robinson (Gunmakers) Ltd.* [1955] Ch. 177. If the demand of cars exceeds the supply and the car dealer can sell all the cars he can get, he has suffered no loss of profit and the damages are nominal only: *Charter v. Sullivan* [1957] 2 Q.B. 117.

A second-hand car does not have a fixed retail price and in such a case the seller can not recover loss of profit for selling one fewer car than he otherwise would have sold. If he manages to find another purchaser of the car at the same or a higher price he will recover no damages from the first buyer who had backed out: *Lazenby Garages Ltd. v. Wright* [1976] 1 W.L.R. 459.

When there is an available market for the goods, prima facie the measure of damages is the difference between the contract price and the market price (s. 50 (3)).

When the seller is ready and willing to deliver the goods and requests the buyer to take delivery, which the buyer does not do within a reasonable time, the seller may recover from the buyer (s. 37)—

(a) any loss occasioned by the buyer's refusal or neglect to take delivery; and

(b) a reasonable charge for the care and custody of the goods.

2. The **buyer** has the following actions against the seller for breach of contract—

For non-delivery

This arises when the seller wrongfully neglects or refuses to deliver the goods to the buyer. The measure of damages is, as in the case of the action for non-acceptance, the estimated loss naturally resulting from the breach of contract which is, prima facie, when there is an available market for the goods, the difference between the contract price and the market price at the time when the goods ought to have been delivered or, if no time for delivery was fixed, from the time of the refusal to deliver (s. 51).

If the buyer purchased the goods for resale and the seller knew of this, the measure of damages will be the difference between the contract price and the resale price, if the goods cannot be obtained in the market. If they can be obtained in the market, the buyer ought to obtain them there and so fulfil his contract of resale, with the result that the damages will be the difference between the market price and the contract price.

P bought Russian wheat for delivery on a named date, and before that date resold it to a third party at a profit. The sellers failed to deliver. There was no market for Russian wheat. The sellers knew that P had bought for resale. *Held*, P was entitled as damages to the difference between the contract price and the resale price: *Patrick* v. *Russo-British Grain Export Co.* [1927] 2 K.B. 535.

Where delivery is delayed, but the goods are ultimately accepted notwithstanding the delay, the measure of damages is the difference between the value of the goods at the time when they ought to have been and the time when they actually were delivered (*Elbinger Actien Gesellschaft* v. *Armstrong* (1874) L.R. 9 Q.B. 477).

For recovery of the price

If the buyer has paid the price and the goods are not delivered he can recover the amount paid.

For specific performance

A buyer can only get his contract specifically performed, *i.e.* obtain an order of the court compelling the seller to deliver the goods he has sold, when the goods are specific or ascertained. The remedy is discretionary and will only be granted when damages would not be an adequate remedy. If, therefore, the goods are ordinary articles of commerce which can readily be obtained in the market, specific performance will not be granted; but it will be granted if the goods are of special value or are unique, *e.g.* a picture, a rare book or a piece of jewellery.

For breach of condition

On breach of condition the buyer is entitled to reject the goods. If he was not entitled to reject, a contract would be forced upon him which he never agreed to make. He cannot reject the goods, however, if (s. 11, as amended by the Misrepresentation Act 1967, s. 6 (1))—

    (a) he waives the breach of condition, and elects to treat it as a breach of warranty; or

    (b) the contract is not severable and he has accepted the goods or part of them.

Merely taking delivery will not amount to acceptance (see p. 253, *ante*).

L, in 1944, bought from I a picture of Salisbury Cathedral said by I to be by Constable. In 1949 L found it was not by Constable and claimed to rescind the contract and recover the purchase price. *Held*, as the picture had been accepted, it could not later be rejected: *Leaf* v. *International Galleries* [1950] 2 K.B. 86.

In all these cases the breach of condition can only be treated as breach of warranty.

Contracts frequently contain a clause prohibiting the rejection of goods by the buyer. Such a clause has no effect unless the goods are within the contract description.

Timber of different sizes was sold under a contract which provided that "buyers shall not reject the goods herein specified, but shall accept or pay for them in terms of contract against shipping documents." The timber delivered was not, in respect of quantity, the specified timber. *Held*, the buyer could reject the timber as the clause did not operate when the goods tendered were not the specified goods which the buyer contracted to buy: *Green* v. *Arcos Ltd.* (1931) 47 T.L.R. 336. Furthermore a clause which prohibits rejection of goods for breach of the conditions implied by sections 12–15 of the Sale of Goods Act is likely to be void or unenforceable (s. 55 of the Sale of Goods Act as amended by the Supply of Goods (Implied Terms) Act 1973, see p. 241, *ante*).

For breach of warranty

On breach of warranty, the buyer can either—

    (a) set up against the seller the breach of warranty in diminution or extinction of the price; or

    (b) maintain an action against the seller for breach of warranty.

The measure of damages for breach of warranty is the estimated loss arising directly and naturally from the breach, which is prima facie the difference between the value of the goods as delivered and the value they would have had if the goods had answered to the warranty (s. 53).

N sold to B sulphuric acid warranted to be commercially free from arsenic. B used the acid for making glucose, which he sold to brewers for the purpose of brewing beer. Owing to the poisonous nature of the acid the beer was poisonous and killed people who drank it. B sued N for damages. *Held*, he could recover (i) the price paid for the acid, (ii) the value of the beer spoilt by being made from the acid, but not (iii) the damages B had had to pay the brewers for injury to the goodwill of their business: *Bostock & Co. Ltd.* v. *Nicholson & Sons Ltd.* [1904] 1 K.B. 725.

EXPORT SALES

The Uniform Laws on International Sales Act 1967

This Act gives effect to two Conventions signed at a conference at the Hague in 1964, which were designed to achieve some uniformity in the laws which in different states apply to contracts for the international sale of goods. The two Conventions are incorporated in the Act as Schedules. The first Convention, the Uniform Law on the International Sale of Goods, is in Schedule 1 and the second Convention, the Uniform Law on the Formation of Contracts for the International Sale of Goods is in Schedule 2. The Act is part of English law and whenever a contract of sale of goods is governed by English Law as the law governing the contract (see p. 159, *ante*), the Uniform Law in Schedule 1 will apply to that contract, provided the parties to the contract have expressly chosen the Uniform Law as the law of the contract (s. 1 (3) and Uniform Laws on International Sales Order 1972 (S.I. 1972 No. 973), art. 2 (*b*)).

The Uniform Laws and home transactions

Although the Uniform Laws are conceived of as applying to contracts of international sale, there is nothing to stop the parties to a home transaction expressly adopting them (Sched. 1, art. 4). The only limitation is that the parties can not in the case of a home transaction avoid the mandatory provisions of English law (Sched. 1, art. 4). The only such mandatory provisions are those which in the case of a consumer sale make it impossible, and in any other case make it difficult, for the seller to rely on a clause excluding or restricting liability for breach of the terms implied by sections 12–15 of the Sale of Goods Act (see p. 241, *ante*). Thus, where in a home transaction the parties expressly adopt the Uniform Laws, the latter will apply except in so far as they are inconsistent with those mandatory provisions of the Sale of Goods Act 1893, as amended by the Supply of Goods (Implied Terms) Act 1973. Apart from that restriction relating to home sales, the parties are free to contract out of any of the provisions of the Uniform Laws (Sched. 1, art. 3).

The Uniform Law on the international sale of goods

The Uniform Law (Sched. 1) contains provisions governing the seller's obligations as to the time and place of delivery, the insurance and carriage of the goods, the conformity of the goods with the contract, and the giving of good title. Other provisions govern the passing of risk and the buyer's obligations as to payment and the taking delivery of the goods. These rules are in several respects different from ordinary English law. In particular, the Uniform Laws do not recognise the concept of the "condition" which exists in English law, for the breach of which the buyer can reject the goods even though the breach causes him no loss (see p. 233, *ante*). The Uniform Laws instead introduce a concept of "fundamental breach" which is similar to the approach which the English courts have adopted in cases such as *Hongkong Fir Shipping Co. Ltd.* v. *Kawasaki Kisen Kaisha Ltd.* (p. 26, *ante*) and *Cehave N.V.* v. *Bremer Handelsgesellschaft m.b.h.* (p. 234, *ante*). Thus, in order to determine whether the buyer has the right to reject, one must examine the breach that has actually occurred together with its consequences. He will be able to reject the goods only if the breach is "fundamental," *i.e.* if a reasonable person in the position of the buyer "would not have entered into the contract if he had foreseen the breach and its effects" (Sched. 1, art. 10).

The Uniform Law does not prevent a contract of a well recognised type (*e.g.* c.i.f. or f.o.b., see p. 264, *post*) taking effect as such, because the parties are "bound by any usage which they have expressly or impliedly made applicable" (Sched. 1, art. 9).

The Uniform Law on the formation of contracts for the international sale of goods

Schedule 2, which contains that Uniform Law, applies to the formation of contracts of sale which if they were concluded would be governed by the Uniform Law in Schedule 1. Its provisions relate to offer and acceptance. In particular, it contains the following rules. An offer is in general revocable until the offeree has despatched his acceptance. However, an offer is not revocable if it either states a fixed time for acceptance or else indicates that it is irrevocable (Sched. 2, art. 5). A qualified acceptance will normally be construed as a rejection of the offer and a counter offer. However, if the qualification consists of additional or different terms which do not materially alter the terms of the offer, it will constitute a binding acceptance unless the offeror promptly objects to the discrepancy (Sched. 2, art. 7). A late acceptance may be treated by the buyer as having arrived in time, provided the offeror promptly informs the acceptor that he regards it as binding. A late acceptance which suffers an unusual delay in transit and which would in normal transit have arrived in time is regarded as being in time unless the offeror promptly informs the acceptor that he considers his offer has lapsed (Sched. 2, art. 9).

F.o.b. contracts

Under an f.o.b. (free on board) contract it is the duty of the seller to put the goods on board a ship for the purpose of their transmission to the buyer. The contract of carriage by sea has to be made by, or on behalf of, the buyer, and the cost of insurance has likewise to be borne by the buyer if the buyer wishes to insure the goods.

The cost of putting the goods on board must be borne by the seller, but once the goods are shipped they remain at the risk of the buyer. Delivery is complete when the goods are put on board the ship, but the seller should give notice of the shipment to the buyer so as to enable him to insure; if the seller fails to do this, the goods will be at his risk: *Wimble, Sons & Co.* v. *Rosenberg & Sons* [1913] 3 K.B. 743, holding that section 32 (3) (see p. 247, *ante*) applies to f.o.b. contracts.

The property in the goods does not pass to the buyer until after shipment. If, therefore, the seller is prevented from putting them on board by the failure of the buyer to nominate an effective ship, *i.e.* a ship able and ready to carry the goods, the proper remedy of the seller is an action for damages for non-acceptance and not an action for the price (*Colley* v. *Overseas Exporters*, p. 259, *ante*).

There is no general rule that, in the absence of a specific provision in an f.o.b. contract, the duty of obtaining an export licence falls on the buyer: the obligation depends in each case on the construction of the contract and the surrounding circumstances and, if there are no indications to the contrary, will fall on the seller (*A. V. Pound and Co. Ltd.* v. *M. W. Hardy and Co. Inc.* [1956] A.C. 588).

C.i.f. contracts

A c.i.f. (cost, insurance, freight) contract is a contract for the sale of goods to be performed by the delivery of documents representing the goods, *i.e.* of documents giving the right to have the goods delivered or the possible right, if they are lost or damaged, of recovering their value from the shipowner or from insurers. The duties of a seller under such a contract are—

1. To ship at the port of shipment goods of the description contained in the contract.

2. To procure a contract of carriage by sea, under which the goods will be delivered at the destination contemplated by the contract.

3. To arrange for an insurance upon the terms current in the trade which will be available for the benefit of the buyer.

4. To make out an invoice of the goods.

5. To tender, within a reasonable time after shipment, the bill of lading, the policy or certificate of insurance and the invoice to the buyer so that he may obtain delivery of the goods, if they arrive, or recover for their loss if they are lost on the voyage (Hamilton J. in *Biddell Bros.* v. *E. Clemens Horst Co.* [1911] 1 K.B. 214). The bill of lading tendered must correctly state the date of shipment, otherwise the buyer can reject the goods (*Finlay* v. *Kwik Hoo Tong* [1929] 1 K.B. 400).

Under a c.i.f. contract the buyer has a right to reject the documents and also a right to reject the goods. These rights are quite distinct.

B sold goods to K, who were merchants, shipment to be made by
October 31. The goods were shipped on November 3. The date of shipment shown on the bill of lading was forged to show a shipment in October,
but B was ignorant of and not a party to the forgery. In ignorance of the
forgery K paid the price and received the documents, but before the goods
arrived K discovered it. K took delivery, but as the market had fallen
was unable to sell the goods. *Held*, (a) the bill of lading, though forged,
was not a nullity as the forgery did not go to the essence of the contract;
(b) K, although he had not rejected the documents, still had a right to
reject the goods and could recover the difference between the contract
price and the market price: *Kwei Tek Chao* v. *British Traders & Shippers
Ltd.* [1954] 2 Q.B. 459.

But if the buyer accepts the documents knowing that they are
not in order he is estopped from later trying to reject them.

P sold a quantity of Brazilian yellow maize to E. The contract was
c.i.f. Antwerp and provided that shipment had to take place from Brazilian
ports "during the period of June/July 1965" and that "bill of lading to be
considered proof of date of shipment in the absence of evidence to the
contrary." The goods were, in fact, shipped on August 11 and 12, 1965
but the bill of lading was antedated and, falsely, gave as the date of shipment July 31, 1965. However, a certificate of shipment issued by a super-
intendent company in Brazil stated as date of shipment August 10 to 12,
1965, and this certificate was tendered together with the bill of lading.
Held, by taking up the documents and paying for them, the buyers were
aware that the goods were shipped later than provided in the contract and
were estopped from complaining of the late shipment or the defect of the
bill of lading: *Panchaud Frères S.A.* v. *Etablissement General Grain Co.*
[1970] 1 Lloyd's Rep. 53.

The duties of the buyer are—

1. To pay the price, less the freight, on delivery of the documents. He cannot defer payment until after he has inspected the
goods (*Clemens Horst Co.* v. *Biddell Bros.* [1912] A.C. 18).

2. To pay the cost of unloading, lighterage and landing at the
port of destination according to the bill of lading.

3. To pay all import duties and wharfage charges, if any.

During the voyage the goods are at the risk of the buyer. This
risk will in ordinary cases be covered by the insurance, but if the
goods are lost from a peril not covered by the ordinary policy of
insurance current in trade, the buyer must nevertheless pay the full
price on delivery of the documents.

B sold to G 100 bales of cloth on c.i.f. terms. B shipped the goods,
insuring them under a policy which did not cover war risks. This was
customary. The ship carrying the goods was sunk by a German cruiser.

Held, G was bound to pay the price on tender of the shipping documents, notwithstanding that the policy did not cover the risk by which the goods were lost: *C. Groom Ltd.* v. *Barber* [1915] 1 K.B. 316.

Even if the seller knows that the goods have been lost at the time the shipping documents are tendered, he can still compel the buyer to take and pay for them (*Manbre Co.* v. *Corn Products Co.* [1919] 1 K.B. 198).

The property passes when the documents are taken up by the buyer, but "what the buyer obtains, when the title under the documents is given to him, is the property in the goods, subject to the conditions that they revest if upon examination he finds them to be not in accordance with the contract" (*per* Devlin J. [1954] 2 Q.B. 459 at p. 487).

Arrival and ex ship contracts

Under an arrival contract the goods themselves must arrive at the place of destination and it is insufficient that documents evidencing the shipment of the goods to that destination are made available to the buyer. When examining whether a particular contract is a c.i.f. contract or an arrival contract, attention has to be paid to the intention of the parties, as contained in their agreement; the designation of the contract used by the parties is not decisive.

In April 1940 a Belgian company bought 500 tons of La Plate rye from an Argentine company. The terms were c.i.f. Antwerp. The goods were part of a larger consignment, and the documents tendered to the buyers included a delivery order addressed to the sellers' agents in Antwerp and instructing them to release 500 tons to the buyer. The buyers paid against the documents, but the ship carrying the goods, the s.s. *Julia*, was diverted to Lisbon because Antwerp had fallen into enemy hands. At Lisbon the goods were sold cheaply. This was one of some 900 transactions concluded by the parties before on similar terms. *Held*, the contract, despite its designation, was an arrival contract because the delivery order, unlike a bill of lading, passed neither possession nor property to the buyers but was merely a note from one agent of the sellers to another. Since, owing to the non-arrival of the goods in Antwerp, the consideration had wholly failed, the buyers were entitled to recover the whole purchase price paid by them from the sellers: *Comptoir d'Achat* v. *Luis de Ridder* [1949] A.C. 293.

When goods are sold ex ship, the duties of the seller are—

1. To deliver the goods to the buyer from a ship which has arrived at the port of delivery at a place from which it is usual for goods of that kind to be delivered.

2. To pay the freight or otherwise release the shipowner's lien.

3. To furnish the buyer with a delivery order, or some other effectual direction to the ship to deliver.

The goods are at the seller's risk during the voyage and there is no obligation on the seller to effect an insurance on the buyer's behalf (*Yangtsze Insurance Association* v. *Lukmanjee* [1918] A.C. 585).

Export finance

Special arrangements are made in contracts of export sale for the payment of the price. Payment is normally arranged at the seller's place under a **documentary credit** or at the buyer's place under a **collection arrangement**.

The most important of these methods is the documentary credit which "involves the practice of raising money on the documents so as to bridge the period between the shipment and the time of obtaining payment against the documents" (*per* Lord Wright in *Ross T. Smyth & Co. Ltd.* v. *T. D. Bailey Son & Co.* [1940] 3 All E.R. 60).

The principal methods of payment of the price in an export sale are discussed in the section on Documentary Credits in the chapter on Bills of Exchange (see p. 352, *post*).

SALES BY AUCTION

The following rules apply to auction sales (s. 58)—

1. Each lot is prima facie deemed to be the subject of a separate contract of sale.

2. The sale is complete when the auctioneer announces its completion by the fall of the hammer or in other customary manner. Until such announcement any bidder may retract his bid.

D sold a motor-car by auction. It was knocked down to K, who was only allowed to take it away on giving a cheque for the price and signing an agreement that ownership should not pass until the cheque was cleared. The cheque was not cleared. Meanwhile, K sold to S. *Held*, the property passed on the fall of the hammer and the subsequent agreement did not retransfer it from K, so that S had a good title: *Dennant* v. *Skinner* [1948] 2 K.B. 164.

3. The seller himself or any person employed by him cannot bid, and it is not lawful for the auctioneer knowingly to take any such bid, unless notice is given beforehand that the sale is subject

to a right on the part of the seller to bid. A sale contravening this rule may be treated as fraudulent by the buyer.

4. The sale may be made subject to a reserve price, and a right to bid may also be reserved by the seller.

On a sale by auction announced to be subject to a reserve price, each bid is accepted conditionally on the reserve being reached (*McManus* v. *Fortescue* [1907] 2 K.B. 1).

When an auctioneer sells goods, he impliedly undertakes the following obligations—

1. He warrants his authority to sell.

2. He warrants that he knows of no defect in his principal's title.

3. He undertakes to give possession against the price paid into his hands.

4. He undertakes that such possession will not be disturbed by his principal or himself (*per* Salter J. in *Benton* v. *Campbell, Parker & Co. Ltd.*, below).

Where an auctioneer, disclosing the fact that he is acting as agent but not disclosing the name of his principal, sells specific goods he does not warrant his principal's title to the goods.

B bought a motor-car at an auction sale conducted by C, an auctioneer. The car was sold on behalf of X, who had no title to it, and the true owner subsequently recovered it from B. B sued C for the return of the price. *Held*, he could not recover as he knew C was an agent, and the sale was a sale of specific goods: *Benton* v. *Campbell, Parker & Co. Ltd.* [1925] 2 K.B. 410.

Subject to contrary agreement, the auctioneer has the following rights (*Chelmsford Auctions Ltd.* v. *Poole* [1973] 1 Q.B. 542):

1. He is entitled himself to sue the purchaser for the price. The purchaser can not avoid this liability to the auctioneer by paying the vendor direct without telling the auctioneer.

2. He has against the seller a lien over the proceeds of sale for his commission and charges.

Auction sales are usually conducted in accordance with printed conditions contained in the sale catalogue. The conditions frequently contain provisions limiting the liability of the seller in respect of the goods sold (see *Couchman* v. *Hill*, p. 233, *ante*). An express oral warranty given at the time of the sale, however, overrides an exemption clause in the printed conditions of sale (*Harling* v. *Eddy* [1951] 2 K.B. 739).

Auctions (Bidding Agreements) Acts 1927 and 1969

An agreement by a dealer to give any person any consideration for abstaining from bidding at an auction sale is a criminal offence on the part of the dealer and of the person receiving the consideration. A dealer is a person who, in the normal course of his business, attends sales by auction for the purpose of purchasing goods with a view to reselling them (s. 1 of the 1927 Act). The effect of this Act is to make a "knock-out" agreement illegal when it is entered into by a dealer (see *Rawlings* v. *General Trading Co.* [1920] 3 K.B. 30). In case of a conviction the court may order that the convicted person or any representative of him shall not, without consent of the court, enter upon premises where goods intended to be auctioned are on display, or participate in an auction, for a period not exceeding one year in the case of a summary conviction or not exceeding three years on conviction on indictment; contravention of the court prohibition is punishable (s. 2 of the 1969 Act).

A civil remedy is provided in favour of a seller whose goods have been sold at an auction to a person who is a party to a prohibited bidding agreement, provided that one of the parties to that agreement is a dealer. Such a seller may avoid the contract and if restitution of goods is not made to him, may recover any loss sustained by him from any party to the prohibited bidding agreement, not only from the buyer (s. 3 of the 1969 Act). This remedy is available irrespective of whether a party to the prohibited bidding agreement has been convicted in a criminal court.

A copy of the Act must be affixed in some conspicuous part of any room in which an auction sale takes place.

The Act does not interfere with bona fide agreements to purchase goods on a joint account, where the agreement is deposited with the auctioneer before the sale.

Mock Auctions Act 1961

It is a criminal offence to promote or conduct, or to assist in the conduct of, a mock auction at which one or more lots to which the Act applies are offered for sale. A sale of goods by way of competitive bidding is taken to be a mock auction if during the course of the sale—

(a) any lot to which the Act applies is sold to a person bidding for it, and either it is sold to him at a price lower than the amount of his highest bid for that lot, or part of the price at which it is sold to him is repaid or credited to him or is stated to be so repaid or credited; or

(b) the right to bid for any lot to which the Act applies is restricted, or is stated to be restricted, to persons who have bought or agreed to buy one or more articles: or

(c) any articles are given away or offered as gifts.

The Act applies to any lot which consists of or includes plate, plated articles, linen, china, glass, books, pictures, prints, furniture, jewellery, articles of household or personal use or ornament or any musical or scientific instrument or apparatus.

THE TRADE DESCRIPTIONS ACTS 1968 AND 1972

The object of these Acts is to prevent, by way of criminal sanctions, the use of false or misleading trade descriptions. The Acts which have taken the place of, and considerably extended the regulation formerly contained in, the Merchandise Marks Acts, do not provide any civil remedies. The 1968 Act provides, on the contrary, that "a contract for the supply of any goods shall not be void or unenforceable by reason only of a contravention of any provision of this Act" (s. 35). In any case the consumer has extensive civil remedies: they are, in particular, the rules relating to misrepresentation, reinforced by the Misrepresentation Act 1967 (see p. 75, *ante*), and the provisions of the Sale of Goods Act 1893, as amended by the Supply of Goods (Implied Terms) Act 1973, particularly those on implied terms (see p. 234, *ante*). Although the Trade Descriptions Acts do not affect the consumer's civil remedies, the criminal court has power, on convicting an offender, to order him to pay compensation to the victim (Powers of Criminal Courts Act 1973, s. 35). This is so irrespective of whether it was the public prosecutor or the victim who brought the prosecution.

The Act of 1968 creates three principal offences—

1. Any person who, in the course of a trade or business—

(a) applies a false trade description to goods; or

(b) supplies or offers to supply any goods to which a false trade description is applied,

shall be guilty of an offence (s. 1 (1)).

A trade description is any indication, direct or indirect, of (s. 2 (1))—

(a) a quantity, size, or gauge;

(b) method of manufacture, production, processing or reconditioning;

(c) composition;

(d) fitness for purpose, strength, performance, behaviour or accuracy;

(e) any physical characteristics not included in the preceding paragraphs;

(f) testing by any person and results thereof;

(g) approval by any person or conformity with a type approved by any person;

(h) place or date of manufacture, production, processing or reconditioning;

(i) person by whom manufactured, produced, processed or reconditioned;

(j) other history, including previous ownership or use.

The offence under section 1 (1) is committed only if the application of the false trade description was associated with the sale or supply of goods (*Wickens Motors (Gloucester) Ltd.* v. *Hall* [1972] 1 W.L.R. 1418). While most offenders will be sellers, a buyer could commit the offence, *e.g.* a car dealer who when negotiating to buy a second-hand car wrongly informs the seller that it can not be repaired and is fit only for scrap (*Fletcher* v. *Budgen* [1974] 1 W.L.R. 1056).

The trade description is false when it is false to a material degree (s. 3 (1)).

Under a contract to supply a new car, the manufacturers supplied to the dealer a car which had been damaged in a collision in a compound, which damage had been repaired. The manufacturers were convicted. *Held*, on appeal, the conviction should be quashed because if damage is perfectly repaired making the car as good as new, it is not false to describe the car as "new": *R.* v. *Ford Motor Co. Ltd.* [1974] 1 W.L.R. 1220.

It is a defence that the defendant displayed a disclaimer which was as bold, precise and compelling as the description itself (*Norman* v. *Bennett* [1974] 1 W.L.R. 1229). A car dealer would be wise to display such a disclaimer adjacent to a speedometer, which otherwise will amount to a trade description as to the mileage covered by the vehicle.

2. It is an offence to make misleading statements as to the price of goods, *e.g.* to state, contrary to the truth, that goods are sold at less than the recommended price or that the price has been reduced

(s. 11). It is the duty of the defendant to resolve ambiguities in his indicated price. Thus to indicate a price which fails to state that V.A.T. will be added to it may well be misleading and therefore amount to an offence (*Richards* v. *Westminster Motors Ltd.* [1975] Crim. L.R. 528).

3. Certain false or misleading statements relating to services are punishable, *e.g.* if it is claimed that the purchased goods are repaired free of charge during a guarantee period, when the guarantee provides for a charge for labour (s. 14 (1), (3)).

The Act admits certain defences when a prosecution is initiated. In particular, it shall be a defence for a person to prove (s. 24 (1))—

   (a) that the commission of the offence was due to a mistake or to reliance on information supplied to the defendant or to the act or default of another person, an accident or some other cause beyond his control; and

   (b) that he took all reasonable precautions and exercised all due diligence to avoid the commission of such an offence by himself or any person under his control.

Both the requirements under (a) and (b) have to be proved if the defence is to succeed.

The defendants sold a car with an odometer reading of 14,000 miles. They made enquiries about the car's history from its previous owner and learnt nothing suggesting that the odometer reading was false. *Held*, the defendants had no defence under section 24 because they had, in failing to display a disclaimer, failed to take all reasonable precautions to avoid the commission of the offence: *Simmons* v. *Potter* [1975] R.T.R. 347.

If a person intends to rely on the defence that the commission of the offence was due to the act or default of another person, he must notify the prosecutor of his intention seven clear days before the hearing (s. 24 (2)), thus enabling him to prosecute the other person (s. 23); the court has power to dispense with that time limit. The shop manager of a company is "another person" within the meaning of section 24 (1) and the company can rely on the defence that the contravention was due to his act or default (*Tesco Supermarkets Ltd.* v. *Nattrass*, below).

At one of the defendants' supermarkets a large advertisement stated that Radiant washing powder was 2*s*. 11*d*. a packet. In fact some packets marked 3*s*. 11*d*. were available on the shelves. A customer took one of these and was charged 3*s*. 11*d*. The defendants pleaded that this was due to the default of the store manager in failing to carry out the system laid down by the defendants for the operation of the store. *Held*, the defendants had a good defence since the store manager was "another person" and the defendants had taken all reasonable precautions under section 24 (*b*) by devising a proper system for the store and doing all they could to see that it was implemented: *Tesco Supermarkets Ltd.* v. *Nattrass* [1972] A.C. 153.

Another defence admitted by the Act is (s. 24 (3))—
> for the person charged to prove that he did not know, and could not with reasonable diligence have ascertained, that the goods did not conform to the description or that the description had been applied to the goods.

The Trade Descriptions Act 1972 makes it an offence for someone in the course of a business to supply imported goods which have a clearly visible name or mark which is (or is likely to be taken as) a United Kingdom name or mark, unless the goods bear a conspicuous indication of the country where they were in fact made.

The Unsolicited Goods and Services Act 1971

The main provision of this Act is that in certain circumstances a person who has received unsolicited goods other than goods reasonable to be used in his trade or business may treat them as an unconditional gift. He may do so if either the sender fails to collect the goods within six months or if the sender fails to collect the goods within 30 days after the recipient has served on the sender a written statement that the goods were unsolicited (s. 1).

The Act also contains provisions requiring the written form for orders relating to entries in trade or business directories (s. 3) and making it an offence to send out unsolicited books describing or illustrating human sexual techniques (s. 4).

The Fair Trading Act 1973

This Act established the office of Director General of Fair Trading. Apart from its provisions relating to monopolies, mergers and restrictive practices (see pp. 314, 319 *post*), it confers certain consumer protection functions upon the Director-General. In conjunction with the Consumer Protection Advisory Committee which also was established by the Act, he can recommend that the Secretary of State for Prices and Consumer Protection makes orders for the control or prevention of consumer trade practices which adversely affect the economic interests of consumers (s. 17). The orders so far made by the Secretary of State under this procedure (under s. 22) include one prohibiting the display of an exemption clause which is void by virtue of the Sale of Goods Act 1893, as amended by the Supply of Goods (Implied Terms) Act 1973 (see p. 241, *ante*). Orders made under the Fair Trading Act do not affect civil rights (s. 26). Infringement is a criminal offence. Defences are available similar to those in s. 24 of the Trade Descriptions Act 1968 (see p. 273, *ante*).

The Director-General has powers in relation to anyone who appears to be persisting in breaking the law (civil or criminal) in a way detrimental to the interests of consumers in respect of health, safety or other matters. He can ask for an assurance from the offender as to future conduct (s. 34 (1)). If that fails to achieve the desired result, he can take proceedings against him in the Restrictive Practices Court (s. 35).

(For the functions of the Director General under the Consumer Credit Act 1974 see p. 297, *post*).

SELECT BIBLIOGRAPHY
Books

P. S. Atiyah, *The Sale of Goods* (4th ed., 1971).
M. Mark, *Chalmers' Sale of Goods Act 1893*, (17th ed., 1975).
C. M. Schmitthoff, *The Sale of Goods* (2nd ed., 1966).
C. M. Schmitthoff, *The Export Trade* (6th ed., 1975).

Articles

Atiyah, P. S., "Transfer of Title by Non-owners" [1965] J.B.L. 130–141.
Battersby, G. and Preston, A. D., "The Concepts of 'Property,' 'Title' and 'Owner' used in the Sale of Goods Act 1893" (1972) 35 M.L.R. 268.
Carr, C., "Supply of Goods (Implied Terms) Act 1973" (1973) M.L.R. 519–528.
Davies, C., "Merchantability and Fitness for Purpose: Implied Conditions of the Sale of Goods Act 1893" (1969) 85 L.Q.R. 74–91.
Feltham, J. D., "Appropriation to a.C.I.F. Contract of Goods Lost or Damaged at Sea" [1975] J.B.L. 273–280.
Feltham, J. D., "The Sale by Description of Specific Goods" [1969] J.B.L. 16–25.

Greig, D. W., "Misrepresentations and Sales of Goods" (1971) 87 L.Q.R. 179–213.

Hall, C., "International Sales and the Supply of Goods (Implied Terms) Act 1973" (1973) 22 I.C.L.Q. 740–748.

Henderson, McN., "Of Merchantable Quality" (1970) 86 L.Q.R. 169–171.

Koh, K. L., "Sale by Description" [1968] C.L.J. 11–14.

Lagergreen, G., "The Uniform Law on the Formation of Contracts for the International Sale of Goods" [1966] J.B.L. 22–30.

Mann, F. A., "Amended Sale of Goods Act 1893 and the Conflict of Laws" (1974) 90 L.Q.R. 42–54.

Patient, I., "More Lore on Section 14" (1970) M.L.R. 565–570.

Sassoon, D. M., "The Origin of F.o.b. and C.i.f. Terms and the Factors Influencing Their Choice" [1967] J.B.L. 32–37.

Szakats, A., "Sale of Goods Act 1893 and the Uniform Law on the International Sale of Goods: Some Points of Contrast and Contract" [1968] J.B.L. 235–242.

Thornely, J. W. A., "Effects of Resale by Unpaid Sellers of Goods" [1967] C.L.J. 168–170.

Treitel, G. H., "Specific Performance in the Sale of Goods" [1966] J.B.L. 211–231.

Waddams, S. M., "The Strict Liability of Suppliers of Goods" (1974) 37 M.L.R. 154–174.

Whincup, M., "Reasonable Fitness of Cars" (1975) 38 M.L.R. 660.

Yates, David, "The Supply of Goods (Implied Terms) Act 1973" [1973] J.B.L. 135.

CHAPTER 16

HIRE-PURCHASE

THE HIRE-PURCHASE TRANSACTION

Definition of the hire-purchase contract

A HIRE-PURCHASE contract is a contract by which goods are
delivered to a person who agrees to make periodical payments by
way of hire, with an option of buying the goods after the stated
hire instalments have been paid. The goods may be returned to the
owner at any time before the option is exercised, on payment of the
sum stated in the contract. Until the option is exercised there is no
agreement to buy the goods.

The hire-purchase contract thus consists of three parts: a **contract
of bailment** under which the hirer obtains possession of the goods,
which remain in the ownership of the owner, and is thus enabled to
use them before they are fully paid; an **option** in favour of the hirer
entitling him, after payment of the periodical instalments and usually
for a nominal consideration, to purchase the goods; and, if the hirer
exercises the option, a **contract of sale** making him the owner of the
goods already in his possession.

Hire-purchase and other instalment sales

The hire-purchase transaction, as described above, is a complex
form of instalment sale which is adopted by commercial practice in
order to protect the owner's title to the goods if the instalment
buyer, in breach of his undertaking, sells them to a third party
acquiring them in good faith before the payment of all instalments.
A reservation of property would not protect the seller in this case
because the Factors Act 1889, s. 9, and the Sale of Goods Act 1893,
s. 25 (2) provide that, if the buyer is in possession of the goods with
the consent of the seller and then resells them to a good faith purchaser who has no notice of the original seller's right, the title of the
good faith purchaser prevails over that of the original seller. If, on
the other hand, the instalment purchaser has possession under a
contract of bailment (hire) and is merely given the option of purchasing the goods or returning them, the provisions of the Factors Act
and of the Sale of Goods Act do not apply and the original owner

277

can recover them from a good faith purchaser to whom the hire-purchaser has sold them before the payment of the last instalment (*Helby* v. *Matthews*, below).

The owner of a piano agreed to let it on hire, the hirer to pay a rent in monthly instalments, on the terms that the hirer might terminate the hiring by returning the piano to the owner but remaining liable for all arrears of hire; also that the piano should remain the property of the owner but if the hirer had punctually paid all monthly instalments, the piano should become his property. The hirer, after having paid a few instalments, pledged the piano to a pawnbroker. *Held*, the hirer was under no legal obligation to buy but had an option either to return the piano or to become its owner by payment in full; consequently, he had not "agreed to buy" it within the meaning of the Factors Act 1889, s. 9, and the owner could recover it from the pawnbroker: *Helby* v. *Matthews* [1895] A.C. 471.

It is important to distinguish between three different types of instalment agreement. First, a **hire-purchase agreement** does not involve the customer in a legal obligation to buy and therefore does not attract the application of the Factors Act 1889, s. 9, or the Sale of Goods Act 1893, s. 25 (2). Secondly, a **credit sale agreement** does involve the customer in a legal obligation to buy and contains no express provision as to the transfer of property, with the result that property transfers to the buyer at the time the contract is made (Sale of Goods Act, s. 18, rule 1; see p. 243, *ante*). Thus, anyone purchasing from the buyer will obtain good title. Third, a **conditional sale agreement** involves the buyer in a legal obligation to buy but contains an express provision preventing the property from passing to the buyer until he has paid his instalments. At common law, if before completing his instalments under a conditional sale agreement the buyer sold the goods to a good faith purchaser, the latter obtained a good title by virtue of the Factors Act 1889, s. 9, and the Sale of Goods Act 1893, s. 25 (2). However, these sections do no longer apply where the conditional sale agreement is a consumer credit agreement within the meaning of the Consumer Credit Act 1974 (see that Act, Sched. 4; p. 297, *post*). Thus in this case, as in the case of a hire-purchase agreement, the original owner can recover the goods from the good faith purchaser.

In view of the variety of hire-purchase terms which can be arranged, an agreement that "the balance of purchase price can be had over a period of two years" is too vague (*Scammell* v. *Ouston* [1941] A.C. 251, see p. 21, *ante*); such an arrangement does not even indicate whether hire-purchase terms are "to be granted by the [owners] or on the other hand by some finance company acting in collaboration with the [owners]" (*per* Viscount Maugham, *ibid.*, on p. 256).

The social implications of instalment sales have made it necessary for the legislator to intervene, with a view to protecting persons acquiring goods by way of instalment sales because these persons are often members of the economically weaker strata of society. The main enactment is the Consumer Credit Act 1974 (see p. 296, *post*).

A different object is pursued where in time of economic need the Government fixes a minimum deposit and other details of the instalment transaction. The aim here is to operate credit restrictions in the interest of the national economy. Contravention of these regulations is punishable but a valid title could pass under a contract contravening them. (*Belvoir Finance Co. Ltd.* v. *Stapleton* [1971] 1 Q.B. 210; see p. 115, *ante*).

The finance company

In many instances the owner of the goods does not dispose of the resources necessary to finance his hire-purchase transactions. This is particularly true in the car trade. In these cases the services of a finance company are used which will finance the transaction for a consideration (the finance charges) that is included in the total hire-purchase price and thus has to be borne by the hire-purchaser.

If the services of a finance company are used, the hire-purchase transaction takes on the following triangular form—

1. The original owner of the goods, *e.g.* the car dealer, sells the goods to the finance company under an outright **contract of sale.** Property is transferred at once to the finance company which becomes the owner of the goods. The finance company pays the cash price of the goods to the original owner. If the goods are a car and the dealer accepts the buyer's car in part exchange, he will give the finance company credit for the car taken in part exchange.

2. The finance company, as owner of the goods, then enters into a **hire-purchase contract** with the person intent to purchase the goods. The purchaser pays the instalments which include the finance charges to the finance company directly and if, after payment of the last instalment, he exercises his option to acquire the goods, title to them will pass from the finance company to the purchaser.

3. No contract of sale or of hire-purchase exists between the
original owner (car dealer) and the purchaser. But their
relationship might not be entirely devoid of legal effect. It is
possible that a **collateral contract of warranty** may exist by
virtue of which the original owner has undertaken a warranty
relating to the goods to the hire-purchaser in consideration
of the latter entering into the hire-purchase contract with the
finance company (see p.282, *post*).

The finance company often enters into a **recourse agreement** with
the dealer. By such an agreement the dealer agrees to be liable to the
finance company if the purchaser defaults on his obligations. The
ordinary recourse agreement is in the form of an indemnity (*Goulston
Discount Co. Ltd.* v. *Clark* [1967] 2 Q.B. 493, see p. 293, *post*), but it
may also take the form of a guarantee. An arrangement similar in
purpose but different in legal effect is a **re-purchase agreement**
whereby the dealer offers to re-purchase the goods from the finance
company if the purchaser defaults. The re-purchase agreement is a
unilateral contract subject to certain conditions; two conditions
precedent are that the hire-purchase contract is terminated before all
the instalments are paid and that the finance company exercises its
option to claim the re-purchase within a reasonable time.

Eagle, dealers in aircraft, intended to sell a Vickers Viscount to Orion,
one of their customers, on hire-purchase terms. Eagle sold the aircraft
outright to United Dominions Trust, a finance company, which granted
Orion hire-purchase terms. Eagle also entered into a re-purchase agreement with the finance company whereby they offered to re-purchase the
aircraft if the hire-purchase agreement should be terminated before the
total hire-purchase price was paid. Orion defaulted on the instalments
and the finance company terminated the hire-purchase agreement. The
finance company did not call on Eagle to re-purchase the aircraft until
nearly five months after termination of the hire-purchase agreement.
Held, Eagle's offer to re-purchase was in the nature of a unilateral contract
and was subject to the implied condition precedent that the call to re-
purchase should be made within a reasonable time from the termination
of the hire-purchase contract. The call of the finance company was too
late and consequently the obligation of Eagle to re-purchase the aircraft
never arose: *United Dominions Trust (Commercial) Ltd.* v. *Eagle Aircraft
Services Ltd.* [1968] 1 W.L.R. 74.

Under a hire-purchase agreement in which the hirer has only an
option to purchase, a guarantor is not entitled, on paying the
amount he has guaranteed, to have possession of the article hired
(*Chatterton* v. *Maclean* [1951] 1 All E.R. 761).

Refinancing arrangements

An extension of the concept of hire-purchase agreement is the refinancing arrangement. The essence of such an arrangement is that the owner of goods, such as a car, sells them to a dealer who resells them under an outright contract of sale to a finance company which grants the original owner hire-purchase terms.

The validity of this type of transaction is not free from doubt. If the goods never leave the possession of the original owner and only property is transferred to the finance company, the economic effect of the transaction is that the original owner has obtained a loan on the security of goods retained in his possession. This transaction may well infringe the Bills of Sales Acts 1878 and 1882 (see pp. 382–383 *post*) and be void as an unregistered bill of sale.

The courts draw here the following distinction.

1. If all the parties to the transaction, including the finance company, are aware that the real object of the transaction is to provide a loan on the security of goods remaining in the possession of the borrower, the hire-purchase transaction is a sham intended to disguise the true intention of the parties and the transaction is void as an unregistered bill of sale (*Polsky* v. *S. and A. Services* [1951] 1 All E.R. 185, 1062). "For acts or documents to be a 'sham,' with whatever legal consequences follow from this, all the parties thereto must have a common intention that the acts or documents are not to create the legal rights and obligations which they give the appearance of creating" (*per* Diplock L.J. in *Snook* v. *London and West Riding Investments Ltd.* below).

2. If the parties intend the transaction to be a genuine hire-purchase transaction and, in particular, the finance company accepts the proposed hire-purchase transaction unaware of any irregularity, the refinancing agreement is not a sham but is valid (*Stoneleigh Finance Ltd.* v. *Phillip* [1965] 2 Q.B. 537). The original owner is estopped from denying that the dealer had authority to transfer the title in the goods to the finance company (*Eastern Distributors Ltd.* v. *Goldring* [1957] 2 Q.B. 600).

Snook bought a new MG car from a dealer for £935. He paid £735 by way of deposit. The balance of £200 was financed by hire-purchase with Totley Investments Ltd. Later Snook went to another company, Auto Finance, which contracted with Totley to pay off the remaining instalments of £160, and arranged new hire-purchase terms with the defendants who thought that the transaction was a genuine hire-purchase transaction relating to a car belonging to Auto Finance. Auto Finance stated in the proposal form that the cash price which Snook was to pay was £800 and that they had received £500 by way of deposit but these figures were fictitious. They received £300 from the defendants of which they paid £160 to Totley, £125 to Snook, and kept £15. Totley declared themselves to be satisfied and purported to transfer the property in the car to Auto Finance which purported to transfer it to the defendants. The defendants entered into a hire-purchase contract with Snook who began to pay instalments to them. All the time the car remained in the possession of Snook. Snook defaulted on the instalments and Auto Finance seized the car. Snook then offered the instalments to Auto Finance but they refused to accept them and resold the car for £575. They paid the defendants £280 (which satisfied them) and kept the balance of £295 as their profit. Snook sued for damages. *Held* (by the Court of Appeal, Lord Denning M.R. dissenting), (1) the plaintiff was estopped from denying that the defendants had acquired the property in the car; (2) since the defendants were unaware of any irregularity in the transaction, it was not a sham and the hire-purchase contract between the defendants and the plaintiff was valid. The action was dismissed: *Snook* v. *London and West Riding Investments Ltd.* [1967] 2 Q.B. 786.

The liability of the dealer

The normal hire-purchase transaction involves, as has been explained earlier, three parties, the seller, the finance company and the hire-purchaser. In this type of transaction, the hire-purchase contract is concluded between the finance company and the hire-purchaser, and no contract of sale or of hire-purchase exists between the original seller and the hire-purchaser. It follows that if the goods are not fit for the particular purpose for which they are required the hire-purchaser has no claim against the original seller under section 14 (1) of the Sale of Goods Act 1893, his only claims being under the hire-purchase agreement against the finance company (*Drury* v. *Victor Buckland Ltd.* [1941] 1 All E.R. 269).

But if the original seller, *e.g.* the car dealer, gives the hire-purchaser an express warranty, *e.g.* that a second-hand car is in good working order, a collateral contract of warranty is concluded between the original seller and the hire-purchaser. The consideration supporting the warranty is the willingness of the hire-purchaser to conclude the hire-purchase contract with the finance company and to accept liability under its terms. If the original seller's warranty is broken, the hire-purchaser can sue the seller for breach of the contract of warranty (*Brown* v. *Sheen and Richmond Car Sales Ltd.* [1950] 1 All E.R. 1102, applied in *Shanklin Pier Ltd.* v. *Detel Products*

Ltd. [1951] 2 K.B. 854, and *Andrews* v. *Hopkinson* [1957] 1 Q.B. 229, see p. 27, *ante*).

Furthermore, the correct measure of damages as between the hire-purchaser and the dealer whose warranty has induced him to enter into the agreement is the whole damage suffered by the hirer, including his liability under the hire-purchase contract, and is not limited to the difference in value between the goods as warranted and as in·fact they are (*Yeoman Credit Ltd.* v. *Odgers* [1962] 1 W.L.R. 215).

The liability of the finance company

Under a hire-purchase agreement the creditor can be made liable to the debtor (the customer as hire-purchaser) under the terms of the Supply of Goods (Implied Terms) Act 1973. In the triangular arrangement already described the finance company is the creditor, but where the retailer finances his own hire-purchase agreements the retailer will be the creditor. The effect of the 1973 Act is to extend to the customer acquiring goods on hire-purchase the same protection as it provides for a customer buying for cash. Thus in a hire-purchase contract there are implied terms as to title (s. 8), description (s. 9), merchantable quality (s. 10 (2)), fitness for purpose (s. 10 (3)) and sample (s. 11). These terms are virtually identical to those implied in a contract of sale of goods (see p. 234, *ante*). The condition that the goods be reasonably fit for a particular purpose is implied only if that particular purpose for which the goods are required is made known before the contract is made. It is sufficient if the customer makes known to the dealer the purpose for which the goods are required (s. 10 (3)).

A clause in a hire-purchase agreement which purports to exclude or restrict the creditor's liability under these implied terms is subject to exactly the same rules as it would be in a contract of sale (s. 12 and see p. 241, *ante*).

The Consumer Credit Act 1974

This Act replaces the Hire-Purchase Act 1965. It is wider in scope and applies to many other agreements besides hire-purchase contracts. In this chapter reference will be made to sections of the Act which are particularly applicable to hire-purchase contracts. However, these contracts are subject to the provisions of the Act as a whole and those are set out in the next chapter. The Act is the main enactment governing hire-purchase, although there are certain others which relate to particular aspects of the subject, namely the Hire-Purchase Act 1964, Pt. III (p. 294, *post*), the Bills of Sales Act 1878 and 1882 (p. 382, *ante*) and the Supply of Goods (Implied Terms) Act 1973 (see p. 234, *ante*).

The main definition in the Consumer Credit Act is that of a regulated consumer credit agreement. A hire-purchase agreement is such a regulated agreement if it fulfils two conditions: (i) the hirer (termed by the Act, debtor) is not a company or body corporate, and (ii) the amount of the credit does not exceed £5,000 (ss. 8 and 9). The credit consists of the capital amount borrowed, not the deposit and not the interest or finance charges. Thus if an individual (or a partnership) enters a hire-purchase agreement to acquire a car having a cash price of £11,000, the agreement could be a regulated one, *e.g.* if there was an initial payment of £6,000 plus 22 instalment payments of £250 monthly, £500 amounting to the interest and finance charges. The amount of the credit here is exactly £5,000, *i.e.* the difference between the initial payment of £6,000 and the amount needed to acquire the car for cash (£11,000). The fact that the subsequent instalments will total £5,500 is irrelevant (see also the example on p. 297, *post*). In this chapter references to regulated agreements are references to agreements which are regulated consumer credit agreements and, unless otherwise indicated, references to sections are references to sections of the Consumer Credit Act 1974. This is despite the fact that, at the time of writing, this Act is not yet fully in force and, until it is, the Hire-Purchase Act 1965 will remain in force. However, the 1974 Act is expected soon to be fully implemented and this chapter and the following one are written as if it had been.

The Act introduces new terminology. In the past it has been customary to refer to the customer, the hire-purchaser, as the "hirer" and to the other party to the hire-purchase agreement (often a finance company) as the "owner." They are termed by the Act "debtor" and "creditor" respectively and that practice will be followed in the rest of this chapter.

The protection provided by the Act can not be contracted out of (s. 173).

Is the dealer an agent of the finance company?

Normally the dealer, when negotiating with the customer or receiving the deposit from him, does so in his own right. Thus at common law he is generally not regarded as agent of the creditor, the finance company. "There is no rule of law that in a hire-purchase transaction the dealer never is, or always is, acting as agent for the finance company or as agent of the customer. In a typical hire-purchase transaction the dealer is a party in his own right, selling his car to the finance company on his own behalf and not as general agent for either of the other two parties" (*per* Pearson L.J. in *Mercantile Credit Co. Ltd.* v. *Hamblin* [1965] 2 Q.B. 242, 269).

Although the dealer is not the agent of the customer, there is a rule of law that normally someone who signs a document is bound by that document even though he may be mistaken about its contents (*Saunders* v. *Anglia Building Society* [1971] A.C. 1004, see p. 67, *ante*). It has been held that this applies to an intending hire-purchaser who signs a hire-purchase proposal form in blank and leaves the dealer to fill in the details. If, after the dealer has fraudulently filled in inflated figures (to which the customer never agreed) in respect of the total price and the size of instalments, the finance company accepts that proposal, the customer is bound by that document and those figures (*United Dominions Trust Ltd.* v. *Western* [1976] Q.B. 513).

That is the position at common law. For agreements regulated by the Consumer Credit Act, it is very different. The dealer is regarded as agent of the finance company during the negotiations between the dealer and customer (s. 56). Those negotiations include representations made by the dealer to the customer and "any other dealings between them." Thus where the dealer fills in figures different from those agreed to by the customer, the latter is not bound by the document. Furthermore, if on signing the form the customer had paid a deposit to the dealer, he is entitled to recover the amount of that deposit from the finance company because in receiving it the dealer was doing so as agent of the finance company. That is so irrespective of whether the dealer had passed the deposit on to the finance company or not. The fact that representations made by the dealer are made by him also as agent for the finance company means that in addition to any liability under the Supply of Goods (Implied Terms) Act 1973, the finance company could be liable to the customer for misrepresentation if the goods do not live up to the statements made by the dealer about them (as to liability for misrepresentation see p. 81, *ante*). In the case of a regulated agreement the dealer is also agent of the finance company for the purpose of receiving from the debtor a notice withdrawing an offer to enter the agreement (s. 57); notice of cancellation of the agreement (s. 69); or notice rescinding the agreement (s. 102).

Form and contents of agreement

A regulated agreement must comply with the Act's requirements as to its legibility, information to be given in it, the state of the agreement when signed, and the giving of copies to the debtor. If these requirements are not complied with, the creditor may be unable to enforce the agreement against the debtor (see generally p. 303, *post*).

Right of cancellation

Certain regulated agreements are cancellable (ss. 67–73). These rights of cancellation last for only a few days after the agreement has been made and the intention behind them is to provide the victim of doorstep salesmanship with a short period for second thoughts during which he is still free to escape from the agreement at no cost to himself. These rights extend also to regulated consumer credit agreements other than hire-purchase agreements and will be dealt with in the next chapter (see p. 304, *post*).

Termination of agreement

A hire-purchase agreement can either be terminated in accordance with the terms of the agreement or it may be broken. It is terminated in accordance with its terms if the hire-purchaser exercises his option (essential in the hire-purchase transaction of the normal type) to return the goods to the owner. It is broken if the hire-purchaser defaults on his instalments; normally the agreement provides that in this case the owner may terminate the agreement by notice to the hirer. Sometimes the agreement provides that the creditor has the right to terminate it on some event other than a breach of it by the debtor (*e.g.* on the debtor's death or bankruptcy or on his being sent to prison).

In the case of a regulated agreement there are restrictions on the creditor's right of termination. If he wishes to terminate the agreement for some reason other than a breach of it by the debtor, he can not do so without first serving on the debtor a written notice giving at least seven days warning (ss. 76 and 98; see p. 309, *post*). Where the debtor's death is the reason for the creditor wishing to terminate a regulated agreement, he probably will be unable to do so at all (s. 86; see p. 310, *post*). Where a breach of the agreement by the debtor is the reason for the creditor wishing to terminate a regulated agreement, he can not do so without first serving a **default notice** giving the debtor at least seven days warning and allowing the debtor in that time to put right his default (s. 87; see p. 309, *post*).

For the debtor who is in arrears (by far the most common breach) and whose agreement is a regulated one, there are three ways in which he can escape the undesirable consequences of termination. First, he can bring his payments up to date by paying off his arrears before the expiry date of the default notice. Secondly, after receiving the default notice, he can apply to the court for a time order allowing him extra time to pay (s. ·129 and see p. 309, *post*). Thirdly, he may be able to take advantage of the protected goods provisions (see p. 291, *post*) thereby forcing the creditor to sue him in order to recover possession of the goods (or a money sum) and, when sued, he can ask the court to make a time order (s. 129; see p. 309, *post*). If the court decides to make a time order, it can thereby alter the whole instalment pattern and extend the repayment period (s. 130). If the debtor is unable to avoid the consequences of termination, the creditor in addition to recovering possession of the goods will usually claim a minimum payment or damages.

The minimum payment clause

It is customary for a hire-purchase agreement to contain a minimum payment clause whereby the purchaser undertakes to pay the owner a calculable amount in the event of the agreement being terminated or broken. The economic justification of the minimum payment clause is that, if the owner is repossessed of the goods, they have often depreciated in value, particularly if he can resell them only as used and no longer as new goods.

Sometimes, however, the sum fixed by the minimum payment clause is excessive. Here the question arises, whether the contractual rules relating to penalties apply (see p. 143, *ante*).

1. If the hire-purchase agreement is terminated by *breach* on the part of the debtor, it is clear that the distinction between penalties and liquidated damages applies. It may be recalled that if the fixed amount is a genuine pre-estimate of the damages likely to be suffered, it is treated as liquidated damages and can be recovered irrespective of the actual amount of the damages suffered; but if it is a penalty, it is disregarded and only the actual amount of damages can be recovered (see p. 143, *ante*).

It follows that, if the agreement is terminated by breach, a stipulated minimum payment which is inserted *in terrorem* of the debtor, is a penalty and is not recoverable.

Lamdon Trust Ltd. v. *Hurrell* [1955] 1 W.L.R. 391, see p. 144, *ante.*

Bridge acquired a Bedford Dormobile from the finance company on hire-purchase terms. The total hire-purchase price was £482. The deposit was £105 which was accounted for by a car given in part exchange to the value of £95 and a cash payment of £10. The monthly instalments were £10 each. The agreement provided in clause 6 that the debtor might terminate the hiring at any time by giving the creditor written notice of termination, and thereupon the provisions of clause 9 should apply. Clause 9 was the minimum payment clause according to which in case of termination the debtor had to pay all arrears of hire rent and as "agreed compensation for depreciation" two-thirds of the hire-purchase price. After eight weeks Bridge wrote to the finance company apologising that "owing to unforeseen personal circumstances" he would not be able to pay further instalments and returned the Dormobile. The finance company sued him for £206 which were two-thirds of the purchase price, less the payments received from Bridge. *Held*, (1) the letter by which Bridge informed the finance company of his unwillingness to pay further instalments was not an exercise of his option under clause 6 but was a notification of his intention to break the agreement; (2) since the agreement was terminated by breach, the rules relating to penalties applied; (3) the minimum payment clause provided a penalty which was not enforceable; (4) the case had to be remitted to the county court to determine the amount of actual damages suffered by the finance company: *Bridge* v. *Campbell Discount Co. Ltd.* [1962] A.C. 600.

2. If the hire-purchase agreement is terminated, not by breach, but by exercise of the debtor's option *in accordance with the terms of the contract*, the position is less clear. Older authorities have held that the rules relating to penalties do not apply in this case because their application presupposes a breach of contract (*Associated Distributors Ltd.* v. *Hall* [1938] 2 K.B. 83). The result would be that the debtor is bound by the minimum payment clause even though the stipulated sum is excessive.

The problem was discussed, *obiter*, in *Bridge's* case (above) in the House of Lords. Viscount Simonds and Lord Morton of Henryton thought that the older cases were decided correctly but Lord Denning and Lord Devlin expressed the view that the rules relating to penalties likewise applied to the termination of the contract in accordance with its terms. While the question thus remains open, there is, it is thought, much strength in Lord Denning's observation that, if the present distinction between breach and termination in accordance with the terms of the contract is maintained, the paradox result is that equity "will grant relief to a man who breaks his contract but penalises the man who keeps it." It is thought that the rules relating to penalties should apply, irrespective of the manner in which the contract is terminated.

In any event, a debtor is not to be taken to exercise his option to terminate the agreement unless he does so consciously knowing of its consequences (*United Dominions Trust (Commercial) Ltd.* v. *Ennis* [1968] 1 Q.B. 54).

A minimum payment clause which escapes the doctrine of penalties, may nevertheless be caught by the provisions of the Consumer Credit Act relating to extortionate credit agreements. These apply not only to regulated agreements but also to credit agreements involving credit in excess of £5,000, provided the debtor is not a body corporate (see p. 310, *post*). Furthermore, in the case of a regulated agreement the Act stipulates the amount payable when the debtor exercises an option to terminate (see p. 290, *post*).

The owner's claim for damages

If the hire-purchase agreement is terminated by a breach on the part of the debtor or by notice of the creditor, after the debtor has committed a breach, and the creditor cannot rely on the minimum payment clause because it stipulates a penalty or he does not wish to rely on it, the question arises what the measure of damages is to which the creditor is entitled. Here the following distinction is made.

1. If the breach of contract by the debtor amounts to a *repudiation* of the contract which has been accepted by the creditor, the measure of damages is the loss which the creditor has suffered owing to the debtor's failure to carry out the contract; this loss is due to the debtor's repudiation and not to the retaking of the goods by the creditor (*Yeoman Credit Ltd.* v. *Waragowski* [1961] 1 W.L.R. 1124; *Overstone Ltd.* v. *Shipway* [1962] 1 W.L.R. 117).

Such a repudiation takes place, *e.g.* where the debtor fails to pay several instalments and it is clear that he does not intend to be bound by the contract any longer, or where he writes to the creditor that he cannot or will not make any further payments. *Bridge* v. *Campbell Discount Co. Ltd.* (see p. 288, *ante*) was a case of repudiation.

2. Different from repudiation is the case in which the debtor is

slightly in arrear with the instalments but has every intention of up-
holding the contract and carrying out his obligations. If the creditor
terminates the agreement in this situation, as he may well be entitled
to under its terms, the measure of damages is only the amount of
instalments which the debtor has not paid to the date of termination.
In this case the principle applies that "when an agreement of hiring
is terminated by virtue of a power contained in it, and the owner
retakes the vehicle, he can recover damages for any breach up to the
date of termination but not for any breach thereafter, for the simple
reason that there are no breaches thereafter" (*per* Lord Denning
M.R. in *Financings Ltd.* v. *Baldock*, below).

Baldock agreed to hire a Bedford truck from the plaintiff finance
company. The debtor failed to pay the first two instalments amounting
together to £56. The finance company terminated the agreement and
repossessed the truck. The debtor told them that he would raise the money
in the next three days but he could not do so and the finance company sold
the truck. They sued Baldock for £538, claiming this sum as the loss they
had suffered owing to the non-execution of the contract. *Held*, in the
present case the contract was not terminated by repudiation on the part
of the debtor but by notice by the creditor, following the debtor's failure
to pay the rentals, a failure which by itself did not amount to repudiation.
Consequently, the finance company was only entitled to recover £56:
Financings Ltd. v. *Baldock* [1963] 2 Q.B. 104.

Debtor's statutory right of termination

The debtor under a regulated agreement has a statutory right to
terminate the agreement at any time by giving notice to the creditor
(s. 99) (the references on this and the following pages are to the Consumer Credit Act 1974). In that case the debtor must, as well as
returning the goods, pay (s. 100)

  (i) all arrears of instalments due before termination, and
 (ii) damages for any loss caused by any failure of the debtor to
      take reasonable care of the goods, and
(iii) the smallest of the three following amounts:
      (a) the amount of the minimum payment stipulated in the
          agreement,
      (b) the amount necessary to bring his payments up to half
          the total hire-purchase price (the total hire-purchase
          price includes the deposit and all the instalments and
          the option money payable under the agreement),
      (c) the loss sustained by the creditor in consequence of the
          termination.

An alternative method of premature termination is open to the debtor under a regulated agreement who can afford to pay off all his instalments. He has the right to pay them off early and thereby become the owner of the goods that much earlier as well as earning a rebate of some of his interest charges (ss. 94 and 95; see p. 308, *post*).

Protected Goods

Goods let under a regulated hire-purchase agreement are protected goods if the debtor is in breach of the agreement and has paid or tendered at least one-third of the total hire-purchase price (s. 90). The creditor is not entitled otherwise than by court action to recover possession of protected goods from the debtor. If he does recover possession in contravention of that rule, the agreement is terminated and the debtor is released from all liability under it and can even recover all sums which he has already paid (s. 91). In two situations the creditor can recover possession of protected goods without court action and without contravening the rule. First, he can obtain possession of the goods with the debtor's consent (s. 173 (3), *Mercantile Credit Co. Ltd.* v. *Cross* [1965] 2 Q.B. 194). Secondly, if the debtor has permanently disposed of the goods to a third party or has abandoned them, the creditor will not be in contravention of the rule if he seizes possession of them. This is because the rule prevents him from obtaining possession only "from the debtor" (s. 90).

The debtor paid the deposit and a few instalments. After a crash in which the car was damaged, he left it at a garage but gave no instructions for repairs to be effected. He paid no more instalments and nine months later he had disappeared without trace, having on the last occasion he was contacted given a false telephone number. The creditor, a finance company, took the car from the garage where it had been left nine months earlier. *Held*, the debtor had abandoned the car and, although he had paid more than one-third of the total price, the finance company had not contravened the rule against taking possession from the debtor: *Bentinck Ltd.* v. *Cromwell Engineering Co.* [1971] 1 Q.B. 324.

The hire-purchaser of a car had paid more than one-third of the total price but then fell into arrears. The creditor, a finance company, took possession of the car without his consent. A few hours later, realising their mistake, they took the car back and left it outside the debtor's house. The creditor, treating the hire-purchase contract as being still in force, sued for the outstanding instalments and the return of the car. *Held*, that the hire-purchase agreement had been terminated by the creditor taking possession of the car without a court order and without the consent of the debtor and that the debtor was released from his liability; moreover, he was entitled to a return of the moneys paid by him under the agreement. Further on the facts of the case, the debtor was not liable to the creditor in detinue for not returning the car to them: *Capital Finance Co. Ltd.* v. *Bray* [1964] 1 W.L.R. 323.

The creditor is entitled to take court action to recover possession of protected goods, once the agreement has terminated. However, in that case the court may grant a time order allowing the debtor extra time to pay (see below).

The court's powers in relation to a regulated agreement

Any court action brought by the creditor should be brought in the county court and any guarantor should also be made a party to the proceedings (s. 141). The creditor's claim will usually be for possession of the goods together with a money claim for the minimum payment or damages. Broadly speaking, the court has three options as to the order it makes. It may decide to give the debtor extra time to pay and therefore grant him a **time order,** very possibly extending the repayment period (s. 129). It may decide not to give extra time and therefore make an **immediate return order** requiring the immediate return of the goods to the creditor (s. 133). In this case, the creditor may well ask for the minimum payment or damages as well as the return of the goods. The third possibility open to the court is in an appropriate case to make a **transfer order** (s. 133). A transfer order is possible if the goods are divisible and the debtor has paid enough of the total price to cover both the cost of a part of them and also at least one-quarter of the rest of the total price. In that case the court can make a transfer order which, (i) allows the debtor to keep as his own the part of the goods for which he has paid, and (ii) requires him to return the rest of the goods to the creditor.

Contracts of guarantee

Contracts of guarantee relating to hire-purchase, credit-sale or conditional sale agreements and any securities given by a guarantor are likewise enforceable only if copies of the main and the guarantee agreements are supplied to the guarantor in the prescribed manner (s. 22).

An ordinary recourse agreement between a finance company and a car dealer, by which the latter undertakes to indemnify the former if the hire-purchaser defaults on the hire-purchase contract, is an indemnity and not a guarantee; consequently the finance company can recover from the dealer under such an agreement the whole amount of damages suffered, and not only the equivalent of the instalments with which the hire-purchaser was in arrear before the termination of the hire-purchase contract (*Goulston Discount Co. Ltd.* v. *Clark*, below).

A customer, through the defendant car dealer, entered into a hire-purchase agreement with the plaintiff finance company in respect of a Jaguar car. The total hire-purchase price was £458. The plaintiffs paid the dealer £300 and the latter gave the customer credit for £100 for an old car taken in part exchange. The dealer then signed a recourse agreement in respect of the Jaguar by which he undertook to indemnify the plaintiffs against any loss which they might suffer if the customer did not pay the total hire-purchase price. The customer paid the first two or three instalments and then defaulted. The plaintiffs retook the Jaguar and resold it for £155. The claimed £157 from the dealer under the recourse agreement. If that agreement was a guarantee, they were entitled to claim from the customer only £74, *viz.* the instalments due prior to the termination of the hire-purchase agreement, by virtue of the rule in *Financings Ltd.* v. *Baldock* [1963] 2 Q.B. 104, and the dealer, who would only be liable for the amount recoverable from the customer as principal debtor, would only be liable in that amount. But if the recourse agreement was an indemnity, the dealer was liable for the whole of the £157. *Held*, the recourse agreement was an indemnity: *Goulston Discount Co. Ltd.* v. *Clark* [1967] 2 Q.B. 493.

Where the principal credit agreement (*i.e.* the hire-purchase agreement) is a regulated agreement, certain contracts of guarantee and indemnity are subject to provisions of the Consumer Credit Act. They are those contracts of guarantee or indemnity which are entered by the surety (*i.e.* the guarantor or indemnifier) at the request, express or implied, of the debtor. A recourse agreement would therefore not be affected since it is not entered at the request of the debtor, whereas a contract of guarantee or indemnity entered by the debtor's friend or relative would be. Those agreements that are affected are subject to the following rules—

(i) Unless the hire-purchase agreement is in the prescribed form and the contract of guarantee or indemnity is in the prescribed form and unless copies of both have been given to the surety, the contract of guarantee or indemnity can be enforced against the surety only if the court considers it fair and just that it should be (ss. 105 and 127—see p. 304, *post*).

(ii) The agreement can not be enforced against the surety to any extent greater than the hire-purchase agreement is enforceable against the debtor (s. 113—see p. 310, *post*).

Conditional sale and credit sale agreements

The provisions of the Consumer Credit Act 1974 apply to conditional sale agreements in exactly the same way as they apply to hire-purchase contracts. Thus, the debtor's statutory right of termination is the same in both cases, as are the protected goods provisions and court's power to grant time orders, return orders and transfer orders. Credit sale agreements are not treated in the same way. They are subject to most of the Act's provisions, including the formality and cancellation provisions but the debtor has no statutory right of termination and, since ownership is transferred to the debtor at the time the contract is made, the creditor has no right to recover possession of the goods if the debtor falls into arrears. It follows that the protected goods and return order and transfer order provisions have no application to agreements other than hire-purchase and conditional sale agreements. Also it is only with respect to hire-purchase and conditional sale agreements that the court, in making a time order, can allow extra time for the payments which have not yet fallen due (*e.g.* by extending the future instalments to later dates) (s. 130).

HIRE-PURCHASE ACT 1964

The provisions of this Act which are not repealed relate to the protection of a private purchaser of a motor vehicle which is subject to a hire-purchase or conditional sale agreement. These provisions apply even if the private purchaser is a company and even if the hire-purchase or conditional sale agreement involved credit in excess of the statutory limit (£5,000) for the application of the Consumer Credit Act.

Protection of private purchaser of motor vehicle

A private purchaser who can claim this protection is a purchaser who is not a car dealer or a car finance house (s. 29 (2) of the Act of 1964). A car dealer does not obtain the protection even if he is buying the vehicle for his own private purposes and not for his business purposes (*Stevenson* v. *Beverley Bentinck Ltd.* [1976] 1 W.L.R. 483). The protection is available where the debtor under a hire-purchase agreement or conditional sale agreement disposes of a motor vehicle, before the payment of the price and the transfer of property to him, to a private purchaser who acquires it in good faith and without notice of the hire-purchase or conditional sale agreement. In that case the disposition has effect as if the debtor had the title to the vehicle immediately before the disposition; in other words, the title of the purchaser is protected against a claim by the creditor (s. 27 (2) of the Act of 1964).

The provisions of the Act aimed at the protection of the private purchaser of a motor vehicle do not affect the civil or criminal liability of a debtor who sells the vehicle contrary to his contractual undertakings to the creditor (s. 27 (6) of the Act of 1964).

SELECT BIBLIOGRAPHY
Books

A. L. Diamond, *Introduction to Hire-Purchase Law* (2nd ed., 1971).

A. P. Dobson, *Sale of Goods and Consumer Credit* (1975), chaps. 15–22.

R. M. Goode, *Hire-Purchase Law and Practice* (2nd ed., 1970).

Articles

Fitzpatrick, P. G., "Hire-Purchase Agreements and The Bills of Sale Acts" [1969] J.B.L. 211–219.

Harding, R. W., "Hire-Purchase Act 1964" [1965] J.B.L. 15–21.

Hughes, A. D., "Hire-Purchase in Modern Britain" [1967] J.B.L. 307–317.

CHAPTER 17

CONSUMER CREDIT

THE Consumer Credit Act 1974 was passed in the wake of the Report in 1971 (Cmnd. 4569) of the Crowther Committee on Consumer Credit and it effects a wide-ranging reform of the law. Its scheme is to bring under one Act all forms of consumer credit. Thus, it repeals certain earlier Acts which dealt with particular forms of credit, the Pawnbrokers Acts 1872 and 1960, Moneylenders Acts 1900–1927, Hire-Purchase Act 1965 and Advertisements (Hire-Purchase) Act 1967. However, two earlier enactments remain—the Hire-Purchase Act 1964, Pt. III (see p. 294, *ante*) and the Bills of Sales Acts 1878 and 1882 (see p. 281, *ante*). Much of the new Act is modelled on the Hire-Purchase Act 1965. It does not so much alter the general structure of the statutory law relating to hire-purchase as improve it and extend it to all other forms of consumer credit. The transactions which are governed by it therefore include: loans by finance companies and banks, bank overdrafts, credit card agreements, *e.g.* Barclaycard and Access, which allow the holder to pay off the debt in instalments, credit sale agreements, conditional sale agreements, hire-purchase agreements, check trading agreements and certain rental agreements, *e.g.* of television sets.

The Act introduces a whole new range of terminology. In particular, the **creditor** is the person who provides the finance and who is to be repaid, *e.g.* the bank or finance company, and the **debtor** is the customer, the borrower, the person who is to do the repaying. Where the terms **owner** and **hirer** are used, reference is being made not to the parties to a hire-purchase agreement but only to the parties to certain rental agreements, termed by the Act consumer hire agreements (see p. 298, *post*).

A framework is provided by the Act, but many details are to be provided by regulations under the Act. Many of these have still to be made and therefore the Act is not yet fully in force. It is expected to be implemented fully fairly soon. Until it is, the Acts to be repealed (including the Hire-Purchase Act 1965) will remain in force. This chapter is written as if the 1974 Act were already fully in force and, unless otherwise indicated, references to the Act and to sections are references to the Consumer Credit Act 1974 and to sections of it.

Director-General of Fair Trading

The Director General is given additional functions (s. 1). These include administering the licensing system (see p. 301, *post*), superintending the working and enforcement of the Act and keeping under review developments in the field of consumer credit at home and abroad.

AGREEMENTS WITHIN THE ACT

Regulated agreements

Agreements regulated by the Act fall into two categories, **consumer credit agreements** and **consumer hire agreements**. Such agreements, provided they are not exempt agreements (s. 16), are **regulated agreements**. A consumer credit agreement is an agreement by which the creditor provides an individual (the debtor) with credit not exceeding £5,000 (s. 8). "Credit" includes a cash loan and "any other form of financial accommodation" (s. 9 (1)). An agreement where the debtor is a company or other body corporate is not a consumer credit agreement because such a body is not an individual. An unincorporated body, *e.g.* a partnership, is an individual (s. 189 (1)). Consumer credit agreements include all those types of agreements mentioned earlier in this chapter, except for rental agreements (which fall within the definition of consumer hire agreements). However, no agreement is a consumer credit agreement if the credit exceeds £5,000 and for this purpose a distinction has to be made between **fixed-sum credit** and **running-account credit** (s. 10). Fixed-sum credit is one where the actual amount of the credit is fixed from the start, *e.g.* a single loan of £100. It is still fixed-sum credit if it is to be received or repaid in instalments. Thus credit sale, conditional sale and hire-purchase agreements are all examples of fixed-sum credit agreements. A fixed-sum credit agreement is within the £5,000 limit if the credit does not exceed £5,000. The credit is the capital amount borrowed. It does not include anything else, such as the deposit or interest (or "finance") charges on the advance. The latter are part of the total charge for credit (s. 20) and are not part of the credit itself (s. 9 (4)). In the case of fixed-sum credit the relevant figure is the credit, not what it costs to have it.

Example: C agrees to let D (an individual) have possession of a car in return for periodical payments. The agreement provides for the property in the goods to pass to D on payment of a total of £7,500 and the exercise

by D of an option to purchase. The sum of £7,500 includes a down payment of £1,000 and includes also finance charges amounting to £1,500.
The price for which D could have bought the car for cash was £6,000.

This agreement is one which provides fixed-sum credit of exactly £5,000
(*i.e.* £7,500—(£1,500 + £1,000)). It is therefore a consumer credit agreement (Example 10, Schedule 2 to the Act).

Running-account credit is credit the amount of which is not fixed
by the agreement, though the agreement may (in fact it usually will)
fix a credit limit, *i.e.* a maximum to the amount to which the debtor's
debit balance is allowed to rise. An agreement by which a bank
authorises its customer to overdraw if he needs or wishes to do so, is
an example. Another is the credit card agreement which allows the
debtor to keep using his card to obtain credit provided his total
indebtedness under the agreement does not exceed his credit limit.
A running-account credit agreement is within the £5,000 limit, *i.e.* it
is a consumer credit agreement, if the debtor's credit limit does not
exceed £5,000 (s. 10 (3)). If there is a term of the agreement allowing
the credit limit to be exceeded merely temporarily, it is disregarded
and the agreement is still within the definition (s. 10 (2)). If there is
no credit limit or if the credit limit exceeds £5,000, the agreement is
still within the definition: (i) if there is a limit of £5,000 or less to the
amount of credit (ignoring finance charges) that can be drawn on
any one occasion; or (ii) if the finance charges become more onerous
on the debtor's indebtedness exceeding a figure of £5,000 or less; or
(iii) if it is probable that his indebtedness will not exceed £5,000
(s. 10 (3)).

A consumer hire agreement is one which provides for the hire of
goods, is capable of lasting more than three months and does not
require the hirer to make payments exceeding £5,000 (s. 15). An
agreement where the hirer is a body corporate is not within the
definition. Neither is any hire-purchase agreement because a hire-
purchase agreement falls within the definition of a consumer credit
agreement.

A consumer credit agreement or a consumer hire agreement which
is an exempt agreement is not regulated by the Act (s. 16). By way of
exception to that, the court has power to re-open extortionate credit
bargains if they are exempt agreements (s. 16 (7) and see p. 310, *post*).
Agreements where credit is secured on land, *i.e.* mortgage agreements, and granted by a local authority or building society, are
exempt (s. 16 (1)). The Secretary of State has made orders exempting

land mortgages granted by certain other bodies. These exemptions so far mentioned apply only to mortgage agreements which provide the finance for the buying of land or of dwellings on land already owned (s. 16 (2)). Also exempt are: certain low-cost consumer credit agreements where the rate of interest is below a certain level; certain consumer credit agreements where the number of repayments does not exceed four; consumer hire agreements for the hire of telephones and gas and electricity meters.

Sub-categories of consumer credit agreement

A regulated consumer credit agreement is either a restricted-use credit agreement or an unrestricted-use credit agreement (s. 11). It falls within the latter category if the credit is in fact provided in such a way as to leave the debtor free to use it as he chooses. Thus a bank loan will usually be an example of an unrestricted-use credit unless for example the loan agreement is for the loan to finance a particular transaction and the loan is provided in such a way that it could be used by the debtor only for that transaction. Hire-purchase, conditional sale and credit sale agreements are all restricted-use credit agreements.

A regulated consumer credit agreement is either a **debtor–creditor–supplier agreement** (s. 12) or a **debtor–creditor agreement** (s. 13). It will fall into the first category:

(i) if it is a restricted-use credit agreement where the creditor and supplier are in fact the same person, *e.g.* where the retailer enters as creditor into a hire-purchase agreement with the customer (the debtor); or

(ii) if it is a restricted-use credit agreement "made by the creditor under pre-existing arrangements, or in contemplation of future arrangements, between himself and the supplier," *e.g.* where a customer buys goods from a shop and, instead of paying cash, makes payment by using his Access credit card; or

(iii) if it is an unrestricted-use credit agreement made by the creditor under pre-existing arrangements between himself and the supplier in the knowledge that the credit is to be used to finance a transaction between the debtor and supplier, *e.g.* where the supplier sells the goods directly to the customer for cash but does so only after having put the customer in touch with a firm (the creditor) with which the supplier had a relationship and which agreed to lend the customer the money for this purpose.

Where part of an agreement falls into a category of agreement defined in the Act and part either does not do so or else falls within a different category of agreement mentioned in the Act, the whole agreement is a **multiple agreement,** the two parts of it being treated as separate agreements (s. 18).

Example: A issues to B (an individual) a credit card for use in obtaining goods or cash from suppliers or banks who have agreed to honour credit cards issued by A. The credit limit is £300.

This is a consumer credit agreement for running-account credit. So far as it related to goods it provides restricted-use credit and it is a debtor–creditor–supplier agreement. So far as it relates to cash it provides unrestricted-use credit and is a debtor–creditor agreement. It is therefore a multiple agreement (based on Example 16, Schedule 2 to the Act).

The reason for the distinction between debtor–creditor–supplier agreements and debtor–creditor agreements is that the former are agreements where there is some business connection between the creditor and the supplier. In that case the creditor as well as the supplier will often be answerable to the debtor for defects in the goods or services provided by the supplier (see p. 307, *post*).

Further definitions

A **small agreement** is a regulated agreement (other than a hire-purchase or conditional sale agreement) for the provision of credit not exceeding £50 (s. 17). The rules for determining whether an agreement is within this limit are the same as they are in relation to the £5,000 limit, *mutatis mutandis* (see p. 297, *ante*). A **non-commercial agreement** is a consumer credit or consumer hire agreement not made by the creditor or owner in the course of any business carried on by him (s. 189 (1)). Many small agreements and non-commercial agreements are not subject to certain provisions of the Act, in particular the formality and cancellation provisions (see p. 303, *post*).

LICENSING AND SEEKING BUSINESS

Licensing

Part III of the Act (ss. 21–42) establishes a comprehensive system of licensing for those who conduct business dealing with regulated agreements. There are two types of businesses which need to be licensed. They are, firstly, consumer credit businesses and consumer hire businesses and, secondly, ancillary businesses. Into the first category falls someone who carries on a business which provides under regulated agreements either credit or goods on hire. Thus, not only must finance companies be licensed but so also, *e.g.* must the ordinary retailer who enters into credit sale, conditional sale or hire-purchase agreements with some of his customers, thereby providing them with credit. The second category, ancillary businesses, comprises (s. 145 (1)) the businesses of credit brokerage, debt-adjusting, debt-counselling, debt-collecting and operating a credit reference agency. Thus, the retailer who does not enter into credit agreements with his customers but who instead arranges finance for them through the familiar triangular transaction (see p. 279, *ante*) must be licensed as a credit-broker, *i.e.* someone effecting introductions of potential customers to someone carrying on a consumer credit business. Mortgage or finance brokers also need to be licensed as credit-brokers. Debt-counselling is giving advice to debtors or hirers about the liquidation of debts due under consumer credit or consumer hire agreements. Thus, solicitors require a licence. Businesses which do more than counselling or advising, which negotiate with the creditor on behalf of the debtor or which will actually take over the debt and pay it off for the customer (usually giving the customer longer time in which to pay them off) need to be licensed as debt-adjusters. Persons carrying on a business of procuring payment of debts due under consumer credit or consumer hire agreements need to be licensed as debt-collectors. Credit reference agencies are businesses which collect and then provide (usually to finance companies) information about the financial standing of individuals.

The Director-General of Fair Trading is responsible for administering the licensing system. He has powers to vary, suspend, renew and withdraw licences and can thereby clamp down on malpractices. Anyone who without a licence carries on a business requiring one, commits an offence (s. 39). A regulated agreement made by an unlicensed business (s. 40) or after an introduction by an unlicensed credit-broker (s. 149) will generally be unenforceable against the customer. Similarly, any agreement for the services of an unlicensed ancillary business will be unenforceable against the client (s. 148). In each of these cases, someone who is unable to enforce agreements can apply to the Director-General for an order allowing the agreements to be enforced.

Advertising and canvassing

An advertiser of credit commits an offence if his advertisement:
  (i) infringes regulations made under section 44. These regulations will be designed to achieve truth in lending and are likely to require advertisements either to give a clear indication of the true cost of the credit by stating a true annual percentage rate or else to indicate that such information is available.
 (ii) advertises the supply of goods or services on credit when those goods or services are not also offered for cash (s. 45).
(iii) is false or misleading in a material respect (s. 46). Further offences are: sending someone under 18 a document inviting him to seek information about credit or to obtain credit (s. 50); issuing an unsolicited credit-token (*e.g.* a credit card) other than as a renewal or replacement (s. 51); infringing regulations as to the contents and form of a quotation of credit terms (s. 52); failing to comply with regulations as to information to be displayed at premises of credit businesses (s. 53).

It is an offence to canvass debtor–creditor agreements off trade premises (s. 49). This is to prevent the doorstep "selling" of ordinary loans and second mortgages. The offence would be committed for example if the canvasser without being requested in writing to do so, deliberately visited someone at the person's home and tried to persuade him to apply for debtor–creditor credit. It is not an offence to canvass debtor–creditor–supplier agreements, provided the canvasser is acting under a licence which specifically authorises that activity (s. 23). It is an offence to canvass off trade premises someone to make use of the services of a credit-broker, debt-adjuster or debt-counsellor (s. 154).

RIGHTS AND OBLIGATIONS BETWEEN THE PARTIES

Section 173 prevents the parties contracting out of the protection provided by the Act for the debtor or hirer.

Formalities

A creditor or owner under a regulated agreement can enforce the agreement only if it satisfies certain statutory requirements (in ss. 55 and 60–65). Non-commercial agreements, certain small agreements and, if the Director-General so decides, certain bank overdraft agreements are exempt from the formalities requirements (s. 74).

The requirements are—

(i) Specified information, *e.g.* as to the true annual cost of the credit, expressed both as an annual percentage rate and as a total sum, must be disclosed (in the prescribed manner) to the prospective customer before he enters the regulated agreement (regulations to be made under s. 55).

(ii) All the terms, other than implied terms, of the agreement must be embodied in the written agreement (or in another document referred to in the written agreement) (s. 61 (1) (*b*)). All the terms of the written agreement must be readily legible (s. 61 (1) (*c*)). It must contain details of the debtor's right, if any, of cancellation (s. 64 (1) (*a*)). It must comply with regulations as to its form and contents, *e.g.* requiring it to indicate the names and addresses of the parties, the amounts and due dates of payments required of the debtor, the true cost of the credit—regulations to be made under section 60.

(iii) The agreement must be signed by the customer (*i.e.* the debtor or hirer) in person and by or on behalf of the creditor or owner (s. 61 (1) (*a*)).

(iv) The customer must receive one copy of the agreement when he is given or sent the agreement to sign (ss. 62 (1) and 63 (1)). If, as is common, the agreement is not actually made when he signs it, then he must be given a second copy later (s. 63 (2)). The agreement will not be made on the occasion of his signing it, if it is in the form of a proposal or offer by him which is sent to (or left with) the creditor or owner for him to decide whether to accept it. That is the situation in the common triangular hire-purchase transaction (see

p. 297, *ante*). The agreement is made when the offer is accepted, *i.e.* often on the posting of an acceptance addressed to the customer. The second copy must be given to the customer within seven days of the making of the agreement (s. 63 (2)). In the case of a cancellable agreement it must be sent by post (s. 63 (3)). In the case of a credit-token agreement (*e.g.* a credit card or trading check agreement) the second copy is given in time if it is given before or at the time the credit-token is given to the customer (s. 63 (4)). Further, each time a new credit-token is given to the customer, a copy of the agreement must also be given to him (s. 85).

(v) In the case of a prospective regulated agreement which is proposed to be secured by a mortgage on land, the customer must receive a copy of the agreement at least seven clear days before he is sent by post the actual agreement for him to sign (s. 61 (2)). During that time and for a further period of seven days the prospective creditor must stay away from the customer so as to allow him a consideration period free from sales pressure. The only situation in which he may do so is if during the consideration period the customer specifically asks the creditor to contact him. These rules, however, do not apply where the customer wants the credit to buy the land which it is proposed to mortgage or for a bridging loan in connection with the purchase of land.

In an action the court may grant dispensation with most of these requirements if it is just and fair to do so in the light of the degree to which the customer has been prejudiced by the failure to comply with them and the degree of culpability of the creditor or owner (s. 127). There are similar requirements as to the contents, form, copies and signatures of security agreements (*e.g.* of guarantee and indemnity) entered by or at the request of the customer (s. 105).

Cancellation

Certain regulated agreements are cancellable by the customer (ss. 67–73). The object of this right is to allow him a short **cooling off** period to think over the concluded bargain and, on second thoughts, to rescind it. The agreement is cancellable (s. 67) if, (i) the antecedent negotiations included oral representations by the creditor or owner or the dealer made in the customer's presence, and, (ii) the customer signed the agreement elsewhere than at certain trade premises (*i.e.* the trade premises of persons such as the creditor or owner or, in the case of a debtor–creditor–supplier agreement, the dealer). Thus the agreement could be cancellable if the customer signed it in the street, at home or at his own trade premises, provided oral representations had been made in his presence. An agreement is not cancellable if it is not subject to the formalities requirements (see p. 303, *ante*) or if it involves a land mortgage or finance to purchase land (or bridging finance for such a purpose).

The cooling off period begins at the time of the customer's signature and lasts until the end of the fifth clear day after he receives his second copy of the agreement (s. 68). He cancels the agreement if during that time he gives (or posts) to the creditor or owner (or, in the case of a debtor–creditor–supplier agreement, the dealer) a written notice to that effect (s. 69).

The effect of cancellation depends upon whether the agreement was, on the one hand, a debtor–creditor–supplier agreement for restricted-use credit or consumer hire agreement or, on the other hand, a debtor–creditor or unrestricted-use credit agreement. The first category includes all hire-purchase, conditional sale and credit sale agreements. Here the effect is that the customer is entitled to recover payments already made (s. 70). He is obliged to return the goods, but he need not take them back; he can wait until they are collected from him in pursuance of a written request (s. 72); he has a lien on them for the return of his payments (s. 70 (2)); he has to take reasonable care of the goods for 21 days after serving his notice of cancellation. By way of exception to what has just been said, the customer is under no duty to return perishable goods, goods supplied to meet an emergency or goods which before cancellation were consumed or incorporated in something else (*e.g.* plants in a garden or spare parts in a car). In two of these cases, namely, where goods or services were supplied to meet an emergency or where the customer has incorporated goods into something else, the customer is liable after cancellation to pay for those goods or services (s. 69 (2)).

The effect of cancellation is different in the case of an agreement in the second category (*e.g.* an ordinary loan). Here, the customer must repay (usually with interest) any credit he has already received (s. 71).

Credit reference agencies

Someone who is refused credit may wonder if he has been black-listed by a credit reference agency. Certain courses of action are open (ss. 157–159). He is entitled to discover from any creditor or owner to whom he has applied to enter a regulated agreement, the name and address of any credit reference agency consulted (s. 157). He is entitled on making a written request and a payment of 25 pence to demand from any credit reference agency a copy of the file that that agency has on him (s. 158). He can then take steps, if necessary, to add a correction to the file (s. 159).

Dealer as agent of creditor

A negotiator in antecedent negotiations is deemed in conducting those operations to be the creditor's agent (s. 56). Section 56 can make someone a negotiator in antecedent negotiation (*i.e.* an agent) only in respect of a debtor–creditor–supplier agreement. There are two such types of section 56 agent. First, there is the credit-broker negotiating with the customer in relation to goods sold or proposed to be sold to the creditor before forming the subject-matter of a debtor–creditor–supplier agreement. Into this category falls the dealer in the common triangular hire-purchase transaction. Secondly, there is the supplier negotiating with the customer in relation to a transaction to be financed by a debtor–creditor–supplier agreement. Into this category falls the retailer negotiating with a customer who is proposing to pay with his Access card or Barclay-card. The antecedent negotiations include any representations made by the negotiator to the customer and any other dealings between them (s. 56). The effect of the negotiator being an agent of the creditor is to make the creditor liable for misrepresentations made by the negotiator as if the creditor had made them; also any money paid by the customer to the negotiator will be regarded as received by the creditor. The negotiator is also the creditor's agent for the purpose of receiving certain written notices from the customer: notice withdrawing an offer to enter a regulated agreement (s. 57); notice of cancellation of the regulated agreement (s. 69); notice rescinding the regulated agreement (s. 102).

"Any person who, in the course of a business carried on by him, acts (or acted) on behalf of the debtor or hirer in any negotiations for the agreement" is not, unless he falls within the definition of a negotiator in antecedent negotiations, generally agent of the creditor or owner. However, he is the agent of the creditor or owner for the purpose of receiving the notices mentioned in the last paragraph. The customer's solicitor who negotiates a loan for him would, for example, fall within this category.

Liability of creditor for supplier's default

Where the customer acquires goods or services from one person (the supplier) and the credit to pay for them from another (the creditor), the latter can be liable in respect of the supplier's default in two situations:

(i) where the creditor himself contracts with the customer to supply the customer with the goods or services.

This occurs in the triangular hire-purchase, conditional sale or credit sale transaction. Here the creditor will himself be liable for breach of implied terms as to title, description, quality, etc, in the hire-purchase agreement or contract of sale (see p. 283, *ante*). He will also normally be liable in respect of misrepresentations made by the dealer to the customer (s. 56).

(ii) where s. 75 applies.

This section applies to debtor–creditor–supplier agreements other than those where the creditor himself contracts to supply the goods or services to the customer. If the debtor has a claim against the supplier in respect of a misrepresentation or breach of contract, he has a like claim against the creditor who with the supplier is jointly and severally liable to the debtor (s. 75 (1)). Thus, if the customer has used a Barclaycard or Access card to pay for goods or services and has a claim against the supplier, he can also or alternatively bring his claim against the credit card company. However, this rule does not apply to any item to which the supplier had attached a cash price not exceeding £50 or more than £10,000 (s. 75 (3)).

Misuse of credit facilities

The general rule is that the debtor under a regulated agreement is not liable for any use of credit facilities by another person who is not the debtor's agent or authorised by the debtor to use them (s. 83). That rule does not apply in the case of the misuse of a cheque or other negotiable instrument. A further limited exception applies in the case of a credit-token, *e.g.* a trading check or credit card. Here the holder can be liable up to a maximum of £50 on any occasion when he has lost it, although he is not liable for any misuse occurring after he has given the creditor notice (confirmed in writing within 7 days) of the loss of the card (s. 84).

Early and late payment by debtor

A debtor under a regulated agreement has the right, after giving written notice to the creditor, to complete his payments ahead of the due time (s. 94). He may then qualify for a rebate of his interest charges (regulations to be made under s. 95).

Where he is late making payments under the agreement, he may well in accordance with the agreement have to pay extra interest to take account of the delay in payment. However, he can not be obliged to pay interest at a rate higher than that payable under the agreement as a whole (s. 93).

Consumer hire agreements

These agreements are for the most part subject to provisions governing regulated consumer-credit agreements—hence the frequent use of the expressions "creditor or owner" and "debtor or hirer." However, there are some provisions which do not apply to consumer hire agreements, *e.g.* the extortionate credit bargain provisions (see p. 310, *post*) and sections 93 and 94 dealing with early and late payment. On the other hand certain sections apply only to consumer hire agreements. Thus after 18 months the hirer has, subject to certain exceptions, a statutory right, after giving notice of either 3 months or of the length of the shortest interval between his rental payments, to terminate the agreement (s. 101). Also, where the owner recovers possession of goods which have been the subject of a consumer hire agreement, the court can grant the hirer financial relief by excusing him from some payments or even requiring some money to be repaid to him (s. 132).

ENFORCEMENT OF AGREEMENT BY CREDITOR OR OWNER

Any court action by the creditor or owner to enforce a regulated agreement must be brought in the county court and the debtor or hirer and also any surety (guarantor or indemnifier) must be made parties to the action (s. 141).

Default and non-default notices

Where the creditor or owner wishes merely to sue for payments already due, he has an unfettered right to commence proceedings. However, if because the debtor or hirer is in breach of the agreement, the creditor or owner wishes,—

"(a) to terminate the agreement, or
(b) to demand earlier payment of any sum, or
(c) to recover possession of any goods or land, or
(d) to treat any right conferred on the debtor or hirer by the agreement as terminated, restricted or deferred, or
(e) to enforce any security,"

he must serve a default notice on the debtor or hirer (s. 87). If the creditor or owner wishes to do one of those things for a reason other than a breach of the agreement by the debtor or hirer and if the agreement is one of specified duration (*e.g.* a hire-purchase agreement) he must serve a notice of his intention (ss. 76 and 98). These notice requirements do not apply if the creditor merely wishes to prevent the debtor making further drawings of credit (*e.g.* on his credit card). The notice served under one the above mentioned provisions must give the debtor or hirer at least seven days notice before the creditor or owner can pursue any of the remedies listed above. In the case of a default notice (s. 87), the notice must make clear what, if anything, can be done by the debtor or hirer to rectify his breach and if he then does that, the breach is regarded as never having occurred (s. 89).

Time orders

If the debtor or hirer has been served with a default or non-default notice or if any action is brought by the creditor or owner to enforce a regulated agreement, the debtor or hirer can ask the court for a time order (s. 129). The court can in making a time order, allow the debtor or hirer extra time to rectify any breach of the agreement and it can allow him extra time to make payments which have already fallen due. Only in the case of hire-purchase and conditional sale agreements (see p. 292, *ante*) can the court alter the pattern of future payments or allow extra time for them to be made. The court can at a later date revoke, vary or extend a time order.

Extortionate credit bargains

The debtor can at any time ask the court to re-open the agreement as being extortionate (ss. 137–140). The court's powers to do so, extend to exempt agreements and also to credit agreements which exceed the £5,000 limit. An agreement is extortionate if it requires payments that are grossly extortionate or if it grossly contravenes ordinary principles of fair dealings (s. 138). If it finds the agreement extortionate the court has wide powers to alter its terms, even extending to being able to require the repayment to the debtor of sums already paid.

Death of debtor or hirer

In the event of the death of the debtor or hirer, the creditor or owner can not terminate the agreement if it is of specified duration (*e.g.* a hire-purchase agreement) and is a fully secured agreement (s. 86 (1)). If it is of specified duration but is not fully secured, he still can not do so unless the agreement gives him the power to do so and he is able on an application to the court to show that the obligations of the debtor or hirer under the agreement are unlikely to be carried out (s. 86 (2)). The object is to enable the deceased's relatives to continue with his hire-purchase agreements and others of specified duration if they wish to do so. This right does not extend to agreements of unspecified duration (such as credit card agreements).

Security

The creditor or owner can not enforce any security given by or at the request, express or implied, of the debtor or hirer, to any extent greater than he can enforce the regulated agreement (s. 113). Thus for example a guarantor can not be made to pay an amount from which the debtor has been excused under the extortionate credit provisions. By way of exception, an indemnifier can be made liable when the only reason that the debtor or hirer is not liable is that he is under 18 (s. 113 (7)).

SELECT BIBLIOGRAPHY

Books

A. P. Dobson, *Sale of Goods and Consumer Credit* (1975).
R. M. Goode, *Introduction to the Consumer Credit Act, 1974* (1974).

Articles

Dobson, A. P., "Consumer Credit—Finance Company's Liability for Dealer's Default" [1975] J.B.L. 208.
Goode, R. M., "The Consumer Credit Act 1974" [1975] C.L.J. 79.
Schofield, P. J., "Consumer Credit Law Reformed" [1975] J.B.L. 1.

PART 4: COMPETITION

CHAPTER 18

MONOPOLIES, RESTRICTIVE TRADE PRACTICES AND RESALE PRICES

THE purpose of the enactments dealing with these topics is to control attempts of private manufacturers or suppliers to misuse their economic power by reducing or abolishing free competition amongst themselves.

A distinction is drawn between monopolies and mergers, which are the subject of government control with the aid of the Monopolies and Mergers Commission, an administrative body, and restrictive trade practices and resale price maintenance, which are subject to judicial control, exercised by the Restrictive Practices Court. The law governing monopolies and mergers is now contained in the Fair Trading Act 1973, which consolidates and amends earlier legislation. Until December 15, 1976 the enactments dealing with restrictive trade practices were the Restrictive Trade Practices Acts of 1956 and 1968 and the Fair Trading Act 1973, whilst the 1956 Act and the Resale Prices Act 1964 dealt with resale price maintenance. The Restrictive Trade Practices Act 1976 and the Resale Prices Act 1976 which came into operation on December 15, 1976 respectively repeal and re-enact the law of restrictive trade practices and resale price maintenance. The law in these areas is thereby consolidated and with it, by virtue of the Restrictive Practices Court Act 1976, the procedure of the relevant judicial body, the Restrictive Practices Court.

MONOPOLIES AND MERGERS

Legislation passed in 1948 provided for the investigation of monopoly situations by the Monopolies Commission at the direction of Government. Broadly speaking, a monopoly situation existed where at least one-third of the market in the supply, processing or export of goods of any description was in the hands of a single firm (or a connected group of firms) or in the hands of several firms who, whether by agreement or not, prevented or restricted the operation of a free market in the goods in question. Provision was also made for the Commission to report on the general effect on the public interest of particular classes of practices. Although the test of a **monopoly situation** is now **control of one-quarter** of the market in question, the principles described above remain valid.

The Commission can be required to report to Government whether the monopoly situation or the things done as a result of or to preserve that situation operate against the public interest and to make recommendations. The Commission is an independent advisory body with no executive powers. The recommendations made in the Commission's report, which is laid before Parliament and published, may be implemented by Government which may make an order for the purpose of remedying or preventing any mischiefs reported to them by the Commission. This power is rarely exercised; in nearly all cases those concerned agree to comply with suitable undertakings at the instance of Government.

Criminal proceedings do not lie for the contravention of such an order. On the other hand, the Crown may enforce it by civil proceedings for an injunction, and an individual injured as a result of the infringement of such an order may institute a civil action.

Furthermore, where a recommendation has been made as to action to be taken by the parties, Government may at any time refer to the Commission for investigation and report whether they have complied with it.

The effect of Part III of the Act of 1956 was to exclude from the Commission's activities restrictive trading agreements, *i.e.* cartels. These agreements were to be dealt with under Part I of the Act of 1956 (p. 316, *post*).

Legislation in 1965 provided, *inter alia*, for:

   (a) the enlargement of the Monopolies Commission to a maximum of 25 members, with further powers to allow for the appointment of additional members for particular references;

   (b) the investigation by the Monopolies Commission of restrictive practices and monopoly situations in the supply of services;

   (c) extension of the power to require general reports from the Monopolies Commission;

   (d) the investigation of mergers by the Monopolies Commission at the reference of Government where the merger would either lead to or strengthen a monopoly situation or where the gross value of the assets taken over would exceed £5 million. There was also special provision for the control of newspaper mergers;

(e) Government, on the basis of a Monopolies Commission report, to take action against monopoly situations which were incompatible with a treaty to which the United Kingdom was a party.

It should be noted that:

(i) there is no duty to pre-notify mergers although informal prenotification is usual;

(ii) there is no presumption that monopolies or mergers are harmful *per se*: each case is considered on its merits in the light of the public interest. In consequence, control is discretionary. For the period from the 1965 Act until the end of 1976 only about three per cent. of mergers considered for reference to the Commission were so referred. In the calendar year 1975, 157 mergers or merger proposals (excluding newspapers) falling within the monopolies and mergers legislation were considered but of these only four merger references were made. Referral often leads to abandonment of the parties' plans.

Fair Trading Act 1973 (as regards monopolies and mergers)

Broadly speaking, the monopoly and merger provisions of the earlier legislation described above were repealed and re-enacted in the Fair Trading Act 1973 but there were changes both of substance and of detail. The 1973 Act is complex and the following survey of some of the main changes is necessarily selective.

The 1973 Act provides for a reduction in the monopoly test from one-third to one-quarter of the supply of goods or services concerned in the United Kingdom. The geographical area may be a substantial part of the United Kingdom (as under the 1948 legislation) or, according to the nature of the monopoly, a lesser area, *e.g.* a single city. The gross asset value test of £5 million remains the same. As before, a monopoly may be either **simple** (concentration of power in the hands of a single firm or company) or **complex** (where several firms or companies share such power).

The 1973 Act was of primary importance in establishing a new post independent of government, the Director General of Fair Trading, who has, in addition to looking after consumer interests, a wide discretion in supervising monopolies, mergers and restrictive practices (p. 315, *post*). His duties include the monitoring of commercial activities in the United Kingdom, so as to ascertain circumstances relating to monopoly and merger situations or uncompetitive practices and, in this connection, the provision of information, assistance and recommendations to the Government (the Secretary of State for Prices and Consumer Protection). He may require information to be provided to him and whilst only the Department of Prices and Consumer Protection (on the advice of the **merger panel** which the Director chairs) may initiate merger references to the Commission (now renamed the Monopolies and Mergers Commission) the Director General may make monopoly references, subject to government veto where relevant. His duties also include assistance to the Commission and after report of the Commission, obtaining undertakings from the parties if appropriate. The Director General will monitor the observance of such undertakings.

As regards monopolies and mergers, the establishment of the Fair Trading Office under the Director General means the separation of the investigation or prosecutory function, *i.e.* fact finding (formerly conducted by the Commission but now undertaken by the Director) from that of adjudication, *i.e.* providing assessment and advice to the Secretary of State, which remains with the Commission.

The Commission's report must, as before, have express regard to the public interest which is now defined (s. 84 of the Fair Trading Act 1973) with emphasis on the need to promote competition. The Government must accept a Commission report that the matters on reference have operated in the public interest but an adverse report is not binding. The Government may impose a time limit for Commission reports, which is always a requirement for merger cases. The Commission may now investigate restrictive labour practices, an interesting addition, given co-operation from the Trade Unions, to the Commission's purview on a reference to the Commission for a **general report.**

There is no change in the powers exercisable by the Department of Prices and Consumer Protection after the Commission's report, except that under the 1973 Act The Secretary of State may now ban the recommending of prices (Pt. I of the Eighth Schedule to the Fair Trading Act 1973).

The wide range of activities in the monopolies and mergers field of the Director General's staff at the Office of Fair Trading, is evidenced by the second report of the Director General for 1975. Thus, for example, in that year the Director General submitted to the Commission two general references on pet foods and ceramic sanitary ware. He also submitted a reference on a partial merger situation, where the proposal by a Swiss company to acquire and consolidate in a United Kingdom subsidiary company certain Swiss shareholdings in an English company, amounting to 33·4 per cent. of that company's equity, was held not to be expected to operate against the public interest. The Office of Fair Trading also kept under review a variety of goods and services which had been the subject of previous Commission reports, ranging from plasterboard to petrol. A settlement was reached in the dispute between the Hoffman–La Roche Group and the Government in connection with the Commission's report on the supply of Librium and Valium and the subsequent litigation which had ensued.

RESTRICTIVE TRADE PRACTICES

The remainder of this chapter seeks to cover, on a historical basis, the development of some important features of restrictive trade practices law which was consolidated but unchanged by the Restrictive Trade Practices Act 1976.

The Restrictive Trade Practices Act 1956 required restrictive trade agreements to be registered in a public register, except if they referred to exports, in which case they were filed with Government but are now held by the Director General. They are not published. Restrictive trade agreements are agreements under which producers, suppliers or exporters restrict the manufacture, supply or distribution of goods, for example, by arranging minimum selling prices or the same conditions for the supply of goods. The Fair Trading Act 1973 amended the 1956 Act to include restrictive agreements relating to the supply of services within the scope of this legislation. (See p. 325, *post*). The general rule is that a restrictive trade agreement is presumed to be invalid as being contrary to the public interest, unless the parties can justify the restriction before the Restrictive Practices Court on any one of eight specified grounds (p. 320, *post*).

Duty to register restrictive agreements

Registrable agreements

Part I of the Act of 1956 as amended by the Act of 1973 provided that any agreement made between two or more persons carrying on business in the United Kingdom must be registered by any of them with the Director General (before the 1973 Act with the Registrar of

Restrictive Trading Agreements) if restrictions are accepted by two or more parties in respect of the following matters (now s. 6 (1) of the 1976 Act):

    (a) the prices to be charged, quoted or paid for goods, supplied, offered or acquired, or for the application of any process of manufacture to goods;

    (b) the prices to be recommended or suggested as the prices to be charged or quoted in respect of the resale of goods supplied;

    (c) the terms or conditions on or subject to which goods are to be supplied or acquired or any such process is to be applied to goods;

    (d) the quantities or descriptions of goods to be produced, supplied or acquired;

    (e) the processes of manufacture to be applied to any goods, or the quantities or descriptions of goods to which any such process is to be applied; or

    (f) the persons or classes of persons to, for or from whom, or the areas or places in or from which, goods are to be supplied or acquired, or any such process applied.

Sub-paragraph (b) covers recommended prices for resale, which may well overlap with the contents of sub-paragraph (a). A single manufacturer, however, has freedom to recommend resale prices provided he enters into no agreement with another party as to such prices.

The term "agreement" includes any agreement or arrangement, whether or not it is or is not intended to be legally enforceable. All that is required to constitute an arrangement not enforceable in law is that the parties to it shall have communicated with one another in some way and that as a result of the communication each has intentionally aroused in the other an expectation that he will act in a certain way (see *Re British Basic Slag Ltd.'s Agreement* (1962) L.R. 4 R.P. 155, and *Re Mileage Conference Group of the Tyre Manufacturers Conference Ltd.'s Agreement* (1967) L.R. 6 R.P. 66).

The phrase "an agreement for the supply of goods," where it appears in Part I of the Act of 1956, is to be construed as a reference to any agreement whereby one party agrees to supply goods to another, notwithstanding that it may contain agreement on other related or unrelated matters (*Registrar of Restrictive Trading Agreements* v. *Schweppes and Others* (1971) L.R. 7 R.P. 336).

Excepted agreements

Various exceptions to the need for registration are set out in the Restrictive Trade Practices Act 1976 (s. 9 and Sched. 3). These include agreements containing only restrictions relating exclusively to the goods supplied thereunder, agreements expressly authorised by statute, sales agency agreements between two parties, and agreements between two parties for the use of patents, registered designs or trade marks.

Sections 9 (7) and 43 (2) of the 1976 Act, which provide that a company and its subsidiary are to be treated as a single person, are concerned only with the counting of heads and are not directed to treating the persons to which they relate as the one and the same person so that, for the purposes of section 9 (4) of the 1976 Act, one must look at the agreement as it stands, and if, after counting as one any parties to it which are inter-connected bodies corporate, one still finds that restrictions relating exclusively to the goods supplied are accepted as between two or more persons by whom the goods are to be supplied, section 9 (4) does not apply. (The *Schweppes* case, above.) One cannot rely within the same agreement on more than one of the exceptions set out in section 9 (the *Schweppes* case, above).

In one case X and Y undertook to sell their entire production of citrus concentrates to a joint sales company in quota proportions; the parties were held to have accepted registrable restrictions with the 1956 Act. X and Y accordingly entered into new arrangements whereby Y undertook to purchase X's production up to a maximum and to compensate X for any shortfall. Y might only purchase elsewhere after allowing X to match a third party's lower price. *Held*, that Y's obligation was not a restriction on Y's own production. A shortfall might indeed arise through Y's own sales but this was no restriction on Y as to production. It was a restriction relating only to the goods, supplied under the agreement which could therefore be ignored in considering whether the agreement was registrable. Nor was there any implied restriction on Y's production to be inferred from X's obligation to Y. The agreement did not require registration under the 1956 Act: *Cadbury Schweppes Ltd. and J. Lyons & Co. Ltd.'s Agreement* [1975] 1 W.L.R. 1018.

Export agreements

These agreements are not registrable with the Director General if all the restrictions relate exclusively to:

(a) the supply of goods by export from the United Kingdom;

(b) the production of goods or the application of any process of manufacture to goods, outside the United Kingdom;

(c) the acquisition of goods to be delivered outside the United Kingdom and not imported into the United Kingdom for entry for home use; or

(d) the supply of goods to be delivered outside the United Kingdom otherwise than by export from the United Kingdom.

Such agreements, however, if all the restrictions relate to the supply of goods by export from the United Kingdom, have to be notified to the Director General (s. 25 and paras. 6 (1) and 9 (1) of Sched. 3 to the 1976 Act) and may be referred to the Monopolies and Mergers Commission. So far the Commission has not been asked to investigate any such agreement. References have been made to the Commission to investigate product supply in and export from the U.K. (*e.g.* the reference made in July 1974 relating to U.K. manufacturers of heavy electric cables).

The Director General of Fair Trading

The Director General's functions in respect of monopolies and mergers have already been discussed, (see pp. 314–315, *ante*). In discharging his functions pursuant to the 1973 Act, which remains the authority for his involvement in the field of restrictive trade practices, he retains his independent role. He is appointed by the Secretary of State but is responsible to no minister. He has two main duties: first, to keep the register of agreements subject to registration; and secondly, to bring the registered agreements before the Restrictive Practices Court to declare whether or not they are contrary to the public interest. Both these duties are absolute. He must see that all registrable agreements are put on the register, if necessary using the powers contained in the Act to obtain information; and to bring them before the Court. He has also to enforce orders made by the Court, of which breach is punishable as contempt of court.

The Register

This is kept in two sections, the public section and the special section. The former is open to inspection by anyone on payment of a fee, and copies may be obtained of anything in the register. The special section is secret and contains information the publication of which would be contrary to the public interest, also information about secret processes of manufacture or about the presence, absence,

or location of any mineral or other deposits if government think
publication would substantially damage legitimate business interests.

Judicial investigation of registered agreements

The Restrictive Practices Court, which was established by the
Act of 1956, is a superior court of record presided over by a High
Court judge. The Act provides for both judges and laymen to be
members. Laymen are chosen for their knowledge or experience in
industry, commerce or public affairs.

The main task of the court is to declare on application by the
Director General whether a restriction contained in an agreement is
contrary to the public interest, and if so to declare the agreement
void in respect of that restriction, and the court may, at the request
of the Director General, make an order prohibiting the parties to the
agreement from continuing it or making any other agreement to the
like effect (now s. 2 (2) of the 1976 Act). The test as to whether a
new agreement is *to the like effect* is whether it is intended to operate
in substantially the same way and whether the things it will do or
achieve if it is made effective are the same as those which the first
agreement would have done or achieved: *Re Black Bolt and Nut Association's Agreement (No. 2)* [1962] 1 W.L.R. 75. On the other hand,
where the registrability or otherwise of an agreement is in dispute
between the Director General and a third party, it will be a matter
for the decision of the High Court and not the Restrictive Practices
Court.

The onus is placed on the parties to the agreement to satisfy the
court that the restrictions are not contrary to the public interest. A
restriction will be deemed to be contrary to the public interest
unless it satisfies one or more of the following circumstances
(commonly known as **gateways**) (now s. 10 (1) (*a*)—(*h*) of the 1976
Act):

(a) that the restriction is reasonably necessary, having regard to
the character of the goods, to protect the public against injury;

(b) that the removal of the restriction would deny to the public as
purchasers, consumers or users other specific and substantial
benefits or advantages;

(c) that the restriction is reasonably necessary to counteract
measures taken by a person not party to the agreement;

(d) that the restriction is reasonably necessary to enable the persons party to the agreement to negotiate fair terms with a person not party to it who controls a preponderant part of the trade, business or market in the goods concerned;

(e) that the removal of the restriction would be likely to have a serious and persistent adverse effect on the general level of unemployment;

(f) that the removal of the restriction would be likely to cause a reduction in the volume or earnings of the export business which is substantial either in relation to the whole export business of the United Kingdom or in relation to the whole business (including export business) of the trade or industry;

(g) that the restriction is reasonably required for purposes connected with the maintenance of any other restriction accepted by the parties.

(h) that the restriction does not directly or indirectly restrict or discourage competition to any material degree in any relevant trade or industry and is not likely to do so. (This additional gateway was added by the Restrictive Trade Practices Act 1968.)

Even if the court is satisfied on one or more of these circumstances it must further be satisfied that the restriction is not unreasonable, having regard to the balance between those circumstances and any detriment to the public or to persons not parties to the agreement resulting or likely to result from the operation of the restriction.

The Court has power to vary previous orders it has made if the relevant circumstances can be shown to have materially changed (now s. 4 of the 1976 Act.) The Court has in several cases accepted undertakings on behalf of the parties to an agreement which it has declared void that they will inform the Registrar, now the Director General, if they intend to make an agreement to the like effect, so that he can apply for an Order before they do so. The Director General can apply to the Court for an Order at any time if parties to an agreement which has been found objectionable continue to operate their arrangements, or to operate new arrangements having the same effect as those condemned.

On a motion on behalf of the Registrar alleging contempt of court the Court imposed fines totalling £103,000 on eight companies members of the Galvanised Tank Manufacturers Association for breach of undertakings given to the Court in earlier proceedings: *Re Galvanised Tank Manufacturers Association's Agreement* [1965] 1 W.L.R. 1074.

A brief analysis of some of the salient features of decisions of the court is set out below.

Section 10 (1) (a)

The test to be applied is "whether a reasonable and prudent man who is concerned to protect the public against injury would enforce the restriction if he could" *per* Devlin J. in *Re Chemists' Federation's Agreement* [1958] 1 W.L.R. 1192.

Section 10 (1) (b)

"The public as purchasers, consumers or users of goods"—means the public viewed as a collective whole in a specified capacity. "The public as purchasers" denotes collectively all persons who purchased the goods: it is not sufficient that some small class of the public benefits by the restriction, but equally it is unnecessary to prove that the ultimate consumers receive a benefit: *Re Black Bolt and Nut Association's Agreement* [1960] 1 W.L.R. 884.

"Any goods." The respondents may choose the particular kind of goods in respect of which they seek to justify the onus of proof cast upon them *Re Black Bolt and Nut Association's Agreement, supra.*

"Specific and substantial benefits or advantages." A benefit is specific if it is "explicit and definable." "Substantial" is not a word which demands a strictly quantitative or proportional assessment, nor is it a term the meaning of which the Court has been prepared to define: *Re Net Book Agreement 1957* (1962) L.R. 3 R.P. 246.

Section 10 (1) (d)

It is not necessary to show that the preponderant buyer is likely to use his powers to negotiate unfair terms. It is sufficient if, in fact, without the restriction the suppliers would not be able to negotiate fair terms, *i.e.* giving a reasonable but no more than a reasonable profit but in the hope of getting an occasional contract are likely to tender at an uneconomic price *Re Water-Tube Boilermakers' Agreement* [1959] 1 W.L.R. 1118.

The Restrictive Trade Practices Act 1968

The Restrictive Trade Practices Act 1968 supplemented and amended Part I of the Act of 1956 so as to make its operation more flexible and to improve its enforcement.

The provisions of the Act of 1968 which modified the operation of the Act of 1956 can be divided into two classes, those which provide for further exemptions from registration and those which affect the position and the judicial examination of registrable agreements.

Further exemption from registration

The principal provision which falls within the first class (now 29 (2) of the 1976 Act) introduces an administrative procedure enabling the Department of Prices and Consumer Protection to exempt from registration for a specified period any agreement which it considers reasonably necessary to promote the carrying out of a project or scheme of substantial importance to the national economy and the aim of which is to promote efficiency in a trade or industry. The Department is required to lay copies of any exemption order and of the exempted agreement before both Houses of Parliament and to make them available for public inspection.

Section 30 of the 1976 Act empowers certain government departments to exempt from registration agreements relating exclusively to prices and designed to prevent or restrict price increases so as to secure restrictions in prices. Exempted agreements under this section are also to be made available for public inspection.

Section 9 (5) of the 1976 Act extends the scope of the existing exemptions from registration of agreements relating to standards of dimension, design or quality or performance and introduces an exemption for agreements relating to certain arrangements to provide information or advice to purchasers, consumers or users.

Information agreements

The principal provision in the second class, designed to strengthen the operation of the restrictive practices legislation, is now section 7 of the 1976 Act which empowers the Department of Prices and Consumer Protection by order to bring agreements for exchange of information within the restrictive trade practices legislation. An information agreement is defined as an agreement between two or more persons carrying on within the United Kingdom any such business as is mentioned in subsection (1) of section 6 of the 1976 Act whether with or without other parties, being an agreement under which provision is made for or in relation to the furnishing by two or more parties to each other or to other persons (whether parties or not) of information with respect to certain matters. These matters are the same as those contained in section 6 (1), with the addition of exchange of information as to costs. However, they differ in one other important respect from those matters set out in section 6 (1) in that section 6 (1) is concerned with restrictions as to future behaviour, *e.g.* the prices to be charged, whereas section 7 (1) of the Act of 1976 is concerned with past behaviour as well, *e.g.* the prices charged or to be charged.

Information agreements are not automatically registrable. The Department of Prices and Consumer Protection may by order call up for registration any class of agreements falling within the definition. So far only one such order has been made; this relates to the matters referred to in section 7 (1) (*a*) and (*b*) of the Act of 1976.

Changes relating to registration

The Act of 1968 made changes in the law relating to registration of agreements with respect to:

    (i) the addition of a new gateway to those already available; (see now section 10 (1) of the 1976 Act, see p. 321, *ante*);

    (ii) the time within which particulars of agreements and certain variations must be furnished to the Director General (see now s. 24 and Sched. 2 to the 1976 Act);

    (iii) the relaxation of the requirement to furnish particulars of certain variations (see now s. 27 (1) (*c*) of the 1976 Act);

    (iv) the effect of failure to furnish particulars within the proper time (see now s. 35 of the 1976 Act).

The last-mentioned deserves separate consideration. It is provided that if particulars of any registrable agreement (whether made before or after the commencement of the 1968 Act) are not duly furnished within the time required, the agreement shall be void in respect of all relevant restrictions accepted thereunder and it will be unlawful for any party who carries on business within the United Kingdom to give effect to or to enforce or purport to enforce any such restrictions. It is not a criminal offence to give effect to a void restriction, but the Director General may take proceedings in the Restrictive Practices Court for an injunction restraining the continuance or repetition of any such unlawful action (see also the *Flushing Cisterns* case [1973] I.C.R. 654.) and any person who has suffered a loss through the operation of the void restrictions may bring civil proceedings for damages.

What is now section 21 (1) (*b*) of the 1976 Act gives the Director General a discretion whether to refer to the Restrictive Practices

Court for adjudication a restrictive agreement which has been determined (under the Act of 1956 he was under a statutory duty to refer all registered agreements to the Court, whether they had been determined or not). Section 21 (2) of the 1976 Act allows the Department of Prices and Consumer Protection, on the representation of the Director General, to discharge him from the duty of referring agreements to the Court where it is considered that the restrictions are not of such significance (whether on economic or other grounds) as to call for investigation by the Restrictive Practices Court. (Under the Act of 1956 this could only be done where the agreements were considered to be of no substantial economic significance.)

Fair Trading Act 1973 (as regards restrictive trade practices)

The Act of 1973 contained various amendments to the previous restrictive trade practices legislation which are re-enacted in the Act of 1976. Some have already been noted. A most significant addition was the extension of the legislation to services pursuant to Part X of the 1973 Act.

Services

Part X of the Act of 1973 adapted the Acts of 1956 and 1968 and the information agreements Order for application to services (either by category or as a whole). This new law became operative after order of the Secretary of State on March 22, 1976 (see below). The combined effect of what are now sections 11–13 of the 1976 Act (and see generally Pt. III, of the 1976 Act) is that the restrictive trade practices legislation which previously applied only to goods, is applied to any agreement:

  (i) between two or more parties carrying on business in the UK in the supply of services brought under control by the Order mentioned above;

 (ii) under which two or more parties accept restrictions relating to certain **matters,** *e.g.* charges to be made for supplying **designated services.**

The Restrictive Trade Practices (Services) Order 1976 brought all commercial services under control (*i.e.* (i) above) with the exception of certain services already subject to supervision, *e.g.* by the Civil Aviation Authority, or Traffic Commissioners and designated all services, (*i.e.* (ii) above) except for those specified in Schedule 4 to the 1973 Act, *i.e.* professional services, which may however be reviewed by the Monopolies and Mergers Commission. "Services brought under control" relates to the business of the parties: contrast "designated services" which covers services in respect of which restrictions are accepted. The matters mentioned above which are included in the Order are those listed in section 107 (3) of the 1973 Act (s. 11 (2) of the 1976 Act) which resemble (but with necessary changes) those listed in s. 6 (1) of the 1956 and 1976 Acts (see p. 319, *ante.*).

The Order of March 1976 referred to above required parties to restrictive agreements relating to the supply of services to register their agreements with the Director General by June 21, 1976 or to terminate such agreements. Over 500 service agreements were submitted of which, at the time of writing,[1] 102 have been placed on the Register. Their coverage extends to nearly all commercial services, from finance to sport and entertainment. A similar Order may be made by the Secretary of State bringing under control information agreements relating to services. The mechanism for control closely follows sections of the 1968 Act (see p. 323, *ante.*).

Trade associations fall within the legislation, so that restrictions accepted by an association are deemed to be accepted by its members and recommendations made by an association are deemed to be restrictions accepted by the members. Section 16 of the 1976 Act extends the control of the 1956 Act and section 5 of the 1968 Act to trade associations as regards restrictions relating to the supply of services.

Section 18 of and the Third Schedule to the 1976 Act respectively set out exceptions to the need for registration (along the lines of the exceptions relating to the supply of goods).

As to the definition of **services**, what is now section 20 of the 1976 Act provides that the term includes all engagements undertaken for gain except for the production or supply or processing of goods. The professional services listed in the Fourth Schedule of the 1973 Act (First Sched. of the 1976 Act) are, however, excluded (see p. 325, *ante.*).

Although comprised in the one consolidating Act of 1976, the legislation applies separately to the supply of goods and services. This means that two parties engaged in the supply of goods only may freely accept restrictions in relation to services and vice versa.

[1] February 1977.

Other changes

Although detailed consideration of other amendments to the restrictive trade practices legislation, brought about by the Act of 1973, is outside the scope of this book, one or two points may be noted:

(i) The Director General's powers to require cross examination in court of executives of companies suspected of operating an unregistered agreement have been strengthened and now extend to all persons employed by the company in question (now s. 37 of the 1976 Act).

(ii) What are now sections 2 (2) and 2 (3) of the 1976 Act strengthen the court's powers in regard to trade associations where the court has pronounced against an agreement to which the members are deemed to be parties.

RESALE PRICE MAINTENANCE

The position is now covered by the Resale Prices Act 1976. Arrangements for the **collective enforcement** of price maintenance arrangements are, on principle, prohibited, thus the Act operates so as to prevent manufacturers and other suppliers from imposing conditions for the maintenance of minimum prices at which goods are to be resold and to prohibit enforcement of such prices by withholding supplies from dealers who do not observe them. The Act also prevents, on principle, collective arrangements between suppliers for recommending minimum prices, although an **individual** supplier is free to **recommend** minimum prices for his goods.

Certain classes of goods may be exempted by the Restrictive Practices Court from the general prohibition if they pass through certain gateways but only two exempting orders have been made by the Court, *viz.* in the case of books in 1969 and ethical and proprietary drugs in 1970. The Director General of Fair Trading is now responsible for enforcement of the ban on resale price maintenance.

EEC TREATY RULES OF COMPETITION

Articles 85–90 of the EEC Treaty, which contain widely drawn rules for the conduct of business in the common market now form part of English law by virtue of the European Communities Act 1972. The

EEC Treaty provisions which emphasise economic effect and substance rather than legal form are susceptible of interpretation, whereas under the restrictive trade practices legislation the "effects doctrine" is inapplicable and the emphasis is more towards a strictly legalistic approach.

Space does not permit a detailed consideration of the EEC Treaty rules of competition. The relationship between these rules and the restrictive trade practices legislation should, however, be noted.

Article 85 of the EEC Treaty and the Restrictive Trade Practices Act 1976 each has provision for exemptions. There is thus the possibility of conflict. Broadly speaking, the 1976 Act still applies even though an agreement may be void under Article 85 (1) or authorised under Article 85 (3) of the EEC Treaty. But in these circumstances the Restrictive Practices Court, if seized of the matter, has a discretion to decline or postpone the exercise of its jurisdiction (s. 5 of the 1976 Act). Alternatively, the Court may review its former decision in the light of the operation of a Community provision, *e.g.* refusal to grant exemption under Article 85 (3). The Director General may also refrain from taking proceedings before the Court in the light of any authorisation or exemption granted under Community law (s. 21 (1) (*a*) of the 1976 Act).

Regulations have been made under section 10 (2) of the European Communities Act 1972 under which details of any notification to the European Commission or any Commission decision or exemption in relation to an agreement or agreements are to be registered with the Director General.

Section 99 of the 1973 Act (ss. 9 (1) and (2) of the 1976 Act) provide that restrictions in agreements between coal and steel undertakings which relate to coal and steel are to be ignored. This fulfills the United Kingdom's obligations under the Treaty of Paris under which only the European Commission has jurisdiction in these matters.

SELECT BIBLIOGRAPHY

Books

D. Barounos, D. F. Hall and J. Rayner James, *EEC Anti Trust Law* (1975).

C. Bellamy and G. D. Child, *Common Market Law of Competition* (1972).

J. P. Cunningham, *The Fair Trading Act* 1973 (1974).

H.M.S.O. Guide, *Mergers* (1969).

V. Korah, *Competition Law of Britain and the Common Market* (1975).

V. Korah, *Monopolies and Restrictive Practices* (1968).

Lord Wilberforce, A. Campbell & N. Elles, *Restrictive Trade Practices and Monopolies* (2nd ed, 1966 with Supplements).

Office of Fair Trading, *Guide to Registration of Restrictive Trading Agreements* (1976).

Annual Reports of the Department of Trade and Industry under the Monopolies and Mergers Acts 1948 and 1965 and of Director General of Fair Trading pursuant to Fair Trading Act 1973; also Reports of Monopolies and Mergers Commission.

Articles

Cunningham, J. P., "Undertakings Under the Restrictive Trade Practices Acts" (1970) 86 L.Q.R. 239–263.

Dashwood, A. A., "New Look at Provisional Validity" (1974) 33 C.L.J. 116–129.

Goyder, D., "Public Control of Mergers" (1965) 28 M.L.R. 654–674.

Kay, M., "Conglomerate Mergers" [1969] J.B.L. 265–275.

Korah, V., "Concerted Practices" (1973) 36 M.L.R. 220–226.

Korah, V., "Registrable Agreements" [1964] J.B.L. 1–17.

Korah, V., "Resale Prices Act 1964" [1963] J.B.L. 6–14, 123–129.

Korah, V., "The Reform of the Restrictive Trade Practices Act 1956" [1967] J.B.L. 210–232.

Lever, J. F., "Bipartite Arrangements and the Restrictive Trade Practices Acts 1956 and 1968" (1969) 85 L.Q.R. 177–179.

Sich, R. L., "Restrictive Trading Agreements and the Public Interest" [1962] J.B.L. 137–145.

Whiteman, P. G., "Exclusive Distributorship Agreements in the Petrol Industry" (1966) 29 M.L.R. 507–521.

Whiteman, P. G., "The New Judicial Approach to the Restrictive Trade Practices Act 1956" (1966) 30 M.L.R. 398–425.

PART 5: NEGOTIABLE INSTRUMENTS

CHAPTER 19

BILLS OF EXCHANGE[1]

A BILL of exchange is an instrument of the class called "negotiable."

The characteristics of a negotiable instrument are—

1. The title to it passes on delivery. This distinguishes it from such things as a fire insurance policy, a bill of sale and a right to recover a debt.

2. The holder for the time being can sue in his own name.

3. No notice of assignment need be given to the person liable thereon.

4. A bona fide holder for value takes free from any defect in the title of his predecessors. This quality distinguishes a negotiable instrument from an assignable contract. Choses in action, for example, can be assigned, either at law under section 136 of the Law of Property Act 1925 or in equity, but in each case the assignee takes subject to any defences available against the assignor. In the case of a negotiable instrument, however, the assignee takes free from any such defences.

Examples of negotiable instruments are: bills of exchange, cheques, promissory notes, dividend warrants, share warrants and debentures payable to bearer. On the other hand, postal orders, share certificates, bills of lading and dock warrants are not negotiable.

A **bill of exchange** is—

—an unconditional order in writing
—addressed by one person to another
—signed by the person giving it
—requiring the person to whom it is addressed
—to pay
—on demand, or at a fixed or determinable future time
—a sum certain in money
—to or to the order of a specified person or to bearer

(s. 3 (1)).

---

[1] References in this chapter are to Bills of Exchange Act 1882 unless the contrary is expressed.

330

The following are common forms of bills of exchange:

Order bill payable on demand

> £400   London, *October* 1, 1977.
> On demand pay John Jones or order the sum of
> £400 for value received.   WILLIAM SMITH.
> *To* Thomas Robinson.

Bearer bill payable at a fixed time

> £300   Newcastle, *October* 1, 1977
> Three months after date pay bearer the sum of
> £300 for value received.   WILLIAM SMITH
> *To* Thomas Robinson.

Bill payable ten days after acceptance

> £200   Manchester, *October* 1, 1977
> Ten days after sight pay to my order £200 for
> value received.   WILLIAM SMITH
> *To* Thomas Robinson.

From these forms it will be seen that there are three parties to a bill:

1. the person who gives the order to pay—the **drawer**;
2. the person to whom the order to pay is given—the **drawee**;
3. the person to whom payment is to be made—the **payee**.

In the examples given, "William Smith" is the drawer, "Thomas Robinson" is the drawee, and "John Jones" is the payee. The drawer and the payee may be the same person, as may also the drawee and the payee. If the drawer and the drawee are the same or the drawee is a fictitious person, the instrument may be treated as a bill of exchange or a promissory note at the holder's option. The holder is the payee or indorsee who is in possession of the bill, or the bearer in the case of a bearer bill.

Both the drawee and the payee must be named or indicated with reasonable certainty. If the payee is a fictitious or non-existing person the bill may be treated as payable to bearer (s. 7 (3)). A bill drawn in favour of an existing person may be in favour of a "fictitious" person if the person named was never intended by the drawer to take under the bill.

X, a clerk employed by V, forged Z's signature to a bill drawn in favour of P, an existing person with whom V did business. The forged bill was accepted by V, the drawee; X forged P's indorsement and, on the maturity of the bill, presented it for payment to V's bank. The bank paid, and V, on learning of the fraud, claimed that the amount of the bill should not be debited against him by the bank. *Held*, as P was never intended by X to take under the bill he was a fictitious person. The bill was therefore payable to bearer, and, as the bank had paid the bearer, V's claim failed: *Bank of England* v. *Vagliano Bros.* [1891] A.C. 107.

If, however, the drawer intends the payee to take under the bill, although he is induced by fraud to form that intention, the payee is not fictitious.

M was induced by the fraud of W to draw a cheque in favour of K. M, when he signed, intended that K should take the money. W forged K's indorsement and paid the cheque into his own bank, which received payment. M sued W's bank for the amount of the cheque. *Held*, he was entitled to succeed, because K, being intended by M to receive the money, was not a fictitious payee, and the cheque was consequently not payable to bearer: *North and South Wales Bank Ltd.* v. *Macbeth* [1908] A.C. 137.

"Cash" cannot be said to be a fictitious or non-existing person and so an instrument made out "cash" cannot be read as payable to bearer. Accordingly, an instrument in the terms "pay cash or order" is not a bill of exchange because it is not to or to the order of a specified person or to bearer; but by virtue of the Cheques Act 1957, s. 4, a banker collecting payment on such a document may be protected (see p. 363, *post*) (*Orbit Mining and Trading Co. Ltd.* v. *Westminster Bank Ltd.* [1963] 1 Q.B. 794).

The bill must be an order, not a request. Accordingly, a document in the terms, "We hereby authorise you to pay on our account to the order of G £6,000," is not a bill of exchange (*Hamilton* v. *Spottiswoode* (1894) 4 Ex. 200).

The order must be unconditional. It must not order any act to be done in addition to the payment of money. If these conditions are not complied with, the instrument is not a bill of exchange. An order for payment out of a particular fund is not unconditional, but an order which is coupled with—

1. an indication of a fund from which the drawee is to refund himself; or
2. a statement of the transaction which gives rise to the bill, is unconditional (s. 3 (3)).

A bill at the end of which is written "provided the receipt form at foot hereof is signed" is not unconditional (*Bavins* v. *London and South Western Bank* [1900] 1 Q.B. 270).

On the other hand, a dividend warrant which ends with the words, "This warrant will not be honoured after three months from date unless specially indorsed by the secretary," is unconditional, the words merely denoting what the company think is a reasonable time for presenting the warrant (*Thairlwall* v. *G. N. Ry.* [1910] 2 K.B. 509).

Similarly, where the words "to be retained" were written on a cheque, it was held that the cheque was unconditional, on the ground that the words merely imported a condition between the drawer and the payee, and did not affect the order on the bankers (*Roberts & Co.* v. *Marsh* [1915] 1 K.B. 42).

A bill is payable on demand if it is expressed to be payable on demand, or at sight, or on presentation, or if no time for payment is expressed (s. 10).

A bill is payable at a determinable future time when it is expressed to be payable at a fixed period after date or sight, or after the occurrence of a specified event which is certain to happen, although the time of happening may be uncertain (s. 11). For example, an order to pay three months after X's death will be a valid bill, but an order to pay three months after X's marriage will not. Even though X does in fact marry, the order will not be a bill. Furthermore, where a document expresses the sum to be payable "on or before" a stated date, the option thus reserved to pay at an earlier date than the fixed date creates an uncertainty and contingency in the time for payment and the document is not a bill (*Williamson and Ors.* v. *Rider* [1963] 1 Q.B. 89).

A sum is certain although it may be payable—

1. with interest;
2. by instalments, with or without a provision that upon default in payment of any instalment the whole shall be due;
3. according to an indicated rate of exchange (s. 9 (1)).

If there is a difference between the sum payable as expressed in words and as expressed in figures, the sum expressed in words is the amount payable (s. 9 (2)).

A bill is **payable to order** when—

1. it is expressed to be payable to order;

    2. it is payable to a particular person and does not contain words prohibiting transfer, *e.g.* a bill in the form "to pay AB £500" is an order bill, but a bill "pay AB only" or "pay AB personally £500" is not an order bill;

    3. it is payable to the order of a particular person. In such a case it is payable either to the person in question or his order (s. 8), *e.g.* a bill payable to "the order of AB" is payable either to AB or to AB's order.

A bill is **payable to bearer** when it is expressed to be so payable or when the only or last indorsement is an indorsement in blank (s. 8 (3)).

An **inland bill** is one which is:

    1. both drawn and payable within the British Isles, or

    2. drawn within the British Isles upon some person resident therein.

A **foreign bill** is any other bill (s. 4).

A bill which is payable at a fixed period after date may be issued undated. In such a case any holder may insert the true date of issue, and if by mistake the wrong date is inserted, the bill is payable as if the date so inserted had been the true date (s. 12). The date on a bill is presumed to be the true date unless the contrary is proved.

A bill may contain words prohibiting its transfer. In such a case it is valid between the parties, but is not negotiable.

D drew a bill on G payable three months after date "to the order of D only" and crossed it "not negotiable." The bill was accepted by G and indorsed for value by D to H. *Held*, H could not sue G for the amount of the bill, because it was not transferable: *Hibernian Bank* v. *Gysin* [1939] 1 K.B. 483.

Incomplete bills (s. 20)

When a bill is wanting in any material particular, the person in possession of it has prima facie authority to fill up the omission in any way he thinks fit.

ACCEPTANCE

After a bill has been issued, the holder should present it to the drawee for acceptance to find out whether the drawee is willing to carry out the order of the drawer. If the drawee agrees to obey the drawer's order he is said to accept the bill, which he does by signing his name on the bill, with or without the word "accepted" (s. 17). Acceptance is defined as the signification by the drawee of his assent to the order of the drawer. After acceptance, the drawee is known as the acceptor. It is not essential for the holder to present the bill for acceptance, although it is to his advantage to do so as he thereby gains the additional security of the acceptor's name and, if acceptance is refused, the antecedent parties become liable immediately. In three cases, however, a bill must be presented for acceptance—

1. When it is payable after sight, presentment for acceptance is necessary to fix the date of payment.

2. When it expressly stipulates that it shall be presented for acceptance.

3. Where it is payable elsewhere than at the place of residence or business of the drawee (s. 39).

A bill may be accepted before it has been signed by the drawer or while otherwise incomplete, and even if it is overdue or has been dishonoured by a previous non-acceptance or non-payment (s. 18).

The rules as to **presentment for acceptance** are—

1. Presentment must be made at a reasonable hour on a business day and before the bill is overdue.

2. When the bill is addressed to two or more drawees who are not partners, presentment must be made to them all, unless one has authority to accept for all.

3. Where the drawee is dead, presentment may be made to his personal representative.

4. Where the drawee is bankrupt, presentment may be made to him or to his trustee.

5. Where authorised by agreement or usage, presentment may be made through the post (s. 41 (1)).

On the presentment the drawee may give either a general or a qualified acceptance, or he may refuse an acceptance.

A **general** acceptance assents without qualification to the order of the drawer.

A **qualified** acceptance in express terms varies the effect of the bill as drawn. An acceptance is qualified which is—

1. conditional;

2. partial, *i.e.* for part only of the amount of the bill;

3. local, *i.e.* to pay only at a particular place. An acceptance to pay at a particular place is a general acceptance, unless

it expressly states that the bill is to be paid there only and not elsewhere;

4. qualified as to time;

5. the acceptance of some of the drawees, but not all (s. 19).

The holder of the bill may refuse to take a qualified acceptance and may treat the bill as dishonoured by non-acceptance (s. 44 (1)). If the holder does take a qualified acceptance, the drawer and indorsers are discharged unless they have assented to it. They are deemed to assent to a qualified acceptance if, after notice, they do not dissent within a reasonable time.

A bill may therefore be treated as dishonoured by non-acceptance when—

1. The drawee does not, after presentment, accept the bill within the customary time, which is generally 24 hours.

2. The drawee gives a qualified acceptance (s. 43 (1)).

3. The drawee is dead or bankrupt, or is a fictitious person or a person not having capacity to contract by bill.

4. Presentment cannot be effected, after the exercise of reasonable diligence.

5. Although the presentment has been irregular, acceptance has been refused on some other ground (s. 41 (2)).

When a bill is treated as dishonoured by non-acceptance, notice of dishonour must be given in the manner stated below, otherwise the holder will lose his right of recourse against the drawer and indorsers.

If the acceptance is procured by fraud, the acceptor is only liable to a holder in due course and not to other holders.

A bill drawn on M in favour of A was accepted by M through the fraud of F. *Held*, M was not liable on the bill to A: *Ayres* v. *Moore* [1940] 1 K.B. 278

ACCEPTANCE FOR HONOUR

If a bill is dishonoured by non-acceptance, the holder may nevertheless allow any other person to accept it for the honour of the drawer. The bill itself sometimes has inserted in it the name of a person to whom the holder may resort in case the bill is dishonoured. Such a person is called **the referee in case of need,** but there is no obligation on the holder to resort to the referee in case of need (s. 15).

To be valid, an acceptance for honour can only take place after the bill has been protested for non-acceptance and is not overdue.

The acceptance for honour *supra protest* must—

1. be written on the bill and indicate that it is an acceptance for honour; and
2. be signed by the acceptor for honour (s. 65).

It may state for whose honour the bill is accepted, but if it does not so state it is deemed to be accepted for the honour of the drawer.

The effect of accepting a bill for honour is that the acceptor for honour becomes liable to pay the bill, provided that—

1. it is presented to the drawee for payment;
2. it is not paid by the drawee;
3. it is protested for non-payment; and
4. he has notice of these facts (s. 66).

Every person who has accepted a bill becomes liable to pay it according to the tenor of his acceptance (s. 54 (1)).

NEGOTIATION

A bill is said to be negotiated when it is transferred from one person to another in such a manner as to constitute the transferee the holder of the bill. It may be negotiated by the holder at any time either before or after acceptance in the following manner—

1. In the case of a bearer bill, by delivery.
2. In the case of an order bill, by indorsement followed by delivery. If an order bill is delivered without indorsement, the transferee acquires such title as the transferor had in the bill, and in addition the right to have the indorsement of the transferor (s. 31).

INDORSEMENTS

An indorsement, in order to operate as negotiation, must be written on the bill itself and signed by the indorser. It must be an indorsement of the entire bill, *i.e.* if the bill is for £100 it is not possible to indorse it as to £25 to X and as to £75 to Y. Where there are two or more indorsements on a bill, they are presumed to have been made in the order in which they appear on the bill, but the liability of an indorser is not affected if he inadvertently puts his signature above instead of below the indorsement of the payee, provided that it is the intention of the parties that the indorser shall be liable on

his signature (*Yeoman Credit Ltd.* v. *Gregory* [1963] 1 W.L.R. 343).
Each indorser is in the nature of a new drawer, so far as those
taking the bill after his indorsement are concerned.

Indorsements are of four kinds—

1. in blank;
2. special;
3. conditional; and
4. restrictive.

Blank indorsement

A blank indorsement is effected by the simple signature of the
payee on the back of the bill. If the payee's name is wrongly spelt,
he may indorse according to the spelling on the bill, adding, if he
thinks fit, his proper signature (s. 32). A blank indorsement specifies
no indorsee and the bill in consequence becomes payable to bearer
(s. 34 (1)).

Special indorsement

A special indorsement is when the payee writes on the back
"pay AB" or "pay AB or order," both of these having the same
meaning. If a bill has been indorsed in blank, any holder may
insert some person's name above the signature and so convert the
indorsement into a special indorsement (s. 34).

Conditional indorsement

A conditional indorsement is where a condition is attached to
the signature, as, for example, where the indorser adds the words
"*sans recours*," which has the effect of negativing his personal
liability on the bill. When a bill is so indorsed, the condition may
be disregarded by the payer and payment to the indorsee is valid
whether the condition has been fulfilled or not (s. 33).

Restrictive indorsement

A restrictive indorsement is one which prohibits further negotiation of the bill, as, for example, "pay D only," or "pay D for
the account of X," or "pay D or order for collection." This gives
the indorsee the right to receive payment of the bill, but no right to
transfer his rights (s. 35).

A holder transferring a bill after indorsement incurs the liabilities
of an indorser as set out below. The transferor of a bearer bill

incurs no liability except that he warrants to his immediate transferee for value—

1. that the bill is what it purports to be;
2. that he has a right to transfer it; and
3. that he is not aware of any fact rendering it valueless (s. 58).

A bill which is negotiable in its origin continues to be negotiable until it has been—

1. restrictively indorsed; or
2. discharged by payment or otherwise (s. 36).

HOLDER IN DUE COURSE

The effect of the negotiation of a bill is to give the transferee, if he took the bill bona fide and for value, a good title to the bill notwithstanding any defects in the title of his predecessors. This attribute is the characteristic of negotiability, and it only attaches to a transferee who is **a holder in due course.**

A holder in due course is a holder who has taken a bill—

1. complete and regular on the face of it;

A bill was drawn in favour of "F. & F. N. Co." It was indorsed "F. & F. N." *Held*, the bill was not complete and regular on the face of it: *Arab Bank Ltd.* v. *Ross* [1952] 2 Q.B. 216.

2. before it was overdue;
3. without notice that it had been previously dishonoured, if such was the fact;
4. in good faith and for value; and
5. without notice, at the time the bill was negotiated to him, of any defect in the title of the person who negotiated it (s. 29 (1)).

Every holder is deemed to be holder in due course until the contrary is proved, but the original payee cannot be such a holder (*R. E. Jones Ltd.* v. *Waring & Gillow Ltd.* [1926] A.C. 670).

The holder of a cheque who had a lien on it is deemed to have taken it for value to the extent of the sum for which he had a lien. Accordingly, provided such a holder satisfies the other conditions of section 29 (1), he can be a holder in due course (*Barclays Bank Ltd.* v. *Astley Industrial Trust Ltd.* [1970] 2 Q.B. 527).

A holder, whether for value or not, who derives his title through a holder in due course has all the rights of a holder in due course as regards the acceptor and all parties prior to such holder if he was not a party to any fraud or illegality affecting the bill.

The rights and powers of the holder of a bill are:

1. He may sue on the bill in his own name.

2. Where he is a holder in due course he holds free from any defect of title of prior parties.

3. Where his title is defective—
    (a) if he negotiates the bill to a holder in due course, that holder obtains a good title;
    (b) if he obtains payment, the person who pays him in due course gets a valid discharge (s. 38).

Valuable consideration

Valuable consideration is presumed in the case of negotiable instruments, but the presumption may be rebutted. Thus, in the case of a cheque the onus is upon the drawer of it to show that it was not for value. The consideration to support a bill is either—

1. any consideration sufficient to support a simple contract; or

2. any antecedent debt or liability.

The antecedent debt or liability must be the debt or liability of the drawer. A cheque drawn to pay an existing debt owed by the drawer is accordingly drawn for valuable consideration, but a cheque drawn to pay another's debt is not.

D owed O £400 for money lent. When payment was due D persuaded W to draw a cheque in favour of O for £400 to discharge the debt. Before the cheque was cashed, W countermanded payment. *Held*, W was not liable to O as there was no consideration for the cheque: *Oliver* v. *Davis* [1949] 2 K.B. 727.

"Where value has at any time been given for a bill the holder is deemed to be a holder for value as regards the acceptor and all parties to the bill who became parties prior to such time" (s. 27 (2)). Consequently the holder may sue the acceptor and all such parties. Further, there is no requirement that the consideration must have passed directly between one party to the bill and another party to the bill. The requirement of the subsection is met if consideration has been given by a third person.

D agreed to lend H £1,650, provided H undertook to procure a cheque for that amount from G by a certain date, so that D would have G's cheque in his possession before his own was presented. D gave H the cheque but because H was unable to get in touch with G in time D stopped it. Soon after, H did obtain the required cheque from G in favour of D, at the same time giving G his own cheque for the same amount. D paid in G's cheque and authorised payment of his cheque in favour of H. G's cheque in favour of D was dishonoured, and so was H's in favour of G. D sued G, but the latter contended that D was not a holder for value as no value had passed between them. *Held*, (1) no requirement existed for value to be given *by the holder of the cheque*; (2) on the facts double value had been given: by H giving G his own cheque in return for G's cheque in favour of D; and by D releasing his cheque in favour of H, after having stopped it; (3) accordingly D was holder for value of G's cheque and was entitled to judgment on it: *Diamond* v. *Graham* [1968] 1 W.L.R. 1061.

From the description of a holder in due course it follows—

1. When an overdue bill is negotiated, the holder takes it subject to any defect of title affecting it at its maturity (s. 36 (2)). A bill payable on demand is overdue when it appears on the face of it to have been in circulation for an unreasonable length of time.

2. When a bill which is not overdue has been dishonoured, any person taking it with notice of dishonour takes it subject to any defect of title attaching to it at the time of dishonour (s. 36 (5)).

PAYMENT

In order to make the drawer and indorsers liable on a bill it must be presented for payment. But presentment for payment is not necessary to make the acceptor liable when the bill is accepted generally (s. 52 (1)). Presentment for payment must comply with the following rules:

1. Presentment is made by exhibiting the bill to the person from whom payment is demanded. On payment the holder must deliver up the bill to the payer.

2. When the bill is payable on demand, presentment must be made within a reasonable time from issue to make the drawer liable, and within a reasonable time from indorsement to make the indorser liable (s. 45 (2)). What is a reasonable time depends on the nature of the bills, the usage of trade with regard to similar bills, and the circumstances of the case.

3. When the bill is not payable on demand, presentment must be made on the date payment is due. Three days of grace must be added to the time of payment, but when the last day of grace is a non-business day, the bill is payable on the succeeding business day. Non-business days are: Saturday, Sunday, Good Friday,

Christmas Day, a day declared to be a non-business day by an order made under the Banking and Financial Dealings Act 1971, s. 2, and a day appointed by Royal proclamation as a public fast or thanksgivings day (s. 92, as amended by the Banking and Financial Dealings Act 1971, ss. 3 and 4).

4. Presentment must be made at a reasonable hour on a business day to the payer or some person authorised to make payment on his behalf (s. 45 (3)).

5. Presentment must be made—

(a) at the place of payment specified in the bill;

(b) if no place is specified, at the address of the drawee or acceptor as given in the bill;

(c) if neither of these are present, at the acceptor's place of business, if known, and, if not, at his ordinary residence;

(d) in any other case, if presented to the acceptor wherever he can be found or at his last known place of business or residence (s. 45 (4)).

6. Presentment may be made through the post where agreement or usage authorises that course.

7. Delay in making presentment will be excused if it is imputable to circumstances beyond the holder's control, and presentment is effected with reasonable diligence after the cause of the delay has ceased to operate.

Presentment for payment may be dispensed with—

1. where, after the exercise of reasonable diligence, it cannot be effected;

2. where the drawee is a fictitious person;

3. as regards the drawer, where the drawee is not bound as between himself and the drawer to accept or pay the bill, and the drawer has no reason to believe that the bill would be paid if presented. This occurs when the bill is an accommodation bill (see p. 348, *post*);

4. as regards an indorser, where the bill was accepted or made for the accommodation of that indorser, and he has no reason to expect that the bill would be paid if presented;

5. by waiver of presentment, express or implied (s. 46).

If a bill is not paid when it is presented for payment or if, presentment for payment being excused, it is overdue and unpaid, the bill is said to be dishonoured by non-payment and the holder has an immediate right of recourse against the drawer and indorsers (s. 47). But whether the bill is dishonoured by non-acceptance or by non-payment, the drawer and indorsers cannot be sued until notice of dishonour is given.

Notice of dishonour

This notice must be given by the holder to the last indorser and to everyone on whom he wishes to impose liability. If he merely gives notice to the last indorser, the latter must give notice to any preceding indorsers whom he may wish to make liable, and they in turn must give notice to their predecessors in title. No particular form of notice is essential. The notice may be verbal or in writing or partly one and partly the other, provided that it is given in terms which sufficiently identify the bill and that it intimates that the bill has been dishonoured by non-acceptance or non-payment (s. 49). The return of the dishonoured bill is a sufficient notice of dishonour. The notice may be given as soon as the bill is dishonoured and must be given within a reasonable time.

In the absence of special circumstances, a reasonable time is as follows—

1. Where the parties live in the same place, the notice must be given or sent off in time to reach the recipient on the day after the dishonour of the bill.

2. Where the parties live in different places, the notice must be sent off on the day after the dishonour of the bill, if there be a post on a convenient hour on that day, and if there be none, then by the next post thereafter (s. 49 (12)).

Non-business days (see p. 341, *ante*) are excluded (s. 92). Notice of dishonour which is duly addressed and posted is effective although the letter may be lost or delayed in the post. Further, the notice is effective at the date when it is received, *i.e.* when it is opened or would be opened in the ordinary course of business. The notice must become effective after the bill is dishonoured. If the notice is received before the dishonour of the bill it is bad, but if it is sent out before dishonour and received after that event it is a good notice.

A bill was drawn by Needham Builders on Fir View Furniture. The bill matured on December 31, 1970. It had been accepted by Fir View Furniture and discounted and indorsed to Eaglehill. By December 28, 1970 Eaglehill and Needham knew that Fir View Furniture were in liquidation and that there was no prospect of the bill being honoured on presentation. Eaglehill prepared a notice of dishonour which they intended to send to Needham; the notice was dated January 1, 1971 and was intended to be posted that day. By a clerical error the notice was posted on December 30, 1970 and arrived at Needhams by the first post on December 31. *Held*, the notice was not vitiated by the fact that it was posted before dishonour and on balance of probabilities, as a matter of fact, it was received after dishonour. It was, therefore, a good notice: *Eaglehill Ltd.* v. *J. Needham Builders Ltd.* [1973] A.C. 992.

Delay in giving notice of dishonour will be excused if it is caused by circumstances beyond the control of the giver of the notice and is not imputable to his misconduct or negligence. But when the cause of the delay has ceased to operate, notice must be given with reasonable diligence (s. 50 (1)).

The master of a ship at Colombo drew a bill of exchange on his owners for the price of coal supplied to the ship. The bill was dishonoured on a Saturday, and the holders, after making inquiries, learnt that the vessel was in the Tyne. Not knowing what part of the Tyne, they made further inquiries without success, and finally, on the following Thursday, wrote a letter giving notice of dishonour to "the master of the 'Elmville,' Newcastle-on-Tyne." *Held*, the delay in giving notice of dishonour was excused under section 49 (12) and section 50 (1): *The Elmville* [1904] P. 319.

Notice of dishonour is dispensed with—
1. When after the exercise of reasonable diligence, notice cannot be given or does not reach the person sought to be charged.
2. By waiver, express or implied.
3. As regards the drawer, where—
    (a) the drawer and the drawee are the same person;
    (b) the drawee is a fictitious person or person not having capacity to contract;
    (c) the drawer is the person to whom the bill is presented for payment;
    (d) the drawee is as between himself and the drawer under no obligation to accept or pay the bill;
    (e) where the drawer has countermanded payment.
4. As regards the indorser, where—
    (a) the drawee is a fictitious person or a person not having capacity to contract and the indorser was aware of the fact at the time he indorsed the bill;
    (b) where the indorser is the person to whom the bill is presented for payment;

(c) where the bill was accepted or made for his accommodation (s. 50 (2)).

If a bill has been dishonoured by non-acceptance and notice of
dishonour is given, it is not necessary to give a fresh notice of
dishonour on non-payment of the bill, unless in the meantime it
has been accepted.

Where a foreign bill has been dishonoured by non-acceptance
or non-payment. in addition to notice of dishonour the bill must
be **protested**. If it is not protested, the drawer and indorsers are
discharged. An inland bill need not be protested.

A **protest** is a document drawn up by a notary, or, if no notary
is available at the place of dishonour, by a householder in the
presence of two witnesses, certifying that the bill was duly presented
for payment and that payment was refused. It must be signed by
the notary making it and must specify—

1. the person at whose request the bill is protested;
2. the date and place of protest and the reason for protesting the
   bill;
3. the demand made and the answer given, if any, or the fact
   that the drawee or acceptor could not be found.

The protest must also contain a copy of the bill. It must be
made at the place where the bill was dishonoured, except that—

1. when the bill is presented through the post office and returned
   by post dishonoured, it may be protested at the place to which
   it was returned;
2. when the bill is payable at the place of business or residence
   of some person other than the drawee and has been dishonoured by non-acceptance, it must be protested for non-
   payment at the place where it is expressed to be payable.

Protest may be dispensed with by any circumstances dispensing
with notice of dishonour. It must be made promptly, but it is
sufficient if the bill has been noted for protest within the specified
time, and the formal protest may be extended at any time afterwards as of the date of the noting (s. 93). A bill may be noted on
the day of its dishonour and must be noted not later than the next
succeeding business day (Bills of Exchange (Time of Noting) Act
1917); non-business days (see p. 341, *ante*) are excluded.

Payment for honour

If a bill has been accepted for honour *supra protest* or contains a reference in case of need, it must at maturity be presented to the acceptor for payment. If the acceptor dishonours it, it must be protested for non-payment and then presented to the acceptor for honour or referee in case of need. The presentment must be made in accordance with the following rules—

1. Where the address of the acceptor for honour is in the same place as where the bill is protested for non-payment, the bill must be presented not later than the day following its maturity.

2. Where his address is in some other place, the bill must be forwarded not later than the day following its maturity (s. 67).

When a bill has been protested for non-payment, any person may intervene and pay it. Such a payment, in order not to operate as a mere voluntary payment, must be attested by a notarial act of honour which may be appended to the protest. The notarial act of honour must declare the intention to pay the bill for honour and for whose honour it is paid. The effect of a payment for honour *supra protest* being made is to discharge all parties subsequent to the party for whose honour it is paid and to subrogate the payer for honour for the holder. On paying the bill and the notarial expenses incident to the protest, the payer for honour is entitled to receive both the bill and the protest. If the holder of the bill refuses to receive payment *supra protest*, he loses his right of recourse against any party who would have been discharged by the payment (s. 68).

LIABILITY OF PARTIES

No person is liable on a bill whether as drawer, indorser or acceptor who has not signed it, but the fact of his signing it in a trade or assumed name does not absolve him from liability (s. 23). A signature by procuration operates as notice that the agent has only a limited authority to sign, and therefore the principal will not be bound unless the agent was acting within the scope of his authority (s. 25). Accordingly, if the payee receives payment of a bill drawn by an agent without authority and knows that it is so drawn, he is liable to refund the amount received to the drawer.

T had a power of attorney to draw cheques on R's behalf. He bought a motor car from B and paid for it by a cheque signed "R by T his attorney." B knew the car was bought by T for his own use. *Held,* B must refund the amount of the cheque to R: *Reckitt v. Barnett* [1929] A.C. 176.

If a person signs a bill and adds words to his signature indicating that he signs for or on behalf of a principal or in a representative character, he is not personally liable on the bill; but the words must clearly show that he signs as agent, a mere description of himself as an agent does not negative his personal liability. When it is doubtful whether the signature is that of a principal or of an agent, the construction most favourable to the validity of the instrument is to be adopted (s. 26).

Examples—A signature "for and on behalf of X as agent—Y," Y is not liable as he has negatived personal liability.

A signature "P & W, Churchwardens"; P and W are liable, the word "churchwardens" being merely a description: *Rew v. Pettet* (1834) 1 Ad. & E. 196.

A bill of exchange drawn on the F company was accepted by the company. It was also indorsed on the back "F Co., Ltd., A B and C D, directors." In an action against A B and C D as indorsers, *held*, A B and C D were liable, the addition to their signatures of the word "directors" being a description only, and not a word excluding their liability: *Elliott v. Bax-Ironside* [1925] 2 K.B. 301.

The Companies Act 1948, s. 108 (4) (*b*), provides that an officer of a company or another person who signs or authorises to be signed on behalf of a company a bill of exchange, promissory note or cheque in a name other than the proper name of the company, shall be personally liable. Thus, where the directors of the L. & R. Agencies Ltd. signed a cheque for the company by writing "L.R. Agencies Ltd.," omitting the connecting ampersand, they were held to be personally liable (*Hendon v. Adelman and Others* (1973) 117 S.J. 631). But the use of the abbreviation "Ltd." or a similar abbreviation for "Limited"—or possibly the use of an ampersand for "and" —does not attract personal liability (*Durham Fancy Goods Ltd. v. Michael Jackson (Fancy Goods) Ltd.* [1968] 2 Q.B. 839).

A person who accepts a bill engages to pay it according to the tenor of his acceptance. He is precluded from denying to a holder in due course the existence of the drawer, the genuineness of his signature or his capacity to draw the bill; also he is precluded from denying the capacity of the drawer or payee to indorse the bill, but not the genuineness of their indorsements (s. 54).

The drawer engages that on due presentment the bill shall be accepted and paid according to its tenor, and that if it be dishonoured he will compensate the holder or any indorser who is compelled to pay it, provided that the requisite proceedings on dishonour be taken. He is precluded from denying to a holder in due course the existence of the payee or his capacity to indorse (s. 55).

The indorser engages that on due presentment the bill shall be accepted and paid according to its tenor, and that if it be dishonoured he will compensate the holder or a subsequent indorser who is compelled to pay it, provided that the requisite proceeding on dishonour be taken. He is precluded from denying to a holder in due course the genuineness of the drawer's signature and all previous indorsements, and to his immediate or a subsequent indorsee that the bill was at the time of his indorsement a valid bill and that he had a good title thereto (s. 55).

A bill purports to be drawn by A on B in favour of C. A's signature is forged. The bill is indorsed in blank by C to D for value and eventually is negotiated to X, a holder in due course. C is liable on the bill as indorser; B is only liable if he accepts the bill; D is under no liability unless X is his immediate transferee for value.

Any person who signs a bill otherwise than as drawer or acceptor incurs the liabilities of an indorser. If a person has signed a bill as drawer, acceptor or indorser without receiving value therefor, he is known as an **accommodation party**. He incurs full liability on the bill to a holder for value, and it is immaterial whether, when the holder took the bill, he knew the party to be an accommodation party or not (s. 28).

The **measure of damages** on a dishonoured bill is—
1. the amount of the bill;
2. interest from the time of presentment for payment if the bill is payable on demand and from the maturity of the bill in any other case;
3. the expenses of noting, and, when protest is necessary, the expenses of protest.

When the bill is dishonoured abroad, the measure of damages is the amount of the re-exchange with interest until the time of payment. This is the sum for which a sight bill, drawn at the time and place where the drawer or indorser sought to be charged resides, must be drawn to realise at the place of dishonour the amount of the dishonoured bill and the expenses consequent on its dishonour (s. 57).

Forged Signatures

If any of the signatures on a bill are forged, the signature in question is wholly inoperative and no person, even if acting in good faith, can acquire rights under it (s. 24).

S carried on business in London, and had a branch in Manchester. X, the manager of the Manchester branch, without any authority from S, drew seven bills of exchange, purporting to do so on behalf of S, and signed them "X, Manchester manager." The bills having been dishonoured, K, a holder in due course, sued S as drawer. *Held*, (1) the bills being drawn by X without authority were forgeries and (2) S was not liable on them: *Kreditbank Cassel* v. *Schenkers Ltd.* [1927] 1 K.B. 826.

Exceptions

1. If a banker pays a bill which is drawn on a banker and payable to order on demand, in good faith and in the ordinary course of business, he is protected from liability for his act if the **indorsement** has been forged or made without authority (s. 60).

The person receiving payment will, however, be liable to refund any money received under a forged indorsement to the true owner.

G drew cheques in favour of X. G's clerk forged X's indorsement and negotiated the cheques to C, who took them in good faith and for value. C received payment of the cheques. *Held*, G could recover the amount of the cheques from C: *Goldman* v. *Cox* (1924) 40 T.L.R. 744.

2. If a transferee taking under a forged instrument in a foreign country obtains, by the law of that country, a good title, his title will be treated as good in England (s. 72).

A cheque on a London bank was drawn in Rumania in favour of E. The cheque was stolen and the thief forged the indorsement. It was then presented in Vienna to a bank which paid it in good faith and without negligence, and by Austrian law this gave the Vienna bank a good title. The Vienna bank sent the cheque to the Anglo-Austrian bank, who obtained payment from the bank on which it was drawn. In an action by E to recover the amount of the cheque from the Anglo-Austrian bank, *held*, that as their predecessors in title had by Austrian law a good title to the cheque, the Anglo-Austrian bank also had a good title and E could not succeed: *Embiricos* v. *Anglo-Austrian Bank* [1905] 1 K.B. 677.

Disc+ARGE OF THE BILL

DISCHARGE OF THE BILL

A bill is discharged by—

1. **Payment** in due course by or on behalf of the drawee or acceptor. Payment in due course means payment made at or after the maturity of the bill to the holder in good faith and without notice that his title is defective. Payment by the drawer or an indorser does not discharge the bill, but—

(a) where a bill payable to or to the order of a third party is paid by the drawer, the drawer may enforce payment against the acceptor, but may not reissue the bill;

(b) where a bill is paid by an indorser, or where a bill payable to the drawer's order is paid by the drawer, the party paying it is remitted to his former rights as regards the acceptor or antecedent parties, and he may, if he thinks fit, strike out his own and subsequent indorsements and again negotiate the bill.

When an accommodation bill is paid by the party accommodated the bill is discharged (s. 59).

2. The acceptor of the bill becoming the holder of it at or after maturity in his own right (s. 61).

3. **Waiver,** where the holder renounces his rights under it. Renunciation must be in writing, unless the bill is delivered up to the acceptor (s. 62).

4. **Cancellation,** where it is done intentionally by the holder or his agent and the cancellation is apparent (s. 63).

5. **Alteration** of the bill in a material particular without the assent of all parties liable on it. The following alterations are material: the date, the sum payable, the time of payment, the place of payment, and, where the bill has been accepted generally, the addition of a place of payment without the acceptor's assent. It is also material to alter an inland bill into a foreign bill. The alteration of the number on a bank-note is a material alteration, and avoids the note even in the hands of an innocent holder (*Suffel* v. *Bank of England* (1882) 9 Q.B.D. 555). But if the alteration is made accidentally, the note is not avoided (*Hong Kong and Shanghai Bank* v. *Lo Lee Shi* [1928] A.C. 181).

The effect of a material alteration is only to discharge those who became parties prior to the alteration. The person who made the alteration and all subsequent indorsers are bound by the bill as altered.

If the alteration is not apparent and the bill is in the hands of a holder in due course, the holder may enforce the bill as if it had never been altered (s. 64).

An alteration is apparent if it is of such a kind that it would be noticed by an intending holder scrutinising the document which he intends to take with reasonable care (*Woollatt* v. *Stanley* (1928) 138 L.T. 620).

LOST BILL

If a bill is lost before it is overdue, the holder may apply to the drawer to give him another bill of the same tenor, and the drawer is bound to do so on receiving from the holder security indemnifying the drawer against loss (s. 69).

BILL IN A SET

When a bill is drawn in a set, *i.e.* in duplicate or triplicate, then if each part of the set is numbered and contains a reference to the others, the whole of the parts only constitute one bill. The acceptor should only accept one part, and if he accepts more than one and the different parts get into the hands of different holders in due course, he is liable on each part. On payment, he should require the part bearing his signature to be delivered up to him, because, if he does not do so, he will be liable on it if it is outstanding in the hands of a holder in due course. If the holder indorses two or more parts to different persons, he is liable on each. Except in the cases just mentioned, payment of one part discharges the whole bill (s. 71).

CONFLICT OF LAWS

The form of a bill is determined by the law of the place of issue, but if a bill issued out of the United Kingdom conforms as regards its form to the law of the United Kingdom, it is valid as between all persons who negotiate, hold or become parties to it in the United Kingdom.

The form and the interpretation of the acceptance, indorsement or acceptance *supra protest* and the interpretation of the drawing of a bill is according to the law of the country where it took place.

A bill was drawn by E V in France on K in London to the order of M V. It was indorsed in France by E V with the authority of M V in his own name and without the addition of words to the effect that the indorsement was made on behalf of M V. Such an indorsement was of no effect in English law (s. 32 (1)), but gave a good title to the indorsee by French law. *Held*, the indorsee had a good title, as the validity of the indorsement as regards form was governed by French law: *Koechlin et Cie* v. *Kestenbaum Bros.* [1927] 1 K.B. 889.

But if an inland bill is indorsed abroad, the interpretation of the indorsement is according to the law of the United Kingdom. The duty of the holder with respect to presentment for acceptance or payment is determined by the law of the place where it is to be done. The duty of the holder with regard to protest of notice of dishonour is determined by the law of the country where the bill was dishonoured. When a bill is drawn in one country and is payable in another, the time when it is payable is determined by the law of the place of payment (s. 72).

Where a bill is expressed in foreign currency, the holder, when suing on it, has a choice: he may either sue in sterling, converting, in the absence of some express stipulation, the foreign currency at the date when the bill matured (s. 72 (4)), or he may sue in the foreign currency; in the latter case the English court will give judgment in the foreign currency and the judgment debt will be converted into sterling either at the date of payment of the judgment or at the date of execution (*Barclays Bank International Ltd.* v. *Levin Brothers (Bradford) Ltd.* [1976] 3 W.L.R. 852).

COLLECTION ARRANGEMENTS AND DOCUMENTARY CREDITS

In the export trade payment of the price is normally effected under a collection arrangement or a documentary credit. In both cases the seller draws a bill of exchange. Under a collection arrangement a bank at the buyer's place is instructed to present that bill to the buyer and on his acceptance or payment—depending on the terms of the contract of export sale—to deliver the bill of lading and other shipping documents to him; the bill of lading will enable him to take delivery of the goods when the ship carrying the goods arrives. Under a documentary credit finance is provided for the seller by a bank in his own country on delivery of the shipping documents to the bank; this is done either by the bank discounting or purchasing the seller's bill drawn on the buyer or by the seller drawing directly on the bank for payment. Collection arrangements and the documentary credits are governed by international regulations sponsored by the International Chamber of Commerce and applied by most banks in the world. Collection arrangements are governed by the *Uniform Rules for the Collection of Commercial Paper 1967*, and documentary credits by the *Uniform Customs and Practice for Documentary Credits 1974*.

Documentary credits

Of particular importance is the documentary credit. This method of payment applies only if the parties to an export transaction have adopted it in their contract of sale. The buyer instructs a bank in his country (the issuing bank) to open a credit with a bank in the seller's country (the correspondent bank) in favour of the seller, specifying the documents which the seller has to deliver to the bank if he wishes to receive finance and also the date of expiry of the credit.

Confirmed documentary credits

A documentary credit may be opened by the issuing bank as revocable or irrevocable. If the correspondent bank adds its own **confirmation** of the credit to the seller, the latter has the certainty that a bank in his own locality will provide him with finance if he delivers the correct shipping documents in the stipulated time (*Hamzeh Malas & Sons* v. *British Imex Industries Ltd.*, below). A "reliable paymaster" in his own country has been substituted for the overseas buyer. A confirmed credit constitutes "a direct undertaking by the banker that the seller, if he presents the documents as required in the required time, will receive payment" (*per* Diplock J. in *Ian Stach Ltd.* v. *Baker Bosley Ltd.* [1958] 2 Q.B. 130); the confirmation thus constitutes a conditional debt of the banker, *i.e.* a debt subject to the condition precedent that the seller tenders the specified documents (*W. J. Allan & Co. Ltd.* v. *El Nasr Export and Import Co.* [1972] 2 Q.B. 189). The buyer need not open the credit as confirmed unless he has undertaken to do so in the contract of sale. A confirmed credit which has been notified to the seller cannot be cancelled by the bank on the buyer's instructions.

X sold machinery to Y in Calcutta to be delivered by instalments, payment to be made for each shipment as it took place by means of a confirmed credit with Y's bank in England. Y's bank told X that a

"confirmed irrevocable credit" was open in his favour. After two ship-
ments had been made and paid for, the bank on Y's instructions refused
X's bill. *Held*, the bank was liable in damages to X: *Urquhart Lindsay &
Co. v. Eastern Bank* [1922] 1 K.B. 318.

Jordanian buyers bought a quantity of steel rods from British sellers.
The goods were to be shipped in two instalments and payment was to be
made under two confirmed credits, one for each instalment, to be opened
with the Midland Bank, London. After receipt of the first instalment the
buyers who had already opened the second credit applied for an injunction
restraining the sellers from recovering any money under the second
credit. *Held*, the injunction had to be refused because the bank was under
an absolute obligation to pay, irrespective of any dispute between the
parties to the contract of sale, on tender of the stipulated documents:
Hamzeh Malas & Sons v. British Imex Industries Ltd. [1958] 2 Q.B. 127.

But an irrevocable credit, whether confirmed or unconfirmed,
should not be honoured by the bank if the seller has acted fraudulently or another sufficiently grave cause exists for interfering with
the credit. "I would be slow to interfere with bankers' irrevocable
credits, and not least in the sphere of international banking, unless
a sufficiently grave cause is shown" (*per* Megarry J. in *Discount
Records, Ltd. v. Barclays Bank Ltd.*, below, 320).

Discount Records, an English company, ordered records and cassettes
from Promodisc, a French company. Discount instructed Barclays Bank
to open an irrevocable credit in favour of Promodisc and Barclays Bank
passed on these instructions to Barclays Bank International. Discount
alleged that on arrival of the goods they found them to be a fraudulent
shipment and moved the court for an interlocutory injunction restraining
the banks from paying until final judgment or further order. *Held*, no
fraud was established and no sufficiently grave cause was disclosed for
interfering with the credit; injunction refused: *Discount Records Ltd. v.
Barclays Bank Ltd.* [1975] 1 W.L.R. 315.

The doctrine of strict compliance

The banks which operate the documentary credit act as agents
for the buyer who is the principal. If they exceed his instructions,
they have acted without authority and he need not ratify their act;
the loss would then fall on the bank in question. This has led to the
development of the **doctrine of strict compliance** under which the
correspondent bank will, on principle, refuse documents tendered by
the seller which do not correspond strictly with the instructions.
"There is no room for documents which are almost the same or
which will do just as well" (*per* Lord Sumner in *Equitable Trust Co.
of New York v. Dawson Partners Ltd.* below).

Dawsons bought a quantity of vanilla beans from a seller in Batavia (Jakarta). They opened a credit in his favour through Equitable Trust, instructing them to provide finance on presentation of certain documents, including a certificate of experts. Equitable Trust paid on tender of a certificate by a single expert. The seller was fraudulent and had shipped mainly rubbish but the expert who inspected the cargo had failed to notice it. *Held*, Equitable Trust had paid contrary to Dawsons' instructions and could not debit them: *Equitable Trust Company of New York* v. *Dawson Partners Ltd.* (1926) 27 Lloyd's Law Rep. 49.

Soproma, an Italian company, bought a quantity of Chilian fish full meal from Animal By-Products, a New York company. The contract was c. and f. Savona, and provided that the buyers should open a documentary credit with a New York bank. The documents to be presented by the sellers had to include bills of lading issued to order and marked "freight prepaid" and an analysis certificate showing that the fish meal had a content of at least 70 per cent. protein. The documents tendered to the bank were not correct; the bills of lading were not to order and bore the remark "freight collect" instead of "freight prepaid" and the certificate showed only a minimum protein content of 67 per cent. The bank rejected the documents. After the expiry of the credit the sellers made a direct tender of the correct documents to the buyers who rejected them. *Held*, the second tender was irrelevant and had to be disregarded, and the bank had rightly rejected the first tender of the documents: *Soproma S.p.A.* v. *Marine & Animal By-Products Corporation* [1966] 1 Lloyd's Rep. 367.

Opening of documentary credit

The credit must be made available to the seller at the beginning of the shipment period (*Pavia & Co.* v. *Thurmann-Nielsen* [1952] 2 Q.B. 84). If the parties have not laid down in their contract a time for opening the credit, it must be opened a reasonable time before the seller has to make shipment (*Sinason-Teicher Inter-American Grain Corporation* v. *Oilcakes and Oilseeds Trading Co. Ltd.* [1954] 1 W.L.R. 935). If an intermediary bank has become insolvent, the buyer or another person involved in the transaction may make direct payment to the seller (*Sale Continuation Ltd.* v. *Austin Taylor & Co. Ltd.* [1967] 2 Lloyd's Rep. 403).

SELECT BIBLIOGRAPHY
Books

Chalmers on Bills of Exchange (13th ed., 1964) by D. A. L. Smout.
D. Richardson, *A Simple Guide to Negotiable Instruments and the Bills of Exchange Acts* (3rd ed., 1963).

Articles

Axworthy, C. S., "The Revision of the Uniform Customs on Documentary Credits" [1971] J.B.L. 38.

Hudson, A. H., "Alterations in Bills of Exchange" [1975] J.B.L. 108–113.

Ryder, F. R., "Payment of Cheques—A New Source of Liability" [1975] J.B.L. 195–201.

Silberberg, H., "Personal Liability of Directors on Bills of Exchange" [1967] J.B.L. 116–121.

Thornely, J. W. A., "Consideration for Negotiable Instruments" [1968] C.L.J. 196–198.

Wheble, B. S., "Uniform Customs and Practice for Documentary Credits (1974 Revision)" [1975] J.B.L. 281–286.

CHAPTER 20

CHEQUES AND PROMISSORY NOTES[1]

A **cheque** is
—a bill of exchange
—drawn on a banker
—payable on demand (s. 73).
It therefore follows that the law relating to bills of exchange set out in the preceding chapter applies equally to cheques.

A cheque form was filled up "Pay cash or order," the word "cash" being in writing and "or order" printed. *Held*, not a cheque, because it was not payable to a specified person or to bearer but a direction to pay cash to bearer, the printed "or order" being neglected in favour of the written word "cash": *North and South Insurance Co.* v. *National Provincial Bank* [1936] 1 K.B. 328.

A bank is not bound to honour an undated cheque. The holder of such a cheque is authorised by section 20 (see p. 334, *ante*) to fill in the date, but he must do so within a reasonable time (*Griffiths* v. *Dalton* [1940] 2 K.B. 264).

A cheque may be postdated (s. 13 (2)). A cheque is not usually accepted. Marking or certification is not an acceptance.

A cheque drawn on the B bank on June 13, postdated to June 20, was certified by the manager "marked good for payment on 20.6.39." The P bank became holders in due course and on June 20 presented the cheque for payment, which was refused owing to the state of the drawer's account. *Held*, (1) the certification was not an acceptance of the cheque; (2) the manager had no authority to certify postdated cheques; (3) the B bank was not liable: *Bank of Baroda Ltd.* v. *Punjab National Bank* [1944] A.C. 176.

The holder of a cheque must present it for payment within a reasonable time of its issue, and failure to do this will discharge the drawer to the extent of any damage he may suffer from the delay. Damage will only be suffered when the bank on which the cheque is drawn is unable, for any reason, to honour the cheque.

[1] References in this chapter are to the Bills of Exchange Act 1882 unless the contrary is expressed.

357

Y sent a cheque to W in payment of his rent. W received it on a Friday, and on the Saturday he posted it to his bank, which received it on the Monday. The bank sent it to its head office, which received it on the Tuesday, and present it to Y's bank for payment on the Wednesday. That day Y's bank stopped payment. The jury found that the cheque was not presented within a reasonable time. *Held*, owing to the unreasonable delay on the part of W, Y was discharged from liability on the cheque: *Wheeler* v. *Young* (1897) 13 T.L.R. 468.

In such a case the holder of the cheque is a creditor of the bank to the extent of the discharge of the drawer (s. 74).

If a bank wrongly dishonours a cheque, it is liable to pay damages to its customer, but only nominal damages can be recovered by persons who are not traders.

The relationship of banker and customer is that of debtor and creditor, with the modification that the banker is only liable to repay the customer on payment being demanded, while the ordinary debtor is under an obligation to pay without any demand being made. The consequence of this is that a banker cannot successfully plead the Statutes of Limitation to any action for money standing to a customer's credit, until six years from a demand of payment has elapsed (*Joachimson* v. *Swiss Bank Corporation* [1921] 3 K.B. 111). If, however, the account has not been operated upon for a number of years, payment may be presumed.

In May 1866 F deposited £6,000 with the bank. Transactions were recorded until November 1866, after which there was no record of any payment of principal or interest by the bank. F died in 1893, and in 1927 the deposit receipt was discovered by F's executor. *Held*, payment must be presumed: *Douglass* v. *Lloyds Bank Ltd.* (1929) 34 Com.Cas. 263.

Where a deposit account is kept between a customer and a banker, there is not a new contract every time money is paid in (*Hart* v. *Sangster* [1957] Ch. 329).

An unindorsed cheque—like an indorsed one—which appears to have been paid by the banker on whom it is drawn is evidence of the receipt by the payee of the sum payable by the cheque (Cheques Act 1957, s. 3).

The authority of a banker to pay a cheque is terminated by—

1. Countermand of payment. An oral countermand is sufficient, but whether oral or written it must actually reach the banker.

C drew a cheque on his bank and on the same day, after business hours, countermanded payment by telegram. The telegram was put in the letter-box and, owing to the negligence of the bank's servants, did not reach the manager until two days later. In the meantime the cheque was cashed. *Held*, the cheque was not countermanded because (1) countermanding means actual notice to the banker, there being no such thing as a constructive countermand, and (2) the bank were not, although they reasonably might accept, bound to accept an unauthenticated telegram as authority to stop payment: *Curtice* v. *London City and Midland Bank Ltd.* [1908] 1 K.B. 293.

2. Notice of the customer's death (s. 75).

3. The making of a receiving order against the drawer, whether the banker knows of it or not.

4. Notice of the presentation of a bankruptcy petition against the drawer (Bankruptcy Act 1914, ss. 45, 46).

CROSSED CHEQUES

A cheque is a crossed cheque when two parallel lines are drawn across it; in addition to the parallel lines, words may be written across the cheque.

Crossings are of four kinds—

1. General; consisting only of the parallel lines, or with the addition of the words "and company."

2. Special: when the name of a banker is written between the parallel lines.

3. Not negotiable: when these words are written across the cheque, either with or without the name of a banker.

4. A/c payee: when these words are written across the cheque, whether in addition to the other crossings or not.

The crossing is a material part of the cheque and must not be obliterated or added to or altered except in the following cases—

1. Where a cheque is uncrossed, the holder may cross it generally or specially.

2. Where a cheque is crossed generally, the holder may cross it specially or add the words "not negotiable."

3. A banker to whom a cheque is crossed specially may cross it specially to another banker for collection.

4. Where a cheque is sent to a banker for collection he may cross it specially to himself (s. 77).

When a cheque is crossed it can only be paid to a banker, and if crossed specially, only to the banker named in the crossing. If the banker on whom the cheque is drawn pays it otherwise than in accordance with the crossing, he is liable to the true owner of the cheque for any loss he may sustain owing to the payment (s. 79). But if the cheque does not appear to be crossed or to have had a crossing which has been obliterated or to have been added to or altered, and the banker pays the cheque in good faith and without negligence, he does not incur any liability.

When a cheque is crossed "not negotiable," the person taking it does not have and is not capable of giving a better title to the cheque than that which the person from whom he took it had (s. 81).

W drew a cheque crossed "not negotiable" in blank and handed it to his clerk to fill in the amount and name of the payee. The clerk inserted a sum in excess of her authority and delivered the cheque to P in payment of a debt of her own. *Held*, the clerk had no title to the cheque, P had no better title and W was not liable on the cheque: *Wilson and Meeson* v. *Pickering* [1946] K.B. 422.

The words "account payee" on a cheque are a direction to the bankers collecting payment that the proceeds when collected are to be applied to the credit of the account of the payee designated on the face of the cheque. If, therefore, the bankers credit the proceeds to a different account, they are prima facie guilty of negligence and will be liable to the true owner for the amount of the cheque. This prima facie liability can be displaced on their proving that they made proper inquiry as to the authority of the person, to whose account the cheque was credited, to receive the amount.

A cheque was drawn in favour of "F. S. H. and others or bearer" and crossed "account payee." N, the bearer, paid the cheque into his own account at his bank, and the bank credited him with the proceeds without making any inquiries as to his title to the cheque. N had no title to the cheque. *Held*, having regard to the crossing, the bank were negligent and liable to the true owner of the cheque: *House Property Co.* v. *London County and Westminster Bank* (1915) 84 L.J.K.B. 1846.

If a bank collects the cheque on behalf of another bank, they are not bound to see that the other bank credits the payee with the amount of the cheque.

X drew cheques in favour of Y, crossed "account payee only," and sent them to Z, his agent, to forward to Y. Z forged Y's indorsement and paid the cheques into his own bank in Germany, who forwarded them to their London agents, the W bank, for collection. The W bank collected the proceeds of the cheques and credited the German bank with the amount received. *Held*, the W bank were not liable to X, because they were not bound to inquire to whose account the German bank credited the proceeds of the cheques: *Importers Co. Ltd.* v. *Westminster Bank* [1927] 2 K.B. 297.

The duty of the collecting banker must be carefully distinguished from that of the paying banker.

"A crossing is a direction to the paying bank to pay the money generally to a bank or to a particular bank, as the case may be, and when this has been done the whole purpose of the crossing has been served. The paying bank has nothing to do with the application of the money after it has once been paid to the proper receiving banker. The words "Account A B" are a mere direction to the receiving bank as to how the money is to be dealt with after receipt": *per* Bigham J. in *Akrokerri (Atlantic) Mines Ltd.* v. *Economic Bank* [1904] 2 K.B. at p. 472.

A cheque crossed "account payee" is still negotiable (*National Bank* v. *Silke* [1891] 1 Q.B. 435), but a bill payable to "payee only" is not negotiable (see p. 334, *ante*).

PROVISIONS PROTECTING BANKERS

The Bills of Exchange Act 1882 and the Cheques Act 1957 afford bankers special protection from liability when paying a crossed cheque to a banker; or receiving payment of a crossed cheque for a customer; or paying a cheque that is not indorsed. However, no definition is given of a banker save that it *includes* a body of persons, whether incorporated or not, *who carry on the business of banking.*

Characteristics which are usually found in bankers today were identified in *United Dominions Trust Ltd.* v. *Kirkwood* [1966] 2 Q.B. 431, as follows—

1. they accept money from, and collect cheques for, their customers and place them to their credit;
2. they honour cheques or orders drawn on them by their customers when presented for payment and debit their customers accordingly; and
3. they keep current accounts, or something of that nature, in their books in which the credits and debits are entered.

The Department of Trade is empowered to give a certificate that a company ought to be treated, for the purposes of the Moneylenders Acts, as a banking company and not as a moneylender (see p. 92, *ante*). In issuing such a certificate the Department would no doubt use as a guide the characteristics identified above. Further, production of such a certificate in legal proceedings, whilst not legally conclusive in proceedings under a statute other than the Money-lenders Acts, would be strong evidence of the fact that a company was regarded as a banker and so was a banker (see Companies Act 1967, s. 123).

A banker, but not other persons, is protected—
  1. If, when there is a forged indorsement, the banker pays
      (a) a bill drawn on him payable to order on demand,
      (b) in good faith and in the ordinary course of business, he is deemed to have paid the bill in due course (s. 60).

X drew a cheque in favour of Y or order. Z stole it and forged Y's indorsement. X's bankers paid the cheque in good faith, and in the ordinary course of business. *Held*, the bankers could debit X's account with the amount of the cheque: *Charles* v. *Blackwell* (1877) 2 C.P.D. 151.

A banker can act negligently although he is acting in the ordinary course of business. "The common aphorism that a banker is under a duty to know his customer's signature is in fact incorrect even as between the banker and his customer. The principle is simply that a banker cannot debit his customer's account on the basis of a forged signature, since he has in that event no mandate from the customer for doing so" (*per* Kerr J. in *National Westminster Bank Ltd.* v. *Barclays Bank International Ltd.*, see below). Where a banker, without acting negligently, pays a cheque on which the signature of his customer (the drawer) is forged, he can recover the amount paid from the collecting bank and the payee.

Commander Robert Bill, who lived in Nigeria, was a customer of the National Westminster Bank at one of their branches in London. One of his cheques was stolen in Nigeria. His signature as drawer was so skilfully forged that the forgery was practically undetectable and the cheque was made payable to Mr. Mohamed Ismail, of Nigeria, who was unaware that it was forged and who gave valuable consideration for it; the cheque was not crossed. Mr. Ismail sent the cheque to Barclays Bank International in London, with whom he banked, and instructed them to collect it by way of special collection. National Westminster, to whom Barclays International presented the cheque, did not discover the forgery and paid Barclays who credited the amount to Mr. Ismail's account. Later the forgery was discovered and National Westminster brought an action against Barclays and Mr. Ismail for the recovery of the £8,000. *Held*, (1) National Westminster had not acted negligently in honouring their customer's cheque, (2) they could recover: *National Westminster Bank Ltd.* v. *Barclays International Ltd.* [1975] Q.B. 654.

Further, if, in the absence of an indorsement or where there is an irregular indorsement, a banker pays

(a) a cheque drawn on him,

(b) in good faith and in the ordinary course of business,

he is protected (Cheques Act 1957, s. 1).

2. If, *when a cheque is crossed*, the banker pays

(a) the cheque drawn on him,

(b) in good faith and without negligence,

(c) if crossed generally, to a banker, and, if crossed specially, to the banker to whom it is crossed,

he is placed in the same position as if he had paid the true owner (s. 80).

The drawer is also protected if the cheque has come into the hands of the payee.

3. A banker who receives an unindorsed cheque "for collection" and has given value for, or has a lien on it, has the same rights as if the cheque had been indorsed to him in blank (Cheques Act 1957, s. 2).

Section 2 applies even if the cheque is collected not for the payee's account but for another account, but the banker can successfully sue the drawer of an unindorsed cheque only if he gave value for the cheque or had a lien on it; otherwise the cheque must be indorsed to him (*Westminster Bank Ltd.* v. *Zang* [1966] A.C. 182).

4. If, when a customer has no title or a defective title to a cheque, the banker receives payment of a cheque *whether crossed or not crossed*,

(a) for the customer,

(b) in good faith and without negligence,

the banker does not incur any liability by reason only of having received payment (Cheques Act 1957, s. 4).

This section (which takes the place of the repealed s. 82 of the Act of 1882) applies to cheques and to any document issued by a customer of a banker which, though not a bill of exchange, is intended to enable a person to obtain payment from that banker of the sum mentioned in the document. It therefore applies, *inter alia*, to bankers' drafts, dividend warrants and cheques payable "cash or order" (p. 332, *ante*). Further, where an agent having a customer's ostensible authority to sign and issue an instrument, the instrument is a document "issued by a customer" even where the agent signs it and puts it into circulation in fraud of his principal (*Orbit Mining and Trading Co. Ltd.* v. *Westminster Bank Ltd.* [1963] 1 Q.B. 794).

A banker is not protected if a cheque ceases to be a cheque by reason of a material alteration (*Slingsby* v. *District Bank* [1932] 1 K.B. 544).

A person becomes a customer of a banker when he goes to the banker with money or a cheque and asks to have an account opened, and the banker accepts the money or cheque and agrees to open an account. The duration of the relationship is immaterial. But mere casual acts of service, such as cashing a cheque for a friend of a customer, do not create the relationship of banker and customer (*Commissioners of Taxation* v. *English, Scottish and Australian Bank Ltd.* [1920] A.C. 683).

A bank may be a "customer" of another bank if it has a drawing account with it (*Importers Co.* v. *Westminster Bank* [1927] 2 K.B. 297).

What amounts to negligence depends on the facts of the particular case and the practice of bankers. In *Marfani & Co.* v. *Midland Bank* [1968] 1 W.L.R. 956, Nield J. formulated four principles which should guide a court in such cases, namely—

1. The standard of care required of bankers is that to be derived from the ordinary practice of careful bankers.

2. The standard of care required of bankers does not include the duty to subject an account to microscopic examination.

3. In considering whether a bank has been negligent in receiving a cheque and collecting the money for it, a court has to scrutinise the circumstances in which a bank accepts a new customer and opens a new account.

4. The onus is on the defendant to show that he acted without negligence.

It is negligence—

(a) To open an account without inquiring as to the identity and circumstances of the customer (*Ladbroke & Co.* v. *Todd* (1914) 111 L.T. 43). Among the circumstances to be inquired into are the nature of the customer's employment and the name of his employer.

Lumsden & Co., plaintiff stockbrokers, employed a Mr. Blake as temporary accountant. The practice of the plaintiffs was to draw cheques in favour of their clients in an abbreviated form; thus, where the cheques were payable to Brown Mills & Co., they simply drew them in favour of Brown. Blake, who was fraudulent, opened an account with the defendant bank in the name of a fictitious J.A.G. Brown whose profession he gave as a self-employed chemist. Blake gave the fictitious J.A.G. Brown an excellent reference, describing himself as a "D.Sc., Ph.D." The branch manager of the defendant bank, who thought that he was dealing with two reputable professional men, failed, contrary to his instructions, to make inquiries with Mr. Blake's bank. Mr. Blake then transferred some of the cheques due to Brown Mills & Co. but simply made payable to Brown to the fictitious J.A.G. Brown's account with the defendant bank. *Held*, (1) the defendant bank had acted negligently in opening the account and was not protected by section 4 (1) of the Cheques Act 1957; (2) there was contributory negligence to the extent of 10 per cent. on the part of the plaintiffs and the damages to which they were entitled had to be reduced accordingly: *Lumsden & Co.* v. *London Trustee Savings Bank* [1971] 1 Lloyd's Rep. 114.

(b) To receive payment of a cheque for a customer, when the cheque is drawn in favour of the customer's employer, without inquiring as to his title to the cheque.

U was the sole director and practically the sole shareholder in U Ltd. U had a private account with the L bank, and the company had an account with the X bank, but the L bank knew nothing of this account. Cheques payable to the company were indorsed, "U Ltd.—U, sole director," and paid into the L bank to U's private account. *Held*, U Ltd., were entitled to recover the amount of the cheques, because the L bank were negligent in not inquiring whether U Ltd., had an account, and, if so, why the cheques were not paid into it: *Underwood Ltd.* v. *Bank of Liverpool and Martins Ltd.* [1924] 1 K.B. 775.

If a cheque payable to a customer in his official capacity is paid into the customer's private account, the bank should make similar inquiries (*Ross* v. *London County, etc., Bank* [1919] 1 K.B. 678). The same applies if the instrument bears a clear indication that it is payable to the customer as agent of another person.

M was the manager of three farms in Scotland belonging to B; his duties included the making of applications for and receiving of certain hill sheep subsidies for B. After having left the employment of B, M paid into his personal account three crossed warrants relating to those hill sheep subsidies and made payable to M "(for the Marquess of Bute)." *Held*, the bank had not discharged the onus of proving they had acted without negligence, and therefore they could not claim the protection of section 82[2]: *Bute (Marquess)* v. *Barclays Bank Ltd.* [1955] 1 Q.B. 202.

---

[2] This section is now repealed and section 4 of the Cheques Act 1957 is substituted for it; see p. 363 *ante*.

C, the manager of B bank, was induced to pay out a cheque which, unknown to him, formed part of a species of take-over fraud, whereby those seeking to buy a controlling interest in a certain company stole money from the company in order to pay for their purchase. The circumstances surrounding the tendering of the cheque were unusual and out of the bank's ordinary course of business. Moreover, the amount involved was unusually high. The company to be taken over commenced proceedings claiming replacement by B bank of the amount of the cheque. *Held,* that a reasonable banker, in the interests of his customer, would have made further inquiries before payment, and the bank was liable: *Karak Rubber Co. Ltd.* v. *Burden* (*No. 2*) [1972] 1 W.L.R. 602.

(c) To receive payment of a cheque for a customer, when the cheque is drawn by the customer's employer in favour of a third party or bearer, without inquiring as to the customer's title to the cheque (*Lloyds Bank* v. *Savory* [1933] A.C. 201).

(d) To receive payment of a cheque for a customer, when the cheque is drawn by the customer as agent for a third party in his own favour, without inquiring as to the customer's title to the cheque (*Morison* v. *London County, etc., Bank* [1914] 3 K.B. 356).

T was authorised by a power of attorney to draw cheques on behalf of R. He drew cheques on R's banking account signed "R, by T, his attorney," and fraudulently paid them into his own account with the M bank to reduce his overdraft. *Held,* the bank were negligent, because they had not inquired into T's authority to pay the cheques into his own account and were liable to pay the amount of the cheques to R: *Midland Bank* v. *Reckitt* [1933] A.C. 1.

(e) Not to notice the account of the customer from time to time and consider whether it is a proper or a suspicious one (*Lloyds Bank* v. *Chartered Bank of India* [1919] 1 K.B. 40).

If an open cheque for a large amount payable to bearer is presented to a bank for payment over the counter, it is not negligence for the bank to pay the cheque without making inquiries "in the absence of very special circumstances of suspicion, such as presentation by a tramp, or a postman or an office boy" (*per* Wright J.).

A bill of exchange for £876 9s. 0d., payable to X, was indorsed by X and handed to W to take to the bank for the purpose of collecting through the clearing house. Instead of doing this, W presented the bill for payment over the counter and received cash, which he stole. *Held,* the bank were not liable to X, because such a payment over the counter, though unusual, was made to the bearer in good faith and without notice of any defect in his title: *Auchteroni & Co.* v. *Midland Bank Ltd.* [1928] 2 K.B. 294.

If a banker pays a cheque on the forged signature of his customer he cannot debit his customer with that amount. Similarly, if the amount of a cheque properly drawn by the customer has been fraudulently increased and the banker pays the altered amount, he can only debit his customer with the amount of the cheque as originally drawn. But the customer owes a duty to his banker in drawing a cheque to take reasonable and ordinary precautions against forgery, and, if as the natural and direct result of the neglect of these precautions, the amount of the cheque is increased by forgery, the customer must bear the loss as between himself and the banker.

The firm of M & A entrusted to their clerk the duty of filling up cheques for signature. The clerk presented to one of the partners a cheque payable to the firm or bearer. No sum was written in the space for the writing, and the figures "£2 0s. 0d." were written in the space for the figures. The partner signed the cheque and the clerk then wrote in the space for writing "one hundred and twenty," and altered the figures accordingly. The bank paid £120 out of M & A's account. *Held*, they were entitled to do so, because M & A had been guilty of negligence in signing the cheque in the manner described: *London Joint Stock Bank Ltd.* v. *Macmillan & Arthur* [1918] A.C. 777.

It is not normally a breach of duty on the part of the customer to use reasonable care in leaving a space between the name of the payee and the words "or order" but if the customer abbreviates the name of the payee in a manner which makes forgery more easily possible, that may be contributory negligence (*Lumsden & Co.* v. *London Trustee Savings Bank* [1971] 1 Lloyd's Rep. 114, see pp. 364–365, *ante*).

T drew a cheque in favour of A and handed it to X to be forwarded to A. A space was left between A's name and the words "or order," and X inserted the words "per X" in this space. X indorsed the cheque in his own name and received payment. *Held*, (i) the cheque was not properly indorsed, the proper indorsement being "A per X," so that the bank was not protected by section 60; (ii) the insertion of the words "per X" was a material alteration avoiding the cheque; (iii) there was no negligence on the part of T in the manner in which the cheque was drawn: *Slingsby* v. *District Bank* [1932] 1 K.B. 544.

5. There is no corresponding duty to be careful imposed on the drawer or acceptor of a bill of exchange (*Scholfield* v. *Londesborough* [1896] A.C. 514).

The customer is under a duty to disclose to the bank any forgeries which he has discovered (*Greenwood* v. *Martins Bank* [1933] A.C. 51).

6. In modern practice banks use computers to sort out cheques on which the branch and account number of the customers are printed in magnetic ink. Where a customer alters the printed branch to another one by ordinary ink (which the computer cannot read) and then countermands the cheque but the computer dispatches the cheque to the original branch which pays it, the bank might be liable.

B was a customer of the defendant bank and had accounts at two branches, the Borough and the Bromley Branches. In 1964, many years after the relationship of banker and customer had been established, the bank adopted the system of computer banking and the Borough branch issued B with a cheque book stating his account number in magnetic ink and informing him that he must not use these cheques for another account. B altered one of the cheques by making it payable at the Bromley branch; the alteration was made in ordinary ink which the computer could not read. B then countermanded the cheque by informing the Bromley branch but the computer cleared the cheque to the Borough branch which, being unaware that it had been stopped, paid it. *Held*, that the bank was liable since the notice on the cheque book had not become part of the contract with B, on the principle in *Chapleton* v. *Barry U.D.C.* (p. 33, *ante*). However, the position might have been different if the cheque book bearing the notice had been the first issued to the customer on his opening the account: *Burnett* v. *Westminster Bank Ltd.* [1966] 1 Q.B. 742.

PROMISSORY NOTES

A **promissory note** is
  —an unconditional promise in writing
  —made by one person to another
  —signed by the maker
  —engaging to pay
  —on demand or at a fixed or determinable future time
  —a sum certain in money
  —to or to the order of a specified person or to bearer (s. 83 (1)).
As to certainty of time of payment, it has been held that a document

expressing a sum to be payable "on or before" a stated date introduced uncertainty and so was not a promissory note (*Williamson and Ors.* v. *Rider* [1963] 1 Q.B. 89).

The following is one form of a promissory note—

> Newcastle,
> *June* 1, 1977.
> I promise to pay on demand A B or order the sum of £100 for value received.
>
> X Y.

An instrument, which is void as a bill of exchange because it is not addressed to anyone, may nevertheless be valid as a promissory note.

A document was in the following form—
"On December 31, 1928, pay to my order the sum of £125 7s. 4d. for value received."
It was not signed, but across the face were the words "Accepted payable at Lloyds Bank Ltd., Highgate Branch. J. H. Lack." *Held*, the instrument was a promissory note on which Lack was liable as maker: *Mason* v. *Lack* (1929) 45 T.L.R. 363.

An instrument in the form of a note payable to the maker's order is not a note unless and until it is indorsed by the maker. A note which is made and payable within the British Isles is an inland note: any other note is a foreign note. A promissory note is not complete until it has been delivered to the payee or bearer (s. 84).

A note may be made by two or more makers, who may be liable on it jointly or severally. If it is payable on demand it need not be presented for payment within a reasonable time to render the maker liable; but it must be presented within a reasonable time after indorsement to render the indorser liable.

Even if it appears that a reasonable time has elapsed since the note was issued, the holder is not, on that account, affected by defects of title of which he had no notice (s. 86).

B gave a mortgage on some property to W, and also a promissory note for the amount of the mortgage. W transferred the mortgage to X for the full amount due thereon, and subsequently indorsed the note to G for value. G had no notice of the mortgage. A considerable time later, G sued B. *Held*, although after his transfer of the mortgage W had no right to sue on the note, G was a bona fide holder for value and not affected by the defect in W's title: *Glasscock* v. *Balls* (1889) 24 Q.B.D. 13.

Presentment for payment is not necessary to render the maker liable, but it is necessary to make the indorser liable. If, however, a note is, in the body of it, made payable at a particular place, it must be presented for payment at that place in order to render the maker liable.

The maker of a promissory note by making it—
   1. engages that he will pay it according to its tenor;
   2. is precluded from denying to a holder in due course the existence of the payee and his then capacity to indorse (s. 88).

The law as to bills of exchange applies to promissory notes, the maker of a note corresponding with the acceptor of a bill, and the first indorser of a note corresponding with the drawer of an accepted bill payable to the drawer's order. When a foreign note is dishonoured, protest is unnecessary (s. 89).

SELECT BIBLIOGRAPHY

Books

Chalmers on Bills of Exchange (13th ed., 1964) by D. A. L. Smout.
D. Richardson, *A Simple Guide to Negotiable Instruments and the Bills of Exchange Acts* (3rd ed., 1963).

Articles

Silberberg, H., "Personal Liability of Directors on Bills of Exchange" [1967] J.B.L. 116–121.
Thornely, J. W. A., "Consideration for Negotiable Instruments" [1968] C.L.J. 196–198.

PART 6: COMMERCIAL SECURITIES

CHAPTER 21

BAILMENT, PAWN AND LIEN

BAILMENT

In general

BAILMENT may be constituted by a contract of bailment or otherwise.

Bailment is the delivery of goods by one person, called the bailor, to another, called the bailee, on condition that the same goods are re-delivered by the bailee to or on the direction of the bailor. Examples are the deposit of goods in a cloak-room or left-luggage office for safe custody and the loan, pawn or hire of goods; further examples occur when goods are entrusted to a warehouseman or carrier but special rules apply to the latter case.

Where there is a contract of bailment, the consideration moving from the bailor is his parting with possession of the goods; that from the bailee, the promise to return them. There may also be the additional consideration of a payment on the part either of the bailor, as in the deposit of goods in a left-luggage office, or of the bailee, as in a contract of hire.

But there need not be a contract for the obligations of a bailee to arise. A person may assume the obligations of a bailee in respect of the goods of another by voluntarily taking possession of them, e.g. the finder of goods.

Where the goods of the bailor, while in the possession of the bailee, are lost or damaged by an event for which a third party is responsible, the bailee can recover damages from the third party but has to hold the amount recovered as trustee for the bailor (*The Winkfield* [1902] p. 42). The bailee can also insure the bailor's goods and has an insurable interest in them but again, if the goods are lost or damaged, has to hold the insurance sum as trustee for the bailor (*A. Tomlinson* (*Hauliers*) *Ltd.* v. *Hepburn* [1966] A.C. 451).

Two cases of clocks were shipped from Germany to Australian buyers (the plaintiffs). The ship carrying them was the *Regenstein*. They arrived in Sydney where the defendant stevedores and ship's agents unloaded them in a shed on the wharf under their control. When the plaintiffs wanted to take delivery, one case was missing. *Held*, (1) the absence of a contract of bailment between the plaintiffs and the defendants was irrelevant, (2) the defendants, by voluntarily taking possession of the plaintiff's goods, assumed an obligation to take reasonable care of them, (3) this obligation was the same as that of a bailee, (4) the defendants had become sub-bailees (the shipowners being the main bailees), (5) the defendants were liable: *Gilchrist Watt and Sanderson Pty. Ltd.* v. *York Products Ltd.* [1970] 1 W.L.R. 1262.

Duty of bailee

The bailee is under a duty to take reasonable care of the goods bailed. The standard of care required of a bailee (whether gratuitous or otherwise) is the standard demanded by the circumstances of each particular case. As the burden is on a bailee to show that there has been no negligence, if he fails to return goods or returns them in a damaged condition it is for him to show that the loss or damage occurred in spite of the fact that he took reasonable care of them. It follows that if the cause or the circumstances of loss or damage to goods are unexplained by a bailee, the bailor's claim against him will succeed as the bailee has failed to discharge the burden of proving that this was not due to his negligence (*Houghland* v. *R. R. Low* (*Luxury Coaches*) *Ltd.* [1962] 1 Q.B. 694). For example, if the loss or damage is due to act of God or to robbery with violence, a bailee is not liable, but it is the bailee who has to prove that this was the cause of the loss or damage. If the article bailed is stolen by the employee of a bailee, the latter will be liable if he did not use reasonable care in selecting his employee (*Williams* v. *Curzon Syndicate Ltd.* (1919) 35 T.L.R. 475), or if he omitted to lock up the article bailed while locking up similar articles of his own (*Clarke* v. *Earnshaw* (1818) Gow 30).

M, who was a fee-paying patient, was admitted to hospital where her jewellery was handed over for safe custody. The jewellery was lost. *Held*, the hospital were liable as they were bailees for reward: *Martin* v. *L.C.C.* [1947] K.B. 628.

If, however, the bailee does take reasonable care of the goods, he is not liable for any loss or damage they may sustain.

B left some engraving plates with S as a gratuitous bailee. The plates were stolen from S, but the manner of the theft was unknown. S proved that the plates were kept in a proper place, under the charge of proper persons and under arrangements which were reasonably sufficient. *Held*,

S was not liable: *Bullen* v. *Swan Electric Engraving Co.* (1907) 23 T.L.R. 258.

But it is not sufficient for a bailee to prove that the loss occurred without any negligence on his part; he must also show that he used reasonable care to assist in their recovery.

Some cattle belonging to A were agisted with B. Without any negligence on B's part, the cattle were stolen. B did not inform the owner or the police or make any effort to recover them, because he thought it would be useless to do so. *Held*, B was liable for the loss, unless he could prove that, even if he had reported the loss, the cattle still could not have been recovered: *Coldman* v. *Hill* [1919] 1 K.B. 443.

The bailee is also under a duty to return the goods bailed in accordance with the terms of the contract of bailment. If he fails to do this, he is liable for their loss or damage, notwithstanding the exercise of reasonable care on his part.

A delivered books to B to be bound. He pressed for their return, but B, although more than a reasonable time had elapsed, neglected to return them. A fire accidentally broke out on B's premises, and the books were burnt. *Held*, B was liable for the loss, although he was not negligent, because of his failure to deliver the books within a reasonable time: *Shaw & Co.* v. *Symmons & Sons* [1917] 1 K.B. 799.

The duty of a bailee is generally a duty owed to the bailor, but where the bailor is not himself the owner of the goods bailed the bailee may owe a duty to the owner also.

A, customs and forwarding agents, made one contract with the plaintiffs to clear through customs and deliver goods of the plaintiffs. A made another contract with the defendants, transport contractors, to collect the goods from the docks and deliver them to A's warehouse. The defendants knew from a period of trading with A that A were continuously handling goods owned by their customers, and in the present case the defendants received delivery notes naming the plaintiffs as owners. The defendants' driver collected the goods but left the vehicle unattended, when half the goods were stolen. *Held*, the defendants were bailees for reward of the plaintiffs' goods albeit their contractual duty was owed not to them but to A; since the defendants knew the goods were the plaintiffs', they owed a duty of care to the plaintiffs in respect of their goods, and since, in the circumstances, the defendants could reasonably have foreseen the loss which in fact occurred they were liable to the plaintiffs for the value of the stolen goods: *Lee Cooper Ltd.* v. *C. H. Jeakins and Sons Ltd.* [1967] 2 Q.B. 1.

Duty of bailor

If the goods are to be used for any particular purpose and the bailor knows of it, he is under a duty to the bailee to disclose any defect in the goods rendering them unsuitable for that purpose (*Coughlin* v. *Gillison* [1889] 1 K.B. 145).

Right of bailee to sell

A bailee has no right at common law to sell the goods bailed even if he has incurred expenses in relation to them. Under the Disposal of Uncollected Goods Act 1952, a bailee who has not been paid for services rendered in respect of the goods bailed may sell them. Thus a watch-repairer who, in the course of his business, accepts for repair a watch left with him by the owner, may, if the owner fails to pay for the work done and to collect the watch, subject to giving notice and to other conditions of the Act, sell the watch. Out of the proceeds of sale the watch-repairer may retain his charges, the balance being payable to the owner.

CONTRACTS OF BAILMENT

Deposit

In the contract of deposit, goods are deposited by the bailor with the bailee for safe custody. The bailee is not, as a rule entitled to use the goods bailed; if he, in breach of his contract, does use them, he is liable for the resultant damage. He is bound to take reasonable care of the goods bailed.

X entered a restaurant to dine. His coat was taken by a waiter and hung on a hook behind X. The coat was stolen. *Held*, the restaurant proprietor was liable for the loss: *Ultzen* v. *Nicols* [1894] 1 Q.B. 92.

The contract may, however, exempt the bailee from liability for negligence.

R deposited a motor-car with P, a garage proprietor, for sale on commission, upon the terms of a printed document containing the clause: "Customers' cars are driven by our staff at customers' sole risk." While the car was being sent by P to be shown to a prospective buyer, it was damaged owing to the negligence of P's driver. *Held*, P was protected from liability by the clause in the contract: *Rutter* v. *Palmer* [1922] 2 K.B. 87.

G deposited his bicycle with the railway company. He paid 4d. and received a ticket bearing a condition that the company would not be liable for the loss of any article exceeding £5 in value unless an additional charge was paid. The value of the bicycle exceeded £5, but no extra charge was asked for or paid. The bicycle was put in the booking office and not in the left-luggage office, and when G went to get it, it was missing. *Held*, the railway company was not liable: *Gibaud* v. *G. E. Ry.* [1921] 2 K.B. 426.

Protective conditions will not be effective if the bailee commits a fundamental breach of the contract, such as allowing a third party to enter the left-luggage office and, without the owner's authority, open a locked trunk (*Alexander* v. *Railway Executive* [1951] 2 All E.R. 442).

If the contract is that the goods shall be deposited at one place and they are deposited by the bailee at another, the bailee will be liable for any loss and will not be able to rely on protective terms.

D contracted to warehouse some drapery goods for L at Kingsland Road, but warehoused a portion elsewhere. A fire occurred there, without any negligence on D's part, and the goods were destroyed. *Held*, D was liable for the loss: *Lilley* v. *Doubleday* (1881) 7 Q.B.D. 510.

If goods deposited in a warehouse are stolen, the warehouseman is liable unless he can prove that he took all reasonable precautions against theft: *Brook's Wharf* v. *Goodman Bros.* [1937] 1 K.B. 534.

Loan for use

Under this contract the bailee is entitled to use the goods bailed, and so is not liable for reasonable wear and tear. He must not, however, deviate from the conditions of the loan, otherwise he will be liable for any loss of or injury to the goods.

Hire

In a contract of hire there is an implied warranty on the part of the owner that the goods hired are as fit for the purpose for which they were hired as reasonable care and skill can make them. Even when the hirer has inspected the goods, this warranty applies. The hirer is bound to take reasonable care of the goods and only to use them in accordance with the contract. He is not liable for loss caused by robbery or accidental fire.

The owner cannot claim a return of the goods from the hirer except in accordance with the terms of the contract. If, however, the hirer sells the goods, the contract is terminated and the owner may recover the goods from the purchaser, whether or not he knew of the hiring.

Innkeeper and guest

A "common inkeeper" is one who keeps an inn for the reception of travellers. The liability of the innkeeper is largely regulated by the Hotel Proprietors Act 1956. An hotel is defined in section 1 (3) as "an establishment held out by the proprietor as offering food, drink and, if required, sleeping accommodation, without special contract, to any traveller presenting himself who appears able and willing to pay a reasonable sum for the services and facilities provided and who is in a fit state to be received."

An hotel proprietor's legal position is similar to that of a common carrier. He is bound to receive all travellers who come to his inn, provided that he has sufficient room, that the traveller is able and willing to pay, and that no reasonable objection can be taken to the traveller's personal condition.

Failure to accept a traveller renders the hotel proprietor liable in damages.

If the inn is full, the hotel proprietor is not bound to provide the traveller with accommodation.

X's motor-car broke down and at 2 a.m. he asked Y, an innkeeper, for accommodation. All the beds were occupied and X asked to be allowed to spend the night in the coffee room. Y refused. *Held*, as all the beds were occupied, the inn was full and Y's refusal was justified: *Browne* v. *Brandt* [1902] 1 K.B. 696.

While an hotel proprietor cannot pick and choose his guests, he may reserve tables in his dining-room for prospective guests who have booked them and may refuse to supply a traveller with food if he is keeping it for an evening meal for guests later in the day or for breakfast next morning (*R.* v. *Higgins* [1948] 1 K.B. 165).

The hotel proprietor is only bound to provide such accommodation as he has. If, therefore, his garage is not adequate to prevent the water in his guest's motor-car from freezing, he is not liable (*Winkworth* v. *Raven* [1931] 1 K.B. 652).

The guest must be a "traveller" but only gets the statutory protection for loss or damage to his property if he has engaged sleeping accommodation. For other purposes a local resident going to the inn for a meal or a drink is a traveller (*Williams* v. *Linnitt* [1951] 1 K.B. 565). A traveller is anyone who "uses the inn, either for a temporary or a more permanent stay, in order to take what the inn can give" (*per* Wills J. in *Orchard* v. *Bush* [1898] 2 Q.B. 284, 287).

The guest may lose his character of a traveller and become a lodger by staying on at the inn. In such a case he can be required to leave on reasonable notice (*Lamond* v. *Richard* [1897] 1 Q.B. 541).

Like a common carrier, an hotel proprietor is an insurer of the property brought by the guests to the hotel. Property includes his luggage, but not his motor-car or any property left in it. If, therefore, any of the guest's luggage is lost, damaged or stolen, the innkeeper is liable at common law unless he can prove that the loss was due to—
1. act of God;
2. the King's enemies; or
3. the guest's own negligence.

S brought jewellery worth £600 to an hotel and locked it in her dressing-case. She did not lock her room and this was not the practice at the hotel. The jewellery was stolen. *Held*, the hotel was liable, S's conduct not amounting to negligence. The Innkeepers Liability Act 1863 s. 1 [1] was not exhibited: *Shacklock* v. *Elthorpe Ltd.* [1939] 3 All E.R. 372.

While at common law the amount of damages recoverable from a common innkeeper is not limited, the position is modified by the Hotel Proprietors Act 1956 which provides that an hotel proprietor shall not be liable for the loss of or injury to any property brought to his hotel to a greater amount than £50 for one article or a total of £100 in the case of any one guest unless—
1. the property was stolen, lost or damaged through the neglect or wilful default of the hotel proprietor or his servant; or
2. the property has been deposited expressly for safe custody with the hotel proprietor, in which case he may require them to be deposited in a box fastened and sealed by the person depositing them.

To obtain the protection of the Act, the hotel proprietor must exhibit a copy of the notice set out in the Schedule to the Hotel Proprietors Act 1956 (the effect of which is set out above), in a place where it can be conveniently read by his guests at or near the reception office or desk or, where there is no reception office or desk, at or near the main entrance to the hotel. His liability for articles lost or destroyed up to the value of £50 is the same as at common law.

C stayed at an hotel, bringing with her a diamond ring valued at £45. She put it in an unlocked suitcase and locked the door of her room. On her return the ring was missing. A copy of section 1 of the Innkeepers' Liability Act 1863 [1] was exhibited in the entrance, and in the room was a

---

[1] Repealed by the Hotel Proprietors Act 1956.

notice that all articles of value should be deposited at the office. C claimed £30. *Held*, as there was no negligence on the part of C, the hotel company was liable: *Carpenter* v. *Haymarket Hotel Ltd.* [1931] 1 K.B. 364.

An innkeeper has a lien on all goods brought by the guest to his inn for the price of the food and lodging supplied to him except on articles for which he is no longer responsible in case of loss or damage, *viz.* a guest's motor-car or any property left therein. Further, the innkeeper has no power to detain the guest himself or to take the clothes from his person.

The lien is enforced by detaining the goods and is lost if the innkeeper allows the guest to remove them. The Innkeepers Act 1878 gives a power of sale over goods deposited or left in an inn to satisfy the innkeeper's charges for board and lodging. The sale can only be effected if the goods have been six weeks on the premises, and the sale has been advertised at least one month before it is due to take place.

PAWN

Pawn is the delivery of a chattel by one person, called the pawnor, to another, called the pawnee, as security for a loan. The chattel pawned still remains the property of the pawnor, but its possession is with the pawnee. This distinguishes pawn from mortgage, in which the owner, for example of a house, usually remains in possession. It is distinguished from lien, because the pawnee can, in certain circumstances, sell the chattel pledged, whereas in the case of lien there is no power of sale.

The pawnor has the right to redeem the chattel pawned in the stipulated time or, if no time is stipulated, within a reasonable time after demand for repayment has been made. If he does not redeem, the pawnee has the right to sell the chattel and to pay himself the amount of the loan and expenses, the balance being due to the pawnor.

The pawnee is bound to take reasonable care of the chattel pawned, and if it is not forthcoming when an offer to redeem is made, the burden of proof is on him to show that the loss occurred in spite of his taking due care. The pawnee cannot use the chattel pawned.

The Pawnbrokers Acts 1872 to 1960 governed pledges with pawnbrokers, *i.e.* persons carrying on the business of taking goods and chattels in pawn, when the loan was of £50 or less. The Consumer Credit Act 1974, however, which establishes a comprehensive code of regulation for the supply to individuals of credit not exceeding £5,000, provides for the repeal of the Pawnbrokers Acts, from a date to be, but not yet, appointed.

The provisions of the 1974 Act cover a wider range of transactions than those traditionally associated with the concept of pawnbroking, although the definitions of **pawn** and **pledge** in the Act are unhelpful, being circular—pawn referring to pledge, and pledge to pawn. The requirement for the giving of a pawn-ticket or special contract pawn-ticket under the old Acts is replaced by one for the giving of a pawn-receipt in respect of an article taken in pawn. A pawn is redeemable at any time within six months but, subject to this limitation, the redemption period is that fixed by the parties for the duration of the credit secured by the pledge, or such longer period as they may agree. The imposition of special charges for redemption is prohibited, as are higher charges for safe keeping, after the end of the redemption period. It is not possible to contract out of these provisions. If a pawnee exercises his power to realize the pawn, first he must give notice of such intention to the pawnor and subsequently inform him of the result of the sale and account for the proceeds. It is not necessary for the sale to be by auction but the pawnor is entitled to challenge the price realised or the expenses incurred and if he does so it is for the pawnee to justify the price or expenses in question.

LIEN

There are three kinds of lien—
1. Possessory lien;
2. Maritime lien; and
3. Equitable lien.

Possessory lien

A possessory lien is a right to retain that which is in the possession of the person claiming the lien until a claim is satisfied. For the creation of this lien possession is essential and must be (1) rightful, (2) not for a particular purpose, and (3) continuous.

H, the owner of a motor-car, agreed with a company that they would maintain and garage her car for three years, on being paid an annual sum by H. H was entitled to take the car out of the company's garage as and

when she liked. The annual payment being in arrear, the company detained the car in the garage and claimed a lien. *Held*, as H was entitled
to take the car away as and when she pleased, the company had no lien:
Hatton v. *Car Maintenance Co. Ltd.* [1915] 1 Ch. 621.

A possessory lien may be 1 general, or 2 particular.

1. A general lien is a right to retain possession of the goods
of another until all claims against that other have been satisfied.
It may arise by (a) a course of dealing, (b) continuous and well-
recognised usage, or (c) express agreement.

X imported frozen meat into England. X was financed by J, who paid
for the meat, and reimbursed himself by drawing a bill of exchange in
favour of the bank on X, who accepted it. The bills of lading for the meat
were deposited with the bank as security that the bill of exchange would
be met. On its arrival in England, the meat was stored with the U Co. on
the terms (general in the trade) that they should have a general lien. X
failed to meet his acceptance, whereupon J took up the bills of lading
from the bank and demanded the meat. The U Co. claimed a lien on the
meat for charges due from X in respect of other goods. *Held*, the U Co.
could enforce their general lien against J.: *Jowitt & Sons* v. *Union Cold
Storage Co.* [1913] 3 K.B. 1.

By well-recognised usage, a general lien exists in the case of
solicitors, factors, stockbrokers and bankers.

A banker, in the absence of agreement to the contrary, has a lien on
all securities in his hands for the general balance owing to him on all
accounts of his customer. Although not a right of lien as such—for a
debtor cannot have a lien over his own indebtedness to his customer
—a banker also has the right, again in the absence of agreement to
the contrary, to combine accounts of the customer if the customer is
in credit in one account and in debit in another. This right to combine
accounts may be limited by special agreement so as to exclude certain
accounts of the customer from its operation, although the exclusion
ceases to bind the banker on the death, bankruptcy or liquidation of
the customer (*Halesowen Presswork & Assemblies Ltd.* v. *Westminster
Bank Ltd.* [1972] A.C. 785; see p. 121, *ante*).

2. A particular lien is a right to retain goods until all charges
incurred in respect of those goods have been paid. Common
carriers have a lien in respect of the freight on goods carried. Innkeepers have a lien on most of the luggage and other property
brought to the inn (see p. 378, *ante*).

A person who, at the request of the owner, has done work or

expended money on a chattel has a particular lien in respect of his claim.

G owned a motor car which was let on hire-purchase to X, who agreed to "keep the car in good repair and working condition." The car was damaged, and X sent it to A for repair. The instalments being in arrear, G terminated the hire-purchase agreement and sued A for the car. A claimed a lien for the cost of repair. *Held,* A had a lien, as X had G's authority to have the car repaired: *Green* v. *All Motors Ltd.* [1917] 1 K.B. 625.

If, in the case just quoted, the agreement had been terminated before the car was sent for repair, the repairers would have had no lien as against the owner (*Bowmaker* v. *Wycombe Motors Ltd.* [1946] K.B. 505).

A particular lien does not arise unless (a) the work has been completed, except when the owner prevents completion, and (b) the chattel has been improved by the work or the expenditure. An agreement to maintain a motor-car does not amount to improving it, so that the person responsible for maintenance has no lien (*Hatton* v. *Car Maintenance Co., supra*).

Enforcement of lien

A possessory lien is enforced only by a right of retention. No claim can be made for storage or for any other expense to which the person exercising the lien may be put. There is no general right of sale.

Under particular statutes, a lien may be enforced by sale in the following cases: repairers of goods or persons accepting goods for treatment, under the Disposal of Uncollected Goods Act 1952, and unpaid sellers of goods, under the Sale of Goods Act 1893.

Extinguishment of lien

A possessory lien is extinguished by—
(a) loss of possession of the goods;
(b) payment or tender of the amount claimed;
(c) taking security under such circumstances as to show that the security was taken in substitution for the lien;
(d) abandonment.

Maritime lien

A maritime lien is a right specifically binding a ship, her furniture, tackle, cargo and freight for payment of a claim founded upon the

maritime law. It is distinguished from a possessory lien in two
respects—

1. it is not founded on possession;
2. it is exercised by taking proceedings against the property
itself, *e.g.* by arresting the ship, in the Admiralty Court.

The persons who have a maritime lien are: salvors of the property
saved, seamen for their wages, the master for wages and disburse-
ments, the holder of a bottomry bond for the amount of his bond,
and claimants in respect of damage caused by collision due to the
ship's negligence.

A maritime lien attaches to the ship notwithstanding any sale
or transfer of the ship (*The Bold Buccleugh* (1851) 7 Moore P.C.
267), even to a bona fide purchaser without notice of the lien. It
remains in existence until payment, release, abandonment or loss or
destruction of the ship.

Equitable lien

An equitable lien is a charge upon property, conferred by law until
certain claims have been satisfied. It is distinguished from a possessory
lien in that it attaches independently of the possession of property.

Upon an exchange of contracts for the sale of land an unpaid
vendor's lien arises in favour of the vendor, unless there is something
to exclude it in the contract. Further, if a third person advances
money in payment for land which another is under contract to
purchase, he is entitled by subrogation to the same lien as the vendor
would have had if the price remained unpaid, unless there is evidence
that the parties intended otherwise (*Paul* v. *Speirway Ltd.* [1976]
Ch. 220). Similarly the purchaser of land has a lien on it for the
amount of his deposit.

On a dissolution of partnership owing to the death, bankruptcy
or retirement of a partner, the retiring partner has a lien on the
partnership assets existing at the date of dissolution for payment of
all the partnership debts prior to the date of dissolution.

An equitable lien is binding on all persons who acquire the
property the subject of the lien with notice of the lien. It is enforced
by sale, after a declaration by the court that the lien exists.

Bills of sale

A bill of sale is "a document given with respect to the transfer
of chattels, and is used in cases where possession is not intended to

be given" to the transferee (*per* Lord Esher M.R. in *Johnson* v. *Diprose* [1893] 1 Q.B. 512, 515). The bill of sale may be **absolute,** in which case it is governed by the Bills of Sale Act 1878 or it may be **conditional,** *i.e.* by way of security (when the grantor is entitled to have the property in the goods reconveyed to him on repayment of the loan); a conditional bill is governed by the Bills of Sale Act (1878) Amendment Act 1882.

A bill of sale, whether absolute or conditional, has to be attested by a solicitor and registered at the Central Office of the High Court within seven days of execution; it has to be re-registered every five years. If an absolute bill of sale is not registered in the prescribed manner, it is void as against the trustee in bankruptcy or liquidator of the grantor, but it is valid between the grantor and the grantee. If a conditional bill of sale is not registered, it is void in every respect, and likewise as between grantor and grantee.

CHAPTER 22

GUARANTEE

NATURE OF THE CONTRACT OF GUARANTEE

Guarantee and indemnity distinguished

A CONTRACT of guarantee or suretyship is a contract by one person to answer for the debt, default or miscarriage of another. Whether a particular contractual promise constitutes a guarantee depends upon the words used to express the intentions of the parties. The use of the word guarantee is not in itself conclusive, for it is sometimes used loosely in ordinary commercial dealings to mean a warranty and sometimes used to mis-describe what is in law a contract of indemnity and not of guarantee. Further, where the contractual promise can be correctly classified as a guarantee it is open to the parties expressly to exclude or vary any of their mutual rights or obligations which would otherwise result under the general law from its being classifiable as a guarantee.

The characteristics of a contract of guarantee are—

1. There must be three parties: the principal creditor, the principal debtor, and the guarantor or surety.

2. There must be a primary liability in some person other than the guarantor; the guarantor must be liable only secondarily, *i.e.* to pay **if the principal debtor does not pay.**

Example—A and B go into a shop. B says to the shopkeeper, "Let him (A) have the goods, and if he does not pay you, I will." This is a contract of guarantee, the primary liability being with A, and the secondary liability with B: *Birkmyr* v. *Darnell* (1704) 1 Salk. 27.

The assumption of personal liability is not essential in a guarantee. The provision of security is enough (*Re Conley* (1938) 107 L.J.Ch. 257).

3. The guarantor is totally unconnected with the contract except by means of his promise to discharge the principal debtor's liability if he does not do so.

It is this which prevents a *del credere* agent or a half-commission man employed by a stockbroker from being a guarantor, because each has an interest in the contract by negotiating it.

S & Co., stockholders, agreed with G that in respect of clients introduced by G, G should have half the commission earned as a result of the introductions, and he would pay S & Co. half of any loss sustained in respect of them. *Held*, the contract was not one of guarantee. Lord Esher M.R.: "The test is whether the defendant is interested in the transaction, either by being the person to negotiate it or in some other way, or whether he is totally unconnected with it. If he is totally unconnected with it, except by means of his promise to pay the loss, the contract is a guarantee; if he is not totally unconnected with the transaction, but is to derive some benefit from it, the contract is one of indemnity": *Sutton & Co.* v. *Grey* [1894] 1 Q.B. 285.

But if a large shareholder in a company promises to pay the company's debt in order to prevent its goods from being taken in execution, it is a guarantee, because he has no legal interest in or charge upon the goods (*Harburg India Rubber Co.* v. *Martin* [1902] 1 K.B. 778).

A contract of indemnity, which must be distinguished from a guarantee, differs from a guarantee in all three respects—

1. There are only two parties.

2. The person giving the indemnity is primarily liable and there is no secondary liability.

A and B go into a shop. B says to the shopkeeper, "Let him (A) have the goods, I will see you paid." The contract is one of indemnity: *Birkmyr* v. *Darnell, supra. Goulston Discount Co. Ltd.* v. *Clark* [1967] 2 Q.B. 493; see p. 293, *ante*.

3. The person giving the indemnity has some interest in the transaction apart from his indemnity.

The distinction is of practical importance. If the contract be one of guarantee and the principal contract is discharged without further liability on the part of the principal debtor, the guarantor is discharged. Thus, the guarantor is no longer liable if the principal debtor exercises a contractual option to rescind the contract: *Western Credit Ltd.* v. *Alberry* [1964] 1 W.L.R. 945, or if the principal contract is frustrated and the debtor has not to pay compensation under the Law Reform (Frustrated Contracts) 1943 (p. 135, *ante*). The position is otherwise in the case of an indemnity for the person giving the indemnity is primarily and not secondarily liable.

The distinction between a guarantee and an indemnity is of further importance because a contract of **guarantee is required** by the Statute of Frauds **to be evidenced by a note or memorandum in writing,** while a contract of indemnity is not. The form of the memorandum in writing has been discussed earlier (p. 41, *ante*). There must be consideration for the guarantor's undertaking, but the consideration need not be set out in the memorandum (Mercantile Law Amendment Act 1856).

By the Statute of Frauds Amendment Act 1828 (Lord Tenterden's Act), no action can be brought in respect of a representation given by one person as to the credit of another to the intent that such person may obtain credit or money, unless the representation is in writing signed by the party to be charged. The memorandum under this statute must conform to the requirements of the Statute of Frauds, except that (1) the consideration need not be stated, and (2) the signature cannot be made by an agent.

Guarantee is not a contract **uberrimae fidei.** Disclosure of all material facts by the principal debtor or the principal creditor to the guarantor before the contract is entered into is not required. Fraud on the part of the principal debtor is not enough to set aside the contract, unless the guarantor can show that the creditor or his agent knew of the fraud and was a party to it. When a guarantee is given to a bank there is no obligation on the bank to inform the intending guarantor of matters affecting the credit of the debtor or of any circumstances connected with the transaction which render the position more hazardous (*Wythes* v. *Labouchere* (1859) 3 De G. & J. 593).

G guaranteed the account of C with the bank. C afterwards drew on this account in order to pay off an overdraft he had with another bank. *Held*, the fact that the bank were suspicious that C was defrauding G, and did not communicate their suspicions to G, did not discharge the guarantee: *Nat. Prov. Bank of England Ltd.* v. *Glanusk* [1913] 3 K.B. 335.

If the guarantee is in the nature of an insurance, as in fidelity guarantee, all material facts must be disclosed, otherwise the guarantor can avoid the contract.

In 1903 G employed L as a clerk, and in 1905 L misappropriated £29 of their money. This sum was made good by L's relations and G agreed to retain L in their service on having fidelity guarantee. H gave the guarantee without being informed of L's previous dishonesty. In 1909 L misappropriated £100, and G claimed against H under the guarantee. *Held*, the guarantee could not be enforced against H owing to the non-disclosure of L's previous dishonesty: *London General Omnibus Co.* v. *Holloway* [1912] 2 K.B. 72.

LIABILITY OF THE GUARANTOR

The guarantor is a favoured debtor, and can insist on a strict adherence to the terms of his obligation. His liability does not arise until the principal debtor has made default, although notice of the default need not be given to him unless it is expressly agreed to be given. It is not necessary for the creditor to request the debtor to pay or to sue the debtor, unless this is expressly stipulated for, before taking proceedings against him.

If the transaction is void as between the principal debtor and the creditor, the guarantor is not bound.

B guaranteed a minor's overdraft at his bank. The minor's debt to the bank was void under the Infants Relief Act. *Held*, B was not liable: *Coutts & Co.* v. *Browne-Lecky* [1947] K.B. 104.

Similarly the guarantor is not bound if the principal debtor is discharged, *e.g.* by statute (*Unity Finance Ltd.* v. *Woodcock* [1963] 1 W.L.R. 455).

Any conditions precedent to the guarantor's liability must be fulfilled before recourse can be had to him. For example, if the guarantor agrees to be only one of several co-sureties, he will not be under any liability unless the others execute the guarantee.

B signed a guarantee to the bank which, on the face of it, was intended to be the joint and several guarantee of A, B, H and J. J did not sign, and he afterwards died. The bank never agreed with A, B and H to dispense with J's signature, and J was willing to sign, although by an accident his signature was not obtained. *Held*, B was under no liability on the guarantee: *Nat. Prov. Bank of England* v. *Brackenbury* (1906) 22 T.L.R. 797.

Again, if several guarantors have agreed to become co-sureties for definite amounts, and the creditor allows the amounts to be altered by one guarantor without the consent of the others, the guarantee will not be binding.

A firm of brewers employed C and required him to execute a bond with sureties for the faithful discharge of his duties. The bond was drawn up with four sureties, N and E being liable to the extent of £50 each, and P and B to the extent of £25 each. P, B and E all signed, but N, who was the last to sign, added "£25 only" to his signature. The brewers accepted the bond so signed. *Held*, none of the guarantors was liable on the bond: *Ellesmere Brewery Co.* v. *Cooper* [1896] 1 Q.B. 75.

If the contract is an instalment contract and it is broken by
a wrongful repudiation on the part of the principal debtor, *e.g.* by
persistent failure to pay the instalments, acceptance of this repudiation by the creditor does not release the guarantor from liability to
pay either the past instalments, due and unpaid before acceptance
of the repudiation, or the future instalments, due and payable thereafter (*Lep Air Services* v. *Rolloswin Investments Ltd.* [1973] A.C.
331).

CONTINUING GUARANTEES

A guarantee may be intended to cover a single transaction only, or
may be a continuing guarantee. A continuing guarantee may be
defined as "one which extends to a series of transactions, and is
not exhausted by or confined to a single credit or transaction."
The liability of the guarantor in such a case extends to all the
transactions contemplated until the revocation of the guarantee.

Whether a guarantee is continuing or not depends on the
language of the guarantee, the subject-matter and the surrounding
circumstances.

"I agree to be answerable to K for the amount of five sacks of flour,
to be delivered to T, payable in one month." *Held*, a guarantee for five
sacks delivered at one time, but not a continuing guarantee to cover
subsequent deliveries, though not exceeding in the whole five sacks: *Kay*
v. *Groves* (1829) 6 Bing. 276.

When a guarantee is continuing it is not exhausted by the first
advance or credit up to the pecuniary limit.

A guarantees B's overdraft up to £100. If B overdraws up to £100 and
then reduces his overdraft to £50 and subsequently increases it to £100
again, A is still liable if his guarantee is a continuing one.

GUARANTOR'S RIGHTS AGAINST THE CREDITOR

The rights of a guarantor against the creditor arise at the time of
his becoming guarantor, and not merely when he discharges the
obligation of the principal debtor.

"It certainly is not the law that a surety has no rights until he pays
the debt due from his principal": Cozens-Hardy J. in *Dixon* v. *Steel*
[1901] 2 Ch. at p. 607.

The rights of the guarantor are—

1. At any time after the guaranteed debt has become due, and before he has been asked to pay it, to require the creditor to sue for and collect the guaranteed debt.

"A surety is entitled at any time to require the creditor to call upon the principal debtor to pay off the debt, or himself to pay off the debt, and when he has paid it off he is at once entitled in the creditor's name to sue the principal debtor": A. L. Smith L.J. in *Rouse* v. *Bradford Banking Co.* [1894] 2 Ch. at p. 75.

The surety must, however, in such a case, undertake to indemnify the creditor for the risk, delay and expense he thereby incurs, and in any event he cannot compel the creditor to sue the debtor before he sues the surety himself (*Wright* v. *Simpson* (1802) 6 Ves. 714).

2. On being sued by the creditor, to rely on any set-off or counterclaim which the debtor possesses against the creditor (*Bechervaise* v. *Lewis* (1872) L.R. 7 C.P. 372).

3. On payment of what is due under the guarantee, to be subrogated to all the rights of the creditor in respect of the debt to which the guarantee relates.

X, the director of a company in voluntary liquidation, guaranteed and paid the poor rates due from the company before the date of liquidation. *Held*, X was entitled to all the rights of the creditor whose debt he had paid, and consequently he was a preferential creditor of the company for so much of the payment as was in respect of rates due and payable within twelve months of the liquidation: *Re Lamplugh Iron Ore Co. Ltd.* [1927] 1 Ch. 308.

4. On payment of what is due under the guarantee, to have assigned to him every judgment or security held by the creditor in respect of the debt (Mercantile Law Amendment Act 1856, s. 5).

This right to have securities assigned to him extends to all securities, whether known by the guarantor or not at the time when he entered into the contract, whether the creditor received them before, at, or after the creation of the guarantee, and whether they existed at the time the guarantee was created or not.

S mortgaged leasehold premises and a policy of assurance to W to secure £200 and interest, F joining in as surety. Subsequently, S borrowed further sums amounting to £530 from W and charged them on the same leasehold premises. F knew nothing of these further advances. On S making default, F paid the £200 and interest, and claimed to have the policy and the leasehold premises assigned to him. W refused to assign the premises unless G also paid him the £530. *Held*, on payment of the £200, F was entitled to have both securities handed to him: *Forbes* v. *Jackson* (1882) 19 Ch.D. 615.

When a guarantor has only guaranteed part of a debt he is, on paying the amount for which he is liable, entitled to all the rights of a creditor in respect of that amount, and to share in the security held by the principal creditor for the whole debt (*Goodwin* v. *Gray* (1874) 22 W.R. 312).

5. On payment of what is due under the guarantee, to all equities which the creditor could have enforced not only against the debtor himself, but also against persons claiming through him.

Goods belonging to C were sold by D, a broker acting as agent for buyer and seller, to B & Co. D gave B & Co. a delivery order, which B & Co. indorsed to the bank. B & Co. stopped payment and D, who was personally liable for the purchase price to C, paid C and obtained a second delivery order. At the time he paid C, D had no notice of the bank's title. *Held*, D was in the position of a surety, and, having paid the vendor, could exercise the unpaid vendor's lien against the goods: *Imperial Bank* v. *London and St. Katherine Docks Co.* (1877) 5 Ch.D. 195.

Guarantor's Rights against the Debtor

Against the debtor, the guarantor has the following rights—

1. Before the payment has been made, to compel the debtor to relieve him from liability by paying off the debt. This right can be exercised by one of several co-sureties without consulting the others.

A and four others guaranteed the T company's overdraft to the extent of £20,000. A died and the bank closed the old account and opened a new one. The company's liability at the time of A's death was £17,000. A's executors, being anxious to wind up A's estate, called on the company to pay off the overdraft and relieve them from liability. The company refused. *Held*, A's executors could compel them to do so: *Ascherson* v. *Tredegar Dry Dock Co.* [1909] 2 Ch. 401.

But before the guarantor can compel the debtor to pay, the debt must be an ascertained one, and there must be an existing liability to pay on behalf of the guarantor.

M guaranteed the B Co.'s overdraft up to £5,000, the guarantee to be determinable on the bank's closing the account and demanding payment by M, and on M's giving three months' notice to determine the guarantee. In the absence of either of these steps, *held*, M had no immediate right to compel B & Co. to relieve him of his liability: *Morrison* v. *Barking Chemicals Co. Ltd.* [1919] 2 Ch. 325.

Once the debtor's liability has become due as a fixed sum, the guarantor is entitled to ask the debtor to exonerate him, irrespective of whether the creditor, under the guarantee, had to make a demand on the guarantor or not (*Thomas* v. *Nottingham Incorporated Football Club Ltd.* [1972] Ch. 596).

2. After payment has been made, to be indemnified by the principal debtor against all payments properly made.

The right of indemnity may be an express one contained in the instrument of guarantee, in which case the rights of the parties are governed by the express agreement, or an implied one. An implied right of indemnity arises in every case when the guarantee has been undertaken at the request, actual or implied, of the debtor, but not otherwise.

A right to indemnity arises immediately a payment has been made under the guarantee, and on payment the guarantor becomes a simple contract creditor of the principal debtor. He is entitled to recover the amount he has paid with interest, and if he has sustained damage beyond that, he is entitled to recover that damage also.

"If a surety could prove that by reason of the non-payment of the debt he had suffered beyond the principal and interest which he had been compelled to pay, he would be entitled to recover that damage from the principal debtor": Stirling J. in *Badeley* v. *Consolidated Bank* (1887) 34 Ch.D. at p. 556.

The guarantor cannot recover the costs of an action brought against him on the guarantee from the principal debtor, unless he was authorised by the principal debtor to defend the action, and the defence was based on reasonable grounds (*Mors le Blanch* v. *Wilson* (1873) L.R. 8 C.P. 227).

3. When sued by the principal creditor, the guarantor can issue a third party notice against the principal debtor and claim an indemnity.

RIGHTS OF CO-GUARANTORS AMONG THEMSELVES

A guarantor who has paid more than his share under the guarantee is entitled to contribution from his co-guarantors, whether they are bound by the same or different instruments, and whether he knew or not of the existence of co-guarantors at the time he became bound. This is because the doctrine of contribution is not founded on contract, but is the result of general equity on the ground of equality of burden and benefit.

To obtain contribution, all the guarantors must have guaranteed the same debt. There is, therefore, no right of contribution—

1. When each guarantor has expressly agreed only to be liable for a given portion of one sum of money.

A borrows £100 from B and X guarantees one-half of the debt and Y the other half. There is no right to contribution between X and Y. If X and Y had each guaranteed the £100 there would have been a right to contribution.

2. When guarantors are bound by different instruments for equal portions of a debt due from the same principal, and the guarantee of each is a separate and distinct transaction (*Coope* v. *Twynam* (1823) Turn. & R. 426).

The right to contribution can be enforced before or after payment of the amount guaranteed. To enforce the right **before payment** the guarantor should make the principal creditor a party to the action, when he will obtain an order on his co-guarantor to pay his proportion to the principal creditor (*Wolmershausen* v. *Gullick* [1893] 2 Ch. 514).

After payment, the guarantor can only recover contribution if he has paid more than his proportion under the guarantee.

S and B by deed guaranteed payment of £15,000 advanced on mortgage, interest and the premiums on an insurance. The £15,000 was not to be called in for 10 years. Before 10 years had elapsed, S had paid more than his proportion of the interest and premiums and sued B for contribution. *Held*, the £15,000 interest and premiums constituted one debt, that until S had paid more than his proportion he could not obtain contribution from B, and that it was immaterial that S had paid more than his proportion of what had become due: *Stirling* v. *Burdett* [1911] 2 Ch. 418.

The proportion due from each guarantor is regulated by the number of solvent guarantors.

A, B and C guarantee X's debt of £150. A becomes insolvent and B pays the full amount. He can recover £75 from C.

If the guarantors have not guaranteed equal amounts, contribution can be claimed from each of them in proportion to the amount guaranteed.

Before recovering contribution, the guarantor who has paid the debt must bring into account all securities he has received from the creditor in respect of the debt.

H and A guaranteed C's debt with D, who had as security three policies on C's life. H later on paid off the debt and took an assignment of the policies. In an action for contribution against A, *held*, H was entitled to contribution from A, on bringing into account the value of the policies: *Re Arcedeckne* (1883) 24 Ch.D. 709.

Similarly, if a guarantor only consented to give the guarantee on condition of receiving security from the principal debtor, he must nevertheless account for the security if he sues to obtain contribution from his co-guarantors. It is not necessary, in an action for contribution, to join the principal debtor if the rights of the parties can be finally decided in his absence.

DISCHARGE OF THE GUARANTOR

The guarantor will be discharged in the following events—

1. If the contract between the principal debtor and the principal creditor is varied without the consent of the guarantor. The rule is stated by Cotton L.J. in *Holme* v. *Brunskill* (1877) 3 Q.B.D. 495 to be "if there is any agreement between the principals with reference to the contract guaranteed the surety ought to be consulted, and if he has not consented to the alteration, although in cases where it is without inquiry evident that the alteration is unsubstantial, or that it cannot be otherwise than beneficial to the surety, the surety may not be discharged; yet, if it is not self-evident that the alteration is unsubstantial, or one which cannot be prejudicial to the surety, the court will not, in an action against the surety, go into an inquiry as to the effect of the alteration or allow the question, whether the surety is discharged or not, to be determined by the finding of a jury as to the materiality of the alteration or on the question whether it is to the prejudice of the surety, but will hold that in such a case the surety himself must be the sole judge whether or not he will consent to remain liable notwithstanding the alteration, and that if he has not so consented he will be discharged."

X as surety for Y joined in a mortgage by Y of his property to Z. X guaranteed the loan made by Z and brought in some of her own property as additional security. Y later borrowed further sums from Z, who eventually consolidated his advances by a deed in which Y entered into a fresh covenant for payment of all the sums advanced. *Held*, X was discharged from liability and her property which she had brought in was released: *Bolton* v. *Salmon* [1891] 2 Ch. 48.

T owed a bank a considerable amount of money. His uncle A undertook, in consideration of the bank continuing the existing account with T, to guarantee T's liabilities to the bank to the amount of £10,500. Without knowledge and consent of A, the bank opened a No. 2 account for T and received considerable payments from him on that account. *Held*, the opening of the No. 2 account was, on the construction of the terms of the guarantee, an unauthorised variation of the principal contract and the guarantee and consequently the liability of A as guarantor was discharged: *National Bank of Nigeria Ltd.* v. *Awolesi* [1964] 1 W.L.R. 1311.

It is immaterial whether the variation be prejudicial to the guarantor or not, the principle being, "If the creditor does intentionally violate any rights which the surety had when he entered into the suretyship, even though the damage be nominal only, he shall forfeit the whole remedy" *(per* Blackburn J. in *Polak* v. *Everett* (1876) 1 Q.B.D. 669).

2. If the creditor makes a binding contract to give time to the principal debtor. Mere omission to press the debtor or delay in suing him is not such conduct as to release the guarantor. The contract, to have this effect, must be one which is legally enforceable.

P and C guaranteed the performance by D of his contract with the gas company. Under that contract D undertook to pay for each month's supply within 14 days. In July the gas company, not being paid within 14 days, took a promissory note from D. *Held*, this was a binding agreement to give time and discharged P and C from liability for the July account: *Croydon Gas Co.* v. *Dickinson* (1876) 2 C.P.D. 46.

If the contract is one contract, and not a series of monthly contracts, a binding contract to give time to the debtor will discharge the guarantor from the whole contract.

T bought from M a motor-car under a hire-purchase agreement, by which he was to pay £14 a month. N guaranteed these payments. T fell into arrear with his instalments, and it was agreed between T and M that T should give a cheque for £20 and pay the rest of the arrears at the end of the month. *Held*, N was discharged from the whole contract, because M had agreed to give time to T, and the contract was one contract and not a series of monthly contracts: *Midland Motor Showrooms* v. *Newman* [1929] 2 K.B. 256.

If the creditor when giving time to the debtor expressly reserves his rights against the guarantor, the guarantor is not discharged. The effect of this is to leave untouched the guarantor's rights against the debtor and, therefore, if the guarantor is pressed by the creditor, the agreement to give time to the debtor becomes of small value.

3. If the creditor omits to do something which he is bound to do for the protection of the surety. For example, if he omits to take up an award until the time for its performance is past (*Re Jones* (1863) 2 H. & C. 270), or if he omits to register a deed giving security so that the deed becomes inoperative and the creditor unsecured (*Wulff* v. *Jay* (1872) L.R. 7 Q.B. 756).

4. If the creditor relinquishes any security held by him in respect of the guaranteed debt. On payment of the debt the guarantor is entitled to have handed over to him all the securities held by the creditor in respect of the debt in the same condition as he received them. If the creditor, by any act or neglect on his part, is unable to hand over the securities in their unimpaired condition, the guarantor will be, to that extent, discharged.

X and Y held partly paid shares in a company and D and P guaranteed the payment of their unpaid calls to the company. The company called upon X and Y to pay the calls and, on default being made, forfeited the shares under a power given in the articles. *Held*, the company by forfeiting the shares had deprived D and P of the lien on the shares to which they would have been entitled had they been compelled to pay the calls, and they were therefore discharged from their liability as sureties under the guarantee: *Re Darwen and Pearce* [1927] 1 Ch. 176.

5. If the creditor expressly or impliedly discharged the debtor. An express discharge of the debtor by the creditor will always discharge the surety, unless the creditor expressly reserves his rights against the surety. Also, if the creditor does some act which, by implication, releases the debtor from his liability, the surety will be discharged.

X let some chattels to Y under a hire-purchase agreement, Z guaranteeing the instalments payable under the agreement. On the instalments being in arrear, X determined the contract and seized the chattels; he then sued Z on his guarantee. *Held*, as X had determined the contract, he could not recover from Z: *Hewison* v. *Ricketts* (1894) 63 L.J.Q.B. 711.

Similarly, a guarantor for rent payable under a lease is discharged from liability if the lease is determined before the expiration of the term (*Hastings Corpn.* v. *Letton* [1908] 1 K.B. 378).

The bankruptcy of the debtor and his subsequent discharge do not release a guarantor for him (Bankruptcy Act 1914, ss. 16 and 28).

6. If the creditor discharges a co-guarantor or does any act whereby the right of contribution between the co-guarantors is destroyed or prejudiced. The discharge of one guarantor from whom his co-guarantors could have obtained contribution is a discharge of those co-guarantors (*Mayhew* v. *Crickett* (1818) 2 Swan. 185, *per* Lord Eldon L.C.).

W guaranteed the overdraft of a company, and 12 persons deposited the deeds of their various properties with W and charged their properties with the repayment to W of any sum he might pay under the guarantee. X, one of the 12, persuaded W to hand over her deeds to her, and she mortgaged her property to Y. The company went into liquidation and W paid under his guarantee. *Held*, W's action in handing back her deeds to X had released a property which might have been taken towards the satisfaction of the bank's debt; this increased the burden on the remaining properties and thereby brought about a substantial alteration of the rights of the 11 parties among themselves, and they were therefore discharged: *Smith* v. *Wood* [1929] 1 Ch. 14.

7. If the guarantee is revoked. In the absence of an express provision for revocation in the contract itself, the question whether a guarantee can be revoked or not depends on the question whether the consideration for the guarantee is entire and indivisible and given once for all.

B appointed X his agent to collect his rents, and required him to execute a fidelity bond in which C was surety. C died. In an action by B against C's executors, *held*, C could not revoke his liability under the bond during his lifetime, and consequently his death did not release his estate from liability.

"The right to determine or withdraw a guarantee by notice forthwith cannot possibly exist, in my opinion, when the consideration for it is indivisible, so to speak, and moves from the person to whom the guarantee is given once for all, as in the case of the consideration being the giving or conferring an office or employment upon any person whose integrity is guaranteed" *per* Joyce J. in *Balfour* v. *Crace* [1902] 1 Ch. 733.

A continuing guarantee can be revoked as to future transactions by notice of revocation or by notice, actual or constructive, of the death of the guarantor. In such cases, however, liability for previous transactions remains.

W let a cottage to X, who was C's gardener, and C thereupon guaranteed the payment of X's rent for three months and thereafter from week to week. After four months X left C's employment, and C gave notice to W terminating his guarantee. X remained in the cottage and became liable to W for rent. *Held*, C was not liable for the rent which became due after he had revoked his guarantee: *Wingfield* v. *de St. Croix* (1919) 35 T.L.R. 432.

On the bankruptcy of the surety, the principal creditor can prove for the whole amount due at the date of the receiving order notwithstanding that he may, since that date, have received sums on account from a co-surety, provided that he does not receive more than 100 new pence in the pound (*Re Houlder* [1929] 1 Ch. 205). On the other hand, on the bankruptcy of the principal debtor, the surety cannot prove unless he has paid off the debt or the principal creditor has renounced his right to prove while preserving his rights against the surety; otherwise there would be a double proof in respect of the same debt (*Re Fenton* [1931] 1 Ch. 85).

SELECT BIBLIOGRAPHY
Articles

Blair, M., "The Conversion of Guarantee Contracts" (1966) 29 M.L.R. 522–536.

Steyn, J., "Guarantees: The Co-Extensiveness Principle" (1974) 90 L.Q.R. 246–266.

CHAPTER 23

LIFE, FIRE AND ACCIDENT INSURANCE

NATURE OF CONTRACT OF INSURANCE

THE owner of a ship or of a house can never be certain that his ship will not be damaged or lost or his house not damaged or destroyed. To cover himself against this contingency, he may enter into a contract providing for a sum of money to be paid upon the happening of such an event. A contract of insurance is a contract for the payment of a sum of money, or for some corresponding benefit such as the repairing of a ship or the rebuilding of a house, to become due on the happening of an event, which event must have some degree of uncertainty about it, and must be of a character more or less adverse to the interest of the person effecting the insurance. Thus there are three elements in a contract of insurance—

1. For some consideration, usually but not necessarily by way of periodical payments called **premiums** a contract of insurance secures some benefit, usually but not necessarily the payment of a sum of money, upon the happening of some event.
2. The event must be one which involves some degree of **uncertainty.** There must be either uncertainty whether or not the event will ever happen, or if the event is one which is bound to happen at some time there must be uncertainty as to the time at which it will happen.
3. The uncertain event which is necessary to make the contract one of insurance—rather than a wager—must be an event which is prima facie adverse to the interest of the assured. That requirement is expressed by the law stipulating that there shall be an **insurable interest** in the assured at the time of the making of the contract.

Each member of an association paid an annual sum so that if an event occurred which prevented the member from driving, due to disqualification or injury, the association would provide him with a chauffeur, and if necessary a car and chauffeur, for up to 40 hours a week for a maximum of 12 months. The Department of Trade contended that the association was carrying an insurance business and was an insurance company to which the Insurance Companies Act 1958 (then in force) applied. *Held*, there was no difference in substance between the association paying for a chauffeur for a member and its agreeing to pay him the cost of providing himself with a chauffeur; accordingly, the contracts between the members and the association were contracts of insurance; insurance business was being carried on: *Dept. of Trade* v. *St. Christopher Motorists' Assn. Ltd.* [1976] 1 W.L.R. 99.

REGULATION AND PROTECTION

There are elaborate statutory provisions for the regulation of insurance companies which carry on business in Great Britain. The principal Act is the Insurance Companies Act 1974 which with certain exceptions consolidates the Insurance Companies Acts 1958 to 1973.

The Act applies whether a company is established within or outside Great Britain, provided it carries on business within Great Britain. Insurance business is carried on where the contracts of insurance are made and the policies are issued, not where the risks are situated (*Re United General Commercial Insurance Corpn. Ltd.* [1927] 2 Ch. 51). The following are exceptions: an insurance company registered under the Acts relating to friendly societies; a trade union or employer's association carrying on insurance business if that business is limited to the provision for its members of provident or strike benefits; a member of Lloyds or of any other approved association of underwriters.

The Secretary of State for Trade has extensive powers, including power—

> to control entry into the insurance business, needing to be satisfied that the value of the company's assets exceed its liabilities by a certain amount and that every director, controller or manager of a company is a fit and proper person to be in such a position; and
> to intervene in the affairs of a company where he considers it desirable for protecting policy holders or potential policy holders, having regard to what appears to be the financial stability or solvency of the company.

Further protection for policyholders is afforded by the Policyholders Protection Act 1975. The main purposes of this Act are—

> to provide for the protection of policyholders who have been or may be prejudiced because of the inability of authorised insurance companies to meet their liabilities; and

to provide for the imposition of levies on the insurance industry in order to finance this protection.

The Policyholders Protection Board is the body which administers the Act.

The extent of the indemnity provided differs according to the type of insurance and other factors. Thus, *e.g.* the Board is required to secure payment of—

the full amount that a company in liquidation is liable to pay to a United Kingdom policyholder in respect of a liability subject to compulsory insurance;

the full amount, to a person entitled to the benefit of a judgment under the Road Traffic Act 1972;

90 per cent. of the amount, to a United Kingdom policyholder, who is an individual or partnership, under a policy which is not one for marine, aviation or transport insurance, reinsurance or under a requirement for compulsory insurance.

LIFE INSURANCE

Life insurance is a contract by which the insurer agrees, upon the death of a person whose life is insured, to pay a given sum in consideration of the payment of certain sums called premiums.

The insurable interest

By the Life Assurance Act 1774, s. 1, any insurance made by one person on the life of another is null and void unless the person making the insurance has an insurable interest in the life insured. An insurable interest means that the person effecting the insurance will sustain some pecuniary loss on the death of the person whose life is insured. The interest, however, need only subsist when the insurance is effected, and the policy does not become void if it has ceased before the death of the insured. But no more than the amount of the insurable interest at the time of effecting the insurance can be recovered under the policy.

A creditor has an insurable interest in the life of his debtor to the extent of the debt, and the policy money is recoverable even though the debt be paid before the maturity of the policy (*Dalby* v. *India and London Life Assurance Co.* (1854) 15 C.B. 365). A surety has an insurable interest in the principal debtor's life, and so have joint debtors in each other's lives to the extent of half the debt (*Beauford* v. *Saunders* (1877) 25 W.R. 650). A theatrical manager has an insurable interest in the life of an actor engaged by him, and so has a servant engaged for a term of years in his employer's life (*Hebden* v. *West* (1863) 3 B. & S. 597). A person always has an insurable interest in his own life, and one spouse has an insurable interest in the life of the other spouse.

A husband and wife made a contract of insurance whereby the policy money was payable, on the death of either of them, to the survivor. The premiums were paid by them jointly. The wife died first and the husband sued for the policy money. *Held*, it was not necessary for him to prove pecuniary interest in his wife's life: *Griffiths* v. *Fleming* [1909] 1 K.B. 805.

A parent has no insurable interest in his child's life, nor has the child in the life of the parent, unless the parent is supporting the child (*Howard* v. *Refuge Friendly Society* (1886) 54 L.T. 644). Sisters have no insurable interest in each other's lives (*Evanson* v. *Crooks* (1911) 106 L.T. 264).

Whenever one person effects an insurance on the life of another there must be inserted in the policy the name of the person interested therein, or for whose use, benefit or on whose account the policy is made, otherwise the policy will be void (Life Assurance Act 1774, s. 2). By the Married Women's Property Act 1882, s. 11, a husband or wife may insure his or her own life, and if the policy is expressed to be for the benefit of the other, or for the children, a valid trust of the policy money will be created, and the policy money will not form part of the insured's estate or be liable for his debts.

A husband insured his life for £500, the money to be paid to his wife if living at his death, otherwise to his personal representatives. Under a clause in the policy the husband elected to have the present value of the policy paid. *Held*, as a trust was created in the wife's favour in a certain event, the money could only be paid to the husband and wife jointly: *Re Fleetwood's Policy* [1926] 1 Ch. 48.

Insurance as contract uberrimae fidei

Life insurance, like all other forms of insurance, is a contract uberrimae fidei, and therefore full disclosure must be made to the insurer of every material circumstance which is known to the insured and which would influence the judgment of a prudent insurer in fixing, or determining whether to take the risk. In the event of failure to disclose any such circumstance the policy is voidable.

In making a proposal for insurance, M, in reply to questions asking whether previous proposals on his life had been made to any other office, and, if so, whether they had been accepted at the ordinary rates, said that he was then insured at two offices at the ordinary rates. He omitted to disclose that his life had been declined by several other offices. *Held*, this was a material failure to disclose and the policy could be set aside: *London Assurance* v. *Mansel* (1879) 11 Ch.D. 363.

Whether the omission to disclose any particular circumstance is material so as to render the contract voidable is a question of fact in each case.

A proposal form asked the name of any physician whom the proposer had consulted in the last five years. The proposer said "none," though in fact, he had consulted a doctor and received tonics, but he had never been away from his work. The insurer's doctor said that if he had known of this he would still have recommended the acceptance of the risk at the ordinary premium. *Held*, there was no material concealment and the policy was not avoided: *Mutual Life Insurance Co. of New York* v. *Ontario Metal Products Co.* [1925] A.C. 344.

If between the date of the proposal and the making of the contract there is a material alteration of the risk, disclosure of this alteration must be made, otherwise the contract will be voidable (*Looker* v. *Law Union and Rock Insce. Co. Ltd.* [1928] 1 K.B. 554).

If the insured makes a statement containing certain information, and the policy contains a term to the effect that the statement is to be taken as the basis of the contract, then the policy is voidable if any part of the statement is untrue, whether it is material or not (*Dawsons Ltd.* v. *Bonnin*, p. 405, *post*).

Return of the premium

If the policy is voidable owing to fraudulent misrepresentation, the insurer can have the policy set aside without having to return the premiums. But if the insurer can have the policy set aside on the ground that it is void *ab initio* from some cause not amounting to fraud or illegality, *e.g.* if the policy is expressed to be void on a misstatement of fact in a declaration which is the basis of the contract, the premiums can be recovered back from the insurer. In such a case no risk is run by the insurer. The policy may, however, contain a term that if the policy is void the premium shall be forfeited, and this term will prevent the premiums from being recoverable (*Sparenborg* v. *Edinburgh Life Assurance Co.* [1912]

1 K.B. 195). If the policy is voidable on the ground of the fraud of the insurer, the insured can recover back the premiums.

If the policy is illegal, whether because there is no insurable interest, or from any other cause, no premiums can be recovered back.

The insurer's agent in good faith represented to H that an insurance effected by H on his mother's life would be valid. H, relying on the representation, insured his mother's life and paid premiums. In an action to recover the premiums, *held*, the policy was illegal for want of an insurable interest, but, as the representation was made innocently, both parties were *in pari delicto* and the premiums could not be recovered: *Harse* v. *Pearl Life Assurance Co.* [1904] 1 K.B. 558.

Where the parties are not *in pari delicto* the insured, if he is the innocent party, can recover the premiums.

T effected five policies with the L company, and then decided not to keep them up. The L company's agent fraudulently represented to H, who had no insurable interest in the lives insured, that if she paid the arrears on the policies and paid the premiums in the future, she would be entitled to the policy moneys. T knew nothing of this arrangement. On learning that the policies were illegal, H sued to recover the premiums she had paid. *Held*, the parties not being *in pari delicto*, H succeeded: *Hughes* v. *Liverpool Victoria Legal Friendly Society* [1916] 2 K.B. 482.

Assignment of life policies

By the Policies of Assurance Act 1867, s. 1, the person entitled by assignment to a policy of life insurance may sue in his own name to recover the policy moneys. The assignment of a policy may be made either by indorsement on the policy or by a separate instrument in the form or to the effect set out in the Schedule to the Act (s. 5), but it must be followed by notice in writing to the insurer (s. 3). The date on which notice is received by the insurer regulates the priority of all claims under the assignment as between the insurer and the assignees, and the insurer is bound, on the request in writing of the person giving the notice, and on being paid a fee not exceeding 25p, to give a written acknowledgment of the notice (s. 6). The notice does not, however, regulate the rights of the various claimants to the policy moneys among themselves, and consequently an assignee who has given notice with knowledge of a prior incumbrance does not thereby obtain priority (*Newman* v. *Newman* (1885) 28 Ch.D. 674). In any action on a life policy a defence on equitable grounds may be relied on (s. 2).

If, in the opinion of the board of directors of an insurance company, no sufficient discharge for the policy moneys can be otherwise obtained, the company may pay the moneys into court (Life Insurance Companies (Payment into Court) Act 1896).

FIRE INSURANCE

A contract of fire insurance differs from a contract of life insurance in that it is a contract of indemnity. The contract is to indemnify the assured up to a certain amount from loss or injury by fire to specified property during a specified time. The contract is usually embodied in a policy.

Although the Life Assurance Act 1774 refers in its title to life assurance only, it is not in its terms limited to such insurance. As a result, it has been held to apply, for example, to personal accident insurance. On the other hand, section 4 expressly excludes from its operation insurance on ships, merchandise and goods, goods for this purpose including money.

The PS Union took out a policy covering their members against the loss of money collected by them for the P by burglary. A member sustained a loss by burglary and the Union sued under the policy. *Held*, the money was "goods" and the Union need not have an insurable interest under the Act: *Prudential Staff Union* v. *Hall* [1947] K.B. 685.

By section 1 of the Act an insurance of any kind is null and void unless the person for whose benefit it is made has an interest in the subject matter; and by section 2 the name of the person for whose benefit the policy is made must be inserted in the policy.

Usually, when the insured has no insurable interest the policy will be void by Gaming Act 1845 as a wagering contract.

A person has an insurable interest if he is liable to sustain any loss by the fire. The following are examples of persons who have an insurable interest: tenants who are liable to pay rent after a fire; carriers, innkeepers and wharfingers for goods entrusted to them, by virtue of their responsibility for loss, their lien or their possession; a mortgagee; an insurer, who may reinsure and so cover himself against loss. The insurable interest in the case of fire insurance must exist at the date of the loss.

Since a contract of fire insurance is a contract of indemnity, if the insured suffers no loss as a result of the fire he is not entitled to any money under the contract.

X agreed to sell his house to Y. Before completion the house was destroyed by fire, and X received its value from the insurance company. On completion X also received the price from Y. *Held*, the insurance company could recover from X the money they had paid: *Castellain* v. *Preston* (1883) 11 Q.B.D. 380.

Any money received by the vendor under a policy of insurance relating to the property sold has to be paid by the vendor to the purchaser on the completion of the contract, but this is subject to (1) any stipulation to the contrary contained in the contract, (2) any requisite consents of the insurers, and (3) the payment by the purchaser of a proportionate part of the premium (Law of Property Act 1925, s. 47). The insurers are not under an obligation to consent. By section 83 of the Fires Prevention (Metropolis) Act 1774—a statute which extends to all England and Wales—any person interested in any buildings destroyed by fire can compel the insurer to expend the insurance money in reinstatement of the buildings. Under this Act a mortgagee can insist on the insurance money being used to rebuild the mortgaged premises (*Sinnott* v. *Bowden* [1912] 2 Ch. 414).

Assignment

A contract of fire insurance can only be assigned with the consent of the insurers. If the insurers refuse to consent, the attempted assignment is of no effect.

The policy

In order to effect an insurance, the person wishing to insure fills in a proposal form. This is his offer, and when it is accepted the policy is issued. If the answers to the questions in the proposal form are untrue in a material particular, the policy is voidable at the option of the insurers. Sometimes in the policy it is stated that the statements in the proposal form shall be the basis of the contract. In such a case, if any of the statements are untrue, whether in a material particular or not, the policy may be avoided by the insurers.

D insured his lorry with B. The policy recited that the proposal should be the basis of the contract. One question in the proposal form asked where the lorry was usually garaged, and to this D replied that it was garaged at his address in Glasgow, whereas in fact it was garaged outside Glasgow. The answer was given inadvertently and had no effect on the acceptance of the risk. *Held*, B could avoid the policy, as a misstatement, although not material, was a breach of the conditions on which the policy was issued: *Dawsons Ltd.* v. *Bonnin* [1922] 2 A.C. 413.

If, however, the statement in the proposal form is only a description of the risk, the policy cannot be avoided.

M, in answer to a question in a proposal form for the insurance of a lorry, stated that the lorry was to be used for the purpose of carrying coal. The answers were made the basis of the contract. The lorry was damaged in a collision when it was carrying coal, but earlier on the same day it had been carrying timber. *Held*, the insurers were liable, as the question was only to define the risk insured against: *Provincial Insurance Co.* v. *Morgan* [1933] A.C. 240.

Where a policy makes a particular term a condition precedent to the insured's right to recover, it is for the insurer to prove the insured has not complied with that term.

An insurance policy against loss of or damage to an aeroplane provided that it should be a condition precedent for a claim under it that the pilot had observed all statutory regulations relating to air navigation. The plane crashed and its owners claimed to be indemnified under the policy. *Held*, the burden of proving that the pilot had not complied with the regulations was on the insurers: *Bond Air Services* v. *Hill* [1955] 2 Q.B., 417.

The person making the proposal is also under a duty, as in the case of all insurances, of disclosing to the insurers all facts material to the risk which are likely to affect the insurer's judgment, whether or not any questions are asked on the point in question.

Fire policies sometimes contain an average clause, the effect of which may be illustrated as follows:

A insures property worth £8,000 with B for £4,000. If £2,000 worth of the property is destroyed, then under an average clause A will only be able to recover one-quarter of £4,000 from B. If the whole is destroyed, he will recover £4,000.

Perils covered

Fire policies cover loss by fire. Ignition is necessary to fire; heating, unaccompanied by ignition, is not fire. The cause of the fire is immaterial, unless it was the deliberate act of the insured himself or someone acting with his knowledge or consent. Loss by fire caused by the insured's negligence is covered.

H hid her jewellery in her grate under the coal. Later, having forgotten this, she lit the fire and the jewellery was damaged. *Held*, H could recover under a fire policy: *Harris* v. *Poland* [1941] 1 K.B. 462.

The usual excepted perils in a fire policy are riot, civil commotion, war and explosion. To recover under a fire policy it must be proved that the loss claimed was proximately caused by fire, that is, that it was actually caused by fire, as where a building is burnt down, or that it was the reasonable and probable consequence of fire, as if property is damaged by water in extinguishing a fire or destroyed to prevent the spread of a fire. Consequential loss is not covered, and must form the subject of a separate policy. Such a policy will cover loss of profit from the interruption of a business carried on at premises damaged by fire, standing charges which continue to be payable although the business is interrupted, and increased cost of carrying on the business.

Subrogation

The doctrine of subrogation applies to those contracts of insurance which are contracts of indemnity, *e.g.* fire, motor and contingency insurance covering non-payment of money, but not life or personal accident insurance. The doctrine is a corollary of the principle of indemnity. By requiring any means of reducing or extinguishing a loss to be taken into account or prevents the assured from recovering more than a full indemnity.

Subrogation means that the insurer is entitled to enforce any remedy which the assured himself might have enforced against any third party. This applies to rights both in contract and in tort, and if the assured renounces any benefit or rights of action against third parties, the insurer is discharged to that extent.

S insured buildings against fire with P. During the currency of the policy the Plymouth Corporation served a notice to treat on S for the compulsory purchase of the buildings. Thereafter the buildings were destroyed by fire. P paid S £925 under the policy. S subsequently agreed with the corporation to receive a sum which took into account the £925 received from P. *Held*, as the buildings were at the corporation's risk from the date of the notice to treat, S was entitled to the full purchase-money from them notwithstanding the fire, and as P were subrogated to S's rights, they were entitled to recover from her the £925 they had paid: *Phoenix Assurance Co.* v. *Spooner* [1905] 2 K.B. 753.

The right arises only in so far as the insurer has admitted his liability to the assured and paid him the amount of the loss, although the loss itself may be total or partial. The insurer can sue in his own name only if there is a formal assignment of the right of action;

otherwise he must bring the action in the name of the assured who is under an obligation to permit his name to be used in this way.

An insurer who has indemnified an assured is entitled to sue the wrongdoer to recover not only the loss but also interest on the whole or any part; further, in order to give efficacy to the contract of insurance and to ensure that the assured is not over-compensated for the loss and the insurer not under-compensated it is necessary to imply a term into the contract of insurance to the effect that the assured can retain any interest which accrued before the date of settlement but that interest awarded in respect of any period subsequent to that must go to the insurers (*H. Cousins and Co. Ltd.* v. *D. & C. Carriers Ltd.* [1971] 2 Q.B. 230).

When construing a policy of insurance regard should be had to the general doctrine of subrogation only if there is ambiguity in the policy: the terms of the policy itself should be considered first and may exclude the application of the doctrine of subrogation (*L. Lucas Ltd.* v. *Export Credit Guarantee Dept.* [1974] 1 W.L.R. 909).

ACCIDENT, BURGLARY AND OTHER FORMS OF INSURANCE

Burglary insurance resembles fire insurance in that it is a contract to indemnify the assured against loss from the risk insured against. Accident insurance, on the other hand, is not a contract of indemnity, but is an agreement to pay a specified sum of money upon the happening of certain events. The usual form of accident insurance is a contract to pay a certain sum to the executors of the assured in the event of his death by accident, and a smaller sum in the event of his disablement, total or partial, and a weekly sum during his incapacity from following his usual employment.

The principles previously explained in the case of life and fire insurance apply equally to all insurances. In particular, a full disclosure must be made by the assured to the insurer of all facts that are likely to influence the insurer's judgment in deciding whether or not to accept the risk. The fact that the proposal form has a question on any particular point shows that the insurer attaches importance to that point, but the mere fact of there being no question on a point does not dispense with the necessity of disclosing anything material. Examples of things which must be disclosed are—

The fact that another insurance company has declined to accept the proposed insurance. This applies to all classes of insurance except marine insurance. If a partnership makes a proposal for insurance, the non-disclosure by one partner of the refusal of an insurance company to accept his proposal renders the policy voidable.

G and H were partners and made a proposal on the firm's behalf with L for a burglary insurance. G had been previously refused, but the firm had never been refused. *Held*, the omission to disclose that G had been refused was a concealment of a material fact, and the policy was voidable: *Glicksman* v. *Lancashire and General Insurance Co.* [1927] A.C. 139.

In a burglary insurance, the non-disclosure by the proposer that he was a Rumanian, although he had been in England since the age of 12, was held to be an omission which entitled the insurer to avoid the policy (*Horne* v. *Poland* [1922] 2 K.B. 364).

In January 1956 a company took out a policy of insurance against loss or damage from whatever cause arising to, *inter alia*, skins and furs. When the policy was effected, the fact was not disclosed that the chairman of the insured company had been convicted and sentenced in 1933 for receiving stolen furs. *Held*, there had been a wrongful non-disclosure of a material fact, *viz*, the previous conviction of the chairman, and the underwriters were entitled to avoid the policy: *Regina Fur Co. Ltd.* v. *Bossom* [1957] 2 Lloyd's Rep. 466.

Diamond merchants insured their diamonds against all risks. They failed to disclose that their sales manager had been convicted eight years before in America for smuggling diamonds into the U.S.A., since they considered that fact to be immaterial. Later the director of the diamond merchants was robbed of diamonds with violence and the diamond merchants made a claim under the policy. *Held*, the manager's offence and conviction were material facts which should have been disclosed and the claim was dismissed: *Roselodge Ltd.* v. *Castle* [1966] 2 Lloyd's Rep. 113.

The deliberate overvaluation of the property insured will avoid the policy, as also will the valuation of the property on the basis of a reasonable prospect of appreciation, unless the proposer makes it plain to the insurer that the value is not immediate, but speculative (*Hoff Trading Co.* v. *Union Insce. Co. of Canton* (1928) 45 T.L.R. 164).

In car insurance the proposer should disclose previous accidents he has had in driving, whether he was driving on his own behalf or on behalf of others (*Furry* v. *Eagle Star and British Dominions Insce. Co.* (1922) W.C. & Ins. Rep. 225).

In a proposal form, false answers which are material make the policy voidable at the insurers' option; if the false answers are not material, the policy will be voidable when the proposer has warranted the truth of his answers, but not otherwise.

Role of agents and brokers

The general rule is that the "agent" is not the agent of the insurance company. He is paid a commission on the business he introduces and is supplied with information about the company's terms of business and rates of premiums and also given a supply of insurance forms, but the acceptance or rejection of business he introduces rests with the company. If, as a matter of convenience, he fills up the proposal form he is acting as agent for the proposer. The result is that if he fills in false answers and the proposal form is signed by the proposer without reading the answers, the policy is voidable at the option of the insurer.

The R Co.'s agent filled in a proposal form for the insurance of N's motor-omnibuses. Many of the answers were false, although N had given the correct answers to the agent. N signed the form containing the false answers without reading it. *Held*, the policy was voidable, as the knowledge of the true facts by the agent could not be imputed to the R Co.: *Newsholme Bros.* v. *Road Transport and General Insce. Co.* [1929] 2 K.B. 356.

In all matters relating to the placing of insurance, of whatever kind, the insurance broker is the agent of the assured, and of the assured only. It has been contended that while this applies to the placing of the policy, when a claim arises under it the broker who placed it may thereupon become the agent of both parties in some respects. But this contention was rejected by Megaw J. in *Anglo-African Merchants Ltd.* v. *Bayley* [1970] 1 Q.B. 311, when he said: "Even if it were established to be a practice well known to persons seeking insurance—not merely to insurers and brokers—I should hold the view . . . that a custom will not be upheld by the courts of this country if it contradicts the vital principle that an agent may not at the same time serve two masters—two principals—in actual or potential opposition to one another: unless, indeed, he has the explicit, informed, consent of both principals. An insurance broker is in no privileged position in this respect."

Perils covered

A burglary policy usually covers loss by burglary, house-breaking and larceny committed on the property described in the policy. A loss from these causes on other property is not covered. An accident policy covers personal injury or death by accident, meaning something not due to natural causes, but brought about by chance. It will include such intentional acts as murder, which is something brought about by chance as far as the deceased is concerned, and also accidents caused by negligence, even of the insured himself.

Accident and burglary policies usually contain a condition that notice of the accident or loss must be given "immediately," "as soon as possible," or within a fixed number of days. Such conditions are almost always conditions precedent to liability, so that there is no liability on the insurers unless the term as to notice is complied with (*Re Williams and Thomas and L. & Y. Accident Insce. Co.* (1902) 19 T.L.R. 82). "Immediately" means "with all reasonable speed considering the circumstances of the case" (*per* Fletcher Moulton L.J., in *Re Coleman's Depositories Ltd. and Life and Health Assurance Association* [1907] 2 K.B. 798). Notice of death by accident is given "as soon as possible" if it is given by the executors of the deceased as soon as possible after they learn that the deceased had an insurance against accidental death (*Verelst's Adm.* v. *Motor Union Insce. Co.* [1925] 2 K.B. 137).

A motor insurance policy which excludes liability if "car is conveying any load in excess of that for which it is constructed" does not prevent the insured from recovering for damage to a private car carrying an extra passenger beyond its ordinary seating capacity (*Houghton* v. *Trafalgar Insce. Co.* [1954] 1 Q.B. 247).

Where a bailee insures the goods of the bailor it is a matter of the interpretation of the policy whether he has insured only his own interest as bailee or the interest of the bailor as owner of the goods.

T, carriers, claimed on a policy on goods owned by IT. The goods were taken to IT's warehouse where they were taken into the charge of IT's night-watchman and were to have been unloaded the following morning, but they were stolen in the night. *Held*, T, as bailees, had an insurable interest in the goods, and consequently were entitled to insure them for their full value; they could retain so much as would recover their own interest as bailees; and they would be trustees for the owners for the rest: *A. Tomlinson (Hauliers) Ltd.* v. *Hepburn* [1966] A.C. 451.

Public policy

In considering a claim under a contract of insurance, a court will consider whether allowing the claim in respect of a particular event would be contrary to public policy, having regard to the nature of that event. The broad principle is that no man should be allowed to profit at another's expense from his own criminal act (see p. 97, *ante*). Thus the murderer *In the Estate of Crippen* [1911] P. 108, and the felonious suicide in *Beresford* v. *Royal Insurance Co. Ltd.* [1938] A.C. 586 (see p. 98, *ante*) or those claiming through them, have had their claims defeated on the grounds that it would be contrary to public policy to assist a personal representative to recover what were in fact the fruits of the crime committed by the assured person. First, the law aims to deter the intending criminal by ensuring that no one shall indemnify him against loss he may incur as a result of his crime. Secondly, it is no part of the court's function to assist those who do commit deliberate crime to recover money to which they can lay claim only by proving the commission of that crime. On the other hand, it was held in *Tinline* v. *White Cross Insurance Association Ltd.* [1921] 3 K.B. 327, that a man who pleaded guilty to a charge of manslaughter arising from the negligent driving of a motor car was entitled to enforce an indemnity against the defendants who had insured him in respect of accidental injury. It was, however, made clear in that decision that if the occurrence had been due to an intentional criminal act on the part of the assured, the policy would not have protected him.

Where death has occurred, the logical test, in the judgment of Geoffrey Lane J., is "whether the person seeking the indemnity was guilty of deliberate, intentional and unlawful violence or threats of violence; if he was, and death resulted therefrom, then, however unintended the final death of the victim may have been, the court should not entertain a claim for indemnity" (*Gray* v. *Barr* [1970] 2 Q.B. 626, see p. 97, *ante*).

Liability of insurers to persons other than the insured

Before the Third Parties (Rights Against Insurers) Act 1930, when an injured person obtained judgment against a wrongdoer who was insured, and the wrongdoer then went bankrupt, the injured person had no direct claim against the insurance moneys. He could only prove in the bankruptcy, the insurance moneys going into the pool for the benefit of the general body of creditors. In the

Act of 1930 the injured person was given a right against the insurance company. Section 1 says that: "Where under any contract of insurance a person . . . is insured against liabilities to third parties which he may incur," then in the event of the insured becoming bankrupt if he is an individual, or, in the case of the insured being a company, in the event of a winding-up, if, either before or after that event, any such liability as aforesaid is incurred by the insured, his rights against the insurer under the contract in respect of the liability shall, notwithstanding anything in any Act or rule of law to the contrary, be transferred to and vest in the third party to whom the liability was so incurred."

Under that section the injured person steps into the shoes of the wrongdoer. There are transferred to him the wrongdoer's "rights against the insurers under the contract." As the insurers' obligation under the contract of insurance is to indemnify the insured in respect of what the latter is legally liable to pay the injured third party, the insurers' obligation to indemnify cannot arise until the insured's own obligation to pay the injured third party has been established, either by judgment of a court or by an award in arbitration or by agreement (*Post Office* v. *Norwich Union Fire Insurance Society Ltd.* [1967] 2 Q.B. 363).

It is not all the rights and liabilities of the insured under the contract of insurance which are transferred to the third party, only the particular rights in respect of the liability incurred by the insured to the third party. Rights which are not referable to the particular liability of the insured to the particular third party are not transferred. So, insurers are not entitled to set-off against the sum due to an injured third party moneys owing to them by the insured as unpaid premium (*Murray* v. *Legal and General Assurance Society Ltd.* [1970] 2 Q.B. 495).

Every driver of a motor vehicle is required to be insured against liability in respect of the death of or bodily injury to any person, including passengers, caused by the use of the vehicle on the road. A judgment against the insured in respect of such liability can be enforced against the insurer (Road Traffic Act 1972, ss. 149 and 150). The insurance must not contain a provision that liability shall cease if some specified thing is done or omitted *after* the accident. Further, any restriction on the insurance by reference to the age or condition of the driver, the condition of the vehicle, or the number of persons or weight of goods carried, is void.

If the policy is expressed to indemnify persons driving the motor vehicle with the consent of the insured, such persons, although not parties to the contract or named in the policy as being parties interested, can sue for an indemnity under the policy (*Tattersall* v. *Drysdale* [1935] 2 K.B. 174).

Motor Insurer's Bureau

Over the past 40 years procedures have evolved, outside the terms of any statute, whereby a person injured by a road vehicle but who cannot recover damages from the driver of the vehicle, can in certain circumstances and subject to certain conditions recover compensation from the Motor Insurers' Bureau, if necessary by action in the courts, although he has not given consideration to the Bureau.

In 1937 a Departmental Committee made recommendations to secure compensation to third party victims of road accidents in cases where, notwithstanding the provisions of the Road Traffic Acts relating to compulsory insurance, the victim was deprived of compensation by the absence of insurance, or of effective insurance. In accordance with an agreement made in 1945 between the Minister and insurers transacting compulsory motor vehicle insurance business the Motor Insurers' Bureau was formed and in 1946 it entered into a further agreement with the Minister to give effect to the recommendations made in 1937.

The 1946 agreement—described by Lord Denning M.R. as being "as important as any statute"—provided for compensation to be payable by the Bureau to a victim who had obtained a judgment which remained unsatisfied in respect of a known driver who had been negligent and ought to have been insured, but was not. The agreement did not, however, cover cases where the negligent driver was not known and could not be traced. As this gave rise to hardship, for many years the Bureau in such circumstances made payments on an *ex gratia* basis. This practice was formally recognised in an agreement in 1969, which also provided for an appeal against the Bureau's decisions in such cases, and in 1971 modifications were made to the provisions relating to compensation in the case of uninsured drivers. In 1972 two new agreements were entered into and these now constitute the current arrangements.

One agreement—*Compensation of Victims of Uninsured Drivers*—provides for payment of compensation, provided judgment is obtained against the driver and the Bureau is informed within seven days of the commencement of proceedings. The agreement became effective on December 1, 1972 and, reflecting the Road Traffic Act 1972, includes passengers in its provisions. In the notes published with the agreement it is emphasised that there is nothing in the agreement affecting any obligations imposed on a policyholder by his policy. Policyholders are not released from their contractual obligations to their insurers, although the scheme protects third party victims from the consequences of failure to observe them. Thus, the failure of a policyholder to notify claims to his insurers as required by his policy, although not affecting a victim's right to benefit under the scheme, may leave the policyholder liable to his insurers.

Under the other agreement—*Compensation of Victims of Untraced Drivers*—the Bureau accepts liability in this regard but by clause 4 the Bureau will not include in any payment awarded "any amount in respect of any damages for loss of expectation of life or for pain or suffering which the applicant might have had a right to claim under the Law Reform (Miscellaneous Provisions) Act 1934." Applications for a payment under the agreement must be made in writing to the Bureau within three years of the accident giving rise to the death or injury.

It is the publicly declared policy of the Bureau not to rely on the absence of privity of contract.

SELECT BIBLIOGRAPHY
Books

R. Colinvaux, *The Law of Insurance* (3rd ed., 1971).

E. R. Hardy Ivamy, *Casebook on Insurance Law* (1969).

E. R. Hardy Ivamy, *Fire and Motor Insurance Law* (2nd ed., 1973).

E. R. Hardy Ivamy, *General Principles of Insurance Law* (3rd ed., 1975).

E. R. Hardy Ivamy, *Personal Accident, Life and other Insurances* (1973).

MacGillivray & Parkington on Insurance (6th ed., 1975) Gen. Ed. M. Parkington.

Articles

Cockerell, H. A. J., "Accumulation of Claims, Payments, Recourse and Subrogation in Private and Social Insurance" [1973] J.B.L. 214–225.

Hasson, R. A., "Basis of the Contract Clause In Insurance Law (1971) 34 M.L.R. 29–41.

Hasson, R. A., "The Doctrine of Uberrima Fides in Insurance Law —A Critical Evaluation" (1969) 32 M.L.R. 615–637.

Hodgin, R. W., "Subrogation in Insurance Law" [1975] J.B.L. 114–121.

Hudson, A. H., "Problems in Insurance Law" [1975] 38 M.L.R. 212–217.

Powles, D. G., "Subrogation-Equity, Implied Terms and Exclusion" (1974) 90 L.Q.R. 34–41.

CHAPTER 24

MARINE INSURANCE[1]

A CONTRACT of marine insurance is a contract whereby the insurer undertakes to indemnify the assured against marine losses, that is to say, the losses incident to marine adventure (s. 1). There is a marine adventure when—

1. any ship or goods are exposed to maritime perils;
2. the earning or acquisition of any freight, passage money, commission, profit, or other pecuniary benefit or the security for any advances is endangered by the exposure of insurable property to maritime perils;
3. liability to a third party may be incurred by the owner of or a person interested in insurable property by reason of maritime perils.

"Maritime perils" means the perils consequent on or incidental to the navigation of the sea, but a marine insurance contract may, by express terms or by useage of a trade, be extended to protect the assured against losses on inland waters (s. 2).

Insurable interest

A contract of marine insurance where the assured has no insurable interest is a gaming or wagering contract and is void. Policies are void when they are made—

1. interest or no interest; or
2. without further proof of interest than the policy itself; or
3. without benefit of salvage to the insurer, except where there is no possibility of salvage (s. 4).

A person has an insurable interest if he is interested in a marine adventure in consequence of which he may benefit by the safe arrival of insurable property or be prejudiced by its loss, damage or detention. The following persons have an insurable interest—

1. The lender of money on bottomry or *respondentia*, to the extent of the loan. Bottomry is a pledge of the ship and freight to secure a loan to enable the ship to continue the voyage. It is named after the bottom or keel of the ship, which is figuratively

---

[1] References in this chapter are to the Marine Insurance Act 1906 unless the contrary is expressed.

used to express the whole ship. *Respondentia* is a pledge of the cargo only and not of the ship.

2. The master and crew to the extent of their wages.

3. A person advancing freight to the extent that the freight is not repayable in case of loss.

4. A mortgagor, to the extent of the full value of the property, and a mortgagee for the sum due under the mortgage.

5. The owner, to the extent of the full value, notwithstanding that a third party has agreed to indemnify him from loss.

6. A reinsurer, to the extent of his risk.

Defeasible, contingent and partial interests are insurable.

The assured must have the insurable interest at the time of the loss, although he need not have it when the insurance is effected. If he insures property "lost or not lost" the insurance is good although the property may in fact be lost at the date when the insurance is effected, provided the assured did not know that it was lost. If the assured assigns his interest in the property insured he does not transfer his rights in the insurance to the assignee, unless there is an agreement to that effect.

Disclosure and representations

A contract of marine insurance is one in which the utmost good faith (*uberrima fides*) must be observed, and if it is not, the contract is voidable by the insurer. The assured must disclose to the insurer every material circumstance which is known to him, and he is deemed to know everything which he ought to know in the ordinary course of business. A circumstance is material if it would influence the judgment of a prudent insurer in fixing the premium or determining whether to take the risk (s. 18). The following are examples of the concealment of facts, which have been held to be material—

The fact that the ship had grounded and sprung a leak before the insurance was effected (*Russell* v. *Thornton* (1859) 20 L.J. Ex. 9).

A merchant, on hearing that a vessel similar to his own was captured, effected an insurance without disclosing this information (*De Costa* v. *Scandret* (1723) 2 P. Wms. 170).

The nationality of the assured concealed at a time when his nationality was important (*Associated Oil Carriers Ltd.* v. *Union Insce. Socy. of Canton Ltd.* [1917] 2 K.B. 184).

In an insurance on a ship, the fact that the goods carried were insured at a value greatly exceeding their real value (*Ionides* v. *Pender* (1874) L.R. 9 Q.B. 531).

In every case, however, whether a circumstance is material or not depends on the particular facts. The following circumstances need not be disclosed—

1. Those diminishing the risk.
2. Those known or presumed to be known by the insurer in the ordinary course of his business.
3. Those which are waived by the insurer.

If the insurance is effected by an agent, the agent must disclose to the insurer every fact which the assured himself ought to disclose and also every material circumstance known to the agent. The agent is deemed to know every fact which he ought to know in the ordinary way of business or which ought to have been communicated to him (s. 19).

In addition to his duty to make a full disclosure, the assured is under a duty to see that every material representation made during the negotiations for the contract is true. If any material representation be untrue the insurer may avoid the contract (s. 20).

The policy

The contract of marine insurance is made as soon as the proposal is accepted by the insurer, although the policy may not be issued until later. Before the policy is issued it is usual to issue a document called "the slip," which is a short memorandum of the contract evidencing the date of the commencement of the insurance (s. 21). No action can be brought until the policy is issued; the slip cannot be sued upon, but where there is a duly stamped policy reference may be made to the slip in any legal proceeding (s. 89). The policy must be signed by the insurer, or, if the insurer is a corporation, it may be sealed, and must specify—

1. The name of the assured or of some person who effects the insurance on his behalf.
2. The subject-matter insured and the risk insured against.
3. The voyage or period of time or both, as the case may be, covered by the insurance.
4. The sum or sums insured.
5. The name or names of the insurers.

The subject-matter of the insurance must be described with reasonable certainty, regard being had to any trade usage. The

Marine Insurance

nature and extent of the assured's interest in the subject-matter need not be specified (s. 26).

The policy usually takes the form known as Lloyd's S.G. policy, set out in the Marine Insurance Act 1906. The Act also contains rules for the construction of the policy.

Policies are of the following kinds—

1. **Voyage policies,** where the contract is to insure "at and from" or from one place to another. The subject-matter is then insured for a particular voyage only.

2. **Time policies,** where the contract is to insure for "a definite period of time" (s. 25 (1)). A policy for a period of time and not for a voyage does not cease to be a time policy merely because that period may thereafter be extended or curtailed pursuant to one of the policy's provisions. The duration of the policy is defined by its own times and is thus for "a definite period of time" (*Compania Maritima San Basilio S.A.* v. *Oceanus Mutual Underwriting Assn. (Bermuda) Ltd.* [1976] 3 W.L.R. 265). By the Stamp Act 1891, s. 93, no time policy can be made for a period exceeding 12 months, but by virtue of section 11 of the Finance Act 1901 a time policy may contain a "continuation clause" providing that if at the end of the period the ship is at sea the insurance shall continue until the ship's arrival at her port of destination or for a reasonable time thereafter. A time policy sometimes contains restrictions as to locality, *e.g.* "from June 1, 1948, to April 1, 1949, no Baltic." A contract for both voyage and time may be included in the same policy (s. 25). This is known as a **mixed policy.** The underwriter is only liable under it when the loss occurs within the insured period and while the ship is on the described voyage.

3. **Valued policies,** where the policy specifies the agreed value of the subject-matter insured. In the absence of fraud, this value is conclusive as between the insurer and the assured, whether the loss be partial or total; but it is not conclusive in determining whether there has been a constructive total loss (s. 27). Mere over-valuation is not fraudulent unless it is of a very gross nature. Without fraud, over-valuation is not a ground for repudiation as such (*Berger & Light Diffusers Pty.* v. *Pollock* [1973] 2 Lloyd's Rep. 442).

4. **Unvalued policies,** where the value of the subject-matter is not specified, but is left to be subsequently ascertained, subject to the limit of the sum insured. The insurable value is ascertained as follows—

(a) As to the ship, the value includes her outfit, provisions and stores, money advanced for wages and disbursement to make the ship fit for the voyage, plus the charges of insurance on the whole. In the case of a steamship, it also includes the machinery, boilers, coals and engine stores.

(b) As to the freight, the value is the gross freight at the risk of the assured, plus the charges of insurance.

(c) As to the goods and merchandise, the value is the prime cost of the property insured, plus the expenses of and incidental to shipping and the charges of insurance (s. 16).

5. **Floating policies,** where the insurance is described in general terms, leaving the name of the ship and other particulars to be defined by subsequent declaration. The subsequent declarations may be made by indorsement on the policy or in other customary manner and must be made in order of shipment. They must, in the case of goods, comprise all consignments within the terms of the policy and the value of the goods must be stated. If the value is not stated until after notice of loss or arrival, the policy must be treated as unvalued as regards those goods (s. 29).

Open cover is not a policy, but is an agreement by the underwriter to issue an appropriate policy within the terms of the cover. To this extent it resembles a floating policy.

Reinsurance is where the insurer himself insures the whole or part of the risk he has undertaken with another insurer. In such a case the ordinary law as to insurer and assured applies as between the reinsurer and the insurer. Unless the policy provides otherwise, the original assured has no right or interest in the reinsurance (s. 9). When a constructive total loss occurs, the insurer need not give notice of abandonment to the reinsurer (s. 62 (9)).

Double insurance is where two or more policies are effected by or on behalf of the assured on the same adventure and interest and the sums assured exceed the indemnity allowed by the Act, *e.g.* if X insures property worth £1,000 with Y for £750 and Z for £500, there is a double insurance, because the measure of X's indemnity, *viz.* £1,000, has been exceeded. If X had insured with Y for £450 and Z for £550 there would be no double insurance.

Where the assured is over-insured by double insurance he may, unless the policy otherwise provides, claim payment from the insurers in such order as he may think fit, provided he does not recover more than his indemnity. If the policy is a valued policy, the assured must give credit as against the valuation for any sum received under any other policy without regard to the value of the subject-matter insured. If the policy is unvalued, the assured must give credit, as against the full insurable value, for any sum received under any other policy. If the assured receives any sum in excess of his indemnity, he is deemed to hold it in trust for the insurers according to their rights amongst themselves (s. 32).

As between the insurers, each is liable to contribute to the loss in proportion to the amount for which he is liable. If any insurer pays more than his proportion he can sue the others for contribution (s. 80).

Warranties

In contracts of marine insurance the term "warranty" has a different meaning from that in the Sale of Goods Act 1893. In the Marine Insurance Act 1906 it means that the assured undertakes that some particular thing shall or shall not be done, or that some condition shall be fulfilled, or whereby he affirms or negatives the existence of a particular state of facts. A warranty must be exactly complied with whether it be material or not. The effect of non-compliance is to discharge the insurer from liability as from the date of the breach (s. 33). A breach of warranty may be waived by the insurer.

The following warranties are implied—

1. In a voyage policy, that at the commencement of the voyage the ship is seaworthy for the purpose of the particular adventure insured. A ship is deemed to be seaworthy when she is reasonably fit in all respects to encounter the ordinary perils of the seas of the adventure insured (s. 39 (1), (4)).

2. In a voyage policy, where the voyage is to be performed in stages, during which the ship requires different kinds of or further equipment or preparation, that at the commencement of each stage the ship is seaworthy in respect of such preparation or equipment for the purpose of that stage.

A ship was insured for a round voyage from the U.K. to South America and back. During the voyage the master left Monte Video without enough coal to take the ship to St. Vincent, the next port of call, and in consequence some of the ship's fittings and spars had to be burnt, otherwise the ship would have been a total loss. In an action against the insurers to recover the value of the fittings and spars, *held*, as the vessel was not fit when she left Monte Video to meet the ordinary perils of the voyage, there was a breach of an implied warranty and the policy did not attach: *Greenock SS. Co.* v. *Maritime Insce. Co. Ltd.* [1903] 2 K.B. 657.

3. Where the policy attaches while the ship is in port, that the ship shall, at the commencement of the risk, be reasonably fit to encounter the ordinary perils of the port (s. 39 (2)).

4. In a voyage policy on goods or other movables, that at the commencement of the voyage the ship is not only seaworthy as a ship, but also that she is reasonably fit to carry the goods to the destination contemplated by the policy.

5. That the adventure is a legal one and will be carried out in a lawful manner (s. 41).

There is **no** implied warranty in the following cases—

1. As to the nationality of the ship or that her nationality shall not be changed during the risk (s. 37).

2. In a time policy, that the ship shall be seaworthy at any stage of the adventure, but where, with the privity of the assured, the ship is sent to sea in an unseaworthy state, the insurer is not liable for any loss attributable to seaworthiness (s. 39 (5)).

If the loss is not attributable to the unseaworthiness to which the assured was privy, the insurer will be liable on the policy.

A ship which was insured under a time policy, was sent to sea unseaworthy in two respects; her hull was in an unfit state for the voyage and her crew was insufficient. The assured knew of the insufficiency of the crew but not of the unfitness of the hull. The ship was lost because of the unfitness of the hull. *Held*, the insurers were liable: *Thomas* v. *Tyne and Wear SS. Freight Insce. Assn.* [1917] 1 K.B. 938.

3. In a policy on goods or other movables, that the goods or movables are seaworthy (s. 40 (1)).

The voyage

In a voyage policy, if the voyage is altered, the insurer is discharged from liability. If, when the contract is made, the ship is said to be at a particular place, it is not necessary that it should be at that place, but the voyage must be commenced within a reasonable time (s. 42). If the ship does not sail from the place of departure specified in the policy or does not go to the destination so specified or does not prosecute the voyage with reasonable dispatch, in all these cases the insurer is not liable on the policy.

If the ship deviates from the voyage contemplated by the policy, the insurer is discharged from liability as from the time of deviation, and it is immaterial that the ship may have regained her route before any loss occurs (s. 46). Deviation, however, is excused in the following cases—

1. Where authorised by the policy.
2. Where caused by circumstances beyond the control of the master and his employer.
3. Where reasonably necessary to comply with an express or implied warranty.
4. Where reasonably necessary for the safety of the ship or subject-matter insured.
5. For the purpose of saving human life or aiding a ship in distress where human life may be in danger; but not for saving property (*Scaramanga* v. *Stamp* (1880) 5 C.P.D. 295).
6. Where reasonably necessary to obtain medical aid for any person on board the ship.
7. Where caused by the barratrous conduct of the master or crew if barratry be one of the perils insured against.

When the cause excusing the deviation ceases to operate, the ship must resume her course and prosecute her voyage with reasonable dispatch (s. 49).

If the policy specifies several ports of discharge, the ship must proceed to such of them as she goes to in the order designated by the policy; if she does not, there is a deviation (s. 47).

Assignment of policy

A marine policy is assignable by indorsement, and the assignee can sue on it in his own name subject to any defence which would have been available against the person who effected the policy. The assignment may be made either before or after loss, but an assured who has parted with or lost his interest in the subject-matter assured cannot assign.

The premium

The insurer is not bound to issue the policy until payment of the premium. If the insurance is effected through a broker, the broker is responsible to the insurer for the premium. He has, however, a lien on the policy for the premium and his charges. If he has dealt with the person who employs him as a principal, he has a lien on the policy for his general balance of insurance account. When a broker effects the insurance and the policy acknowledges the receipt of the premium, the acknowledgment is, in the absence of fraud, conclusive as between the insurer and the assured, but not as between the insurer and the broker (s. 54).

Perils covered

The risks insured against usually include perils of the seas (p. 454, *post*), collisions between ships up to three-fourths of the damage sustained (this is not a peril of the seas), loss by fire, pirates (p. 454, *post*) thieves (does not cover clandestine theft or a theft committed by one of the ship's company, whether crew or passengers), barratry (p. 454, *post*), and the risk of "all other perils, losses and misfortunes, that have or shall come to the hurt, detriment or damage" of the subject-matter of the insurance. The last risk includes only marine damage of a kind similar to the foregoing.

War risks are excluded and are covered separately.

Burden of proof

Whether the burden of proof is upon the insured or the insurer is often a matter of practical importance in that a case may be determined one way or the other according to where the burden lies owing to the paucity of evidence. Thus, when a plaintiff claims for loss under a policy of marine insurance asserting that the loss was caused by perils of the sea, the onus is on him to prove that the loss was accidental. Accordingly, if on the available evidence the loss is equally consistent with accidental loss by perils of the sea as with scuttling, the plaintiff fails. The basis of this principle is that the words in the policy "loss . . . by perils of the sea" necessarily connote some accidental or fortuitous loss. It follows therefore that if the plaintiff in such a case does not disprove scuttling on a balance of probabilities, he has failed to prove his loss was caused by "perils of the sea."

The position is different, however, in the case of a claim under a policy for "loss by fire." The risk of fire insured against is not confined to an accidental fire. Thus, if a ship has been set alight by some mischievous person but without the plaintiff's connivance, the plaintiff will be entitled to recover. The plaintiff cannot, of course, recover if he was the person who fired the ship or was a party to the ship being fired, because of the principle of insurance law that no man can recover for a loss which he himself has deliberately or fraudulently caused. As to the burden of proof, once it is shown that the loss has been caused by fire, the plaintiff has made out a prima facie case and the onus is upon the defendant to show on a balance of probabilities that the fire was caused or connived at by the plaintiff. Accordingly, if the court comes to the conclusion that the loss is equally consistent with arson as it is with an accidental fire, the onus being on the defendant, the plaintiff will succeed (*Slattery* v. *Mance* [1962] 1 Q.B. 676).

Loss and abandonment

The insurer is only liable for those losses which are proximately caused by a peril insured against.

The fact that the loss would not have happened but for the negligence of the master or crew does not relieve the insurer from liability, but he is not liable for loss attributable to the wilful misconduct of the assured. He is not liable for loss through delay, even though caused by a peril insured against, or for wear and tear, leakage or breakage, or inherent vice of the subject-matter insured (s. 55).

A loss may be either **total** or **partial.** A partial loss is any loss other than a total loss. A total loss may be actual or constructive.

An **actual total loss** is where the subject-matter insured is (1) destroyed, (2) so damaged as to cease to be a thing of the kind insured against, or (3) where the assured is irretrievably deprived thereof.

A ship was insured against perils of the sea and not loss from capture. During the Russo-Japanese war she was captured and, whilst being navigated towards a Court of Prize, was wrecked. *Held*, the loss was a loss by capture and not by perils of the sea: *Andersen* v. *Marten* [1908] A.C. 334.

A ship on which dates had been loaded was sunk during the voyage and subsequently raised. The dates still retained the appearance of dates, and were of value for distillation into spirits, but were no longer merchantable as dates. *Held*, there was an actual loss of the dates: *Asfar & Co.* v. *Blundell* [1896] 1 Q.B. 123.

An actual total loss may be presumed if a ship is missing and, after a reasonable time, no news of her has been received (s. 58).

A **constructive total loss** is where the subject-matter insured is reasonably abandoned because its actual total loss appears to be unavoidable, or because the expenditure to prevent an actual total

loss would be greater than the value of the subject-matter when
saved. For example, there is a constructive total loss where a
ship has sunk and the cost of raising her exceeds her value when
recovered; where a ship is damaged and the cost of repairs exceeds
the value of the ship when repaired; where goods are damaged and
the cost of repair and forwarding them to their destination exceeds
their value on arrival (s. 60).

A ship sank in harbour and notice of abandonment was given to
the insurers. The insurers, by a large expenditure, raised the ship and
claimed that as she could then be repaired for less than her value, the
loss was only partial. *Held*, the insurers could not, by incurring expenditure which an ordinary prudent and uninsured owner would not have
incurred, change a constructive total loss into a partial loss: *SS. "Blair-
more" Co. Ltd.* v. *MacRedie* [1898] A.C. 583.

Where there is a constructive total loss, the assured may either
treat the loss as a partial loss, or abandon the subject-matter to
the insurer and treat the loss as an actual total loss. In the latter
case notice of abandonment must be given. No notice of abandonment need be given in the case of actual total loss.

Notice of abandonment may be either in writing or by word of
mouth, and may take any form as long as it indicates clearly that
the assured abandons unconditionally the subject-matter of the
insurance to the insured. If notice is not given the loss will be considered as partial. The notice must be given with reasonable diligence
after the receipt of reliable information of the loss, time being
allowed to make inquiries in a doubtful case. When notice of
abandonment is accepted the acceptance conclusively admits
liability for the loss, but if the insurer refuses to accept the notice
the assured is not prejudiced if the notice has been properly given
(s. 62).

On abandonment of the subject-matter the insurer is entitled
to take over the interest of the assured in whatever may remain of
the subject-matter insured, and consequently would be entitled to
any freight earned subsequent to the casualty causing the loss (s. 63).

General average (p. 470, *post*)

If a general average loss has been incurred in connection with
a peril insured against, the assured may recover the whole amount
from the insurer without having recourse to the other parties liable

to contribute (s. 66). The insurer can recover this amount from the others.

A **particular average** loss is a partial loss of the subject-matter insured, caused by a peril insured against, which is not a general average loss. It gives no right of contribution from the other parties interested in the adventure. Such a loss can be recovered from the insurers if it is caused in connection with a peril insured against.

Measure of indemnity

Marine insurance being a contract of indemnity, the assured is only entitled to recover from the insurer such loss as he actually sustains. In the case of a **total** loss, the measure of indemnity is the sum fixed by the policy in the case of a valued policy, and the insurable value of the subject-matter in the case of an unvalued policy (s. 68).

In the case of a **partial loss to the ship** the measure of indemnity is—

1. Where the ship has been repaired, the cost of repairs less the customary deductions which are usually one-third of the cost of new materials replacing old.

2. Where the ship has been partially repaired, the cost of repairs as above, and the amount of depreciation arising from the unrepaired damage.

3. Where the damage has not been repaired, the amount of depreciation from the unrepaired damage (s. 69).

In the case of a **partial loss of goods** the measure of indemnity is—

1. Where part of the goods is lost and the policy is valued, such proportion of the fixed value as the value of the lost goods bears to the whole value of the insured goods.

2. Where part of the goods is lost and the policy is unvalued, the insurable value of the part lost.

3. Where the goods have been damaged, such proportion of the fixed value in the case of a valued policy, or of the insurable value in the case of an unvalued policy, as the difference between the gross sound and damaged values at the place of arrival bears to the gross sound value (s. 71).

An insurer is liable for successive losses, although the total amount may exceed the sum insured; but if a partial loss, which has not been made good, is followed by a total loss, the assured can only recover in respect of the total loss (s. 77).

It is the duty of the assured to take reasonable measures to avert or minimise a loss, and to prevent him from being prejudiced by anything he does to preserve the insured property after an accident, the policy usually contains a "suing and labouring" clause. This provides that it shall be lawful for the assured "to sue, labour and travel for, in and about the defence, safeguards, and recovery of the goods, ship, etc., without prejudice to this insurance." Under the clause the assured can recover from the insurer any expenses properly incurred pursuant to the clause, notwithstanding that the insurer has paid for a total loss (s. 78).

Rights of insurer on payment

When the insurer pays for a total loss, he is entitled to whatever remains of the subject-matter insured, but if he pays for a partial loss he is entitled to no part of the subject-matter. In both cases, however, he is subrogated to the rights of the assured, *i.e.* he can bring an action in the assured's name against any person responsible for the loss.

Return of premium

Where the consideration for the payment of the premium totally fails, and there has been no fraud or illegality on the part of the assured, the premium is returnable to the assured, *e.g.* if the assured insured goods on the wrong ship by mistake (*Martin* v. *Sitwell* (1691) 1 Shower 156). If the consideration is apportionable, and there is a total failure of an apportionable part of the consideration, a proportionate part of the premium is returnable.

The premium is returnable in the following cases—

1. Where the policy is void or is avoided by the insurer as from the commencement of the risk, if there has been no fraud or illegality on the part of the assured.

2. Where the subject-matter insured has never been imperilled.

But if a ship is insured "lost or not lost," and has arrived safely when the insurance is effected, the premium is not returnable unless the insurer knew of the safe arrival.

A ship was overdue and the insurers reinsured at a heavy premium. At the date of the insurance, the ship had arrived safely, but neither party knew of it. *Held*, the insurer was bound to pay the premium to the reinsurer: *Bradford* v. *Symondson* (1881) 7 Q.B.D. 456.

3. Where the assured has no insurable interest, unless the policy is a gaming or wagering policy.

4. Where the assured has over-insured under an unvalued policy, a proportionate part of the premium is recoverable.

5. When the assured has over-insured by double insurance, a proportionate part of the several premiums is returnable, except when the double insurance was effected knowingly by the assured (s. 84).

Mutual insurance

Mutual insurance is where two or more persons agree to insure each other against marine losses. In such a case no premium is usually payable, but each party agrees to contribute to a loss in a certain proportion. The rights and duties between the parties depend on agreement, usually embodied in the rules of an association, and the ordinary law of marine insurance applies, subject to any such agreement.

Protection and Indemnity Associations, usually referred to as **P. & I. Clubs,** are a most common example of mutual insurance. It is a usual practice of shipowners to enter their tonnage in a P. & I. Club, contributing to its funds on an agreed basis of mutuality, in return for which the Association, on behalf of its members and within the framework of its rules, undertakes to meet the cost of various kinds of liabilities incidental to shipowning, usually those which would otherwise not be covered by the ordinary form of marine hull insurance policy, *e.g.* liabilities for injuries to passengers and crew, damage to piers, docks and harbours and quarantine expenses.

SELECT BIBLIOGRAPHY

Books

E. R. Hardy Ivamy, *Chalmers' Marine Insurance Act 1906* (8th ed., 1976).

E. R. Hardy Ivamy, *Marine Insurance*, (1969).

PART 8: CARRIAGE BY LAND, SEA AND AIR

CHAPTER 25

COMMON AND PRIVATE CARRIERS

COMMON carriers are now rare but the law relating to them is of importance as a basis to the understanding of current law and conditions of carriage. A common carrier is one who holds himself out as being ready for hire to transport from place to place, either by land, sea or air, the goods of anyone (or for that matter any passengers) wishing to employ him. He must do it as a business and not as a casual operation. He is bound to carry all goods offered to him by persons willing to pay his hire unless—

1. he has no room in his vehicle;
2. the goods offered are not of the kind he professes to carry;
3. the destination is not one to which he usually travels;
4. the goods are offered at an unreasonable hour;
5. the goods are not properly packed; or
6. reasonable charges are not paid in advance.

If he wrongfully refuses to carry any goods or passengers he may be sued for damages in tort.

The defendants who were common carriers by rail refused to accept "packed parcels" from the plaintiffs who were themselves carriers and who were undercutting the defendants' freight rates. *Held*, the defendants were liable for refusal to carry: *Crouch* v. *London and North Western Ry.* (1854) 9 Ex. 556.

Whether a carrier is a common carrier or not depends on the circumstances. If he holds himself out to all and sundry as being prepared to carry he is a common carrier. If he reserves to himself the right of accepting or rejecting offers of goods whether his conveyances are full or empty, being guided by the attractiveness of the offer and not by his ability to carry (*i.e.* whether his vehicle is already full or not), he is not a common carrier.

B was a haulage contractor who owned two lorries. With these and others, which he hired when necessary, he carried sugar from Liverpool to Manchester. At Manchester, he invited offers of goods of all kinds,

431

except machinery, and these he accepted or rejected according as the rate, route and class of goods were or were not satisfactory. *Held*, he was not a common carrier, because he reserved the right to reject goods whether his vehicle was full or not: *Belfast Ropework Co. Ltd.* v. *Bushell* [1918] 1 K.B. 210.

Most carriers nowadays state in their conditions of carriage that they are not common carriers and this is probably effective. Privately owned parcel companies and bus companies who carry passengers and luggage by road may be still common carriers. The courts do not nowadays regularly infer that a carrier is a common carrier (*Webster* v. *Dickson Transport* [1969] 1 Lloyd's Rep. 89).

Nationalised transport undertakings

The organisation of the nationalised transport undertakings is now regulated by the Transport Acts 1962 and 1968 and the Transport (London) Act 1969. The undertakings set up by the Transport Act 1962 that are still in existence, *viz*. the British Railways Board, the British Transport Docks Board and the British Waterways Board, are not to be regarded as common carriers by rail or inland waterway (Transport Act 1962, s. 43 (6)). The London Transport Executive, set up to replace the London Transport Board by the Transport (London) Act 1969, is also stated not to be a common carrier of persons (s. 6 (2) (*g*) of the 1969 Act). Of the undertakings set up by the Transport Act 1968 the National Freight Corporation and its subsidiaries whose duty it is "to provide, or secure or promote ... properly integrated services for the carriage of goods ..." (Transport Act 1968, s. 1 (1)), is stated not to be a common carrier (s. 2 (2) of the 1968 Act). There is, however, no such provision for the other bodies national or local that are created by that Act. Thus, the National Bus Company could be a common carrier of passengers or their luggage.

Carriage by rail, sea and air

Carriers by rail, sea and air are subject to special regulation which will be considered in detail later on. The British Railways Board is, as has been seen (above), not a common carrier and carriage by rail is operated on the basis of the Railway Board's Conditions of Carriage (see p. 440, *post*) which are of a purely contractual nature.

Carriers by sea are in practice not common carriers (see Chap.

27). Carriers by air (Chap. 28) are not normally common carriers because the terms of their contracts of carriage (which are now largely regulated by statute) exclude that quality (see *Alsan* v. *Imperial Airways Ltd.* (1933) 45 Lloyd's Law Rep. 316).

Liability for loss or damage and delay

A contract of carriage of goods is deemed to be made by the owner of goods with the carrier. The consignor is deemed to be acting as agent for the owner if he be not the owner himself.

A common carrier is an insurer of the safety of the goods carried, and therefore he is liable for any damage to or loss of them, whether occasioned by his negligence or not.

The defendant was a common carrier by land. Without any negligence on his part the defendant's warehouse, in which goods were stored, was destroyed by fire. *Held*, the defendant was strictly liable for the loss (*Forward* v. *Pithard* (1785) 1 T.R. 27).

But to this rule of strict liability there are four common law **excepted perils**, *viz.* the carrier is not liable if the loss or damage is caused by—
1. The act of God.
2. The Queen's enemies.
3. Inherent vice in the thing carried.
4. The fault of the consignor.

These common law defences reappear in the modern conditions of carriage of private carriers of goods.

Act of God

The act of God has been explained as "a mere short way in expressing this proposition. A common carrier is not liable for any accident as to which he can show that it is due to natural causes directly and exclusively without human intervention, and that it could not have been prevented by any amount of foresight and pains and care reasonably to have been expected from him" (*per* James L.J. in *Nugent* v. *Smith* (below).

The defendant was a common carrier by barge. Without any negligence on his part a sudden tempest blew the barge into a bridge and the plaintiff's goods were lost. *Held*, the defendant was not liable due to an Act of God (*Amies* v. *Stevers* (1716) 1 Stra. 127).

X, a common carrier by sea, received from Y a mare to be carried from Aberdeen to London. During the voyage the ship encountered rough weather, and the mare received such injuries that she died. The death was due partly to more than ordinary bad weather and partly to the struggling of the mare in fright. *Held*, X was not liable because the direct and irresistible cause of the loss was an act of nature, together with a defect in the thing carried. *Nugent* v. *Smith* (1876) 1 C.P.D. 423.

The Queen's enemies

The Queen's enemies means a hostile foreign sovereign or government. Injury to the goods caused by robbers or through a riot is not within the exception.

Inherent vice in the thing carried

A carrier is not liable for damage caused by something inherent in the nature of the goods carried over which he has no control and against which he cannot guard.

B delivered an engine on a carriage to the defendants. While being hauled to the railway station by the defendants' horses the shaft of the carriage broke and the engine overturned and was damaged. *Held*, the defendants were not liable. (*Lister* v. *Lancashire and Yorkshire Ry.* [1903] 1 K.B. 876.

The fault of the consignor

If the damage is caused by the goods not being properly packed, the carrier is not liable.

B hid money in a consignment of tea which he gave to W a common carrier. The money was stolen. *Held*, W was not liable as "the plaintiff bought this loss on himself by his own manner of conducting his business" (*per* Tenterden C.J.) (*Bradley* v. *Waterhouse* (1828) 3 C.O.P. 318).

Similarly, if delay or non-delivery is caused by inaccurate addressing then the carrier is not liable.

A common carrier cannot rely on the excepted perils if he has been negligent.

It should be emphasised that unlike a common carrier of goods a common carrier of passengers is not strictly liable for the safety of his passengers although he can be sued for refusing to carry.

R was injured in a railway accident which happened without any negligence on the part of the railway company who were common carriers. *Held*, the railway company were not liable (*Readhead* v. *Midland Ry.* (1869) L.R. 4 Q.B. 379).

A private carrier of goods is a **bailee** and as such is only liable for negligence although in the event of loss or damage the burden of disproving negligence is upon him (see p. 372, *ante*). It should be noted that common carriers are not strictly liable for delay as they are for loss or damage. Both common and private carriers are liable for delays caused by their negligence only.

T consigned poultry by rail leaving adequate time for the poultry to reach the market in London in normal circumstances. Transit was, however, delayed by a rail accident caused by the negligence of another railway company over which the defendants had no control. *Held*, the railway company was not liable for the delay even though they were common carriers as there was no lack of diligence on their part and the delay was beyond their control: *Taylor* v. *Great Northern Ry.* (1866) L.R. 1 C.P. 385.

A private or common carrier of passengers is only liable for negligence at common law and does not warrant the safety of his vehicle or craft. The position in relation to carriage of goods depends upon the mode of transport (see Chaps. 26–28).

Modification of common law liability

A common carrier can always be sued for refusal to carry but is not bound to undertake the common carrier's strict liability. He may make a special contract either excluding altogether or restricting his strict liability as a common carrier. When his liability is restricted, he still carries as a common carrier subject to the restriction. If, for example, the contract is that he is not to be liable for damage caused by collision, he will be under the full liability of a common carrier in respect of damage caused in other ways, *e.g.* by fire. Apparently a common carrier cannot put unreasonable exemption clauses in his contract of carriage (*Garton* v. *Bristol and Exeter Ry. Co.* (1859) 6 C.B. (N.S.) 639). Common carriers of goods by land as opposed to common carriers of passengers or common carriers by sea or air are subject to the Carriers Act 1830. This Act, now of little practical importance, provides that where "valuables" worth in excess of £10 are delivered to a carrier by land their nature and value must be declared. If they are not the carrier is not liable for them (see *Casswell* v. *Cheshire Lines Committee* [1907] 2 K.B. 499).

Only the carrier and other parties to the contract can take advantage of any limitation or exemption clauses in the contract (*Scruttons Ltd.* v. *Midland Silicones Ltd.* [1962] A.C. 446, discussed on p. 46, *ante*.

The Carriers Act 1830 only applies to common carriers. The

liability of private carriers at common law is unlimited. If they want to limit or exempt their liability for valuables or for anything else they must do so by contract. It should be noted, however, that some private carriers obtain the protection of the Act as a matter of contract by stating that they will have the benefit of its provisions even though they are not common carriers.

Carrier's duties and liabilities

If dangerous goods are given to a carrier for carriage the consignor is deemed to warrant to the carrier and also to the carrier's servants and other consignors that the goods are fit to be carried. For a breach of this warranty (which is apparently a form of tortious liability rather than contractual) the consignor will be liable in damages even if he were ignorant of the dangerous character of his goods (*Bamfield* v. *Goole and Sheffield Transport Co. Ltd.* [1910] 2 K.B. 94).

The T Co. sent by railway some carboys of corrosive fluid and also some felt hats. During the transit, the fluid escaped from the carboys and damaged the hats. Being common carriers, the railway company were liable for the damage to the hats, and consequently they paid £437, the value of the hats, to their owner. In an action by the railway company to recover this amount from the T Co., *held*, they were entitled to do so, upon an implied warranty that the carboys were fit to be carried: *Great Northern Ry.* v. *L. E. P. Transport Co.* [1922] 2 K.B. 742.

In addition to any contractual or statutory rights a carrier of goods may have the right to sell goods without consulting the owner. This arises where the carrier is an agent of necessity. For this agency to arise it must be commercially impossible to contact the owner and there must be a real emergency, *e.g.* the goods are perishable.

S consigned butter to the railway company. The railway workers went on strike and the butter rapidly started to deteriorate in hot weather. The railway company sold the butter. *Held*, they were not liable because they were agents of necessity: *Sims & Co.* v. *Midland Ry.* [1913] 1 K.B. 103.

A carrier must obey the orders of an unpaid seller of goods who exercises a right of stoppage in transit under sections 44–46 of the Sale of Goods Act 1893 (see p. 257 *ante*).

A carrier is liable during the period of "transit." Transit is defined in relation to carriage by air by the Warsaw Convention 1929.

In relation to carriage by land and sea transit at common law begins at the moment the goods are delivered to the carrier or his agent and the carrier accepts them. Transit does not mean movement and goods can be in transit while being stored in a warehouse (*William Soanes Ltd.* v. *F. E. Walker Ltd.* (1946) 79 Lloyd's Rep. 646). Transit ceases when the goods are delivered to the consignee or when the goods are tendered to the consignee. Where goods are "to be collected" transit ceases a reasonable time after the arrival of the goods at the destination. After transit ceases a carrier is only liable for negligent loss or damage if he charges for warehousing. If he does not then he is an "involuntary bailee" and is only liable for loss or damage caused by an act of deliberate wrongdoing or gross recklessness.

It is the duty of a carrier to deliver the goods to the consignee at the place to which they are directed. If he delivers them at that place in the normal and reasonable course of business the mere fact that the person who receives them is not the consignee is no proof of a breach of duty on his part. The carrier, in the absence of notice to the contrary is entitled to treat the consignee as the owner of the goods and the consignor as his agent to contract with the carrier.

Measure of damages

The measure of damages is often controlled by Act of Parliament (see below). Alternatively many contracts limit the amount of damages payable usually by reference to the weight of the goods. It is also common to exclude liability for "consequential loss." The position in the absence of such provisions is however as follows—

Where goods are lost the measure of damages is the value of the goods. If the value has been declared no higher value can be recovered. In other cases the value is the market value at the place to which they were consigned at the time when they ought to have been delivered. (*C. Czarnikow Ltd.* v. *Koufos* [1969] 1 A.C. 350). *See* p. 140, *ante*.

When there is delay in delivery, the measure of damages is the loss reasonably arising from the breach (see p. 139, *ante*). If the delay has caused the goods to fall in value, for example, because they are perishable or seasonable, the damages will be the difference between the value when actually delivered and the value when they ought to have been delivered. If the article carried is a profit-earning machine, damages may be recovered for loss of use. Loss of profit on resale can only be recovered when the circumstances are brought to the carrier's notice.

Carriage of passengers

As stated above, common carriers of passengers can exist and they can be sued for refusal to carry. All carriers of passengers, whether common or private, are at common law liable only for injury to passengers caused by the carrier's negligence. The liability of carriers of passengers by air is controlled by statute (see Chap. 28) and restrictions on the power to exclude liability are placed by statute on carriers of passengers by land (see Chap. 26). Carriers of passengers by sea are not so controlled by legislation.

The burden of proving negligence falls on the injured passenger but sometimes the circumstances so strongly suggest negligence that it will be presumed in the absence of convincing evidence to the contrary by the carrier. This is known as the doctrine of **res ipsa loquitur** (the thing speaks for itself).

G, a passenger on a railway train, put his hand on a bar across the window. The door immediately flew open and G fell out of the train and was injured. *Held*, negligence on the part of the railway company could be assumed: *Gee* v. *Metropolitan Ry.* (1873) L.R. 8 Q.B. 161.

SELECT BIBLIOGRAPHY

Books

O. Kahn-Freund, *The Law of Carriage by Inland Transport* (4th ed., 1965).

J. Ridley, *The law of Carriage of Goods by Land, Sea and Air* (4th ed., 1976).

CHAPTER 26

CARRIAGE BY LAND

GENERAL

A CARRIER of goods by land does not warrant that his vehicle is road-worthy although the standard of care required is high. Breach of statutory provisions such as the Road Safety Act 1967 is strong evidence of negligence. This is an important difference from the law of carriage of goods by sea where at common law—but not under the Hague Rules relating to Bills of Lading, see p. 456, *post*—there is an absolute warranty of seaworthiness. (See *John Carter Ltd.* v. *Hanson Haulage (Leeds) Ltd.* [1965] 2 Q.B. 495.)

A carrier by land who unjustifiably deviates from the agreed route commits a fundamental breach of contract and is strictly liable for any loss or damage and cannot rely on any contractual term to exclude or limit liability (see p. 34, *ante*.)

The defendant carriers put the plaintiff's cameras on the same lorry as the goods of another customer and delivered the goods of the other customer first, thus deviating from the direct route. *Held*, this deviation was normal commercial practice and was not unjustifiable. The defendants were not therefore strictly liable for a theft that occurred without their negligence (*Mayfair Photographic Ltd.* v. *Baxter Hoare Ltd.* [1972] 1 Lloyd's Rep. 410).

Other unjustifiable acts of a carrier can amount to a fundamental breach and thus lose him the protection of his conditions, *e.g.* giving the goods to a person he ought to know has no right to them; subcontracting without the owner's permission and leaving the goods in an unlocked vehicle in a side street, etc.

Carriage by Rail

As the British Railways Board is no longer a common carrier, the Carriers Act 1830 which is unaffected by the Transport Acts no longer applies to carriage by rail. Similarly there is now no legislation controlling the terms under which the Board may carry goods, *e.g.* there is no limit upon their power to restrict or exclude liability for negligence in the carriage or delivery of goods. The **Railway**

0

440 *Carriage by Land*

Board's Conditions of Carriage therefore operate purely as contractual terms. Four sets have been issued—

    General Conditions for the Carriage of Goods (other than Goods for which Conditions are specially provided);

    Conditions for the Carriage of Live Stock (other than Wild Animals);

    Conditions for the Carriage of Coal, Coke and Patent Fuel; and

    Conditions of Carriage by Water.

These Conditions cover virtually all traffic, the principal exceptions being (a) certain international traffic and (b) special contracts with individual traders.

International Traffic

    Certain international traffic is carried under the International Convention concerning the Carriage of Goods by Rail 1961, known as CIM.[1] This Convention is, in effect, given statutory force by the Carriage by Railway Act 1972. The Convention covers contracts for the carriage of goods by rail under a through consignment note over the territory of at least two contracting states. A similar convention (CIV)[2] covers contracts for the international carriage of passengers by Rail. It also is given statutory effect by the Carriage by Railway Act 1972.

Other Special Contracts

    Special Contracts are made with traders from time to time which generally incorporate the appropriate Standard Conditions with or without amendment.

Board's risk conditions

    The Board is liable for any loss, or misdelivery of, or damage to merchandise during transit, unless the Board can prove that it has arisen from—

    (a) Act of God;

    (b) any consequence of war, invasion, act of foreign enemy, hostilities (whether war be declared or not), civil war,

---

[1] *Convention internationale concernant le transport des marchandises par chemin de fer (CIM)*, see Cmnd. 2187.

[2] *Convention relative à la responsibilité du chemin de fer pour la mort et les blessures de voyageurs (CIV)*.

rebellion, insurrection, military or usurped power or con-
fiscation, requisition, destruction of or damage to property by
or under the order of any government or public or local
authority;
(c) seizure under legal process;
(d) act or omission of the Trader;
(e) inherent liability to wastage in bulk or weight, latent defect
or inherent defect, vice or natural deterioration of the goods;
(f) insufficient or improper packing;
(g) insufficient or improper labelling or addressing;
(h) riot, civil commotion, strikes, lockouts, stoppage or restraint
of labour from whatever cause;
(j) consignee not taking or accepting delivery within a reasonable
time.

When the trader has suffered loss arising from delay or detention
of the goods or unreasonable deviation the Board is liable, unless it
can prove that the loss was not caused by any negligence on the
part of the Board.

The liability of the Board is now limited—
1. where the loss is of the whole of a consignment, to a sum
at the rate of £800 per ton on the gross weight of the consignment;
2. where the loss is of part of a consignment, to the proportion
of the sum calculated under 1 which the actual value of that
part of the consignment bears to the actual value of the whole
of the consignment.

The Board is not liable where the consignor or consignee has been
fraudulent.

It should thus be noted that the Board undertake a liability for
loss, damage or delay somewhere between that of the common and
private carriers at common law. As private carriers they would not,
but at common law they would be liable for the malicious acts of
strangers occurring without their negligence. Under these conditions
it appears that they would.

Owner's risk conditions

In an owner's risk contract the charges are lower than in a
Board's risk contract, and consequently the liability of the Board
is more restricted. Paragraph 5 of the General Conditions (October
1969) provides that the Board shall not be liable for loss, damage,

misdelivery, delay or detention "except upon proof . . . that the same was caused by the wilful misconduct of the Board." But the Board is not exempt from any liability which it would have had under Board's risk conditions for non-delivery of the whole of a consignment or of any separate package forming part of it.

Wilful misconduct means "misconduct to which the will is a party," *i.e.* deliberate or reckless wrongdoing and is something much more than negligence. The person concerned must realise the wrongful nature of the act.

B consigned a large switchback plant to the railway company "at owners risk." The servant responsible made no effort to gauge the goods although it was obvious that they were dangerously large. The goods were damaged when they hit a bridge. *Held*, the railway company were guilty of wilful misconduct and were therefore liable: *Bastable* v. *North British Ry.* [1912] S.C. 555. It should be emphasised that wilful misconduct is not a doctrine of the common law and only arises under these or similar conditions of carriage.

Damageable goods improperly packed

If these are carried, the special conditions provide that in the case of loss or damage the Board is liable only on proof—

(a) of wilful misconduct on the part of the Board or its servants; or

(b) that the damage would still have occurred had the goods been properly packed.

Dangerous goods

The conditions under which the Board now accepts dangerous goods are contained in paragraph 19 of the General Conditions of Carriage of Goods (October 1969). The list of dangerous goods is constantly revised by the Railways Board. The conditions, for example, require prior notice to the Board of the intention to consign dangerous goods.

Liability to pay carriage

The conditions provide that the sender is to be liable to pay carriage but that, if the consignment note states that carriage is payable by the consignee, the sender is not to be required to pay unless the consignee fails to pay after reasonable demands have been made.

Termination of transit

The transit is at an end when the goods are delivered or if the transit is determined by the sender exercising his right of stoppage *in transitu* or otherwise prematurely determining it. If the goods are detained to await order or carried to a private siding, the transit ends one clear day after notice in writing is given to the consignee. After the termination of the transit, the Board holds the goods as a warehouseman, subject to its usual charges.

On the termination of the transit, the Board is given by the conditions a lien on the goods for carriages and other proper charges, and also a power of sale. A power of sale is also given in certain cases of emergency, chiefly in connection with perishable goods.

Time for claims

The general conditions provide that notice of a claim must be made within three days of the termination of the transit, and the claim itself within seven days, both to be in writing. If the claim is for non-delivery of the whole consignment or of a separate package forming part of the consignment, the times are 28 days and 42 days from the commencement of the transit.

Carriage of passengers

The Board is not—because it is no longer regarded as a common carrier—legally obliged to carry any passenger. It is not, however, permitted to impose a term on the carrying of passengers which—

1. excludes or limits its liability in respect of the death of or bodily injury to any passenger; or
2. prescribes the time within which or the manner in which any such liability may be enforced.

(Transport Act 1962, s. 43 (7)).

Apart from these restrictions the Railways Board can impose whatever contractual conditions it likes. The Standard Conditions of Carriage of Passengers and their Luggage are available for inspection at booking offices.

CARRIAGE BY ROAD

As stated above most carriers of goods by road are private carriers and as bailees are only liable for negligence at common law.

There are no statutory restrictions affecting contracts made by road carriers for the carriage of goods within the United Kingdom. Thus carriers by road can, *e.g.* exclude liability for negligence if they see fit. Many carriers use the standard **Conditions of Carriage of the Road Haulage Association,** the latest version of which (1967) is somewhat similar to the Railway Board's Conditions for the carriage of goods. Some companies still use the 1961 conditions which are more in their favour, *e.g.* they are only liable for "wilful negligence."

There is, however, the **Carriage of Goods by Road Act 1965** which incorporates the Convention on the Contract for the International Carriage of Goods by Road (CMR)[1] into British law. It lays down standard conditions for the carriage of goods by road between the territories of its signatories; CMR has thus been given statutory force in this country and carriers cannot contract out of its provisions.

Basically under this Convention and CIM the carrier is liable for loss or damage unless he can bring himself within the scope of listed defences. It should be noted that in the event of ambiguity the judges go to the the French text of the convention and interpret the Acts in accordance with it to give effect to the Convention. Thus in *James Buchanan & Co. Ltd.* v. *Babco Forwarding & Shipping* (*U.K.*) [1977] 2 W.L.R. 107 the carriers were held liable to pay £30,000 to the plaintiffs who had been forced to pay this sum in excise duty for whisky originally destined for export but negligently lost by the carriers in England. This was despite the wording of the English translation which referred to losses "incurred in respect of the carriage of the goods" (art. 23 (4)) which this sum literally was not.

When a passenger is carried by road in a public service vehicle the contract of carriage cannot contain any provision negativing or restricting the liability of the carrier in respect of claims arising out of the death of or bodily injury to any passenger in the vehicle. Any such provision is void (Road Traffic Act 1960, s. 151).

The Carriage of Passengers by Road Act 1974 should also be noted. It gave effect to an international convention concerning the

---

[1] *Convention relative au contrat de transport international de marchandises par route.*

international carriage of passengers by road. It has no application to purely domestic transport.

A free pass issued, for example to an old-age pensioner, by a bus company may, depending on its exact terms, be a contract and not a mere licence; in which case a condition in the pass which purported to absolve the company from liability to the holder for injury would be void by virtue of section 151 (*Gore* v. *Van Der Lann* [1967] 2 Q.B. 31).

PIPE-LINES

The Pipe-Lines Act 1962 relates to—
1. the control of the construction of pipe-lines;
2. the granting of compulsory powers to a person wishing to construct a pipe-line without having to promote a private bill;
3. the regulation of the construction, operation and maintenance of pipe-lines; and
4. the rating of pipe-lines.

The most noteworthy provisions of the Act, from the point of view of commercial law, are those which bestow upon a person the right, subject to certain conditions, to have things conveyed in a pipe-line of which he is not the owner.

A distinction is made in the Act between a "cross-country pipe-line," which is a pipe-line more than 10 miles in length, and a "local pipe-line," which is any other pipe-line.

The construction of a cross-country pipe-line is lawful only if authorised by a "pipe-line construction authorisation" granted by the Secretary of State for Energy. In the case of a local pipe-line, the requirement is merely to notify the Secretary of the intention to construct. The Secretary has, however, power, with the approval of both Houses of Parliament, to direct that local pipe-lines of a certain class or within a certain area shall be subject to the provisions applicable to cross-country pipe-lines.

The Act enables a person to apply to the Secretary of State to be given the right to have things conveyed in a pipe-line already constructed under a pipe-line construction authorisation by some other person (s. 10). If the Secretary of State is satisfied that this can be done without prejudice to the proper and efficient operation of the pipe-line on behalf of the owner he may impose upon the owner certain requirements.

Similarly, from the point of view of commercial law, the note-worthy provisions of the Petroleum and Submarine Pipe-lines Act 1975 are those relating to the use of a pipe-line by a person other than the owner. No person may construct a pipeline in what are termed "controlled waters," which comprise territorial waters and any area designated under the Continental Shelf Act 1964, without the authorisation of the Secretary of State.

The Secretary of State has power, *inter alia*,

—when granting authorisation, to require the owner to increase the capacity of the proposed pipe-line to accommodate use by a third party;

—when granting authorisation or at any time thereafter, to require the owner—to allow connections to be made to his pipe-line;

—to increase the capacity of his pipe-line;

—to allow his pipe-line to be used by a third party.

When thus imposing obligations upon an owner for the benefit of a third party the Secretary of State—

(a) must be satisfied that the efficient operation of the pipe-line on behalf of the owner will not be prejudiced; and

(b) may specify the sums or the method of determining the sums which should be paid to the owner by the third party.

SELECT BIBLIOGRAPHY

Books

G. A. Bonner, *British Transport Law by Road and Rail* (1974).

O. Kahn-Freund, *The Law of Carriage by Inland Transport* (4th ed., 1965).

CHAPTER 27

CARRIAGE BY SEA

A CARRIER by sea may be a common carrier but that would be very unusual; he usually makes a special contract in respect of the goods he carries. Such a contract is called the contract of affreightment and the price of the carriage is called the freight. The contract of affreightment may take the form of—

1. a charterparty; or
2. a bill of lading.

In all contracts of carriage by sea there are implied three undertakings by the shipowner or carrier—

1. That the ship is seaworthy. This undertaking is absolute in common law, *i.e.* the shipowner not only warrants that he has done his best to make the ship fit for the voyage, but that it actually is fit for the voyage. Seaworthiness is a relative term and means that the ship is fit to undertake the particular voyage and to carry the particular cargo.

Lemons were loaded at Naples for London. At Marseilles the ship was required by the French authorities to be fumigated, because she had come from Mombasa, a plague infected port. The fumigation damaged the lemons. *Held*, as the ship was bound to be fumigated at Marseilles, she was not reasonably fit at Naples for the carriage of the lemons and was, therefore, unseaworthy: *Ciampa* v. *British India Steam Navigation Co.* [1915] 2 K.B. 774.

Bad stowage will amount to unseaworthiness if it endangers the safety of the ship, but not if it merely affects the cargo.

A ship was loaded with casks of palm oil, on top of which were placed bags of palm kernels. On arrival, it was found that the palm kernels had crushed the casks and much of the palm oil was lost. *Held*, the ship was seaworthy and the damage was due to bad stowage: *Elder Dempster & Co.* v. *Zochonis & Co.* [1924] A.C. 522.

A ship is unseaworthy if it is not fitted with the required loading and unloading gear (*Hang Fung Shipping & Trading Co. Ltd.* v. *Mullion & Co. Ltd.; The Ardgroom* [1966] 1 Lloyd's Rep. 511) or if its crew is incompetent and inexperienced (*Hongkong Fir Shipping Co. Ltd.* v. *Kawasaki Kisen Kaisha* [1962] 2 Q.B. 26).

If the charterer or shipper discovers the unseaworthiness before the commencement of the voyage, he can repudiate the contract unless the ship can be made seaworthy within a reasonable time. In all other cases, or if he does not repudiate, he can recover such damages as he has suffered by reason of the unseaworthiness.

This implied warranty of seaworthiness may be modified by contract. In bills of lading governed by the Carriage of Goods by Sea Act 1924[1] the warranty of seaworthiness is not absolute, but is only that the shipowner shall use due diligence to make the ship seaworthy.

2. That the ship shall be ready to commence the voyage agreed on and to load the cargo to be carried and shall proceed upon and complete the voyage agreed upon with all reasonable dispatch. A breach of this implied undertaking gives the charterer the right to repudiate the contract if the delay is so serious as to go to the root of the contract, otherwise the remedy is in damages.

3. That the ship shall proceed on the voyage without unnecessary deviation in the usual and customary manner. Deviation to save life is allowed, but not deviation to save property.

A ship was sailing from Kronstadt to the Mediterranean. On the voyage she sighted a vessel in distress and agreed to tow her into Texel, which was out of the direct course. While going there she was stranded. The jury found that the tow was not reasonably necessary to save life, but was reasonably necessary to save the vessel and cargo. *Held*, the deviation was unnecessary, and the shipowners were liable for the cargo: *Scaramanga* v. *Stamp* (1880) 5 C.P.D. 295.

In bills of lading governed by the Carriage of Goods by Sea Act 1924[1] deviation to save property is allowed. Deviation is allowable in case of necessity, *e.g.* to avoid hostile capture, pirates, icebergs, or other dangers of navigation. The effect of deviation is to displace the special contract of carriage, whether charterparty or bill of lading, and to reduce the carrier to the position of common carrier, so that he can no longer rely on the exceptions contained in the contract of carriage.

Goods were shipped under a bill of lading exempting the shipowners from loss through negligence of stevedores. The ship deviated from the

[1] This provision remains unaltered by the Carriage of Goods by Sea Act 1971 which will supersede the 1924 Act as from June 23, 1977 (Position: May 1, 1977; see p. 456, *post*).

voyage. In discharging the ship, the stevedores employed by the ship-owners damaged the goods. *Held,* the ship having deviated, the contract evidenced by the bill of lading was broken, and the shipowners were not entitled to rely on the exception: *Joseph Thorley Ltd.* v. *Orchis SS. Co. Ltd.* [1907] 1 K.B. 660.

Charterparties and bills of lading usually contain a deviation clause giving, *e.g.* liberty to call at any ports in any order. Such a clause is construed in relation to the commercial object of the voyage, and does not sanction deviating from the ordinary route (*Glynn* v. *Margetson* [1893] A.C. 351). Its effect is to give the ship liberty to call at intermediate ports, which might otherwise have amounted to a deviation.

LIABILITY OF SHIPOWNERS

The Merchant Shipping Acts 1894 to 1974 provide that an owner of a British ship, a charterer, any person interested in or in possession of such a ship, and in particular any manager or operator of such a ship, shall not be liable for damage happening without his actual fault or privity in the following cases—

1. Where goods are lost or damaged by fire on board the ship. Unseaworthiness of the ship causing fire does not destroy the protection given by this section (*Louis Dreyfus & Co.* v. *Tempus Shipping Co.* [1931] A.C. 726).

2. Where gold, silver, diamonds, watches, jewels or precious stones are lost by robbery, unless their true nature and value has been declared to the owner or master of the ship at the time of shipment, either in the bill of lading or otherwise in writing.

Also, where, without his actual fault or privity, there occurs—

1. loss of life or personal injury to any person carried in the ship;
2. damage or loss to goods on board the ship;
3. loss of life or personal injury to any person not carried in the ship through the act or omission of any person in the navigation or management of the ship, or any other act or omission of any person on board the ship;
4. loss or damage to any property not on board the ship, through the act or omission of any person in the navigation or management of the ship; or any other act or omission of any person on board the ship;

the shipowner is not liable in damages beyond—
1. in the case of loss of life or personal injury, an amount equivalent to 3,100 gold francs per ton of the ship's tonnage;
2. in the case of damage or loss to goods, an amount equivalent to 1,000 gold francs per ton of the ship's tonnage (s. 503).

A ship of less than 300 tons is treated as though it were of a tonnage of 300 tons.

DANGEROUS GOODS

Dangerous goods must not be sent for carriage or carried unless their nature is distinctly marked on the outside of the package and written notice of their nature is given to the master or owner of the vessel. Penalties are imposed for the breach of this provision (Merchant Shipping Act 1894, s. 446).

The master or owner of a vessel may refuse to take on board any parcel which he suspects contains dangerous goods, and may require it to be opened to ascertain the fact. If dangerous goods are shipped without being marked, or without notice of their dangerous nature having been given, the master may throw them overboard without incurring any liability (s. 448).

CHARTERPARTY

A charterparty is a document by which the owner of a ship either—
1. lets his ship to a person called the charterer for the purpose of carrying a cargo; or
2. undertakes that his ship shall carry a cargo for the charterer.

If the charterparty operates as a lease or demise of the ship (bareboat charter), the charterer becomes for the time being the owner of the vessel and the master and crew become his servants. If, on the other hand, the charterparty only gives the charterer a right to have his cargo carried by a particular ship, the master and crew, although placed at the charterer's service, do not become the servants of the charterer.

In both cases the charterparty deals with the whole ship and not merely a portion of it. It must be in writing either with or without a seal.

The form of a charterparty usually starts as follows—

"It is this day mutually agreed between A B, agents for the owners of the good ship *Rosa* of 500 tons net register or thereabouts now at the port of Liverpool, and C D merchant."

The statement of the ship's tonnage is not a condition of the contract and, therefore, if the actual tonnage differs from that named in the charterparty the charterer cannot rescind the contract, unless the difference is unreasonably great or such as to be of material importance to the contract. A statement of the position of the ship at the time of making the charterparty or that she will be ready to load at a certain day is usually a condition of the contract, and consequently, if it is untrue it entitles the charterer to rescind (see *Behn* v *Burness* (1863) 3 B. & S. 751).

A charterparty, dated March 29, described the ship as "now sailed or about to sail to the United Kingdom." It provided that the ship should, after discharging, proceed to Quebec and load a cargo. The ship did not sail until April 23, and on learning of this the charterers wrote to the owners saying that they protested against loading, and claimed the extra expense. They ultimately refused to load. *Held*, (1) as the ship did not sail until April 23, the charterers could have repudiated the charterparty, but (2) the letter amounted to a waiver of their right to repudiate, so that they were liable for freight under the charterparty, subject to such damages as they had suffered from the delay: *Bentsen* v. *Taylor, Sons & Co.* [1893] 2 Q.B. 274.

The charterparty then proceeds—

"that the said ship being tight, staunch and strong, and in every way fitted for the voyage, shall with all convenient speed sail and proceed to Sunderland or as near thereto as she may safely get and there load a full and complete cargo of —— which is to be brought to and taken from alongside at merchant's risk and expense, and not exceeding what she can reasonably stow and carry over and above her tackle, apparel, provisions and furniture, and being so loaded shall therewith proceed to Rotterdam or so near thereto as she may safely get and deliver the same on being paid freight."

The form just set out is that of a **voyage charter,** in which the charterer charters the ship for a specified voyage or voyages. Both the port of loading and the port of discharge must be mentioned, although the charterer may be given power to order the ship to proceed to any port within the limits named in the charterparty.

When the ship is chartered for a specified time instead of for a particular voyage or voyages, the charterparty is called a **time charter.** In a time charter the ship may be placed at the charterer's disposal—

1. from a particular date;
2. from the day on which the ship arrives at a named port; or
3. alternatively, from a particular date or from the day on which the ship arrives at a named port.

In case 1 the contract can be repudiated if the ship is not ready by the date in question; in case 2 the ship must arrive at the port within a reasonable time from the date of the charterparty; in case 3 the charterer cannot be compelled to accept the ship before the named date, but the owner is allowed a reasonable time from the date in which to place the ship at his disposal.

The stipulation that the ship shall be fit for the voyage relates to fitness at the date of the charterparty, and not to fitness at the date of loading, which is subject to other considerations. The obligation to provide a seaworthy vessel is not a condition precedent to a shipowner's rights under a charterparty. Breach of that obligation does not, by itself, allow a charterer to escape liability under the charter unless the delays involved in making the vessel seaworthy are so great as to frustrate the commercial purpose of the charter (*Hongkong Fir Shipping Co. Ltd.* v. *Kawasaki Kisen Kaisha Ltd.* [1962] 2 Q.B. 26).

A "full and complete cargo" means as much cargo as the ship can carry with safety, but it does not bind or authorise the charterer to load deck cargo unless—

1. there is a custom binding in the trade or port of loading to stow on deck goods of that class on such a voyage; or
2. there is an express agreement for deck stowage.

Sometimes the charterparty specifies the amount of cargo to be loaded, and in such a case cargo to that approximate amount must be loaded, but the whole ship need not be filled.

A charterparty provided that the ship should load "a full and complete cargo of iron ore, say about 1,100 tons." The charterer provided a cargo of 1,080 tons, the capacity of the ship being 1,210 tons. *Held,* the charterer's contract was not to load the ship to her actual capacity, but that three per cent. was a fair amount of excess over 1,100 tons to allow in estimating what was a full and complete cargo of about 1,100 tons, hence the charterer should have loaded a cargo of 1,133 tons: *Morris* v. *Levison* (1876) 1 C.P.D. 155.

An undertaking to load a full and complete cargo within specified limits binds the charterer to fill the ship within the limits specified.

A charterparty provided that the charterers should load "a cargo of beans not less than 6,500 tons, but not exceeding 7,000 tons." The charterers loaded 6,590 tons. *Held*, that the words "not less than 6,500 tons" were a warranty to the charterers that the ship could take so much cargo, and that the words "but not exceeding 7,000 tons" were a term binding the shipowner not to ask for more than 7,000 tons, but entitling him to receive that amount if the ship could take it: *Jardine, Matheson & Co.* v. *Clyde Shipping Co.* [1910] 1 K.B. 627.

The charterer is entitled to the full benefit of the use of the ship, and the shipowner cannot impair this benefit by loading more bunker coals than are needed for the voyage (*Darling* v. *Raeburn* [1907] 1 K.B. 846).

If the charterer is obliged by the charterparty to load a complete cargo and does not fulfil his obligation, he is liable for **dead freight,** *i.e.* damages for the unoccupied space payable at the same rate as if the space had been occupied by cargo.

The charterparty then continues—

"Restraints of princes and rulers, the act of God, the King's enemies, fire and all and every other dangers and accidents of the sea, rivers and navigation of whatever nature and kind soever, during the said voyage always excepted."

These are known as the excepted perils, and in addition to those set out above there are often excepted negligence of the master and crew, barratry, pirates and breakages. If a loss occurs owing to one of the excepted perils, the shipowner is relieved from liability provided that the charterparty still remains in force. Of the excepted perils, the act of God and the Queen's enemies are excepted by the common law; their meaning is discussed on p. 433, *ante*. "Restraints of princes" means a forcible interruption of the voyage by the action of any state or government.

Cattle sent from London to Buenos Aires became infected with disease during the voyage, and the Argentine Government prohibited their landing. *Held*, a restraint of princes: *Miller* v. *The Law Accident Insurance Co.* [1903] 1 K.B. 712.

The term includes the outbreak of war, which makes commercial relations with alien enemies illegal.

A British ship was proceeding to Hamburg when war broke out. The owners, at the suggestion of the Admiralty, directed the ship to

proceed to a British port. *Held*, the outbreak of war making trading
with Germany illegal was a restraint of princes: *British and Foreign
Marine Insurance Co.* v. *Sanday & Co.* [1916] 1 A.C. 650.

It does not, however, include action taken to avoid loss by a
possible capture.

A German ship, proceeding to Hamburg, learnt of the outbreak of
war during the voyage, put into a neutral port and abandoned the voyage.
If the voyage had been continued, the ship would probably have been
captured. *Held*, the loss of the voyage was caused by the voluntary act of
the captain in putting into a port to avoid risk of capture and not to a
restraint of princes: *Becker, Gray & Co.* v. *London Assurance Corporation*
[1918] A.C. 101.

Perils of the sea means some accident of the seas beyond the
ordinary action of wind and waves. It includes damage caused by
violence of the winds or waves, and also damage caused in calm
weather by striking a sunken rock or icebergs, collision due to
negligence on the part of the other ship, the unexplained heeling of
the ship resulting in loss of cargo when loading, the entry of water
into the ship through a hole made by rats or swordfish, or through
the engineer opening the sea cock with the intention of filling the
ballast tank and accidentally opening the wrong valves. It does
not include sea water entering by reason of ordinary decay or wear
and tear of the ship, bad stowage, unseaworthiness of the vessel,
and damage to the cargo by rats or vermin. A storm, though not
of exceptional violence, is a peril of the seas.

Barratry means any wilful act of wrongdoing by the master or
mariners against the ship and goods. Examples are, boring holes
in the ship to scuttle it, smuggling and mutiny. Pirates include passengers who mutiny and rioters who attack the ship from the shore.

The charterparty usually contains terms as to payment of the
freight, and as to the time allowed for loading, with a provision for
payment of demurrage. A usual clause is—

"Charterer's liability to cease under this charterparty on
the cargo being loaded, the master and owners having a lien
on cargo for freight and demurrage."

The first part of this clause is known as a **cesser clause,** and the
second part as a **lien clause.** These two clauses proceed on the
assumption that the charterer has made available the chartered
ship as a general ship to a consignor, who is not identical with the

charterer, to have the consignor's goods carried in the ship. The two clauses have to be construed together; they mean that the charter shall be relieved from his obligation to pay demurrage if that obligation falls on the consignor but that in this case the shipowner shall have a lien on the consignor's goods (*Fidelitas Shipping Co. Ltd.* v. *V/O Exportchleb* [1963] 2 Lloyd's Rep. 113). Consequently, no liability imposed on the charterer will be destroyed by the cesser clause unless it is recreated in someone else by the lien clause having become effective. (*Overseas Transportation Co.* v. *Mineralimportexport; The Sinoe* [1972] 1 Lloyd's Rep. 201). The cesser clause relieves the charterer from liability as to the future, but whether it also relieves him from past liabilities depends on the construction of the clause in each particular case.

At the end of the charterparty is usually the clause—

> "Penalty for non-performance of this agreement estimated amount of freight."

This is entirely inoperative, and does not confer upon the parties any rights which they otherwise would not have. It is said in *Scrutton on Charterparties*, Art. 189: "It is a mystery why this clause survives, except upon the supposition that chartering brokers regard it as a piece of sacred ritual."

A charterparty may contain a clause paramount, embodying the provisions of the Hague Rules on Bills of Lading (see p. 456, *post*). Although these Rules are designed for bills of lading and not for charterparties, the effect of such incorporation is to limit the liability of the owner to the charterer in the manner stated in the Hague Rules (*Adamastos Shipping Co. Ltd.* v. *Anglo-Saxon Petroleum Co. Ltd.* [1959] A.C. 133; p. 23, *ante*).

BILL OF LADING

A bill of lading is a document signed by the shipowner, or by the master or other agent of the shipowner, which states that certain goods have been shipped on a particular ship, and sets out the terms on which those goods have been delivered to and received by the shipowner. It is used generally when the goods shipped form part only of the intended cargo of the ship, a charterparty being employed if the goods form the complete cargo. On being signed by or on behalf of the carrier, it is handed to the shipper and it answers three purposes—

1. It is a receipt for the goods shipped, containing the terms on which they have been received.

2. It is evidence of the contract for the carriage of the goods.

3. It is a document of title to the goods specified therein.

When goods are delivered to the ship, a receipt is usually given, called **the mate's receipt.** This may be qualified, if the goods are in a damaged condition, but otherwise it is a clean receipt. The mate's receipt is not normally a document of title. By local custom it may have that character, but not if it is marked "non-negotiable" (*Kum* v. *Wah Tat Bank Ltd.* [1971] 1 Lloyd's Rep. 439).

A document which is not signed by or on behalf of the carrier is not a bill of lading in the legal sense (*The Maurice Desgagnes* [1977] 1 Lloyd's Rep. 290; a Canadian case). Receipts issued by freight forwarders, although sometimes described as "bills of lading," do not have the legal character of a bill of lading and, in particular, are not documents of title.

Possession of the bill of lading entitles the holder to delivery of the goods, and the property in the goods passes to a transferee or an indorsee. It is not a negotiable instrument, and consequently a transferee will receive no title unless his transferor was competent to transfer it to him, but as the mechanism of negotiability—indorsement and delivery—is employed it has been described as quasi-negotiable. A transfer, however, to a bona fide purchaser of the goods for value without notice of the insolvency of the transferor defeats the original owner's right to stoppage in transitu (*Lickbarrow* v. *Mason* (1794) 5 Term Rep. 683).

Bills issued under the Carriage of Goods by Sea Act 1924[1]

Bills of lading issued in connection with the carriage of goods by sea in ships **from** any port in Great Britain or Northern Ireland must conform to the Carriage of Goods by Sea Act 1924 which, in its Schedule, adopts the **Hague Rules on Bills of Lading.**

Whenever a contract for the carriage of goods by sea is made to

This Act will be superseded by the Carriage of Goods by Sea Act 1971 which it is intended to bring into operation on June 23, 1977. The 1924 Act will continue to apply to bills of lading issued before June 23, 1977 and to bills of lading issued on or after that date but before December 23, 1977, pursuant to contracts entered into before June 23, 1977 (position: May 1, 1977). The salient points of the 1971 Act are summed up on p. 463, *post.*

which the Act applies, there is no absolute warranty of seaworthiness implied (s. 2).

Every bill of lading governed by the Act must contain an express statement that it is to have effect subject to the rules in the Schedule to the Act (s. 3); this statement is known as "the clause paramount." By Article III (3) of the rules, the shipper, after delivering the goods into the charge of the owner, charterer, or the master of the ship or other agent, can demand a bill of lading giving the following particulars—

1. The leading marks necessary for identification of the goods, as the same are furnished in writing by the shipper before the loading of such goods starts, provided such marks are stamped or otherwise shown clearly upon the goods if uncovered, or on the cases or coverings in which such goods are contained, in such a manner as should ordinarily remain legible until the end of the voyage.

2. The number of packages or pieces, or the quality or weight, as the case may be, as furnished in writing by the shipper.

3. The apparent order and condition of the goods. Such a bill of lading is prima facie evidence of the receipt by the carrier of the goods therein described.

As regards the particulars which he has to furnish in writing, the shipper is deemed to have guaranteed their accuracy and to have undertaken to indemnify the carrier from any inaccuracy, but where carriers issued clean bills of lading, when both parties knew that the goods were not in good order and condition, and the shippers agreed to indemnify the carriers, it was held that the carriers had committed the tort of deceit and the indemnity was accordingly unenforceable (*Brown Jenkinson & Co. Ltd.* v. *Percy Dalton* (*London*) *Ltd.* [1957] 2 Q.B. 621). On the other hand, whilst a carrier who delivers without production of the bill of lading does so at his peril, an indemnity given to the carrier in order to induce him to deliver the goods to the consignee without production of the bill of lading is valid and enforceable by the carrier (*Sze Hai Tong Bank Ltd.* v. *Rambler Cycle Co. Ltd.* [1959] A.C. 576).

The bill of lading when signed is prima facie evidence of the facts stated therein, except that where under any trade custom the weight of any bulk cargo is a weight ascertained by some third party other than the shipper or the carrier, the accuracy of the weight is not guaranteed by the shipper (s. 5).

A statement in the bill of lading that the goods are in apparent

good order and condition refers only to their external appearance.
Thus, if they arrive damaged, the shipowner is liable on proof—
1. that the goods were shipped in good condition internally; or
2. that the damage resulted from some external cause within the
   control of the shipowner.

Such a statement estops the shipowner from denying to an
indorsee for value of the bill that the goods were in good order and
condition externally, if the indorsee acquired the bill in good faith.

Bags of zinc ashes were shipped at Buenos Aires for Liverpool. The
upper layers of the bags were wet externally, but the bill of lading stated
that the bags were shipped in good order and condition. Owing to the
wet the ashes became heated, and had to be discharged and dried. They
were then reshipped and arrived in Liverpool three months late. Meanwhile, the price of zinc ashes had fallen. An indorsee for value of the bill
of lading sued the shipowners for damages for delay. *Held*, he succeeded,
because the shipowners were estopped from denying that the goods were
shipped in good order and condition: *Brandt* v. *Liverpool etc., Navigation
Co.* [1924] 1 K.B. 575.

The bill of lading, however, must be construed as a whole and if
the statement is not sufficiently clear there will be no estoppel.

A bill of lading stated that a cargo of sugar was "received in apparent
good order and condition." It also had an indorsement "signed under
guarantee to produce ship's clean receipt." The sugar as delivered was
damaged. The ship's receipt stated "many bags stained, torn and resewn."
Held, estoppel: *Canadian Sugar* v. *Canadian Steamships* [1947] A.C. 46.

Although the bill of lading is only prima facie evidence of the
receipt by the carrier of the goods therein named, yet as against the
master or other person signing it, it is in the hands of a consignee or
indorsee for value conclusive evidence that the goods were shipped
notwithstanding that the goods were not shipped (Bills of Lading
Act 1855, s. 3). The only way in which the person signing the bill of
lading can escape liability is by showing either—
1. that the holder took the bill with actual notice that the goods
   were not on board; or
2. that the mistake was not due to his, the signer's fault, but
   was due to the fraud of the shipper, holder, or some person
   under whom the holder claims.

The shipowner is not estopped by the master's signature from
proving that the goods were not in fact shipped, or that the master
has signed for a greater quantity of goods than has actually been
put on board, or that he has delivered all the goods which were

put on board. The burden of proving that the bill of lading is false rests on the shipowner. Where the shipowner is not liable because he can prove that the agent signing the bill of lading acted without authority, *e.g.* because he signed for a greater quantity than was actually shipped, the agent himself might be liable for breach of an implied warranty of authority (*V/o Rasnoimport* v. *Guthrie and Co. Ltd.* [1966] 1 Lloyd's Rep. 1).

A shipper has the right, after the goods are loaded, to a "shipped" bill of lading, *i.e.* a bill which says that the goods have been shipped on board and not merely received for shipment by the shipowner, and if he has previously received another bill of lading he can exchange it for the "shipped" bill (Art. III (7)).

In all bills of lading to which the Carriage of Goods by Sea Act 1924 applies, the following provisons are implied—

1. An obligation on the carrier, before and at the beginning of the voyage, to exercise due diligence to—

    (a) make the ship seaworthy;

    (b) properly man, equip and supply the ship;

    (c) make the holds, refrigerating and cold chambers and all other parts of the ship in which goods are carried fit and safe for their reception, carriage and preservation.

The word "voyage" in this context means the contractual voyage from the port of loading to the port of discharge as declared in the bill of lading. There is therefore an obligation on the carrier to exercise due diligence before and at the beginning of sailing from the loading port to have the vessel adequately bunkered for the first stage of the voyage, and to arrange for adequate bunkers of a proper kind at the first and other intermediate ports on the voyage so that the contractual voyage might be performed (*The Makedonia* [1962] P. 190).

If loss or damage arises from unseaworthiness, the burden of proof is on the carrier to show that due diligence has been exercised. The carrier does not discharge this burden merely by showing that the negligence in repairing the ship was that of an independent contractor to whom he delegated the work because it called for technical or special knowledge or experience (*Riverstone Meat Co. Pty. Ltd.* v. *Lancashire Shipping Co. Ltd.* [1961] A.C. 807).

2. An obligation on the carrier properly and carefully to load, handle, stow, carry, keep, care for and discharge the goods carried.

3. Removal of the goods by the person entitled to delivery

is prima facie evidence of delivery by the carrier. In the event of loss or damage to the goods, **notice in writing** must be given to the carrier before or at the time of removal, unless at the time of their receipt the goods have been the subject of joint survey or inspection. If the loss or damage be not apparent, the notice must be given within three days. In any event, the carrier is discharged from all liability in respect of the goods unless action is brought within one year after delivery or the date when the goods should have been delivered.

4. The carrier is not responsible for loss or damage arising from the following excepted perils—

(a) Act, neglect or default of the master, mariner, pilot or the servants of the carrier in the navigation or in the management of the ship.

The effect of this exception is that the shipper has to bear risks incident to navigation and management of the ship, but the carrier bears risk incident to loading under 2, above. The operation of management is not restricted to the period during which the vessel is at sea; it extends to the period during which the cargo is being loaded or discharged (*The Glenochil* [1896] P. 10). The expression "management of the ship" means management of the entire ship, and a distinction has to be drawn between want of care of the cargo and want of care of the vessel indirectly affecting the cargo. "Some one or, perhaps, every subordinate part of the ship or its equipment may be the object which is immediately dealt with negligently, but neglect in regard to that object must still be neglect in the management of the ship, if it is to avail the shipowner as a defence" (*per* Lord Sumner).

A ship with a cargo of tinplates sustained damage during the voyage, and had to be kept in dock for repairs. During the execution of the repairs, workmen were frequently in and out of the hold, and the hatches were in consequence left open. Owing to the negligence of the shipowners' servants the hatches were not covered up, and rain fell into the hold and damaged the tinplates. *Held*, the shipowners were liable because (1) they had failed properly and carefully to "carry, keep and care for" the tinplates, and (2) the negligence in the management of the hatches was not negligence "in the management of the ship" so as to protect them from liability: *Gosse Millard Ltd.* v. *Canadian Government Merchant Marine* [1929] A.C. 223.

(b) Fire, unless caused by the actual fault or privity of the carrier.

(c) Perils, dangers and accidents of the sea or other navigable waters.

(d) Act of God.

(e) Acts of war or of public enemies. Arrest or restraint of princes, rulers, or people, or seizure under legal process. Quarantine restrictions.

(f) Act or omission of the shipper or owner of the goods or his agent.

(g) Strikes or lock-outs.

(h) Riot and civil commotions.

(i) Saving or attempting to safe life or property at sea.

(j) Wastage in bulk or weight or any other loss or damage arising from inherent defect, quality or vice of the goods.

(k) Insufficiency of packing or insufficiency or inadequacy of marks. Insufficiency of packing cannot be relied upon if a reasonable inspection would have disclosed it, and the bill of lading acknowledges the receipt of the goods in apparent good order and condition (*Silver* v. *Ocean Steamship Co.* [1930] 1 K.B. 416).

(l) Latent defects not discoverable by due diligence.

(m) Any other cause arising without the actual fault or privity of the carrier or his servants or agents. The burden of proof is on the carrier to show that neither he nor his servants or agents have contributed to the loss. Stevedores are the servants or agents of the shipowner for this purpose.

H shipped cloth from Liverpool to Shanghai under a bill of lading governed by the Carriage of Goods by Sea Act 1924. While the cargo was being unloaded at Shanghai, some of the cloth was stolen. *Held*, (1) the shipowner was liable unless he could show that the cloth was stolen by someone who was not his servant or agent; (2) on the probabilities, the stevedores' men had stolen the cloth, and as the shipowner's duty was to discharge the cargo, the stevedores he employed to fulfil that duty were his servants or agents: *Heyn* v. *Ocean SS. Co. Ltd.* (1927) 43 T.L.R. 358.

A consignment of tea was shipped in *The Chyebassa* from Calcutta to Rotterdam under bills of lading incorporating the Hague Rules. When other goods in the ship's hold in which the tea was stowed were unloaded at an intermediate port, the stevedores stole the cover plate of a storm valve and on the further voyage sea-water damaged the tea. The officers and the crew were not negligent in the supervision of the stevedores in the intermediate port. *Held*, the carriers were exempt from their liability because the damage was caused by "any other cause" without the actual fault of the carriers' servants: Art. IV, r. 2 (*q*). The stevedores who normally were the ship's agents had acted outside their authority when stealing the storm valve cover plate: *Leesh River Tea Co. Ltd.* v. *British India S.N. Co. Ltd.* [1967] 2 Q.B. 250.

5. The carrier is not liable for any loss or damage resulting from any deviation in saving or attempting to save life or property at sea or any reasonable deviation. Reasonable deviation is one which is reasonable having regard to the terms of the contract and the interest of all persons concerned in the voyage (*Stag Line* v. *Foscolo Mango & Co.* [1932] A.C. 328, 343).

6. The carrier is not liable for loss or damage to goods exceeding £100 per package or unit, unless the nature and value of the goods is declared before shipment and inserted in the bill of lading, but under the *British Maritime Law Association Agreement* 1950 British ship-owners and British insurers accept liability to the amount of £200 instead of £100; this agreement is sometimes referred to as the Gold Clause Agreement. If the nature or value of the goods has been knowingly misstated, the carrier is not liable for their loss or damage in any event.

A stevedore engaged as independent contractor by a carrier in the discharge of goods cannot rely on these limitations of liability as he is not a party to the contract of carriage (*Scruttons Ltd.* v. *Midland Silicones Ltd.* [1962] A.C. 446, see p. 46, *ante*).

7. If goods of an inflammable, explosive or dangerous character have been shipped without disclosure of their nature to the carrier, the carrier may discharge or destroy them without paying compensation. Even if the carrier was told of the nature of the goods, they may be discharged or destroyed if they become a danger to the ship or cargo. In such a case the shipper may have a claim to general average.

The carrier cannot contract out of the liability imposed upon him under heads 1 and 2 above. He may, however, increase his liability or contract out of any immunities given to him, provided the terms of the contract are set out in the bill of lading.

The provisions set out above do not apply to—
1. contracts of carriage between one port in Great Britain or Northern Ireland and another port in Great Britain or Northern Ireland or the Irish Republic (s. 4). This excepts persons engaged in the coasting trade;
2. contracts of carriage of "particular goods," *i.e.* not ordinary commercial shipments made in the ordinary course of trade;
In both these cases no bill of lading must be issued, but the

terms agreed must be embodied in a receipt, which is a non-negotiable document and should be marked as such.

    3. charterparties, but if a bill of lading is issued in the case of a ship under charterparty it must conform to the provisions of the Act.

    4. The Hague Rules do not apply to the carriage of live animals and deck cargo which is carried as such by virtue of the contract of carriage (Art. I (*c*)).

When the Carriage of Goods by Sea Act 1924 does not apply to a bill of lading the parties may insert any terms agreed upon.

    5. The carrier and the ship are discharged from all liability in respect of loss of or damage to the goods unless suit is brought within one year after delivery of the goods or the date when they should have been delivered (Art. III, r. 6). By the *British Maritime Law Association Agreement 1950* the period of one year is extended to two years, provided that the cargo-owner has given the carrier notice of his claim within the first year and has acted without delay.

The Carriage of Goods by Sea Act 1971

This Act is intended to give effect to the Hague Rules as amended by the Brussels Protocol 1968. The Act is intended to be brought into operation by an Order in Council as from June 23, 1977 (position: May 1, 1977). When the Act comes into operation, it will supersede the Carriage of Goods by Sea Act 1924 (see p. 456, *post*).

The following is a brief summary of the main changes which will be introduced by the 1971 Act:

1. The scope of the Rules is extended. As before, they apply only to outward bills of lading, but not only if the shipment is from a British port, but also if the bill of lading is issued in a contracting state or shipment is made from the port of a contracting state (art. X).

2. The Act applies to coasting trade, if carried out under bills of lading.

3. The Act applies not only to shipments under bills of lading but also to shipments under "any similar document of title" (s. 1(4)), and even to non-negotiable receipts if the Rules are expressly stated therein to apply, as if such receipts were bills of lading (s. 1(6)).

4. The bill of lading shall be conclusive evidence when transferred to a third party acting in good faith (art. III (4)).
5. The maximum limits of liability of the carrier are raised to 10,000 gold francs (at present equal to £238) per package or unit or 30 gold francs per kilo of gross weight, whichever is higher (art. IV (5)).
6. The amended Rules contain a container clause (art. IV (5) (*c*)). It is provided that where packages or units which form the contents of the container are enumerated in the bill of lading separately, they are deemed to be the packages or units for the purposes of the Rules, but otherwise the whole container is the package or unit within the meaning of the Rules.
7. The Act further provides that a servant or agent of the carrier, but not an independent contractor, shall be entitled to avail himself of the same defences and limits of liability as the carrier (art. IV *bis* (2)). This provision overrules *Adler* v. *Dickson* [1955] 1 K.B. 158, known as the *Himalaya* case.

DEMURRAGE AND DISPATCH MONEY

Demurrage is a sum agreed to be paid by a charterer to a shipowner as liquidated damages for delay beyond a stipulated or a reasonable time for loading and unloading; **dispatch money** is the amount agreed to be paid by the shipowner to the charterer for time saved in loading or unloading.

Sometimes a certain number of days is fixed within which the cargo is to be loaded or unloaded. These are known as **lay days,** and for time taken beyond these days demurrage must be paid either at the agreed rate or at a rate to be ascertained as damages for detention. The lay days commence when the ship is an **arrived ship,** *i.e.* when she has arrived at her place of destination, ready to load. If the charterparty names a particular berth (berth charter), or dock area (dock charter) the ship must have arrived there; if it names a port, the ship must have arrived in the commercial area of the port (port charter), as close to the actual loading spot as circumstances permit (*Leonis Steamship Co.* v. *Rank Ltd.* [1908] 1 K.B. 499). In the case of a port charterparty, if the ship cannot proceed immediately to a berth because the port is overcrowded, she is an arrived ship when she has reached a position *within* the port where she is at the immediate and effective disposition of the charterer; that would normally be the place where waiting ships usually lie in the port before being able to proceed to an empty berth.

Under a port charterparty the owners of the m.v. *Johanna Oldendorff* chartered her to carry grain to one of six ports at the charterers' option. The charterparty provided that time for discharge was to count "whether in berth or not." Following instructions by the charterers, the ship proceeded to Liverpool/Birkenhead. On January 3, 1968 she anchored at the Mersey Bar which is within the legal limits of the Port of Liverpool and the usual waiting place for grain ships discharging at that port. The port authorities had ordered her to that place as no berth was available. Notice of readiness was given the same day. The ship waited at the bar until January 20, 1968 when she proceeded to a berth. *Held*, the ship was an arrived ship when anchored at the bar (*E. L. Oldendorff & Co. GmbH* v. *Tradax Export S.A.; The Johanna Oldendorff* [1974] A.C. 479.

If the currency in which freight and other monetary obligations arising under the charterparty have to be paid is a foreign currency, the English courts have jurisdiction to give judgment for payment of demurrage in foreign currency, even though the contract constituted by the charterparty is governed by English law (*Federal Commerce and Navigation Co. Ltd.* v. *Tradax Export S.A.: The Maratha Envoy* [1977] 2 W.L.R. 122).

Sometimes the charterparty requires the shipowner to give **notice of readiness** when the ship has become an arrived ship at the port of loading or discharge, or both. In the absence of an express stipulation in the charterparty, notice of readiness must be given at the loading port but not at the port of discharge. If the shipowner, contrary to his undertaking in the charterparty, fails to tender notice of readiness at the port of discharge before he begins to discharge the cargo, the lay days run from the (later) date of notice of readiness, and not from the (earlier) date of actual discharge (*Pteroti Compania Naviera* v. *National Coal Board* [1958] 1 Q.B. 469).

If the charterer has agreed to load or unload within a fixed time, his obligation is absolute and he will not be released by delay resulting from the crowded state of the docks, bad weather or a strike of dock labourers (*Budgett* v. *Binnington* [1891] 1 Q.B. 35). If no fixed time is stipulated he is allowed a reasonable time, in calculating which the circumstances above mentioned will be taken into account.

Demurrage is payable under a charterparty by the charterer, unless he has been freed by the cesser clause; under a bill of lading it is payable by (1) the shipper or consignor; (2) the person presenting the bill and demanding delivery under it, if the court is satisfied that there was an agreement to pay it; (3) under the Bills of Lading Act 1855 every consignee named in or indorsee of the bill of lading to whom the property in the goods has passed. The effect of the cesser clause and the lien clause on the payment of demurrage has been discussed earlier (see p. 454, *ante*).

Where delay is due to the detention of the vessel as the result of exceeding the lay days and the demurrage provisions, according to their terms, cover such a delay, no damages in excess of the demurrage payments can be claimed (*Suisse Atlantique Société d'Armement Maritime S.A.* v. *N.V. Rotterdamsche Kolen Centrale* [1967] 1 A.C. 361, see pp. 35–36, *ante*).

<h2 style="text-align:center">FREIGHT</h2>

Freight is the consideration paid to the carrier for the carriage of the goods. It is only payable if the carrier has delivered the goods, or is ready to deliver them but is prevented from doing so by the default of the consignee. Even if delivery cannot be effected because of the happening of one of the excepted perils, the carrier, though relieved of liability for the goods, cannot recover the freight.

Cement was shipped under a bill of lading which stipulated for payment of freight within three days after the ship's arrival. On arrival, a fire broke out on board and the ship had in consequence to be scuttled. When the ship was raised it was found that the cement was useless. *Held*, the shipowners, not being ready to perform their part of the contract, were not entitled to freight: *Duthie* v. *Hilton* (1868) L.R. 4 C.P. 138.

The fact that the goods can only be delivered in a damaged condition does not prevent the carrier from recovering freight, unless it can be shown that the thing delivered is not the same thing in a business sense as the thing shipped. The remedy of the consignee is an action for damages, unless the damage to the goods was caused by the excepted perils or the vice of the goods themselves.

Coal shipped under a charter was, through the negligence of the captain, so deteriorated as not to be worth its freight. The charterer, therefore, abandoned it to the shipowner. *Held*, he was liable for freight, his remedy being by cross-action: *Dakin* v. *Oxley* (1864) 15 C.B.(N.S.) 646.

The carrier is entitled to his freight if the consignee refuses to name a safe port to which the ship can proceed and enter.

Advance freight

Advance freight is where freight is payable before the delivery of the goods. It must be paid even if the goods are lost by excepted perils after the agreed date of payment.

C chartered a ship from Liverpool to Archangel, freight payable in Liverpool before sailing on signing bills of lading. Before the vessel was completely loaded, and all the bills of lading signed, fire broke out and the vessel sank with the cargo. *Held*, freight could be recovered from C for the amount of cargo for which bills of lading had been signed: *Coker & Co. Ltd.* v. *Limerick SS. Co. Ltd.* (1918) 34 T.L.R. 296.

In this case freight was not recoverable in respect of cargo already loaded when the ship sank but for which no bill of lading had been signed.

When freight is payable on the signing of the bill of lading the charterers must present the bills for signature within a reasonable time, even though the ship has been lost after the goods have been supplied (*Oriental Steamship Co.* v. *Tylor* [1893] 2 Q.B. 518).

Lump sum freight

Lump sum freight is where the charterer agrees to pay a lump sum for the use of a ship. It is payable if the shipowner is ready to perform his contract though no goods are shipped. When goods are shipped, the whole freight becomes payable on delivery of part of the cargo only if the non-delivery of the remainder is due to an excepted peril.

T chartered a ship to carry a cargo of timber for a specified lump sum, the charterparty containing an exception of perils of the seas. The ship arrived outside the port, but owing to heavy weather was driven ashore and wrecked. Part of the cargo was washed ashore and was collected by the captain and delivered to T. The remainder was lost by the perils of the seas. *Held*, the whole of the freight was payable: *Thomas* v. *Harrowing SS. Co.* [1915] A.C. 58.

Pro rata freight

Pro rata freight is that amount of freight recoverable by the carrier when the owner of the goods voluntarily agrees to take delivery of the goods at a port short of the original destination. It is only payable if the carrier is able and willing to carry the goods to their destination, and not if he abandons the ship and cargo or unreasonably delays the voyage. If he insists on leaving the goods at an intermediate port and the owner is consequently obliged to accept them there, no freight is payable.

A ship agreed to take cargo from Florida to Hamburg. During the voyage war broke out making delivery at Hamburg illegal. The cargo was therefore discharged at Runcorn and delivered to the owners. *Held*, the shipowners were not entitled to freight, either in whole, since they had not completed the voyage, or in part, because no new contract could be inferred with the owners of the goods to take delivery at Runcorn instead of at Hamburg: *St. Enoch SS. Co.* v. *Phosphate Mining Co.* [1916] 2 K.B. 624.

By whom payable

The person liable to pay freight is prima facie the shipper of the goods, unless the bill of lading or other contract frees him from this liability, as, for example, when there is a cesser clause. In addition, the fact of taking delivery of the goods is evidence of an implied promise to pay the freight. The Bills of Lading Act 1855, s. 1 provides:—

> "Every consignee of goods named in a bill of lading, and every indorsee of a bill of lading to whom the property in the goods therein mentioned shall pass upon or by reason of such consignment or indorsement, shall have transferred to and vested in him all rights of suit, and be subject to the same liabilities in respect of such goods as if the contract contained in the bill of lading had been made with himself."

This provision imposes liability to pay freight upon every consignee of goods named in a bill of lading and every indorsee of a bill of lading to whom the property in the goods has passed by reason of the consignment or indorsement. By section 2 of the same Act, this does not relieve the original shipper or owner of any liability to which he may be subject.

Right of suit

Where section 1 of the Bills of Lading Act 1855, which has just been quoted, applies, the right of suit is vested exclusively in the consignee or the indorsee to whom the property in the goods has passed by virtue of the consignment or indorsement. This means that in these cases the consignor, who has concluded the contract of carriage with the shipowner, cannot claim by way of damages the loss which the consignee or indorsee has suffered (*The Albazero* [1976] 3 W.L.R. 419). This is anomalous and solely due to the operation of section 1 of the 1855 Act. In cases in which the Act does not apply, the consignor can recover those damages from the shipowner but has to hold the amount recovered as trustee for the person who suffered the loss, *i.e.* the consignee or indorsee (*Dunlop* v. *Lambert* (1839) 9 Cl. & F. 600).

The charterers chartered *The Albacruz* from the shipowners. They shipped a cargo of crude oil from La Salina in Venezuela to Antwerp. The carriage was covered by a bill of lading issued pursuant to the charter-party naming the charterers as consignees. *The Albacruz* and her cargo became a total loss owing to breaches by the shipowners of the charter-party. Before the ship and cargo were lost, the charterers had indorsed the bill of lading to the indorsees in whom the property in the cargo was vested at the time of the loss. The indorsees (as cargo-owners) had lost their right of action under the bill of lading owing to expiry of the one year prescription period provided by article III, rule 6, of the Hague Rules. The charterers as consignors claimed from the shipowners by way of damages the loss suffered by the cargo-owners, and arrested the *Albazero*, a ship belonging to the same shipowners. *Held*, (1) the Bills of Lading Act 1855, s. 1, applied; (2) although privity of contract existed between the charterers and shipowners, by virtue of section 1 of the 1855 Act the right of action was vested solely in the indorsees; (3) the charterers were not entitled to sue: *Albacruz* v. *Albazero*; *The Albazero* [1976] 3 W.L.R. 419.

Shipowner's lien

At common law the carrier has a possessory lien for freight, that is, he can withhold delivery until he is paid. This lien only attaches when freight is payable on delivery and does not exist in the case of—

1. advance freight; or
2. freight agreed to be paid after delivery of the goods.

It can be exercised against all goods coming to the same consignee on the same voyage for the freight due on all or any part of them, but not to goods on different voyages under different contracts. Lien may be waived by accepting a bill of exchange for the freight or by making delivery without requiring payment. At common law there is no lien for dead freight, but such a lien may be granted by express agreement. The charterparty and the bill of lading often contain special provisions dealing with lien, and in such a case the common law lien will be modified.

The lien can be enforced at common law merely by retaining the goods. By the Merchant Shipping Act 1894, s. 497, if the lien is not discharged, a power of sale is given after the goods have been warehoused for 90 days, subject to the conditions laid down in the section.

GENERAL AVERAGE

During the course of a sea voyage there are three interests which are risked: the ship, the cargo, and the freight. As a general rule any loss which any of these interests sustains must be borne by that interest alone; this is known as particular average, *i.e.* loss to be borne by the particular interest incurring it. If, for example, one of the ship's boats is carried away in a storm, this is a particular average loss and must be borne by the shipowner alone. Where, however, extraordinary sacrifices are made or expenditure is incurred for the benefit of the whole adventure, the loss is borne by all in proportion and is known as a general average loss. In such a case the particular interest which has suffered the loss is entitled to contribution, called a general average contribution, from the other interests. The conditions under which a general average contribution can be claimed are—

1. There must have been a common danger. An interest which was never in peril cannot be compelled to contribute.

2. The danger must not be due to the default of the interest claiming contribution; *e.g.* if goods are thrown overboard because they are dangerous their owner cannot claim for general average contribution.

3. The danger must be a real one. Where, therefore, the master of a ship believed that the ship was on fire and caused steam to be turned into the hold to extinguish it and the ship was never in fact on fire, it was held that the resulting damage to the cargo was not a general average loss (*Joseph Watson & Son Ltd.* v. *Fireman's Fund Insurance Co.* [1922] 2 K.B. 355).

4. There must have been a voluntary and reasonable sacrifice of the property in respect of which contribution is claimed. This occurs when cargo is thrown overboard to lighten the ship in heavy weather.

5. The interest called upon for contribution must have been saved.

Extraordinary expenditure incurred by the shipowner for the benefit of the adventure will be the subject of general average contribution. "Extraordinary expenditure must to some extent be connected with an extraordinary occasion. For example, an abnormal user of the engines and an abnormal consumption of coal in endeavouring to refloat a steamship stranded in a position of peril is an extraordinary sacrifice and an extraordinary expenditure (*The Bona* [1895] P. 125). A mere extra user of coal, however, in order to accelerate the speed of the vessel would not be a general average act" (*per* Sankey J. in *Société Nouvelle d'Armement* v. *Spillers and Bakers Ltd.* [1917] 1 K.B. 865).

General average contribution is made by all who have benefited by a general average act. These are—

1. the shipowner in respect of his ship and the freight payable under the charterparty, if any, and, if not, under the bills of lading.
2. The charterer in respect of freight payable under the bills of lading.
3. The cargo owner in respect of the cargo.

The liability is enforced by the shipowner on behalf of all interests by exercising his lien over the cargo, and if he fails to exercise his lien, he may be sued by those entitled to contribution (*Crooks* v. *Allan* (1879) 5 Q.B.D. 38).

The amount of contribution payable by each interest is settled by average adjusters, and is borne by the owners of each interest rateably. The adjustment is made on the basis of the York–Antwerp Rules 1974, if the parties have adopted them, as they do frequently. If the York–Antwerp Rules are not adopted, adjustment is made according to the law of the country where the port of destination is situated or, if the ship does not reach that port, at the port where the voyage ends.

SELECT BIBLIOGRAPHY
Book
Carver's Carriage by Sea (12th ed., 1971, 2 vols.), by R. P. Colinvaux.

Articles
Cadwallader, F. J. J., "Uniformity in the Regulation of Combined Transport" [1974] J.B.L. 193–201.
Davies, A. G., "Incorporation of Charterparty Terms into a Bill of Lading" [1966] J.B.L. 326–334.
Lord Diplock, "Combined Transport Document" [1972] J.B.L. 269.
Fitzpatrick, D. G., "Combined Transport and the C.M.R. Convention" [1968] J.B.L. 311–319.
Giles, O. C., "Combined Transport" (1975) 25 I.C.L.Q. 379–392.

Grönfors, K., "Container Transport and the Hague Rules" [1967] J.B.L. 298–306.

Hill, D. J., "Loss in Transit" [1969] J.B.L. 100–112.

Mankabady, S. M., "Some Legal Aspects of the Carriage of Goods by Container" (1974) 23 I.C.L.Q. 317–338.

Marston, G., "The Cancelling Clause in Charterparties" [1969] J.B.L. 187–203.

Marston, G., "The Near Clause in Charterparties" [1966] J.B.L. 42–54.

Powles, D. G., "Reversing the Arrived Ship" [1974] J.B.L. 282–293.

Rainberg, J., "Combined Transport Operators" [1968] J.B.L. 132–141.

Sassoon, D. M., "Deterioration of Goods in Transit" [1962] J.B.L. 351–362.

CHAPTER 28

CARRIAGE BY AIR

History of statutory provisions

THERE is substantial uniformity, internationally, in the law relating to the carriage of goods by air. This is because over a period of years there has been international negotiation of international conventions. The three British statutes, of which the earliest is now repealed, were all related to such agreements.

The **Carriage by Air Act 1932** gave statutory effect in the United Kingdom to the Warsaw Convention of 1929. In contrast with the Carriage of Goods by Sea Act 1924, which deals only with the carriage of goods, the Act of 1932 dealt with the carriage of persons as well as goods. The 1932 Act applied to all "international carriage" of persons, luggage or goods performed by aircraft and to the air portion of a "combined carriage," *i.e.* a carriage partly performed by air and partly by another mode of carriage, provided the air portion qualified as an "international carriage." The general effect of the Act was to make it relatively easy for a plaintiff passenger, consignor or consignee to establish legal liability on the part of the defendant air carrier for loss, damage, injury or death occurring during the carriage by air. This was done by providing that the carrier was liable unless he could establish one or more specified defences. In return for this shift in the burden of proof on to the carrier, *i.e.* to prove that he was *not* liable, the liability of the carrier was subject to maximum limitations, specified in terms of the gold franc.

Over the years it became clear that the Warsaw Convention required amendment, more particularly with regard to the limitation of liability in the event of death of a passenger which was regarded as too low. Amendment was therefore agreed upon at The Hague on September 28, 1955 in the Hague Protocol. The Warsaw Convention, as amended at The Hague, 1955 was enacted in the **Carriage by Air Act 1961** which came into force on June 1, 1967. The 1961 Act repealed the Act of 1932, but by section 10 provision is made to give effect to the unamended Warsaw Convention in applicable cases.

The third stage in the development of the statutory provisions was reached because neither the original nor the amended Warsaw Convention makes it clear whether the "carrier" referred to is the carrier in contractual relationship with the passenger or consignor, or whether the "carrier" is the carrier who actually performs the carriage. It was therefore necessary to supplement the Warsaw Convention by a further convention, signed in 1961 at Guadalajara in Mexico. This supplementary convention aims at the unification of certain rules relating to international carriage performed by a person other than the contracting carrier. The Guadalajara Convention was enacted by the **Carriage by Air (Supplementary Provisions) Act 1962**, which applies to carriage governed by the original Warsaw Convention as well as to carriage governed by the Warsaw Convention as amended.

By virtue of the three statutes and the orders made under them there is a comprehensive, although complex, regulation of reasonable uniformity for the carriage of goods by air, so far as actions in the English courts are concerned. The fact remains however that there are three different regimes, namely—

1. carriage governed by the original Warsaw Convention;
2. carriage governed by the amended Convention;
3. non-Convention carriage.

The basic elements of carrier's liability are common to all three.

The countries which are parties to the original Warsaw Convention and to the amended Warsaw Convention are listed in the Carriage by Air (Parties to Convention) Order 1975 (S.I. 1975 No. 430), as amended.

Basic elements of liability

The carrier of goods by air is liable for destruction or loss of, or damage to or delay of cargo if it occurs during the carriage by air. He has the right to use specified defences if he can, but he cannot contract out of liability. In return for this liability the carrier can rely on the benefit of maximum limits for his liability, and even that liability arises only if the claimant can prove damage to that extent. The maximum limits of the carrier's liability are—

—250 gold francs per kilogram; or
—the value declared by the consignor for which any supplementary charge has been paid.

The carrier loses the benefit of the limits in the event of certain kinds of technical legal misconduct. The only persons who have rights of action are the consignor and the consignee. Receipt of cargo by the person entitled to delivery without complaint is prima facie evidence of delivery in good condition.

"Carriage by air" comprises the whole period during which the cargo is in the charge of the carrier, whether in an aerodrome or on board an aircraft, or in the case of landing outside an aerodrome in any place whatsoever.

Who may sue

(a) The consignor has a right of action against the first carrier as well as the carrier who actually performed the carriage during which destruction, loss, damage or delay took place (the performing carrier) unless the first carrier has expressly assumed liability for the whole carriage.

(b) The consignee has a right of action against the last carrier and the performing carrier.

The first carrier, the performing carrier and the last carrier are jointly and severally liable respectively to the consignor and the consignee. At the plaintiff's option, written complaints may be made and actions may be brought against either the performing carrier or the contracting carrier or against both together or separately.

Servants and agents of the carrier acting within the scope of their employment can claim the benefit of the limits of liability applicable to the carrier. Acts and omissions of the performing carrier, including his servants and agents, are deemed to be those of the contracting carrier and vice versa.

Who may be sued

(a) *The contracting carrier*, as a principal, makes an agreement for carriage with the consignor or the consignor's agent. In many cases he will be the first or sometimes the only carrier by air, but he may also be one who merely issues a waybill, or an aircraft charterer, or a cargo consolidator or forwarder. He is liable for the whole of the carriage.

(b) *The performing carrier*, by virtue of authority from the contracting carrier, performs the whole or part of the carriage. He is liable only for the part performed by him.

(c) *A successive carrier* is deemed to be a party to the original contract of carriage so far as is relevant to the carriage performed under this supervision.

Defences available

The carrier is not liable if he proves that he and his agents or servants took all necessary measures to avoid the damage or that it was impossible to take such measures.

If the carrier proves that the damage was caused or contributed to by the negligence of the injured person the court may exonerate the carrier wholly or partly.

Application of the regimes

Carriage of cargo for reward by aircraft or gratuitous carriage by an air transport undertaking is governed by the various regimes as follows.

Original Warsaw Convention

When, according to the contract between the parties, the places of departure and destination are located in—
—the territories of two states parties to the Convention; or
—the territory of a single such state with an agreed stopping place anywhere outside that state.

Amended Convention

When, according to the agreement between the parties, the places of departure and destination are located in—
—the territories of two states both of which are parties to the amended Convention; or
—the territory of a single state party to the amended Convention with an agreed stopping place anywhere outside that state.

There is a complication when the place of departure is in the territory of a state party to the original Convention (*e.g.* USA) whilst the place of destination is in the territory of a state which is not only a party to the original Convention but has also become a party to the amended Convention (*e.g.* the United Kingdom). In such circumstances, the only obligations which bind both states are those in the original Convention.

As regards passenger baggage, article 26 (2) of the amended Convention provides that in case of "damage" the person entitled to delivery must complain, at the latest, seven days from the date of receipt of the baggage; this provision does not apply to loss of goods from registered baggage because "loss" is not "damage" to the goods, and the value of the missing goods can be recovered from the carrier though notice is not given within seven days, provided that proceedings are commenced within the time limit of two years laid down by the Convention (*Fothergill* v. *Monarch Airlines Ltd.*, *The Times*, March 19, 1977).

Non-Convention rules

When the carriage of cargo is governed neither by the original nor by the amended Convention, then whatever the place of departure, no part of the contract or agreement for carriage would, as a matter of law, be governed by either of the two Conventions. In an action before the English courts the carriage would be governed by the non-Convention rules, even though the carriage was "international" in the ordinary meaning of the word but not within the technical meaning which is what governs the applicability of the two Conventions. The non-Convention rules are contained in the Carriage by Air Acts (Application of Provisions) Order 1967.

The non-Convention rules also govern—

(a) carriage, wholly within the territory of *any* state, which does not form part of the performance of a Convention contract or agreement for carriage, and without any stopping place outside that state, and regardless of whether that state is a party to either of the Conventions; and

(b) carriage of mail or postal packets.

Each regime involves variation of the basic elements of liability.

Carriage governed by the original Warsaw Convention

Document of carriage

The document of carriage is called the *air consignment note* (ACN). The carrier has the right to require the consignor to make out an ACN and to require a separate one for each package, and the carrier is required to accept it. Nevertheless the absence, irregularity or loss of the document does not affect the validity of the contract or the operation of the Convention rules.

If, however, the carrier accepts goods with an ACN or if the ACN does not contain any of the following particulars, then he cannot take advantage of the provisions of the Convention which would otherwise exclude or limit the carrier's liability—

(a) place and date of execution of the air consignment note;

(b) places of departure and destination;

   (c) agreed stopping places (which the carrier may alter in case of
        necessity);
   (d) name and address of consignor;
   (e) name and address of first carrier;
   (f) name and address of consignee "if the case so requires" [sic];
   (g) nature of the goods;
   (h) number of packages, method of packing and the particular
        marks or numbers on them;
   (i) weight, quantity, volume or dimensions of the goods;
   (j) a statement that the carriage is subject to the rules relating to
        liability established by the Convention.

The ACN and the statements therein are prima facie evidence
of the conclusion of the contract, receipt of the goods, the conditions
of carriage, the weight, dimensions, packing and number of goods.
Statements relating to quantity, volume or condition are not evidence
against the carrier unless expressly stated on the ACN to have been
either checked in the presence of the consignor or they relate to
apparent condition. As to (i), above, the Court of Appeal has held
that only one of these particulars needs be given (*Corocraft Ltd.* v.
Pan American World Airways Inc. [1969] 1 Q.B. 616).

Basic liability

Besides the two basic defences, the carrier is not liable if he can
prove that "the damage was occasioned by negligent pilotage or
negligence in the handling of the aircraft or in navigation and that in
all other respects he and his agents have taken all necessary measures
to avoid the damage." In practice this defence is not used as it is not
available in cases of injury or death of passengers, so to raise this
defence for cargo might give rise to unlimited liability for passengers.

Special rights of consignor and consignee

Unless varied by express provision in the ACN, the consignor
and the consignee have the following rights—
The consignor—
   (a) has the right of disposal prior to delivery to the consignee,
        subject to the production of the consignor's copy of the
        air consignment note to the carrier and payment of all
        expenses involved; and
   (b) may enforce rights in his own name even if acting in the

interests of another, subject to fulfilment of all obligations of the consignor under the contract of carriage.

The consignee—

(a) has the right to require the carrier to hand over goods and on the air consignment note on arrival at the destination on payment of proper charges and compliance with any other conditions set out in the air consignment note; and

(b) may enforce rights in his own name even if acting in the interests of another, subject to the fulfilment of all obligations of the consignee under the contract of carriage.

Carriage governed by the amended Warsaw Convention

Document of carriage

The document of carriage is called an *air waybill* (AWB). All the provisions of the original Convention relating to the ACN apply to the AWB under the amended Convention, with the important exception of the particulars to appear in it and the penalties for omission.

If, **with the consent of the carrier,** cargo is loaded on board without an AWB or if the AWB does not contain a notice to the consignor "to the effect that, if the carriage involves an ultimate destination or stop in a country other than the country of departure, the Warsaw Convention may be applicable and that the Convention governs and in most cases limits the liability of carriers in respect of loss of or damage to cargo," then in either of these circumstances, the carrier cannot take advantage of the limits of liability.

It is stated in the amended Convention that nothing in it "prevents the issue of a negotiable air waybill," although in fact there was nothing in the original Convention to prevent the issue of a negotiable ACN. In practical terms, the speed of air transport has largely eliminated the need for a negotiable document of carriage and waybills are usually printed "not negotiable."

Basic liability

There are no defences other than the two basic ones. The defence of negligent pilotage does not apply. Servants and agents of the carrier enjoy the benefit of the same limits of liability as the carrier. The special rights of the consignor and of the consignee are the same as those under the original Convention.

Non-Convention carriage

The basic system of liability, including limits, is the same as that under the amended Convention, but there are no provisions relating to documents of carriage or to what has been described above as special rights of consignor and consignee.

SELECT BIBLIOGRAPHY

Books

G. A. Seabrooke, *Air Law*, 1964.
Lord McNair, *The Law of the Air* (3rd ed., 1964) by M. R. E. Kerr and A. H. M. Evans.

Articles

Caplan, H., "The Warsaw Convention Revitalised" [1966] J.B.L. 335–338.
Dias, R. W. M., "The Interpretation of the Limiting Clause in the Warsaw Convention 1929" [1969] C.L.J. 40–42.
Mankiewicz, R. H., "Judicial Diversification of Uniform Private Law Conventions: The Warsaw Convention's Days in Court" (1972) 21 I.C.L.Q. 718–757.
Pal, L. T., "Air Trade Terms" [1973] J.B.L. 9–14.

PART 9: BANKRUPTCY

CHAPTER 29

PROCEEDINGS UP TO ADJUDICATION[1]

THE object of bankruptcy is twofold—

1. to enable a person embarrassed with debts to rid himself of his liabilities in a proper manner so that he can make a fresh start; and
2. to provide for equality in the distribution of the debtor's property among creditors of the same rank.

Before a person can be made bankrupt, he must first commit an **"act of bankruptcy,"** that is, some act which shows that it is very probable that he cannot pay his debts. The reason for the necessity of an act of bankruptcy is to prevent solvent persons from being subjected to bankruptcy proceedings. If an act of bankruptcy has been committed, a **bankruptcy petition** may be presented, on which a **receiving order** will be made. After the receiving order the creditors of the debtor meet to decide whether to accept a composition or whether to make the debtor bankrupt; if they decide on the latter course, the debtor will be **adjudicated bankrupt**. On bankruptcy, his property will pass to his trustee in bankruptcy, who will collect all his property and distribute it among such of the creditors as have proved their debts. The bankrupt will undergo his **public examination** unless the court makes an order dispensing with it. Subject to that the bankrupt can apply for his **discharge**, which will be granted or refused according to his conduct before and during the bankruptcy, and the amount of the dividend distributed among his creditors. Alternatively there is now provision for (a) an order for automatic discharge by the court after the conclusion of the public examination or dispensation with such examination to take effect on the fifth anniversary of the date of adjudication of bankruptcy, and (b) discharge on the application of the official receiver in the sixth year after the adjudication. On discharge the bankrupt is freed from his former debts and liabilities (subject to certain exceptions) and can commence business again.

[1] References in this chapter are to the Bankruptcy Act 1914 unless the contrary is expressed.

481

The early Bankruptcy Acts, which date from the reign of Henry VIII, applied only to traders, but at the present time all persons can be made bankrupt. The following particular cases should be noted.

A minor can be made bankrupt if he has incurred debts which are legally enforceable against him.

A minor carrying on business as a manufacturer of cosmetics, failed to pay purchase tax for which she was liable. The Commissioners of Customs and Excise recovered judgment against her and on non-payment applied for a receiving order. *Held*, a receiving order should be made: *Re a Debtor, ex p. Commissioners of Customs and Excise* [1950] Ch. 282.

Mentally disordered persons

Where it appears to be for the benefit of such a person that he should be made bankrupt, the court may direct the receiver or other person duly appointed to file a declaration of insolvency or present a bankruptcy petition in his name or to consent to a receiving order or an adjudication on his behalf (*Re James* (1884) 12 Q.B.D. 332 and Mental Health Act 1959, ss. 103 and 105).

Corporations

A corporation or a company registered under the Companies Act 1948 cannot be made bankrupt. Liquidation by reason of insolvency in the case of a company corresponds to bankruptcy in the case of an individual.

BEFORE RECEIVING ORDER

Acts of bankruptcy (s. 1)

Before any bankruptcy proceedings can be taken, a debtor must have committed an act of bankruptcy.

A debtor may be any person, whether or not a British subject, who at the time any act of bankruptcy was done—

(a) was personally present in England; or
(b) ordinarily resided or had a place of residence in England; or
(c) was carrying on business in England, personally, or by means of an agent or manager; or
(d) was a member of a firm or partnership which carried on business in England.

The following are acts of bankruptcy—

1. If the debtor in England or elsewhere makes a conveyance or assignment of his property to a trustee for the benefit of his creditors generally.

The conveyance must be of all, or substantially all, the debtor's property and must be for the benefit of the creditors generally and not of a particular class, *e.g.* trade creditors (*Re Phillips* [1900] 2 Q.B. 329).

A creditor who has assented to the assignment cannot rely on it as an act of bankruptcy. The assent may be express, by executing the deed of assignment, or implied from conduct, as by taking a benefit under the deed or by selling goods to the trustee under the deed. Mere attendance at a meeting of creditors does not amount to assent (*Re Sunderland* [1911] 2 K.B. 658).

If a deed of arrangement becomes void because of non-registration, a creditor who assented to it can nevertheless rely on it as an act of bankruptcy (Deeds of Arrangement Act 1914, s. 24 (2)).

2. If the debtor in England or elsewhere makes a fraudulent conveyance, gift, delivery or transfer of his property, or of any part thereof.

A conveyance may be fraudulent either (a) under section 172 of the Law of Property Act 1925, or (b) under the bankruptcy law. Under section 172 the actual intention to defraud creditors must be proved, whether the conveyance is voluntary or for valuable consideration. In bankruptcy law the word "fraudulent" is used in a sense different from that in which it is ordinarily used. There need not be moral fraud; it exists if there is no more than an intention to defeat or delay creditors generally which will prevent the distribution of the insolvent debtor's property in accordance with the bankruptcy laws (*Re Sinclair* (1884), 26 Ch.D. 319).

An assignment of the whole, or substantially the whole, of a debtor's property in consideration of a past debt is an act of bankruptcy, whatever the motives of the parties may have been (*Re Ellis* (1876) 2 Ch.D. 797). If the consideration for the transfer is partly a past debt and partly a further advance, the question is whether there was a genuine intention to enable the debtor to continue his business. If the further advance was merely a device for obtaining payment or security, the assignment will be fraudulent. The amount of the further advance is immaterial, except as evidence of the intention of the parties.

If the assignment is by way of sale or charge made in good

faith for a fair present equivalent, it will not necessarily be fraudulent; but, if it has the effect of defeating or delaying creditors, it will be fraudulent. On this principle, an assignment by an insolvent debtor of his business to a company formed to take it over, may be an act of bankruptcy.

S had creditors for £28,000 and an overdraft of £6,500. He assigned his assets to a company for £17,000 to be satisfied by the issue of 17,000 £1 shares, and the bank was granted debentures in the company. *Held*, the assignment was void. "A transfer by a debtor of substantially the whole of his property, whether by way of charge or by way of sale, will be an act of bankruptcy, if the necessary consequence of the transfer will be to defeat or delay his creditors; and . . . I feel no difficulty in holding that the substitution in place of a going business and substantial business assets of (a) shares in a private company which has taken over the debtor's assets and liabilities, together with (b) a right of action by the debtor against that company of its covenant to discharge his liabilities, must necessarily have the result of delaying the creditors, and cannot be treated as providing something which the creditors can reach just as easily as the assets which have been transferred": *per* Clauson J., *Re Simms* [1930] 2 Ch. 22.

The transfer of the assets of a defaulter on the Stock Exchange to the official assignee is fraudulent, as it withdraws the debtor's property from the general creditors: *Tomkins* v. *Saffery* (1877) 3 A.C. 213.

When the assignment is void as being fraudulent, the transferee, even if he takes in good faith and for value, has no title to the property if a bankruptcy petition is presented within three months (*Re Gunsbourg* [1920] 2 K.B. 426). An assignment which is voidable under section 172 of the Law of Property Act 1925 may be set aside at any time, except as against a purchaser in good faith and for value who has no notice of the intent to defraud creditors.

3. If in England or elsewhere the debtor makes any conveyance or transfer of his property, or any part thereof, or creates any charge thereon which would be void as a fraudulent preference if he were adjudged bankrupt.

What amounts to a fraudulent preference is explained in section 44 (see p. 514, *post*).

4. If, with intent to defeat or delay his creditors, the debtor departs out of England, or being out of England remains out, or departs from his dwelling-house, or otherwise absents himself, or begins to keep house.

An intent to defeat or delay creditors may be presumed if the debtor avoids his creditors and omits to pay his debts. But if he resides abroad, no presumption can be drawn from his remaining out of England (*Ex p. Brandon* (1884) 25 Ch.D. 500).

5. If execution against the debtor has been levied by seizure of his goods, and the goods have either been sold by the sheriff or held by him for 21 days.

If any petition is presented on this act of bankruptcy, it must be presented within three months of the completion of the 21 days, notwithstanding that the sheriff continues in possession beyond 21 days (*Re Beeston* [1899] 1 Q.B. 626).

6. If the debtor files in the court a declaration, in prescribed form, of his inability to pay his debts, or presents a bankruptcy petition against himself.

7. If the debtor, within the appropriate period of service on him of a bankruptcy notice, fails to comply with it or to satisfy the court that he has a counterclaim, set-off or cross-demand which equals or exceeds the amount to be paid.

The following conditions must be met—

(a) The creditor in whose name the bankruptcy notice is served must have obtained a final judgment or order against the debtor for a sum of money, and there must have been no stay of execution.

(b) The notice must be served on the debtor in England, although it may, with leave of the court, be served on him elsewhere.

(c) The time for compliance, if served in England, is within 10 days of service, and if served elsewhere then within such time as may be laid down when leave is so given.

(d) Only one judgment debt can be included in a bankruptcy notice, which must be in the prescribed form.

(e) A notice calls upon the debtor to pay the judgment debt or to compound for it to the creditors' satisfaction, and states the consequences of non-compliance (s. 2).

(f) If the debtor does not pay or compound the debt, he can avoid an act of bankruptcy only by setting up a counterclaim or set-off; but such counterclaim or set-off must not be one which he could have set up in the action in which the judgment was obtained.

(g) Once a bankruptcy notice is not complied with, then any creditor can present a petition founded on this act of bankruptcy, even though he was not the creditor in whose name the notice was served.

8. If the debtor gives notice to any of his creditors that he has suspended, or that he is about to suspend, payment of his debts.

The notice need not be in writing, but it must be a deliberate and intentional act applying to all creditors. It usually takes the form of a circular letter addressed by the debtor to his creditors; a letter merely summoning a meeting of creditors is not a notice of suspension of payment. The test to be applied in such a case is: What effect would the circular produce on the mind of a creditor receiving it as to the intention of the debtor with regard to his creditors?

A debtor sent this letter to his creditors: "Being unable to meet my engagements as they fall due, I invite your attendance at" [a specified time and place], "where I will submit a statement of my position for your consideration and decision." *Held*, this was a notice by the debtor that he was about to suspend payment of his debts: *Crook* v. *Morley* [1891] A.C. 316.

9. If any person has a criminal bankruptcy order made against him he shall be treated as a debtor who has committed an act of bankruptcy on the date on which the order is made (Powers of Criminal Courts Act 1973, Sched. 2, para. 1).

10. Where a debtor fails to make any payment under an administration order and the court revokes such order and makes a receiving order instead. In such a case the debtor shall be deemed to have committed an act of bankruptcy at the time when the latter order is made (s. 11 (1) and (5) of the Insolvency Act 1976).

The petition (ss. 4–6)

A bankruptcy petition may be presented by the debtor or by a creditor.

A debtor's petition alleges that the debtor is unable to pay his debts. It is only debts presently payable which have to be considered, not debts payable in the future (*Re a Debtor* [1967] Ch. 590). Presentation of such a petition is an act of bankruptcy without the previous filing by the debtor of a declaration of inability to pay his debts.

A creditor is not entitled to present a bankruptcy petition against a debtor unless—

1. The debt owing to him is at least £200. Two or more creditors

may join together to present the petition if the aggregate amount of their debts is £200.

2. The debt is a liquidated sum, payable either immediately or at some certain future time. It must be liquidated at the date of the act of bankruptcy, and it is not sufficient that it has become liquidated after the act of bankruptcy but before the presentation of the petition (*Re Debtors* [1927] 1 Ch. 19).

3. The act of bankruptcy on which the petition is founded has occurred within three months before the presentation of the petition.

4. The debtor—

(a) is domiciled in England; or

(b) within a year before the date of the presentation of the petition—

 (i) has ordinarily resided in England, or

 (ii) had a dwelling-house or place of business, in England, or

 (iii) has carried on business in England, personally or by means of an agent or manager; or

(c) is, or within a year before the date of the presentation of the period has been, a member of a firm or partnership of persons which has carried on business in England by means of a partner or partners, or an agent or manager.

The petition asks that a receiving order be made against the debtor, and sets out (a) the address at which the debtor has been carrying on business; (b) the amount of the petitioning creditor's debt; (c) the security, if any, which he holds for the debt (if the petitioning creditor does not disclose his security, the receiving order will be rescinded (*Re a Debtor* [1943] Ch. 213)), and (d) the act of bankruptcy on which the petition is founded. It must be verified by the affidavit of the creditor or of some person on his behalf who has knowledge of the facts, and must be served on the debtor. It is presented to the county court of the district in which the debtor has resided or carried on business for the longest period during the six months immediately preceding the presentation of the petition, or if the debtor is not resident in England, or his residence is unknown, or he resides within the London bankruptcy district, the petition must be presented in the High Court.

The hearing of the petition takes place eight days after service. During this the petitioning creditor must prove his debt, the service of the petition, and the act of bankruptcy, and the court may thereupon make a receiving order. If any of these things are not proved, or if the court is of opinion for other sufficient cause that no order should be made, the petition will be dismissed.

There is sufficient cause for dismissing a petition if the debtor's sole asset is a life interest which will cease on bankruptcy (*Re Otway* [1895] 1 Q.B. 812), but not that there are no assets to distribute (*Re Leonard* [1896] 1 Q.B. 473), or that the petitioning creditor is actuated by some motive other than a desire to obtain a distribution of the debtor's assets in bankruptcy, *e.g.* a desire to prevent the carrying out of a proposed deed of assignment because the petitioning creditor did not get an improper advantage from it (*Re Sunderland* [1911] 2 K.B. 658).

Effect of petition

After a petition is presented steps may be taken to protect the debtor's estate.

1. The court may, if it is necessary for the protection of the estate, before the receiving order is made, appoint the official receiver to be interim receiver of the debtor's property (s. 8).

2. The court may stay any action, execution or other legal process against the person or property of the debtor (s. 9).

3. The petition must be entered in the register of pending actions at the Land Charges Registry (s. 5 of the Land Charges Act 1972). In the case of registered land a creditor's notice is also entered on the register of title.

Receiving order

Unless the petition is dismissed or stayed, a receiving order is made. The effect of the receiving order is to constitute the official receiver the receiver of all the debtor's property, and no action can thereupon be begun against the debtor without the leave of the court (s. 7). Where the nature of the debtor's business demands it, the official receiver may, on the application of a creditor, appoint a special manager of the debtor's business at such remuneration as the creditors may determine (s. 10).

When a receiving order is made it must be advertised in the *London Gazette* and in a local paper (s. 11). It should also be registered in the register of writs and orders affecting land under section 6 (1) (*c*) of the Land Charges Act 1972. This is so whether or not it is known to affect land. Registration of a receiving order lapses after five years unless renewed (*ibid.* s. 8). As regards registered land registration of the receiving order in the register of writs and orders affecting land is not in itself effective as a protection but operates merely as the initiating machinery leading to the entry of a bankruptcy inhibition on the register of title (Land Registration Act 1925, s. 61 (3), (4)).

A receiving order may be **rescinded** in the following cases—

1. If a majority of the creditors in number and value are resident in Scotland or Ireland and, from the situation of the debtor's property or other causes, his estate ought to be distributed according to the bankruptcy law of Scotland or Ireland (s. 12). The court has a discretion to rescind the order, and will have regard to the assets and the creditors in England. The exercise of a foreign bankruptcy does not debar an English bankruptcy (*Re a Debtor* [1922] 2 Ch. 470).

2. When a composition or scheme is sanctioned by the court under section 16 (see rules 197–216).

3. Under section 108 the court has a general discretion under which it can rescind a receiving order. The discretion can be exercised when the court is satisfied that the order should not have been made, or that the debts will be paid in full, and only in special circumstances can it be exercised where there has been no misconduct on the debtor's part, and the recission is for the benefit of the creditors (*Re Izod* [1898] 1 Q.B. 241; *Re a Debtor (D.C.)* [1971] 1 W.L.R. 261). When exercising its discretion on special grounds, the court has to take into account the public interest and the effect of its decision on future creditors and on those creditors who abstained from taking proceedings because a receiving order was already made (*Re a Debtor (D.C.)* [1971] 1 W.L.R. 261). The fact of the debtor's having arranged to pay his creditors in full does not entitle him to have the order rescinded, even if the creditors agree, if the court is of opinion that, owing to the debtor's conduct, a public examination is necessary (*Re Leslie* (1887) 18 Q.B.D. 619).

AFTER RECEIVING ORDER

Within three days of the receiving order, if it is made on his own petition, or seven days if made on a creditor's petition, the debtor must submit to the official receiver his **statement of affairs**. This statement must be verified by affidavit, and contain a list of the debtor's assets and liabilities, and the names and addresses of his creditors with the securities (if any) they hold (s. 14). If the debtor cannot himself prepare a proper statement of affairs, the official receiver may, at the expense of the estate, employ some person to assist in its preparation (s. 74). If the debtor fails to submit a statement, he may be adjudged bankrupt on the application of the official receiver or a creditor.

The statement of affairs is open to the inspection of anyone stating himself in writing to be a creditor.

Meeting of creditors

As soon as may be after the receiving order, and not more than 14 days from that date, the official receiver must summon a meeting of creditors.

There is sent to the creditors a summary of the statement of affairs, including the causes of the debtor's failure, and any observations the official receiver may think fit to make. The first meeting is presided over by the official receiver, and the procedure at the meeting is laid down in the Bankruptcy Act 1914, and Rules.

The object of the first meeting of creditors is to decide whether a composition or scheme of arrangement is to be accepted, or whether the debtor is to be adjudicated bankrupt (s. 13).

Composition or scheme (s. 16)

If a debtor has any proposal to make for the arrangement of his affairs, he must, within four days of submitting his statement of affairs, submit his proposal in writing to the official receiver. The latter then sends each of the creditors a copy of the proposal and summons a creditors' meeting.

Any creditor who has proved his debt may attend the meeting and vote, or may assent or dissent to the scheme by letter in the the day before the meeting.

The scheme will only become binding if—

1. a majority in number and three-fourths in value of the creditors resolve to accept it; and
2. it is approved by the court.

The application for the court's approval may be made by the debtor or by the official receiver, and may be opposed by any of the creditors, even though they may have voted for its acceptance at the meeting. Before approving, the court hears a report from the official receiver on the scheme and on the debtor's conduct. The application cannot be made until after the conclusion of the public examination of the debtor or an order has been made dispensing with a public examination.

The court is **bound to refuse** to approve the scheme when—

1. The terms of the proposal are not reasonable.

2. The proposal is not calculated to benefit the general body of creditors.

3. The circumstances would require the court to refuse the debtor's discharge if he were bankrupt.

4. The circumstances would require the court to refuse, suspend or attach conditions to the debtor's discharge if he were bankrupt, unless reasonable security for payment of not less than 25 new pence in the pound on his unsecured debts is provided. Here "reasonable security" does not mean such a security as it would be reasonable for a prudent man to invest money upon, but only that there should be a reasonable probability that the amount named will be realised having regard to the state of affairs presented to the creditors (*per* Cross J. in *Re Murray, a Debtor* [1969] 1 W.L.R. 246, 251).

5. The scheme does not provide for the payment in priority of the preferential debts.

In all other cases the court may approve or refuse to approve the scheme in its discretion. In exercising its discretion the court will have regard, not only to the wishes of the creditors, but also to the interests of the public, the requirements of commercial morality and the conduct of the debtor (*Re Beer* [1903] 1 K.B. 628).

The scheme, when approved, is binding on **all** the creditors so far as it relates to debts due from the debtor and provable in bankruptcy. As far as other debts are concerned, they are not discharged unless the creditor assents to the scheme (s. 17). When a scheme is approved, the court discharges the receiving order.

A scheme may be **annulled** if—

1. default is made in payment of any instalment due under the scheme;

2. the scheme cannot, in consequence of legal difficulties or for any sufficient cause, proceed without injustice or undue delay to the creditors or to the debtor;

3. the approval of the scheme was obtained by fraud.

Public examination (s. 15)

As soon as conveniently may be after the receiving order is made and subject to what is said below, the debtor is publicly examined as to his conduct, dealings and property. The examination is taken before the registrar, when the debtor is examined on oath and his answers taken down in writing and signed by him. The debtor may be questioned by the official receiver, any creditor, his trustee in bankruptcy and the court, and the notes of his examination are open to the inspection of the creditors and may be used in evidence against him.

The object of the public examination is not merely to obtain a full and complete disclosure of the debtor's assets and the facts relating to his bankruptcy in the interests of his creditors, but is also for the protection of the public. A debtor cannot, therefore, refuse to answer a question on the ground that by doing so he may incriminate himself (*Re Paget* [1927] 2 Ch. 85).

Judgment was obtained against X for selling lamps in infringement of a patent, and he was afterwards adjudicated bankrupt. In his public examination he was asked where he had obtained the lamps and he refused to answer. *Held*, he could be compelled to answer, because (1) the answer might lead to the discovery of further assets, and (2) the answer might be in the public interest by enabling the supply of infringing lamps to be stopped at the source: *Re Jawett* [1929] 1 Ch. 108.

If the debtor fails to attend his public examination after being required by notice to attend, a warrant for his arrest may be issued.

When a debtor's affairs have been sufficiently investigated, the court may declare that his examination is concluded, but it may not do so until after the first meeting of creditors has been held.

In a number of cases, however, a public examination may not be necessary and power is given to the court under section 6 (1) of the Insolvency Act 1976 to make an order dispensing with it. In determining whether to make such an order the court shall have regard to all the circumstances of the case including, in particular—

(a) whether the debtor has made a full disclosure of his affairs;
(b) whether he has been adjudged bankrupt on a previous occasion;
(c) the number and nature of his debts;
(d) whether his bankruptcy would for any reason be a matter of public concern; and

(e) such other matters as may be prescribed for the purposes of section 6 (1) by rules made under section 132 of the Bankruptcy Act 1914.

An order under section 6 (1) can only be made on the application of the official receiver although the court's power to review or rescind any such order may be exercised either on the application of the official receiver or on the application of the debtor, a creditor or the trustee (s. 6 (2)). These provisions are without prejudice to the existing power under section 15 (10) of the Bankruptcy Act 1914 to dispense with a public examination in the case of a debtor suffering from mental or physical disability. Where an order is made under either section the effect is the same as if the debtor's public examination had taken place and been concluded on the date on which the order is made (s. 6 (4)).

Adjudication of bankruptcy

Where a receiving order has been made a debtor may be adjudicated bankrupt if—

1. he applies to be made bankrupt (rule 217).
2. he fails to submit a statement of affairs (s. 14 (3)).
3. he fails to pay any instalment due under a composition (s. 16 (16)).
4. his creditors by ordinary resolution resolve that he be adjudicated bankrupt.
5. his creditors do not meet.
6. a composition or scheme is not approved within 14 days of the debtor's examination (or the order dispensing with it), or such further time as the court allows (s. 18).
7. the public examination is adjourned *sine die* (rule 220).

Notice of the adjudication must be advertised in the *London Gazette* and in a local paper (s. 18 (2)).

On adjudication, the property of the bankrupt vests in a trustee and becomes divisible among his creditors.

Appointment of trustee (s. 19)

The trustee may be a creditor, but need not be, and is appointed by—

1. ordinary resolution of the creditors, or
2. the committee of inspection, if the creditors resolve to leave the appointment to the committee, or

3. the Department of Trade, if the creditors do not appoint a trustee within four weeks of adjudication. In such a case the creditors may subsequently appoint a trustee instead of the trustee appointed by the Department.

The official receiver is not appointed trustee unless—

1. The value of the estate is not likely to exceed £4,000 (s. 129).
2. There is a vacancy in the trusteeship, and then only until a new trustee is appointed (ss. 74 (1) (*g*) and 78 (4)).

The appointment of the trustee is not complete until he has given security to the satisfaction of the Department of Trade and his appointment has been certified by the Department. The Department may refuse to certify the appointment if—

1. it was not made in good faith by a majority of the creditors voting;
2. the person appointed is not fit to act as trustee, *e.g.* because he has been previously removed from the office of trustee for misconduct;
3. the proposed trustee's connection with or relation to the bankrupt or his estate or any particular creditor makes it difficult for him to act with impartiality in the interests of the creditors generally, *e.g.* if he has acted as trustee under a deed executed by the debtor within three months of the petition (*Re Mardon* [1896] 1 Q.B. 140).

If the Department refuses to consent to the appointment they must, if so requested by a majority of the creditors, notify their objection to the High Court, who will decide on its validity (s. 19 (3)).

When the appointment is certified, the Department advertises it in the *London Gazette*, and the trustee must advertise his appointment in a local paper (r. 331).

Committee of inspection (s. 20)

The creditors may appoint a committee of inspection to superintend the trustee. Where a committee is appointed its consent is necessary to enable the trustee to do certain things. The trustee may, however, act without a committee being appointed; in such a case the necessary consent is given by the Department of Trade.

The committee consists of not more than five nor less than three persons who are creditors or persons to whom a creditor has given or intends to give a general proxy or power of attorney.

Every creditor must have proved his debt before he can be a member himself or give a proxy to enable another person to be a member.

The committee meets at least once a month—more often if required—and a majority must be present to form a quorum.

A person ceases to be a member of the committee if he—
1. resigns;
2. becomes bankrupt or compounds with his creditors;
3. is absent from five consecutive meetings;
4. is removed by an ordinary resolution of the creditors.

A member of the committee is in a fiduciary position and so cannot buy any of the property of the bankrupt.

Annulling adjudication

An adjudication of bankruptcy may be annulled if—
1. a composition or scheme is accepted after adjudication (s. 21);
2. the debtor ought not to have been adjudicated bankrupt (s. 29);
3. the debts of the bankrupt are paid in full (s. 29).

As to 1, a composition or scheme may be accepted after adjudication under the same conditions as before adjudication, *i.e.* with the consent of a majority in number of the creditors and three-fourths in value, subject to the approval of the court. There is a similar provision for a fresh adjudication if the debtor fails to pay any instalment under the scheme.

As to 2 and 3, the power to annul an adjudication on the ground of payment in full is discretionary, and regard is paid to the conduct of the debtor and the interests of commercial and public morality. A release of debts without payment is not payment in full (*Re Keet* [1905] 2 K.B. 666).

On annulment, the property of the debtor vests in such person as the court may appoint, or, in default of appointment, in the debtor. Notice of the order of annulment must be inserted in the *London Gazette* and a local paper.

The word "debts" in section 29 extends to all debts properly proved in bankruptcy but does not cover provable debts which have not been so proved. So, an annulment on payment in full of the proved debts or on the ground that the debtor ought not to have been made bankrupt revives the right of a creditor, who did not prove, to sue the debtor as soon as the bankruptcy is annulled (*More* v. *More* [1962] Ch. 424).

Summary of proceedings up to adjudication

1. Act of bankruptcy.
2. Presentation of petition within three months.
3. Receiving order.
    Official receiver becomes receiver of the debtor's property.
4. Debtor's statement of affairs.
5. First meeting of creditors.
    Decision taken as to whether composition to be accepted or debtor to be made bankrupt.
    If the latter, trustee and committee of inspection appointed.
6. Public examination of debtor unless dispensed with. Not to be concluded until after first meeting of creditors.
7. Adjudication order.

SELECT BIBLIOGRAPHY

Books

G. H. L. Fridman, I. Hicks and E. C. Johnson, *Bankruptcy Law and Practice* (1970).
Halsbury's Laws of England (4th ed., 1973), vol. 3, "Bankruptcy."

Reports

Report of the Committee on Bankruptcy Law and Deeds of Arrangement Law Amendment Cmnd. 221 (1957) and *Bankruptcy—A Report by Justice* (1975).

CHAPTER 30

DEBTS PROVABLE AND PROPERTY DIVISIBLE[1]

Debts Provable

Before a creditor is entitled to any share in the property of the bankrupt he must first prove his debt. Debts which are provable in bankruptcy are "all debts and liabilities, present or future, certain or contingent, to which the debtor is subject at the date of the receiving order, or to which he may become subject before his discharge by reason of any obligation incurred before the date of the receiving order" (s. 30 (3)). No debt is provable unless the obligation to pay it was incurred before the date of the receiving order.

Although a contingent creditor can prove in the bankruptcy of his debtor, a surety who has not paid off the principal creditor cannot prove in the bankruptcy of the principal debtor, unless the principal creditor has renounced his right to lodge a proof himself, while preserving his rights against the surety (*Re Fenton* [1931] 1 Ch. 85). Consequently, if the principal creditor has already lodged a proof the surety cannot also prove, because there would then be two proofs in the bankruptcy in respect of the same debt (*Re Oriental Commercial Bank* (1871) L.R. 7 Ch. 99). When a surety for a debt has become bankrupt, the creditor may prove for the whole of the debt due at the date of the receiving order, notwithstanding that he may have subsequently received sums from some source other than the principal debtor—as, for example, a co-surety—provided that he does not recover more than 100 pence in the pound (*Re Houlder* [1929] 1 Ch. 205). Again, an annuity payable to a woman during her life, but subject to determination on her marrying again, may be proved for (*Re Blakemore* (1877) 5 Ch.D. 372).

In the case of a contingent debt the trustee must estimate the value of the contingent liability. If the creditor is aggrieved he may appeal to the court, which may itself value the liability. If, in the opinion of the court, the liability cannot be fairly estimated, the debt will not be provable in the bankruptcy (s. 30).

---

[1] References in this chapter are to the Bankruptcy Act 1914 unless the contrary is expressed.

There **cannot** be proved in bankruptcy—

1. Demands in the nature of unliquidated damages arising otherwise than by reason of a contract, promise or breach of trust. Such demands can be proved against the estate of a deceased insolvent (Law Reform (Miscellaneous Provisions) Act 1934, s. 1). This covers damages for tort, such as personal injuries. If the damages have become liquidated by judgment, award or compromise, they will be provable generally.

2. Arrears of alimony or maintenance payable by a debtor to his wife which accrued before the making of a receiving order against the debtor. The reason for this is that such arrears are under the control of the court and it is entirely at the discretion of the court how far arrears shall be enforced (*James* v. *James* [1964] P. 303).

3. Debts contracted by any person after notice of any available act of bankruptcy (s. 30).

Mutual dealings (s. 31)

To prevent a creditor from paying his debt in full while only receiving a dividend in respect of the debt owed him by the bankrupt, it is provided that where there have been mutual credits, mutual debts or other mutual dealings between a debtor and one of his creditors, an account shall be taken of what is due from one to the other, and the balance of the account and no more shall be paid or claimed.

A company's sales representatives who were independent contractors were supplied by the company with goods for sale to customers. When the company became insolvent, it owed C, one of its sales representatives, £246 in commission and money held in his name. *Held*, there were "mutual dealings" between the company and C under section 31 of the Bankruptcy Act 1914 (which, by virtue of s. 317 of the Companies Act 1948, applied to the winding up of an insolvent company) and C was entitled to a set-off with the money received by him on behalf of the company and the goods held by him for the purpose of selling them to the customers: *Rolls Razor Ltd.* v. *Cox* [1967] 1 Q.B. 552.

No creditor can claim the benefit of any set-off if he had, at the time of giving credit to the debtor, notice of an available act of bankruptcy. There can be no set-off unless the debts are due in the same right. On the other hand it is not possible to contract out of the statutory right of set-off conferred by section 31 if it applies. *National Westminster Bank Ltd.* v. *Halesowen Presswork and Assemblies Ltd.* [1972] A.C. 785, see p. 121, *ante*.

In the winding up of a company, the liquidator sought to set off against a debt due by the company to a creditor a debt due to the company by a firm in which the creditor was a partner. *Held*, he could not do so, as the several debt of the partner could not be set off against the joint debt of the firm: *Re Pennington & Owen Ltd.* [1925] Ch. 825.

A contingent liability can be set off against a liquidated amount.

The holder of a life policy in an insurance company mortgaged the policy to the issuing company. On the company's going into liquidation the policy holder claimed to set off the value of the policy against his mortgage debt. *Held*, he was entitled to do so: *Re City Life Assurance Co. Ltd.* [1926] Ch. 191.

Proof of debts

Debts should be proved as soon as may be after the receiving order by delivering or sending through the post in a pre-paid letter to the official receiver or, if a trustee has been appointed, to the trustee—

    (a) in any case in which the official receiver or trustee so requires, an affidavit verifying the debt;

    (b) in any other case, an unsworn claim to the debt (s. 5 (1) of the Insolvency Act 1976).

The official receiver or trustee examines every proof and may call for the vouchers specified, and then within 28 days he must in writing admit it, reject it, or require further evidence in support of it. If he rejects it, he must state his reasons in writing, and the creditor may then, within 21 days, appeal to the court.

Secured creditors

A secured creditor is one who holds some security for his debt, such as a mortgage of some part of the debtor's property or a bill of sale on his goods. He must disclose his security in his proof, otherwise he will lose the benefit of his security by having to surrender it to the trustee for the general body of creditors (Bankruptcy (Amendment) Act 1926, s. 11).

The court in such a case may grant relief if satisfied that the omission has arisen from inadvertence.

A secured creditor may—

1. Realise his security and prove for the balance due to him after deducting the amount realised.

2. Surrender his security to the trustee and prove for the whole debt.

3. Value his security and rank for dividend in respect of the balance due after deducting the value of his security.

If a secured creditor has valued his security the trustee may (a) redeem the security at that value, or (b) require the security to be sold. The creditor may, on the other hand, serve notice in writing on the trustee requiring him to elect whether or not he will exercise either of these powers, and if the trustee does not within six months signify his intention to elect, he loses his right to exercise the powers.

If the creditor has made a mistake in the valuation of his security he may amend it by application to the court. If he subsequently realises his security, the amount realised must be substituted for the amount in the proof.

Preferential debts (s. 33 as amended)

The costs and charges of the bankruptcy proceedings, including the petitioning creditor's costs and the trustee's remuneration, are payable out of the estate in priority to the debts in the order set out in rule 115. Subject to the payment of these charges, the estate must be applied in payment of the following debts in priority to all other debts—

1. Rates payable within a year of the receiving order, and taxes assessed up to April 5 next before that date and not exceeding one year's assessment.

The Crown need not choose the last year, but may claim preferential payment for any one year before the receiving order: *Re Pratt* [1951] Ch. 225.

2. Wages or salary of a clerk or servant, whether or not earned wholly or in part by way of commission, and wages of a labourer or workman, whether payable for time or for piece work, in respect of services rendered to the bankrupt during four months before the date of the receiving order not exceeding £800. Included within this figure are guarantee payments, remuneration on suspension on medical grounds, payment for time off and remuneration under a protective award under the Employment Protection Act 1975 (ss. 22, 29, 57 (4), 61 (3), 63 and 101).

3. Accrued holiday remuneration payable to a clerk, servant, workman or labourer on the termination of his employment before or by the effect of the receiving order: Companies Act 1947, s. 115.

4. Contributions payable under the Social Security Act 1975 and the Social Security Pensions Act 1975 during 12 months before the date of the receiving order. This also includes redundancy fund contributions.

5. Sums due to the Crown for income tax deducted by the bankrupt under the "pay as you earn" system for the twelve months before the date of the receiving order (Finance Act 1952, s. 30).[1]

6. General betting duty, gaming licence duty and bingo duty due within 12 months before the date of the receiving order.

If the estate of a deceased person is administered in bankruptcy funeral and testamentary expenses have priority over all other debts.

These debts rank equally among themselves, and if the assets are insufficient to pay them in full they abate in equal proportions between themselves.

Special priorities are also given by the Friendly Societies Act 1974, and the Trustee Savings Banks Act 1969.

A person **apprenticed or articled** to the bankrupt may give notice in writing to the trustee and thereby terminate his contract. If he has paid any fee or premium, the trustee may, subject to an appeal to the court, return to him such part of the premium as he may think fit having regard to the length of time served and the general circumstances. Instead of repaying any such sum the trustee may, on the application of the apprentice or articled clerk, transfer the agreement of apprenticeship or clerkship (s. 34).

In the case of certain debts an employee can apply to the Secretary of State for payment and upon payment the Secretary of State is subrogated to the employee's rights and remedies (ss. 64 and 67 of the Employment Protection Act 1975). The relevant debts are up to eight weeks' arrears of pay; liabilities of the employer under section 1 of the Contracts of Employment Act 1972; up to six weeks' holiday pay in the previous 12 months; any basic award of compensation for unfair dismissal and any reasonable sum by way of reimbursement of any fee or premium paid by an apprentice or articled clerk.

Landlord

If a landlord has distrained on the bankrupt's goods within three months of the receiving order, the amount he has recovered is subject

---

[1] This provision is not repealed by the Income and Corporation Taxes Act 1970, see Sched. 16.

to a first charge in favour of the preferential creditors. If any money is paid under this charge the landlord becomes a preferential creditor himself to the extent of his loss (s. 33 (4)).

A landlord cannot distrain after the commencement of the bankruptcy for more than six months' rent accrued due prior to the bankruptcy. He can prove for any balance due to him after the distress (s. 35).

Other debts

Subject to the payment of the preferential debts and to the postponement of the deferred debts, all debts proved in the bankruptcy rank equally among themselves. Any surplus after paying the debts is applied in paying interest at four per cent. on all debts proved (s. 33).

Deferred debts

The following debts can only be paid after all other debts proved in the bankruptcy have been paid in full—

1. An advance of money to a person engaged or about to engage in business at a rate of interest varying with the profits (Partnership Act 1890, s. 3).

2. An amount due to the vendor of the goodwill of a business under a contract whereby the vendor is to receive from the purchaser a portion of the profits by way of annuity or otherwise (Partnership Act 1890, s. 3).

3. Loans by a wife to her husband or by a husband to his wife for the purpose of his or her trade or business (s. 36).

4. Interest exceeding five per cent. under a moneylending contract.

Subsequent bankruptcy (s. 39)

If a second or subsequent receiving order is made against a bankrupt, the trustee in the last preceding bankruptcy is to be deemed a creditor in respect of any unsatisfied balance of debts. He can accordingly prove in the subsequent bankruptcy. If the subsequent receiving order is followed by an adjudication of bankruptcy, then—

1. Property acquired by the bankrupt since his last adjudication which had not been distributed among his creditors in his last bankruptcy vests in the trustee in the subsequent bankruptcy.

2. On notice being received by the trustee of a subsequent receiving order, the trustee must transfer all property acquired by the bankrupt since the last adjudication to the trustee in the subsequent bankruptcy (Bankruptcy (Amendment) Act 1926).

Dividends

The trustee must distribute dividends with all convenient speed, subject to the retention of sums necessary for the costs of administration. He must distribute all money in hand, after making provision for disputed claims, all necessary expenses and the claims of creditors residing at such a distance as to prevent them from having had time to tender their proofs.

The first dividend must be distributed within four months of the first meeting of creditors, unless the committee of inspection are satisfied that there is good reason for postponing it, and subsequent dividends at intervals of not more than six months (s. 62).

Before declaring a dividend, the trustee must give notice of his intention to the Department of Trade and to all creditors mentioned in the bankrupt's statement who have not proved their debts. Notice of his intention is also gazetted. After declaring a dividend, the trustee must send to each creditor who has proved a notice showing the amount of the dividend and when and how it is payable, and a statement giving particulars of the estate (s. 62).

If a creditor has not proved before the declaration of a dividend he may be paid the dividend he would have received out of any money in the hands of the trustee, but he cannot disturb the distribution of a dividend declared before he proved his debt (s. 65).

The final dividend is declared when all the bankrupt's property has been realised. Before declaring it, the trustee must give notice to all creditors whose proofs he has not admitted that if they do not, within the time limited by the notice, establish their claims to the satisfaction of the court, he will proceed to make a final dividend without regard to their claims (s. 67).

Any surplus remaining after payment of all the creditors in full with interest and of the cost of the bankruptcy is the property of the bankrupt (s. 69).

The trustee cannot be sued for not paying a dividend, but the court may, in a proper case, order him to pay it (s. 68).

Bankruptcy of partnerships

A receiving order may be made against a firm, but it operates as if it were a receiving order against each partner in the firm. The partners submit a statement of the partnership affairs and each partner submits a statement of his separate affairs. The first meeting of creditors is attended by the joint and the separate creditors, and the joint creditors may agree to accept a composition while the separate creditors refuse to do so and vice versa. Only one trustee is appointed for the joint estate and the separate estates, but the joint creditors and each set of separate creditors may appoint their own committee of inspection.

The joint estate is applicable in the first instance in payment of the joint debts and the separate estates in payment of the separate debts. A joint creditor is not entitled to receive any dividend out of the separate estate until the separate creditors have been paid in full. Any surplus of the separate estates is dealt with as part of the joint estate. Any surplus of the joint estate is dealt with as part of each partner's separate estate in proportion to each partner's interest in the joint estate.

When joint and separate estates are being administered, dividends of the joint and separate properties are declared together, unless the Department of Trade otherwise directs (s. 63 (see p. 222, *ante*)).

A person jointly liable with the bankrupt may not prove so as to compete with outside creditors. Therefore a retired partner cannot prove in the bankruptcy of the continuing partners in competition with joint creditors of the old firm. This rule, however, has no application where—

1. there are no proofs by creditors in the old firm. The mere possibility there may be proofs is not enough (*Ex p. Andrews* (1884) 25 Ch.D. 505);
2. the debt of the creditor of the old firm is set off by a larger debt due from him to the firm, so that he is not in fact a creditor at all (*Re Douglas* [1930] 1 Ch. 342).

One partner's claim against another in respect of a joint liability will be postponed to the creditors of the firm for interest.

H and C were partners. H was adjudicated bankrupt and C then paid off the firm's overdraft. H's separate creditors were paid in full, leaving £3,025 for the firm's creditors and C. £1,250 was due to the firm's creditors and £1,540 to C, but, if these were paid in full, the assets would be insufficient to pay interest, amounting to £450, to the separate creditors and £90 to the joint creditors. *Held*, the joint and separate creditors were entitled to receive interest in full before any payment was made to C: *Re Howes* [1934] 1 Ch. 49.

Bankruptcy of limited partnership

A receiving order made against a limited partnership operates as a receiving order against each general partner. The Bankruptcy Act 1914 applies to limited partnerships as if they were general partnerships (s. 127).

In the bankruptcy of a limited partnership, the partnership assets are applied (1) in discharging the partnership debts, (2) in repaying the actual contributions of the limited partners, (3) in discharging the separate debts of the general partners (*Re Barnard* [1932] 1 Ch. 269).

PROPERTY DIVISIBLE

On bankruptcy a debtor's property becomes liable to be divided among his creditors. In certain circumstances, however, property not belonging to the bankrupt may be divisible among his creditors, while, not all his property may be so divisible.

The following property is **divisible** amongst the bankrupt's creditors (s. 38)—

1. All property belonging to the bankrupt at the commencement of the bankruptcy.

2. All property acquired by or devolving on him before his discharge.

3. The capacity to exercise powers over property which the bankrupt might have exercised for his own benefit, except the right of nomination to a vacant ecclesiastical benefice.

4. Goods in the bankrupt's reputed ownership.

5. Property comprised in certain voluntary settlements made by the bankrupt (s. 42).

6. Property used by the bankrupt to give a fraudulent preference to any of his creditors (s. 44).

The following property is **not divisible** amongst the bankrupt's creditors—

1. Property held by the bankrupt on trust for any other person. Money in a solicitor's client's account comes under this head (*Re a Solicitor* [1952] 1 All E.R. 133).

2. The tools (if any) of his trade and the necessary wearing apparel and bedding of himself, his wife and children to an inclusive value of £250 (s. 38).

3. Rights of action in respect of personal injuries or of annoyance or injury to the personal feelings of the bankrupt where his property is not injured (*Rose* v. *Buckett* [1901] 2 K.B. 449, contracts involving the bankrupt's personal skill).

1. Property belonging to the bankrupt at the commencement of the bankruptcy

The property of the bankrupt at the "commencement of the bankruptcy" passes to the trustee in the condition in which the bankrupt had it, subject to all charges and other incidents affecting it.

A deserted wife continuing to live in the matrimonial home is not in the technical sense a licensee; her right to remain in occupation is purely personal as against her husband and does not bind his trustee in bankruptcy (*National Provincial Bank Ltd.* v. *Hastings Car Mart Ltd.* [1965] A.C. 1175). But by the Matrimonial Homes Act 1967, s. 2, a spouse's right to occupation is made a charge on the estate or interest of the spouse who owns the house; this charge is brought to an end on death or termination of the marriage for another reason unless the court orders otherwise. The charge is, however, void against the husband's trustee in bankruptcy (s. 2 (5) Matrimonial Homes Act 1967 and s. 18 and Sched. 3, para, 8 (1) of the Land Charges Act 1972).

The "commencement of the bankruptcy" is the first act of bankruptcy committed by the bankrupt in the three months immediately preceding the presentation of the bankruptcy petition (s. 37). Accordingly, payments made to the bankrupt after the commencement of the bankruptcy are not a good discharge to the person making them, unless they come within the protected transactions, and property which the bankrupt owned between the date of bankruptcy and the receiving order passes to his trustee in bankruptcy, notwithstanding that he may have assigned or parted with some of it. This is called the **doctrine of relation back.**

P consulted a solicitor about his affairs, and paid him £15 for future costs. The solicitor then called a meeting of P's creditors, and prepared a deed of assignment, which P executed. Within three months P was adjudicated bankrupt. *Held*, the solicitor could not retain any part of the £15 for costs incurred after the execution of the deed: *Re Pollitt* [1893] 1 Q.B. 455.

The bankrupt's contracts are not determined by the bankruptcy: the rights pass to the trustee if not disclaimed or rescinded, subject to the rights of the persons with whom the bankrupt has contracted, and to the rights of third persons which have been created in respect of them. But where the personal skill or conduct of the bankrupt forms a material part of the consideration, the contract does not pass (*Lucas* v. *Moncrieff* (1905) 21 T.L.R. 683, contract to publish a book). The trustee has power to disclaim contracts.

Property may be given to or settled on a person with a provision that his interest shall cease on bankruptcy. Care must be used to employ proper words of limitation to ensure that it does pass away from him in the event of his bankruptcy. In such a case there is then no property which is capable of passing to the trustee. An owner cannot settle his own property on himself, subject to such a provision (*Mackintosh* v. *Pogose* [1895] 1 Ch. 505).

The doctrine of relation back of the trustee's title is subject to important exceptions. These are—

1. Where an execution against a debtor's property has been completed by seizure and sale of the property before (a) the date of the receiving order, and (b) notice of the presentation of a bankruptcy petition or of any available act of bankruptcy, it is valid as against the debtor's trustee in bankruptcy (s. 40). If, therefore, there is an act of bankruptcy on September 8, presentation of a bankruptcy petition on November 11, execution is completed on November 11 without notice of either of them, and the receiving order is made on December 14 followed by adjudication, the judgment creditor can retain the benefit of the execution (*Re Love* [1951] 2 All E.R. 1016).

When the execution is for a debt exceeding £250, the sheriff must retain the proceeds of sale for 14 days, and if, within that time, he receives notice of any bankruptcy petition on which a receiving order is subsequently made, he must hand over the proceeds to the trustee (s. 41). The rights given by sections 40 and 41 may be set aside by the court.

2. **Protected transactions.** The following transactions are protected, *i.e.* are valid as against the trustee in bankruptcy although they take place after the commencement of the bankruptcy—

    (a)—(i) Any payment *by* the bankrupt to any of his creditors and any conveyance or assignment *by* the bankrupt for valuable consideration.

   (ii) Any payment or delivery *to* the bankrupt.
   (iii) Any contract by or with the bankrupt for valuable
       consideration (s. 45).
These are valid as against the trustee if made—
   (A) before the date of the receiving order; and
   (B) without notice of any available act of bankruptcy.

S had two banking accounts, No. 1 overdrawn and covered by a
guarantee, and No. 2 not overdrawn. After the presentation of the
petition, S obtained a loan from a moneylender, paid off the overdraft on
No. 1 and released the guarantor. The bank had no knowledge of the
presentation of the petition. The trustee claimed the amount of the
payment into No. 1 under the doctrine of relation back. *Held*, the bank
was protected by section 45: *Re Seymour* [1937] 1 Ch. 668.

X owed a bank £1,352. The bank received a cheque of £3,000 payable
to X for collection and credited her account with that amount. On the
following day, November 16, the bank received the proceeds of the
cheque, being unaware that on the same day a receiving order was made
against X founded on an act of bankruptcy committed on October 5.
Held, the bank's lien arose out of a contract with the bankrupt for valuable
consideration (s. 45) and the bank was, by virtue of its lien, a secured
creditor: *Re Keever, ex p. The Trustee* v. *Midland Bank Ltd.* [1967] Ch.
182.

(b) Any payment of money or delivery of property *to* a bankrupt
is valid as against the trustee if made—
   (i) before the date of the receiving order; and
   (ii) without notice of the presentation of a bankruptcy petition;
       and
   (iii) either pursuant to the ordinary course of business or other-
       wise bona fide (s. 46).
In none of these cases is there any protection for transactions
between the making of the receiving order and the adjudication
(*Re Wigzell* [1921] 2 K.B. 835). If, however, the receiving order
has not been gazetted and a person in possession of the bankrupt's
property pays it to a third party without notice of the receiving
order, the trustee in bankruptcy can only recover the money from
that person if it is not reasonably practicable to obtain it from the
third party (Bankruptcy (Amendment) Act 1926, s. 4).
   3. A purchaser of the legal estate in land in good faith and for
money or money's worth without notice of an available act of
bankruptcy is not deemed to have notice of a bankruptcy petition
unless it is registered (Land Charges Act 1972, s. 5 (8)). Such a

purchaser is therefore protected if he completes his purchase before—

(i) the date of the receiving order; and

(ii) the date of registration of the petition.

If the bankrupt is insured against third party risks, his rights against the insurer vest, on bankruptcy, in the third party (see p. 412, *ante*).

2. Property acquired by or devolving on the bankrupt before his discharge

All property belonging to the bankrupt at the commencement of the bankruptcy or which he acquires between that date and his adjudication vests in the trustee, and no claim is necessary to complete the trustee's title. Property acquired *after adjudication* is divisible among the creditors, but the trustee must intervene and claim it. The trustee's right to claim such property is subject to the following restrictions—

1. The personal earnings of the bankrupt belong to the trustee, except such part of them as is necessary for the maintenance of the bankrupt and his family (*Re Roberts* [1900] 1 Q.B. 122).

W was adjudicated bankrupt. He later earned a salary, out of which he had saved £655 at the date of his death. He had also incurred debts for £300. *Held*, in so far as the debts were for necessaries to enable W to earn his salary, they were payable in full out of the £655. "The trustee, if the bankrupt was alive, could not claim anything more than that which was over after the bankrupt had provided for what was reasonably necessary, having regard to his occupation and station": *per* Tomlin J. in *Re Walter* [1929] 1 Ch. 647.

2. When the bankrupt is a beneficed clergyman, the trustee may apply for a sequestration of the profits of the benefice but must allow the bankrupt, if he performs his duties, such stipend as the bishop may allow (s. 50).

3. When the bankrupt is an officer in H.M. Forces or is in the civil service, the trustee receives such part of the bankrupt's salary as the head of the department under which the pay is enjoyed may allow (s. 51 (1)).

4. When the bankrupt is in receipt of a salary or income or is entitled to any half pay, or pension, or to any compensation by the Treasury, the court may order any part to be paid to the trustee (s. 51 (2)). However, income from the life interest of a bankrupt

under his father's will is not comprised in the term "income" in the subsection (*Re Cohen, A Bankrupt* [1961] Ch. 246). Further, a bankrupt's entitlement to a return of contributions under a teachers superannuation scheme is not "compensation" within the subsection (*Re Duckett* [1964] Ch. 398).

5. The trustee cannot claim any property, acquired by the bankrupt after adjudication, from a person who has acquired it in good faith and for value before the trustee's claim is made (s. 47). The property may be acquired in good faith, even if the purchaser knows of the bankruptcy (*Cohen* v. *Mitchell* (1890) 25 Q.B.D. 262).

Dealings between a bankrupt and his banker are also protected under section 47 when they take place *after* adjudication, but there is no protection for transactions between the receiving order and adjudication otherwise than under section 4 of the Bankruptcy (Amendment) Act 1926 (see p. 508, *ante*).

3. The capacity to exercise the bankrupt's powers over property

This calls for no explanation.

4. Goods in the bankrupt's reputed ownership

All goods at the commencement of the bankruptcy—
1. in the possession, order or disposition of the bankrupt in his trade or business;
2. with the consent of the true owner;
3. under such circumstances that he is reputed the owner thereof;

pass to the trustee in bankruptcy (s. 38 (*c*)).

The term "goods" includes all chattels personal (s. 167), but not choses in action, except debts growing due to the bankrupt in the course of his trade or business. If the bankrupt has, prior to his bankruptcy, assigned any of his book debts, the assignee, to avoid the inference of reputed ownership, should give notice of the assignment to the debtors (*Re Collins* [1925] Ch. 556).

The consent of the true owner of the goods must be given to the use of those goods in the bankrupt's business, and not merely to use generally.

L owned a motor-car which he let on hire to P. P used the car for business purposes, but L did not know this. *Held*, P's trustee in bankruptcy could not claim the car: *Lamb* v. *Wright & Co.* [1924] 1 K.B. 857.

The consent must also be to possession under circumstances necessarily leading to an inference of ownership (*Re Watson & Co.* [1904] 2 K.B. 753). But where goods are in the bankrupt's possession and used by him in his business, such an inference does arise, in the absence of special circumstances (*Re Kaufmann* [1923] 2 Ch. 89). A builder is the reputed owner of building materials in his yard but not of loose material on the site (*Re Fox* [1948] Ch. 407). Possession by the bankrupt's agent is sufficient.

Goods in an absolute bill of sale which is duly registered are not in the reputed ownership of the grantor (Bills of Sale Act 1878, s. 20). If, however, the bill of sale is by way of security, registration will not of itself prevent the trustee in bankruptcy from claiming the goods.

Goods may be within the reputed ownership of the bankrupt, although they are comprised in a hire-purchase agreement, but the service of a default notice under the Consumer Credit Act 1974 negatives the owner's consent to their being in the bankrupt's possession. (See Bankruptcy Act 1914, s. 38 A (1) added by Sched. 4 of the Consumer Credit Act.) Also the prevalence of hire purchase in relation to many classes of goods may operate to rebut reputed ownership. *Halsbury's Laws of England* (4th ed.), Vol. 3, para. 657 states ". . . the hire-purchase system may now have extended so far as to deprive the doctrine of reputed ownership of most of its value to a trustee in bankruptcy."

An established custom in a trade for a trader to have the goods of others in his possession negatives the reputation of ownership; *e.g.* the custom of hotel-keepers to hire the furniture of their hotels is so notorious that the hotel-keeper does not get the reputation of ownership (*Re Parker* (1885) 14 Q.B.D. 636). Again, the stock of a farmer is not in his reputed ownership, as it is well established that he might have it on a contract of agistment (*Re James* (1907) 24 T.L.R. 15). A trade custom for wholesale dealers in antique furniture to send articles of furniture to retail dealers "upon sale or return" is notorious so as to exclude the operation of the doctrine of reputed ownership (*Re Ford* [1929] 1 Ch. 134).

If goods are taken by the trustee as being in the reputed ownership of the bankrupt, the true owner can prove in the bankruptcy for their value (*Re Button* [1907] 2 K.B. 180).

5. Property comprised in certain voluntary settlements (s. 42)

All settlements of property which are not made—
1. before and in consideration of marriage; or
2. in favour of a purchaser or incumbrancer in good faith and for value; or
3. for the wife or children of the settlor in respect of property which has accrued to the settlor after marriage in right of his wife;

are void on the bankruptcy of the settlor within **two** years after the date of the settlement. If the bankruptcy occurs after two years but within **ten** years, the settlement is void, unless it can be proved that—
1. the settlor was, at the time of the settlement, able to pay his debts without the aid of the property settled;
2. the interest of the settlor in the property passed to the trustee of the settlement on the execution thereof.

A settlement in this connection means that there should be an intention on the part of the settlor that the property should be retained. For example, a gift of diamonds by a husband to a wife will be a settlement (*Re Vansittart* [1893] 1 Q.B. 181), but a gift of money to a son to enable him to commence business is not a settlement (*Re Player* (1885) 15 Q.B.D. 682).

To fall within the marriage exception the settlement must have been conditioned only to take effect on the marriage taking place and be for the purpose of or with view to encouraging or facilitating the marriage. In *Re Densham* [1975] 3 All E.R. 726 it was held that an implied agreement that a wife should have a half share in the matrimonial home was void under section 42 since it did not fall within the exceptions. The wife, however, had an interest in the property based on her contributions which amounted to less than half.

Property coming to a husband by reason of his wife's dying intestate is property accruing to him in right of his wife (*Re Bower Williams* [1927] 1 Ch. 441).

A purchaser for value of the property comprised in a voluntary settlement who buys in good faith and without notice of any act of bankruptcy will have a good title as against the trustee in bankruptcy, although he knows that his title is derived through a voluntary settlement (*Re Carter & Kenderdine's Contract* [1897] 1 Ch. 776). Valuable consideration here means a *quid pro quo*. However, it does not have to replace anything in the bankrupt's estate for it may be something which he has bargained shall be provided for a third party, nor does it have to be equal to what is taken out. Where property subject to a mortgage is transferred by a debtor a covenant by the transferee to indemnify the debtor against liability under the mortgage was held not to be valuable consideration (*Re Windle* [1975] 3 All E.R. 970), but where the equity of redemption has no real value then such a covenant may constitute valuable consideration (*Re Charters* [1923] 3 B. & C.R. 94).

Covenants in marriage settlements to settle after-acquired property, not being property accruing to the settlor in right of the settlor's wife or husband, **are void** as to property which has not been settled under the covenant at the commencement of the bankruptcy.

Payments made and property transferred under such covenants before the commencement of the bankruptcy are void as against the trustees unless made—

1. more than two years before the commencement of the bankruptcy; or
2. at a date when the settlor could pay his debts without the aid of the property settled; or
3. in pursuance of a contract to transfer property expected to come to the settlor on the death of a particular person named in the contract and made within three months after the property came under the control of the settlor (s. 42).

The persons entitled under any such covenant can prove in the bankruptcy for their loss, but their claim is postponed until all the creditors for value have been paid in full.

Assignments of book debts, existing or future, by a person engaged in trade or business are void as against his trustee in bankruptcy as to debts not paid at the commencement of the bankruptcy, unless they are registered under the Bills of Sale Act 1878. But an assignment of (1) book debts due at the date of the assignment from specified debtors; (2) debts growing due under specified contracts; (3) books debts included in a transfer of a business made bona fide and for value or in any assignment of assets for the benefit of creditors generally, is not void (s. 43). In cases (1) and (2), however, the debts will be in the possession, order and disposition of the bankrupt unless notice of the assignment is given to the debtor (*Re Neal* [1914] 2 K.B. 910).

6. Property used by the bankrupt to give a fraudulent preference to any of his creditors

If a person unable to pay his debts as they become due makes any payment or any transfer of his property to a creditor in the six months prior to his becoming bankrupt, with a view of giving that creditor a preference over the other creditors, the payment or transfer is void (s. 44, as amended by the Companies Act 1947, s. 115).

Whether any transaction constituted a fraudulent preference or not depends on the circumstances of the case, but a fraudulent preference must satisfy the following conditions—

1. There must be an intention on the part of the debtor to prefer the creditor. The mere fact that the payment has the effect of preferring him is not sufficient.

The intention may be inferred from the circumstances.

K and his wife were sole directors and shareholders in K, Ltd., which had an overdraft at the bank guaranteed by K. On May 12, K was told the company was insolvent. Between May 12 and 21, payments were made into the bank extinguishing the overdraft. On May 23, a resolution for winding up was passed. *Held*, the payments made after May 12 constituted a fraudulent preference: *Re Kushler Ltd.* [1943] Ch. 248.

2. The payment or transfer must be the voluntary act of the debtor. It must not be done under pressure by the creditor (*Sharp* v. *Jackson* [1899] A.C. 419).

If a payment is made to correct an error, the debtor believing himself under an obligation to make the payment, there is no fraudulent preference: as where a debtor shortly before his bankruptcy assigned his furniture by a bill of sale to his wife to secure advances bona fide made by her, and afterwards discovered that the bill of sale was void for some technical defect and issued another a fortnight before the receiving order was made, it was held that the second bill of sale was valid (*Re Tweedale* [1892] 2 Q.B. 216).

A payment is not a fraudulent preference if it is made—

1. Under a belief that legal proceedings will be taken or that the debtor is under a legal obligation to make it (*Re Vautin* [1900] 2 Q.B. 325).

2. To repay trust money misapplied by the debtor (*Ex p. Taylor, re Goldsmid* (1886) 18 Q.B.D. 295).

3. To save the debtor from exposure or criminal proceedings.

4. To revive a debt barred by limitation (*Re Lane* (1889) 23 Q.B.D. 74).

5. By a trader in the ordinary course of business to enable him to carry on business although he knows he is insolvent (*Re Clay & Sons* (1895) 3 Mans. 31).

The burden of proof is on the trustee in bankruptcy to show that the dominant motive of the debtor was to prefer the creditor. The creditor's motive is immaterial.

If a creditor has received property from the bankrupt under circumstances making it a fraudulent preference and afterwards transfers the property to a third party, the third party, if he takes in good faith and for value, will get a good title (s. 44 (2)). The burden of proving good faith is upon the person seeking to establish it.

Discovery of the property of the debtor

The trustee has extensive powers of obtaining discovery of the debtor's property.

1. The statement of affairs must be submitted by the debtor within seven days of the receiving order. This must disclose all his assets.

2. The public examination (if held) is an examination into the debtor's affairs and property. He can be compelled to answer on oath all questions tending to disclose his assets.

3. The debtor must, if required, attend meetings of his creditors and make a full disclosure of his property to them. If he fails to make such disclosure or to deliver his property to the trustee, he is guilty of contempt of court and may be punished accordingly (s. 22).

4. A private examination on oath may be ordered by the court of the debtor, his wife, any person known or suspected to have in his possession any of the property of the debtor, or any person capable of giving information as to the debtor's affairs (s. 25). As a result of the examination, an order for the delivery up of property may be made. An order for a private examination may be made even after the bankrupt's discharge (*Re Coulson* [1934] Ch. 45); it can even be made after the bankrupt's discharge and subsequent death, in which case the order is made against the bankrupt's personal representatives (*Re a Debtor, ex p. Trustee of the Property of the Bankrupt* v. *Clegg* [1968] 1 W.L.R. 788). The purpose of such an examination is to enable the trustee to obtain information relevant

to the recovery of assets and the practice of keeping depositions off the file by means of a "stop order" is justified in cases where immediate publication of the information will be likely to jeopardise the overall purpose of the bankruptcy proceedings. Assuming the deposition to be notionally on the file a stranger to the bankruptcy will only be allowed to inspect and take copies in exceptional circumstances. The fact that the stranger has brought an action against some other party is not a sufficiently special circumstance (*Re Poulson ex parte Granada Television Ltd.* v. *Maudling* [1976] 1 W.L.R. 1023).

5. The court has power to order that, for a period not exceeding three months, letters and telegrams addressed to the debtor be directed to the official receiver or the trustee (s. 24).

Realisation of property

On the receiving order being made, the debtor's property passes to the official receiver, but after adjudication and on the appointment of a trustee it vests in the trustee. The trustee's certificate of appointment is deemed to be a conveyance or assignment of property for all purposes in which registration or enrolment are required (s. 53).

It is the trustee's duty to take possession as soon as may be of the property of the bankrupt. For the purpose of acquiring possession he is in the same position as if he were a receiver appointed by the High Court. He can transfer stock, shares in ships, shares, and choses in action to the same extent as the bankrupt could have done (s. 48).

Disclaimer (s. 54)

When any part of the bankrupt's property consists of—
   1. land burdened with onerous covenants;
   2. shares or stock in companies;
   3. unprofitable contracts; or
   4. property that is unsaleable or not readily saleable because it binds the owner to the performance of an onerous act or the payment of money;

the trustee may disclaim the property. The disclaimer must be made—
   1. In writing signed by the trustee.

2. Within 12 months of the first appointment of a trustee or such extension as the court may grant.

3. If the trustee was not aware of the property within a month of his appointment, within 12 months after he has become aware, or such extended period as the court may allow.

Disclaimer of leaseholds

Subject to important exceptions, a lease cannot be disclaimed without the leave of the court. Before granting leave the court may require notices to be served on persons interested and may impose terms and make orders as to the fixtures, tenant's improvements and other matters arising out of a tenancy (s. 54 (3)).

Any person claiming under the bankrupt in respect of the lease, whether as underlessee or mortgagee, may apply to the court for an order vesting the property in him, but the order will only be made—

1. subject to the same liabilities and obligations as the bankrupt was subject to under the lease at the date of the filing of the bankruptcy petition; or
2. if the court thinks fit, subject to the same liabilities and obligations as if the lease had been assigned to the person applying at that date.

The trustee may disclaim **without leave**—

1. Where the bankrupt has not sublet or charged the lease; and
   (a) the rent and value are less than £20 a year; or
   (b) the estate is being administered summarily; or
   (c) the trustee has served the lessor with notice of intention to disclaim, and the lessor has not within seven days given notice requiring the matter to be brought before the court.

2. Where the bankrupt has sublet or charged the lease, and the trustee has served the parties interested with notice of his intention to disclaim, and none of them have within 14 days required the matter to be brought before the court.

A disclaimer of leaseholds must be filed in court, and until it is filed it is inoperative.

The trustee cannot disclaim any property if notice in writing is served on him by a person interested requiring him to decide whether he will disclaim or not within 28 days and he does not disclaim within that time. In the case of a contract, if the trustee does not

disclaim within the time he is deemed to have adopted the contract
(s. 54 (4)).

Rescission of contracts

A person who is, as against the trustee, entitled to the benefit
or subject to the burden of a contract with the bankrupt may apply
to the court for an order rescinding the contract. The court may
grant rescission on such terms as it thinks fit, including the payment
of damages for breach of contract. Any damages ordered by the
court may be proved for in the bankruptcy (s. 54 (5)).

A person injured by the disclaimer of any property may—
1. prove for the damage he has suffered as a debt under
   the bankruptcy (s. 54 (8)).
2. apply to the court for an order vesting in him any disclaimed property in which he has an interest (s. 54 (6)).

Effect of disclaimer

A disclaimer operates to terminate the bankrupt's interest in
the property disclaimed as from the date of the disclaimer, and
discharges the trustee from personal liability in respect of the
property disclaimed as from the date when the property vested in
him (s. 54 (2)).

If the trustee does not disclaim property held by the bankrupt
under a lease or tenancy agreement, he will be personally liable for
rent due after his appointment.

> T leased a wharf to M for 21 years. M filed his petition on December 8,
> and C was appointed trustee on January 3. C never entered into possession
> of the wharf, but unsuccessfully tried to assign the lease. T served notice
> on C requiring him to disclaim, but C did not disclaim. T sued C for two
> quarters' rent, one due on December 25, and the other on March 25.
> *Held*, C was personally liable for the second quarter's rent, but not for the
> first, as it had accrued due before he became trustee: *Titterton* v. *Cooper*
> (1882) 9 Q.B.D. 473.

Even when a trustee does disclaim a tenancy, he will be personally
liable for the rates charged upon the premises during his occupation.

> A receiving order was made against a debtor on February 8, and he
> was later adjudicated bankrupt. He had a tenancy of a small dwelling-
> house, of which the trustee took possession until May. On June 1 the
> trustee disclaimed the tenancy. *Held*, the trustee was personally liable
> for the rates during the period of his occupation, because liability for

rates was not "a liability in respect of the property disclaimed," but a liability arising out of the trustee's voluntary occupation of the premises: *Re Lister* [1926] Ch. 149.

In both the last-mentioned cases the trustee will be entitled to an indemnity out of the bankrupt's estate.

Powers of the trustee

The trustee can, without any further permission, do the following acts—

1. Sell the bankrupt's property, by public auction or private contract, with power to transfer it to any person or company.

2. Give receipts which will effectually discharge the person making a payment to him.

3. Prove, rank, claim and draw a dividend in respect of any debt due to the bankrupt (s. 55).

With the permission of the committee of inspection the trustee can (s. 56)—

1. Carry on the bankrupt's business so far as is necessary for beneficially winding it up. He cannot, however, carry on business for any other purpose, *e.g.* to make a profit or to benefit the bankrupt, but if he does so under a guarantee for a third party he can enforce the guarantee, because his conduct is not necessarily contrary to the policy of the Bankruptcy Acts (*Clark* v. *Smith* [1940] 1 K.B. 126).

2. Bring and defend actions relating to the bankrupt's property.

3. Employ a solicitor or other agent to do any business which may be sanctioned by the committee.

4. Accept as the consideration for the sale of any property money payable at a future time subject to such security as the committee think fit.

5. Mortgage or pledge any part of the bankrupt's property to raise money for the payment of his debts.

6. Refer disputes to arbitration, and compromise any claims by or against the bankrupt on such terms as may be agreed on.

7. Divide in its existing form among the creditors, according to its estimated value, any property which from its peculiar nature or other special circumstances cannot be readily or advantageously sold.

The permission given by the committee of inspection must not be a general permission, but only a permission to do a particular thing.

In addition to the above powers the trustee may, with the permission of the committee of inspection—

1. appoint the bankrupt to carry on his business for the benefit of his creditors (s. 57);
2. make an allowance to the bankrupt for the support of himself and his family, or in consideration of his services if he is engaged in winding up his estate, but any such allowance may be reduced by the court (s. 58).

If a trustee has seized any property in the possession or on the premises of the bankrupt, and the property either belongs to another person or some other person has a claim against it, the trustee will not be liable for any loss the other person has sustained, unless in the opinion of the court he has been guilty of negligence (s. 61).

SELECT BIBLIOGRAPHY

Books

G. H. L. Fridman, I. Hicks and E. C. Johnson, *Bankruptcy Law and Practice* (1970).
Halsbury's Laws of England (4th ed., 1973), Vol. 3, "Bankruptcy."

Reports

Report of the committee on Bankruptcy Law and Deeds of Arrangement Law (*Amendment*) (Cmnd. 221).
Bankruptcy—A Report by Justice (1975).

CHAPTER 31

DISCHARGE FROM BANKRUPTCY[1]

THE **official receiver** is an official appointed by the Department of Trade; he is appointed for a particular district and is attached to the court; he is an officer of the court to which he is attached, and he has duties in relation to (1) the debtor's conduct, (2) the debtor's estate.

1. His duties as to the debtor's conduct are—
    (a) To investigate his conduct and to report to the court whether the debtor has committed any offence or has done any act which would justify the court in refusing, suspending or qualifying his discharge.
    (b) To take part in the debtor's public examination or if appropriate to apply for it to be dispensed with.
    (c) To assist in the prosecution of a fraudulent debtor.
    (d) To apply to the court where appropriate for rescission of an order for automatic discharge at any time before the fifth anniversary of the date of adjudication (*i.e.* before it takes effect).
    (e) To make an application to the court in respect of the adjudication of bankruptcy within 12 months after the fifth anniversary of the adjudication to enable the court to consider whether an undischarged bankrupt should be given his discharge.

2. His duties as to the debtor's property are—
    (a) Until the appointment of a trustee, to act as interim receiver and manager.
    (b) To summon and preside at the first meeting of creditors.
    (c) To issue forms of proxy for use at the meetings of creditors.
    (d) To report to the creditors any proposal made by the debtor to liquidate his affairs.
    (e) To advertise the receiving order and any other matters it may be necessary to advertise.
    (f) To act as trustee during any vacancy in the office of trustee.

[1] References in this chapter are to the Bankruptcy Act 1914 unless the contrary is expressed.

While acting as interim receiver or manager the official receiver has the same powers as a receiver and manager appointed by the High Court, but he must consult the wishes of the creditors (ss. 70–75 of the Bankruptcy Act 1914 and ss. 6 and 8 of the Insolvency Act 1976).

Special manager

If the nature of the debtor's business or the interests of the creditors generally require the appointment of a special manager, the official receiver may appoint one to act until a trustee is appointed. The appointment can only be made at the request of a creditor and if the official receiver is satisfied that the appointment is required.

The special manager must give security and account to the Department of Trade; he is remunerated as the creditors may by ordinary resolution determine; and his powers are such as are entrusted to him by the official receiver.

The trustee

The trustee must use his own discretion in the management of the estate and its distribution among the creditors. His discretion, however, is controlled and assisted in the following ways—

1. He must have regard to directions given by (a) the creditors in general meeting, and (b) the committee of inspection. In case of conflict, the creditors' directions override those of the committee of inspection.

2. He must summon meetings of the creditors (a) when the creditors by resolution direct him to do so, and (b) when one-sixth in value of the creditors request him to do so. He may summon meetings of creditors at any other time.

3. He may apply to the court for directions.

4. He must answer any inquiry made by the Department of Trade and his conduct generally is under the supervision of the Department (ss. 79–81).

Remuneration of trustee (s. 82)

The trustee's remuneration is fixed by an ordinary resolution of the creditors, or, if the creditors so resolve, by the committee of inspection. It takes the form of a commission or percentage on the amount realised by the trustee and on the amount distributed as dividend. The Department of Trade may fix the remuneration if—

1. one-fourth in number or value of the creditors dissent from the resolution; or
2. the bankrupt satisfies the Department that the remuneration is unnecessarily large.

The resolution should express what expenses the remuneration is to cover. If the trustee acts without remuneration he is allowed such expenses as the creditors, with the consent of the Department, approve.

The trustee must not, under any circumstances, accept any other benefit or share any part of his remuneration with any person who may be employed about a bankruptcy. Any arrangement by a trustee with a creditor to apply part of his remuneration to increase the creditor's dividend is illegal (*Farmers' Mart Ltd.* v. *Milne* [1915] A.C. 106).

Trustee's accounts

A trustee must keep accounts and must furnish a statement of accounts at any time if called upon by one-sixth of the creditors (s. 85). He must keep—

1. A record book, recording all minutes, proceedings and resolutions of creditors, and of the committee of inspection.
2. A cash book, containing receipts and payments made from day to day.
3. A trading account, when he carries on the business of the debtor.

These books may be inspected by the creditors or their agents (s. 86). The debtor has no right to inspect the record book (*Re Solomons* [1904] 2 K.B. 917).

The record book must be submitted to and the cash book audited by the committee of inspection not less than once in every three months. The trading account must be examined and certified by the committee not less than once a month. Six months after the making of the receiving order and every subsequent six months the cash book, with vouchers, must be transmitted to the Department of Trade for audit. A copy of the audited account is then filed with the registrar.

Once a year, and more often if required, the trustee must send to the Department a statement showing the proceedings in the bankruptcy (s. 87). He must also twice a year send an account of his receipts and payments to the Department. These may be required by the Secretary of State to be audited and copies are filed with the Department and the court. They are then open to the inspection of any creditor or of the bankrupt or of any person interested (s. 92 as amended by s. 2 of the Insolvency Act 1976).

The trustee must not pay any money received by him as trustee into his private banking account (s. 88). He must pay it into the Insolvency Services Account at the Bank of England, unless—

1. the Department of Trade, on the application of the committee of inspection, authorises him to make payments into a local bank;
2. the Department, where there is no committee of inspection, on the application of the trustee authorises him for special reasons to make payments into a local bank.

If the trustee retains for more than 10 days a sum exceeding £100 without satisfactorily explaining the retention to the Department he becomes liable to (a) pay interest at 20 per cent.; (b) lose his remuneration, and (c) be removed from his office (s. 89 as amended by Sched. 1 to the Insolvency Act 1976).

Any balance on the Insolvency Services Account which, in the opinion of the Department, is not required to answer demands in respect of bankrupts' estates is transferred to the Insolvency Services Investment Account and managed and invested in accordance with the provisions of the Insolvency Services (Accounting and Investments) Act 1970.

Vacation of office by trustee

A trustee may vacate his office by (1) resignation; (2) removal; (3) release.

1. Resignation is effected by calling a meeting of creditors and placing the resignation before them. The creditors may either accept it or reject it.

2. Removal (s. 95) is effected by an ordinary resolution of the creditors passed at the meeting called for that purpose. In addition, the Department of Trade has power to remove a trustee when—

(a) he is guilty of misconduct or fails to perform his duties under the Bankruptcy Act;
(b) his trusteeship is being needlessly protracted without any probable advantage to the creditors;

  (c) he is, by reason of illness or absence, incapable of performing his duties;

  (d) his connection with the bankrupt or any creditor makes it difficult for him to act with impartiality in the interest of the creditors generally;

  (e) he has previously been removed for misconduct.

The making of a receiving order against the trustee also vacates his office (s. 94).

3. Release is granted by the Department when the property of the bankrupt has been realised and the final dividend declared. To obtain a release, application must be made by the trustee. The Department then causes a report on his accounts to be prepared, and, after considering the report and any objections raised by any creditor, they grant or refuse the release. If the release is refused, the trustee may appeal to the High Court.

A release discharges the trustee from all liability in respect of any act done during his administration of the bankrupt's affairs (s. 93).

The discharge of the bankrupt

There are three procedures under which a bankrupt may be discharged. These are—

  (a) on his own application (s. 26 of the Bankruptcy Act 1914);

  (b) automatic discharge by the court on the conclusion of the public examination or the making of an order dispensing with it to take effect on the fifth anniversary of the date of adjudication (s. 7 of the Insolvency Act 1976); or

  (c) discharge on the application of the official receiver after the fifth anniversary of the date of adjudication (s. 8 of the Insolvency Act 1976).

Under section 26 of the Bankruptcy Act 1914 as amended by section 6 of the Insolvency Act 1976 the bankrupt may, at any time after adjudication, apply to the court for an order of discharge, but the application cannot be heard until the bankrupt's public examination is concluded or dispensed with.

The application is heard after 14 days' notice to the creditors, and the court may hear the official receiver, the trustee and any creditor. The court takes into account a report of the official receiver as to the bankrupt's conduct and affairs and may (s. 26 (2))—

  1. grant the discharge;

2. refuse the discharge;

3. suspend the discharge for a specified time; or

4. grant the discharge subject to any conditions as to the bankrupt's future earnings or property.

The discharge may be both conditional and suspensive.

In the cases set out below the court has a discretion to do one of four things, but cannot grant an unconditional discharge. The court may—

1. refuse the discharge; or

2. suspend it for such a period as the court thinks proper; or

3. suspend it until a dividend of not less than 50 pence in the pound is paid; or

4. require the bankrupt, as a condition of his discharge, to consent to judgment being entered against him for any part of the balance of debts proved against him.

The cases to which the foregoing apply are—

1. That the bankrupt's assets are not equal to 50 pence in the pound, unless this is due to circumstances for which he cannot justly be held responsible.

2. That the bankrupt has omitted to keep proper books of account in his business within three years of the bankruptcy.

3. That the bankrupt has continued to trade after knowing himself to be insolvent.

4. That he has contracted a debt provable in the bankruptcy without, at the time of contracting it, any reasonable expectation of being able to pay it.

5. That he has failed to account satisfactorily for any loss or deficiency of assets to meet his liabilities.

6. That he has brought on or contributed to his bankruptcy by rash and hazardous speculations, or by unjustifiable extravagance in living, or by gambling, or by culpable neglect of his business affairs.

7. That he has put any of his creditors to unnecessary expense by defending an action, or that he has brought on or contributed to his bankruptcy by incurring unjustifiable expense in bringing a frivolous or vexatious action.

8. That he has, within three months of the receiving order, when unable to pay his debts as they became due, given an undue (not necessarily a fraudulent) preference to any of his creditors.

9. That he has, within three months before the receiving order

incurred liabilities with a view to making his assets equal to 50 pence in the pound on the amount of his unsecured liabilities.

10. That he has previously been adjudicated bankrupt, or made a composition or arrangement with his creditors.

11. That he has been guilty of fraud or fraudulent breach of trust.

12. That he has committed any offence in connection with the bankruptcy (Bankruptcy (Amendment) Act 1926, s. 1).

The procedure for automatic discharge under section 7 of the Insolvency Act 1976 is as follows. Where the court makes an order that the debtor's public examination is concluded or is dispensed with it may if it thinks fit make a further order that "the same results shall ensue as if the court had" granted him an absolute order of discharge under section 26 of the Bankruptcy Act 1914. An order under section 7 can only take effect (a) if the bankrupt has not been discharged under section 26 before the fifth anniversary of the date of his adjudication and (b) the adjudication has not been annulled before that date. In considering whether to make an order under section 7 the court shall have regard to all the circumstances of the case including the matters stated in section 26 (3) of the 1914 act. The order takes effect on the fifth anniversary of the bankrupt's adjudication. Before that date it can be rescinded on the application of the official receiver or trustee (s. 7 (3)).

Section 8 of the Insolvency Act 1976 contains a long stop provision. If five years have elapsed since the date of adjudication and the bankrupt has not been discharged or his adjudication annulled the official receiver shall make an application to the court within 12 months after the fifth anniversary of the bankrupt's adjudication. The court must then fix a date for the hearing and notice of this must be published in *The London Gazette* and a local newspaper and sent to the bankrupt at least 14 days before the hearing (s. 8 (3)). At the hearing the official receiver presents a report as to the bankrupt's conduct and affairs including his conduct during the bankruptcy. The report is prima facie evidence of the statements contained in it (s. 8 (4)). Except where the court otherwise directs the application may be heard in the bankrupt's absence and the court may hear the trustee and any creditor, receive such other evidence as it thinks fit and if the bankrupt is present put questions to him (s. 8 (5)).

On any application under section 8 the court may—

(a) grant or refuse an absolute order of discharge; or

(b) suspend the discharge for such period as the court thinks proper or until a dividend of not less than 50 pence in the pound has been paid to the creditors; or

(c) require the bankrupt as a condition of his discharge to consent to judgment being entered against him by the official receiver or trustee for any balance or part of any balance of the debts provable under the bankruptcy which is not satisfied at the date of the discharge. Such balance or part will then be paid out of future earnings or after acquired property on such conditions as the court may direct (s. 8 (6)).

At any time after two years from the date of an order under section 8 the bankrupt can apply to the court for a modification of the order if there is no reasonable probability of him being in a position to comply with it (s. 8 (9)).

Effect of discharge (s. 28)

An order of discharge releases the bankrupt from all debts provable in the bankruptcy.

It does not release him from—

1. debts due to the Crown;
2. debts or liabilities incurred by means of fraud or fraudulent breach of trust;
3. liability under an affiliation order, unless the court otherwise orders (s. 28).

It also frees him from the disabilities of an undischarged bankrupt, which are—

1. Property acquired after the bankruptcy may be claimed by the trustee.
2. The bankrupt must not obtain credit for £50 or upwards without informing the person giving credit that he is an undischarged bankrupt (s. 155).
3. The bankrupt must not engage in trade or business under another name without informing persons with whom he does business of the name he was under when he was made bankrupt (s. 155).
4. The bankrupt cannot be a company director without leave of the court.

Annulment of bankruptcy (s. 29)

The court may annul an adjudication of bankruptcy when—

1. In the opinion of the court the debtor ought not to have been adjudged bankrupt.

2. The debts of the bankrupt are paid in full.

Notice of the order of annulment is then gazetted and published in a local paper.

Any sale or other disposition of the debtor's property by the trustee before annulment is valid, but after annulment the debtor's property vests in such person as the court may appoint.

Administration orders and bankruptcy

An application by a debtor to the county court for an administration order under section 21 of the Administration of Justice Act 1965 and an order by the county court requiring a debtor to furnish a list of creditors with a view to the making of an administration order under section 29 of the Administration of Justice Act 1970 constituted acts of bankruptcy. These provisions have now been repealed by section 13 of the Insolvency Act 1976. Where, however, an administration order has been made and the debtor fails to make any payment under it the appropriate court may if it thinks fit revoke the administration order and make a receiving order against the debtor (s. 11 (1)). Where such a receiving order is made the debtor shall be deemed to have committed an act of bankruptcy at that date (s. 11 (5)). The minimum debt for this purpose is £400 (Sched. 1 to the Insolvency Act 1976).

Criminal bankruptcy

Criminal bankruptcy was introduced by the Criminal Justice Act 1972 but the relevant provisions are now contained in the Powers of the Criminal Courts Act 1973, ss. 39–41 and Schedule 2. The policy of the legislation is to make available to those who have suffered at the hands of a person convicted of an offence loss or damage not attributable to personal injury, the machinery of bankruptcy to facilitate the recovery of assets to make good the loss or damage. In certain respects the provisions are wider reaching than those of the Bankruptcy Act 1914. Criminal bankruptcy represents an extension of the penal system and as such is outside the scope of this book. For a detailed discussion see *Halsbury's Laws of England* (4th ed.), Vol. 3, paras. 1053–1100 read in the light of the 1973 Act.

Deeds of arrangement

An insolvent person, without becoming bankrupt, may make an arrangement with his creditors. The arrangement may be either (1) a composition with creditors, by which an agreement is made between the debtor and his creditors that the creditors shall accept a proportion of their claims in satisfaction of the whole, or (2) an assignment by the debtor of his property to a trustee for the benefit of his creditors. If the arrangement is embodied in a document, whether under seal or not, it is void unless—

   (a) it is registered within seven days of its first execution with the registrar appointed by the Department of Trade;
   (b) within 21 days of its execution it has received the assent of the majority in number and value of the creditors.

The High Court has power to extend the time for registration. If the deed affects land, it must be registered under section 7 of the Land Charges Act 1972 otherwise it will be void as against a purchaser for value.

The Deeds of Arrangement Act 1914 requires registration of all instruments made by a *debtor* for the benefit of his creditors generally, or made by an *insolvent debtor* for the benefit of three or more of his creditors. These instruments include (a) an assignment of property; (b) a deed of composition; (c) a deed of inspectorship for carrying on or winding up a business; (d) a letter of licence authorising a debtor or any other person to carry on or dispose of a business with a view to the payment of debts; (e) any agreement for carrying on or winding up a debtor's business with a view to the payment of his debts.

A creditor expresses his assent by executing the deed, or by sending to the trustee his assent in writing attested by a witness. The trustee under the deed must, within 28 days of registration, file a statutory declaration that the requisite majority of creditors have assented to the arrangement (Deeds of Arrangement Act 1914, ss. 2, 3).

The deed when registered is open to the inspection of any person on payment of the prescribed fee. A copy must be sent to the county court of the district in which the debtor carries on business, and it is also open to inspection there.

The registration of a deed of arrangement does not make it binding on creditors who have not assented to it. If it is made for the benefit of creditors generally, it is an act of bankruptcy, and a bankruptcy petition may be presented against the debtor within three months of its execution. The trustee under such a deed may, however, give notice to any creditor of the execution of the deed and of the filing of the statutory declaration as to the creditor's assents, and may intimate to the creditor that he will not, after the expiration of a month from the notice, be able to present a bankruptcy petition founded on the deed. If the creditor does not present a petition within the month he loses his right to petition (Deeds of Arrangement Act 1914, s. 24).

If a deed has become void through non-registration or otherwise, a creditor can present a bankruptcy petition founded on it, notwithstanding that he has assented to the deed.

Position of trustee under void deed

The trustee should not act under the deed for three months after its execution, unless all the creditors have assented to it. If he does, and the debtor becomes bankrupt, the title of the trustee in bankruptcy will relate back to the date of the execution of the deed, and the trustee under the deed must account fully for what he has received. If the deed becomes void through the debtor's bankruptcy, the trustee in bankruptcy may treat the trustee under the deed as his agent, or he may treat him as a trespasser, when he must account for the value of the estate he has received. The trustee in bankruptcy has a discretion to allow remuneration for services which have benefited the estate. But if a deed never becomes effective, *e.g.* because a majority of the creditors do not assent to it, the court only can allow remuneration (*Re Zakon* [1940] 1 Ch. 253). Any expenses incurred by the trustee under the deed in complying with the provisions of the Deeds of Arrangement Act 1914 are a first charge on the estate.

If the deed is void only because it has not received the assent of the requisite number of creditors, and the trustee does not know and had no reason to suspect that it was void, then on a receiving order being made within three months, the trustee is not liable for any dealings with the debtor's property which would have been proper had the deed been valid (Deeds of Arrangement Act 1914, s. 19).

When a deed is void for any reason except non-registration, the trustee, as soon as he knows that it is void, must give written notice to each creditor and file a copy of the notice with the Department of Trade: Deeds of Arrangement Act 1914, s. 20.

Payments made to a trustee, as assignee of the bankrupt, are protected transactions if the conditions of section 46 of the Bankruptcy Act 1914 (see pp. 507–509, *ante*) are complied with.

Security

The trustee under a deed of arrangement must give security to the registrar of the court, unless a majority in number and value of the creditors, either by resolution or by notice in writing, dispense with the giving of security.

Accounts

The trustee must transmit an account of his receipts and payments, verified in the prescribed manner, to the Department of Trade when required. The rules provide that the accounts must be rendered every 12 months from the date of registration, and, if a business is carried on, a separate trading account must be rendered. These accounts are open to the inspection of any person interested. He must also, every six months, send to every creditor who has assented to the deed a statement of his accounts and of the proceedings under the deed. Money received by the trustee must be banked to an account in the name of the debtor's estate (Deeds of Arrangement Act 1914, s. 11 (4)).

The Department of Trade may order the trustee's accounts to be audited on the written application of a majority in number and value of the creditors who have assented to the deed, if the application is made within 12 months from the rendering of the final accounts to the Department. The expenses of the audit are to be borne as decided by the Department.

Duties of trustee

The trustee must carry out the trusts of the deed and distribute the property assigned to him in accordance with the provisions of the deed. He must pay all creditors equally, except those entitled to enforce their claims by distress, or those who are entitled to preferential payment in bankruptcy. If any questions arise in the course of administering the trusts, the trustee, the debtor, or any creditor may apply to the court to have them determined.

The bankruptcy rules which go to swell the assets, *i.e.* those dealing with reputed ownership, the avoidance of voluntary settlements, and fraudulent preference, have no application to deeds of arrangement. The trustee can only distribute the property actually assigned to him by the debtor.

If the deed contains a covenant by the creditors not to sue the debtor, but reserving their rights against sureties, a surety who has been compelled to pay a creditor is not prevented by the deed from enforcing his right to be indemnified by the debtor (*Cole* v. *Lynn* [1942] 1 K.B. 142).

A trustee acting under a deed which is void to his knowledge exposes himself to heavy penalties.

SELECT BIBLIOGRAPHY

Books

G. H. L. Fridman, I. Hicks and E. C. Johnson, *Bankruptcy Law and Practice* (1970).
Halsbury's Laws of England (4th ed., 1973), Vol. 3, "Bankruptcy."

Reports

Report of the Committee on Bankruptcy Law and Deeds of Arrangement Law (Amendment) (Cmnd. 221).
Bankruptcy—A Report by Justice (1975).

PART 10: ARBITRATION

CHAPTER 32

ARBITRATION[1]

The Arbitration Acts 1950 and 1975

THE statutory regulation of the law relating to arbitration [is contained in the Arbitration Acts 1950 and 1975.

The Arbitration Act 1950 is the principal Act. It also gives effect to two international measures, *viz.* the Geneva Protocol on Arbitration Clauses of 1923 and the Geneva Convention on the Execution of Foreign Arbitral Awards of 1927, appended to the 1950 Act as Schedules 1 and 2. The two Geneva measures are in the process of being superseded by the New York Convention on the Recognition and Enforcement of Foreign Arbitral Awards of 1958, which was promoted by the United Nations. The object of the Arbitration Act 1975 is to give effect to the New York Convention in the United Kingdom. The 1975 Act came into operation on December 23, 1975 (S.I. 1975, No. 1662).

At present the law is in a transitional stage and awards can be classified into three categories—

(a) *ordinary awards.* They do not contain a foreign element.

(b) *foreign awards.* They are made in pursuance of an arbitration agreement in a country which is a party to the Geneva Convention of 1927 but not to the New York Convention of 1958. Here Part II of the 1950 Act applies.

(c) *Convention awards.* They are made in pursuance of an arbitration agreement in a country which is a party to the New York Convention of 1958 (For a list of these countries see the Arbitration (Foreign Awards) Order 1975 (No. 1709), as amended.) Here the Arbitration Act 1975, ss. 2 to 6, applies.

---

[1] References in this chapter are to the Arbitration Act 1950 unless the contrary is expressed.

534

As more and more countries will give effect to the New York Convention, category (b) will be reduced in course of time and category (c) correspondingly enlarged.

Reference to arbitration

A reference to arbitration may be made in one of three ways—
1. Under order of the court.
2. Under an Act of Parliament.
3. By agreement of the parties.

Under order of the court

The court may refer any question arising in any matter before it to an official or special referee for inquiry or report. It may also refer the whole question before it to be tried by an official or special referee if—
1. all the parties consent;
2. the case requires prolonged examination of documents or scientific or local investigation;
3. the question in dispute consists wholly or in part of matters of account.

Under an Act of Parliament

Various Acts of Parliament provide for the settlement of disputes arising out of their provisions by arbitration. These Acts usually describe how the arbitration is to be conducted; but in all other cases the Arbitration Acts 1950 and 1975 apply.

By agreement of the parties

A reference by agreement of the parties must originate in arbitration agreement. Such an agreement may be made verbally or in writing, but the Arbitration Acts 1950 and 1975 only apply to written agreements.

An arbitration agreement is defined by section 32 as "a written agreement to submit present or future differences to arbitration, whether an arbitrator is named therein or not."

An arbitration must be distinguished from a valuation. It is an arbitration if the parties intend that any dispute between them shall be settled by an inquiry held in a quasi-judicial manner, usually but not necessarily, after hearing argument or evidence.

On the other hand, it is a **valuation** if the object of the activity of the appointed person is to value or appraise something but no dispute exists between the parties on the facts or the law. Examples of valuers are an architect who certifies the sums payable by the building owner to the builder, as the work performed by the builder progresses; or an accountant who, in accordance with the agreement between shareholders of a company, fixes the "fair value" of the shares sold by one of them to another. A valuer is liable for negligence in the performance of his duties but an arbitrator enjoys the same immunity as a judge and cannot be held liable in negligence.

Mr. Sutcliffe was the building owner of land on which he wished to have built a high class dwelling-house. He employed Mr. Thackrah and his partners as architects and the David Walbank Company as builders. The architects negligently issued interim certificates for the work defectively done by the builders who were paid by the building owner on the strength of the certificates. The builders then became insolvent. *Held*, the architects were liable to the building owner in negligence: *Sutcliffe* v. *Thackrah and Others* [1974] A.C. 727.

Archy Arenson was the controlling shareholder of a private company, A. Arenson Ltd. He had agreed with his nephew Ivor Arenson who likewise held shares in the company to purchase Ivor's shares at a fair value to be determined by the company's auditors. Messrs. Casson Beckman Rutley & Co., a firm of chartered accountants, who were the company's auditors, valued Ivor's shares at £4,916 for which sum they were transferred to the uncle. A few months later, in the course of the company going public, the shares of the company were revalued and under the revaluation Ivor's shares would have been worth £29,500 i.e. six times the value which Ivor had received. *Held*, if auditors had acted as valuers they may be a proper party to be sued in negligence. *Arenson* v. *Casson Beckman Rutley & Co.* [1975] 3 W.L.R. 815.

However, it should not be inferred from the *Arenson* case that an accountant is a valuer in all circumstances; if a dispute on facts or a legal question has arisen and is referred by the parties to their accountant, the latter would act as an arbitrator even if in the course of his arbitration he has to make an appraisal, and he would enjoy quasi-judicial immunity unless he has acted fraudulently.

EFFECT OF ARBITRATION AGREEMENT

No ouster of jurisdiction of the court in questions of law

The jurisdiction of the courts in England in questions of law cannot be excluded—ousted—by agreement of the parties. "There must be no Alsatia in England where the King's writ does not run," said Scrutton L.J. in *Czarnikow* v. *Roth, Schmidt & Co.* [1922] 2 K.B. 478, 488.

Consequently, a party cannot be deprived by the arbitration agreement of his right to ask the arbitrator or the court for stating a special case for the opinion of the court on a question of law (*Czarnikow* v. *Roth, Schmidt & Co.*, see p. 547, *post*). However, the agreement may be framed in such a manner as to prevent any right of action from accruing under the contract until an award is first made. In such a case an award is a condition precedent to a right to sue.

A policy of insurance on a ship provided that in the event of loss the amount of the loss should be referred to arbitration. It provided that the award of the arbitrators was to be a condition precedent to the maintaining of an action. *Held*, until an award was made, no action was maintainable: *Scott* v. *Avery* (1856) 5 H.L.C. 811.

It is provided by section 25 (4) that if the court orders that the agreement to refer the dispute to arbitration shall cease to have effect, it may also order that the condition precedent shall cease to have effect.

Power of court to break arbitration agreement

If a party to an arbitration agreement commences proceedings in court, contrary to his undertaking to submit to arbitration, the court, on the application of the other party, may either order a stay of court proceedings, thus allowing the arbitration to proceed, or refuse the application for a stay, thus breaking the arbitration agreement (s. 4). If the only point in issue is a point of law, the court will usually refuse a stay of proceedings.

Two cases have to be distinguished here: if the arbitration agreement is a domestic arbitration agreement, the discretion of the court to order or refuse a stay of court proceedings is wide (s. 4 (1)), but if it is a non-domestic arbitration agreement its discretion is limited (Arbitration Act 1975, s. 1).

An arbitration agreement is domestic if—

1. it does not provide, expressly or by implication, for arbitration in a state other than the United Kingdom, and
2. all parties to it are—
   (a) United Kingdom citizens or natural persons habitually resident in the United Kingdom; or

(b) corporations incorporated in the United Kingdom or having their central management and control exercised in the United Kingdom (1975 Act, s. 1 (4)).

Both conditions must be satisfied for an arbitration agreement to be classified as domestic.

1. *Domestic arbitrations*

A stay of court proceedings **may** only be granted if all the following requirements are satisfied (s. 4 (1))—

(a) The matter in question must be within the scope of the arbitration agreement;

(b) The applicant must have taken no step in the court proceedings. If he delivers a defence, makes an application to the court, or does anything else of a like nature, he cannot have the proceedings stayed;

(c) The applicant must have been ready and willing from the commencement to do everything necessary for the proper conduct of the arbitration; and

(d) There must be no sufficient reason why the dispute should not be referred to arbitration.

The burden of proof is upon the party opposing the stay to satisfy the court there is good reason for proceeding with the action and not granting the stay, because when parties have agreed that their disputes are to be decided by a particular tribunal the court is inclined to hold them to their agreement, unless there is some strong reason why they should not be so held.

A cargo of turpentine was loaded at a Russian port into a German vessel. The bills of lading were held by an English company which claimed that the turpentine was contaminated in transit and brought an action against the German vessel in the English courts. The owners of the German vessel applied for a stay on the ground that the bills of lading provided that all disputes should be judged in the U.S.S.R. *Held*, that the stay should be refused because the dispute had little connection with the U.S.S.R. None of the parties had Soviet nationality and virtually all the witnesses and other evidence was to be found in England: *The Fehmarn* [1957] 1 W.L.R. 815.

The court may, in particular, refuse a stay (s. 24)—

(a) After a dispute has arisen, if the arbitrator is or may not be impartial by reason of his relation to one of the parties or of his connection with the subject referred.

J A did work for the B Corporation under a contract by which disputes were to be referred to the corporation's engineer. Disputes arose involving a probable conflict of evidence between J A and the engineer. *Held*, the action must proceed, because the engineer would, in an arbitration, be placed in the position of a judge and witness: *Bristol Corpn.* v. *John Aird & Co.* [1913] A.C. 241.

(b) If the dispute involves the question whether any of the parties have been guilty of fraud, so far as necessary to enable that question to be determined.

2. *Non-domestic arbitrations*

Here the court **must** order a stay of proceedings, unless it is satisfied—

(a) that the arbitration agreement is null and void, inoperative or incapable of being performed, or

(b) that there is not in fact any dispute between the parties with regard to the matters agreed to be referred (1975 Act, s. 1 (1)).

A party who wishes the court to stay court proceedings so that the arbitration will proceed, must apply to the court after entering an appearance and before delivering any pleadings or taking any other step in the court proceedings (1975 Act, s. 1 (1)).

In 1970 the plaintiffs Nova, an English company, entered into a partnership agreement with the defendants Kammgarn, a German company, whereby the plaintiffs were to supply the defendants with knitting machines. The contract contained an arbitration clause and there was also a separate arbitration agreement. In 1972 the plaintiffs sold 12 machines to the defendants and received 24 bills of exchange for a total of £173,558. The first six of these bills of exchange were honoured by the defendants but the others were not paid on the ground, as the defendants alleged, of fraud. The defendants commenced arbitration proceedings in Germany and the plaintiffs issued a writ in the English courts for service out of the jurisdiction claiming payment of the outstanding bills of exchange. The defendants applied for a stay of the court proceedings. *Held*, the court was bound by section 1 (1) of the Arbitration Act 1975 to order a stay because the dispute between the parties concerned the issue whether the bills should or should not be paid: *Nova (Jersey) Knit Ltd.* v. *Kammgarn Spinnerei GmbH.* [1976] 2 Lloyd's Rep. 155.

Whether the arbitrator can determine the validity of the arbitration agreement

The question whether or not an arbitrator has power to determine the validity of the agreement by virtue of which he has been appointed as arbitrator is determined in accordance with the following principles—

(a) An arbitration clause is a written submission, agreed to by the parties to the contract, and like other written agreements, must be construed according to its language and in the light of the circumstances in which it is made.

(b) If the dispute is whether the contract which contains the clause has ever been entered into at all, that issue cannot go to arbitration under the clause, for the party who denies that he has ever entered into the contract is thereby denying that he has ever joined in the submission.

(c) Similarly, if one party to the alleged contract contends that it is void ab initio (because, for example, the making of such a contract is illegal), the arbitration clause cannot operate, for on this view the clause itself is also void.

(d) But where the parties are at one in asserting that they entered into a binding contract, but a difference arises between them whether there has been a breach by one side or the other, or whether circumstances have arisen which have discharged one or both parties from further performance, the arbitration clause is binding (*Heyman* v. *Darwins Ltd.*, below).

(e) Where there is an application to the court to stay proceedings, if the agreement is on the face of it perfectly valid and effective, the application will generally be granted as the court will be unwilling to treat the agreement or the submission to arbitration as void until the matter has been decided by a court or by an arbitrator (*The Tradesman* [1962] 1 W.L.R. 61).

D Ltd., appointed H their selling agent under a contract containing a clause agreeing to refer disputes "in respect of this agreement" to arbitration. A dispute arose and H claimed that D Ltd., had repudiated the contract. He accepted the repudiation, claimed that the contract was at an end and issued a writ. *Held*, the action should be stayed, as the alleged repudiation only amounted to a breach of contract and therefore left the arbitration clause binding: *Heyman* v. *Darwins Ltd.* [1942] A.C. 356.

Whether the arbitrators can determine claims in tort connected with the contract

If a contract contains an arbitration clause and a claim is made in negligence—a tort—which is coextensive with a claim for breach of the contract containing the clause, the claim in tort is within the jurisdiction of the arbitrators who can dispose of it (*Woolf* v. *Collis Removal Service* [1948] 1 K.B. 11). The position is the same in other cases in which a sufficiently close connection exists between the tort and the breach of contract.

Charterers thought that they had a claim for damages against the shipowners who had stopped the discharge of goods from the ship. In pursuance of their claim, the charterers arrested the ship. The shipowners claimed that the arrest was wrongful and demanded damages. The charter-party contained an arbitration clause and the arbitrators decided the claim for damages for wrongful arrest in favour of the shipowners. *Held*, (1) the claim for damages for wrongful arrest of the ship was founded in tort, (2) the arbitrators had jurisdiction to dispose of the claim as the arrest of the ship was only the sequel to the claim of the charterers and so closely connected with the alleged breach of charterparty that it was within the scope of the arbitration: *Astro Vencedor Compania Naviera S.A. of Panama* v. *Mabanaft GmbH; The Damianos* [1971] 2 Q.B. 588.

In other cases the arbitrators have no jurisdiction to entertain claims which are not submitted to them explicitly.

Arbitration agreement in apprenticeship deed

An arbitration clause in an apprenticeship deed between a minor and his employer is for the minor's benefit (see p. 54, *ante*), and is binding on the minor (*Slade* v. *Metrodent Ltd.* [1953] 2 Q.B. 112).

Assignment of contract containing arbitration agreement

When a contract is assignable, the benefit of an arbitration clause contained in it is assignable as part of the contract (*Shayler* v. *Woolf* [1946] Ch. 320). But an assignment of all money due under a contract does not include an arbitration clause in the contract.

THE ARBITRATION AGREEMENT

Every arbitration agreement is assumed to include the following provisions, unless a contrary intention is expressed in it—

1. If no other mode of reference is provided, the reference is to a single arbitrator (s. 6).

2. If the reference is to two arbitrators, they shall appoint an umpire immediately after they are themselves appointed (s. 8 (1)).

3. If the arbitrators have delivered to any party or to the umpire a notice in writing stating that they cannot agree, the umpire may enter on the reference (s. 8 (2)).

4. The parties to the arbitration must submit to be examined on oath before the arbitrator or umpire and must produce all books, deeds, papers, accounts, writings and documents in their possession which may be called for, and must do all other things which, during the reference, the arbitrators or umpire may require (s. 12 (1)).

5. The witnesses on the reference must, if the arbitrators or umpire think fit, be examined on oath (s. 12 (2)).

6. The award to be made by the arbitrators or umpire is final and binding on the parties (s. 16).

7. The costs of the reference and award are in the discretion of the arbitrators or umpire, who can direct who shall pay the costs and can tax or settle the amount of costs to be paid (s. 18 (1)). A provision in the submission that a party shall pay his own costs in any event is void (s. 18 (3)).

8. The arbitrators or umpire can order specific performance of any contract, except a contract relating to land (s. 15).

9. An interim award may be made (s. 14).

An arbitration agreement may be altered or amended by consent of the parties, but the arbitrator or umpire has no power to alter it.

The authority of an arbitrator or umpire appointed under an arbitration agreement is irrevocable except by leave of the court (s. 1). An arbitration agreement is not discharged by the death of any party to the agreement, and the authority of an arbitrator is not revoked by the death of the party appointing him (s. 2). On the bankruptcy of a party, an arbitration clause in a contract is enforceable by or against his trustee in bankruptcy if he adopts the contract (s. 3). There is no similar provision dealing with the liquidator of a company. The court may revoke an agreement, after a dispute has arisen, on the ground that the arbitrator is not impartial by reason of his relation to one of the parties to the agreement, or of his connection with the subject referred, or when a question of fraud arises (s. 24).

Where an international contract contains an arbitration clause but does not define the proper law of the contract, the presumption is that the law of the place at which the arbitration is to be held is the proper law of the contract (*Tzortzis* v. *Monark Line A/B* [1968] 1 W.L.R. 406, see p. 160, *ante*) but this presumption may be rebutted by the surrounding circumstances (*Cie Tunisienne de Navigation S.A.* v. *Cie d'Armement Maritime S.A.*, see p. 161, *ante*).

The law applicable to the arbitration procedure may be different from the substantive law governing the contract (*Whitworth Street Estates (Manchester) Ltd.* v. *James Miller & Partners Ltd.* [1970] A.C. 583). But the provision of the Arbitration Act 1950 which gives the court power to extend the time for commencing arbitration proceedings in case of undue hardship (s. 27) forms part of the substantive law governing the contract and can be invoked if the contract is governed by English law even though the arbitration procedure is governed by a foreign law (*International Tank and Pipe S.A.K.* v. *Kuwait Aviation Fuelling Co. K.S.C.* [1975] Q.B. 224).

APPOINTMENT OF ARBITRATOR

The parties may refer their dispute to a single named arbitrator, to two arbitrators—one to be appointed by each party—or to two arbitrators and an umpire or chairman. A High Court judge may be appointed arbitrator (Administration of Justice Act 1970, s. 4).

In the following cases—

1. where the reference is to a single arbitrator and the parties do not concur in the appointment of an arbitrator;
2. if the appointed arbitrator dies or refuses to act and the parties do not supply the vacancy;
3. where the parties or two arbitrators are at liberty to appoint an umpire and do not appoint him:
4. where the umpire dies or refuses to act and the parties do not supply a vacancy;

any party may serve the others with a written notice to make an appointment, and if the appointment is not made within seven days the court will make the appointment (s. 10).

The m.v. *Tanais* was under charter for a voyage between Canada and Italy. The charterparty provided, *inter alia*, for "arbitration to be settled in London." A dispute arose between the shipowners and the charterers and the shipowners requested the charterers to agree on the arbitrator, but the latter refused to co-operate. *Held*, that the dispute should be settled by arbitration and an arbitrator be appointed by the court: *Tritonia Shipping Inc.* v. *South Nelson Forest Products Corpn.* [1966] 1 Lloyd's Rep. 114.

Sometimes the arbitrator is to be appointed by a third person, *e.g.* by a chamber of commerce or the president of a professional association. If the organisation or person who is to make the appointment, declines to do so, the court has normally no jurisdiction under section 10 (*a*) of the Arbitration Act 1950 to appoint the arbitrator and the arbitration cannot take place.

National Enterprises, the plaintiffs, a company incorporated in Pakistan, were appointed by Racal, the defendants, an English company, to act as Racal's agents for the sale of military equipment in Pakistan. The agency contract provided for arbitration by an arbitrator appointed by the Federation (now Confederation) of British Industries. The CBI refused to appoint an arbitrator. *Held*, the court had no jurisdiction under the Arbitration Act 1950, s. 10 (*a*), to appoint an arbitrator where the third party had failed to make the appointment, unless there was an express or implied agreement, which there was not in the present case, that, if the third person failed to appoint, an arbitrator should be agreed upon by the parties: *National Enterprises Ltd.* v. *Racal Communications Ltd.* [1975] Ch. 397.

A clause worded "suitable arbitration clause" in an English contract is not void on the ground of uncertainty but means an arbitration which reasonable men in this type of business would consider suitable, the court being empowered to appoint an arbitrator under the Arbitration Act 1950 (*Hobbs Padgett & Co. (Reinsurance) Ltd.* v. *J. C. Kirkland Ltd.* [1969] 2 Lloyd's Rep. 547). Where the arbitration clause provides for the appointment of "commercial men" as arbitrators and umpire, a practising member of the Bar cannot be appointed umpire by the arbitrators (*Rahcassi Shipping Co. S.A.* v. *Blue Star Ltd.* [1969] 1 Q.B. 173).

Where the agreement provides that the reference shall be to two arbitrators, one to be appointed by each party, and one party appoints an arbitrator who subsequently dies or refuses to act, such party may appoint a new arbitrator. If he fails to do so or fails to appoint an arbitrator in the first instance, the other party may serve notice on him to make an appointment within seven days, and, in default of such appointment, the arbitrator appointed by the other party will be the sole arbitrator and his award will be binding on both parties. An appointment made under these circumstances may be set aside by the court (s. 7).

If the agreement for reference is to three arbitrators the award of any two is binding. If the reference is to three arbitrators, one to be appointed by each party and the third by the arbitrators, the effect is the same as a reference to two arbitrators and an umpire (s. 9).

The appointment of an arbitrator is constituted by (1) nominating the arbitrator to the other party, (2) informing the arbitrator of his nomination, and (3) an intimation by him that he is willing to accept the nomination.

The plaintiffs chartered the defendants' motor vessel *La Loma*. The charterparty contained an arbitration clause providing for the appointment of an arbitrator by the claimants within three months from the final discharge of the goods from the ship, and further providing that in the absence of such an appointment the claimants' claim should be absolutely barred. A dispute arose between the parties and the plaintiffs, who were the claimants, indicated the name of their arbitrator to the defendants but failed to inform him of his nomination. After the expiry of the three months from the final discharge the plaintiffs notified the arbitrator and he accepted. *Held*, the appointment of the arbitrator was not completed within the time stated in the arbitration clause and consequently the plaintiffs' claim was absolutely barred: *Tradax Export S.A.* v. *Volkswagenwerk* [1970] 1 Lloyd's Rep. 62.

Removal of arbitrator or umpire

The court may remove an arbitrator or umpire who fails to use reasonable dispatch in proceeding with the reference and making an award. No remuneration is payable to an arbitrator or an umpire who is removed.

CONDUCT OF AN ARBITRATION

The duty of an arbitrator is to make an award on the matters of dispute or difference between the parties submitted for his decision. If the reference is to two arbitrators, and, if they fail to agree, to an umpire, the umpire has the same powers and duties as an arbitrator. An arbitrator or an umpire cannot delegate the powers conferred on him by the agreement.

A lay arbitrator may in a proper case, in the absence of an objection by the parties, hear the arbitration with a legal assessor. In all cases he may employ legal assistance in drawing up his award.

The arbitrator should fix a time and place for the hearing of the arbitration and give notice to all parties. Should one of the parties fail to attend after notice, the arbitrator can proceed with the reference, notwithstanding his absence. The arbitrator can administer oaths to the witnesses appearing before him (s. 12 (3)), and with respect to their testimony he is bound to observe the rules of evidence. Unless the submission provides to the contrary he should hear the witnesses tendered in the presence of both parties. He has no power to call a witness himself without the consent of the parties (*Re Enoch & Zaretsky's Arbn.* [1910] 1 K.B. 327).

A commercial arbitrator is entitled to rely on his own knowledge and experience in deciding on the quality of the goods which form the subject-matter of the arbitration, and can also assess the damages, even though there has been no evidence before him as to the amount of the damages (*Mediterranean & Eastern Export Co.* v. *Fortress Fabrics Ltd.* [1948] 2 All E.R. 186). But if intending to rely on his own knowledge of the trade, he must not take the parties by surprise but invite them, if he thinks they have missed a point, to deal with it; further, if he has knowledge of facts which do not appear to be known to the parties, he must disclose those facts to them and give them an opportunity to plead to them (*Thomas Borthwick* (*Glasgow*) *Ltd.* v. *Faure Fairclough Ltd.* [1968] 1 Lloyd's Rep. 16).

In commercial arbitrations where an umpire has been appointed the arbitrators can give evidence before the umpire.

A dispute arose between buyers and sellers of meat as to its quality. The buyers sent K to examine the meat, and on the dispute being referred to arbitration, appointed K their arbitrator. The arbitrators having failed to agree, an umpire was appointed. *Held*, K could give evidence before the umpire as to the state of the meat: *Bourgeois* v. *Weddell & Co.* [1924] 1 K.B. 539.

Stating a special case

An arbitrator has power to state his award in the form of a special case for the opinion of the court, and can be compelled to do so by the court (s. 21). This is done by stating the facts which he has found in the arbitration and formulating questions of law based on those facts for the opinion of the court. The award should be so stated that the answers of the court to the questions of law formulated will enable the result of his award to be ascertained without sending the award back to him. A clause in the arbitration agreement prohibiting the parties from requiring the arbitrator to state his award in the form of a special case for the opinion of the court is contrary to public policy and void (*Czarnikow* v. *Roth, Schmidt & Co.* [1922] 2 K.B. 478).

When any question of law arises in the course of a reference the arbitrator may state a special case for the opinion of the court and may be directed by the court to do so. When a case is stated on a question of law arising in the course of the reference, the court gives its opinion in a consultative capacity, and there is no appeal from its decision without leave of the court or of the Court of Appeal.

A special case should be stated, according to Lord Denning M.R. in *Halfdan, Grieg & Co. A/S* v. *Sterling Coal & Navigation Corp.* [1973] Q.B. 843, 862, if three conditions are satisfied. The point of law should be—

1. real and substantial and such as to be open to serious argument and appropriate for decision by a court of law;
2. clear cut and capable of being accurately stated as a point of law—as distinct from the dressing up of a matter of fact as if it were a point of law; and
3. of such importance that the resolution of it is necessary for the proper determination of the case—as distinct from a side issue of little importance.

Where there is no request for a special case and the arbitrator has not misconducted himself (see p. 551, *post*), the court has no jurisdiction to interfere with an award which does not embody reasons (a so-called non-speaking award), for in such a case the arbitrator is the sole judge of questions of fact and law (*Prodexport State Company for Foreign Trade* v. *E. D. & F. Man Ltd.* [1973] Q.B. 389).

The arbitrator must decide according to the law; the parties cannot give him power to decide according to an equitable rather than a strictly legal interpretation because the adoption of such an extra-legal criterion would make it impossible for the court, when a special case is stated, to ascertain whether the arbitrator had fallen into an error when deciding a question of law (*Orion Compania Espanola de Seguros* v. *Belfort Maatschappij Voor Algemene Verzekgringeen* [1962] 2 Lloyd's Rep. 257).

THE AWARD

The award may be in writing or made verbally, unless the arbitration agreement provides that it must be in writing. To be valid, the award should comply with the following—

1. It must follow the agreement and not purport to decide matters not within the agreement. An award on something outside the agreement is void, and if the void part cannot be severed from the rest of the award, the whole award is void (*Buccleuch* (*Duke*) v. *Metropolitan Board of Works* (1870) L.R. 5 Ex. 221).

2. It must be certain. If it is uncertain it cannot be enforced. For example, an award that A or B shall do a certain act is void for uncertainty (*Lawrence* v. *Hodgson* (1826) 1 Y. & J. 16).

3. It must be final. An award, therefore, that a third party shall certify the loss arising from a breach of contract is void for want of finality (*Dresser* v. *Finnis* (1855) 25 L.T.(o.s.) 81). An award is not void, however, if it is made in the form of a special case, if notice is given by either party within a specified time that he intends to take the opinion of the court, and if such notice is not given within the time, then in the form of a final award (*Re Olympia Oil and Cake Co. and MacAndrew, Moreland & Co.* [1918] 2 K.B. 771).

4. It must be reasonable, legal and possible. An award that one of the parties should do something beyond his power, as to deliver up a deed which is in the custody of X, is void (*Lee* v. *Elkins* (1701) 12 Mod. Rep. 585).

5. It must dispose of all the differences submitted to arbitration. If, however, all matters in dispute between the parties are submitted to arbitration, the award is good if it deals with all matters submitted to the arbitrator, although there may be other differences between the parties.

An arbitrator has jurisdiction to make his award in a foreign currency where that currency is the currency of the contract (*Jugoslavenska Oceanska Plovidba* v. *Castle Investment Co. Inc.* [1974] Q.B. 292).

An arbitrator is entitled to award interest on the sum he finds to be due (*Chandris* v. *Isbrandtsen-Moller Co.* [1950] 2 All E.R. 618).

In a commercial arbitration, interest should always be awarded, except for good reason (*Panchaud Frères S.A.* v. *R. Pagnan & Fratelli* [1974] 1 Lloyd's Rep. 394,411).

When the award is ready the arbitrator gives notice to the parties, who can take it up on paying the arbitrator's costs. After the award is made the arbitrator is *functus officio*, and cannot alter or vary his award. He may, however, correct any clerical mistake or error arising from any accidental slip or omission (s. 17).

Effect of the award

When an award is made it is final, and no appeal can be made to the courts, except in the limited cases when the award can be remitted to the arbitrator or set aside by the court (see p. 550, *post*). The agreement for arbitration may provide for an appeal to an appeal committee or other tribunal, but except when it does so, the arbitrator's decision on the facts is final and conclusive, and it is his duty to state the facts, as found by him, in the award; a mere reference to the evidence, *e.g.* to the transcript of evidence is insufficient (*Tersons Ltd.* v. *Stevenage Development Corpn.* [1965] 1 Q.B. 37).

THE COSTS OF THE ARBITRATION

The costs of the arbitration, unless a contrary intention is expressed in the agreement, are in the discretion of the arbitrator (s. 18). This discretion must be exercised judicially (*Lloyd del Pacifico* v. *Board of Trade* (1930) 46 T.L.R. 476). In the absence of special circumstances, it is settled practice that the successful party should be awarded costs. If there are special circumstances before the arbitrator justifying the exercise of his discretion in favour of the unsuccessful party, he need not follow the settled practice (*Dineen* v. *Walpole* [1969] 1 Lloyd's Rep. 261), and in this case need not give his reasons (*Perry* v. *Stopher* [1959] 1 W.L.R. 415). The arbitrator may award a lump sum for costs, or may direct that the costs shall be taxed in the High Court or by himself. The costs include all the costs of the arbitration including the arbitrator's own costs.

The arbitrator may fix the amount of his own remuneration and include it in the award. It is then payable on the taking up of the award. The fees of an arbitrator and an umpire may be taxed, and only so much as is found to be reasonable on taxation need to be paid (s. 19). If the reference is to two arbitrators and an umpire and the umpire, owing to the disagreement of the arbitrators, draws up the award, he should include the fees of the arbitrators as well as his own fees, specifying the amount of each (*Gilbert* v. *Wright* (1904) 20 T.L.R. 164). In exceptional cases if it is apparent that the umpire, when settling his own and the arbitrators' remuneration, misunderstood his duties and settled it in a wholly extravagant manner, this might amount to misconduct and the whole award be set aside (*Government of Ceylon* v. *Chandris* [1963] 2 Q.B. 327).

ENFORCEMENT OF AWARDS

An award on an arbitration agreement may, by leave of the court, be enforced in the same manner as a judgment (s. 26). Leave will be granted unless it can be shown that the award is a nullity, or is bad on the face of it, or is ultra vires (*Re Stone and Hastie* [1903] 2 L.B. 463).

An alternative method of enforcing an award is to bring an action on it. If the submission is oral, or the person against whom the award is to be enforced is out of the jurisdiction, an action is the only method of enforcing the award.

REMISSION TO ARBITRATOR

In all cases of reference to arbitration, the court may remit the whole or part of the matter for reconsideration by the arbitrators or umpire. When an award is remitted the award must be made within three months of the order of remission (s. 22).

An award will be remitted for reconsideration on the following grounds—

1. Where the arbitrator has made a mistake.

The arbitrator was not given the submission but, thinking he understood the matters in dispute, made an award. When the award was taken up, it was found that it did not deal with the matters in dispute. The arbitrator thereupon read the submission, destroyed his award and made a new one. *Held*, the arbitrator, having made an award, was *functus officio* and had no power to make a new award, but that the case should be remitted to the arbitrator for reconsideration: *Re Stringer and Riley Bros.* [1901] 1 Q.B. 105.

2. Where, since the making of the award, material evidence has been discovered which might have affected the arbitrator's

decision (*Re Keighley, Maxted & Co.* v. *Durant & Co.* [1893] 1 Q.B. 405).

3. Where there has been misconduct on the part of the arbitrator. In such a case the court may either set the award aside or remit it to the arbitrator.

Misconduct, sometimes called technical misconduct, does not imply a moral reprobation. It occurs if the arbitrator has failed "to act fairly and to be seen to act fairly. This is not to say that [the arbitrator] intended to be unfair or was aware that [he] might appear to have acted unfairly. Such cases are, happily, very rare because the commercial community is fortunate in the skill and conscientiousness of those who devote time to the resolution of commercial disputes by arbitration" (*per* Donaldson J. in *Thomas Borthwick (Glasgow) Ltd.* v. *Faure Fairclough Ltd.* [1968] 1 Lloyd's Rep. 29).

SETTING ASIDE THE AWARD

Where an arbitrator or umpire has misconducted himself, or any arbitration or award has been improperly procured, the court may set aside the award (s. 23). An award is improperly procured if it is obtained by fraud or by concealment of material facts.

An award can be set aside for misconduct if the arbitrator has received bribes, or if he is secretly interested in the subject-matter of the dispute. Misconduct, however, may exist where no improper motives are imputed to the arbitrator. It is misconduct, for example, to refuse to state a case for the opinion of the court on a point of law material to the case which is substantial, and not frivolous or vexatious (*Re Fischel & Co. and Mann and Cook* [1919] 2 K.B. 431), or to make an award on an illegal contract (*David Taylor & Son* v. *Barnett* [1953] 1 W.L.R. 562). It is also misconduct to make his award before hearing all the evidence, or allowing a party to finish his case; to examine a witness in the absence of either of the parties; to inspect property, the subject of the arbitration accompanied by only one party (*Re Brien and Brien's Arbn.* [1910] 2 Ir.R. 84); to fail to give notice to the parties of the time and place of meeting (*Oswald* v. *Grey* (1855) 24 L.J.Q.B. 69); or to hear the evidence of each party in the absence of the other (*Ramsden & Co.* v. *Jacobs* [1922] 1 K.B. 640).

FOREIGN AWARDS

Foreign awards, as defined in section 35, can be enforced in England
either by action or in the same manner as the award of an arbitrator
under section 26, provided that the conditions laid down in section 37
are complied with.

One of these conditions is that the award has become final in
the country in which it was made. Whether an award has become
final in this way is a matter of English law when enforcement is
being sought in England and it matters not, for example, if the
award could not be enforced in the country where it was made
until some further step had been taken, such as an order of the
local court (*Union Nationale des Cooperatives Agricoles de Céréales*
v. *Robert Catterall and Co. Ltd.* [1959] 2 Q.B. 44).

CONVENTION AWARDS

A Convention award is an award made in pursuance of an arbitration
agreement in the territory of a foreign state which is a party to the
New York Convention on the Recognition and Enforcement of
Foreign Arbitral Awards of 1958 (see p. 534, *ante*). These awards
are subject to the Arbitration Act 1975, ss. 2 to 6.

A Convention award is enforced in the same manner as an
English award (1976 Act, s. 3). Enforcement of such an award can
be refused only if the party against whom it is made proves—

(a) that a party to the arbitration agreement was (under the law
applicable to him) under some incapacity; or

(b) that the arbitration agreement was not valid under the law
to which the parties subjected it or, failing any indication
thereon, under the law of the country where the award was
made; or

(c) that he was not given proper notice of the appointment of the
arbitrator or of the arbitration proceedings or was otherwise
unable to present his case; or

(d) that the award deals with a difference not covered by the
arbitration agreement; or

(e) that the composition of the arbitral authority or the arbitral
procedure was not in accordance with the agreement of the
parties, or failing such agreement, with the law of the country
where the arbitration took place; or

(f) that the award has not yet become binding on the parties, or has been set aside or suspended by a competent authority of the country in which, or under the law of which, it was made (1975 Act, s. 5 (1)).

The enforcement of a Convention award may also be refused if the subject-matter of the award is not capable of settlement by arbitration or it would be contrary to public policy to enforce it (1975 Act, s. 5 (3)).

INTERNATIONAL INVESTMENT DISPUTES

Legal disputes arising directly out of an investment between a state (or a department or agency of a state) and a national of another state may be settled by arbitration under the rules of the International Centre for Settlement of Investment Disputes, established at the International Bank for Reconstruction and Development in Washington. The Centre has jurisdiction only if both parties have consented in writing to submit the dispute to the Centre.

The provisions relating to arbitration over international investment disputes are contained in an international convention which is set out in the Schedule to the **Arbitration (International Investment Disputes) Act 1966.** A person seeking recognition or enforcement of such an award is entitled to have the award registered in the High Court (s. 1 (2)). If the award is in a foreign currency, the currency is converted on the basis of the rate of exchange prevailing at the date when the award was rendered (s. 1 (3)). The Act came into force on January 18, 1967.

SELECT BIBLIOGRAPHY

Books

Gill, W. H., *The Law of Arbitration* (2nd ed., 1975).
Russell on Arbitration (18th ed., 1970) by A. Walton.

Articles

Cawley, C., "Forum Selection Clauses" [1973] J.B.L. 340–346.
Lew, J. D. M., "Arbitration Act 1975" (1975) 24 I.C.L.Q. 870–878.
Marshall, E. A., "Arbitral Immunity" [1976] J.B.L. 313.
Polonsky, M., "Arbitration of International Contracts" [1971] J.B.L. 1–11.

Schmitthoff, C. M., "The Supervisory Jurisdiction of the Courts" [1967] J.B.L. 318–333.

Schmitthoff, C. M., "Defective Arbitration Clauses" [1975] J.B.L. 9–22.

Weinreb, A., "Arbitration Clauses in Multilateral International Agreements" [1975] J.B.L. 287–291.

"Note on *James Millar & Partners Ltd.* v. *Whitworth Street Estates (Manchester) Ltd.*" (1970) 86 L.Q.R. 289–291.

INDEX

556 *Index*